Programming in Parallel with CUDA

CUDA is now the dominant language used for programming GPUs; it is one of the most exciting hardware developments of recent decades. With CUDA, you can use a desktop PC for work that would have previously required a large cluster of PCs or access to an HPC facility. As a result, CUDA is increasingly important in scientific and technical computing across the whole STEM community, from medical physics and financial modelling to big data applications and beyond.

This unique book on CUDA draws on the author's passion for and long experience of developing and using computers to acquire and analyse scientific data. The result is an innovative text featuring a much richer set of examples than found in any other comparable book on GPU computing. Much attention has been paid to the C++ coding style, which is compact, elegant and efficient. A code base of examples and supporting material is available online, which readers can build on for their own projects.

RICHARD ANSORGE is Emeritus University Senior Lecturer at the Cavendish Laboratory, University of Cambridge and Emeritus Tutor and Fellow at Fitzwilliam College, Cambridge. He is the author of over 170 peer-reviewed publications and co-author of the book *The Physics and Mathematics of MRI* (2016).

Programming in Parallel
with CUDA

A Practical Guide

Richard Ansorge

CAMBRIDGE
UNIVERSITY PRESS

CAMBRIDGE
UNIVERSITY PRESS

University Printing House, Cambridge CB2 8BS, United Kingdom

One Liberty Plaza, 20th Floor, New York, NY 10006, USA

477 Williamstown Road, Port Melbourne, VIC 3207, Australia

314–321, 3rd Floor, Plot 3, Splendor Forum, Jasola District Centre, New Delhi – 110025, India

103 Penang Road, #05–06/07, Visioncrest Commercial, Singapore 238467

Cambridge University Press is part of the University of Cambridge.

It furthers the University's mission by disseminating knowledge in the pursuit of
education, learning, and research at the highest international levels of excellence.

www.cambridge.org
Information on this title: www.cambridge.org/9781108479530
DOI: 10.1017/9781108855273

First published 2022

Printed in the United Kingdom by TJ Books Limited, Padstow Cornwall

A catalogue record for this publication is available from the British Library.

ISBN 978-1-108-47953-0 Hardback

To Catherine and Lydia

Contents

Figures

Appendix Figures

Tables

Appendix Tables

Examples

Appendix Examples

Preface

This book has been primarily written for people who need lots of computing power, including those engaged in scientific research who need this power to acquire, process, analyse or model their data. People working with medical data who need to process ever-larger data sets and more complicated image data are also likely to find this book helpful.

Complicated and demanding computations are something I have been doing for my entire research career, firstly in experimental high-energy physics and more recently in various applications of medical imaging. The advent of GPU computing is one of the most exciting developments I have yet seen, and one reason for writing this book is to share that excitement with readers.

It seems to be a corollary of Moore's law that the demand for computing power increases to always exceed what is currently available. Since the dawn of the PC age in the early 1980s, vendors have been providing supplementary cards to improve the speed of rendering displays. These cards are now known as graphics processing units or GPUs, and, driven by the demands of the PC gaming industry, they have become very powerful computing engines in their own right. The arrival in 2007 of the NVIDIA CUDA Toolkit for writing software that exploits the power of GPUs for scientific applications was a game changer. Suddenly we got a step up in computing power by a factor of 100 instead of the usual doubling every 18 months or so. Since then, the power of GPUs has also continued to grow exponentially over time, following and even exceeding Moore's law. Thus, knowing how to program GPUs is just as useful today as it was in 2007. In fact, today, if you want to engage with high-performance computing (HPC) perhaps on world-class supercomputers, knowing how to use GPUs is essential.

Up till about 2002 the exponential growth in PC computing power was largely due to increasing clock speeds. However, since then, clock speeds have plateaued at around 3.5 GHz, but the number of cores in a CPU chip has steadily increased. Thus, *parallel programming*, which uses many cooperating cores running simultaneously to share the computing load for a single task, is now essential to get the benefit from modern hardware. GPUs take parallel programming to the next level, allowing thousands or even millions of parallel threads to cooperate in a calculation.

Scientific research is difficult, and competitive, available computing power is often a limiting factor. Speeding up an important calculation by a factor of, say, 200 can be a game changer. A running time of a week is reduced to less than one hour, allowing for same-day analysis of results. A running time of one hour would be reduced to 18 seconds, allowing for exploration of the parameter space of complex models. A running time of seconds is reduced to milliseconds, allowing for interactive investigation of computer models. This book should be particularly useful to individual researchers and small groups who can equip their own in-house PCs with GPUs and get these benefits. Even groups with good access to large HCP facilities would benefit from very rapid tools on their own desktop machine to explore features of their results.

Of course, this book is also suitable for any reader interested in finding out more about GPUs and parallel programming. Even if you already know a little about the subject, we think you will find studying our coding style and choice of examples rewarding.

To be specific, this book is about programming NVIDIA GPUs in C++. I make no apology for concentrating on a specific vendor's products. Since 2007 NVIDIA have become a dominant force in HPC and, more recently, also AI. This is due to both the cost-effectiveness of their GPUs and, just as importantly, the elegance of the C++-like CUDA language. I know that some scientific programming is still carried out in various dialects of Fortran (including Fortran IV, a language I was very fond of in the early 1980s). But C++ is, in my opinion, more expressive. Fans of Fortran may point out that there is a technical problem with optimising C++ code using pointers, but that problem was overcome in C++11 with the introduction of the restrict keyword in C11. This keyword is also supported by modern C++ compilers, and it is used in many of our examples.

The examples are one feature that distinguishes this book from other current books on CUDA. Our examples have been carefully crafted from interesting real-world applications, including physics and medical imaging, rather than the rather basic (and frankly boring) problems often found elsewhere. Another difference between this book and others is that we have taken a lot of care over the appearance of our code, using modern C++ where appropriate, to reduce verbosity while retaining simplicity. I feel this is really important; in my experience most scientific PhD students learn computing by modifying other people's code, and, while much of the CUDA example code currently circulating works, it is far from elegant. This may be because in 2007 CUDA was launched as an extension to C, not C++, and most of the original SDK examples were written in a verbose C style. It is unfortunate that that style still persists in many of the online CUDA tutorials and books. The truth is that CUDA always supported some C++, and nowadays CUDA fully supports up to C++17 (albeit with a few restrictions). In November 2019 the venerable "NVIDIA C Programmers Guide" was renamed the "NVIDIA C++ Programmers Guide", and, although then there was no significant change to the content of the guide, it did signal a change in NVIDIA's attitude to their code, and since 2020 some more advanced uses of C++ have started to appear in the SDK examples.

This book does not aim to teach you C++ from scratch; some basic knowledge of C++ is assumed. However Appendix I discusses some of the C++ features used in our examples. Modern C++ is actually something of a monster, with many newer features to support object-orientated and other high-level programming styles. We do not use such features in this book, as, in our view, they are not appropriate for implementing the algorithmic code we run on GPUs. We also favour template functions over virtual functions.

To get the most out of our book, you will need access to a PC equipped with an NVIDIA GPU supporting CUDA (many of them do). The examples were developed using a Windows 10 PC with a 4-core Intel CPU and an NVIDIA RTX 2070 GPU (costing £480 in 2019). A Linux system is also fine, and all our examples should run without modification. Whatever system you have, you will need a current version of the (free) NVIDIA CUDA Toolkit. On Windows, you will also need Visual Studio C++ (the free community version is fine). On Linux, gcc or g++ is fine.

Sadly, we cannot recommend CUDA development on macOS, since Apple do not use NVIDIA cards on their hardware and their drivers do not support recent NVIDIA cards. In addition, NVIDIA have dropped support for macOS starting with their Toolkit version 11.0, released in May 2020.

All of the example code can be downloaded from https://github.com/RichardAns/CUDA-Programs. This site will also contain errata for the inevitable bugs that some of you may find in my code. By the way, I welcome reader feedback about bugs or any other comments. My email address is rea1@cam.ac.uk. The site will be maintained, and I also hope to add some additional examples from time to time.

I hope you enjoy reading my book as much as I have enjoyed writing it.

1

Introduction to GPU Kernels and Hardware

This book aims to teach you how to use graphics processing units (GPUs) and Compute Unified Device Architecture (CUDA) to speed up your scientific or technical computing tasks. We know from personal experience that the best way to learn to speak a new language is to go to the relevant country and immerse yourself in the culture. Thus, we have chosen to start our book with a complete working example of an interesting problem. We present three versions of the code, firstly a standard C++ implementation for a single central processing unit (CPU) thread, and secondly a multithread CPU version suitable for running on one or two threads on each core for a multicore CPU, say between 4 and 16 threads. The third version uses CUDA to run with thousands of simultaneous threads. We don't expect readers to immediately grasp all the nuances in the CUDA code – that is what the rest of this book is for. Rather I hope you will see how similar the code is in all three versions and be encouraged that GPU programming is not difficult and that it brings huge rewards.

After discussing these introductory examples, we go on to briefly recap the architecture of traditional PCs and then introduce NVIDIA GPUs, introducing both their hardware features and the CUDA programming model.

1.1 Background

A modern PC processor now has two, four or more computing CPU cores. To get the best from such hardware, your code has to be able to run in parallel on all the resources available. In favourable cases, tools like OpenMP or the C++11 thread class defined in `<thread>` allow you to launch cooperating threads on each of the hardware cores to get a potential speed-up proportional to the number of cores. This approach can be extended to clusters of PCs using communication tools like Message Passing Interface (MPI) to manage the inter-PC communication. PC clusters are indeed now the dominant architecture in high-performance computing (HPC). A cluster of at least 25 PCs with 8-core CPUs would be needed to give a factor of 200 in performance. This is doable but expensive and incurs significant power and management overheads.

An alternative is to equip your PC with a modern, reasonably high-specification GPU. The examples in this book are based on an NVIDIA RTX 2070 GPU, which was bought for £480 in March 2019. With such a GPU and using NVIDIA's C++-like CUDA language, speed-ups of 200 and often much more can be obtained on a single PC with really quite modest effort. An additional advantage of the GPU is that its internal memory is about 10 times faster than that of a typical PC, which is extremely helpful for problems limited by memory bandwidth rather than CPU power.

At the heart of any CUDA program are one or more *kernel* functions, which contain the code that actually runs on the GPU. These kernel functions are written in standard C++ with a small number of extensions and restrictions. We believe they offer an exceptionally clear and elegant way of expressing the parallel content of your programs. This is why we have chosen CUDA for this book on parallel programming. One feature that distinguishes the book from other books on CUDA is that we have taken great care to provide interesting real-world problems for our CUDA examples. We have also coded these examples using features of modern C++ to write straightforward but elegant and compact code. Most of the presently available online tutorials or textbooks on CUDA use examples heavily based on those provided by the NVIDIA Software Development Kit (SDK) examples. These examples are excellent for demonstrating CUDA features but are mostly coded in a verbose, outdated C style that often hides their underlying simplicity.[1]

To get the best from CUDA programs (and, indeed, any other programming language), it is necessary to have a basic understanding of the underlying hardware, and that is the main topic of this introductory chapter. But, before that, we start with an example of an actual CUDA program; this is to give you a foretaste of what is to come – the details of the code presented here are fully covered in later chapters.

1.2 First CUDA Example

Here is our first example showing what is possible with CUDA. The example uses the trapezoidal rule to evaluate the integral of `sin(x)` from 0 to π, based on the sum of a large number of equally spaced evaluations of the function in this range. The number of steps is represented by the variable `steps` in the code. We deliberately choose a simple but computationally expensive method to evaluate `sin(x)`, namely, by summing the Taylor series for a number of terms represented by the variable `terms`. The sum of the sin values is accumulated, adjusted for end points and then scaled to give an approximation to the integral, for which the expected answer is 2.0. The user can set the values of `steps` and `terms` from the command line, and for performance measurements very large values are used, typically 10^6 or 10^9 steps on the CPU or GPU, respectively, and 10^3 terms.

Example 1.1 cpusum single CPU calculation of a sin integral

```
02 #include <stdio.h>
03 #include <stdlib.h>
04 #include "cxtimers.h"

05 inline float sinsum(float x, int terms)
06 {
      // sin(x) = x - x^3/3! + x^5/5! ...
07    float term = x;     // first term of series
08    float sum  = term; // sum of terms so far
09    float x2   = x*x;
10    for(int n = 1; n < terms; n++){
```

```
11       term *= -x2 / (float)(2*n*(2*n+1));
12       sum += term;
13   }
14   return sum;
15 }

16 int main(int argc, char *argv[])
17 {
18   int steps = (argc >1) ? atoi(argv[1]) : 10000000;
19   int terms = (argc >2) ? atoi(argv[2]) : 1000;

20   double pi = 3.14159265358979323;
21   double step_size = pi/(steps-1); // n-1 steps

22   cx::timer tim;
23   double cpu_sum = 0.0;
24   for(int step = 0; step < steps; step++){
25     float x = step_size*step;
26     cpu_sum += sinsum(x, terms);    // sum of Taylor series
27   }
28   double cpu_time = tim.lap_ms(); // elapsed time

29   // Trapezoidal Rule correction
30   cpu_sum -= 0.5*(sinsum(0.0,terms)+sinsum(pi, terms));
31   cpu_sum *= step_size;
32   printf("cpu sum = %.10f,steps %d terms %d time %.3f ms\n",
                             cpu_sum, steps, terms, cpu_time);
33   return 0;
34 }

D:\ >cpusum.exe 1000000 1000
cpu sum = 1.9999999974,steps 1000000 terms 1000 time 1818.959 ms
```

We will show three versions of this example. The first version, cpusum, is shown in Example 1.1 and is written in straightforward C++ to run on a single thread on the host PC. The second version, ompsum, shown in Example 1.2 adds two OpenMP directives to the first version, which shares the loop over steps between multiple CPU threads shared equally by all the host CPU cores; this illustrates the best we can do on a multicore PC without using the GPU. The third version, gpusum, in Example 1.3 uses CUDA to share the work between 10^9 threads running on the GPU.

Description of Example 1.1

This is a complete listing of the cpusum program; most of our subsequent listings will omit standard headers to save space. Notice that we chose to use 4-byte floats rather than 8-byte doubles for the critical function sinsum. The reasons for this choice are discussed later in this chapter, but briefly we wish to exploit limited memory bandwidth and to improve calculation speed. For scientific work, the final results rarely need to be accurate to more than a few parts in 10^{-8} (a single bit error in an IEEE 4-byte float corresponds to a fractional error of 2^{-24} or $\sim 6 \times 10^{-8}$). But, of course, we must be careful that errors do not propagate as calculations progress; as a precaution the variable cpusum in the main routine is an 8-byte double.

- Lines 2–4: Include standard headers; the header cxtimers.h is part of our cx utilities and provides portable timers based on the C++11 chrono.h library.
- Lines 5–15: This is the sinsum function, which evaluates sin(x) using the standard Taylor series. The value of x in radians is given by the first input argument x, and the number of terms to be used is given by the second input argument terms.
- Lines 7–9: Initialise some working variables; term is the value of the current term in the Taylor series, sum is the sum of terms so far, and x2 is x^2.
- Lines 10–13: This is the heart of our calculation, with a loop where successive terms are calculated in line 11 and added to sum in line 12. Note that line 11 is the single line where all the time-consuming calculations happen.

The main function of the remining code, in lines 16–35, is to organise the calculation in a straightforward way.

- Lines 18–19: Set the parameters steps and terms from optional user input.
- Line 21: Set the step size required to cover the interval between 0 and π using steps steps.
- Line 22: Declare and start the timer tim.
- Lines 23–27: A for loop to call the function sinsum steps times while incrementing x in to cover the desired range. The results are accumulated in double cpusum.
- Line 28: Store the elapsed (wall clock) time since line 22 in cpu_time. This member function also resets the timer.
- Lines 30–31: To get the integral of sin(x), we perform end-point corrections to cpusum and scale by step_size (i.e. dx).
- Line 31: Print result, including time, is ms. Note that the result is accurate to nine significant figures in spite of using floats in the function sinsum.

The example shows a typical command line launch requesting 10^6 steps and 10^3 terms in each step. The result is accurate to nine significant figures. Lines 11 and 12 are executed 10^9 times in 1.8 seconds, equivalent to a few GFlops/sec.

In the second version, Example 1.2, we use the readily available OpenMP library to share the calculation between several threads running simultaneously on the cores of our host CPU.

Example 1.2 ompsum OMP CPU calculation of a sin integral

```
02    #include <stdio.h>
03    #include <stdlib.h>
03.5  #include <omp.h>
04    #include "cxtimers.h"
```

```
05    float sinsum(float x, int terms)
06    {
      . . . same as (a)
15    }

16    int main(int argc, char *argv[])
      . . .
19.5  int threads = (argc >3) ? atoi(argv[3]) : 4;
      . . .
23.5  omp_set_num_threads(threads);              // OpenMP
23.6  #pragma omp parallel for reduction (+:omp_sum)   // OpenMP
24    for(int step = 0; step < steps; step++){
      . . .
32    printf("omp sum = %.10f,steps %d terms %d
         time %.3f ms\n", omp_sum,steps,terms,cpu_time);
33    return 0;
34    }

D:\ >ompsum.exe 1000000 1000 4    (4 threads)
omp sum = 1.9999999978, steps 1000000 terms 1000 time 508.635 ms
D:\ >ompsum.exe 1000000 1000 8    (8 threads)
omp sum = 1.9999999978, steps 1000000 terms 1000 time 477.961 ms
```

Description of Example 1.2

We just need to add three lines of code to the previous Example 1.1.

- Line 3.5: An extra line to include the header file `omp.h`. This has all the necessary definitions required to use OpenMP.
- Line 19.5: An extra line to add the user-settable variable `threads`, which sets the number of CPU threads used by OpenMP.
- Line 23.5: This is actually just a function call that tells `openMP` how many parallel threads to use. If omitted, the number of hardware cores is used as a default. This function can be called more than once if you want to use different numbers of cores in different parts of your code. The variable `threads` is used here.
- Line 23.6: This line sets up the parallel calculation. It is a compile time directive (or pragma) telling the compiler that the immediately following `for` loop is to be split into a number of sub-loops, the range of each sub-loop being an appropriate part of the total range. Each sub-loop is executed in parallel on different CPU threads. For this to work, each sub-loop will get a separate set of the loop variables, `x` and `omp_sum` (N.B.: We use `omp_sum` instead of `cpu_sum` in this section of the code). The variable `x` is set on each pass through the loop with no dependencies on previous passes, so parallel execution is not problematic. However, that is not the case for the variable `omp_sum`,

which is supposed to accumulate the sum of all the `sin(x)` values. This means the sub-loops have to cooperate in some way. In fact, the operation of summing a large number of variables, held either in an array or during loop execution, occurs frequently and is called a *reduce* operation. Reduce is an example of a *parallel primitive*, which is a topic we discuss in detail in Chapter 2. The key point is that the final sum does not depend on the order of the additions; thus, each sub-loop can accumulate its own partial sum, and these partial sums can then be added together to calculate the final value of the `sum_host` variable after the parallel `for`. The last part of the pragma tells OpenMP that the loop is indeed a reduction operation (using addition) on the variable `omp_sum`. OpenMP will add the partial sums accumulated by each thread's copy of `omp_sum` and place the final result into the `omp_sum` variable in our code at the end of the loop.

- Line 32: Here we have simply modified the existing `printf` to also output the value of `threads`.

Two command line launches are shown at the end of this example, the first using four OMP threads and the second using eight OMP threads.

The results of running `ompsum` on an Intel quad-core processor with hyper-threading are shown at the bottom of the example using either four or eight threads. For eight threads the speed-up is a factor of 3.8 which is a good return for little effort. Note using eight cores instead of four for our PC means running two threads on each core which is supported by Intel hyper-threading on this CPU; we see a modest gain but nothing like a factor of 2.

In Visual Studio C++, we also have to tell the compiler that we are using OpenMP using the properties dialog, as shown in Figure 1.1.

In the third version, Example 1.3, we use a GPU and CUDA, and again we parallelise the code by using multiple threads for the loop in lines 24–27, but this time we use a separate thread for each iteration of the loop, a total of 10^9 threads for the case shown here. The code changes for the GPU computation are a bit more extensive than was required for OpenMP, but as an incentive to continue reading, we will find that the speed-up is now a factor of 960 rather than 3.8! This dramatic gain is an example of why GPUs are routinely used in HPC systems.

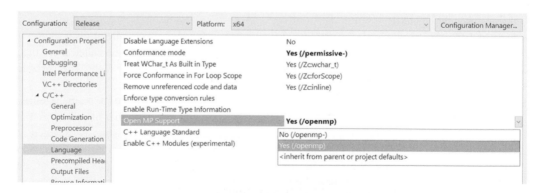

Figure 1.1 How to enable OpenMP in Visual Studio

Example 1.3 gpusum GPU calculation of a sin integral

```
01   // call sinsum steps times using parallel threads on GPU
02   #include <stdio.h>
03   #include <stdlib.h>
04   #include "cxtimers.h"              // cx timers
04.1 #include "cuda_runtime.h"          // cuda basic
04.2 #include "thrust/device_vector.h"  // thrust device vectors

05   __host__ __device__ inline float sinsum(float x, int terms)
06   {
07     float x2 = x*x;
08     float term = x;   // first term of series
09     float sum = term; // sum of terms so far
10     for(int n = 1; n < terms; n++){
11       term *= -x2 / (2*n*(2*n+1));   // build factorial
12       sum += term;
13     }
14     return sum;
15   }

15.1 __global__ void gpu_sin(float *sums, int steps, int terms,
      float step_size)
15.2 {
       // unique thread ID
15.3   int step = blockIdx.x*blockDim.x+threadIdx.x;
15.4   if(step<steps){
15.5     float x = step_size*step;
15.6     sums[step] = sinsum(x, terms);  // store sums
15.7   }
15.8 }

16   int main(int argc, char *argv[])
17   {
       // get command line arguments
18     int steps = (argc >1) ? atoi(argv[1]) : 10000000;
19     int terms = (argc >2) ? atoi(argv[2]) : 1000;
19.1   int threads = 256;
19.2   int blocks = (steps+threads-1)/threads;  // round up

20     double pi = 3.14159265358979323;
21     double step_size = pi / (steps-1); // NB n-1
       // allocate GPU buffer and get pointer
21.1   thrust::device_vector<float> dsums(steps);
21.2   float *dptr = thrust::raw_pointer_cast(&dsums[0]);
22     cx::timer tim;
```

```
22.1 gpu_sin<<<blocks,threads>>>(dptr,steps,terms,
                          (float)step_size);
22.2 double gpu_sum =
             thrust::reduce(dsums.begin(),dsums.end());
28   double gpu_time = tim.lap_ms(); // get elapsed time
29   // Trapezoidal Rule Correction
30   gpu_sum -= 0.5*(sinsum(0.0f,terms)+sinsum(pi, terms));
31   gpu_sum *= step_size;
32   printf("gpusum %.10f steps %d terms %d
           time %.3f ms\n",gpu_sum,steps,terms,gpu_time);
33   return 0;
34   }

D:\ >gpusum.exe 1000000000 1000
gpusum = 2.0000000134 steps 1000000000 terms 1000 time 1882.707 ms
```

Description of Example 1.3

This description is here for the sake of completeness. If you already know a bit of CUDA, it will make sense. If you are new to CUDA, skip this description for now and come back later when you have read our introduction to CUDA. At this point, the message to take away is that potentially massive speed-ups can be achieved and that, to my eyes at least, the code is elegant, expressive and compact and the coding effort is small.

The details of the CUDA methods used here are fully described later. However, for now you should notice that much of the code is unchanged. CUDA is written in C++ with a few extra keywords; there is no assembly to learn. All the details of the calculation are visible in the code. In this listing, line numbers without dots are exactly the same lines in Example 1.1, although we use gpu instead of cpu in some of the variable names.

- Lines 1–4: These include statements are the same as in Example 1.1.
- Line 4.1: This is the standard include file needed for all CUDA programs. A simple CUDA program just needs this, but there are others that will be introduced when needed.
- Line 4.2: This include file is part of the Thrust library and provides support for thrust vectors on the GPU. Thrust vector objects are similar to the std::vector objects in C++, but note that CUDA has separate classes for thrust vectors in CPU memory and in device memory.
- Lines 5–15: This is the same sinsum function used in Example 1.1; the only difference is that in line 5 we have decorated the function declaration with __host__ and __device__, which tell the compiler to make two versions of the function, one suitable for code running on the CPU (as before) and one for code running on the GPU. This is a brilliant feature of CUDA: literally the same code can be used on both the host and device, removing a major source of bugs.[2]
- Lines 15.1–15.8: These define the CUDA kernel function gpu_sin that replaces the loop over steps in lines 24–27 of the original program. Whereas OpenMP uses a small number of host threads, CUDA uses a very large number of GPU threads. In this case we use 10^9 threads, a separate thread for each value of step in the original for loop. Kernel functions are declared with the keyword __global__ and are launched by the host code. Kernel functions can receive arguments from the host but cannot return values – hence they must be declared as void. Arguments can either

be passed to kernels by value (good for single numbers) or as pointers to previously allocated device memory. Arguments cannot be passed by reference, as in general the GPU cannot directly access host memory.

Line 15.3 of the kernel function is especially noteworthy, as it encapsulates the essence of parallel programming in both CUDA and MPI. You have to imagine that the code of the kernel function is running simultaneously for all threads. Line 15.3 contains the magic formula used by each particular instance of an executing thread to figure out which particular value of the index step that it needs to use. The details of this formula will be discussed later in Table 1.1. Line 15.4 is an out-of-range check, necessary because the number of threads launched has been rounded up to a multiple of 256.

- Lines 15.5 and 15.6 of the kernel: These correspond to the body of the for loop (i.e. lines 25–26 in Example 1.1). One important difference is that the results are stored in parallel to a large array in the global GPU memory, instead of being summed sequentially to a unique variable. This is a common tactic used to avoid serial bottlenecks in parallel code.
- Lines 16–19 of main: These are identical to the corresponding lines in Example 1.1.
- Lines 19,1–19.2: Here we define two new variables, threads and blocks; we will meet these variables in every CUDA program we write. NVIDIA GPUs process threads in blocks. Our variables define the number of threads in each block (threads) and the number of thread blocks (blocks). The value of threads should be a multiple of 32, and the number of blocks can be very large.
- Lines 20–21: These are the same as in Example 1.1.
- Line 21.1: Here we allocate an array dsum in GPU memory of size cteps. This works like std::vector except we use the CUDA thrust class. The array will be initialised to zero on the device.
- Line 21.2: Here we create a pointer dptr to the memory of the dsum vector. This is a suitable argument for kernel functions.
- Lines 22.1–22.2: These two lines replace the for loop in lines 23–27 of Example 1.1, which called sinsum steps times sequentially. Here line 22.1 launches the kernel gpu_sin, which uses steps separate GPU threads to call sinsum for all the required x values in parallel. The individual results are stored in the device array dsums. In line 22.2 we call the reduce function from the thrust library to add all the values stored in dsums, and then copy the result from the GPU back to the host variable dsum.[3]
- Lines 28–34: These remaining lines are identical to Example 1.1; notice that the host version of our sinsum function is used in line 30.

As a final comment we notice that the result from the CUDA version is a little less accurate than either of the host versions. This is because the CUDA version uses 4-byte floats throughout the calculation, including the final reduction step, whereas the host versions use an 8-byte double to accumulate the final result sum over 10^6 steps. Nevertheless, the CUDA result is accurate to eight significant figures, which is more than enough for most scientific applications.

The sinsum example is designed to require lots of calculation while needing very little memory access. Since reading and writing to memory are typically much slower than performing calculations, we expect both the host CPU and the GPU to perform at their best efficiencies in this example. In Chapter 10, when we discuss profiling, we will see that the GPU is delivering several TFlops/sec in the example. While the sinsum function used in this example is not particularly interesting, the brute force integration method used here could be used for any calculable function spanned by a suitable grid of points. Here we used 10^9 points, which is enough to sample a function on a 3D Cartesian grid with 1000 points along each of the three coordinate axes. Being able to easily scale up to 3D versions of problems that can only be reasonably done in 2D on a normal PC is another great reason to learn about CUDA.

In order to write effective programs for your GPU (or CPU), it is necessary to have some feeling for the capabilities of the underlying hardware, and that is our next topic. So, after this quick look at CUDA code and what it can do, it is time to go back to the beginning and remind ourselves of the basics of computer hardware.

1.3 CPU Architecture

Correct computer code can be written by simply following the formal rules of the particular language being used. However, compiled code actually runs on physical hardware, so it is helpful to have some insights into hardware constraints when designing high-performance code. This section provides a brief overview of the important features in conventional CPUs and GPUs. Figure 1.2 shows a simplified sketch of the architecture of a traditional CPU.

Briefly the blocks shown are:

- Master Clock: The clock acts like the conductor of an orchestra, but it plays a very boring tune. Clock-pulses at a fixed frequency are sent to each unit causing that unit to execute its next step. The CPU processing speed is directly proportional to this frequency. The first IBM PCs were launched in 1981 with a clock-frequency of 2.2 MHz; the frequency then doubled every three years or so peaking at 4 GHz in 2002. It turned out that 4 GHz was the fastest that Intel was able to produce reliability, because the power requirement (and hence heat generated) is proportional to frequency. Current Intel CPUs typically run at ~3.5 GHz with a turbo boost to 4 GHz for short periods.
- Memory: The main memory holds both the program data and the machine code instructions output by the compiler from your high-level code. In other words, your program code is treated as just another form of data. Data from memory can be read from memory by either the load/save unit or the program fetch unit but normally only the load/save unit can write data back to the main memory.[4]

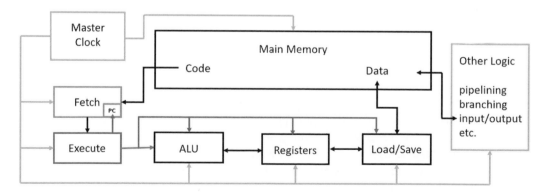

Figure 1.2 Simplified CPU architecture

- Load/Save: This unit reads data from and sends data to the main memory. The unit is controlled by the Execute logic which at each step specifies if data is to be read or written to main memory. The data in question is transferred to or from one of the registers in the register file.
- Register File: This is the heart of a CPU; data must be stored in one or more registers in order to be operated on by the ALU.
- ALU or Arithmetic Logic Unit: This device performs arithmetic and logical operations in data stored in registers; at each step the required operation is specified by the execute unit. This is the piece of hardware that actually computes!
- Execute: This unit decodes the instruction sent by the instruction fetch unit, organises the transfer of input data to the register file, instructs ALU to perform the required operation on the data and then finally organises the transfer of results back to memory.
- Fetch: The fetch unit fetches instructions from main memory and passes them to the execute unit. The unit contains a register holding the program counter (PC)[5] that contains the address of the current instruction. The PC is normally incremented by one instruction at each step so that the instructions are executed sequentially. However, if a branch is required, the fetch unit changes the PC to point to the instruction at the branch point

1.4 CPU Compute Power

The computing power of CPUs has increased spectacularly over time as shown in Figure 1.3.

The transistor count per chip has followed Moore's law's exponential growth from 1970. The CPU frequency stopped rising in 2002. The performance per core continues to rise

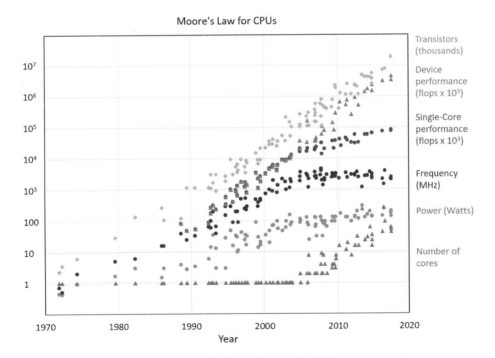

Figure 1.3 Moore's law for CPUs

slowly but recent growth has been due to innovations in design rather than increase in frequency. The major contribution to performance per chip since 2002 has been from multicore technology. GPUs are excluded from this plot although recent Intel Xeon-phi designs with hundreds of cores are becoming quite GPU-like. Remarkably the power used by a single device has also not increased since 2002. The data are from https://github.com/karlrupp/microprocessor-trend-data.

It is really worth taking a moment to contemplate the story told in this figure. The compute power of individual devices has increased by a factor of more than 10^6 in the last 30 years and also the number of devices has grown at an even faster rate. Many people now own numerous devices in their smartphones, laptops, cars and household gadgets while the internet giants run vast server farms each of which must have a processor count running into millions. Likewise, for scientific computing the most powerful systems in the recent TOP500 list of supercomputers also have millions of processing cores. These developments, particularly in the last 15 years or so, have transformed society – and the process has only just begun, there is no sign that the trends shown in the figure are about to stop.

One hope I have in writing this book, is that learning about GPUs and parallel programming will be a small help in keeping up with the changes to come.

1.5 CPU Memory Management: Latency Hiding Using Caches

Data and instructions do not move instantly between the blocks shown in Figure 1.1; rather they progress clock-step by clock-step through various hardware registers from source to destination so that there is a *latency* between issuing a request for data and the arrival of that data. This intrinsic latency is typically tens of clock-cycles on a CPU and hundreds of clock-cycles on a GPU. Fortunately, the potentially disastrous performance implications of latency can be largely hidden using a combination of caching and pipelining. The basic idea is to exploit the fact that data stored in sequential physical memory locations are mostly processed sequentially in computer code (e.g. while looping through successive array elements). Thus, when one element of data is requested by the memory load unit, the hardware actually sends this element and a number of adjacent elements on successive clock-ticks. Thus, although the initially requested element may arrive with some latency, thereafter successive elements are available on successive clock-ticks. Thinking of data flows along the lines shown in Figure 1.1 just like water flows through pipes in your house is a valid comparison – when you turn on a hot tap, it takes a little while for the hot water to arrive (latency) and thereafter it stays hot.

In practice PCs employ a number of memory cache units to buffer the data streaming from multiple places in main memory as shown in Figure 1.4.

Note that in Figure 1.4 all three caches are on-chip and there are separate L1 caches for data and instructions. The main memory is off chip.

Program instructions are also streamed in a pipeline from main memory to the instruction fetch unit. This pipeline will be broken if a branch instruction occurs, and PC hardware uses sophisticated tricks such as *speculative execution* to minimise the effects. In speculative execution the PC executes instructions on one or more of the paths following the branch before the result of the branch is known and then uses or discards results once the branch path is known. Needless to say, the hardware needed for such tricks is complex.

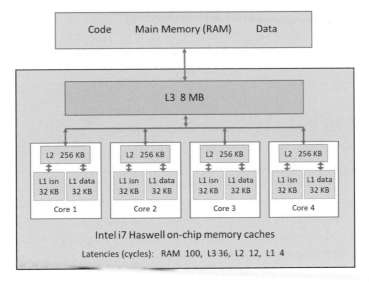

Figure 1.4 Memory caching on 4-core Intel Haswell CPU

The caching scheme shown in Figure 1.4 is typical for modern CPU multi-core chips. There are three levels of caching memories, all integrated into the CPU chip. First the level-3 (L3) cache is large at 8 MB and is shared by the 4 CPU cores. Each core also has progressively faster L2 and L1 caches, with separate L1 caches for data and instructions.

The hardware transfers cache data in packets called *cache lines* of typically 64 or 128 bytes. On current Intel processors the cache line size is 64 bytes, but the hardware usually transfers two adjacent lines at once giving an effective size of 128 bytes. The data in a cache line corresponds a contiguous region of the main memory beginning at an address that is a multiple of the cache line size.

1.6 CPU: Parallel Instruction Set

Before discussing the powerful parallel capabilities of GPUs, it is worth noting that Intel CPUs also have some interesting parallel capabilities in the form of vector instructions. These first appeared around 1999 with the Pentium III SSE instruction set. These instructions used eight new 128-bit registers each capable of holding 4 4-byte floats. If sets of 4 such floats were stored in sequential memory locations and aligned on 128-byte memory boundaries they can be treated as a 4-element vector and these vectors can be loaded to and stored from the SSE registers in a single clock-cycle and likewise enhanced ALUs could perform vector arithmetic in single clock-cycles. Thus, using SSE could potentially speed up some floating-point calculations by a factor of four. Over the years SSE has evolved and many recent Intel CPUs support AVX2 which uses 256-bit registers and can support many data types. Currently Intel's most recent version is AVX-512 which uses 512-byte registers capable of holding vectors of up to 16 floats or 8 doubles. The use of AVX on Intel CPUs is discussed in detail in Appendix D.

1.7 GPU Architecture

In this section we give more details of the evolution of GPU computing in general and specifically on NVIDIA hardware.

1.7.1 First a Little Bit of History

GPUs were designed for high-performance computer graphics; in modern gaming a screen size of say 1920×1080 pixels refreshed at 60 Hz is normal. Each pixel needs to be computed from the instantaneous state of the game and the player's viewpoint – about 1.25×10^8 pixel calculations per second. While this might just about be possible with a modern processor, it certainly was not possible one or two decades ago when interest in PC gaming emerged. Note this is a massively *parallel* computing problem as the pixel values can all be calculated independently. Gaming cards emerged as dedicated hardware with a large number of simple processors to perform the pixel calculations. An important technical detail is that the pixel array representing the image is stored in a 2D array in a digital frame buffer as data, with typically 3-bytes per pixel representing the red, green and blue (RGB coding) intensities of the pixel. The frame buffer is specialised computer memory (video ram) that can be read or written as normal but has an additional port allowing dedicated video hardware to independently scan the data and send suitable signals to a monitor.

It was quickly noticed that an inexpensive card doing powerful parallel calculations and sending the results to computer memory might have applications beyond gaming and in around 2001 the acronym GPGPU (general purpose computing on graphics processing units) and website gpgpu.org were born. In 2007 NVIDIA launched their GPU programming toolkit which changed GPU programming from being a difficult niche activity to mainstream.

1.7.2 NIVIDA GPU Models

NVIDIA produces three classes of GPU:

1. The GeForce GTX, GeForce RTX or Titan branded models, e.g. GeForce GTX 1080; these are the least expensive and are aimed at the gaming market. Typically, these models have less FP64 support than the equivalent scientific versions and do not use EEC memory. However, for FP32 calculations their performance can match or exceed the scientific card. The Titan branded models are the most powerful and may have more capable GPUs. The RTX 3090 has the highest FP32 performance of any NVIDIA card released up to March 2021.
2. The Tesla branded models, e.g. Tesla P100; these are aimed at the high-end scientific computing market, have good FP64 support and use EEC memory. Tesla cards have no video output ports and cannot be used for gaming. These cards are suitable for deployment in server farms.
3. The Quadro branded GPUs, e.g. Quadro GP100; these are essentially Tesla model GPUs with added graphics capabilities and are aimed at the high-end desktop workstation market.

Between 2007 and the time of writing in 2020 NVIDIA have introduced 8 different GPU generations with each successive generation having more software features. The generations are named after famous scientists and within each generation there are usually several models which themselves may differ in software features. The specific capability of a particular GPU is known as its Compute Capability or CC, which is specified by a monotonically increasing number. The most recent generation is Ampere with a CC value of 8.0. The examples in the book were developed using a Turing RX 2070 GPU with a CC of 7.5. A fuller account can be found in Appendix A.

1.8 Pascal Architecture

NVIDIA GPUs are built up in a hierarchical manner from a large number of basic compute-cores, the arrangement for the Pascal generation GTX1080 is shown in Figure 1.4:

1. The basic unit is a simple compute-core; it is capable of performing basic 32-bit floating point and integer operations. These cores do not have individual program counters.
2. Typically, groups of 32 cores are clustered together form what NVIDIA call "32-core processing blocks" – I prefer to use the term "warp-engine". This is because, as explained in the software sections, in a CUDA kernel program the executing threads are grouped into 32-thread groups which NVIDIA calls "warps" which can be considered as the basic execution unit in CUDA kernel programs. All threads in a given warp run in lock-step executing the same instruction at every clock-cycle. In fact, all threads in a given warp are run on the same warp-engine which maintains a single program counter that is used to send a common instruction sequence to all the cores belonging to that warp-engine.[6]

   Importantly, the warp-engine adds additional compute resources shared by its cores. These include special function units (SFUs) which are used for fast evaluation of transcendental functions such as `sin` or `exp`, and double precision floating point units (FP64). In Pascal GPUs, warp-engines have eight SFUs and either 16 or one FP64 unit.
3. Warp-engines are themselves grouped together to form what NVIDIA calls symmetric multiprocessors or SMs. In the Pascal generation a GPU has either two (Tesla GP100 only) or four warp-engines (all others). Thus, an SM has typically 128 compute cores. The threads in a CUDA kernel program are grouped into a number of fixed size thread blocks. Each thread block in fact runs on a single SM, but different thread blocks may run on different SMs. This explains why threads in the same thread block can communicate with each other, for example using shared memory or `__syncthreads()`, but threads in different thread blocks cannot.

   The SM also adds texture units and various on chip memory resources shared equally between warp-engines, including a register file of 64K 32-bit words, shared memory of 96 KB and L1/texture cache of 24 KB or 48 KB.
4. Finally, a number of SMs are grouped together to make the final GPU. For example, the GTX 1080 has 20 SMs containing a total of $20 \times 128 = 2560$ compute-cores. Note all these cores are on the same hardware chip. An L2 cache of either 4 GB or 2 GB shared by all SMs is also provided at this level.

For the gaming market NVIDIA make a range of GPUs which differ in the number of SM units on the chip, for example the economy GTX 1030 has just 3 SM units. Gaming cards may also have different clock-speeds and memory sizes.

   In Figure 1.5 a single compute core is shown on the left; it is capable of performing 32-bit floating point or integer operations on data which flows through the core. The hardware first

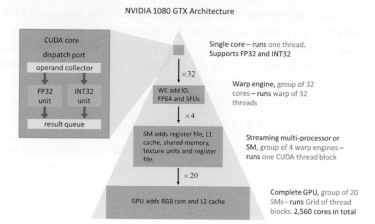

NVIDIA 1080 GTX Architecture

Figure 1.5 Hierarchical arrangement of compute cores in an NVIDIA GTX1080

groups the cores into "warps" of 32 cores processed by a "Warp Engine" (WE) which adds shared resources including IO, double precision units (either 1 or 16), and eight special function units (SFUs). The SFUs evaluate 32-bit transcendental functions such as sin or exp. All the threads in any particular CUDA warp run together on a single warp engine. Small groups of WEs, usually two or four, are then grouped together into one SM unit. Finally, multiple SMs are grouped together to make the GPU.

1.9 GPU Memory Types

GPU memory is also organised in a hierarchical fashion similar to cores, with the main GPU memory at the bottom of the pyramid and various specialised memories and caches above. This is also indicated in Figure 1.5. The memory types are as follows:

- **Main memory:** This is analogous to the main memory of a CPU; the program itself and all data resides here. The CPU can write and read data to and from the GPU main memory. These exchanges go via the PCI bus and are relatively slow and therefore CUDA programs should be designed to minimise data transfers. Helpfully data in the GPU main memory is preserved between kernel calls so that it can be reused by successive kernel calls without the need to reload. It is also possible for memory transfers to proceed in parallel with kernel execution (i.e. asynchronous transfers), this can be helpful in data processing tasks such as manipulating frames of a movie, where the next frame can be transferring to the GPU while the present frame is being processed. Notice that because texture and constant data are stored in the GPU main memory they can be written to by the CPU even though they are read only on the GPU.
- **Constant Memory:** A dedicated 64 KB of GPU main memory is reserved for constant data. Constant memory has a dedicated cache which bypasses the L2 cache so if all threads from a warp read the same memory location this can be as fast as if the data was in a register. In practice recent versions of the NVCC compiler can often detect this situation in your code and automatically place variables in constant memory. The use of `const` and `restrict` where appropriate will be helpful. It is probably not worthwhile worrying too

much about explicitly using constant memory. Notice also that this memory is quite limited and therefore not useful for large tables of parameters.

- **Texture memory:** This feature is directly related to the graphics processing origins of GPUs. Texture memory is used to store arrays of up to three dimensions and is optimised for local addressing of 2D arrays. They are read only and have their own dedicated caches. Textures are accessed by the special lookup functions, `tex1D`, `tex2D` and `tex3D`. These functions are capable of performing very fast 1D interpolation, 2D bilinear interpolation or 3D trilinear interpolation for arbitrary input positions within the texture. This is a massive help for image processing tasks and I highly recommend using texture lookup wherever helpful. A number of our examples will illustrate how to use textures.

Recent versions of CUDA support additional texture functionality, including layered textures (indexable stacks of 1D or 2D textures) and surfaces which can be written to by the GPU.

- **Local memory:** These are memory blocks private to each individual executing thread; they are used as overflow storage for local variables in intermediate temporary results when the registers available to a thread are insufficient. The compiler handles the allocation and use of this resource. Local memory is cached via the L2 and L1 caches just like other data.
- **Register file:** Each SM has 64K 32-bit registers which are shared equally by the thread blocks concurrently executing on the SM. This can be regarded as a very important memory resource. In fact there is a limit of 64 on the maximum number of concurrent warps (equivalent to 2K threads) that can execute on a given SM. This means that if the compiler allows a thread to use more than 32 registers, the maximum number of thread blocks running on the SM (i.e. occupancy) is reduced, potentially harming performance. The NVCC compiler has a switch, `--maxrregcount <number>`, that can be used to tune overall performance by trading occupancy against thread computational performance.
- **Shared memory:** Each SM provides between 32 KB and 64 KB of shared memory.[7] If a kernel requires shared memory the size required can be declared either at kernel launch time or at compile time. Each concurrently executing thread block on an SM gets the same size memory block. Thus if your kernel requires more than half of the maximum amount of shared memory, the SM occupancy will be reduced to a single thread block per SM. Realistic kernels would usually ask for no more than half that available memory.

Shared memory is important because it is very fast and because it provides the best way for threads within a thread block to *communicate* with each other. Many of our examples feature the use of shared memory.

Many early CUDA examples emphasise the faster memory access provided by shared memory compared to the poor performance of the (then poorly cached) main memory. Recent GPUs have much better memory caching so using shared memory for faster access is less important. It is important to balance the performance gain from using shared memory against reduced SM occupancy when large amounts of shared memory are needed.

Current GPUs use their L1 and L2 caches together with high occupancy to effectively hide the latency of main memory accesses. The caches work most effectively if the 32 threads in a warp access 32-bit variables in up to 32 adjacent memory locations and the starting location is aligned on a 32-word memory boundary. Using such memory addressing patterns is called *memory coalescing* in CUDA documentation. Early documentation places great emphasis on

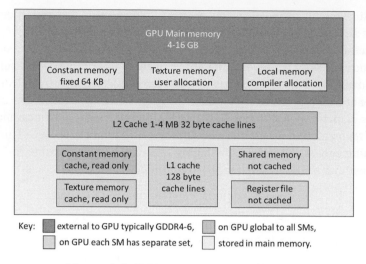

Figure 1.6 GPU memory types and caches

this topic because early GPUs had poor or no caching. Modern GPUs are more forgiving so you probably just need to stick to the golden rule: adjacent threads (or indices on CPUs) address adjacent memory locations. The memory arrangement is shown in Figure 1.6.

1.10 Warps and Waves

The GPU architecture is reflected in the way a CUDA kernel is designed and launched by host software. Designing good kernels to match particular problems requires skill and experience and is essentially what the rest of this book is about. When you get it right, it is very satisfying to see your code speed up by a large factor. First you have to decide how many threads, Nthreads, to use. Choosing a good value for Nthreads is one of the most important choices you make when designing CUDA kernels. The choice of Nthreads is of course problem specific. For our example for the gpusum program in Example 1.3 we used a value of Nthreads equal to the number of steps. So for 10^9 steps we used 10^9 threads which is huge compared to the eight that can be run in parallel on our CPU. In later chapters we will say a lot about image processing. To process a 2D image having nx × ny pixels, a good choice is to put Nthreads = nx × ny. The key point is that Nthreads should be *big*, arguably as big as possible.

If you are new to CUDA you might expect that setting Nthreads equal to Ncores, the number of cores in your GPU, would be enough to keep the GPU fully occupied. In fact, this is far from correct; one of the very neat features on NVIDIA GPUs is that the hardware can hide the latencies in memory accesses or other hardware pipelines by rapidly switching between threads and use the data for particular threads as soon as it becomes available.

To be specific the GPU used for most of our examples is a RTX 2070 which has 36 SM units (Nsm = 36) and each SM has hardware to process two warps of 32 threads (Nwarp = 2). Thus, for this GPU Ncores = Nsm × Nwarp × 32 = 2304. What is less obvious is that during kernel processing each SM unit has a large number of *resident* threads, Nres, for the RTX 2070; Nres =1024 equivalent to 32 warps. At any given instant two of these 32 warps will be *active* and the remainder will be suspended, possibly waiting for pending memory requests to be satisfied. This is how the latency hiding is implemented in NVIDIA hardware. When we launch a kernel with say 10^9 threads these threads are run in *waves* of Nwave = Nres × Nsm threads; this is actually 27127 waves on the 2070 GPU with Nwave = 36864, with the last wave being incomplete. Ideally the minimum number of threads in any kernel launch should be Nwave, and if more threads are possible it should be a multiple of Nwave.

Note that although the Turing generation of GPUs have Nres = 1024 this is unusual; all the other recent NVIDIA GPU generations have Nres = 2048, twice the Turing value. Since for these GPUs Nwarp = 2 is the same as for Turing, Nwaves will be twice the Turing value. Note that for any particular GPU generation Nsm will vary with model number, e.g. Nsm = 46 for the RTX 2080 GPU, but Nwarp will not. Thus, Nwave will vary like Nsm with GPU model for a given GPU generation.

1.11 Blocks and Grids

In CUDA the thread block is a key concept; it is a group of threads that are batched together and run on the same SM. The size of the thread block should be a multiple of the warp size (currently 32 for all NVIDIA GPUs) up to the hardware maximum size of 1024. In kernel code, threads within the same thread block can communicate with each other using shared or global device memory and can synchronise with each other where necessary. Threads in different thread blocks cannot communicate during kernel execution and the system cannot synchronise threads in different thread blocks. Note it is common for the thread block size to be a sub multiple of 1024; often it is 256. In that case warps from up to four (or eight for non-Turing GPUs) different thread blocks will coexist on the SMs during kernel execution. Even though these blocks may coexist on the same SM they will still not be able to communicate.

When we launch a CUDA kernel we specify the *launch configuration* with two values, the thread block size and the number of thread blocks. The CUDA documentation refers to this as launching a *grid* of thread blocks and the grid-size is just the number of thread blocks. In our examples we will consistently use the variable names threads and blocks for these two values. Thus, the total number of threads is specified implicitly as Nthreads = threads × blocks. Notice Nthreads must be a multiple of threads the thread block size. If the number of threads you actually want our kernel to run is N, then blocks must be large enough so that Nthreads ≥ N. This is the purpose of line 19.2 in Example 1.3; it is to round up blocks to ensure there will be at least steps threads. Because of rounding up we must include an out-of-range check in the kernel code to prevent threads of rank ≥ N from running. That is the purpose of the test in line 15.4 of Example 1.3.

The CUDA documentation does not explicitly talk about waves very much; about the only reference we found was in the 2014 blog post by Julien Demouth at https://developer.nvidia .com/blog/cuda-pro-tip-minimize-the-tail-effect/. This is interesting because it implies that threads are dispatched to SMs for execution in complete waves when possible, which in turn means that it is important for blocks to be a multiple of the number of SMs on the GPU being used.

Table 1.1 *CUDA built-in variables. NB the first 4 are structs containing x, y and z members*

variable	comment
`threadIdx`	`id = threadIdx.x` is thread rank in thread block
	`id = blockDim.x*blockIdx.x+threadIdx.x` is thread rank in grid
`blockIdx`	`blockIdx.x` is block rank in grid of blocks
`blockDim`	`blockDim.x` is number of threads in one block
`gridDim`	`gridDim.x` is number of blocks in the grid
	`threads = gridDim.x*blockDim.x` is total number of threads in launch
`warpSize`	Number of threads in warp, set to 32 on all current GPUs

1.12 Occupancy

NVIDIA define occupancy as the ratio of the number of threads actually resident in the SM units compared to the maximum value `Nres`. Occupancy is usually expressed as a percentage. Full occupancy of 100 per cent is the same as saying that complete waves are running on the SMs of the GPU.

Even if we launch a kernel with sufficient threads to achieve 100 per cent occupancy we might not actually achieve full occupancy. The reason for this is that each SM has a limited total shared memory size and a limited number of registers. If our thread block size is 256 then full occupancy will only be achieved if four (or eight) threads bocks are resident on each SM which reduces the resources available to each thread block by the same factor. NVIDIA GPUs have enough registers for each thread to use up to 32 registers while maintaining full occupancy. Shared memory is more difficult as it is typically limited to 64 or 96 KB per SM which is equivalent to only 32 or 48 bytes per thread at full occupancy for non-Turing GPUs. On the latest Ampere GPUs this is increased to 80 bytes.

Less than full occupancy is not necessarily bad for performance, especially if the kernel is compute bound rather than memory bound, you may have to accept lower occupancy if your kernel needs significant amounts of shared memory. Experimentation may be necessary in these cases; using global memory instead of shared memory and relying on L1 caching for speed may by a good compromise on modern GPUs.

Kernel code can use the built-in variables shown in Table 1.1 to determine the rank of a thread in its thread block and in the overall grid. Only the 1D case is shown in this table the 2D and 3D cases are discussed in the next chapter.

This is the end of our introductory chapter. In Chapter 2 we introduce the more general ideas behind parallel programming on SIMD machines and GPUs. We then give some more detailed examples, including the classic problem of parallel reduction. We also discuss kernel launches in more detail.

Endnotes Chapter 1

1 For example, the Nvidia plugin for Visual Studio C++ helpfully generates a sample program to get you started but unfortunately that program is full of `goto` statements. The use of `goto` has of course been deprecated since the early 1980s.

2 Both the Nvidia documentation and their example code mostly refer to the CPU as the *host* and to the GPU as the *device*. We often but not always follow this convention.

3 Later we will discuss reduce operation in some detail as an example of a parallel primitive. Our best CUDA code for this operation will turn out to be a bit faster than using thrust.

4 Computers which store instructions and data in a common memory are said to have *von Neumann architecture*, after the physicist John von Neumann who worked on the design of the early 1945 ADVC machine. Arguably the idea of treating computer instructions as data can also be credited to Ada Lovelace in the 1840s. The alternative *Harvard architecture* uses separate hardware to store data and instructions. Examples include the Colossus computers, used at Bletchley Park from 1943, which were programmed using switches and plugs. Paper tape could also be used to hold instructions. In a curious case of nominative determinism, the English mathematician, Max Newman played an important role in the design of Colossus – truly these "new men" ushered in our digital age. Today Harvard architecture is still used for specialised applications, e.g. embedded systems running fixed programs stored in read only memory units (ROMs).

5 Unfortunately, the acronym PC for program counter is the same as for personal computer. Actually, the former use predates the introduction of personal computers by at least 20 years, thus we will use PC for both. This should not be confusing as we will rarely use PC for program counter.

6 Recently the Volta/Turing generation of GPUs launched in 2017 has relaxed this restriction somewhat. This is discussed later as an advanced topic.

7 This depends on the compute capability of a particular device. Most devices can be configured to have at least 48 KB.

2

Thinking and Coding in Parallel

Computers have always been very good at giving users the impression that they can perform multiple tasks at the same time. For example, even a single core PC will allow you to browse the web while running a lengthy calculation in the background. However, this is accomplished by fast task switching – the user gets CPU cycles when active, otherwise the CPU cycles are given to the calculation. This is resource sharing not true parallel programming.

If you have a more recent 4-core PC, you might launch four instances of your lengthy calculation with different parameter values to genuinely perform parallel computation without any extra programming effort. Problems that can be solved with this approach are sometimes called "*trivially parallel*". In spite of the name, this approach is perfectly valid if it gets your job done effectively and has the enormous advantage of requiring little extra programming effort. If the potential number of jobs is large, a simple script file might be useful to automate the launching of new jobs and collecting their results. A nice example is the CERN data centre which has more than 200,000 cores mostly running event data processing or Monte Carlo simulation using the same program but different event data or different random numbers.

Unfortunately, the trivial programming approach does not work on GPUs which have very simple processing cores designed to work together on a single task. True parallel programming requires just this – many processing cores working together to complete a single task. It turns out that writing effective parallel code is often rather straightforward – as hopefully we demonstrate in this book.

2.1 Flynn's Taxonomy

Computer scientists recognise a small number of serial and parallel computer architectures described by 4-letter acronyms summed up in Flynn's taxonomy shown in Table 2.1.[1]

The first, SISD case, represents a "normal" single processor running a single thread. Computers with this architecture can still be relatively fast and by employing rapid switching between tasks they can give human beings the illusion that they are multitasking but in fact they only execute one operation on one data item in a clock-cycle.

The second, SIMD case, covers architectures where the hardware can execute the same instruction on multiple data items at the same time. This can be achieved by have multiple ALUs fed with different data items but using a common instruction decoder. To overcome memory access bottlenecks the data items are fed to the ALUs in a vector format. Hence these architectures are often known as vector processors. The fondly remembered CRAY supercomputers, dating from the 1970s, were early and very effective examples of this approach. In 1999 Intel CPUs introduced their so-called Streaming SIMD Extensions (SSE)

Table 2.1 *Flynn's taxonomy*

acronym	Name	comment
SISD	Single Instruction Single Data	Single-core system running one thread.
SIMD	Single Instruction Multiple Data	Multiple processors running the same task on multiple data streams.
MIMD	Multiple Instruction Multiple Data	Multi-core system with each core running a different task, also multiple connected systems.
MISD	Multiple Instructions Single Data	Rare, possible application in fault tolerant designs.
SIMT	Single Instruction Multiple Threads	Variation on SIMD implemented in CUDA.

instruction set into the Pentium III architecture; these instructions could perform operations on vectors of four 32-bit floating point numbers using what were effectively 128-bit registers. Over the years the capabilities of Intel SIMD operations have increased; currently Intel supports advanced vector extensions using 512-bit registers (AVX-512), enough for up to 16 32-bit numbers. We discuss this topic in more detail in Appendix D.

The third, MIMD, is effectively just a set of separate CPUs performing separate tasks. This case includes both modern multicore PCs running Linux or Windows and clusters of PCs connected by a network. In both cases suitable software, for example, MPI or OpenMP, can be used to allow the multiple independent processors to work together on a single computing task.

The fourth, MISD, is included for the sake of completeness and is rarely used. It might be used in specialised embedded systems requiring redundancy against failure; for example, satellites.

The final, SIMT, was introduced by NVIDIA as a variation of SIMD to describe their GPU architecture. Although both are used to tackle similar scientific computations, there are differences between them. In the SIMD model a relatively small number of threads use vector hardware to process data. In the SIMT model a large number of threads are used to process individual data items. If a common instruction is used by all threads then SIMD behaviour is replicated, but the SIMT architecture also permits threads to perform divergent operations which, while it may lead to a drop in performance, also allows for more versatile code. In the recent Volta and Turing generations of GPU, NVIDIA have extended the capabilities for programming individual threads.

It is the SIMD/T case that is of interest for parallel programming. We look for sections of our code where the same operation is performed on multiple data items – obvious candidates are `for` loops. However, if we want to share the computation of a loop across multiple threads it is important that there are no dependencies between passes through the loop, for example the order in which the loop traversals are executed should not matter.

Consider again the loop in the Example 1.1

```
23    double sum_host = 0.0;
24    for (int step = 0; step <= steps; step++){
25       float x = step_size*step;
26       sum_host += sinsum(x, terms);
27    }
```

The loop statements shown in lines 25–26 are independent of other passes through the loop, because the order in which we sum the values in the variable sum_host does affect the final result.[2] Thus, this loop is a good candidate for parallel code, particularly so if the evaluation of the function sin_host is computationally expensive. Before we proceed there is a subtle technical problem to resolve. Either the variable sin_host must be global – therefore, visible to all the threads participating in the parallel calculation or some other means must be found to get the correct final sum.

Making sin_host global to all threads, while straightforward to implement, introduces yet another complication – if two or more threads try to update the variable simultaneously the result will be undefined! With CUDA, one thread will succeed and the attempts by other threads at simultaneous update will be ignored, so the final answer will be wrong. There is a fix for this problem, which is actually a generic issue for all parallel computing platforms; it is to use so-called *Atomic* operations to perform the required operation serially. Atomic operations are usually implemented by calling platform specific functions, and their use in CUDA code is discussed in Appendix B. For now we note that using atomics might slow down a calculation and we choose an alternative approach, which is to simply store the individual values returned by the sinsum function in separate elements of a large array. The elements of the array will be summed together in a separate step once they have all been calculated. This is an example of parallel thinking; we separate a serial loop into a part that can be done in parallel – calling the simsum many times, and a part which cannot be done in parallel – the reduce operation of adding up all the individual stored values. These two steps are the only parts of the calculation that will be done on the GPU; code running on the CPU takes care of everything else.

Now it is time to look in more detail at our first CUDA program emphasising the steps necessary to convert the serial version in Example 1.1 to the parallel version in Example 1.3.

The first step is to add the header files needed for CUDA

```
04.1 #include "cuda_runtime.h"        // cuda basic
04.2 #include "thrust/device_vector.h" // thrust device vectors
```

The headers added are cuda_runtime.h which provides basic support for CUDA and thrust/device_vector.h provides a container class like std::vector for 1D arrays in GPU memory. Most of the examples in this book use these headers.

We then convert the function sinsum into a function that can be used on both the CPU and the GPU. This is simply done be adding a CUDA keyword to the function declaration.

```
05  __host__ __device__ inline float sinsum(float x, int terms)
```

The keyword __device__ tells the compiler to compile a version of the function that runs on the GPU and can be called by kernels and other functions running on the GPU. Likewise, __host__ tells the compiler to create a version of the function for the CPU code to use. The inline keyword is part of standard C++ and tells the compiler to generate function code embedded in the caller's code, removing the overhead of a function call at the price of increasing the size of the final exe file. In CUDA inline is the default for __device__ functions. The __host__ keyword is only needed if the function is to be used on both the host and device; for device only functions just __device__ is needed. The entire body of the function in lines 6–15 is unchanged. This is a very powerful feature of CUDA.

It is also possible to have two different versions of a function, one declared with __device__ and one declared with __host__. The __host__ prefix could be omitted from the host version as this is the default, but we recommend using it to make your intentions clear. Obviously this prefix is not needed (or recommended) for functions which are only used by the host.

The __device__ version of sinsum is simply a GPU function and is not callable directly from the host. We need to write a separate CUDA kernel function which runs on the GPU and can be called from the host. CUDA kernels are declared using __global__ instead of __device__ this reflects their dual nature – callable by the host but running on the GPU. In the CUDA world people talk about "launching" kernels rather than "calling" them so that is what we shall do from now on. Our first kernel gpu_sum in lines 15.1–15.8 is all new code which replaces most of lines 23–27 in the original program.

```
15.1  __global__ void gpu_sin(float *sums, int steps, int terms,
                                float step_size)
15.2  {
15.3    int step = blockIdx.x*blockDim.x+threadIdx.x;
15.4    if(step<steps){
15.5      float x = step_size*step;
15.6      sums[step] = sinsum(x,terms);   // store values
15.7    }
15.8  }
```

The kernel declaration in line 15.1 looks very much like a normal C++ declaration except for the prefix __global__. There are, however, some restrictions based on the fact that although the kernel is called from the host it cannot access any memory on the host. All kernels must be declared void and their arguments are restricted to scalar items or pointers to previously allocated regions of device memory. All kernel arguments are passed by value. In particular, references are not allowed. It is not a good idea to try and pass large C++ objects to kernels; this is because they will be passed by value and there may be significant copying overheads. Also any changes made by the kernel will not be reflected back in the host's copy after the kernel call. Additionally, any C++ classes or structs passed to a kernel must have __device__ versions of *all* their member functions.

- Line 15.3 declares a variable step equivalent to the for loop index variable of the same name in line 24 of Example 1.1. It is set to a value defined by the built-in variables blockDim.x, blockIdx.x and threadIdx.x. The values of these variables depend on the launch parameters used in the host call to the kernel as follows:

- blockDim.x will be set to threads, i.e. the thread block size used by the kernel.
- blockIdx.x will be set to the rank of the thread block to which the current thread belongs and will be in the range [0,blocks-1].
- threadIdx.x will be set to the rank of the current thread within its thread block and will be in the range [0,threads-1].
- step = blockDimx.blockIdx.x+threadIdx.x is in range [0, threads × blocks - 1].

The key point is that the system will run threads × blocks instances of the kernel on the GPU covering all possible combinations of values for threadIdx and blockIdx. Thus, when we look at a kernel listing we must imagine that we are looking at the contents of a loop which is executed for all possible values of these built-in variables. In this case step takes all values in the range [0,size-1] where size = threads × blocks. When looking at a kernel code, you must imagine that the code is being run simultaneously by all the threads. Once you have mastered this concept, you will be a parallel programmer![3]

- Line 15.4: This is an out-of-range check on the value of step, the kernel will exit at this point for threads that fail the check.
- Line 15.5: Calculate the x value corresponding to step.
- Line 15.6: Call sinsum with the thread dependant value of x. The result is stored in the array sums using step as an index.
- Line 15.7: The kernel exits at here; recall that return statements are not required for void functions in C++.

The changes to the main routine are as follows:

```
19.1 int threads = 256;
19.2 int blocks = (steps+threads-1)/threads; // round up
```

- Lines 19.1–19.2: The two lines are added to define the kernel launch configuration parameters threads and blocks. In this our first example, we use a fixed value of 256 for threads and a calculated value for blocks which is set to be just big enough to get the total number of threads in the launch to satisfy threads × blocks ≥ steps.

```
21.1 thrust::device_vector<float> dsums(steps); // GPU buffer
21.2 float *dptr = thrust::raw_pointer_cast(&dsums[0]);
```

- Line 21.1: This line creates the array dsums of size steps in the device memory using the thrust device_vector class as a container. By default the array will be initialised to zeros on the device. This array is used by the `gpu_sin` kernel to hold the individual values returned by calls to the `sinsum` function.

- Line 21.2: We cannot pass `dsums` to the kernel directly as thrust was not designed to make this possible,[4] but we can pass a pointer to the memory array managed by the class. For `std::vector` objects, the member function `data()` does this job. While this function does work for thrust `host_vector` objects it does not work for `device_vector` objects. Therefore we have to use the more complicated `cast` shown in this line. As an alternative you could instead use the undocumented `data().get()` member function of `device_vectors`.

```
22.1 gpu_sin<<<blocks,threads>>>
                (dptr,steps,terms,(float)step_size);
```

- Line 22.1: This line shows our first CUDA kernel launch; this is basically just a function call with a weird extra bit `<<<blocks, threads>>>` inserted between the function name and its argument list. The `int` variables that appear here specify the number of threads in each thread block (`threads`) and the number of thread blocks (`blocks`). Note these values can be defined at *run time* and if you have multiple kernel launches in your code each launch can use different values. As discussed above, `threads` should be a multiple of 32 and has a maximum allowed value of 1024 for all current GPUs.[5] The second parameter `blocks` should be large. These values affect the performance of the kernel and "tuning" them to get the best performance involves trying different combinations and choosing the combination that runs the kernel fastest. To aid this in most of our subsequent example code we will make these launch parameters user settable command line parameters. For most kernels a good starting point is `<<<4*Nsm, 256>>>` where Nsm is the number of SMs on the target GPU.[6] In this book we often use `<<<288, 256>>>` as our GPU has 36 SM units. For testing or debugging purposes using `<<<1, 1>>>` is sometimes interesting and is allowed. That version has the effect of running just a single thread on one SM unit.

```
22.2 double gpu_sum =
            thrust::reduce(dsums.begin(),dsums.end());
```

- Line 22.2: Here we use the host callable reduce function in the thrust library to sum all the elements of the array `dsums` in GPU memory. This call involves two steps, firstly we perform the required additions on the GPU and secondly we copy the result from GPU memory to CPU memory. This is often referred to as a D2H (device to host) transfer.

That is the end of our detailed description of our first kernel. We have deliberately kept this code as simple as possible.

It is worth looking at line 15.1 of the code in more detail. For any particular thread at line 15.1 of the kernel function the CUDA system variable `blockIdx.x` is set to the number of the currently executing thread block and the variable `threadIdx.x` is set to the rank of that current thread within its thread block. Thus, in the present case where `steps` is set to 10^9 and threads is set to 256, `blocks` will be set to 3906251 and `blockIdx.x` will be in the range [0,3906250], `threadIdx.x` will be in [0,255] and `blockDim.x` will be 256. Thus, for each thread the calculation, line 15.1 produces a unique value for `step` in the range $0-10^9$ - 1. This is exactly what we need to replicate the behaviour of the original `for` loop from Example 1.1. You will find something like line 15.1 in every CUDA kernel function – it allows each thread to determine what specific task it has to do. In fact, the variable `step` is nothing more than a unique thread id; this is often referred to as the *rank* of the thread. NVIDIA also use the term *lane* to refer to the rank of a thread within its particular 32-thread warp.

There is another important point to make about line 15.1. The GPU hardware allocates all the threads in any particular thread block to a single SM unit on the GPU, and these threads are run together very tightly on warp-engines as warps of 32 threads. The variable `threadIdx.x` is set so that threads in the *same* warp have *consecutive* values of this variable; specifically `threadIdx.x%32` is the rank or lane of a thread within its warp (range 0–31) and `threadIdx.x/32` is the rank of the warp within the thread block (range 0–7 in our case). Thus, in line 15.6 of the kernel where we store a value in `sums[step]`, the adjacent threads within a given warp have adjacent values of `step` and so they will address adjacent memory locations in the array `sums`. This is vital to make efficient use of the GPU memory caching. Had we not known this we might have used the formula:

$$\text{step = threadIdx.x*gridDim.x+blockIdx.x;}$$

in line 15.1. Since the variable `gridDim.x` is set to the number of thread blocks the alternative would have given us the same range of values for the variable `step` but now adjacent hardware threads have values of `step` separated by 3906251 – resulting in a serious loss of memory performance.

In case you were wondering about the .x decoration, these variables are actually all `dim3` structs defined by the CUDA SDK (in vector_types.h). The type `dim3` is a struct with three `const uint` members x, y and z. In the next example we will see how they are used in 3D grids of threads to best fit the needs of a particular problem. The CUDA SDK defines a number of structs like this with up to four elements. For example, `uint3` is similar to `dim3` except that `uint3` defines overloaded operators to support basic arithmetic operations whereas `dim3` does not. Also, `dim3` has a default constructor that initialises all unspecified values to one so that it is always safe to use all components of the variables even if the user has not explicitly set them. Although we used simple integers for our kernel launch, the compiler will silently and safely promote them to type `dim3` for the actual kernel launch.

The values of threads and blocks are defined in lines 19.1 and 19.2 of the example to ensure that there are at least `steps` threads so that we use a separate thread for each call to `sinsum`. This may well be optimal here because the `sinsum` function does a great deal of computation. But this code gives the user no chance to experiment to find out if that is true. A more general approach is to allow the user to specify values for threads and blocks and to modify the `gpu_sin` kernel to allow individual threads to make more than one call to `gpu_sin` if necessary. Both modifications are very straightforward as shown in Example 2.1.

Example 2.1 Modifications to Example 1.3 to implement thread-linear addressing

```
. . .
15.1  __global__ void gpu_sin(float *sums, int steps,
                                int terms, float step_size)
15.2  {
15.3     int step = blockIdx.x*blockDim.x+threadIdx.x; // ID
15.4     while(step<steps){
15.5        float x = step_size*step;
15.6        sums[step] = sinsum(x,terms);  // store value
15.65      step += gridDim.x*blockDim.x;  // grid size stride
15.7     }
15.8  }
. . .    // NB ternary operator (test) ? a : b used here
19.1     int threads = (argc > 3) ? atoi(argv[3]) : 256;
19.2     int blocks  = (argc > 4) ? atoi(argv[4]) :
                                (steps+threads-1)/threads;
      . . .
```

Our modifications to the kernel are changing the `if` in line 15.4 to `while` and inserting an extra line `15.65` at the end of the while loop. In line 15.65 we increment `step` by the total number of threads in the grid of thread blocks. The while loop will continue until steps values have been calculated for all (non-zero) user supplied values of `blocks` and `threads`. Moreover, and importantly for performance reasons, on each pass through the `while` loop adjacent threads always address adjacent memory locations. Other ways of traversing through the data could be devised but the one shown here is the simplest and best. This technique of using a while loop with indices having a grid-size stride between passes through the loop is called "thread-linear addressing" and is common in CUDA code. It should always be considered as an option when porting a loop in host code to CUDA.

The added lines 19.1 and 19.2 of the main routine now also use the C/C++ ternary operator (`?:`) and set the values of threads and blocks according to whether or not the user has supplied extra command line arguments. If the user does not specify these arguments then `argc` will be set to three or less and both tests will fail so both default values (after the :) will be used. If the user specifies just one extra argument argc will be set to four so the first test will succeed and `threads` will be set using the expression before the : which will be the user supplied value. The second test will still fail and a default value for `blocks` will be used in the calculation. Finally, if the user supplies both extra arguments then both `threads` and `blocks` will be set using the user's values.

We confess to being ambivalent about the (`?:`) operator; it is very terse and was introduced in the early days of C in the 1970s when it was desirable to minimise keystrokes on heavy mechanical teletype machines when inputting code. Careless use of this operator can make code hard to read. However, crucially it *returns a value* whereas `if` statements do not. Using (`?:`) allows us to declare and initialise a variable in the *same statement* which is in line with modern C++ RAII practices. In our view this trumps the terse syntax of the operator. We do use it in our examples when initialising a variable to one of two alternatives.

One drawback of this approach to reading command line arguments for setting program options is that the user has to know the order in which the options are defined and cannot set a given option without also specifying all the previous options. For production code we would of course recommend something better.

For thread-linear addressing it is possible to replace the `while` loop Example 2.1 with a `for` loop as shown in Example 2.2.

Example 2.2 `gpu_sin` kernel alternative version using a for loop

```
.  .  .
15.1 __global__ void gpu_sin(float *sums, int steps,
                             int terms, float step_size)
15.2 {
15.3   for(int step = blockIdx.x*blockDim.x+threadIdx.x;
                 step<steps; step += gridDim.x*blockDim.x){
15.5     float x = step_size*step;
15.6     sums[step] = sinsum(x,terms);   // store value
15.7   }
15.8 }
```

Feel free to use either version but for me the first version using `while` seems clearer; there is so much going on in the `for` statement in the second version that I find the code harder to follow. A good compiler will generate identical code from either version.

2.2 Kernel Call Syntax

The general form of a call to a CUDA kernel uses up to four special arguments in the `<<< >>>` brackets and the kernel itself can have a number of function arguments. The four arguments inside the `<<< >>>` brackets in order are:

First: defines the dimensions of the grid of thread blocks used by the kernel. Either an integer (or unsigned integer) for linear block addressing or a `dim3` type defining a 2D or 3D grid of thread blocks.

Second: defines the number of threads in a single thread block. Either an integer (or unsigned integer) for thread-linear addressing within a block or a `dim3` type to define a 2D or 3D array structure for the threads within a thread block.

Third: An optional argument of type `size_t` (or `int`) defining the number of bytes of dynamically allocated shared memory used by each thread block of the kernel. No shared memory is reserved if this argument is omitted or set to zero. Note that as an alternative the kernel itself can declare static shared memory. The size of a static shared memory allocation must be known at compile time but the size of dynamically allocated shared memory can be determined at run time.

Fourth: An optional argument of type `cudaStream_t` specifying the CUDA stream in which to run the kernel. This option is only needed in advanced applications running multiple simultaneous kernels. CUDA streams are discussed in Chapter 7.

2.3 3D Kernel Launches

Only the first 2 arguments specified as simple integers have been used in our examples so far. Our next Example 2.3 shows the use of dim3 variables to run a kernel on a 3D grid. This example is really just for illustrative purposes and most of the code is concerned with printing grid related quantities.

Example 2.3 grid3D using a 3D grid of thread blocks

```
01  #include "cuda_runtime.h"
02  #include "device_launch_parameters.h"
03  #include <stdio.h>
04  #include <stdlib.h>

05  __device__   int   a[256][512][512];  // file scope
06  __device__   float b[256][512][512];  // file scope

07  __global__ void grid3D(int nx, int ny, int nz, int id)
08  {
09    int x = blockIdx.x*blockDim.x+threadIdx.x; // find
10    int y = blockIdx.y*blockDim.y+threadIdx.y; // (x,y,z)
11    int z = blockIdx.z*blockDim.z+threadIdx.z;
12    if(x >=nx || y >=ny || z >=nz) return;     // range check

13    int array_size = nx*ny*nz;
14    int block_size = blockDim.x*blockDim.y*blockDim.z;
15    int grid_size  = gridDim.x*gridDim.y*gridDim.z;
16    int total_threads = block_size*grid_size;
17    int thread_rank_in_block = (threadIdx.z*blockDim.y+
              threadIdx.y)*blockDim.x+threadIdx.x;
18    int block_rank_in_grid = (blockIdx.z*gridDim.y+
              blockIdx.y)*gridDim.x+blockIdx.x;
19    int thread_rank_in_grid = block_rank_in_grid*block_size+
              thread_rank_in_block;
20    // do some work here
21    a[z][y][x] = thread_rank_in_grid;
22    b[z][y][x] = sqrtf((float)a[z][y][x]);
23    if(thread_rank_in_grid == id) {
24      printf("array size    %3d x %3d x %3d = %d\n",
              nx,ny,nz, array_size);
25      printf("thread block %3d x %3d x %3d = %d\n",
              blockDim.x, blockDim.y, blockDim.z, block_size);
26      printf("thread  grid %3d x %3d x %3d = %d\n",
              gridDim.x,  gridDim.y, gridDim.z, grid_size);
27      printf("total number of threads in grid %d\n",
              total_threads);
```

```
28          printf("a[%d][%d][%d] = %i and b[%d][%d][%d] = %f\n",
                    z, y, x, a[z][y][x], z, y,  x, b[z][y][x]);
29          printf("for thread with 3D-rank %d 1D-rank %d
                    block rank in grid %d\n", thread_rank_in_grid,
                    thread_rank_in_block,block_rank_in_grid);
30      }
31  }

32  int main(int argc, char *argv[])
33  {
34      int id = (argc > 1) ? atoi(argv[1]) : 12345;
35      dim3 thread3d(32,  8,  2); // 32*8*2     = 512
36      dim3  block3d(16, 64,128); // 16*64*128 = 131072
37      grid3D<<<block3d,thread3d>>>(512,512,256,id);
38      return 0;
39  }
```

Description of Example 2.3

- Lines 1–4: Basic include statements for CUDA.
- Lines 5–6: Declare two large 3D arrays which have file scope and so can be used by any of the functions declared later in the same file. This is standard C/C++ but with an extra CUDA feature. By declaring the arrays with the __device__ prefix we are telling the compiler to allocate these arrays in the GPU memory not in the host memory. Thus, the arrays a and b are usable by kernel functions but not host functions. Notice the array dimensions are in order z, y, x going from left to right, where memory is allocated so the adjacent x values are adjacent in memory. This is standard in C/C++ but opposite to Fortran which uses x, y, z order. Apart from array subscripts we will use "natural" x, y, z ordering in our code. This follows CUDA practice where for example a float4 variable a has members a.x, a.y, a.z, a.w which are ordered from x to w in memory.

Using a global declaration is actually an easy way to create GPU arrays of known size, but we will rarely use it – there are two important disadvantages. Firstly, the array dimensions must be set at compile time not run time and secondly declaring variables with file scope is a deeply depreciated programming style because it leads to unstructured code where functions can easily cause unwanted side effects. In our subsequent examples we will allocate arrays in code and then pass them as pointer arguments to called functions as necessary.

- Line 7: The kernel grid3D is declared with four arguments which are the array dimensions and id which specifies the thread whose information will be printed.
- Lines 9–11: Here we calculate the thread's x, y and z coordinates within its thread block. The launch parameters defined in lines 35–36 set the block dimensions to 32, 8 and 2 and the grid dimensions to 16, 64 and 128 for x, y and z respectively. This means that in line 9 the built-in variables blockDim.x and gridDim.x are set to 32 and 16 respectively. Thus threadIdx.x and blockIdx.x will have ranges [0,31] and [0,16] and the desired coordinate x will have the range [0,511] which is required to index the global arrays a and b. Similarly, y and z have ranges of [0,511] and [0,255]. Within any particular thread block the threadIdx values will have ranges of [0,31], [0,7] and [0,1] for x, y and z; note the x range corresponds to one

complete warp of threads; this is a design choice not chance. Having decided to use an x range of 32 we are restricted to smaller ranges for y and z as the product of all three is the thread block size which is limited by hardware to a maximum of 1024.

- Line 12: This is an out-of-range check on the calculated indices. This check is not strictly necessary here as we have carefully crafted the launch parameters to exactly fit the array dimensions. In general, this will not always be possible and it is good practice to always include range checks in kernel code.
- Lines 13–19: Calculate some values derived from the launch parameters. Most of these values would not be needed in a real-world problem, but we want to print them to illustrate the detail of 3D addressing in kernels.
  - ○ Lines 13–15: The 3D array, thread block and grid sizes are simply calculated as the product of their dimensions.
  - ○ Line 16: Similarly the total number of threads is the product of the thread block size `block_size` and the number of thread blocks `grid_size`.
  - ○ Line 17: The rank of the thread within its 3D thread block is calculated using the standard 3D addressing rank formula:

> **3D Rank Formula**
> ```
> rank = (z*dim_y + y)*dim_x + x
> ```

for a 3D array of dimensions (`dim_x`, `dim_y`, `dim_z`) laid out sequentially in memory with the x values adjacent, the y values are separated by stride of `dim_x` and the z values are separated by a stride of `dim_x*dim_y`. We will use versions of this formula very often in our examples, often encapsulated in a lambda function.
  - ○ Line 18: Here we also use the rank formula to calculate the rank of the thread block within the grid of thread blocks.
  - ○ Line 19: Here we use the 2D version of the rank formula to calculate the rank of the thread within the entire thread grid.
  - ○ Lines 21–22: Here we actually do some real work storing values into the array a and b using indices derived from the threads position in the 3D thread grid.
  - ○ Lines 23–29: Here, for one thread, chosen by the user, we print some of the calculated quantities.
- Lines 32–39: Here is the complete short main routine. Basically, we get a user settable value for `id` in line 34, set the kernel launch parameters in lines 35–36 and launch the kernel in line 37.

The results of running Example 2.3 are shown in the box below. There are 2 cases shown.

- Case `id=511`: This is the last thread in the first block which spans the range: [0-31,0-7, 0-1] and the last point in this range is (31,7,1) which is shown correctly as the index [1][7][31] in the figure.
- Case `id=1234567`: To understand this we need to realise that a set of 16 blocks will span the complete x range for eight consecutive y and two consecutive z values. Hence the first 1024 blocks will span the range [0-511,0-511,0-1] which is two complete x-y slices of the array, The next 1024 blocks will span the slices with z in range [2-3] and so on. Since 1234567 = 512*2411+135 we have picked the 135th thread in the 2412th block. The first 4 x-y slices account for 2048 blocks so our pick is in the 364th block in the

4–5 slice pair. Next since $364 = 22*16 + 12$ we conclude that our thread is in the 12th block in the set of 16 blocks that spans the index range $[0-511,168-175,5-6]$. This 12th block spans $[352-383,176-183,5-6]$ and since the 135th thread is offset by $[7,4,0]$ from this position we find an index set of $[359,180,5]$ or a C/C++ 3D vector index address of $[4][180][359]$.

Case 1 Last thread in first thread block:

```
D:\ > grid3D.exe 511
array size    512 x 512 x 256 = 67108864
thread block  32 x   8 x   2 = 512
thread  grid  16 x  64 x 128 = 131072
total number of threads in grid 67108864
a[1][7][31] = 511 and b[1][7][31] = 22.605309
rank_in_block = 511 rank_in_grid = 511 rank of block_rank_in_grid = 0
```

Case 2 Thread 135 in block 2411

```
D:\ grid3d.exe 1234567
array size    512 x 512 x 256 = 67108864
thread block  32 x   8 x   2 = 512
thread  grid  16 x  64 x 128 = 131072
total number of threads in grid 67108864
a[4][180][359] = 1234567 and b[4][180][359] = 1111.110718
rank_in_block = 135 rank_in_grid = 1234567 rank of
  block_rank_in_grid = 2411
```

Results from running grid3D

As our second case illustrates 3D thread blocks are somewhat complicated to visualise but their unique selling point is that they group threads spanning 3D subregions of the array into a single SM unit where the threads can cooperate. In many volume processing applications, for example, automatic anatomical segmentation of 3D MRI scans, this is a key advantage. In practice, addressing such a subregion directly from the GPU main memory is often inefficient due to the large strides between successive y and z values. In such cases caching a 3D subregion in shared memory on the SM is an important optimisation.

However, if threads in your kernel only process individual elements of the array with little collaboration between threads then 1D thread-linear address is simpler to implement and offers more scope for tuning the launch configuration. Example 2.4 shows a version of the grid3D kernel with 1D thread-linear addressing.

Example 2.4 `grid3D_linear` thread-linear processing of 3D array

```
01  #include "cuda_runtime.h"
02  #include "device_launch_parameters.h"

03  #include <stdio.h>
```

```
04   #include <stdlib.h>

05   __device__   int    a[256][512][512];   // file scope
06   __device__   float b[256][512][512];    // file scope

07   __global__ void grid3D_linear(int nx, int ny, int nz, int id)
08   {
09     int tid = blockIdx.x*blockDim.x+threadIdx.x;

10     int array_size = nx*ny*nz;
11     int total_threads = gridDim.x*blockDim.x;
12     int tid_start = tid;
13     int pass = 0;

14     while (tid < array_size){   // linear tid => (x, y, z)
15       int x =  tid%nx;           // tid      modulo nx
16       int y = (tid/nx)%ny;       // tid/nx modulo ny
17       int z =  tid/(nx*ny);      // tid/(x-y slice size)
18       // do some work here
19       a[z][y][x] = tid;
20       b[z][y][x] = sqrtf((float)a[z][y][x]);
21       if(tid == id) {
22         printf("array size    %3d x %3d x %3d = %d\n",
                  nx,ny,nz,array_size);
23         printf("thread block %3d\n",blockDim.x);
24         printf("thread  grid %3d\n",gridDim.x);
25         printf("total number of threads in grid %d\n",
                  total_threads);
26         printf("a[%d][%d][%d] = %i and b[%d][%d][%d] = %f\n",
                  z,y,x,a[z][y][x],z,y,x,b[z][y][x]);
27         printf("rank_in_block = %d rank_in_grid = %d
                  pass %d tid offset %d\n", threadIdx.x,
                  tid_start, pass, tid-tid_start);
28       }
29       tid += gridDim.x*blockDim.x;
30       pass++;
31     }          // end while
32   }

33   int main(int argc, char *argv[])
34   {
35     int id      = (argc > 1) ? atoi(argv[1]) : 12345;
36     int blocks  = (argc > 2) ? atoi(argv[2]) : 288;
37     int threads = (argc > 3) ? atoi(argv[3]) : 256;
38     grid3D_linear<<<blocks,threads>>>(512,512,256,id);
39     return 0;
40   }
```

```
D:\ > grid3d_linear.exe 1234567 288 256
array size    512 x 512 x 256 = 67108864
thread block 256
thread  grid 288
total number of threads in grid 73728
a[4][363][135] = 1234567 and b[4][363][135] = 1111.110718
rank_in_block = 135 rank_in_grid = 54919 rank of
 block_rank_in_grid = 214 pass 16
```

Results from example 2.4 using the `grid3D_linear` kernel to process 3D arrays with thread-linear-addressing. The displayed array element has different 3D indices as compared to example 2.2 even though its linear index is the same as used in that example.

Description of Example 2.4

- Lines 1–8: These lines are unchanged from Example 2.3 except we have renamed the kernel.
- Line 9: The variable `tid` is set to the current thread's rank in the grid of threads blocks using the standard formula for 1D thread and grid-blocks.
- Lines 10–13: We set some variables used in the later print statements here. Note the formula for the `total_threads` is now the simple 1D case.
- Lines 14–31: These lines are the `while` loop used for thread-linear addressing.
- Lines 15–17: These lines show how to convert a thread-linear address into 3D coordinates with x the most rapidly varying coordinate and z the least rapidly varying. Note the division and modulus (%) operators are expensive and could be replaced by masking and shifting operations if `nx` and `ny` are known powers of 2. This gives better performance at the price of a less general kernel. For the case where both `nx` and `ny` are 512 we could use:

```
int x =  tid & 0x01ff;          // x = bits 0-8
int y = (tid >> 9) & 0x01ff;    // y = bits 9-17
int z =  tid >> 18;             // z = bits 18 and above
```

Calculation of 3D coordinates by extraction of bit fields from thread-linear address. The two 9-bit masks are for case where both nx and ny are equal to 512.

The formulae used to convert between a 3D `(x,y,z)` index triad and a linear index are shown in the box. Lines 15–17 here are an example of this:

```
Relations Between Linear and 3D indices
index = (z*ny+y)*nx+x

x = index % nx
y = (index / nx) % ny
z = index / (nx*ny)
```

- Lines 19–28: This is similar to the previous example except we are using the variable name `tid` instead of `thread_rank_in_grid`.
- Line 29: Here we increment `tid` using a stride equal to the length of the entire thread-grid
- Line 30: Here we increment a counter `pass` and continue to the next pass of the while loop. The variable `pass` is only used as part of the information printed. The actual linear address being used by a given `tid` within the `while` loop is `rank_in_grid+pass*total_threads`.
- Lines 33–40: The `main` routine now accepts two additional user arguments `blocks` and `threads`, which define the kernel launch parameters.

The results for the thread with a linear index of 1234567, the same value as used in Example 2.2, shows that this linear index corresponds to a 3D element [4][363][135] whereas in Example 2.2 using 3D grid and thread blocks it corresponded to the element [4][180][359]. Neither result is "wrong". The difference merely reflects the different order in which elements of the arrays are encountered.

Next we return to the CUDA topic of occupancy.

2.4 Latency Hiding and Occupancy

When a new kernel begins execution, a 32-thread warp will begin execution on each of the warp-engines on the GPU. These warps become *active-warps* and will remain *resident* until all warps in their thread block are complete. A likely early step will be loading an item of data from global memory but loading this data from global memory has a latency of several hundred clock-cycles. Thus, the active threads have to wait for their data to arrive before they can proceed – while waiting they are termed *stalled* threads. In fact, the hardware is quite sophisticated and the threads will not stall until an instruction that actually uses the pending data is reached. This means that a programmer can hide some of the latency by doing work independent of the data between requesting that data and using it. While useful, there may be limited scope for this in practice, and writing instructions in an unnatural order makes code harder to debug and maintain – probably it's best to rely on the compiler to do this job for you.

A key feature of the GPU design is that each warp engine can process several active warps in an interleaved fashion, if one of its active warps stalls, a warp-engine will switch to another active warp capable of running with no loss of cycles. Efficient switching between warps is possible because each thread in an active warp maintains its own state and set of registers. This is in dramatic contrast to the standard CPU architecture where a single set of registers is shared by all active threads making task switching an expensive operation. Thus, a warp-engine can continue executing instructions until all its active-warps have stalled waiting for memory access. Such a multiple stall may occur once at the start of a kernel but, provided each thread does "enough" computation between each global memory access, any further stalls are avoided. Note, enough computation is the number of instructions that could be executed in the time taken for a "typical" memory access. This can be several hundred instructions on a modern GPU. Latency hiding is illustrated in Figure 2.1.

Figure 2.1 shows four thread blocks, T1–T4. On the left they each run briefly and then stall waiting for a memory access. The access requests are shown as vertical arrows. The dispatch of the requested data is shown by the slanted dashed lines. Most of the latency

Table 2.2 *Kernel launch configurations for maximum occupancy*

Thread Block Size	Blocks per SM	Blocks per Grid if GPU has 20 SMs	Registers per Thread	Bytes of shared memory per Thread Block
32	64	1280	32	1 KB
64	32	640	32	2 KB
128	16	320	32	4 KB
256	8	160	32	8 KB
512	4	80	32	16 KB
1024	2	40	32	32 KB

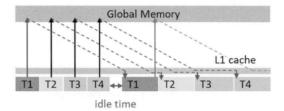

Figure 2.1 Latency hiding on GPUs

from T1's first memory request is hidden by the initial running of T2–T4. After a small amount of additional idle time T1's data arrives in L1 cache and T1 resumes execution using this data, T1 then stalls again with a second memory access shown as the grey vertical line. However, now there is no further idle time as data will now reach the L1 cache before it is needed.

On the Pascal architecture each SM has four warp-engines each capable of running up to 16 active warps, or equivalently 64 warps or 2048 threads on the SM. Thus, if the global memory latency is 400 cycles, each thread would need to do only 25 cycles worth of computation between memory accesses to fully hide this latency. This is a best-case situation because the kernel launch configuration may restrict the maximum number of active warps to less than 16. The *occupancy* of a kernel is defined as:

$$\text{occupancy} = \frac{\text{Actual number of active warps}}{\text{Maximum number of active warps}}.$$

The factors which may limit occupancy are the thread block size, the number of thread blocks, the number of registers used by each thread and the amount of shared memory used by a thread block. The number of thread blocks should be an integer multiple of the number of SMs in the GPU sufficient to give 2048 threads per block. There are also limits of 64K 32-bit registers and 64 KB of shared memory per SM. These limits are illustrated in Table 2.2 for a Pascal GPU with 20 SMs. Note, the number of registers allocated to each thread is determined by the compiler and depends on the complexity of the code. For full occupancy, the hardware has sufficient registers for 32 registers per thread. This value can be inspected and/or overridden by using NVCC compiler switches `--maxrregcount` and `--resource-usage`.

Full occupancy is more important for memory bound kernels than it is for compute bound kernels but it is always a good idea to keep your kernel code compact and straightforward as this will allow the compiler to allocate registers more effectively. It is also a good idea to split long calculations into stages and use separate kernels for each stage. Remember that the contents of GPU global memory is preserved between kernel launches.

It is now time to move on to more interesting GPU code where threads have to actively cooperate to perform a calculation.

2.5 Parallel Patterns

Parallel programming for GPUs running vast numbers of threads does require some rethinking of your approach to coding. Methods that work well in single CPUs or codes running a small number of independent threads may need to be rethought.

2.5.1 Avoid If Statements

One big difference is that branch statements are problematic in CUDA code, for example consider a CUDA kernel containing the following code:

```
if (flag == 0) function1(a1,a2,...);
else           function2(b1,b2,...);
```

If all the 32 threads in a particular warp have flag=0, then all threads will call function1 and there is very little performance loss, the same is true if none of the 32 threads have flag set to zero. However, if even just one of these threads has flag set to a non-zero value while the other 31 threads have flag=0 then we get a so-called *branch-divergence*. The system handles this by serializing the calls to the two functions, that is, the subset of threads in the warp with flag=0 execute the call to function1 while the threads having flag non-zero stay idle. Then, when the function has returned for all active threads, the else clause calling function2 is executed by the previously idle threads while previously active threads are now idle.[7]

> **CUDA Coding tip**
>
> - Avoid diverging if statements
> - But only within 32-thread warps
> - Modest conditional execution, e.g.:
>
>   ```
>   if(flag==0) x= x+1;
>   ```
>
>   is less harmful.

If the functions concerned are modest and require only a small fraction of the kernel's execution time, no great harm is done, but otherwise there can be up to a factor two drop in performance. If the called functions also have branch divergences the performance penalty is even worse.

If you have not encountered parallel programming on GPUs before, the need to remove all `if` statements from your code may seem like a deal breaker – but as we shall see in our examples this can be achieved quite straightforwardly in many cases. I also have to confess that I enjoy the intellectual challenge of designing good GPU code.

2.6 Parallel Reduce

The parallel reduce operation, mentioned in Chapter 1, is a good place to begin our discussion of parallel coding patterns. This is a good example of the more general problem of performing the same operation on a large set of numbers. Reduce itself involves finding the arithmetic sum of the numbers, but other operations such as max or min would require similar code.

As a specific case, consider the problem of summing N floating point numbers stored in the GPUs global memory. The first point to recognise is that each data item just requires a single add; thus we will be limited by memory access speed not arithmetic performance. This is the exact opposite to the situation in Example 1.3. We want to use as many threads as possible in order to hide memory latency efficiency so our basic algorithm is as shown in the box and illustrated in Figure 2.2.

Reduce Algorithm 1: Parallel sum of N numbers

- Use N/2 threads to get N/2 pairwise sums
- Set N = N/2 and iterate till N=1

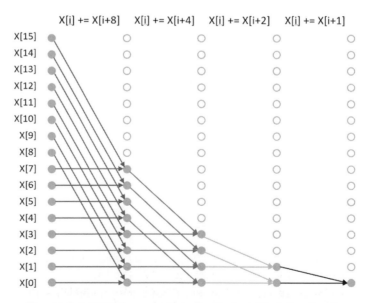

Figure 2.2 Pairwise reduction for the last 16 elements of x

The GPU implementation of this algorithm is shown in Example 2.5. The host code which initialises the data and manages most of the calculation is also shown and discussed in this example.

Description of Example 2.5

- Lines 1–3: All the necessary includes are here. The file cx.h is part of our example set and contains all the standard includes and some helpful definitions; it is fully described in Appendix G. The header cxtimers.h defines a portable C++ based timer object.
- Lines 4–8: Show the reduce0 kernel which is very simple; each thread finds its rank, tid, in the grid and, making the tacit assumption that tid is in the range 0 to m-1, adds the appropriate element from the top half of the array to the bottom half. At this point, it is worth pausing to admire the simplicity of the kernel code. We have been able to directly express the idea for implementing a parallel reduction with a 2-line kernel. The method is illustrated in Figure 2.2 and shows the last few steps. Another thing to think about when looking at kernel code is the sheer power of the GPU; line 7 which does the additions will be executed in parallel by all the cores on the GPU, potentially delivering one or more operations for each core on each clock-cycle. My RTX 2070 GPU has 2304 cores running at about 1.1 GHz and can deliver several 10^{12} operations per second.
- Line 11: Here we set the array size N to a user supplied value or a default of 2^{24}.
- Lines 12–13: Here we allocate thrust host and device vectors x and dev_x to hold the data.
- Lines 15–17: These lines initialise a C++ random number generator and use it to fill x. The use of generators from <random> is much preferred over the deprecated rand() function from ancient C.

Example 2.5 reduce0 kernel and associated host code

```
01   #include "cx.h"
02   #include "cxtimers.h"
03   #include <random>

04   __global__ void reduce0(float *x, int m)
05   {
06     int tid = blockDim.x*blockIdx.x+threadIdx.x;
07     x[tid] += x[tid+m];
08   }

09   int main(int argc, char *argv[])
10   {
11     int N = (argc >1) ? atoi(argv[1]) : 1 << 24; // 2²⁴

12     thrust::host_vector<float>        x(N);
13     thrust::device_vector<float> dev_x(N);

14     // initialise x with random numbers and copy to dx
15     std::default_random_engine gen(12345678);
16     std::uniform_real_distribution<float> fran(0.0,1.0);
17     for(int k = 0; k<N; k++) x[k] = fran(gen);
```

```
18      dx = x;   // H2D copy (N words)

19      cx::timer tim;
20      double host_sum = 0.0;    // host reduce!
21      for(int k = 0; k<N; k++) host_sum += x[k];
22      double t1 = tim.lap_ms();

23      // simple GPU reduce for N = power of 2
24      tim.reset();
25      for(int m = N/2; m>0; m /= 2) {
26        int threads = std::min(256,m);
27        int blocks  =  std::max(m/256,1);
28        reduce0<<<blocks, threads>>>(dev_x.data().get(), m);
29      }
30      cudaDeviceSynchronize();
31      double t2 = tim.lap_ms();

32      double gpu_sum = dev_x[0];   // D2H copy (1 word)
33      printf("sum of %d random numbers: host %.1f %.3f ms,
                  GPU %.1f %.3f \n", N, host_sum, t1, gpu_sum, t2);
34      return 0;
35    }


D:\ > reduce0.exe
sum of 16777216 random numbers: host 8388314.9 14.012 ms
                                 GPU 8388315.0  0.535 ms
```

- Line 18: The contents of x are copied from the host to dev_x on the GPU. The details of the transfer are handled by thrust.
- Lines 19–22: A timed loop to perform the reduction on the host using a simple for loop.
- Lines 24–31: Implement the GPU-based parallel iteration of Algorithm 1. For each pass through the for loop the reduce0 kernel called in line 28 causes the top half of the array dev_x to be "folded" down to an array of size m by adding the top m elements to the bottom m elements. The last pass through the loop has m=1 and leaves the final sum in dev_x[0]; this value is copied back to the host in line 35. Lines 28–29: Within the for loop the kernel launch parameters blocks and threads are set so that the total number of threads in the grid is exactly m. This code will fail if N is not a power of 2 due to rounding down errors at one or more steps in the process.

In CUDA programs a kernel launch such as that used in line 28 will not block the host which will proceed to the next line of the host program without waiting for the kernel call to finish. In this case that means all the kernel calls (23 in all for N=2^{24}) will be rapidly queued to run successively on the GPU. In principle the host can do other CPU work while these kernels are running on the GPU. In this case we just want to measure the duration of the reduction operation so before making the time measurement we must use a cudaDeviceSynchronize call in line 30 which causes the host to wait for all pending GPU operations to complete before continuing. This kind of synchronisation issue often occurs in parallel code.

- Lines 32–33: Here we copy the final sum in the dev_x[0] back to the host, again using thrust, and print results.

The bottom line shows the results obtained running this program with the default value of 2^{24} for the number of values to be summed. Note the kernel execution time of 0.535 ms is too short a single measurement to be reliable. The values shown in these reduce examples were in fact obtained as averages of 10,000 runs using a for loop around kernel calls. An alternative method would be to use the Nsight Compute profiling tool, but our simple host-based method using cx::timer is a good starting point.

An interesting feature of the results obtained is that the host calculation uses a 64-bit double variable to accumulate the sum of the x values but the GPU does not. However, the results differ by only 1.1 parts in 10^{-8} – this is about the best that can be expected from a 32-bit floating point calculation; rounding errors have not accumulated in the GPU calculation. On the other hand, if we change the variable host_sum (line 23 of the host calculation in Example 2.4) to a float instead of a double the accuracy of the host calculation falls to only about 3 parts in 10^{-5} thus rounding errors do accumulate in the host calculation. This difference is due to the fact that the GPU accumulates many intermediate partial sums and thus tends to be always adding numbers of similar sizes. Although this improvement is data dependent, this is encouraging to see, as we plan to use 32-bit floats in our GPU calculations whenever possible.

While accurate, our kernel is very inefficient and unlike the compute bound problem in Chapter 1, reduction is a memory bound problem and the reduce0 kernel does not handle this well.

Firstly, the only calculation done by each thread is a single addition, and secondly the statement:

$$x[tid] \; += \; x[tid+m],$$

triggers three global memory operations, namely loading both the values stored in x[tid] and x[tid+m] into GPU registers and then storing the sum of these values back into x[tid]. If we could accumulate partial sums in local registers, that would reduce the number of global memory accesses needed for each addition down to one, which offers a speed-up by a potential factor of three.

Secondly, the host calls the kernel iteratively, halving the array size at each step to complete the reduction process, leaving the final sum in the first array element. The effect of this is to double the number of times the x[tid] += x[tid+m] statement is performed. If we could instead perform the iteration inside the kernel that could also reduce the number of memory accesses required.

Finally, the kernel of Example 2.5 is not general enough, the array size must be a power of 2 and the host has to make multiple calls to the kernel using a carefully crafted sequence of launch parameters. A better solution is to use thread-linear addressing, with user defined values of blocks and threads to get something like Example 2.6:

Example 2.6 `reduce1` kernel using thread-linear addressing

```
04   __global__ void reduce1(float *x, int N)
05   {
06     int tid = blockDim.x*blockIdx.x+threadIdx.x;
06.1   float tsum = 0.0f;
06.2   for(int k=tid; k<N; k += gridDim.x*blockDim.x)
                                         tsum += x[k];

07     x[tid] = tsum; // store partial sums in first
08   }              // gridDim.x*blockDim.x elements of x
       . . .
24     tim.reset();
25     reduce1<<< blocks, threads >>>(dx.data().get(),N);
26     reduce1<<< 1, threads >>>(dx.data().get(),blocks*threads);
27     reduce1<<< 1,1 >>>(dx.data().get(),threads);
30     cudaDeviceSynchronize();
31     double t2 = tim.lap_ms();
32     double gpu_sum = dx[0];   //D2H copy (1 word)

D:\ > reduce1.exe
sum of 16777216 numbers:  host 8388889.0 14.012 ms
                          GPU 8388315.5  0.267 ms
```

Description of Example 2.6

- Lines 5–10: This is the reduce1 kernel, now 4 lines long. We use thread-linear addressing to sum all the N values contained in x into lower `block*threads` elements. Each thread accumulates its own partial sum in its copy of the register variable `tsum` and then stores the final result in `x[tid]` where `tid` is the thread's unique rank in the grid. In this example we have used a `for` loop instead of a `while` clause to keep the code compact.

  Note line 7, where we change the value of an element of x, requires thought. Not all threads actually run at the same time so using the same array for a kernel's input and output is always potentially dangerous. Can we be sure no thread other than `tid` needs the original value in `x[tid]`? If the answer is no, then the kernel would have a *race condition* and the results would be undefined. In the present case we can be sure because every thread uses a separate disjoint subset of the elements of x. If in doubt you should use different arrays for kernel input and output.

- Lines 28–30: Replace the for loop in lines 28–32 of the original. Now we make three calls to reduce1, the first uses the full thread-grid defined by the user set variables blocks and threads. After this call the lower `blocks*threads` elements of x contain partial sums. The second kernel call uses just 1 thread block of size threads, after this call the partial sums are in the first threads elements of x. The third call uses just 1 thread to sum threads elements of dx and leave to total sum in the first element. Clearly the last two kernel calls do not make efficient use of the GPU.

The bottom line shows the time required for the reduce1 kernel; the host time is unchanged but the GPU time is about half that required for reduce0.

Table 2.3 *Features of GPU generations from Kepler to Ampere*

GPU Generation	Kepler		Maxwell			Pascal			Volta	Turing	Ampere
Compute Capability	3.5	3.7	5.0	5.2	5.3	6.0	6.1	6.2	7.0	7.5	8.0
Shared Mem per SM (KB)	48	112	64	96	64	64	96	64	96	64	164
Max Resident Threads per SM					2048					1024	2048
Shared Mem per Thread (bytes)	24	56	32	48	32	32	48	32	48	64	82
4-byte Registers per Thread	32	64	32	32	32	32	32	32	32	64	32

The `reduce1` is about twice as fast as `reduce0` which is not a bad start but we can do more. Our `reduce1` kernel is also much more user friendly, it can cope with any value of the input array size N and the user is free to tune the launch configuration parameters `blocks` and `threads`.

Notice that in the last reduce step, line 27 of Example 2.6, we used a single thread running alone to sum `threads` values stored in x. We can do better than this by getting the threads in each thread block to cooperate with each other.

A key feature of NVIDIA GPUs is shared memory which allows the threads within a thread block to cooperate efficiently. A thread block running on the GPU can reserve an allocation of shared memory, and all threads in the thread block can then read from and write to that memory. Threads in different thread blocks of a kernel get different allocations of shared-memory and cannot read or write to each other's allocations. Each SM unit has a pool of shared memory which is divided between all the currently resident thread blocks that request shared memory. Of course, device global memory is also visible to all threads on all thread blocks but accessing shared memory is much faster and can be as fast as using registers.

NVIDIA GPUs have at least 48 KB of shared memory per SM unit and more recently 64K. The precise amount depends on the CC level and is summarised in Table 2.3. It is clear from the table that at the thread level shared memory is a scarce resource; there is enough for only 8 or 16 4-byte words per thread. If more is required one can try using more shared memory per thread at the expense of lower occupancy. The runtime system will automatically run fewer kernels per SM if necessary. If a kernel requests more shared memory than the total available on an SM then the kernel launch will fail. Shared memory featured very prominently in early CUDA tutorials and books because these GPUs had little or no caching capability for global memory accesses. More recent GPUs have good L1 and L2 caching and in particular L1 caching can sometimes work well as an alternative to using shared memory. Interestingly devices with CC 7.0 and above have a single fast memory resource that can be shared between L1 and shared memory partitions in different proportions for different kernels.

In our next Example 2.7 we use shared memory to enable the threads in each thread block to sum their individual accumulated totals and then write a single word with the block-sum to external memory. The scheme of Figure 2.2 is again used for this intra-block reduction.

Example 2.7 reduce2 kernel showing use of shared memory

```
01   __global__ void reduce2(float *y, float *x, int N)
02   {
03     extern __shared__ float tsum[]; // Dynamic Shared Mem

04     int id = threadIdx.x;
05     int tid = blockDim.x*blockIdx.x+threadIdx.x;
06     int stride = gridDim.x*blockDim.x;
07     tsum[id] = 0.0f;
08     for(int k=tid;k<N;k+=stride) tsum[id] += x[k];
09     __syncthreads();
       // power of 2 reduction loop
10     for(int k=blockDim.x/2; k>0; k /= 2){
11       if(id<k) tsum[id] += tsum[id+k];
12       __syncthreads();
13     }
       // store one value per thread block
14     if(id==0) y[blockIdx.x] = tsum[0];
15   }

16   int main(int argc, char *argv[])
17   {
18     int N = (argc > 1) ? atoi(argv[1]) : 1 << 24;
19     int blocks  = (argc > 2) ? atoi(argv[2]) : 256;
20     int threads = (argc > 3) ? atoi(argv[3]) : 256;
21     thrust::host_vector<float>    x(N);
23     thrust::device_vector<float>  dx(N);
23     thrust::device_vector<float>  dy(blocks);

24     // initialise x with random numbers
25     std::default_random_engine gen(12345678);
26     std::uniform_real_distribution<float> fran(0.0,1.0);
27     for(int k = 0; k<N; k++) x[k] = fran(gen);
28     dx = x;   // H2D copy (N words)

29     cx::timer tim;
30     double host_sum = 0.0;    // host reduce!
31     for(int k = 0; k<N; k++) host_sum += x[k];
32     double t1 = tim.lap_ms();

33     // simple GPU reduce for any value of N
34     tim.reset();
35     reduce2<<<blocks,threads,threads*sizeof(float)>>>
                    (dy.data().get(),dx.data().get(),N);
36     reduce2<<<1, blocks, blocks*sizeof(float)>>>
                    (dx.data().get(),dy.data().get(),blocks);
```

```
37      cudaDeviceSynchronize();
38      double t2 = tim.lap_ms();
39      double gpu_sum = dx[0];   // D2H copy (1 word)
40      printf("sum of %d numbers: host %.1f %.3f ms
41           GPU %.1f %.3f ms\n",N,host_sum,t1,gpu_sum,t2);
42      return 0;
43  }


D:\ > reduce2.exe 16777216 256 256
sum of 16777216 numbers: host 8388314.9 14.012 ms
                          GPU 8388314.5 0.202 ms
```

Description of Example 2.7

- Lines 1–9: This is the reduce2 kernel which uses shared memory.
- Line 1: This kernel uses y as an output array and x as the input array with N elements. The previous reduce1 kernel used x for both input and output.
- Line 3: Here we declare the float array tsum to be a shared memory array of size determined by the host at kernel launch time. Shared memory is on-chip and very fast. Each SM has its own block of shared memory which has to be shared by all the active thread blocks on that SM. All threads in any given thread block share tsum and can read or write to any of its elements. Inter-block communication is not possible using tsum because each thread block has a separate allocation for its tsum. For this kernel, an array size of blockDim.x is assumed for y and it is up to the host code to ensure that the correct amount has been reserved. Incorrectly specified kernel launches could cause hard-to-find bugs.
- Lines 4–6: To prepare for thread-linear addressing we set id to the rank of the current thread in its thread block, tid to the rank of the current thread in the whole grid and stride to the number of threads in the whole grid.
- Line 7: Each thread "owns" one element of tsum, tsum[id] for this part of the calculation. Here we set the element to zero.
- Line 8: Here each thread sums the subset of elements of x corresponding to x[id+n*stride] for all valid integers $n \geq 0$. Although there is a large stride between successive elements, this is a *parallel* calculation and adjacent threads will simultaneously be reading adjacent elements of x so this arrangement is maximally efficient for reading GPU main memory. Note that for large arrays, most of the kernel's execution time is used on this statement and very little calculation is done per memory access.
- Line 9: The next step of the algorithm requires threads to read elements of tsum that have been updated by *different* threads in the thread block. Technically that's fine – this is what shared memory is for. However, not all threads in the thread block run at the same time and we must be sure that *all* threads in the thread block have completed line 8 before *any* of the threads proceed. The CUDA function __syncthreads() does exactly this; it acts as a barrier, all (non-exited) threads in the thread block must reach line 9 before any of them can proceed. Note that __syncthreads only synchronises threads in a single thread block. This is in contrast to the host function cudaDeviceSynchronize() which ensures that all pending CUDA kernels and memory transfers have completed before allowing the host to continue. If you want to ensure that all threads in all thread blocks have reached a particular point in a kernel then in most cases your only option is to split the kernel into two separate kernels and use cudaDeviceSynchronize() between their launches.[8]

- Lines 10–13: This is the implementation of the power of 2 reduction scheme of Figure 2.2 implemented to sum the values in tsum on a thread block. This section of code assumes that blockDim.x is a power of 2. Note that the number of active threads reduces by a factor of 2 on each pass through the for loop. Older tutorials tend to dwell on further optimisation of this loop by explicitly unrolling and exploiting synchronicity within 32-thread warps. This will be discussed in the next chapter on cooperative groups. For now, note further optimisation of this loop is only important for smaller datasets.
- Line 14: The final block sum accumulated in tsum[0] is stored in the output array y using blockIdx.x as an index.
- Lines 16–45: This is the main routine; much of it is similar to the previous example and here we will just mention differences.
- Lines 18–20: Here we give the user the option to set the array size N and the launch parameters blocks and threads. Note blocks needs to be a power of 2 for the reduce2 kernel to work properly.
- Line 23: We now allocate a device array dy having dimension blocks. This new array will hold the individual block wide reduction sums.
- Line 35: Here we call the reduce2 kernel for the first time to process the whole dx array with the block sums being stored in the output array dy. Note the third kernel argument requesting a shared memory allocation of threads 4-byte floats for each active thread block. A large value here may result in reduced occupancy.
- Line 36: Here we call reduce2 again but with the array arguments swapped round. This has the result of causing the values stored in y by the previous kernel call, to themselves be summed with the total placed in x[0]. This requires a launch configuration of a single thread block of size blocks threads.

The result at the end of the listing shows that reduce2 is about 2.65 times faster than reduce0.

A worthwhile optimisation of the reduce2 kernel would be to drop the restriction that blocks must be a power of 2. This is because in many GPUs the number of SM units is not a power of 2. For example, my GPU has 36 SMs so to keep all SMs equally busy it is better to use 288 rather than 256 for the number of user set value of blocks. We can do this by replacing blockDim.x in line 10 of the reduce2 kernel by the smallest power of 2 greater than or equal to blocks. For blocks = 288 this would be 512. The effect of doing this is that in the first pass when k=256, threads with rank 0 to 31 will add values from tsum[256] to tsum[287] to their tsum values. We also have to add an out-of-range check to prevent threads 32-255 from attempting out-of-range additions. The modified reduce3 kernel is shown in Example 2.8.

Example 2.8 reduce3 kernel permitting non-power of two thread blocks

```
01   __global__ void reduce3(float *y,float *x,int N)
02   {
03     extern __shared__ float tsum[];

04     int id = threadIdx.x;
05     int tid = blockDim.x*blockIdx.x+threadIdx.x;
06     int stride = gridDim.x*blockDim.x;
07     tsum[id] = 0.0f;
08     for(int k=tid;k<N;k+=stride) tsum[id] += x[k];
09     __syncthreads();
```

```
        // next higher power of 2
10.1    int block2 = cx::pow2ceil(blockDim.x);
        // power of 2 reduction loop
10.2    for(int k=block2/2; k>0; k >>= 1){
11          if(id<k && id+k < blockDim.x) tsum[id] += tsum[id+k];
12          __syncthreads();
13      }
        // store one value per block
14      if(id==0) y[blockIdx.x] = tsum[0];
15  }


D:\ >reduce3.exe 16777216 288 256
sum of 16777216 numbers: host 8388314.9 14.012 ms
                          GPU 8388314.5  0.196 ms
```

Description of Example 2.8

In this example the kernel and main routine (not shown) are the same as in Example 2.7 except for lines 10 and 11 of the kernel.

- Line 10.1: Here we add a new variable block2 which is set the value of blockDim.x rounded up to the lowest power of 2 greater than or equal to blockDim.x. We use the cx utility function pow2ceil for this. That function is implemented using the NVIDIA intrinsic function __clz(int n) which returns the number of the most significant non-zero bit in n. This is a device-only function.
- Line 10.2: This is the same as line 10 in reduce2 except we use the rounded up block2/2 as the starting value of k.
- Line 11: This corresponds to line 11 of reduce2 with an added out-of-range check on id+k.

In the last line we see that launching this kernel with exactly 8 thread blocks per SM gives a speed-up of 2.73 compared to reduce0, slightly better than reduce2.

The reduce3 kernel is about 70 times faster than the single core host version. While this is not quite as spectacular as our Chapter 1 result for a CPU bound calculation, reduction is a memory bandwidth bound calculation with just one add per read of 4-bytes of memory so we expect reduced performance. Given that the GPU memory bandwidth is only about 10 times that of the CPU the factor 70 improvement shows that other GPU features including the latency hiding are helping speed up this memory bound problem. The last trick to try is explicitly unrolling the loop in lines 10–13.

Example 2.9 reduce4 kernel with explicit loop unrolling

```
01  __global__ void reduce4(float * y, float * x,int N)
02  {
03      extern __shared__ float tsum[];

04      int id = threadIdx.x;
```

```
05      int tid = blockDim.x*blockIdx.x+threadIdx.x;
06      int stride = gridDim.x*blockDim.x;
07      tsum[id] = 0.0f;
08      for(int k=tid;k<N;k+=stride) tsum[id] += x[k];
09      __syncthreads();

10      if(id<256 && id+256 < blockDim.x)
                    tsum[id] += tsum[id+256]; __syncthreads();
11      if(id<128) tsum[id] += tsum[id+128]; __syncthreads();
12      if(id< 64) tsum[id] += tsum[id+ 64]; __syncthreads();
13      if(id< 32) tsum[id] += tsum[id+ 32]; __syncthreads();

14      // only warp 0 array elements used from here
15      if(id< 16) tsum[id] += tsum[id+16]; __syncwarp();
16      if(id< 8)  tsum[id] += tsum[id+ 8]; __syncwarp();
17      if(id< 4)  tsum[id] += tsum[id+ 4]; __syncwarp();
18      if(id< 2)  tsum[id] += tsum[id+ 2]; __syncwarp();
19      if(id==0)  y[blockIdx.x] = tsum[0]+tsum[1];
20    }

D:\ >reduce4.exe 16777216 288 256
sum of 16777216 numbers: host 8388314.9 14.012 ms
                          GPU 8388314.5  0.195 ms
```

Description of Example 2.9

- Line 1–9: These are the same as in the previous example.
- Lines 10–19: These replace the for loop and last line of the previous example. Here we have unrolled the loop on the explicit assumption that the number of threads per block, blockkDim.x, is in the range [256,511]. In practice we used 256 threads and 288 blocks for the first call to reduce4 and 288 threads and 1 block for the second call to reduce4. This kernel could easily be generalised to work with a larger range of thread block sizes, for example, by making the thread block size a template parameter. You can find such generalisations in many tutorials; for example, the very early blog by Mark Harris: "Optimizing Parallel Reduction in CUDA, November 2 2007" downloadable from https://developer.download.nvidia.com/assets/cuda/files/reduction.pdf.
- Line 10: This is the first step in the parallel reduction chain; values in tsum[256-511] (if any) are added to those in tsum[0-255]. This line is needed for second kernel call with blockDim.x=288. The if statement is then necessary to avoid out of range errors for threads 32-255.
- Lines 11–13: These lines are the next three steps in the parallel reduction. No out-of-range checks are needed here on the assumption blockDim.x is at least 256.

Note there is a __syncthreads after each step in lines 10–13. These calls are necessary to ensure that all threads in the thread block have completed their addition before any of them proceed to the next step.

- Lines 15–19: These lines are the final five steps in the parallel reduction tree. In these lines only the first 32 threads participate. These threads are all in the same warp so we can replace __syncthreads with the much faster __syncwarp. For devices of CC < 7 all threads in the same warp act in strict lockstep so here it is possible to rely on implicit warp synchronisation and omit the __syncwarp calls entirely. You will find this done in early (now deprecated) tutorials. Even if you only have access to older devices, we strongly recommend that you always use syncwarp where it would be necessary on newer devices to maintain code portability.

The result shown in the last line shows at best a tiny improvement compared to reduce3.

The performance difference between reduce3 and reduce4 is small but reduce4 has introduced us to warp level programming. We will return to the reduce problem in the next chapter and show how warp-based programming can be taken much further.

Next we will discuss shared memory in more detail and then explore another application, namely matrix multiplication.

2.7 Shared Memory

Shared memory is a fast access memory pool of size typically 64 KB available on each SM. Kernels can elect to use shared memory by declaring one or more array or scalar variables as prefixed with the decoration __shared__.

Each thread block running on an SM gets a separate allocation of the required size from the shared memory pool. If a kernel has thread blocks requiring more than 32 KB (i.e. more than half the total available) then only one thread block can run on the SM at once which severely reduces occupancy. Thus, shared memory use is one of the factors to be considered when optimising occupancy.

As the name implies, shared memory is shared by all the threads in a thread block, i.e. any part of it can be read or written by any thread in the thread block. Note that, while this is extremely useful in many situations, the sharing is local – shared memory is not shared between thread blocks. The contents of the shared memory belonging to a given thread block are lost when that thread block exits.

Shared memory allocation can be either *static* or *dynamic*. For static shared memory allocation the required sizes are declared in the kernel code using values known a compile time, for example using:

```
__shared__ float data[256];
```

This is arguably the simplest method but lacks flexibility. Shared memory array sizes typically depend on the number of threads in the thread block, thus if they are fixed at compile time then so is the size of the thread block.

Dynamic shared memory allocation is an alternative where the kernel does not specify the size of an array but declares an externally allocated shared pointer, for example:

```
extern __shared__ float *data; or equivalently extern __shared__
    float data[];
```

In this case the actually required memory size is specified by the host at kernel launch time using the value (in bytes) as third kernel launch third parameter. Since this value can be a variable determined during program execution this method of memory allocation known as dynamic. Examples 2.4 and 2.5 use this method.

Static memory declarations are usually placed at the start of your kernel code, but this is not mandatory; obviously like all variables, their declaration needs to precede their use.[9] More than one shared array or variable can be declared in a single kernel, the static allocation case is straightforward, for example:

```
__shared__ float sx[256];
__shared__ unsigned short su[256];
```

will work as expected creating separate arrays with a total memory requirement of 1024+512 bytes. However, the corresponding dynamic allocation in kernel code:

```
extern __shared__ float sx[];
extern __shared__ unsigned short su[];
```

will compile successfully without warnings but both arrays will start at the *same* address – namely the starting address of the reserved block of shared memory that is allocated when the kernel is runs. Although annoying and bug prone, this is the only possible thing the compiler can do since it does not know the array sizes at compile time. Thus, during execution, writing to either array will write to both, leading to kernel failure or (worse) hard to find bugs. In order to fix this problem, we need to modify the kernel code so that only one array is declared `extern` and all other arrays are declared as pointers with appropriately calculated offsets from the `extern` array as shown in Example 2.10.

Example 2.10 `shared_example` kernel showing multiple array allocations

```
01  __global__ void shared_example(float *x,float *y,int m)
02  {
03      // notice order of declarations,
04      // longest variable type first
05      // shortest variable type last
        // NB sx is a pointer to the start of the shared
06      extern __shared__ float sx[]; // memory pool

07      ushort* su = (ushort *)(&sx[blockDim.x]); // start after sx
08      char*   sc =   (char *)(&su[blockDim.x]); // start after su

09      int id = threadIdx.x;

10      sx[id] = 3.1459*x[id];
11      su[id] = id*id;
12      sc[id] = id%128;
        // do useful work here
        . . .
30      int threads = (argc >1) ? atoi(argv[1]) : 256;
31      int blocks =   (size+threads-1)/threads;
32      int shared = threads*(sizeof(float) +
                          sizeof(ushort) + sizeof(char));
33      shared_example<<< blocks, threads, shared >>>
                          (dx_ptr,dy_ptr,size);
```

Description of Example 2.10

The start of the kernel using three dynamic shared memory arrays is shown in lines 1–12 of this example. Here we will assume that the required size of each array is the number of threads in the thread block, i.e. `threadDim.x` for 1D thread grids.

- In line 6: A single dynamically allocated shared memory array `sx` of type `float` is declared. Note that sx is just a C style pointer to an array of floats. We could have used "`float *sx;`" instead of "`float sx[]`"
- Lines 7–8: Here pointers to two additional arrays, `su` and `sc`, are declared using pointer arithmetic to calculate their offsets from the start of sx. In line 7 the `su` pointer is set to the address after `blockDim.x` floating point elements of the array `sx` and then cast to the `ushort` pointer type. Similarly, in line 8 the `sc` pointer is set to the address after `blockDim.x` `ushort` elements of the array `su` and then cast to the `char` type.
- Lines 9–12: Here we demonstrate use of the arrays, the variable `id` is set to the current threads's rank in the thread block and then used normally to index the three arrays.
- Lines 30–33: These show a fragment of the corresponding host code containing the kernel.
  - Line 30: The launch parameter `threads` is set using an optional user supplied value.
  - Line 31: The parameter `blocks` is then set as usual. in lines 30–31.
  - Line 32: A third launch parameter `shared` is set in line 32. The value stored in `shared` is calculated as the total number of *bytes* necessary for the three arrays.
  - Line 33: This shows the kernel launch using three parameters in the launch configuration.

One subtle detail of this example is that the calculation made in line 32 makes no allowance for memory "gaps" between the arrays that might be needed for natural alignment of each array on memory boundaries. However, because the declarations and assignments in lines 5–8 of the kernel go from the longest variable type (4-byte `float`s) to the shortest variable type (1-byte `char`s), natural alignment will be achieved for all three arrays without the compiler needing to introduce gaps.[10]

Simple variables can also appear in dynamically allocated shared memory, but since their size, namely `sizeof(variable type)`, is known at compile time, static allocation is the best choice. If the variable is intended to contain some parameter which is read but not changed by the threads, then using `constant` memory might be a better choice. Note that `constant` memory will be automatically used for most kernel arguments.

2.8 Matrix Multiplication

Our next example is a naturally 2D problem – matrix multiplication. Matrix multiplication has in fact been featured as an early example of the use of shared memory in all releases of the CUDA SDK and our final version is closely based on the that SDK code. A matrix **M** is simply a 2D rectangular array of numbers, if the matrix **M** has n rows and m columns we say it is an n by m (or n × m) matrix and M_{ij} denotes the element in row i and column j. Note the order of the suffices is significant, in general M_{ij} and M_{ji} are different values in different positions in the matrix. In the special case where $M_{ij} = M_{ji}$ for all values of i and j the matrix is *symmetric* and *square* meaning that its dimensions n and m are the same. Matrices are multiplied using the formula:

Formula for Matrix Multiplication

If **A** is n × m and **B** is m × p then **C** = **A**×**B** is a n × p matrix with elements given by:

$$C_{ij} = \sum_{k=1}^{m} A_{jk}B_{kj}.$$

Note the number of columns of **A** must be equal to the number of rows of **B**

As mentioned above 2D arrays can be implemented in numerous ways, but the most efficient method is to use a single contiguous memory block and address elements using the 2D version of the rank formula given above, namely:

2D linear addressing for matrices

The expression:

```
A[i*Ncols+j]
```

gives the element A_{ij} of the matrix held in the 1D array **A**, Ncols is the number of columns in **A**. The number of rows Nrows is not explicit here but the size of **A** must be at least Nrows*Ncols. This notation is correct if **A** is either a thrust or std vector or a simple pointer.

In this scheme the column index j is the "hot" index, j and j+1 refer to adjacent memory locations whereas i and i+1 refer to memory locations separated by a stride Ncols. In most of our examples we will use thrust as a container class for both host and device arrays.

We are fully aware that C++ provides nice tools to create beautiful containers for vectors and matrices with support for more elegant addressing schemes such as the Fortran like A(i,j) or the C multidimensional A[i][j] style. Indeed we had intended to adopt one of these wrappers when we began this project. However at the time of writing any attempt to pass any object other than a bare pointer to a CUDA kernel prevents any optimisations based on using __restrict and since our goal is fast code we will stick with the simple explicit address calculation as shown in the box.[11] Example 2.11 shows a straightforward implementation of matrix multiplication on the host.

Example 2.11 hostmult0 matrix multiplication on host CPU

```
01    #include "thrust/host_vector.h"
02    #include "cxtimers.h"
03    #include <random>

04    int hostmult0(float *C, float A, float * B, int Ay,
                                              int Ax, int Bx)
05    {
06       // compute C=A*B for matrices (assumes Ax = By)
07       for(int i=0;i<Ay;i++) for(int j=0;j<Bx;j++){
08         C[i*Bx+j] = 0.0;        // row.col dot product
```

```
09        for(int k=0;k<Ax;k++)C[i*Bx+j] += A[i*Ax+k]*B[k*Bx+j];
10      }
11      return 0;
12    }

13    int main(int argc, char *argv[])
14    {
15      int Arow = (argc > 1) ? atoi(argv[1]) : 1024;
16      int Acol = (argc > 2) ? atoi(argv[2]) : Arow;
17      int Brow = Acol;
18      int Bcol = (argc > 3) ? atoi(argv[3]) : Brow;
19      int Crow = Arow;
20      int Ccol = Bcol;

21      thrust::host_vector<float> A(Arow*Acol);
22      thrust::host_vector<float> B(Brow*Bcol);
23      thrust::host_vector<float> C(Crow*Ccol);

24      // initialise A and B with random numbers
25      std::default_random_engine gen(12345678);
26      std::uniform_real_distribution<float> fran(0.0,1.0);
27      for(int k = 0; k<Arow*Acol; k++) A[k] = fran(gen);
28      for(int k = 0; k<Brow*Bcol; k++) B[k] = fran(gen);
29      cx::timer tim;

30      hostmult0(C.data(),A.data(),B.data(),Arow,Acol,Bcol);
31      double t1 = tim.lap_ms();
32      double flops = 2.0*(double)Arow*(double)Acol*
                                      (double)Bcol;
33      double gflops= flops/(t1*1000000.0);
34      double gbytes = gflops*6.0; // 12 bytes per term
35      printf("A %d x %d B %d x %d host time %.3f ms
                Gflops/sec %.3f\n",Arow,Acol,Brow,Bcol,t1,gflops);
36      return 0;
37    }

D:\ >hostmult0.exe
A 1024 x 1024 B 1024 x 1024 host time 2121.046 ms
                 GFlops 1.013 GBytes 6.076
```

Description of Example 2.11

- Line 1: Here we include the thrust host_vector header, std::vector could have been used instead for this host only code.
- Lines 4–12: This is the host matrix multiply function hostmult0, it takes standard pointers to the data for the matrices C, A and B as the first three arguments. The next three arguments define the

sizes of all three matrices. Note we use y and x instead of row and col to denote the first and second dimensions of the matrices. Thus, A is ay × ax, B is ax × bx and C is ay × bx, we infer the first dimension of B and both dimensions of C from the properties of matrix multiplication.

- Lines 7: These for loops over i and j cover all the elements of the desired product C.
- Line 9: The inner loop over k implements the summation from the standard formula. You can think of this summation as a dot product between the ith row of A and the jth column of B. Notice how the array indices vary with the for loop index k. The factor A[i*Ax+k] behaves "nicely" because as k increments, it addresses elements of A which are adjacent in memory, this is optimal for caching. On the other hand, the factor B[k*Bx+j] addresses memory with a stride of Bx words between successive values of k, which gives poor cache performance. This problem is inherent in matrix multiplication and has no simple fix.

Notice also that a triple for loop is needed for matrix multiplication. If the matrices have dimensions of 10^3 then a total of 2×10^9 arithmetic operations are required – multiplication of big matrices is slow!

You might worry that the expressions like i*Bx+j used for the array indices add a significant computational load for each step through the loop. In fact, this sort of index expression is so common that compilers are very good at generating the best possible code for indexing such arrays efficiently.

- Lines 13–36: This is the main routine:
  - Lines 15–20: Here we set the matrix sizes using optional user inputs for the dimensions of A (Arow & Acol) and the number of columns of B (Bcol). The dimensions of C and number of rows of B are set to be compatible with matrix multiplication.
  - Lines 21–23: Here we allocate thrust vectors to hold the matrices.
  - Lines 24–28: Here A and B are initialised with random numbers.
  - Lines 29–31: A timed call the hostmult0 to perform the multiplication.
  - Lines 32–35: Print some results, the performance in GFlops/sec assumes two operations per iteration in line 9 and ignores all overheads.

The timing result in the last line shows that this calculation runs at about 1 GFlops/sec and is clearly memory bound. The memory bandwidth achieved is about 6 GBytes/sec (8 bytes read and 4 bytes written per term).

The performance of this code is quite poor but we can improve it significantly by adding the C++11 __restrict keyword to the pointer argument declarations in line 9. This is shown in Example 2.12 where only line 9 from Example 2.11 has been changed.

Example 2.12 hostmult1 showing use of restrict keyword

```
      . . .
04    int hostmult1(float * __restrict C, float * __restrict A,
                    float * __restrict B, int Ay, int Ax, int Bx)
      . . .
D:\ > hostmult1.exe
A 1024 x 1024 B 1024 x 1024 host time 1468.845 ms
                GFlops 1.462 GBytes 8.772
```

We have improved the performance by 44% making this simple change! If you are not familiar with the history of C/C++ this requires some explanation. When a function is declared with a simple pointer argument, the compiler has no way of being certain that there are no other pointers to the same memory location elsewhere in the code. This is called pointer aliasing and in the early days of C when computer memory was a scarce resource, people would deliberately use pointer aliasing to use the same piece of memory for different purposes at different stages in the program. Needless to say, this practice often resulted in hard-to-find bugs. On modern systems with 64-bit memory addressing pointer aliasing is completely unnecessary yet the memory of old practice lingers on in modern compilers which are still reluctant to fully optimise code involving simple pointers. Specifically, they will tend to unnecessarily store intermediate results back to main memory rather than using registers. Adding the `restrict` qualifier to a pointer declaration tells the compiler that the pointer is not aliased and aggressive optimisation is safe.[12]

The CUDA NVCC compiler also supports `restrict` and the performance of many kernels does indeed improve when it is used. Thus, we come to the conclusion shown in the box:

> Always use **`restrict`** with pointer arguments.

As mentioned above, in practice C++ compiler support for restrict is quite shallow; if the restrict pointer is passed as a function argument wrapped in even a simple C++ class then restrict has no effect. In fact, while restrict is officially part of modern C11, it is not part of any C++ standard up to C++17. Fortunately, most recent C++ compilers including Visual Studio and g++ do support restrict, albeit in a shallow form. Another issue is that while the C standard uses `restrict` without decoration, C++ compilers may use `_restrict` or `__restrict` instead.

At this point we should mention another qualifier, `const`; many books on C++ get very excited about this. We discuss it in more detail in our C++ coding appendix. In principle use of `const` can allow the compiler to further optimise code. In practice we find using `const` does not usually give much or any performance gain; its use is actually more important as a safeguard to prevent accidental overwriting of variables and to make a programmer's intentions clear. In the case of pointers there are four possibilities shown in Table 2.4.

Table 2.4 *Possible combinations of const and restrict for pointer arguments*

declaration	cx wrapper	effect
float * __restrict A	r_Ptr<float>	A pointer variable, data variable
const float * __restrict A	cr_Ptr<float>	A pointer variable, data constant
float * const __restrict A	cvr_Ptr<float>	A pointer constant, data variable
const float * const __restrict A	ccr_Ptr<float>	A pointer constant, data constant

Example
```
int hostmult1(r_Ptr<float> C, cr_Ptr<float> A, cr_Ptr<float> B, int Ay,
int Ax, int Bx)
```

The middle column of the table shows templated wrappers defined in cx.h that can be used to hide the gory details in the first column. An example of their use is shown in the bottom row. These wrappers can be used in both host and kernel code and the first two will be used in most of our examples from now on.

It is now time to look at a GPU version of matrix multiply; to get the best performance is actually quite complicated but we will start with a simple approach as shown in Example 2.13.

Example 2.13 gpumult0 kernel simple matrix multiplication on the GPU

```
04   __global__ void gpumult0(float * C, const float * A,
                   const float * B, int Ay, int Ax, int Bx)
05   {
06     int tx = blockIdx.x*blockDim.x + threadIdx.x;   // col j
07     int ty = blockIdx.y*blockDim.y + threadIdx.y;   // row i
08     if(ty >= Ay || tx >= Bx) return;
09     C[ty*Bx+tx] = 0.0;
10     for(int k=0;k<Ax;k++) C[ty*Bx+tx] +=
                            A[ty*Bx+k]*B[k*Bx+tx];
11   }
     . . .
13   int main(int argc, char *argv[])
14   {
15     int Arow = (argc > 1) ? atoi(argv[2]) : 1024;
16     int Acol = (argc > 2) ? atoi(argv[3]) : Arow;
17     int Brow = Acol;
18     int Bcol = (argc > 3) ? atoi(argv[4]) : Brow;
19     int Crow = Arow;
20     int Ccol = Bcol;
20.1 uint tilex = (argc > 4) ? atoi(argv[5]) : 32;   // tile x
20.2 uint tiley = (argc > 5) ? atoi(argv[6]) : 8;    // tile y

21     thrust::host_vector<float>      A(Arow*Acol);
22     thrust::host_vector<float>      B(Brow*Bcol);
23     thrust::host_vector<float>      C(Crow*Ccol);
23.1 thrust::device_vector<float> dev_C(Crow*Ccol);
23.2 thrust::device_vector<float> dev_A(Arow*Acol);
23.3 thrust::device_vector<float> dev_B(Brow*Bcol);

24     // initialise A and B with random numbers
25     std::default_random_engine gen(12345678);
26     std::uniform_real_distribution<float> fran(0.0,1.0);
27     for(int k = 0; k<Arow*Acol; k++) A[k] = fran(gen);
28     for(int k = 0; k<Brow*Bcol; k++) B[k] = fran(gen);
28.1 dev_A = A;   // H2D copy
28.2 dev_B = B;   // H2D copy

28.3 dim3 threads ={tilex, tiley, 1};
```

```
28.4    dim3 blocks ={(Bcol+threads.x-1)/threads.x,
                      (Arow+threads.y-1)/threads.y, 1};
29      cx::timer tim;
30      gpumult0<<<blocks,threads>>>(dev_C.data().get(),
                 dev_A.data().get(), dev_B.data().get(),
                 Arow, Acol, Bcol);
30.1    cudaDeviceSynchronize();  // wait for kernel
31      double t2 = tim.lap_ms();
31.1    C = dev_C;                // D2H copy

32      double flops = 2.0*Arow*Acol*Bcol;
33      double gflops = flops/(t2*1000000.0);
34      double gbytes = gflops*6.0; // 12 bytes per term
35      printf("A %d x %d B %d x %d gpu time %.3f ms
                 GFlops %.3f GBytes %.3f\n",Arow,Acol,Brow,
                 Bcol,t2,gflops,gbytes);
36      return 0;
37  }

D:\ >gpumult0.exe 1024 1024 1024 32 32
A 1024 x 1024 B 1024 x 1024 gpu time 6.685 ms
             GFlops 321.233 GBytes 1927.400
```

Description of Example 2.13

Much of the code in this example is identical to the host version shown in Example 2.11. Here we comment on the differences.

- Lines 4–11: The GPU kernel gpumult0 replaces the previous hostmult0 function here. The kernel is designed to use one thread to calculate one element of the matrix product. The kernel expects to be called with a 2D grid of thread blocks with sufficient threads in the x and y dimensions to span all the elements of C. As before x is the column index and y is the row index.
- Lines 6–7: Here we set tx and ty from the built-in variables to determine which element of C this thread will calculate. These lines effectively replace the loops over i and j used in the host version, we can think of the kernel as effectively calculating *all* the elements of C in parallel.
- Line 8: This is an out-of-range check on tx and ty. It is necessary because the dimensions of each thread block may have been rounded up.
- Lines 9–10: Here we calculate one element of C using the standard formula. Notice the factor B[k*Bx+tx] in line 10 still uses a memory stride of Bx words on successive passes through the for loop over k. But now in this parallel kernel *adjacent threads* will use adjacent elements of B because adjacent threads have adjacent values of tx. Thus L1 caching will be efficient for both factors in the multiplication – this is an interesting example of how parallel CUDA code can provide efficient memory access in situations where single threaded code struggles.
- Lines 20.1–20.2: We add two additional user settable parameters tilex and tiley which define the x and y dimensions of the thread blocks used by the kernel launch. These are equivalent to the threads and blocks parameters we use in many 1D examples.

- Lines 23.1–23.3: Here we allocate device arrays to hold copies of the matrices A, B and C.
- Lines 28.1–28.2: Copy A and B to the device.
- Line 28.3: Set `threads` to a dim3 triad representing a 2D tile on the matrix C.
- Line 28.4: Set blocks as a dim3 with x and y dimensions sufficient for the thread block tiles in threads to span the matrix C. Notice the integer rounding up for cases where the dimensions of C are not exact multiples of `tilex` and `tiley`. The out-of-range test in line 8 is necessary for cases where rounding up was needed. Rounding up and consequent testing in kernels are very common in CUDA code written to process general cases where not everything is a power of 2.
- Lines 29–31: This timed loop is similar to that of Example 2.9 but performs a kernel launch instead of a host function call. The use of `cudaDeviceSynchronize` is necessary for timing purposes.
- Line 31.1: Here we copy the result back to the host. Although C is not used in the code shown here, it would obviously be used in real-world code. Indeed, we have used C to compare the results from the host and GPU versions and find the calculated C_{ij} agree to about 6 significant figures.

The timing result in the last line shows that there is an impressive speed-up of about 220 times compared to the host calculation in Example 2.12.

If we change the `gpumult0` declaration in line 4 to use restrict we get the `gpumult1` kernel declaration shown in Example 2.14. This example shows two alternative methods of declaring restrict arrays in kernel code; the first method just uses C++ keywords and is quite verbose; the second method uses cx defined abbreviations for the same result. Note that `cr_Ptr` and `r_Ptr` are defined with templated `using` statements in `cx.h`. We will use the abbreviated versions in all our later examples.

Example 2.14 `gpumult1` kernel using restrict keyword on array arguments

```
    . . .
04    __global__ void gpumult1(float * __restrict C,
         const float * __restrict A, const float * __restrict B,
         int Ay, int Ax, int Bx)
or:
04    __global__ void gpumult1(r_Ptr<float> C, cr_Ptr<float> A,
         cr_Ptr<float> B, int Ay, int Ax, int Bx)

D:\ > gpumult1.exe
A 1024 x 1024 B 1024 x 1024 gpu time 2.536 ms
          GFlops 846.813 GBytes 5080.878
```

We can see that simply using restrict on our GPU matrix multiply code gives a dramatic speed-up of more than a factor of 2.6 (compared to about 1.4 for host code). The effective memory bandwidth is also much greater than the hardware limit of about 400 GBytes/sec separately for read and write, demonstrating that memory caching is playing an important role.

Finally, if you really hate the explicit address calculations in line 10 of Example 2.13 they can be hidden using a lambda function as shown in Example 2.15.

Example 2.15 `gpumult2` kernel using lambda function for 2D array indexing

```
04 __global__ void gpumult2(r_Ptr<float> C, cr_Ptr<float> A,
        cr_Ptr<float> B, int Ay, int Ax, int Bx)
05 {
06    int j = blockIdx.x*blockDim.x + threadIdx.x;  // col j
07    int i = blockIdx.y*blockDim.y + threadIdx.y;  // row i
08    if(i >= Ay || j >= Bx) return;

      // lambda function
09    auto idx = [&Bx](int i,int j){ return i*Bx+j; };

10    C[idx(i,j)] = 0.0;
11    for(int k=0;k<Ax;k++)
              C[idx(i,j)]+= A[idx(i,k)]*B[idx(k,j)];
12 }
```

In Example 2.15 we have added a new line 9 which defines a local function `idx` that performs the standard 2D address calculation needed for this function. The span needed step to successive rows of B and columns of C is `Bx`, the number of columns of B and (necessarily) also the number of rows of C. The value is captured by the lambda function using the `[&Bx]` syntax to indicate that the variable `Bx` used in the body of the lambda function is the same variable as used in the main body of the surrounding function. Moreover, by prefixing `&` to `Bx` we indicate that the variable is to be used by reference with no copy required. This should lead to the compiler generating code identical to Example 2.14, and indeed we find no performance difference between these two versions. Using a lambda function in this way is modernising the old trick of using a macro; in this case:

$$\#define \ idx(i,j) \ (i)*Bx+(j)$$

which achieves the same effect. However, we deeply deprecate the use of macros in this way because even if the macro occurs inside a function its definition will persist throughout the code which risks hard-to-find bugs and greatly complicates code where different 2D spans are needed in different parts of the code. Note also the precautionary brackets around `i` and `j` in the macro definition, these are need for correctness if say `i` is passed as `i+1`.

2.9 Tiled Matrix Multiplication

Matrix multiplication is often used to demonstrate the use of shared memory in many CUDA tutorials and books. This is based on the observation that A_{ik} and B_{kj} for fixed k are read from main memory many times for each possible combination of the values of i and j. This was a major problem on early GPUs which had poor memory caching and it is still an issue on recent GPUs which have much better caching.

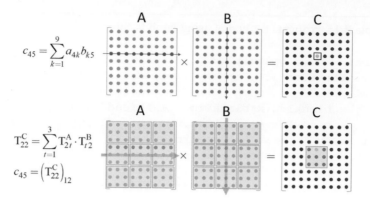

$$c_{45} = \sum_{k=1}^{9} a_{4k} b_{k5}$$

$$T_{22}^{C} = \sum_{t=1}^{3} T_{2t}^{A} \cdot T_{t2}^{B}$$

$$c_{45} = \left(T_{22}^{C} \right)_{12}$$

Figure 2.3 Tiled matrix multiplication

To exploit shared memory, we can use each thread in a thread block to store different elements of A and B in shared memory and then let all the threads in the block use all the cached values to calculate contributions to the product. This is relatively straightforward because matrix multiplication can be represented as a sum over products of 2D tiles defined over the matrices as shown in the following equation:

$$\mathbf{T}_{I,J}^{C} = \sum_{t=1}^{M_T} \mathbf{T}_{I,t}^{A} \cdot \mathbf{T}_{t,J}^{B},$$

where the **T**s are rectangular tiles defined over the matrices and · represents matrix multiplication between tiles. The summation index, t, represents a summation over contributing M_t pairs of tiles; the matrix product implies further summations over the individual matrix elements within the tiles. The idea is shown in Figure 2.3 where we use a set of 3×3 tiles to perform the multiplication of 9×9 matrices.

Tiled matrix multiplication can be readily implemented in CUDA kernels by using a 16×16 or 32×32 thread blocks to represent a pair of tiles from A and B. Each thread then first copies one element of its thread block's allocated A and B tiles into shared memory arrays. Once this process is complete, the same threads can then compute the elements of the tiled matrix multiplication to obtain that tile-pair's contribution to a tile in C. In this way each element of A and B is only read once from external memory instead of 16 or 32 times. Our implementation is the `gputiled` kernel shown in Example 2.16. In Figure 2.3 the element c_{45} is shown calculated conventionally in the top row and by tiled matrix multiplication in the bottom row.

Example 2.16 `gputiled` kernel: tiled matrix multiplication using shared memory

```
01   #include "cx.h"
02   #include "cxtimers.h"
03   #include <random>
     . . .
```

```
13   int main(int argc, char *argv[])
14   {
         . . .
28.3   dim3 threads = {tilex,tilex,1};   // square
28.4   dim3 blocks = {(Bcol+threads.x-1)/threads.x,
                      (Arow+threads.y-1)/threads.y, 1};
         . . .
29     cx::timer tim;
30     if(tilex == 8) gputiled< 8><<<blocks,threads>>>(
            dev_C.data().get(),dev_A.data().get(),
            dev_B.data().get(),Arow,Acol,Bcol);
30.1   else if(tilex == 16) gputiled<16><<<blocks,threads>>>(
            dev_C.data().get(),dev_A.data().get(),
            dev_B.data().get(),Arow,Acol,Bcol);
30.2   else if(tilex == 32) gputiled<32><<<blocks,threads>>>(
            dev_C.data().get(),dev_A.data().get(),
            dev_B.data().get(),Arow,Acol,Bcol);
30.3   cudaDeviceSynchronize();
31     double t3 = tim.lap_ms()
         . . .
37   }


40   template <int TS> __global__ void gputiled(
            float * __restrict C, float * __restrict A,
            float * __restrict B, int Ay, int Ax, int Bx)
41   {
42     __shared__ float Atile[TS][TS];   // tile A e.g. [16][16]
43     __shared__ float Btile[TS][TS];   // tile B e.g. [16][16]
44     int tx  = threadIdx.x;            // tile col index j
45     int ty  = threadIdx.y;            // tile row index i
46     int ocx = blockDim.x*blockIdx.x;  // tile x origin in C
47     int ocy = blockDim.y*blockIdx.y;  // tile y origin in C

48     int ax = tx;        // j or x in first tile on A
49     int ay = ocy+ty;    // i or y in first tile on A and C
50     int bx = ocx+tx;    // j or x in first tile on B and C
51     int by = ty;        // i or y in first tile on B

52     float csum = 0.0f;
53     for(int t=0; t<gridDim.x; t++){
54       Atile[ty][tx] = A[ay*Ax+ax];   // copy A to shared mem
55       Btile[ty][tx] = B[by*Bx+bx];   // copy B to shared mem
56       __syncthreads();
57       for(int k=0;k<TS;k++) csum += Atile[ty][k]*Btile[k][tx];
58       __syncthreads();
59       ax += TS;        // step A tiles along rows of A
60       by += TS;        // step B tiles down  cols of B
```

```
61    }
62    C[ay*Bx+bx] = csum; // store complete result
63  }

D:\  > gputiled.exe  1024 1024 1024 32
A 1024 x 1024 B 1024 x 1024 gpu time 1.945 ms
                GFlops 1104.284 GBytes 6625.701
```

Description of Example 2.13

The kernel is shown in full as here the changes are significant. For the main routine only changes from Example 2.13 are shown.

- Line 28.3: We use `tilex` to set both dimensions of the 2D thread blocks used to represent tiles. While it is possible to use non-square tiles, that would complicate the kernel code.
- Lines 29–31: As before this is the timed block that launches a kernel and waits for completion. The kernel launch itself is now changed because the `guptiled` kernel is written to use the value of `tilex` as a template parameter. Here we use a 3-way if-else tree to allow values of 32, 16 or 8 for this parameter. The kernel argument list is the same as before.
- Line 40: This is the start of our new `guptiled` kernel; the arguments are as before and we are now using the `restrict` keyword by default for all pointers. Note that this is a templated kernel; thus the tile size parameter `TS` is known at compile time.
- Lines 42–43: We declare two statically allocated shared memory arrays to hold square tiles copied from A and B to `Atile` and `Btile`.
- Lines 44–45: Here we set the position of the current thread in the local `TS` x `TS` tiles. This depends only on the thread block dimensions.
- Lines 46–47: Here we set `ocx` and `ocy` to the origin of the target tile in C using grid-block quantities. These values are the same for all threads in the thread block.
- Lines 48–51: In the first two lines we set `ax` and `ay` to the current thread's position in A based on the first tile to be used. Similarly, in the second pair of lines we set `bx` and `by` for matrix B. Notice that as we step to different tiles along the rows of A and down the columns of B `ay` and `bx` are constant whereas `ax` and `by` change. In fact `ay` and `bx` are the i and j values of the c_{ij} element being evaluated by the current thread.
- Line 51: The local variable `csum` is used to accumulate the current thread's c_{ij} value; here we set it to zero.
- Lines 53–61: Each pass through this loop performs matrix multiplication on one pair of tiles from A and B and accumulates the result in `csum`.
  - Lines 54–55: Here we copy the current tiles from A and B to shared memory. Each thread copies one element from A and one from B to `Atile` and `Btile` and will later read `TS` values back from these arrays.
  - Line 56: An essential `syncthreads` here; no thread in the block can safely proceed until all the elements of `Atile` and `Btile` have been set.
  - Line 57: Matrix multiplication of `Atile` and `Btile`; each thread computes one element of the product.
  - Line 58: A second essential `syncthreads`; no thread can proceed to the next pass through the for loop until all threads have reached this point.

○ Lines 59–60: Here we increment ax and by to point to the required position in the next tiles from A and B.

• Line 62: Here we store the final result in C.

The result in the last line shows that gputiled delivers more than 1 TFlop/sec of processing. A tile size of 32 × 32 works best on the RTX 2070 GPU used for this test.

We note that using shared memory as shown in Example 2.16 gives a significant performance boost of about 250 GFlops/sec amounting to about 1.1 TFlops/sec overall. Although not shown here, we did try running this example without using restrict in kernel arguments and found only a small drop in performance. This is presumably because we now read from A and B fewer times and hence the performance gain from using restrict on the pointers to these arguments is less important.

There is one last trick we can try to squeeze a bit more performance from our code and that is explicit loop unrolling:

Example 2.17 gputiled1 kernel showing explicit loop unrolling

```
      .  .  .
52    float csum = 0.0f;
52.1  #pragma unroll 16
      // step A tiles along rows of A
53    for(int t=0;t<gridDim.x;t++){
      .  .  .

D:\ gputiled1.exe  1024 1024 1024 32
A 1024 x 1024 B 1024 x 1024 gpu time 1.765 ms
            GFlops 1216.958 GBytes 7301.748
```

As shown in the last line of Example 2.17 we have gained another 100 GFlops/sec of performance by using loop unrolling. The optimal depth of unrolling can only be found by experiment; on our RTX 2070 the value 16 seems to give the best result. On other GPUs you may find a different optimum. Tuning GPU code always involves some experimentation. Note the NVCC compiler will often automatically perform loop unrolling and especially in cases where the number of passes is known at compile time. For this reason, making the loop counter a template parameter can be worthwhile. Here this is done for the inner loop over TS but not for the outer loop over gridDim.x which is therefore not known at compile time. Interestingly, we find that explicit unrolling over the outer loop helps but in experiments (not shown) we found explicit unrolling over the inner loop does not help.

2.10 BLAS

Matrix multiplication is a classic problem in computational linear algebra and the results of more than 50 years of development are encapsulated in the BLAS (basic linear algebra subprograms) function libraries that are available for all serious computing platforms. BLAS is used by calling appropriate functions to perform the desired operations. Matrix multiplication of float-4 matrices can be performed by calling the sgemm (single precision general matrix multiplication) routine which implements the saxpy-like operation $\mathbf{C} = \alpha\mathbf{AB} + \beta\mathbf{C}$ for matrices $\mathbf{A}$, $\mathbf{B}$ and $\mathbf{C}$. The good news is that BLAS is available for CUDA code. The NVIDIA cuBLAS library is a set of host callable routines that run BLAS functions on the GPU using vectors and matrices in GPU memory. In fact, although cuBLAS provides its own routines to allocate and transfer arrays between host and GPU memories it is also perfectly possible to use thrust (or any other method) to manage these arrays. Thus cuBLAS can be used in our matrix multiply example with just a few modifications. Example 2.18 shows how BLAS routines can be used in host code to replace the kernel calls used in our previous examples.

Example 2.18 Host code showing matrix multiplication using cuBLAS

```
     . . .
05   #include "cublas_v2.h"
     . . .
10   int main(int argc, char *argv[])
11   {
     . . .
20     thrust::host_vector<float>        A(Arow*Acol);
21     thrust::host_vector<float>        B(Brow*Bcol);
22     thrust::host_vector<float>        C(Crow*Ccol);
23     thrust::device_vector<float> dev_A(Arow*Acol);
24     thrust::device_vector<float> dev_B(Brow*Bcol);
25     thrust::device_vector<float> dev_C(Crow*Ccol);
26     thrust::device_vector<float> dev_D(Crow*Ccol);

27     // initialise A and B with random numbers, clear C
28     std::default_random_engine gen(12345678);
29     std::uniform_real_distribution<float> fran(0.0,1.0);
30     for(int k = 0; k<Arow*Acol; k++) A[k] = fran(gen);
31     for(int k = 0; k<Brow*Bcol; k++) B[k] = fran(gen);
32     for(int k = 0; k<Crow*Ccol; k++) C[k] = 0.0f;

33     dev_A = A;  // H2D copy
34     dev_B = B;  // H2D copy
35     dev_C = C;  // clear

36     float alpha = 1.0f;
37     float beta  = 1.0f;
38     cublasHandle_t handle; cublasCreate(&handle);
       // enable tensor cores
39     cublasSetMathMode(handle,CUBLAS_TENSOR_OP_MATH);

40     cx::timer tim;    // C = alpha*(A*B) + beta*C
```

```
41    cublasSgemm(handle, CUBLAS_OP_T, CUBLAS_OP_T,
              Crow, Ccol, Arow, alpha, dev_A.data().get(),
              Acol, dev_B.data().get(), Bcol, &beta,
              dev_C.data().get(), Crow);
42    beta = 0.0f;
      // D = transpose(C) from C = alpha*A+beta*B
43    cublasSgeam(handle, CUBLAS_OP_T, CUBLAS_OP_T,
              Crow, Ccol, &alpha, dev_C.data().get(),
              Crow, &beta, dev_C.data().get(),
              Crow, dev_D.data().get(), Ccol);
44    cudaDeviceSynchronize();
45    double t3 = tim.lap_ms()/(double)(nacc);

46    C = dev_D; // D2H copy
47    double flops = 2.0*(double)Arow*(double)Acol*(double)Bcol;
48    double qflops = flops/(t3*1000000.0);
49    double gbytes = gflops*6.0; // i.e 12 bytes per term
50    printf("A %d x %d B %d x %d gpu time %.3f ms
              GFlops %.3f GBbytes %.3f\n", Arow, Acol, Brow,
              Bcol, t3, gflops, gbytes);
51    return 0;
52  }

D:\ > blasmult.exe 1024
A 1024 x 1024 B 1024 x 1024 time 0.318 ms
            GFlops 6747.1 GBytes 40482.8 (no TC)
A 1024 x 1024 B 1024 x 1024 time 0.242 ms
            GFlops 8882.3 GBytes 53293.9 (with TC)
```

Description of Example 2.18

- Line 5: The include file `cublas_v2.h` is necessary to use the NVIDIA BLAS library. It is also necessary to use the include file `cublas.lib` in the linking stage on Windows. An older version `cublas.h` file is also supplied for backward compatibility but that version is now deprecated for new code.
- Lines 12–18 (not shown): Set the sizes of the A, B and C matrices using optional user supplied values as before.
- Lines 20–26: Create thrust containers for the matrices for the host and device. An additional device matrix dev_D the same size as the result matrix C is created here. It will be needed to hold the transpose of dev_C as explained below.
- Lines 27–35: Initialise the matrices A and B to random numbers and set C to zeros. (Clearing C is technically unnecessary as this is thrust's default allocation option, but we like to make our intentions clear). The host vectors are then copied to the corresponding device vectors.
- Lines 36–37: The parameters alpha and beta are declared and set to one.
- In line 38: A `cublasHandle_t` object handle is created; this is a necessary first argument to nearly all of the library functions. It is useful in multithreaded applications where separate threads use different handles.

- Line 39: Because we are using a GPU equipped with tensor cores (i.e. having a CC of 7.0 or above) we tell cuBLAS to use them where possible. Although originally realised as a tool for mixed precision operations on 2 and 4-byte floats, recent versions of cublas can also use tensor cores to speed up pure 4-byte float calculations. In a test we see a speed-up of about 30% using 1024 × 1024 matrices and speed-ups of up to a factor of two using larger matrices.
- Lines 40–45: This is the timed loop where the matrix product is calculated. The BLAS library is great for performance but the functions have a dreadful user interface essentially unchanged from their early Fortran origins in the 1950s. Also, they keep to the Fortran convention of expecting matrices in column major format (i.e. elements in the same column are stored in adjacent memory locations). This means that default C/C++ style matrices, in row major format, are treated as if they had been transposed. While this does not matter for simple operations such as addition, it does matter for matrix multiplication. Fortunately, the matrix functions such as cublasSgemm (the cuBLAS version of sgemm), used in line 41, have flag arguments specifying whether the input matrices A and B should be transposed before use. This results in correct matrix multiplication but the resulting matrix C is still left in column major format. We correct this in line 43 by calling the cuBLAS function cublasSgeam to transpose C back to row major format.
- Line 41: The call the cubalsSgemm function has many arguments as follows:
  1. The mandatory cuBLAS handle
  2. Transpose A if CUBLAS_OP_T or not if CUBLAS_OP_N
  3. Transpose B if CUBLAS_OP_T or not if CUBLAS_OP_N
  4. The number of rows of A (after transposition if done) and C; we use Crow here.
  5. The number of columns of B (after transposition if done) and C; we use Ccol here.
  6. The number of columns of A (after transposition if done) and rows of B (after transposition if done), we use Arow here. This is the index that is summed in matrix multiplication.
  7. Pointer to the scaling factor alpha.
  8. Pointer to the matrix A.
  9. Leading dimension of array used to hold A; we use Acol here.
  10. Pointer to the matrix B.
  11. Leading dimension of the array used to hold B; we use Bcol here.
  12. Pointer to the scaling factor beta.
  13. A pointer to the matrix C.
  14. Leading dimension of the array used to store C.

For square matrices all the dimensions are the same and the interface is relatively forgiving; in other cases significant care is required to get everything correct. We have allowed for the transposition of A and B in our choice for argument 6 but not arguments 9 and 11. We have tacitly assumed that C is in column major format for our choice of arguments 5, 6 and 14.

- Line 42: Set beta to zero before calling cublasSgeam.
- Line 43: Here we use the cublasSgeam function which evaluates $\mathbf{C} = \alpha\mathbf{A} + \beta\mathbf{B}$ to transpose C. This function is an NVIDIA extension to the standard set of BLAS functions. By setting $\alpha = 1$ and $\beta = 0$ we cause A to be copied to C with optional transposition of A if requested. The arguments for cublasSgeam are as follows:
  1–5. Same as cublasSgemm.
  6.   Pointer to alpha.
  7.   Pointer to the matrix A; we use C here.
  8.   Leading dimension of array used to hold first matrix; we use Crow here.
  9.   Pointer to beta. Note beta is set to zero in line 42.
  10. Pointer to the matrix B; we use C here.

11. Leading dimension of array used to hold B matrix; we use `Crow` here.
12. Pointer to the matrix C; we use `D` here.
13. Leading dimension of array used to hold C matrix; we use `Ccol` here. (This would be `Dcol` in cases where C and D had different sizes).

- Lines 44–52: These are similar to before.

The results at the end of the example show performances of 6.7 and 8.9 TFlops for the RTX2070 and 1024×1204 matrices. The latter result was obtained using the tensor core processors available on devices of CC ≥ 7.0.

The performance of the `cublasSgemm` is a factor of 6 or more better than our best kernel. Moreover, tensor cores, if available, can be used to give further impressive speed-ups of ~30% or more. Thus, while matrix multiplication is an excellent and much used calculation for demonstrating the use of shared memory in CUDA kernels, if you really need lots of fast matrix multiplication, use the NVIDA library not your own kernels. Similar advice applies to other standard problems such as FFT for which NVIDIA also has a good library. We discuss NVIDIA's full range of libraries in Appendix F.

Figure 2.4 shows how the performance of our matrix multiply routines varies as a function of matrix size. The peak performance for the largest matrix sizes is over 15 TFlops for `cublasSgemm` with tensor cores. The curve labelled kernel corresponds to the `gputiled1` kernel. The curves labelled blas and blas+TC correspond to the two BLAS routines. Note the peak performance achieved by the TC version of cuBLAS for the largest matrices is over 15 TFlops; this is an astonishing performance from a £400 PC card.

In Chapter 11 we show you how to write your own matrix multiply kernels using tensor cores; the shared memory version achieves about 5.6 TFlops compared to the 8.9 achieved by cuBLAS. This is actually not bad as the cuBLAS library routines will contain many

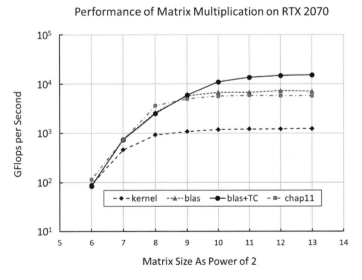

Figure 2.4 Performance of matrix multiplication on an RTX 2070 GPU

detailed optimisations. The performance of this kernel is shown as the chap11 curve on Figure 2.4.

The fact that fast libraries for standard calculations like matrix multiplication are available does not mean that learning to write your own kernels in CUDA is unnecessary; there are many situations where an out of the box solution is not readily available. For example, simulation is very important in many areas. Models of your particular problem often have to be hand-crafted and could gain enormously in speed if you are able to include code that exploits the raw power of GPUs. We also note from Figure 2.4 that our matrix multiply kernels are more competitive with cuBLAS for smaller matrices which might be useful when many small matrix multiplications are required as part of a bigger program.

This concludes our second introductory chapter. In the next chapter we discuss warp level programming which will provide important insights into how to get the best performance from your GPU. The examples in Chapter 3 include further improvements to the reduce kernels.

Endnotes Chapter 2

1 Flynn, Michael J. "Some computer organizations and their effectiveness." *IEEE transactions on computers* 100, no. 9 (1972): 948–960.

2 In practice the addition of floating-point numbers is not precisely commutative because the accumulation of rounding errors can depend on the order in which the terms are added together. Once the sum gets large, the contribution from subsequent small numbers is inaccurate or completely lost. This is a particular issue for F32 where only about 7 significant figures are useful. Interestingly parallel reduction techniques, where a number of partial sums are accumulated in parallel, are likely to be more robust than a single serial evaluation.

3 I first encountered this approach to parallel programming when learning MPI in the mid-1990s and it was a revelation. My previous encounters with trying to program multiple devices to run in parallel had involved writing different programs for each device and hand tuning at the assembly level to make the execution times identical on each device (MIMD) – a nightmare task compared to the common code SIMD model of CUDA and MPI.

4 Specifically, the member functions the host and device vector class do not have __device__ definitions. Thrust was designed as a suite of host callable functions which ran on the GPU for speed. Users of thrust were not expected to write their own kernels.

5 Our recommendation that threads should be a multiple of 32 is for performance reasons. Any value in [1,1024] is allowed, it is just that values which are multiples of the warp size are more efficient. For example, if you specified 48 then every thread block would be run with one full warp of 32 threads and one ½ full warp of 16 threads leading to a 25% performance loss.

6 If you want your compiled code to run on different GPU models you can use the device query functions in CUDA to find the value of Nsm at run time.

7 As a technical aside, we mention that the GPU hardware manages branch divergence at the warp-engine level by maintaining a 32-bit active-thread bit mask for each active warp, the bits are turned on or off to determine with threads execute in the currently scheduled instruction.

8 The Cooperative Groups feature does allow grid-wide synchronisation of all threads in a grid during kernel execution but only if a number of restrictions are applied including having all thread blocks resident on the device at once.

9 The modern C++ practice of declaring and initialising objects in the same statement (RAII) cannot be applied to shared memory objects in CUDA kernels because the declaration is the same for all threads in the kernel, but the initialisation is usually thread dependent.

10 Actually, it should be second nature for you as a C++ programmer to always use longest first/shortest last ordering in variable declarations for all your classes and structs as well as special cases like CUDA dynamically declared arrays. This will achieve natural alignment for all your variables without the compiler having to insert "hidden" padding.

11 Giving up on containers for kernel arguments means that we have to pass array dimensions explicitly as separate arguments. This is a genuine loss and is a potential source of bugs. One advantage of containers is that objects know their sizes.

12 Of course, if you use `restrict` it is your responsibility to ensure that aliasing does not occur – the compiler still cannot actually check this.

3

Warps and Cooperative Groups

The 32-thread warp has been a stable feature of NVIDIA GPU architecture since the early Fermi generation.[1] The GPU hardware processes all threads in a warp together using a dedicated subunit of a GPU SM.[2] From the Fermi to Pascal GPU generations, each warp was processed using a single program counter and a 32-bit mask indicating which threads were active for the current instruction. This meant that all active threads within a warp ran in strict lock step with each other and thus were always implicitly synchronised. As a consequence of this design, explicit calls to __syncthreads() in kernel code were only required to synchronise threads in *different* warps but not for threads within the *same* warp. It was actually worthwhile to omit __syncthreads() calls in kernel code when possible, because these calls, which synchronise *all* the threads in the thread block, are expensive – a great deal of code used this implicit intra-warp synchronisation and you may still see this trick used in older tutorial example code.

In 2017 NVIDIA released CUDA SDK version 9.0 with support for the Volta (CC = 7.0) and Turing (CC = 7.5) generations of GPU. These new architectures break the implicit warp synchronisation paradigm because their hardware has separate per thread program counters which means that on these devices the threads within the same warp might not run in lock step. Thus, historic code relying on implicit warp synchronisation might not run correctly on the new GPUs.[3] CUDA 9.0 also introduced cooperative groups as a powerful way of making explicit any assumptions of synchronisation between the threads in a warp and generalising these ideas to other sizes of thread groups. The introduction of cooperative groups promotes warps and thread blocks to first-class C++ objects, allowing programmers to write straightforward code that makes it clear where warp-level ideas are being used.

The May 2020 release of CUDA SDK 11.0 contained a significant improvement to cooperative groups in that grid level objects no longer need special treatment at compile time and work with all CUDA capable cards. Our examples are based on that release. As explained below the previous restrictions continue to apply if the grid.sync member function is used.

To illustrate cooperative groups, we will revisit the reduce kernels of Chapter 2. Example 3.1 shows a modified version of the reduce4 kernel from Chapter 2 which is safe for devices of CC ≥ 7.0. This example uses the new __syncwarp() function to explicitly synchronise threads in a warp whenever implicit warp synchronisation would have been used in the past.

Description of Example 3.1

- Line 10: We declare a template function with one template integer parameter blockSize. This parameter must be a power of 2 between 64 and 1024 and the user must also ensure that the kernel is launched with the number of thread blocks set equal to `blockSize`. That means that the built-in parameter `blockDim.x` will equal `blockSize` during kernel execution. The advantage of this is that the NVCC compiler will delete portions of lines 21–24 *at compile time* keeping only those parts which are necessary. This is a common trick in CUDA programming.

This kernel processes integer data because the types of the arguments `data` and `sums` are both set to `int`, but the kernel can easily be modified to process other arithmetic types, and indeed we could have simply used a second template parameter to generalise the kernel. However, that is not done here to avoid clutter in the example.

- Line 15: This kernel uses statically allocated shared memory of one word per thread. The partial thread sums are stored here.
- Lines 16–17: The variable `id` is set to the thread's rank in its block using `threadIdx.x` and the thread's element of shared memory `s[id]` is set to zero.
- Lines 18–19: Here we accumulate the partial per thread sums in `s[id]`. In this loop each thread uses a stride equal to the total number of threads to pick elements from the input array `data`.
- Line 19: Here `__syncthreads` is used so that all the partial sums will be valid beyond this statement. This statement is necessary.
- Lines 20–23: Here we perform the tree sums necessary for larger block sizes. Notice that at compile time the compiler will completely remove statements that fail the `blockSize` test and remove that part of the test from the statements for which it is true.
- Line 24: For the final stages of the tree sum only threads with `id < 32` participate and as these threads are all in the lowest ranked warp of the thread block, we wrap a single `if` statement around the final lines 26–33 of the kernel. This is warp-level programming and allows threads in other warps to exit the kernel early.
- Lines 25–30: These are the final steps in the tree sum reduction process. Note the use of `__syncwarp()` in these statements. The `__syncwarp()` is part of the warp-level programming support introduced in CUDA version 9.0. A `__syncwarp()` call is cheaper to execute than `__syncthreads()` and in fact does nothing on architectures with CC < 7 because for those GPUs all threads in a warp always run in lockstep.
- Line 31: Here the thread with `id = 0` stores the computed block-wide sum in an element of the output array `sums`.

Example 3.1 `reduce5` kernel using syncwarp for device of CC=7 and higher

```
10  template <int blockSize> __global__ void
        reduce5(r_Ptr<int> sums,cr_Ptr<int> data, int n)
11  {
12    // kernel assumes that blockDim.x = blockSize,
13    // and blockSize is power of 2 between 64 and 1024
14    __shared__ int s[blockSize];
15    int id = threadIdx.x;        // rank in block
16    s[id] = 0;
17    for (int tid = blockSize*blockIdx.x+threadIdx.x;
          tid < n; tid += blockSize*gridDim.x)
                        s[id] += data[tid];
```

```
18    __syncthreads();
19    if(blockSize > 512 && id < 512 && id+512 < blockSize)
                            s[id] += s[id+512];
20    __syncthreads();
21    if(blockSize > 256 && id < 256 && id+256 < blockSize)
                            s[id] += s[id+256];
22    __syncthreads();
23    if(blockSize > 128 && id < 128 && id+128 < blockSize)
                            s[id] += s[id+128];
24    __syncthreads();
25    if(blockSize >  64 && id <  64 && id+ 64 < blockSize)
                            s[id] += s[id+64];
26    __syncthreads();
27    if (id < 32) {
          // syncwarps required for devices of CC >= 7.0
28                    s[id] += s[id + 32]; __syncwarp();
29      if(id < 16) s[id] += s[id + 16]; __syncwarp();
30      if(id <  8) s[id] += s[id +  8]; __syncwarp();
31      if(id <  4) s[id] += s[id +  4]; __syncwarp();
32      if(id <  2) s[id] += s[id +  2]; __syncwarp();
33      if(id <  1) s[id] += s[id +  1]; __syncwarp();

34      if(id == 0) sums[blockIdx.x] = s[0]; // store block sum
35    }
36 }
```

In many tutorial reduction examples predating the introduction of the CC=7.0 architecture, lines 25–30 would have been just the addition statements without either the if clauses or the synchronisation calls. This was possible because all the threads in the warp ran in strict lock step and thus there was no need for explicit synchronisation and also allowing all threads to perform all the additions did not add to the execution time. Moreover, removing the if clauses improved performance without effecting the correctness of the final sum. (Although the final values in s[1-31] will have been corrupted, after they had been correctly used, by subsequent "unnecessary" addition steps.)

In Example 3.1 we have used the relatively fast __syncwarp() calls to ensure the correct behaviour on newer devices. More subtly, the if statements in lines 26–30 are also necessary for CC≥7 correctness. The reason for this is to avoid possible "read after write" errors; consider the statement s[id] += s[id+8] which is part of line 27; if it is made conditional in (id <8) then only s[0-7] will be changed by adding s[8-15]. On the other hand, if the addition is made unconditional and threads do not run in strict lock step then one or more values in s[8-15] may have values from s[16-23] added before they are added to s[0-7] resulting in an incorrect final total. This is sometimes referred to as a "read after write error".

3.1 CUDA Objects in Cooperative Groups

To use NVIDIA cooperative groups, the appropriate header file must be included in your code as shown in the box:

```
#include "cooperative_groups.h"
using cg = cooperative_groups;
```

Here the optional second line defines `cg` as short alias for the namespace `cooperative_groups`. These definitions allow us to create first class C++ objects to represent the familiar, thread block, grid and warp objects defined for any kernel launch. An example is shown in the next box:

```
auto grid  = cg::this_grid();
auto block = cg::this_thread_block();
auto warp  = cg::tiled_partition<32>(block);
```

If you don't like auto, the explicit types of these objects are:

```
cg::grid_group              grid
cg::thread_block            block
cg::thread_block_tile<32>   warp
```

These statements create objects `grid`, `block` and `warp` which represent respectively the grid, thread block and warp to which the particular thread belongs. Notice we are using the built-in objects `this_grid()` and `this_thread_block()` to initialise `grid` and `block` but we use the explicit value of 32 for the warp size in the definition of `warp`.[4] The use of the C++11 keyword `auto` in the declarations is helpful for avoiding mistakes and keeping the code readable. These objects are first class C++ objects and can, for example, be passed as arguments to device functions. There are no default constructors for these objects, and both grid and block must be initialised in the way shown. You can, of course, choose different variable names and copy these objects. Within your kernel code the actual objects are lightweight handles pointing to data shared by all relevant threads.

The block and grid objects encapsulate the familiar properties of the thread block and grid of thread blocks associated with any CUDA kernel launch and in particular provide an alternative way of accessing the same information contained in the CUDA built-in variables like `threadIdx`.[5]

Tiled partitions are more complicated; the example shown above divides the previously created thread block `block` into sub-blocks of 32 contiguous threads representing the individual warps that are used by the hardware. This is by far the most common use of tiled partitions, but it is not the only possibility. Partitions can have sizes which are any power of 2 between 2 and 32 and can be defined on the thread block or on a previously defined larger tiled partition as shown in the next box:

Table 3.1 *Member functions for CG objects*

Function	Grid	Block	Tile	Comment
`void sync()`	√	√	√	Synchronise all threads in object
`ull size()`	√	√	√	Number of threads in object
`ull thread_rank()`	√	√	√	Rank of current thread in object
`dim3 group_dim()`	√	√	–	Same as built-in `blockDim` for block or `gridDim` for grid.
`bool is_valid()`	√	–	–	Availability of grid wide synchronisation
`dim3 group_index()`	–	√	–	Same as built-in `blockIdx`[†]
`dim3 thread_index()`	–	√	–	Same as built-in `threadIdx`[†]
`ull meta_group_size()`	–	–	√	Number of tiles in this partition
`ull meta_group_rank()`	–	–	√	Rank of current tile in this partition
`Cooperative functions`	–	–	√	Additional member functions, see Table 3.2

[†] `blockIdx` and `threadIdx` have type `uint3` whereas the equivalent CG member functions have type `dim3`.

```
auto warp    = cg::tiled_partition<32>(block);
auto warp8   = cg::tiled_partition<8>(block);
auto warp4A  = cg::tiled_partition<4>(warp);
auto warp4B  = cg::tiled_partition<4>(warp8);
```

Here `warp` is the standard partition of a thread-block into warps of 32 threads. `warp8` a partition of the thread-block into groups of 8-thread subwarps. `warp4A` is a partition of warp into 8 4-thread subwarps and `warp4B` is a partition of warp8 into 2 subsets of 4 threads. Although the current thread will have the same rank in `warp4A` and `warp4B`, the values returned by the member functions `meta_group_size()` and `meta_group_rank()` will differ.

If you plan to use sub-warps in an application it is important to remember that cooperative groups only provide software support for this. The GPU hardware will still process threads in units of 32-thread warps; thus if the code in two subwarps, which happen to be in the same GPU warp, diverge there will be an impact on the performance of the code. Table 3.1 shows the member functions available to the three types of group.

CUDA SDK 11.1 released in December 2020 adds the multiwarp `tiled_partion`, to cooperative groups, for example, `cg::tiled_partition<64>(block)`. The thread block size must be a multiple of the warp size, 64 in this case. The implementation implicitly uses shared memory for interwarp communication; there is no new direct hardware support at present.

In the table the member functions in the tile column are available for all tiled partitions, not just 32-thread warps. The member functions of return type `dim3` provide the same information as the familiar CUDA built-in variables such as `threadIdx`. Note that the `sync`, `size` and `thread_rank` functions are available for all three object types. The other member functions are specific to each type. The type `ull` used in the table is an alias for `unsigned long long`, the same alias is defined in `cx.h` and is used in some of our examples.

The grid wide `sync()` function is only available if the kernel code has been compiled under a number of significant restrictions described in Section 3.8. However, since the introduction of

CUDA SDK 11.0 all the other features of grid groups can be used in normal CUDA code. The `is_valid()` member function allows a kernel to test whether or not the `grid.sync()` function is available. Prior to SDK 11.0 in May 2020 *none* of the grid group functionality was available without these restrictions and so many early tutorial examples may not make use of grid groups.

The function `block.thread_rank()` returns the rank of the current thread in its thread block, using the same 3D rank formula as used in Example 2.3 which reduces to the 1D linear thread rank formula in cases where a 1D thread block is used for the kernel launch. The `grid.thread_rank()` function adds `block_rank*block_size` to this result to obtain the rank of a thread within the entire grid of thread blocks. Example 3.2 shows how Example 2.3 can be rewritten using cooperative groups.

Description of Example 3.2

Only lines which differ from Example 2.3 are shown in the example.

- Lines 4.1–4.2: These lines add support for cooperative groups to the code.
- Lines 9–11: These perform the same calculation as before of the thread's 3D rank in the gird but using member functions instead of the corresponding built-in variables. We have still had to remember the correct formulae with arguably a small increase in verbosity.
- Line 14: The member function `block.size()` replaces the previous formula for the thread block size.
- Line 15: There is no member function for the number of blocks in a grid: the ratio of the number of threads in the grid and threads in a block is a simple way to find this quantity.
- Line 16: The member function `grid.size()` gives the total number of threads in the grid directly.
- Line 17: The member function `block.thread_rank()` gives the current thread's rank in the thread block directly. This is a frequently used quantity in kernel code and we have eliminated the formula needed before.
- Line 18: Here we use a simple ratio to calculate the thread block's rank in the grid replacing a more complex formula.
- Line 19: The member function `grid.thread_rank()` gives the current thread's rank in the grid directly. Again, this is a frequently used quantity and we have eliminated the formula needed before.

Example 3.2 `coop3D` kernel illustrating use of cooperative groups with 3D grids

```
      . . .
04.1 #include "cooperative_groups.h"
04.2 namespace cg = cooperative_groups;
05   __device__   int   a[256][512][512];   // file scope
06   __device__   float b[256][512][512];   // file scope
07   __global__   void coop3D(int nx,int ny,int nz,int id)
08   {
08.1   auto grid  = cg::this_grid();
08.2   auto block = cg::this_thread_block();
09     int x = block.group_index().x*block.group_dim().x+
                block.thread_index().x;
```

```
10        int y = block.group_index().y*block.group_dim().y+
                  block.thread_index().y;
11        int z = block.group_index().z*block.group_dim().z+
                  block.thread_index().z;
12        if(x >=nx || y >=ny || z >=nz) return;   // in range?
13        int array_size = nx*ny*nz;
          // threads in one block
14        int block_size =    block.size();
          // blocks in grid
15        int grid_size   =    grid.size()/block.size();
          // threads in whole grid
16        int total_threads = grid.size();
17        int thread_rank_in_block = block.thread_rank();
18        int block_rank_in_grid   =
                  grid.thread_rank()/block.size();
19        int thread_rank_in_grid  = grid.thread_rank();
          . . .
```

Our conclusion from Example 3.2 might be that although there has been some reduction in the need to use error prone formulae there are no really new features so far.

The really interesting new feature is the treatment of warps which we will discuss in two steps. Firstly, in Example 3.3 we show how warps and sub warps can be defined as C++ objects and then we move on to discuss how the additional member functions in Table 3.2 can be used to significantly improve our reduction kernels.

Description of Example 3.3

- Lines 8–15: Define the __device__ function show_tile that takes a thread_block_tile as an input argument and prints information about the current thread.
- Line 8: The template function show_tile is declared here; the first argument is a simple character string used to decorate the printed output. More interestingly the second argument is a thread_block_tile of size defined by the template parameter int T.
- Lines 10–13: Use member functions to obtain rank the rank of the current thread in the tile, size the number of threads in the tile, mrank the rank of the present tile in the parent partition and msize the number of tiles in the parent partition.
- Line 14: Print the parameters and the total number of threads in the partition calculated as size*msize.
- Line 16: Declare the kernel cgwarp; the kernel has a single input argument id, which specifies the rank of the thread that will call show_tile.
- Lines 18–19: Set the CG objects grid and block as usual.
- Lines 20–22: Define a set of tiled partitions defined on the current thread block. These tiles, named warp32, warp16 and warp8 have 32, 16 and 8 threads per tile respectively. The first of these, warp32, with 32 threads represents a standard CUDA warp.
- Line 23: Defines the sub-tile tile8 using tile32 as a parent. Effectively this splits each CUDA warp into 4 tiles of 8 threads.

Example 3.3 cgwarp kernel illustrating use of tiled partitions

```
    . . .
08  template <int T> __device__ void
        show_tile(const char *tag, cg::thread_block_tile<T> p)
09  {
10    int rank = p.thread_rank(); // thread rank in tile
11    int size = p.size();        // number of threads in tile
12    int mrank = p.meta_group_rank(); // rank of tile in parent
                    // number of tiles in parent
13    int msize = p.meta_group_size();

14    printf("%s rank in tile %2d size %2d rank %3d
        num %3d net size %d\n", tag, rank, size,
        mrank, msize, msize*size);
15  }
16  __global__ void cgwarp(int id)
17  {
18    auto grid    = cg::this_grid();          // standard cg
19    auto block   = cg::this_thread_block();  // definitions
                    // 32 thread warps
20    auto warp32  = cg::tiled_partition<32>(block);
                    // 16 thread tiles
21    auto warp16  = cg::tiled_partition<16>(block);
                    // 8 thread tiles
22    auto warp8   = cg::tiled_partition< 8>(block);
                    // 8 thread sub-warps
23    auto tile8 = cg::tiled_partition<8>(warp32);
                    // 4 thread sub-sub warps
24    auto tile4 = cg::tiled_partition<4>(tile8);
25    if(grid.thread_rank() == id) {
26      printf("warps and subwarps for thread %d:\n",id);
27      show_tile<32>("warp32",warp32);
28      show_tile<16>("warp16",warp16);
29      show_tile< 8>("warp8 ",warp8);
30      show_tile< 8>("tile8 ",tile8);
31      show_tile< 4>("tile4 ",tile4);
32    }
33  }
34  int main(int argc, char *argv[])
35  {
36    int id      = (argc >1) ? atoi(argv[1]) : 12345;
37    int blocks  = (argc >2) ? atoi(argv[2]) : 28800;
38    int threads = (argc >3) ? atoi(argv[3]) : 256;
39    cgwarp<<<blocks,threads>>>(id);
40    return 0;
41  }

D:\ >cgwarp.exe 1234567 28800 256
```

```
warps and subwarps for thread 1234567:
warp32 rank in tile 7 size 32 rank  4 num  8 net size 256
warp16 rank in tile 7 size 16 rank  8 num 16 net size 256
warp8  rank in tile 7 size  8 rank 16 num 32 net size 256
tile8  rank in tile 7 size  8 rank  0 num  4 net size 32
tile4  rank in tile 3 size  4 rank  1 num  2 net size 8
```

- Line 24: This defines what is effectively a sub-sub-tile by defining `tile4` as a partition of `tile8`.
- Lines 25–32: Here we print results for the single thread having rank `id` in the grid of thread blocks. The input parameter `id` is a user supplied value.
- Lines 34–41: Here the main routine sets `id` and the launch configuration for optional user input and launches the `cgwarp` kernel.

The sample results shown for Example 3.3 represent different views of the same physical thread regarded as a member of differently defined partitions. The difference between `warp8` and `tile8` is only seen in their "meta" properties with respect to different parents.

3.2 Tiled Partitions

Tiled partitions have the additional member functions shown in Table 3.2.

Table 3.2 *Additional member functions for tiled thread blocks*

Additional member functions for `thread_block_tile` objects. The template parameter `T` for the shuffle functions can be `int`, `long`, `long long` (signed or unsigned) and `float` or `double`. With the `cuda_fp16.h` header included `T` can also be `__half` or `__half2`. These functions implicitly perform all necessary synchronisations with no risk of read after write errors. The `shfl` functions return 0 when referencing values for threads which have exited early. The `match_any` and `match_all` functions are only available for devices with CC ≥ 7.0.

Member Function	Comment (`tid` is the lane of the calling thread)
`T shfl(T var, int src)`	Return value of `val` in lane `scr` to all threads in tile
`T shfl_down(T var, uint sft)`	Return value of `val` in lane `tid+sft` to thread `tid`. If `tid+sft` is out of range return local value of `val`.
`T shfl_up(T var, uint sft)`	Return value of `val` in lane `tid-sft` to thread `tid`. If `tid-sft` is out of range return local value of `val`.
`T shfl_xor(T var, uint msk)`	Return value of `val` in lane (`tid XOR msk`) to thread `tid`. For example, setting `msk` to `size()`−1 or simply −1, reverses the order in which `val`s are held in the threads.
`int any(int pred)`	Returns 1 if `pred` is non-zero for any thread in tile, otherwise returns 0.
`int all(int pred)`	Returns 1 if `pred` is non-zero for all threads in tile, otherwise returns 0.
`uint ballot(int pred)`	Returns a bitmask with bits set to 1 for active threads with non-zero values of `pred`.
`uint match_any(T val)`	Returns a bitmask which has bits set to 1 for active threads having the same value of `val` as this particular thread.
`uint match_all(T val, int &pred)`	If all active threads have the same value of `val`, returns a bitmask of active threads and sets `pred` to 1. Otherwise 0 is returned and `pred` is set to 0.

These functions enable powerful collective operations to be performed by the threads in a tile. The member functions for `thread_block_tile` objects provide for a rich variety of communication between threads in the same group. The various shfl functions are not new but replace older intrinsic functions with similar names. However, the new member functions implicitly include any required synchronisation which is an important simplification when writing warp-level code for new $CC \geq 7$ devices. They also guarantee to perform reads before writes in situations like tree reduction.

The various shfl functions allow threads within the same warp to exchange values in local registers, shared memory or global memory. Example 3.4 shows how Example 3.1 can be modified to use shfl_down to perform the reduction across a warp of threads.

Example 3.4 `reduce6` kernel using `warp_shfl` functions

```
05 #include "cooperative_groups.h";
06 namespace cg = cooperative_groups;
   . . .
10 template <int blockSize> __global__ void
          reduce6(r_Ptr<float> sums,cr_Ptr<float> data,int n)
11 {
12   // This template kernel assumes blockDim.x = blockSize
13   // and that blockSize ≤ 1024
14   __shared__ float s[blockSize];
15   auto grid =  cg::this_grid();            // cg definitions
16   auto block = cg::this_thread_block();       // for launch
17   auto warp =  cg::tiled_partition<32>(block);   // config
18   int id = block.thread_rank(); // rank in block
19   s[id] = 0.0f;   // NB simplified thread linear addressing loop
20   for(int tid=grid.thread_rank();tid < n;
                       tid+=grid.size()) s[id] += data[tid];
21   block.sync();
22   if(blockSize>512 && id<512 && id+512<blockSize)
                              s[id] += s[id + 512];
23   block.sync();
24   if(blockSize>256 && id<256 && id+256<blockSize)
                              s[id] += s[id + 256];
25   block.sync();
26   if(blockSize>128 && id<128 && id+128<blockSize)
                              s[id] += s[id + 128];
27   block.sync();
28   if(blockSize>64 && id<64 && id+64 < blockSize)
                              s[id] += s[id +  64];
29   block.sync();
30   //  just warp zero from here
31   if(warp.meta_group_rank()==0) {
32     s[id] += s[id + 32]; warp.sync();
33     s[id] += warp.shfl_down(s[id],16);
34     s[id] += warp.shfl_down(s[id], 8);
35     s[id] += warp.shfl_down(s[id], 4);
36     s[id] += warp.shfl_down(s[id], 2);
```

```
37       s[id] += warp.shfl_down(s[id], 1);
38       if(id == 0) sums[blockIdx.x] = s[0]; // store sum
39   }
40 }
```

Description of Example 3.4

The kernel shown here is a modification of the `reduce5` kernel shown in Example 3.1.

- Lines 5–6: Here we show the inclusion of the header file needed to access cooperative groups and the definition of `cg` as a shorthand for the cooperative group's namespace.
- Line 10: The new kernel `reduce6` is declared here and has the same interface as `reduce5`.
- Lines 15–17: These additional lines define objects representing the current thread's warp, thread block and also the entire thread-grid.
- Line 18: Equivalent to line 15 of the previous kernel except that we use `b.thread_rank()` instead of `threadIdx.x` to find the rank of the current thread in the thread block.
- Line 20: This line replaces line 17 of `reduce5` and computes the thread based partial sums of the n values stored in the array `data` using thread-linear addressing. Notice how the expressions for the `for` loop start and end values are simplified using the `grid` object.[6]
- Lines 21–29: These are identical to lines 19–26 of `reduce5` except we use `group.sync()` instead of `__syncthreads()`.
- Lines 31–39: This is the code for the last part of the reduction performed by the lowest ranking warp in the thread block; it is equivalent to lines 27–35 of `reduce5`. Notice the warp size of 32 threads is still hard-wired into this part of the code; we could have used `warp.size()` instead of 32 here and replaced lines 29–33 with a `for` loop, but we prefer to use this explicitly unrolled version for clarity and performance.
  - Line 32: We use `warp.sync()` instead of `__syncwarp()` here. Since this code reads data from a different warp we cannot use the `shfl` functions.
  - Lines 33–37: Here we see the important change to the code. We are using the `shfl_down()` member function of `warp` to exchange local values between threads in the same warp. This member function will implicitly perform the necessary intra-warp synchronisation between threads including protection from read after write errors. Thus, we can dispense with both the `if(id<..)` clauses and the `__syncwarp()` statements used in lines 28–33 of the previous example. In fact, not only can we dispense with them – we have to! The `shfl_up`, `_down` and `_xor` instructions shown in Table 3.3 only work if both the sender and receiver threads in the warp execute the instruction. If the sender thread is inactive or exited, the result obtained by the receiver thread is documented as undefined. More details are in Table 3.7 in our section on thread divergence.

In lines 32–37 we have recovered the simplicity and efficiency of older codes with CC<7.0 using lock-step implicit warp-level programming – but with the advantage of making our intentions explicit!

- Line 38: This final line which stores the block sum is identical to line 34 of the previous example.

Looking at the warp-level processing in Example 3.4 we notice that while the `shfl_down` function can use shared memory to hold value being exchanged it does not need to, a local register will work just as well and could be slightly faster. This motivates us to think about dispensing with shared memory entirely and write a third version of the reduction kernel, `reduce7`, shown in Example 3.5; it just uses warp-level code and local registers.

Example 3.5 `reduce7` kernel using solely intra-warp communication

```
10   __global__ void reduce7(r_Ptr<float> sums,
                                  cr_Ptr<float> data,int n)
11   {
12   // This kernel assumes array sums is set to zero
13   // on entry and that blockSize is multiple of 32
14   auto grid  = cg::this_grid();
15   auto block = cg::this_thread_block();
16   auto warp  = cg::tiled_partition<32>(block);

     // accumulate thread sums in register variable v
17   float v = 0.0f;
18   for(int tid=grid.thread_rank(); tid<n;
                       tid+=grid.size()) v += data[tid];
19   warp.sync();
20   v += warp.shfl_down(v,16);   // |
21   v += warp.shfl_down(v, 8);   // |  warp level
22   v += warp.shfl_down(v, 4);   // |  reduce here
23   v += warp.shfl_down(v, 2);   // |
24   v += warp.shfl_down(v, 1);   // |

     //     use atomicAdd to sum over warps
25   if(warp.thread_rank()==0)
          atomicAdd(&sums[block.group_index().x], v);
26   }
```

Description of Example 3.5

This is one of our favourite examples in the entire book; it is very concise and looks different to the standard tutorial reduction examples. In this kernel all the warps are treated symmetrically and are active all the time. There are no restrictions on the size of thread–blocks beyond the natural requirement of being a multiple of 32. We like the fact that shared memory is not required at all as this simplifies kernel launches and allows for maximum L1 cache in GPUs where shared memory and L1 cache are allocated from a common pool. It is a great illustration of what I call *warp-only* kernel coding, which is made easy by CUDA cooperative groups and which I think will become more common.[7]

- Line 10: The declaration of `reduce7` is similar to before except that this is not a template function. The reason for this is that this kernel version works for any thread block size (which is a multiple of 32). All tree reductions will be done in five steps by individual warps.

- Lines 14–16: These define our usual CG objects; notice that there is no preceding shared memory declaration.
- Lines 17–18: Here each thread in the kernel accumulates a sum over a subset of the input data. This corresponds to lines 19–20 of Example 3.4 However, a local register based variable v is used instead of the shared s array indexed by id. Dispensing with shared memory simplifies both the code and the kernel launch; it also allows us to configure the GPU to use maximum L1 cache and minimum shared memory on devices where this is possible.
- Line 19: Here we use `warp.sync()` instead of `__syncthreads()` as was needed in the previous versions. Again, this is slightly faster.
- Lines 20–24: This is a warp-level tree reduction of the 32 local v values held by the threads in each warp. Here we see the real power of the warp-level member functions to share data between threads in the same warp. These lines correspond to lines 33–37 of the previous example.
- Line 25: At this point for each warp, the thread of rank zero in the warp holds that warp's contribution to the total sum. In order to retain the same output interface as the previous version we would like to store just the sum of these individual contributions in a single element of the output array sums. We solve the problem of accumulating multiple values in a single memory location by using atomic addition to update the element of global memory. This is potentially an expensive operation and also requires that the elements of sums to have been present to zero prior to the kernel call. For GPUs of CC=6.0 and above, we could use the new `atomicAdd_block` function which restricts atomic operation to just threads in the same thread block. This newer version should be faster than the older `atomicAdd` which checks all threads in the kernel. However, tests with the RTX 2070 show very little observable performance difference between these two functions.

Notice also that we used `warp.thread_rank() == 0` instead of something like `id%32 == 0` to find the lowest ranking thread in a warp. Again, this makes the programmer's intentions clearer.

The `reduce7` example is not only more compact than the previous version, but it also works for any thread block size that is a multiple of the warp size without the need for template parameters or other tests.

Another interesting point to note about `reduce7` is that, while we used the `shfl_down` intrinsic function, we could equally well have used `shfl_xor` with the same values for the second argument; these values would be interpreted as lane bitmasks for the XOR operations rather than a shift down values. The effect of using these XORs would be to exchange corresponding pairs of values rather than just shift down or return local values when out of range. This in turn would, after five steps, leave *all* the 32 v values in the warp containing the same correct sum, not just thread zero. This takes no extra time and could be helpful in other applications where the sums are part of an ongoing calculation and needed by all threads in the warp.

The topic of reduction has featured in CUDA tutorials from the beginning, mostly as a way of illustrating shared memory. As the final reduce7 example shows, warp-only programming on more recent GPUs can deliver the same or better performance without using shared memory. The May 2020 CUDA SDK 11, which introduced the new CC 8 Ampere generation of GPUs, takes this one step further by adding a new warp-level reduce function to the cooperative group's library.[8] This function can replace lines 19–23 of the `reduce7` kernel. This is shown in our final reduce example `reduce8`.

Example 3.6 `reduce8` kernel showing use of cg::reduce warp-level function

```
05    #include "cooperative_groups/reduce.h"
      . . .
10    __global__ void reduce8(r_Ptr<float> sums, cr_Ptr<float>
                          data, int n)
11    {
12        // This kernel assumes array sums is set to zero
13        // on entry and that blockSize is multiple of 32
14        auto grid =  cg::this_grid();
15        auto block = cg::this_thread_block();
16        auto warp =  cg::tiled_partition<32>(block);

          // accumulate thread sums in register variable v
17        float v = 0.0f;

18        for(int tid=grid.thread_rank(); tid<n;
                          tid+=grid.size()) v += data[tid];
19        warp.sync();
20        v = cg::reduce(warp, v, cg::plus<float>());

21        //atomic add to sum over block
22        if(warp.thread_rank()==0)
              atomicAdd(&sums[block.group_index().x],v);
23    }
```

Description of Example 3.6

- Line 5: This extra include statement is necessary to access the new reduce function.
- Line 20: This function call replaces lines 20–24 of the `reduce7` kernel. The three arguments are the current warp, the data item to be reduced across the warp and the type of reduction operation to be performed. The `cg::reduce` function is a template function for the type of the second argument and C++11 is necessary. The third argument can be any of `plus()`, `less()`, `greater()`, `bit_and()`, `bit_xor()` or `bit_or()`. It is necessary to specify the type of the second argument explicitly in the third argument.

All other lines of the `reduce8` kernel are the same as `reduce7`.

3.3 Vector Loading

A final, but very important, observation we note that these reduction kernels have two steps. Firstly, an accumulation step where partial thread-based sums over the entire input array are found and secondly, a step that reduces the partial thread sums down to a single value per thread block. The time taken by the first step scales with the size of the input array whereas the time for the second step is independent of the size of the input array. Thus, for large input array sizes the time taken for the kernel to execute is dominated by the first step – but our efforts so far have been devoted to optimising the second step.

We note that in the first step each thread reads a single 32-bit word from the input array data on each pass through the read loop (e.g. line 17 of Examples 3.5 and 3.6). The reads are properly coalesced in the sense that consecutive threads read consecutive words from the input array, nevertheless we can improve performance by switching to reading 128-bit items per thread; this is maximally efficient in terms of L1 cache use and allows the compiler to use one 128-bit load and store instruction rather than four 32-bit instructions. This technique is called *vector-loading* and is discussed in the NVIDIA blog https://devblogs.nvidia.com/cuda-pro-tip-increase-performance-with-vectorized-memory-access/.

The modified version of the kernel reduce7_vl is shown in Example 3.7.

Description of Example 3.7

- Line 10: The kernel arguments are unchanged. We will read the input array data as if it were an int4 array, but that detail is hidden from the user.
- Line 17: Here we declare a 128-bit vector variable int4 v4 instead of a scalar variable int v and set each component to zero. This replaces the scalar v used here in the reduce7 kernel.
- Line 18: Since each step of the for loop will now consume 4 constructive values from the input array data, the termination test on tid is now tid < n/4 not tid < n. Note there is a tacit assumption in this code that n is a multiple of four. If this is false, then up to three values from the input array will be ignored due to integer rounding down in the value of n/4. This is a weaker restriction than the need for n to be a multiple of blockSize as in some previous examples.

Here we use a reinterpret_cast to tell the compiler to treat the pointer data as if it were a pointer to a float4 array; this means that the index tid will be treated as an index into an array of 128-bit items and the value returned on the right-hand side is treated as an int4 object. The compiler will use a single 128-bit load instruction to access a complete 128-bit L1 cache line.

The resulting float4 from data is then added component wise to v4 using the overloaded += operator defined in the CUDA SDK header file helper_math.h.

- Line 19: Here we sum the four components of v4 and store the result in the scalar variable v. The scaler v now plays the same role as it did in the reduce7 example. As a subtle detail we note different subsets of values from data will be summed to the v variables in the two versions of this kernel. This could conceivably affect rounding errors.
- Lines 20–26: These are identical to lines 19–25 of reduce7.

Example 3.7 reduce7_vl kernel with vector loading

```
10   __global__ void reduce7_vl(r_Ptr<float> sums,
                                  cr_Ptr<float> data, int n)
11   {
12      // This kernel assumes array sums is set to zero
```

```
13   // on entry and that n is a multiple of 4.
14   auto grid =  cg::this_grid();
15   auto block = cg::this_thread_block();
16   auto warp =  cg::tiled_partition<32>(block);

     // use v4 to read global memory
17   float4 v4 = {0.0f,0.0f,0.0f,0.0f};
18   for(int tid = grid.thread_rank(); tid < n/4;
                               tid += grid.size() ) v4 +=
                 reinterpret_cast<const float4 *>(data)[tid];

     // accumulate thread sums in v
19   float v =  v4.x + v4.y + v4.z + v4.w;
20   warp.sync();
21   v += warp.shfl_down(v,16);  // |
22   v += warp.shfl_down(v,8);   // |  warp level
23   v += warp.shfl_down(v,4);   // |  reduce here
24   v += warp.shfl_down(v,2);   // |
25   v += warp.shfl_down(v,1);   // |

     //  use atomicAdd to sum over warps
26   if(warp.thread_rank()==0)
           atomicAdd(&sums[block.group_index().x],v);
27   }
```

The other kernels can be converted to use 128-bit vector loads in exactly the same way; we will not show the code here but the modified kernels are available in our code repository.

We have run timing tests on the various reduce kernels with and without vector loading for input arrays sizes of powers 2 between 2^{15} and 2^{29}. Since reading global memory is the performance limiting factor, the appropriate metric is the bandwidth in GB/sec calculated as:

$$\text{Bandwidth in GB/sec} = (\text{input array size in bytes})/(10^9 \times \text{time taken})$$

For comparison we also include the result of using the thrust::reduce library function on data already stored in device memory. The results are shown in Figures 3.1 and 3.2 for the RTX 2070 GPU.

Getting good timing information for these fast memory bound kernels is actually quite hard. The results shown here are based on the average times taken to run the kernels in a loop for between 1024 and 65536 iterations using multiple copies of the data buffer data spanning 2^{29} 4-byte words of global memory and rotating through different copies of data on successive iterations in order to defeat memory caching. Without this precaution the execution times for smaller data sizes just reflect the time required to reload data from L1 or L2 cache. We also ran each kernel for several different launch configurations and in each case used the fastest time obtained. The best launch configuration was found to vary between kernels and data size, smaller data sizes required fewer blocks and threads.

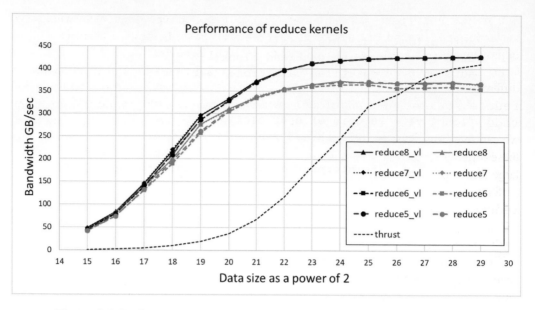

Figure 3.1 Performance of the reduction kernels on a Turing RTX 2070 GPU

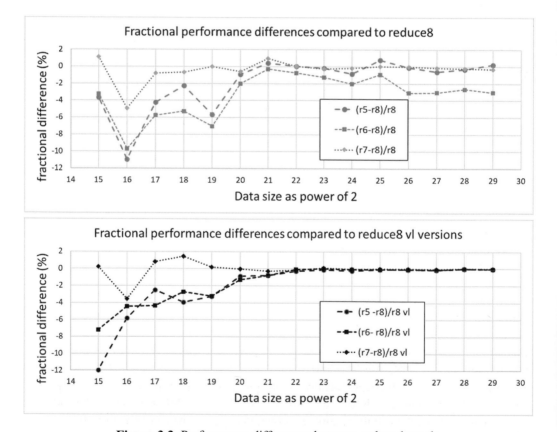

Figure 3.2 Performance differences between reduce kernels

It is clear from Figure 3.2 that by far the most important optimisation is switching to vector loading. Beyond that the `reduce7/8` kernels have the best performance but the improvements over `reduce6` are quite small for larger datasets.

In order to see the difference more clearly Figure 3.3 shows the fractional bandwidth differences between `reduce8` and `reduce5/6/7` and between `reduce8_v1` and `reduce5/6/7_v1`. The differences are calculated as $100(reduce5-reduce8)/reduce8$ for the case of `reduce5` and similarly for the other kernels. From the figure we can see that the `reduce7` versions are better than either `reduce5` or `reduce6`, but these differences become less significant for larger data sets; presumably this is because for large arrays memory access speed dominates the calculation time. The `reduce7` kernel's performance is essentially the same as that of the new CUDA reduce function used in `reduce8`. These results are for our CC 7.5 RTX 2070 Turing GPU. The next generation CC 8 Ampere GPUs have hardware support for warp-level reduce so we might expect `reduce8` to perform better on these devices.

This ends our discussion of reduction operations on GPUs and the remainder of this chapter explores further features of cooperative groups associated with partitioning warps into subsets. This part can be skipped on first reading as you are unlikely to want these more esoteric features of cooperative groups at first. The examples in the rest of this chapter are frankly somewhat artificial, but we think you will find that the more application orientated examples in the rest of the book are more rewarding.

3.4 Warp-Level Intrinsic Functions and Sub-warps

Although CG `tiled_partition` objects are often used with a size of 32 to represent a 32-thread warp, they can also be used to represent power of 2 sized subsets of warps, for example groups of 4 or 16 threads. The `size`, `thread_rank` and all other member functions will reflect the size of the subset defined by the `tiled_partition`. This is a very convenient feature if your problem naturally requires the use of such subsets. Notice, however, that while there is software support for sub-warps, there is no extra hardware support to allow subsets of threads in the *same* warp to perform *different* tasks simultan-eously.[9] Thus if different sub-warps within the same warp perform different operations, then there will be thread divergence with some associated loss of performance. The `sync` member function for any size of `tiled_partition` is always safe to use and will not cause deadlock even in the case of divergent sub-warps in the same warp.

Another benefit of cooperative groups is the ability to handle thread divergence and this is discussed later in the Thread Divergence and Synchronisation section.

The member functions shown in Table 3.2 are not really new. Since the Maxwell CC=3.0 architecture, CUDA has provided a range of intrinsic functions with similar functionality allowing threads to directly share information they hold in registers with other threads in the *same* warp. The available functions are the warp vote and match functions shown in Table 3.3 and the warp shuffle functions shown in Table 3.4. The versions of these functions shown in these tables were introduced with CC 7 and as their names imply, they implicitly perform warp-level synchronisation when necessary. These functions replaced the early CC 3 era functions which had similar names excluding the _sync postfix. Those early functions relied on implicit warp-level lock-step synchronisation and are hence unsafe to use with

Table 3.3 *Warp vote and warp match intrinsic functions*

NB the warp match functions are only available for CC≥7.0

`int __all_sync(uint mask,int pred)`

Evaluate `pred` for all non-exited threads in `mask` and return non-zero if *all* of the participating threads have non-zero values of `pred`.

`int __any_sync(uint mask,int pred)`

Evaluate `pred` for all non-exited threads in `mask` and return non-zero if *any* of the participating threads have non-zero values of `pred`.

`uint __ballot_sync(uint mask,int pred)`

Evaluate `pred` for all non-exited threads in `mask` and return a `uint` with bits set to 1 for participating threads having non-zero values of `pred`.

`uint __activemask()`

Return `uint` with bits set to 1 for all currently active and non-exited threads in the calling warp.

`unsigned uint __match_any_sync(uint mask, T val)`

For each non-exited thread in mask, returns a `uint` with bits set to 1 for those participating threads that have the same value of `val` as the calling thread.

`unsigned uint __match_all_sync(uint mask, T val,int *pred)`

For each non-exited thread in mask, returns a `uint` equal to `mask` if all threads in `mask` have the same value for `val` and set `pred` to non-zero. Otherwise return 0 and set `pred` to 0.

---

modern CC≥7 devices. The `match_all` and `match_any` functions are new with CC=7.0 and only work on devices with CC≥7.0.

The warp-level intrinsic functions shown in the Tables 3.3 and 3.4 are presented mainly for reasons of completeness and because you may well see them in older tutorial examples or existing code. Although they can be used without creating CG objects, we think they are harder to use than the member functions shown in Table 3.2 because of the need to specify the `mask` argument for participating threads. We also think that creating `tiled_partitions` to represent warps is always a good idea for warp-level CUDA code irrespective of whether you need to use the member functions.

Another reason why Tables 3.3 and 3.4 are interesting is that the member functions for `tiled_partions` used in our examples are presumably implemented by calling these older functions with suitably constructed mask and width values.[10]

3.5 Thread Divergence and Synchronisation

In many CUDA programs it is necessary to have branches in code where some threads will take one branch and some take another. A variation on this is that some threads might exit early from the kernel, by using `return`, leaving the remaining subset to continue. In a simple kernel with no divergent branches and no early `returns` we can be sure that all

Table 3.4 *The warp shuffle functions*

Note that T can be any of the 32 or 64-bit integer types, or float or double. If the cuda_fp16.h header is included then __half and __half2 types are also allowed. The shfl functions return 0 when referencing values for threads which have exited early.

T __shfl_sync(uint mask, T val, int src, int width=warpSize)

For each non-exited thread in mask returns the value of val held by the thread whose ID is src. If thread src is inactive the results are undefined. This is a broadcast operation. If width is less than warpSize then each subsection of the warp behaves as a separate sub-warp with lanes in the range [0,width-1]. Also src%width is used for the source lane, thus broadcasts are confined to sub-warps and each sub-warp might use a different src value. Width must be a power of 2≤warpSize.

T __shfl_up_sync(uint mask, T val, uint delta, int width=warpSize)

The same as shfl_sync except that the fixed src lane is replaced by the calling thread's lane minus delta. For example if delta=3, a thread in lane 15 would receive the value from lane 12. If the subtraction results in a negative lane value, the function returns the calling thread's own value of val. Effectively, values are shifted up delta positions within the warp or sub-warp.

T __shfl_down_sync(uint mask, T val, uint delta, int width=warpSize)

The same as shfl_sync except that the fixed src lane is replaced by the calling thread's lane plus delta. For example for delta=3, a thread in lane 15 would receive the value from lane 18. If the subtraction results in a value > width-1, the function returns the calling thread's own value of val. Effectively, values are shifted down delta positions within the warp or sub-warp.

T __shfl_xor_sync(uint mask, T val, uint laneMask, int width=warpSize)

The same as shfl_sync except that the fixed src lane is replaced by the logical XOR of calling thread's lane with laneMask. For example for laneMask=0x1F and width = 32, the values received by the calling threads would be in reverse order to the calling thread's rank in the warp. On present hardware the least 5 significant bits from the result of the XOR are used. Thus, if width is less than warpSize the result of the XOR may be greater than the size of a sub-warp. In this situation threads will not be able to access values in higher ranked sub-warps than their own and return their own value of val but they will be able to access threads in lower ranked sub-warps than their own.

threads are *active*. In other cases we might know that in certain parts of our code that some threads are or might be *inactive* or *exited*.

It is important to distinguish between exited and inactive threads; most CUDA functions deal with exited threads gracefully but may have problems with inactive threads.[11] For example, _syncwarp() might deadlock if there are inactive threads while exited threads are ignored. Inactive threads are a big potential problem if we are writing a general-purpose device *function*. The function might be called by different kernels, and it should not make assumptions about which threads are active when the function is called. In particular, inactive threads cause problems when we use _syncthreads(), syncwarp() or any of the warp shuffle functions. A related issue for the shuffle functions is *out of range* target threads, for example, in the call w.shfl_down(v,16) threads 16–31 in the warp will be out of range whereas threads 0–15 will not. Tables 3.5 and 3.6 summarise the possibilities and outcomes.

Table 3.5 *Return values from warp shuffle functions*

Target Thread State	Return value
Active and in range	target thread value
Out of range	calling thread value
Inactive and in range[12]	undefined (0)
Exited and in range	undefined (0)

NB The non-member warp shuffle functions take a bit mask specifying which threads will participate in the exchange. Only those threads are used for range calculations. Thus if threads 7–10 are excluded by the bitmask, thread 6 will receive its value from thread 11 using shfl_down with a shift of 1.

Table 3.6 *Behaviour of synchronisation functions*

Block level __syncthreads() and b.sync()		
All threads in block active		success
All threads in block either active or exited		success
One or more threads in block inactive	__syncthreads()	deadlock
	b.sync()	undefined
Warp level __syncwarp(mask) and w.sync()		
All non-exited threads in mask reach same __syncwarp() or b.sync().		success
Some non-exited threads in mask reach different __syncwarp() or		success CC≥7.0
b.sync() instructions in divergent code.		undefined CC<7.0
One or more non-exited threads in mask fail to reach any __syncwarp() or		undefined
b.sync()		

In Table 3.5 it is important to note the different return values from active and inactive or exited threads. In a case like our reduction, Example 3.4, where we use addition of the return values from shfl_down, a return value of zero from an inactive thread might not be a problem but if we were to use multiplication instead, an unexpected return value of zero would be catastrophic. If it is known which threads are active then the bitmask used with the intrinsic warp shuffle functions can be set to exclude inactive threads avoiding the problem of undefined return values from inactive threads. In particular, note that the shifts used with shfl_up or shfl_down only use threads included in the bit mask for determining target threads. For example, if threads 7–10 are excluded from the bitmask, thread 6 would receive the value from thread 11 when using shfl_down with a shift of 1. Although you could work directly with the intrinsic functions and manually setting appropriate masks, it is much better to use coalesced groups discussed below.

3.6 Avoiding Deadlock

Sometimes it is necessary to synchronise at the thread block level using __syncthreads(). This function has been available since the launch of CUDA and documented as requiring *all* non-exited threads in the block to reach the *same* __syncthreads() call, otherwise the kernel stalls, waiting forever. If you use shared memory to exchange data between threads in different warps, then you will certainly need at least one __syncthreads() somewhere in the code. This is fine for simple cases, but as soon as there is some thread divergence there is a risk that not all threads will reach a particular `__syncthreads()` call in the code. This is a particular risk when making conditional calls to `__device__` functions that include calls to `__syncthreads()`.

Actually, the CUDA C programming guides for SDK version 9.0 and later explain that pre-Volta hardware actually implemented a weaker form of `__syncthreads()`, to quote from the guide:

> *"Although* `__syncthreads()` *has been consistently documented as synchronizing all threads in the thread-block, Pascal and prior architectures could only enforce synchronization at the warp level. In certain cases, this allowed a barrier to succeed without being executed by every thread as long as at least some thread in every warp reached the barrier. Starting with Volta, the CUDA built-in* `__syncthreads()` *and PTX instruction* `bar.sync` *(and their derivatives) are enforced per thread and thus will not succeed until reached by all non-exited threads in the block. Code exploiting the previous behaviour will likely deadlock and must be modified to ensure that all non-exited threads reach the barrier."*

Example 3.8 shows a kernel, `deadlock`, designed to demonstrate deadlock issues with divergent threads. The kernel partitions the threads in each thread block into three groups using a user settable parameter `gsync`. Group A includes threads with rank in `[0,gsync-1]`, group B threads with ranks in `[gsync,gsync*2-1]` and group C threads with rank≥g-sync*2. The idea is that the group A threads wait at one `__syncthreads()` and group B wait at a different `__syncthreads()`. For CC<7 hardware this is insufficient to cause deadlock – we need a third group of threads that neither calls either of the `__syncthreads()` nor exits. In our example these threads are held at a barrier controlled by the thread of rank zero which is held at the group A's `__syncthreads()`.

Description of Example 3.8

In Example 3.8 lines 10–20 show the C++ `main` function that launches the `deadlock` kernel. The main routine accepts four optional user parameters: `warps`, the number of warps per thread block; `blocks`, the number of thread blocks; the parameter `gsync`, which controls the amount of thread divergence in the kernel; and `dolock` which switches on or off the check on the value of `lock` in line 33.

- Lines 16–18: In line 17 we launch the `deadlock` kernel with user supplied values for the number of thread blocks (`blocks`) and the number of threads per block (`warps*32`). The `int` parameters `gsync` and `dolock` are passed as kernel arguments. (Value of the `blocks` parameter actually makes no difference to whether the kernel deadlocks or not but it is still included here as a user adjustable parameter for consistency with our other examples).
- Line 21: This is the declaration of the `deadlock` kernel which takes two `int` parameters `gsync` and `dolock`. As explained above, the parameter `gsync` controls a 3-way thread divergence; the threads with ranks in the range `[0,gsync-1]` execute lines 26–29 while those with ranks in range `[gsync,2*gsync-1]` execute lines 30–32 and threads with id's ≥2*gsync execute neither of these branches but continue from line 25 straight to line 33.
- Lines 23–25: Here we start the kernel by declaring a shared `int` variable `lock` which is initialised to zero by thread 0. Line 25 is the usual `__syncthreads()` necessary after shared memory has been initialised by one or more threads. After line 25 all threads will see the set value of `lock`. This `__syncthreads()` is executed by all threads and has no potential to cause deadlock.

Example 3.8 `deadlock` kernel showing deadlock on thread divergence

```
10  int main(int argc, char* argv[])
11  {
12    int warps =  (argc > 1)? atoi(argv[1])  :   3; // 3 warps
13    int blocks = (argc > 2)? atoi(argv[2])  :   1; // 1 block
14    int gsync =  (argc > 3)? atoi(argv[3])  :  32; // one warp
15    int dolock = (argc > 4)? atoi(argv[4])  :   1; // use lock?
16    printf("about to call\n");
17    deadlock<<<blocks,warps*32>>>(gsync,dolock);
18    printf("done\n");
19    return 0;
20  }
21  __global__ void deadlock(int gsync, int dolock)
22  {
23    __shared__ int lock;
24    if (threadIdx.x == 0) lock = 0;
25    __syncthreads();  // normal syncthreads

26    if (threadIdx.x < gsync) {   // group A
27      __syncthreads(); // sync A
      // deadlock unless we set lock to 1
28      if (threadIdx.x == 0) lock = 1;
29    }
30    else if (threadIdx.x < 2*gsync) { // group B
31      __syncthreads(); // sync B
32    }
      // group C may cause deadlock here
33    if(dolock) while (lock != 1);
      // see message only if NO deadlock
34    if(threadIdx.x == 0 && blockIdx.x==0)
                      printf("deadlock OK\n");
35  }
```

This code will deadlock if called with default parameters because the threads in the third warp do not call `syncthreads` and cannot exit before thread 0 sets lock to 1.

- Lines 26–29: The statements inside this `if` clause will be executed by threads in group A with ranks less than the user supplied flag `gsync`. For example, this would be just the threads in warp 0 if `gsync=32` or the first half of warp 0 if `gsync=16` or all of warp 0 and half of warp 1 if `gsync=48` and so on.
  - Line 27: Here we perform a `__syncthreads()` inside the `if` clause. If the size of the thread block is greater than or equal to `gsync` (`blockDim.x≥gsync`) the highest-ranking threads will not reach this line of code, leading to potential deadlock.
  - Line 28: If the `__syncthreads()` in the previous line succeeds, then thread zero sets the shared variable `lock` to 1 allowing all threads to eventually progress beyond line 33 and exit.

- Lines 30–31: The __syncthreads() in line 31 is executed for threads in group B with ranks in the range [gsync,2*gsync-1]. If this path is taken by some threads, then there is thread divergence and a strict reading of the early documentation implies that deadlock will occur. In practice, for the GTX 970, there is no deadlock if threads simply execute different __syncthreads().
- Line 33: Threads in group C arrive here directly bypassing both __syncthreads(). Note this is a while statement not an if statement on the test for the value of lock. That means that all threads will idle here waiting for thread zero to execute line 28 and thread zero can only do this if the __syncthreads() in line 27 succeeds; thus we have the potential for deadlock even for older devices with CC<7.

Preventing threads from simply exiting early in divergent code is essential for demonstrating deadlock on CC<7 devices. If the switch dolock in line 33 is set to zero bypassing the check on lock, then all threads with rank ≥2*gsync would simply exit at this point and any pending __syncthreads() would then notice these exits and allow the lower ranking threads to continue past their barriers as the exited threads automatically satisfy sync operations in CUDA.

- Line 34: The thread of rank zero prints a message which will only be seen if the kernel terminates normally.[13]

Some results from running Example 3.8 on two devices are shown in Table 8.3. Entries where the two devices behave differently are shown in bold. looking at the results in Table 3.7 we see the following:

- Row 1: Here there are two warps and all threads in a given warp execute the same __syncthreads() but the two warps execute different __syncthreads(). The are no deadlocks in this case.
- Row 2: Here we have three warps; the first two behave exactly the same as in row 1, but all the threads in the third warp (warp 2) bypass lines 27 and 31 going straight to the check in line 33. In the case dolock=0 all these threads exit and, therefore, do not block the pending __syncthreads(). However, in the case dolock=1 all the threads from the third warp stall at link 33 and block the pending __syncthreads().
- Row 3: Here the lower ranked half of warp 0 is in group A and goes to line 27 and the higher ranked half is in group B and goes to line 31. All threads from warp 1 go straight to line 33. The GTX card behaves as it did for row 2 but the RTX card deadlocks even for dolock=0. This is because for CC≥7 devices the hardware really checks that *all* non-exited threads for a given warp call the *same* __syncthreads.
- Row 4: Here there are 3 warps and all threads are either in group A or group B and reach line 27 or line 31. But half the threads in the middle warp (warp 1) belong to group A and half to group B. Here the value of dolock has no effect because no thread goes directly to line 33. The GTX kernel runs in both cases and the RTX it deadlocks in both cases. The deadlock on the RTX is because threads from warp 1 are held at different __syncthreads().
- Row 5: This is similar to row 4 except that threads from the highest ranked warp go straight to line 33 and for dolock=1 are blocked by pending __syncthreads(). Thus now the CC<7.0 device also deadlocks when dolock=1.

After these experiments we conclude that the following statements appear to apply to avoiding deadlock when using __syncthreads():

Table 3.7 *Results from deadlock kernel in Example 3.8*

warps	gsync	GTX 970 CC=5.2		RTX 2070 CC=7.5	
		dolock = 0	dolock = 1	dolock = 0	dolock = 1
2	32	runs	runs	runs	runs
3	32	runs	deadlock	runs	deadlock
2	16	**runs**	deadlock	**deadlock**	deadlock
3	48	**runs**	**runs**	**deadlock**	**deadlock**
4	48	**runs**	deadlock	**deadlock**	deadlock

> *"For devices of CC≥7 For all warps in each thread-block all non-exited threads in a particular warp must execute the same* `__syncthreads()` *call but different warps can execute different* `__syncthreads()` *calls."*
>
> *"For devices of CC<7 For all warps in each thread-block, at least one thread from each warp having non-exited threads must execute a* `__syncthreads()` *call."*

Notice that avoiding deadlock is a necessary but by no means a sufficient condition for ensuring your code is correct. The best advice is to avoid using `__syncthreads()` in situations of thread divergence. Pay particular care with function calls in divergent code – are you sure those functions do not use `__syncthreads()`?

If all the above looks complicated remember that `__syncthreads()` is fine in non-divergent code but in divergent code, try to use only warp-level synchronisation which is much more flexible because the NVIDIA cooperative groups library includes tools to manage *intra-warp* thread divergence in a simple way.

A final remark on Example 3.8 is to point out that using `__syncthreads()` in sections of divergent code is a clear error! The whole purpose of calling `__syncthreads()` is to synchronise *all* the non-exited threads in the thread block. A more realistic situation that really can occur is where a device function is called in divergent code and that function calls `__syncthreads()`. This is especially true in larger projects where you might not have access to the source code of the device function being called. Ideally writers of such functions should use a weaker version of `__syncthreads()` which just acts on the currently active threads – just this facility is provided by the coalesced groups feature in the NVIDIA cooperative groups library.

3.7 Coalesced Groups

The best way to avoid difficulties with divergent threads is to use the cooperative groups `coalesced_group` object which behaves like a templated `tiled_partition` but contains just the currently active threads in the warp as its members.[14] Unlike the case of `tiled_partitions`, you do not have to specify its size as power of 2, rather the size is automatically set at creation time to be the number of currently active threads. A `coalesced_group` object is created analogously to a `thread_block` using the `coalesced_threads()` object, as shown in the box.

```
          auto a = cg::coalesced_threads(); // a for active
  or
          cg::coalesced_group a = cg::coalesced_threads();
```

Notice the `coalesced_threads` function takes no arguments, unlike the corresponding functions for `tiled_partitions` which need the current thread–block as an argument. The returned object a will contain all the currently active threads in the warp of the calling thread; thus it is a warp-level object. The member function `a.size()` will return the number of active threads and its warp shuffle member functions will implicitly use a mask corresponding to just these active threads. The thread rank values returned by `a.rank()` will be in the range `[0,a.size()-1]`. Most importantly `a.sync()` will perform a warp-level synchronisation of just the active threads hence preventing deadlock and, presumably, implementing the programmer's actual intentions. One caveat is that (obviously) there should not be any further thread divergence between the instantiation of the coalesced group object a and the use of `a.sync()`.

Example 3.9 shows the kernel from the previous example modified to use coalesced groups to perform warp-level synchronisations with the currently active subset of threads in that warp.

This version does not deadlock under any sane combination of parameters. In this example we have replaced the `__syncthreads()` in lines 27 and 31 of Example 3.8 by lines 27 28 and 32–33.

Example 3.9 `deadlock_coalesced` revised deadlock kernel using coalesced groups

```
21   __global__ void deadlock_coalesced(int gsync, int dolock)
22   {
23     __shared__ int lock;
24     if (threadIdx.x == 0) lock = 0;
25     __syncthreads();  // normal syncthreads

26     if (threadIdx.x < gsync) {  // group A
27       auto a = cg::coalesced_threads();
28       a.sync();       // sync A
       // deadlock unless we set lock to 1
29       if (threadIdx.x == 0) lock = 1;
30     }
31     else if (threadIdx.x < 2 * gsync) { // group B
32       auto a = cg::coalesced_threads();
33       a.sync();  // sync B
33     }
     // group C may cause deadlock here
34     if (dolock) while (lock != 1);
     // see message only if NO deadlock
35     if (threadIdx.x == 0 && blockIdx.x == 0)
                   printf("deadlock_coalesced OK\n");
36   }
```

- Lines 27 and 32: These each create a coalesced group object a which is local to the scope of the enclosing conditional statement. This object has all the functionality of a 32-thread `tiled_partition` representing the local warp but adds a hidden bitmask to all member functions selecting just the active threads.

- Lines 28 and 33: Here we use the a.sync() member function to perform a __syncwarp() call restricted to the subset active threads.

Examples 3.8 and 3.9 simply demonstrate how to cause and avoid deadlock in thread divergent code. A useful version of 3.9 would have added code between lines 27 and 28 and between lines 32 and 33 where the added code performs useful warp-level work using the available threads. If such added code calls device functions, then the coalesced group object a could be passed as a function argument or the function itself could create its own version.

Example 3.10 `reduce7_v1_coal` kernel which uses subsets of threads in each warp

```
10   __device__ void reduce7_v1_coal(r_Ptr<float>sums,
                                  cr_Ptr<float>data, int n)
11   {
12     // function assumes that a.size() is a power of 2
13     // and that n is a multiple of 4

14     auto g = cg::this_grid();
15     auto b = cg::this_thread_block();
16     auto a = cg::coalesced_threads(); // active threads in warp

17     float4 v4 ={0,0,0,0};
18     for(int tid = g.thread_rank(); tid < n/4; tid += g.size())
             v4 += reinterpret_cast<const float4 *>(data)[tid];

19     float v = v4.x + v4.y + v4.z + v4.w;
20     a.sync();
21     if(a.size() > 16) v += a.shfl_down(v,16); // NB no new
22     if(a.size() >  8) v += a.shfl_down(v,8);  // thread
23     if(a.size() >  4) v += a.shfl_down(v,4);  // divergence
24     if(a.size() >  2) v += a.shfl_down(v,2);  // allowed
25     if(a.size() >  1) v += a.shfl_down(v,1);  // here

26     if(a.thread_rank() == 0)
             atomicAdd(&sums[b.group_index().x],v);
27   }
       . . .
40   __global__ void reduce_warp_even_odd
     (r_Ptr<float>sumeven, r_Ptr<float>sumodd,
                   cr_Ptr<float>data, int n)
41   {
42     // divergent code here
43     if (threadIdx.x%2==0) reduce_coal_v1(sumeven,data, n);
44     else                  reduce_coal_v1(sumodd, data, n);
45   }
```

As a concrete, albeit somewhat artificial, example consider the modification to our `reduce7_vl` kernel in Example 3.7 where now we want to split the reduce operation into separate sums for the even and odd indexed values in the array `data`. Moreover, we insist on using just the threads with even rank to sum the even values and the threads with odd rank to sum the odd values. A straightforward way to do this is to convert the kernel into a callable device function by changing the `__global__` declaration to `__device__` and to add a simple new kernel that calls the function once for even threads and once for odd threads. We will use separate output buffers `sums_even` and `sums__odd` to hold the results. Otherwise we want to make the minimum number of changes to the code. Example 3.10 shows the result.

Description of Example 3.10

Lines 10–27: These show the device function `reduce_coal_vl` and lines 40–45 show a simple kernel function `reduce_warp_even_odd` which makes thread divergent calls to this device function. The function `reduce7_vl_coal` is equivalent to the kernel `reduce7_vl` except that it only uses active threads in the current warp. Since this is done using a coalesced `tiled_partition` the function is safe to use. The kernel `reduce_warp_even_odd` calls `reduce7_vl_coal` twice with intra-warp thread divergence. Separate output buffers are used for the two divergent calls.

- Lines 10–27: The bulk of the device function `reduce_coal_vl` is identical to that of the kernel `reduce_warp_vl` in Example 3.7. The only difference is that we use a `coalesced_group` object a instead of a `tiled_partition` object w in lines 15 and 20–26. Since line 10 is unchanged only a subset of the values in data will be summed, this is because threads which have diverged from the active coalesced group do not participate.
- Lines 16–21: Here each active thread sums a subset of values in data using a stride equal to the grid size and starting with the true rank of the thread in its thread block. The only difference is the use of `a.sync()` in line 21 to synchronise just the subset of active threads in a warp.
- Lines 21–25: These replace the 5-step tree reduction of lines 22–26 of Example 3.7. The if clauses based on the value of `a.sync()` do not cause any thread divergences but generalise the code to work for size of the coalesced group which is a power of 2. If we just wanted the function to work for the single value of 16, we could remove line 21 and use the `if` clauses in lines 22–25. Note the code will fail if `a.size()` is not a power of 2 because then some of the `shfl_down()` calls will have out of range offsets and hence return the calling thread's value of v.
- Line 26: Here the lowest ranking thread within a is used to add the final group sum to the appropriate element of `sums`.
- Lines 40–45: This is the kernel function called by the host to perform the calculation. The kernel arguments are two arrays `sumeven` and `sumodd` which are used to hold separate block sums from even and odd threads.
- Lines 43–44: Here `reduce_coal_vl` is called for all even ranking threads in the thread blocks in line 43 and a separate call is made in line 44 for all odd threads. Thus, there is intra-warp thread divergence and hence potential for deadlock. On devices with CC<7 for each warp the two function calls will execute sequentially on the GPU because of the thread divergence. On devices with CC≥7 there may be some overlap of execution between these calls.

In testing we find that indeed this kernel does not deadlock and gives correct results. The kernel runs about 1.8 times slower than Example 3.7 using a Turing RTX 2070 GPU. This suggests that for this CC 7.5 card there may be a modest overlap of calculation between the divergent threads of a warp.

We note that line 18 of Example 3.10, where sub-sums of the values in `data` are accumulated by individual threads in the grid, is unmodified from the previous example where all threads in a warp participated. Thus, values in `data` that "belong" to diverged threads are simply not counted and the final values stored in `sums` correspond to just the elements of data which belong to the active threads. This is the behaviour we wanted for this artificial example where even and odd threads accumulate separate sub-sums which can be combined to give the correct total at the end of the calculation.

As a final example in this section in Example 3.11 we show a revised version of 3.10 able to calculate a complete sum with any size of coalesced groups providing that each warp has at least one active thread. In this version it is not necessary for each warp to have the same number of active threads.

Description of Example 3.11

In this example we change our strategy for summing the elements of data. We logically divide data in a number of contiguous sub-blocks with one sub-block for each warp in the grid. The active threads in each warp then act cooperatively to sum the elements of the sub-block belonging to that warp. In the case where warps have different numbers of active threads this approach is not optimal because each warp has the same amount of work to do. However, this is the best we can do as it is difficult or impossible for warps to determine the number of active threads in other warps.

- Line 10: Here we declare the device function `reduce_coal_any_v1` which takes the same argument list as before.
- Lines 14–17: Here we create objects allowing us to access the whole grid, thread block, warp and active threads. Ideally we would like to write functions that just need the local coalesced group `a`, but in this case we need everything in order to properly partition the input data array.[15]
- Line 18: Here we calculate `warps` as the total number of warps in the grid; `g.group_dim()` gives the number of thread blocks in the grid and `w.meta_group_size()` gives the number of warps in a thread block. The member function `a.meta_group_size()` exists but always returns 1 because a coalesced group is regarded as a partition of its containing warp.
- Line 20: Here we set `part_size` to the size of a sub-block handled by the individual warps. We divide the number of elements of `data` by the number of warps, rounding up to the nearest integer. We use `n/4` for the number of elements of data to allow for vector loading.
- Line 21: Here we find the starting element, `part_start`, of the sub-block to be processed by the current warp. The rank of the current warp in the grid is calculated and then multiplied by the sub-block size.
- Line 22: Here `part_end` is set to the last element of the sub-block plus one. Note we add the minimum of `part_size` or `n/4` to do this to avoid overflows in `for` loop of line 26.

Example 3.11 `reduce_coal_any_v1` kernel using coalesced groups of any size

```
10   __device__ void reduce_coal_any_v1(r_Ptr<float>sums,
                                  cr_Ptr<float>data,int n)
11   {
12   // This function works for any value of a.size() in [1,32]
```

```
13     // it assumes that n is a multiple of 4
14     auto g = cg::this_grid();
15     auto b = cg::this_thread_block();
16     auto w = cg::tiled_partition<32>(b); // whole warp
       // active threads in warp
17     auto a = cg::coalesced_threads();
       // number of warps in grid
18     int warps = g.group_dim().x*w.meta_group_size();
19     // divide data into contiguous parts,
       // with one part per warp
20     int part_size =((n/4)+warps-1)/warps;
21     int part_start =(b.group_index().x*w.meta_group_size()+
                          w.meta_group_rank() )*part_size;
22     int part_end =min(part_start+part_size,n/4);

23     // get part sub-sums into threads of a
24     float4 v4 ={0,0,0,0};
25     int id = a.thread_rank();
       // adjacent adds within the warp
26     for(int k=part_start+id; k<part_end; k+=a.size())
             v4 += reinterpret_cast<const float4 *>(data)[k];
27     float v = v4.x + v4.y + v4.z + v4.w;
28     a.sync();

29     // now reduce over a
30     // first deal with items held by ranks >= kstart
       // kstart is max power of 2 <= a.size()
31     int kstart = 1 << (31 - __clz(a.size()));
32     if(a.size() > kstart) {
33       float w = a.shfl_down(v,kstart);
         // only update v for valid low ranking threads
34       if(a.thread_rank() < a.size()-kstart) v += w;
35       a.sync();
36     }
37     // now do power of 2 reduction
38     for(int k = kstart/2; k>0; k /= 2)v+= a.shfl_down(v,k);
39     if(a.thread_rank() == 0)
             atomicAdd(&sums[b.group_index().x],v);
40   }
     . . .
50   __global__ void reduce_any(r_Ptr<float>sums,
                                cr_Ptr<float>data, int n)
51   {
52     if(threadIdx.x%3 ==0) reduce_coal_any_v1(sums,data,n);
53   }
```

- Lines 24–28: This is the summation of the elements of just the current sub-block using the active threads in the warp. This code is equivalent to lines 17–20 of the previous examples which summed over all the elements of `data`. Notice we use `a.sync()` in line 28.
- Lines 31–36: These lines deal with the difficulty that the number of active threads `a.size()` is probably not a power of 2. The idea is to find the greatest power of 2 `kstart` less than or equal to `a.size()`. Then `v` values held by threads with rank greater than `kstart` are added to the `v` values of the lowest ranking threads. After this has been done we can use a simple power of 2 reduction starting with `kstart/2`.
  - Line 31: Here we calculate `kstart` using the CUDA intrinsic function `__clz()` (count leading zeros) which returns the number of leading zero bits in its integer input argument.
  - Line 33: Here we set a temporary variable `w` to the value of `v` held by the thread of rank `kstart` higher than the current thread. This will only be valid for thread of rank less than `a.size()-kstart`.
  - Line 34: Adds `w` to `v` for low-ranking threads where the value of `w` is valid.
  - Line 35: Synchronisation of the coalesced group is necessary here.
- Line 38: The remainder of the power of 2 reduction is now performed using a for loop. Explicitly unrolling this loop, as was done in previous examples, is not possible here as the value of `kstart` is not known at compile time.
- Line 39: This use of `atomicAdd` is the same as for previous examples.
- Lines 50–53: A simple demonstration driver kernel for `reduce_coal_any_v1`. In this case we launch the kernel using every third thread. This means that some warps use 10 threads and some use 11.

The performance of the `reduce_coal_any_v1` function is surprisingly good for a reasonable number of threads as shown in Figure 3.3.

In Figure 3.3 the data size was 2^{24} words and the launch configurations was 288 blocks and 256 threads. In the range 4–16 threads we see roughly linear scaling. At above 16 threads we are close to saturating the memory bandwidth of the device and we see little extra performance gain. Below 4 threads the performance drops further, but more slowly. The GPU used was an RTX 2070.

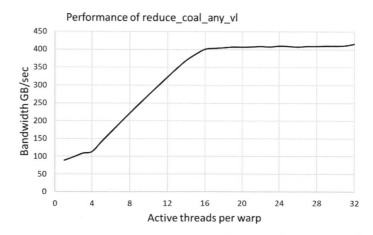

Figure 3.3 Performance of the `reduce_coal_any_v1` device function

3.8 HPC Features

For high-performance computing applications on Linux clusters grid wide synchronisation is possible using the grid group sync member function. As mentioned above, this requires a special compilation and a different kernel launch API. The details are given in the NVIDIA C++ Programming Guide, for example, Section C.7 in the May 2020 version 11 guide.

Unfortunately, at present, grid wide synchronisation has limitations in addition to being complicated to set up. The major limitation is that all thread blocks of the kernel being synchronised, must be co-resident on the GPU – which in practice means that the number of thread blocks should not exceed the number of SM units on the GPU. This limitation could adversely affect the kernel's occupancy. Also, on Windows the device driver must be running in TCC mode which is not available on many GTX cards.

For HPC applications where a kernel might be launched across multiple GPUs there is a multi-grid group created and used in a similar way to the grid level group:

```
Either
    auto mg = this_multi_grid();
or
    multi_grid_group mg = this_multi_grid();

Synchronization across multiple GPUs is possible with

    mg.sync();
```

The SDK 11 release brought in a few new features in addition to the reduce function mentioned previously; we mention them here for the sake of completeness but interested readers are referred to the NVIDIA documentation and examples for more details.

1. A new type of coalesced sub-group is introduced the `labled_partition`:

```
cg::coalesced_group  a = cg::coalesced_threads();
cg::coalesced_group lg = cg::labeled_partition(a,label);

or

auto  a = cg::coalesced_threads();
auto lg = cg::labeled_partition(a,label);
```

Where `label` is an integer that may vary between threads. A separate coalesced group is created for each value of label.

2. A specialised version of the `labeled_partition`, is the `binary_partition` which is similar to the `labeled_partition` except that it is created with a `label` argument that is a Boolean flag so at most two sub-groups are created.
3. A new `memcpy_async` function that speeds the copying of data from global GPU memory to shared memory. On the Ampere architecture this is hardware

accelerated and bypasses the L2 and L1 caches. This feature is intended to improve the flow of matrix data through tensor cores as discussed in Chapter 11 but interestingly it also has the potential to boost the performance of our reduce kernels which use shared memory. More information can be found in the recent blog post at: https://developer.nvidia.com/blog/cuda-11-features-revealed/. An example can be found in the new SDK 11 `globalToShmemAsyncCopy` example in the `0_Simple` directory.

This ends our chapter on CUDA cooperative groups; the main message is that they give strong support to warp-level kernel programming and make explicit and safe some of the tricks that were used for implicit warp-level programming prior to the arrival of CC = 7.0 and CUDA SDK release 9.0. More recent SDKs add additional tools showing NVIDIA's interest in this area.

The next chapter moves on to another topic favoured in many tutorials – parallel stencil calculations for solving partial differential equations and image processing. We think you will find these applications interesting.

Endnotes Chapter 3

1 The first-generation Tesla cards featured 16-thread half-warps.

2 NVIDIA does not seem to have given these subunits a specific name, but they are clearly indicated in the relevant diagrams in the documentation, for cxample Figure 7 in the Pascal Architecture white paper. I like to think of these units as "warp-engines".

3 It should still work on older GPUs but might fail on Volta and later GPUs. Because possible failure depends on a race condition this is potentially a nightmare debugging scenario. We very strongly advise you to upgrade existing code to use the methods described later in this chapter.

4 Unfortunately, we cannot use the built-in parameter warpSize for this purpose because it is not defined as const in the CUDA header files.

5 In fact, if you inspect the header file cooperative_groups.h you will see that many of the member functions are no more than wrappers for the CUDA built-in variables. However, using the cooperative groups leads to clearer, more portable code than using the built-in variables directly.

6 This nice simplification has only been possible in general kernel code since the release of CUDA SDK 11.0.

7 Indeed, since first writing this sentence NVIDIA has introduced a set of "Warp Matrix Functions" to support the powerful new tensor core hardware in CC=7 and above GPUs. See Chapter 11 for more details.

8 For devices of CC 8 and above there are also new intrinsic functions that perform the same operations.

9 CC$\geq$7 architectures do support some intra-warp thread divergence and we might expect such support to improve in future architectures.

10 This can be seen by inspecting the CUDA cooperative_groups.h include file.

11 The GPU hardware maintains a bitmask showing exited threads which allows the hardware to ignore exited threads without additional overheads. (Although of course, the potential work that could have been done by these threads had they not exited is lost.)

12 The return value of zero from inactive and exited threads was found by experiment; the behaviour in these cases is documented as undefined. Therefore, it would be best not to rely on zero values in future.

13 This is a feature of the operating system (at least on Windows), the results of in kernel printfs are buffered by CUDA and are displayed after a kernel's normal exit. If a kernel deadlocks this does not happen.

14 "Currently active" means active at the time the object a is instantiated, for most code that should be good enough. If you have really tricky real-time code, perhaps with program interrupts, then maybe you need to take care – but such situations are beyond the scope of this book.

15 We could have used the old built-in variables such as gridDim and blockDim instead of using CG objects but that really amounts to the same thing and we think it better style not to mix the two notations.

4

Parallel Stencils

In this chapter we discuss the use of 2D and 3D stencils for iterative solution of partial differential equations and image processing. These applications are another classic application of GPUs. We start with the 2D case and then move on to 3D.

4.1 2D Stencils

In numerical computing problems such as the solution of partial differential, the equations can often be approximately solved by replacing the continuous functions involved with discrete approximations using function values evaluated on a grid of equally spaced points.[1] For example, the function $f(x)$ can be replaced by the set of equally spaced points along the x axis $\{\ldots, f_{-2}, f_{-1}, f_0, f_1, f_2 \ldots\}$ where $f_i = f(a + ih)$, a is some convenient origin, h is the spacing between points, and the integer i labels the points. In this notation the derivatives of f can be replaced by their finite difference approximations:

$$\left.\frac{df}{dx}\right|_{x=a+jh} = \frac{f_{j+1} - f_{j-1}}{2h}, \quad \text{and} \quad \left.\frac{d^2f}{dx^2}\right|_{x=a+jh} = \frac{f_{j+2} - 2f_j + f_{j-2}}{h}. \tag{4.1}$$

Or more simply:

$$f_0' = \frac{1}{2}(f_1 - f_{-1}) \quad \text{and} \quad f_0'' = (f_1 - 2f_0 + f_{-1}) \tag{4.2}$$

for the derivatives at the origin in the case where we assume the grid spacing is unity (i.e. $h=1$). In this case Eq. 4.2 can be represented by the *stencils*

$$\frac{df}{dx} \rightarrow \frac{1}{2}[-1, \, 0, \, 1] \quad \text{and} \quad \frac{d^2f}{dx^2} \rightarrow [1, \, -2, 1], \tag{4.3}$$

which show the coefficients required to be applied with respect to a point at the centre of the stencil to calculate the derivates at that point. Similar stencils exist in 2 and 3 dimensions and in particular the Laplacian operator is given by:

$$\frac{\partial^2 f}{\partial^2 x} + \frac{\partial^2 f}{\partial^2 y} \equiv \nabla^2 f \rightarrow \begin{bmatrix} 0 & 1 & 0 \\ 1 & -4 & 1 \\ 0 & 1 & 0 \end{bmatrix} \tag{4.4}$$

and

106

$$\frac{\partial^2 f}{\partial^2 x} + \frac{\partial^2 f}{\partial^2 y} + \frac{\partial^2 f}{\partial^2 x} \equiv \nabla^2 f \rightarrow \begin{bmatrix} 0 & 0 & 0 \\ 0 & 1 & 0 \\ 0 & 0 & 0 \end{bmatrix}_{z=-1} + \begin{bmatrix} 0 & 1 & 0 \\ 1 & -6 & 1 \\ 0 & 1 & 0 \end{bmatrix}_{z=0} + \begin{bmatrix} 0 & 0 & 0 \\ 0 & 1 & 0 \\ 0 & 0 & 0 \end{bmatrix}_{z=+1}.$$

$$(4.5)$$

In 3D the stencil becomes a 3D cube as indicated by the 3 slices shown in Eq. 4.5. We can now use these stencils to find steady state solutions of many standard partial differential equations in physics, for example, Poisson's equation in electrostatics in Eq. 4.6 or the diffusion equation for heat transfer in Eq. 4.7.

$$\nabla^2 \phi = \frac{\rho}{\varepsilon_0}, \tag{4.6}$$

$$\nabla^2 u = \frac{1}{D} \frac{\partial u}{\partial t}. \tag{4.7}$$

In Eq. 4.6 ϕ is the electrostatic potential due to a static electrical charge distribution ρ and in Eq. 4.7 u is the temperature at time t due to a static distribution of heat sources. To solve such equations, we need to apply suitable boundary conditions. For our purposes it is simplest to use Dirichlet boundary conditions where fixed values for ϕ or u are specified on the boundaries of the grids used for the numerical solution. We will seek steady state solutions for Eq. 4.7 where the right-hand side becomes zero. These solutions apply equally to Poisson's equation for the potential inside a closed region with boundaries at fixed potentials.

Our first example uses a 2D square grid with points on the boundaries set to fixed values and where the interior contains no additional charge or heat sources, thus inside the grid we need to solve $\nabla^2 u = 0$ leading to

$$\begin{bmatrix} 0 & 1 & 0 \\ 1 & -4 & 1 \\ 0 & 1 & 0 \end{bmatrix} u = 0 \rightarrow u_{-1,0} + u_{1,0} + u_{0,-1} + u_{0,1} - 4u_{0,0} = 0,$$

$$u_{0,0} = \frac{u_{-1,0} + u_{1,0} + u_{0,-1} + u_{0,1}}{4}. \tag{4.8}$$

We can attempt to solve Eq. 4.8 for any given boundary conditions by setting the interior of our grid to zero and then iterating, replacing each value inside the boundary by the average of the 4 surrounding values. The boundaries themselves are left untouched. This process, known as Jacobi iteration, with suitable boundary conditions turns out to be stable and will converge, albeit slowly, to the correct solution. Example 4.1 shows our code to perform Jacobi iteration inside a rectangle.

Example 4.1 `stencil2D` kernel for Laplace's equation

```
10    __global__ void stencil2D(cr_Ptr<float> a,
                      r_Ptr<float> b, int nx, int ny)
11    {
          // C/C++ ordering of suffices
```

```
12    auto idx = [&nx](int y,int x){ return y*nx+x; };
13    int x = blockIdx.x*blockDim.x+threadIdx.x;
14    int y = blockIdx.y*blockDim.y+threadIdx.y;
      // exclude edges and out of range
15    if(x<1 || y <1 || x >= nx-1 || y >= ny-1) return;

16    b[idx(y,x)] =  0.25f*(a[idx(y,x+1)] +
            a[idx(y,x-1)] + a[idx(y+1,x)] + a[idx(y-1,x)]);
17    }

18    int stencil2D_host(cr_Ptr<float> a, r_Ptr<float> b,
                                        int nx, int ny)
20    {
21      auto idx = [&nx](int y, int x){ return y*nx+x; };
22      // omit edges
23      for(int y=1;y<ny-1;y++) for(int x=1;x<nx-1;x++)
          b[idx(y,x)] = 0.25f*( a[idx(y,x+1)] +
              a[idx(y,x-1)] + a[idx(y+1,x)] + a[idx(y-1,x)] );
24      return 0;
25    }

30    int main(int argc,char *argv[])
31    {
32      int nx =          (argc>1) ? atoi(argv[1]) :  1024;
33      int ny =          (argc>2) ? atoi(argv[2]) :  1024;
34      int iter_host = (argc>3) ? atoi(argv[3]) :  1000;
35      int iter_gpu =  (argc>4) ? atoi(argv[4]) : 10000;
36      int size = nx*ny;

37      thrustHvec<float>     a(size);
38      thrustHvec<float>     b(size);
39      thrustDvec<float> dev_a(size);
40      thrustDvec<float> dev_b(size);

41      // set x=0 and x=nx-1 edges to 1
42      auto idx = [&nx](int y,int x){ return y*nx+x; };
43      for(int y=0;y<ny;y++) a[idx(y,0)] = a[idx(y,nx-1)] = 1.0f;
44      // corner adjustment
45      a[idx(0,0)] = a[idx(0,nx-1)]
                  = a[idx(ny-1,0)] = a[idx(ny-1,nx-1)] = 0.5f;
46      dev_a = a;  // copy to both
47      dev_b = a;  // dev_a and dev_b

48      cx::timer tim;
49      for(int k=0;k<iter_host/2;k++){ // ping pong buffers
50        stencil2D_host(a.data(),b.data(),nx,ny); // a=>b
```

```
51      stencil2D_host(b.data(),a.data(),nx,ny); // b=>a
52    }
53    double t1 = tim.lap_ms();
54    double gflops_host = (double)(iter_host*4)*
                           (double)size/(t1*1000000);

55    dim3 threads = {16,16,1};
56    dim3 blocks ={(nx+threads.x-1)/threads.x,
                    (ny+threads.y-1)/threads.y,1};
57    tim.reset();
58    for(int k=0;k<iter_gpu/2;k++){  // ping pong buffers
59      stencil2D<<<blocks,threads>>>(dev_a.data().get(),
                      dev_b.data().get(), nx, ny); // a=>b
60      stencil2D<<<blocks,threads>>>(dev_b.data().get(),
                      dev_a.data().get(), nx, ny); // b=>a
61    }
62    cudaDeviceSynchronize();
63    double t2 = tim.lap_ms();

64    a = dev_a; // do something with result

65    double gflops_gpu = (double)(iter_gpu*4)*
                          (double)size/(t2*1000000);
66    double speedup = gflops_gpu/gflops_host;
67    printf("stencil2d size %d x %d speedup %.3f\n",
                              nx,ny,speedup);
68    printf("host iter %8d time %9.3f ms GFlops %8.3f\n",
                          iter_host, t1, gflops_host);
69    printf("gpu  iter %8d time %9.3f ms GFlops %8.3f\n",
                          iter_gpu, t2, gflops_gpu);
70    return 0;
71  }
```

Description of Example 4.1

The basic idea of this example is to use two 2D arrays a and b, which have the same size and are initialised to zero everywhere except for the left-hand and right-hand columns which are set to 1.0 as a boundary condition. Likewise, the top and bottom rows are set to zero and are also used as boundary conditions. The Laplacian stencil shown in Eq. 4.8 is then applied to all the non-edge elements of a with the results stored in b. We can then iterate by swapping the roles of a and b on successive iterations in a ping-pong fashion. Note the four edges of a and b are never changed during iteration. The CUDA kernel in this example is designed to use one thread for each element of the arrays and is launched with an appropriate 2D thread grid.

- Line 10: This declares the stencil2D kernel with arguments being pointers to the input array a and output array b and values for their common dimensions nx and ny.

- Line 12: Here we define the helper indexing function `idx` using a stride of `nx`.
- Lines 13–14: Find the array element to be processed by the present thread. It is assumed the kernel launch will use a 2D thread grid of sufficient size to span the arrays.
- Line 15: This is an important check that the current thread is not out of range and also not on any of the edges of the 2D array which are set to the fixed boundary conditions.
- Line 16: Here we implement Eq. 4.8 by summing the 4 elements of a surrounding the current point and storing the average in `b`.
- Lines 18–25: These lines are the equivalent host function `stencil2D_host` which performs the same calculation using a double for loop over the elements of `a`.

The remaining lines show the host code needed to drive the calculation.

- Lines 32–36: Get values for the user supplied parameters; `nx` and `ny` are the array dimensions and `iter_host` and `iter_gpu` are the number of iterations to perform.
- Lines 37–40: Declare the `a` and `b` arrays on the host and device. Note that thrust will automatically set these arrays to zeros.
- Lines 41–45: Initialise the first and last columns of `a` and `b` to the boundary value 1. The corners are then set to 0.5 as they belong to both a vertical and horizontal side. Note the top and bottom rows of `a` and `b` have been set to zero by thrust.
- Lines 46–47: Copy the host arrays to the device arrays.
- Lines 48–54: This is the timed section where the `stencil2D_host` function is called `iter_host` times.
  - Lines 50–51: Here we call the `stencil2D_host` twice within the for loop; the first call processes the values in `a` and stores the results in `b` and the second call does the opposite; thus at the end of the loop the final result is always in `a`. Note there is a tacit assumption the `iter_host` is an even number.
  - Line 54: Here we calculate the performance of the calculation in GFlops/sec noting that 4 floating point operations are used in line 23. The value is stored in `gflops_host`.
- Lines 55–56: Set the kernel 2D launch configuration, using a thread block size of 16 × 16 and a grid size sufficiently large to space arrays of size `nx` × `ny`.
- Lines 57–61: This is the timed section for the `stencil2D` kernel and is similar to the corresponding host section. We use the same ping-pong technique with two calls to the kernel inside the `for` loop.
- Line 64: Copy the final GPU result back to the host vector `a`. In a real-world program further calculation would be done at this point.
- Lines 65–66: Calculate the GPU performance `gflops_gpu` and the host to GPU speed-up.
- Lines 67–69: Print some results.

The stencil calculation is another example of a memory bound problem as 5 global memory accesses (1 write and 4 reads) are required to process each element of the array. The performance of the code is shown in Figure 4.1 below and is modest at around 2–4 GFlops on the host and up to about 125 GFlops on the GPU.

Notice this algorithm would be difficult to perform using only a single array; this is because the update of each element requires the values of four of its neighbours. The strategy of flipping back and forth between two buffers solves this problem and is common for this type of problem and is often called "double buffering". We have paid the price of doubling our memory use to keep the code simple.

On the host we could have saved the (modest) overhead of numerous function calls by adding more `for` loops to `stencil2D_host` to perform an entire calculation using a

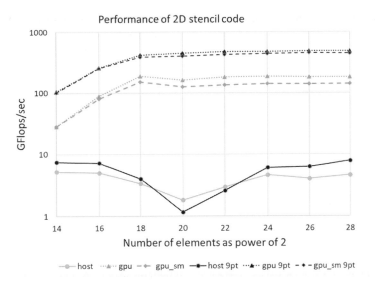

Figure 4.1 Performance of 2D 4-point and 9-point stencil codes

single call from the host. This, however, is *not possible* for the kernel calls. For a typical launch configuration using a thread block of size 16 × 16 and array sizes of 256 × 256, we need 256 thread blocks in launch grid. These blocks can run in any order and, while CUDA provides the `_syncthreads()` call to synchronise the threads within one block, it does not provide a way of synchronizing threads *between* thread blocks. Note the stencil algorithm used to update a given tile requires not just the values in the tile itself but also the values in a one element wide halo around the tile. Hence in the GPU code the only way to ensure all values are kept in step is to wait for the entire kernel to finish one iteration before starting the next.[2]

To use our double buffering method with CUDA kernels we have to ensure that a kernel call using the array a to update the array b has completely finished before the next kernel call using the array b to update a. If it were not for the halo problem, each thread block could have proceeded independently using `_syncthreads()` at the end of each of its passes.

As already mentioned, the amount of calculation done by the stencil functions shown in Example 4.1(a) is small, there are only 4 useful floating-point operations (3 adds and one multiply) in the inner loop for the host version or per thread for the kernel function. One way to attempt to optimise this code is to notice that each element of the input array is read 4 times by different threads in the kernel or different passes through the `for` loops in the host code. Using cache to exploit this should improve performance. Using shared memory is an obvious way to proceed for this kernel and indeed stencil calculations are used as standard examples of shared memory in many CUDA books and tutorials.

It is straightforward to use 2D thread blocks, of, for example, size 16 × 16, and copy tiles from the input array to shared memory as was done for the matrix multiplication example in Chapter 3. However, there is a significant complication in that to perform a stencil calculation for any array element we need to read values from its neighbours. This means that at the edges of the tile we need values not stored in the tile. A simple widely used solution is to use overlapping tiles in shared memory where the tile edges are a "halo" region containing values necessary for the calculation whose corresponding elements are updated by other overlapping thread blocks. This means that for a 16×16 shared memory tile with a halo which is one element wide, only the inner 14×14 values correspond to elements that will be processed by the thread block but these inner elements have access to all of their 8 nearest neighbours in shared memory.[3] A kernel based on the idea is shown in Example 4.2; note the tile size (typically 16×16) is specified at compile time using the template parameters Nx and Ny; this may allow the NVCC compiler to make additional optimisations during compilation.

Example 4.2 `stencil2D_sm` kernel, tiled shared memory version of `stencil2d`

```
10   template <int Nx, int Ny> __global__ void stencil2D_sm
                (cr_Ptr<float> a, r_Ptr<float> b, int nx, int ny)
11   {
        // tile one element includes 1 element wide halo
12      __shared__ float s[Ny][Nx];

13      auto idx = [&nx](int y,int x){ return y*nx+x; };

14      // tiles overlap hence x0 & y0 strides reduced by
        // twice the halo width
15      int x0 = (blockDim.x-2)*blockIdx.x; // x tile origin
16      int y0 = (blockDim.y-2)*blockIdx.y; // y tile origin
17      int xa = x0+threadIdx.x;   // thread x in array
18      int ya = y0+threadIdx.y;   // thread y in array
19      int xs = threadIdx.x;      // thread x in tile
20      int ys = threadIdx.y;      // thread y in tile
21      if(xa >= nx || ya >= ny) return; // out of range check

22      s[ys][xs] = a[idx(ya,xa)];   // fill with halo of width 1
23      __syncthreads();             // (Nx-2) x (Ny-2) active points

        // inside array ?
24      if(xa < 1 || ya < 1 || xa >= nx-1 || ya >= ny-1) return;
        // inside tile ?
25      if(xs < 1 || ys < 1 || xs >= Nx-1 || ys >= Ny-1) return;
26      b[idx(ya,xa)] =  0.25f*(s[ys][xs+1] + s[ys][xs-1] +
                    s[ys+1][xs] + s[ys-1][xs] );
27   }
```

Description of Example 4.2

- Line 10: The kernel function `stencil2D_sm` is declared here as a template function where the template arguments Nx and Ny are the dimensions of the shared memory tile used to buffer elements of a. The other kernel arguments are the same as before.
- Line 12: The 2D shared memory buffer s is declared here as static shared memory.
- Line 13: The index function `idx` is used to improve readability of 2D array indexing.

- Lines 15–20: This set of statements sets up the necessary variables for creating shared memory tiles which map to overlapping regions of the arrays a and b for adjacent thread blocks.
  - Lines 15–16: Then we set the origin (x0,y0) of the tile for the current thread block in the arrays a and b. For non-overlapping tiles we would simply use blockDim.x/y, but here we subtract 2 which is twice the halo width. Thus for overlapping 16 × 16 tiles the stride between adjacent tiles is 14 in both x and y.
  - Lines 17–18: The current thread's position (xa,ya) in the arrays a and b is set here.
  - Lines 19–20: The current thread's position (xs,ys) in the shared memory tiles is set here; this is just the 2D rank of the thread in its thread block.
- Line 21: We perform a necessary check that neither of xa or ya are outside the arrays being processed. Note, unlike stencil2D in Example 4.1, we do not exclude the edges of the arrays at this point.
- Lines 22–23: Here the threads in the entire thread block cooperate in copying the required tile from a to shared memory. This is followed by __syncthreads().
- Line 24: Here we check that we are not attempting to change the boundaries of the output array b. This corresponds to the same check in line 15 of stencil2D.
- Line 25: Here we check that we are not updating an element of b in the halo region of shared memory. These elements will be updated by a different thread block.
- Line 26: Here we calculate the stencil and store the result to b.

Contrary to our expectations, this shared memory kernel 4.2 is about 20% slower than the previous 4.1 version which relied on implicit GPU memory caching. The reason for this is that the new kernel only reuses items in shared memory four times and the savings compared to cached accesses to global memory are too small to compensate for the time required to set up the shared memory tile and halo. Note early generations of NVIDIA GPUs had poorer GPU memory caching and so use of shared memory for stencil calculation was more advantageous.

If we generalise to a 9-point stencil, as shown in Example 4.3, then for larger problem sizes, shared memory version is only about 8% slower for large array sizes. Example 4.3 implements the general 9-point stencil shown in Eq. 4.9:

$$u_{ij} = \sum_{p=-1}^{1} \sum_{q=-1}^{1} c_{pq} u_{i+p,j+q}, \qquad (4.9)$$

where the coefficients c sum to unity. In the kernel code the coefficients are passed from the host as a fifth array argument.

Example 4.3 stencil9PT kernel generalisation of stencil2D using all eight nearest neighbours

```
10   __global__ void stencil9PT(cr_Ptr<float> a,
             r_Ptr<float> b, int nx, int ny, cr_Ptr<float> c)
11   {
12     auto idx = [&nx] (int y,int x) { return y*nx+x; };

13     int x = blockIdx.x*blockDim.x+threadIdx.x;
```

```
14    int y = blockIdx.y*blockDim.y+threadIdx.y;
15    if(x<1 || y <1 || x >= nx-1 || y >= ny-1) return;

16    b[idx(y,x)] =
          c[0]*a[idx(y-1,x-1)] + c[1]*a[idx(y-1,  x)] +
          c[2]*a[idx(y-1,x+1)] + c[3]*a[idx(y  ,x-1)] +
          c[4]*a[idx(y  ,  x)] + c[5]*a[idx(y  ,x+1)] +
          c[6]*a[idx(y+1,x-1)] + c[7]*a[idx(y+1,x  )] +
          c[8]*a[idx(y+1,x+1)];
17   }
```

The use of the idx index function in line 16 of stencil9PT significantly contributes to the clarity of the code. Only lines 10 and 16 differ from stencil2D. The corresponding modifications to Example 4.2 (not shown) are similar.

The performance of the stencil codes for various 2D problem sizes is shown in Figure 4.2. The grey lines correspond to the kernels and host code shown in Examples 4.1 and 4.2 using 4-point stencils and the black lines are for the equivalent 9-points stencils as shown in Example 4.3 for GPU. The GPU version of the 9-point stencils delivers about three times more GFlops/sec than the 4-point equivalents. This is because each thread in a 9-point stencil performs 17 floating point operations compared to four in 4-point versions and as the kernel is memory bound the extra computation is "free". It can be seen that using shared memory never helps on our RTX 2070 although for small array sizes, where kernel performance is poor, the two methods converge.

For the 2D stencil codes considered here the additional complexity introduced by using shared memory is not justified. On earlier GPUs, memory caching was less efficient and so the benefits of using shared memory were much greater and this is reflected in the emphasis placed on shared memory codes in many available tutorials. However, if you are developing new code for modern GPUs, I recommend starting with a simpler version not using shared memory and once that is working consider trying shared memory. The number of times each item in shared memory is used will determine the likely performance gains. Example 4.2 is still a good model for implementing tiled code with halos in suitable problems.

4.1.1 Optimising the Algorithm

After enough iterations, the values in the arrays a and b will converge and then represent the solution of the 2D problem with the given boundary conditions. This solution has several physical interpretations; for example, the 2D potential inside the square when two opposite sides are set to 1 volt and the other two sides are set to 0 volts. Or in heat flow (when multiplied by 100) it is the equilibrium temperature distribution when the sides are set to 100 degrees C and 0 degrees C. By symmetry, the centre of the square must be 50 degrees C in the steady state, and we can use this to check for convergence as iterations proceed. Table 4.1 shows the approximate times taken and numbers of iterations required for convergence using stencil2D with various sizes of square, and Figure 4.2 illustrates the approach to convergence for the case of 512×512 arrays.

Table 4.1 *Convergence rates for the stencil2D kernel*

Array Size	Iterations	Time (ms)
64×64	1×10^4	1.4
128×128	5×10^4	7
256×256	2×10^5	100
512×512	4×10^5	550
1024×1024	1.4×10^6	28,000

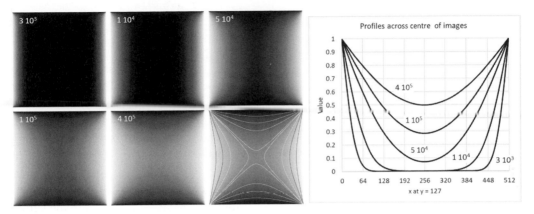

Figure 4.2 Approach to convergence for 512×512 arrays

The first 5 images show the results after 3×10^3, 10^4, 5×10^4, 10^5 and 4×10^5 iterations. The sixth image shows equal value contours on the converged solution shown in the fifth image. The figure on the right shows horizontal profiles across the centres of the five images. This shows that the slow convergence of the Jacobi iteration process is due to the slow rate of propagation of the fixed boundary values inwards to the centre of the array which was initialised to zeros.

A more general convergence test for this problem is to compare the a and b arrays as the iterations proceed and stop once the differences become small enough. In practice, if we keep iterating we find that either a and b become identical or the iterations become trapped in a limit cycle where a becomes b and vice versa on each iteration. In either case this is the best we can do and we can implement a convergence test based on how small the largest absolute difference between any pair of corresponding a and b values. The code for this is shown in Example 4.4.

Example 4.4 `reduce_maxdiff` kernel for finding maximum difference between two arrays

```
10   template <typename T> __global__ void reduce_maxdiff
              (r_Ptr<T> smax,cr_Ptr<T>a, cr_Ptr<T>b, int n)
11   {   // based on reduce6 and using fixed blocksize of 256
```

```
12     auto grid =  cg::this_grid();
13     auto block = cg::this_thread_block();
14     auto warp =  cg::tiled_partition<32>(block);

15     __shared__ T s[256];
16     int id = block.thread_rank();
17     s[id] = (T)0;

18     for(int tid = grid.thread_rank(); tid < n;
                                    tid += grid.size()) {
19       if(b != nullptr) // first pass
              s[id] = fmaxf(s[id],fabs(a[tid]-b[tid]));
20       else  s[id] = fmaxf(s[id],a[tid]); // second pass
21     }

22     block.sync();
23     if(id < 128) s[id] = fmaxf(s[id],s[id + 128]);
       block.sync();
24     if(id <  64) s[id] = fmaxf(s[id],s[id +  64]);
       block.sync();
25     if(warp.meta_group_rank()==0) {
26       s[id] = fmaxf(s[id],s[id + 32]); warp.sync();
27       s[id] = fmaxf(s[id],warp.shfl_down(s[id],16));
28       s[id] = fmaxf(s[id],warp.shfl_down(s[id],8));
29       s[id] = fmaxf(s[id],warp.shfl_down(s[id],4));
30       s[id] = fmaxf(s[id],warp.shfl_down(s[id],2));
31       s[id] = fmaxf(s[id],warp.shfl_down(s[id],1));
         // store block max difference
32       if(id == 0) smax[blockIdx.x] = s[0];
33     }
34   }

35   template <typename T> T array_diff_max
           (cr_Ptr<T> a,  cr_Ptr<T> b, int nx, int ny)
36   {
37     thrustDvec<T> c(256);
38     thrustDvec<T> d(1);
39     reduce_maxdiff<T><<<256,256>>>
           (c.data().get(),a, b, nx*ny);
40     reduce_maxdiff<T><<<  1,256>>>
           (d.data().get(), c.data().get(),nullptr, 256);
41     cudaDeviceSynchronize();
42     return d[0];
43   }
```

Description of Example 4.4

This kernel finds the largest absolute difference between corresponding elements of two arrays using a reduction algorithm. The host function `array_diff_max` returns the absolute value of the maximum difference between corresponding elements of the input arrays a and b. This template function should work for any CUDA type that is supported by the intrinsic functions used.

Lines 35–43: are the host function `array_diff_max` which returns the absolute value of the maximum difference between corresponding elements of the input arrays a and b. Lines 10–24 are the kernel function `reduce_maxdiff` used to perform the calculation. The kernel is based on our previous `reduce6` shown in Example 3.4. We did not use the more compact `reduce7` warp-only kernel because the `atomicMax` function, needed here to replace the `atomicAdd` used in `reduce7`, only works for integers.

- Line 10: The declaration is similar to that of `reduce6` except that we have added a second input array b to the argument list and the data type of the array arguments is now the template parameter T rather than float. The parameter T also replaces explicit float elsewhere in the code.
- Lines 11–17: These are identical to `reduce7`.
- Lines 18–21: This is the main data reading loop where threads accumulate their contributions to the subsequent reduction step. The pointer to the second data array b is used as a flag here to decide if this is an initial call to this function, in which case the maximum of the current value of a[tid] is stored in s[id] or if b is not equal to `nullptr` the absolute value of the difference between a[tid] and b[tid] is stored in s[id].
- Lines 22–32: These lines are the same as lines 26–38 of `reduce6` except that we have replaced the += operators with =fmax(...) in order to find a maximum value rather than perform a summation.
- Line 35: The `array_diff_max` function also has its array arguments templated.
- Lines 37–38: Create two local arrays to hold the set of block-wise maxima from the first pass and the global maximum from the second pass.
- Lines 39–40: Call the `array_diff_max` kernel twice after which the global maximum is stored in d[0].
- Line 42: Return the result.

A call to `array_diff_max` can now be easily incorporated into Example 4.1 as shown in Example 4.5

Example 4.5 Modification of Example 4.1 to use `array_max_diff`

```
           . . .
58     for(int k=0;k<iter_gpu/2;k++){  // ping pong buffers
59         stencil2D<<<blocks,threads>>>(dev_a.data().get(),
                          dev_b.data().get(), nx, ny); // a=>b
60         stencil2D<<<blocks,threads>>>(dev_b.data().get(),
                          dev_a.data().get(), nx, ny); // b=>a
60.1       if(k>0 && k%5000==0){ // check once in 5000 iterations
60.2          cudaDeviceSynchronize();
60.3          float diff = array_diff_max<float>
                   (dev_a.data().get(),dev_b.data().get(),nx,ny);
```

```
60.4        if(diff<1.0e-16){
60.5            printf("converged k=%d diff=%10.3e\n", k*2, diff);
60.6            break;
60.7        }
        }
61    }
62    cudaDeviceSynchronize();
        . . .
```

Example 4.5 shows a modification to the Example 4.1 host code to include a convergence check. In this version the user supplied parameter `iter_gpu` becomes the maximum number of iterations performed. Line 60.4 shows a convergence test using `array_diff_max` with a cut-off value specified as 10^{-16}. In practice, the latter value could be user specifed for tuning tests. Note line 60.1 causes the convergence check to be made once every 5000 passes through the loop, making its effect on performance small.

There is, in fact, an analytic solution to equation $\nabla^2\phi = 0$ with our boundary conditions, it takes the form of a Fourier series in the y coordinate and is given by Eq. 4.10,

$$\phi(x,y) = \sum_{n=1,3,5...}^{\infty} \frac{4}{n\pi} \sin(n\pi y) \frac{\sinh(xn\pi) + \sinh((1-x)n\pi)}{\sinh(n\pi)}, \qquad (4.10)$$

where the summation is over all positive odd integers. We can use this formula to test the accuracy of our stencil calculation. Since we are interested in high performance we will discuss results for a large square of size 1024×1024. In Table 4.2 we show results for both the 4-byte float version of stendcil2D as shown in Example 4.1 and an 8-byte double version.

The fourth column of Table 4.2 shows the maximum difference between corresponding values of the a and b arrays after the indicated number of iterations; a value of zero in this column indicates exact convergence. The fifth column of the table shows the average absolute difference between the final values in a and reference values calculated using Eq. 4.10. These averages are calculated using a central square of size 960×960 as the Fourier series in Eq. 4.10 converges very slowly for values of y near to zero and one. We can see that the best accuracy is (not surprisingly) achieved at convergence and is about two parts in 10^{-3} using floats and four parts in 10^{-7} using doubles. However, the number of iterations required to reach convergence is large and so are the times required: 33 seconds using floats and 260 seconds using doubles. One interesting feature is that the performance in GFlops/sec achieved using doubles is about half of that achieved using floats. This is an unexpectedly good result for the GTX 2070 GPU used here because this gaming card has only 1 64-bit ALU for every 32 32-bit ALUs in the hardware. The fact that stencil calculations are memory bound not CPU bound explains this result.

4.2 Cascaded Calculation of 2D Stencils

Convergence is slow because at each iteration each array element is replaced by the average of its four nearest neighbours. For this to work at all, it is necessary for the sum of the stencil

Table 4.2 *Accuracy of stencil2D for arrays of size 1024 × 1024*

Iterations	Time (secs)	GFlops/sec	Maximum abs(a[i]-b[i])	Accuracy average value of abs(a[i]-ref[i])
10,000	0.28	150	2.43×10^{-5}	4.39×10^{-1}
100,000	2.60	166	2.38×10^{-6}	2.38×10^{-1}
500,000	12.7	165	4.77×10^{-7}	3.50×10^{-2}
1,000,000	25.8	163	1.79×10^{-7}	3.55×10^{-3}
1,290,000	32.9	164	0	1.87×10^{-3}

Accuracy of stencil2D using 8-byte doubles

10,000	0.5	86	2.42×10^{-5}	4.37×10^{-1}
100,000	4.8	88	2.34×10^{-6}	2.38×10^{-1}
500,000	23.4	90	2.62×10^{-7}	3.50×10^{-2}
1,000,000	46.8	90	3.42×10^{-8}	3.31×10^{-3}
2,000,000	93.4	90	3.07×10^{-10}	2.90×10^{-5}
5,000,000	233.8	90	4.44×10^{-16}	4.43×10^{-7}
5,600,000	262.3	90	0	4.43×10^{-7}

coefficients to add up to unity, otherwise the total sum of the array contents would monotonically increase or decrease. If we initialise the inside of the array to zero, then only non-zero boundary values can produce change. These boundary values gradually diffuse into the array travelling inward by at most one element per iteration. At the same time the incorrect starting values diffuse out towards the boundaries, where they are overwritten by the fixed boundary values. Eventually only correct values remain inside the grid and convergence has been reached. Clearly the convergence would be quicker if the grid were initialised with better approximations to the correct answer. Approximate starting values are easily found by solving a smaller grid first and using that result to populate starting values for a bigger grid. We have implemented this method doubling the size of the array dimensions at each step. We refer to this as cascade iterations and our code is shown in Example 4.6.

Example 4.6 zoomfrom kernel for cascaded iterations of stencil2D

```
10   template <typename T> __global__ void Zoomfrom
       (r_Ptr<T> a, r_Ptr<T> b, cr_Ptr<T> aold, int nx, int ny)
11   {
12     int x = blockDim.x*blockIdx.x+threadIdx.x;
13     int y = blockDim.y*blockIdx.y+threadIdx.y;
14     if(x >= nx || y >= ny) return;

14     int mx = nx/2;
15     auto idx = [&nx](int y,int x){ return y*nx+x; };
16     auto mdx = [&mx](int y,int x){ return y*mx+x; };

17     if(x>0 && x<nx-1 && y>0 && y<ny-1)
                 a[idx(y,x)] = aold[mdx(y/2,x/2)]; // interior
```

```
       // top & bottom
18     else if(y==0 && x>0 && x<nx-1)     a[idx(y,x)] = (T)0;
19     else if(y==ny-1 && x>0 && x<nx-1) a[idx(y,x)] = (T)0;
       // sides
20     else if(x==0 && y>0 && y<ny-1)     a[idx(y,x)] = (T)1;
23     else if(x==nx-1 && y>0 && y<ny-1) a[idx(y,x)] = (T)1;
       // corners
24     else if(x==0 && y==0)                    a[idx(y,x)] = (T)0.5;
25     else if(x==nx-1 && y==0)                 a[idx(y,x)] = (T)0.5;
26     else if(x==0 && y==ny-1)                 a[idx(y,x)] = (T)0.5;
27     else if(x==nx-1 && y==ny-1)              a[idx(y,x)] = (T)0.5;
28     b[idx(y,x)] = a[ idx(y,x)];    // copy to b
29   }

30   int main(int argc, char *argv[])
31   {
32     int type =        (argc>1) ? atoi(argv[1]) : 0;
33     int nx =          (argc>2) ? atoi(argv[2]) : 1024;
34     int ny =          (argc>3) ? atoi(argv[3]) : 1024;
35     int iter_gpu =    (argc>4) ? atoi(argv[4]) : 10000;

36     if(type==1)cascade<double>(ny,nx,iter_gpu); // double
37     else       cascade<float> (ny,nx,iter_gpu); // float

38     std::atexit([]{cudaDeviceReset();}); // safe reset
39     return 0;
40   }

50   template <typename T> int cascade(int nx, int ny, int iter)
51   {
52     int nx_start = std::min(nx,32);
53     int size = nx_start*nx_start;  // square array only!
54     thrustDvec<T>  dev_a(size);    // initial buffers
55     thrustDvec<T>  dev_b(size);
56     thrustDvec<T>  dev_aold(size);

57     cx::timer tim;                 // nx is final size, mx is
58     for(int mx=nx_start; mx<=nx; mx *= 2){ // current size
59       int my = mx; // assume square
60       dim3 threads(16,16,1);
61       dim3 blocks((mx+15)/16, (my+15)/16,1);
62       int size = mx*my;
63       if(mx>nx_start){
64         dev_a.resize(size);
65         dev_b.resize(size);
66       }

67       zoomfrom<T><<<blocks,threads>>>
```

```
                dev_b.data().get(),dev_aold.data().get(), mx, my);
                // check frequency and accuracy
68              int check = (mx==nx) ? 5000 : 2500;
69              double diff_cut = (mx==nx) ? 1.0e-14 : 1.0e-09;
70              for(int k=0; k<iter/2; k++){
71                  stencil2D<T><<<blocks,threads>>>
                        (dev_a.data().get(),dev_b.data().get(), mx, my);
72                  stencil2D<T><<<blocks,threads>>>
                        (dev_b.data().get(),dev_a.data().get(), mx, my);
73                  if(k>0 && k%check==0){
74                      cudaDeviceSynchronize();
75                      double diff = array_diff_max<T>
                            (dev_a.data().get(),dev_b.data().get(),mx, my);
76                      if(diff<diff_cut)  break;
77                  }
78              }
79              cudaDeviceSynchronize();
80              if(mx>nx_start) dev_aold.resize(size);
81              if(mx<nx       ) dev_aold = dev_a;
82          }
83          double t1 = tim.lap_ms();

84          thrustHvec<T> a(nx*nx);
85          a = dev_a;
86          char name[256]; sprintf(name,"cascade%d_%d.raw",
                                        nx,(int)sizeof(T));
87          cx::write_raw(name,a.data(),nx*nx); // square
88          printf("cascade time %.3f ms\n",t1);
89          return 0;
90      }
```

Description of Example 4.6

This example is shown in two parts. The first part shows the new kernel zoomfrom and a simple main routine; the second part shows the host function cascade which organises the iteration scheme and calls the stencil2D kernel in a set of increasing resolutions.

Lines 10–28: are the zoomfrom kernel which upscales the current image in aold by a factor of two and copies the result to both a and b. It also resets the boundary values for this specific problem in the edges of the a and b. This is in interesting example of a straightforward but highly problem-specific kernel which some knowledge of CUDA enables you to write quicky and reliably. We think that this is an extremely useful skill in research situations where many problems have novel and perhaps unique features.

- Line 10: The kernel arguments are the arrays a and b of dimensions nx × ny which are to be filled with the upscaled contents of aold. The array aold is assumed to have dimensions of nx/2 × ny/2.

- Lines 12–14: The kernel is designed to be called with a 2D thread grid of size at least nx × ny. Here we find the current thread's x and y in the standard way.
- Lines 14–16: Here we define lambda functions for 2D addressing of the arrays; idx uses a stride of nx between rows and mdx uses a stride mx set to nx/2.
- Lines 17–27: This set of if statements causes each thread to either copy a value from aold to both a and b or to copy the appropriate boundary value instead. Note there is a lot of thread divergence in this kernel but performance is not an issue as this kernel is typically only called once every few thousand iterations. This kernel has been written in a way which makes our intentions clear. Note the upscaling algorithm in line 17 is crude. We did experiment with smoother interpolations but found these did not improve performance.[4]
- Lines 30–40: This is the main routine:
  - Line 32: Set the flag type which is used in lines 36–37 to call the template function cascade as either single precision or double precision. This template choice then propagates down to all subsequent templated functions and kernels. This structure demonstrates how to effectively template an entire program.
  - Lines 33–35: Set the final array size and the maximum number of iterations per size step. Note that nx is assumed to be a power of two and that the array is a square of size nx × nx. The y-dimension ny is not used here but is intended for a future generalisation of this code.

    In a production version of this code additional parameters would be settable by the user. The convergence parameters check and diff_cut which are set in lines 68–69 of the cascade function are prime candidates for performance tuning experiments.

  - Lines 36–37: Call the cascade function with the desired precision.
  - Line 38: Our standard thrust safe CUDA exit for profilers.

  Lines 50–90: This is the cascade function which does all the work; in a non-templated version it could have been part of the main program.

- Line 50: Here are the function arguments at the final array dimensions nx and ny and the required number of iterations iter. Note ny is not actually used in the version which tacitly assumes square arrays.
- Lines 52–53: Here we set nx_start to the value 32 which is the starting array dimension. Pedantically we allow for the case of small starting array sizes by using min, but this would not be a sensible choice. The starting array is as a square array of dimension nx_start.
- Lines 54–56: Here we declare three working device arrays, dev_a and dev_b which are used as before for the flip-flop stencil2D iterations and dev_aold which holds the final result from the previous pass through the main loop in lines 58–82.
- Lines 58–59: This is the for loop over the array sizes; mx holds the current array dimension, which starts at 32 and doubles on each pass up to the final size nx. In line 59 my is set equal to mx.
- Lines 60–61: Set the usual launch parameters blocks and threads to span the current array size using 2D tiles of size 16 × 16.
- Lines 63–66 Here we resize dev_a and dev_b to fit the current array sizes. This step is not needed on the first pass through the loop. The resize member functions of C++ container classes are not particularly efficient but their use is strongly recommended for cases like this – it keeps your code simple and makes your intention clear. Since most of the time will be taken iterating with stencil2D, efficiency elsewhere in this loop is not critical.
- Line 67: The kernel zoomfrom is called here with the three working arrays as arguments. After this call the arrays a_dev and b_dev are initialised with the required boundary conditions on their edges and a scaled-up version of the previous iteration, stored in dev_aold, in their interiors. On the first

Table 4.3 *Results from cascade method using 4-byte floats and arrays of size 1024 × 1024*

Iterations	Time (secs)	GFlops/sec	Maximum abs(a[i]-b[i])	Accuracy average value of abs(a[i]-ref[i])
150	0.011	55	1.94×10^{-4}	1.28×10^{-1}
300	0.018	67	9.13×10^{-5}	4.62×10^{-2}
1000	0.054	74	2.56×10^{-5}	2.11×10^{-3}
5000	0.240	80	5.07×10^{-6}	7.50×10^{-4}
50,000	1.937	103	7.15×10^{-7}	2.34×10^{-4}
Results from cascade using 8-byte doubles				
100	0.014	29	2.42×10^{-5}	4.37×10^{-1}
200	0.024	33	2.34×10^{-6}	2.38×10^{-1}
350	0.036	39	2.62×10^{-7}	3.50×10^{-2}
750	0.071	42	3.42×10^{-8}	3.31×10^{-3}
15,000	1.060	57	1.46×10^{-6}	3.08×10^{-4}
100,000	5.580	72	2.02×10^{-8}	2.50×10^{-5}
300,000	14.891	81	1.38×10^{-11}	3.58×10^{-7}

pass through the loop all three arrays are set to zero so the effect of the call here is to set the correct boundary conditions in a and b while leaving their interiors set to zero. On subsequent passes dev_aold will not yet have been resized from the previous pass and its interior values will be upscaled into a and b.

- Lines 68–69: Here we set the parameters check and diff_max which control the frequency of convergence checks during the stencil iterations and the allowed difference between a and b values used by the convergence test.
- Lines 70–78: This is the iteration loop with pairs of flip-flop calls to stencil2D in lines 71 and 72; after each pair of calls the most recent result is in dev_a.
- Lines 80–81: Here we prepare for the next upscale pass by resizing dev_aold to match the current size of dev_a and then copying dev_a to dev_aold.
- Lines 84–88: Here we finish up by copying the final result back to the host, writing it to disk and printing timing information.

Some results obtained with the cascade version of stencil2d are shown in Table 4.3.

The cascade method is more accurate and faster than simply using all zeros as starting values. In the case of floats, we can achieve an accuracy of $\sim 2 \times 10^{-3}$ in 1000 iterations instead of 1,000,000 required before. The corresponding speed-up is a factor of 500. For the more accurate calculations using doubles the performance gains are more modest; we can achieve a final accuracy of $\sim 3.6 \times 10^{-7}$ in 300,000 iterations compared with over 5,000,000 required before. This is a speed-up of about 16. The rapid convergence of the cascade approach is particularly helpful for 3D stencil calculation which we discuss next.

4.3 3D Stencils

One really important benefit from the increased processing power of GPUs is the ability to tackle 3D versions of problems which are demanding as 2D problems on single processors.

Problems such as stencil calculations are a great example of this. A 2D kernel will typically be written so that each x-y element (grid point of image pixel etc.) is possessed by a separate thread. When converting a CUDA kernel from a 2D to 3D version we have two options:

1. Add a for loop over the z dimension to your existing kernel so that one thread processes all points with a fixed x and y stepping through the full z range.
2. Add more threads to the kernel launch so that each point in the 3D grid is processed by a different thread.

Example 4.7 shows two versions of a stencil3D kernel using these two approaches.

Example 4.7 stencil3D kernels (two versions)

```
10   template <typename T>__global__ void stencil3D_1
         (cr_Ptr<T> a,r_Ptr<T> b,int nx, int ny, int nz)
12   {
13     auto idx = [&nx, &ny](int z, int y, int x)
                         { return (z*ny+y)*nx+x; };

14     int x = blockIdx.x*blockDim.x+threadIdx.x;
15     int y = blockIdx.y*blockDim.y+threadIdx.y;
16     if(x < 1 || y < 1 || x >= nx-1 || y >= ny-1) return;

17     for(int z=1;z<nz-1;z++)  b[idx(z,y,x)] =
          (T)(1.0/6.0)*(a[idx(z,y,x+1)] + a[idx(z,y,x-1)] +
                        a[idx(z,y+1,x)] + a[idx(z,y-1,x)] +
                        a[idx(z+1,y,x)] + a[idx(z-1,y,x)]);
18   }


20   template <typename T>__global__ void stencil3D_2
         (cr_Ptr<T> a, r_Ptr<T> b, int nx, int ny, int nz)
21   {
22     auto idx = [&nx, &ny](int z, int y, int x)
                         { return (z*ny+y)*nx+x; };

23     int x = blockIdx.x*blockDim.x+threadIdx.x;
24     int y = blockIdx.y*blockDim.y+threadIdx.y;
25     int z = blockIdx.z*blockDim.z+threadIdx.z;
26     if(x<1 || y<1 || x>= nx-1 || y>= ny-1 || z<1
                                  || z>= nz-1) return;
27     b[idx(z,y,x)] = (T)(1.0/6.0)*(
                a[idx(z,y,x+1)] + a[idx(z,y,x-1)] +
                a[idx(z,y+1,x)] + a[idx(z,y-1,x)] +
                a[idx(z+1,y,x)] + a[idx(z-1,y,x)] );
28   }
```

Table 4.4 *Performance of 3D kernels for a 256 × 256 × 256 array*

Kernel	Precision	Time (secs)	GFlops	GB/sec
stencil3d_1	Single	6.37	158	738
	Double	13.9	78	678
stencil3d_2	Single	4.18	241	1128
	Double	9.29	108	1012

The times shown are for 10,000 iterations using a 6-point stencil

---

Description of Example 4.7

Both the 3D kernels in this example are based on stencil2D. The stencil3D_1 kernel uses method 1 above:

- Line 13: Here we define a 3D version of our idx lambda function used to address the 3D arrays a and b.
- Line 17: Here we add a for loop over the third array index z; note we exclude z=0 and z=nz-1 from the loop because only interior points are changed by the kernel. This complements line 16 which does the same job for x and y. The single statement in the loop replaces interior elements of b with the average of the six nearest neighbours of the corresponding element in a. (Note the 2D version uses four nearest neighbours.)

  The stencil3D_2 kernel uses method 2 above:
- Line 25: Here we set the z value for the current thread from the kernel launch configuration. For this to work the launch configuration needs to be changed as follows:
  - 2D launch (assumes a for loop over z in 3D kernels)
    dim3 threads = { 16, 16, 1};
    dim3 blocks = {(**nx**+16)/15, (**ny**+15)/16, **1**};
  - 3D launch (assumes one thread per 3D array operation in kernel)
    dim3 threads = { 16, 16, 1};
    dim3 blocks = {(**nx**+15)/16, (**ny**+15)/16, **nz**};
- Line 26: Here we add a check on the range of z to the similar checks on x and y.
- Line 27: This single statement is the only calculation performed by the current thread. The for loop used in stencil3d_1 has gone.

Somewhat to our surprise, using the RTX 2070 GPU and an array size of 256 × 256 × 256 we find stencil3d_2 performs about 33% faster than stencild3d_1 which is a big difference. Once again this demonstrates that modern GPUs really benefit from lots of threads to hide memory latency in memory bound problems. Table 4.4 summarises these results.

We note that the effective memory bandwidths shown in the table exceed the device hardware limits of around 410 GB/sec by up to a factor of three, demonstrating the effective use of local caching.

The details of our 3D host code are not shown here but are available online. For the 3D problem, the boundary conditions are specified on the faces of the 3D cube, in the code we choose to set the faces in the y-z planes at x=0 and x=nx-1 to 1.0 and the remaining faces to zero. The edges and corners of the volume are set to averages of the touching surfaces.

We have also implemented a 3D version of our cascade method to accelerate convergence and again this code is available online. Using the cascade method, we can get convergence to a given accuracy in a 256^3 volume about five times faster than simply starting with the full-size volume initialised to zeros. This is a useful but greatly reduced speed-up compared to the 2D case. The reason for this is that the convergence rate for the Jacobi iteration method depends on the diffusion time and hence on the number of pixels, from the edge to the centre of the area or volume concerned. Going from square to cube hardly changes this value but the number of pixels to be processed per iteration has increased by a factor of 256.

4.4 Digital Image Processing

2D stencil operations are much used for the manipulation of digital image data, for example, smoothing or sharpening operations. In this context the stencil operations are often referred to as image *filtering* and the stencils themselves as *filters* or (confusingly) *kernels*. A simple grey-scale digital image can be represented by a matrix of unsigned 8-bit values where each element represents one image pixel.[5] The values represent the brightness of the element on the display, thus a value of zero corresponds to black and a value of 255 (the maximum) corresponds to white. Colour images are usually represented by a set of three 8-bit numbers giving the brightness of red, green and blue channels (a so-called RGB image). A fourth 8-bit number, A, for attenuation (or transparency) may also be present yielding an RGBA image. An advantage of RGBA images is that the data for each pixel is stored in a 4-byte word and 4-byte words can be manipulated by computer hardware more efficiently than 3-byte words; this often overcomes the disadvantage of needing more memory even if the A field is not needed by the application.

As an annoying complication a 3-byte RGB image can be organised in two different ways, either the 3 bytes corresponding to one pixel can be placed in contiguous memory locations or they can be organised into three separate colour planes. The latter method is more convenient if one wants to inspect each colour as a separate image.

Many image processing tasks can be performed by applying 3×3 of 5×5 stencils to image pixel values. Some well-known examples are shown in Figure 4.3.

The filters shown in Figure 4.3 are as follows:

(a) Identity operation.
(b) Box filter for image blurring by removing high frequencies.
(c) Edge finding filter, a composition of (a) and (b) which removes low frequencies.
(d) Image smoothing filter with approximate Gaussian having standard deviation of one pixel; this 2D filter can be obtained as the outer product of two 1D Gaussian filters.
(e) An image sharpening filter based on a composition of (a) and (b); the parameter α is in the range $[0,1)$ with the image becoming sharper as α approaches 1.
(f) Filters giving approximate derivatives of Gaussian smoothed image; these are used in the Sobel filter discussed below.
(g) A more accurate 5×5 version of the 3×3 Gaussian filter (d).
(h) The result of applying 3×3 Gaussian filter (d) twice; this result is quite similar to (g).
(i) The result of applying box filter (b) twice.

Note all these filters are normalised so that the sum of their coefficients is unity, except for (c) and (f) where the coefficients sum to zero.

(a) Identity

$$\mathbf{I} = \begin{bmatrix} 0 & 0 & 0 \\ 0 & 1 & 0 \\ 0 & 0 & 0 \end{bmatrix}$$

(b) Low Pass

$$\mathbf{L} = \frac{1}{9} \begin{bmatrix} 1 & 1 & 1 \\ 1 & 1 & 1 \\ 1 & 1 & 1 \end{bmatrix}$$

(c) High Pass

$$\mathbf{H} = \mathbf{I} - \frac{1}{9}\mathbf{L} = \begin{bmatrix} -1 & -1 & -1 \\ -1 & 8 & -1 \\ -1 & -1 & -1 \end{bmatrix}$$

(d) 3 x 3 Gaussian

$$\mathbf{G} = \frac{1}{16} \begin{bmatrix} 1 & 2 & 1 \\ 2 & 4 & 2 \\ 1 & 2 & 1 \end{bmatrix} = \frac{1}{16} \begin{bmatrix} 1 \\ 2 \\ 1 \end{bmatrix} \otimes \begin{bmatrix} 1 & 2 & 1 \end{bmatrix}$$

(e) Sharpen Filter

$$\mathbf{S}_\alpha = \mathbf{I} - \frac{\alpha}{9}\mathbf{L} = \frac{1}{9(1-\alpha)} \begin{bmatrix} -\alpha & -\alpha & -\alpha \\ -\alpha & 9-\alpha & -\alpha \\ -\alpha & -\alpha & -\alpha \end{bmatrix}$$

(f) Derivatives of Gaussian

$$\frac{\partial}{\partial x} = \begin{bmatrix} -1 & 0 & 1 \\ -2 & 0 & 2 \\ -1 & 0 & 1 \end{bmatrix}, \quad \frac{\partial}{\partial y} = \begin{bmatrix} 1 & 2 & 1 \\ 0 & 0 & 0 \\ -1 & -2 & -1 \end{bmatrix}, \quad \nabla^2 = \begin{bmatrix} -2 & 1 & -2 \\ 1 & 4 & 1 \\ -2 & 1 & -2 \end{bmatrix}$$

(g) 5 x 5 Gaussian

$$\mathbf{G}_5 = \frac{1}{273} \begin{bmatrix} 1 & 4 & 7 & 4 & 1 \\ 4 & 16 & 26 & 16 & 4 \\ 7 & 26 & 41 & 26 & 7 \\ 4 & 16 & 26 & 16 & 4 \\ 1 & 4 & 7 & 4 & 1 \end{bmatrix}$$

(h) 5 x 5 Gaussian Approximated by G · G

$$\mathbf{G}^2 = \frac{1}{256} \begin{bmatrix} 1 & 4 & 6 & 4 & 1 \\ 4 & 16 & 24 & 16 & 4 \\ 6 & 24 & 36 & 24 & 6 \\ 4 & 16 & 24 & 16 & 4 \\ 1 & 4 & 6 & 4 & 1 \end{bmatrix}$$

(i) Low Pass Filter L·L

$$\mathbf{L}^2 = \frac{1}{81} \begin{bmatrix} 1 & 2 & 3 & 2 & 1 \\ 2 & 4 & 6 & 4 & 2 \\ 3 & 6 & 9 & 6 & 3 \\ 2 & 4 & 6 & 4 & 2 \\ 1 & 2 & 3 & 2 & 1 \end{bmatrix}$$

Figure 4.3 Typical filters used for digital image processing

Figure 4.4 Result of filters applied to reference image

The results of applying some of these filters are shown in Figure 4.4.
In Figure 4.4 the images are as follows:

(a) Unmodified test image.[6]
(b) Close-up showing individual pixels.

(c) Low pass (smoothing) filter L filter applied 10 times.
(d) Sharpening filter S_α for $\alpha = 0.8$.
(e) High pass filter **H**.
(f) Sobel filter discussed below.

The implementation of these filters on a GPU is exactly the same as for the stencils discussed above. In fact, it is often only necessary to implement 3×3 filters, because higher order filters, for example, 5×5, can be simulated by applying a 3×3 filter several times. Figures 4.3 (h) and (i) show the 5×5 filters resulting from applying (d) and (b) twice. Additionally, the 5×5 filters require reading of 25 elements for each pixel whereas a double application of a 3×3 filter requires the reading of only 18 pixels and should thus be faster. The filters shown in (g) are approximate image derivatives applied to Gaussian smoothed images using the filter shown in (d); these behave better than simple one 1D filters (e.g. [−1/ 2,0, 1/2] for d/dx) when applied to noisy images. The Sobel filter discussed below is based on these derivatives.

The kernel `filter_9PT` in Example 4.8 applies a general 3×3 image filter and is designed for 8-bit grey-scale images.

Example 4.8 `filter9PT` kernel implementing a general 9-point filter

```
10   __global__ void filter9PT(cr_Ptr<uchar> a,
         r_Ptr<uchar> b, int nx, int ny, cr_Ptr<float> c)
11   {
12       auto idx = [&nx](int y,int x){ return y*nx+x;  };

13       int x = blockIdx.x*blockDim.x+threadIdx.x;
14       int y = blockIdx.y*blockDim.y+threadIdx.y;
15       if(x<0 || y <0 || x >= nx || y >= ny)return;

         // floor of zero and ceiling of nx/ny-1
16       int xl = max(0,   x-1); int yl = max(0,   y-1);
17       int xh = min(nx-1,x+1); int yh = min(ny-1,y+1);

18       float v =  c[0]*a[idx(yl,xl)] + c[1]*a[idx(yl, x)] +
                    c[2]*a[idx(yl,xh)] + c[3]*a[idx(y ,xl)] +
                    c[4]*a[idx(y , x)] + c[5]*a[idx(y ,xh)] +
                    c[6]*a[idx(yh,xl)] + c[7]*a[idx(yh, x)] +
                    c[8]*a[idx(yh,xh)];

19       uint f = (uint)(v+0.5f);
20       b[idx(y,x)] = (uchar)min(255,max(0,f)); // b in [0,255]
21   }
```

Description of Example 4.8

This kernel is similar to the `stencil2D` kernels shown above; it differs only in that the image data is 8-bit uchar (suitable for grey-scale images) and that the filter coefficients are passed as a kernel argument rather than being built in. For digital image processing these filters are only used once or twice per image so arguably their optimisation is less important, but actually GPUs owe their very existence to the demands of the gaming community for fast image processing at PC display frame rates. The real time filtering of images from CCD cameras is another important application.

- Line 10: The kernel arguments are the input image a and a buffer b to store the results of the filter; these are passed as pointers to arrays of type uchar (unsigned char). The image dimensions are passed as nx and ny and the nine filter coefficients are passed as a third array c of type float. In C++ the type uchar behaves as an unsigned 8-bit integer and is commonly used for image manipulation. Calculations involving 8-bit integers are often done using 16- or 32-bit variables to hold intermediate result which are then either scaled to an 8-bit result or just copied back with a floor and ceiling of 0 and 255 applied.
- Line 12: Defines idx to aid the addressing of 2D arrays.
- Lines 13–14: The kernel is designed for one thread to process one image pixel and hence requires a 2D launch configuration of sufficient size to span the input array. Then we find the x and y pixel coordinates for the current thread.
- Line 15: A standard out-of-range check on the pixel coordinates. This kernel can deal with any size of input image.
- Lines 16–17: Each thread needs to read the eight nearest neighbours of the pixel at (x, y), and we must check that these are also in range. There are various ways of doing this and there is an annoying complication that every thread has to make these checks even though the vast majority of threads process pixels well inside the image boundaries. Here we use xl and yl to index the pixels to the left and above (x,y) and xh and yh pixels to the right and below (x,y). We set these to safe values using the fast CUDA max and min functions. This avoids using if statements which are slower in kernel code. A side effect is the pixels on the edges of the image will have a slightly different filter applied with one of two duplicate image values being used to replace non-existent pixels. Arguably this is as good as any other method of dealing with boundary effects.
- Line 18: This is the general 9-point filter. Note that since the coefficients are of type float, the pixel values will be promoted from uchar to float during the calculation; this is an important detail.
- Line 19: The filter result v is truncated to the nearest uint and stored in f.
- Line 20: The result in f is converted to uchar with a floor of 0 and ceiling of 255 applied and then stored in the output array b.

The `filter9PT` kernel is short and simple and delivers between 100 and 900 GFlops of performance depending on image size. This is equivalent to more than 3000 frames per second for a large image of size 4096 × 4096 and is more than enough for any real time display applications which require at most 120 frames per second. However, many image processing applications are for the analysis of scientific data and for these we may desire more perform-ance at the price of complicating our kernels. Our image filtering kernel is still limited by memory access and can be improved. The first simple step is to notice that the coefficients `c[0]`–`c[8]` used in line 18 are being read from global memory by each thread. A faster solution is to store these parameters in GPU constant memory as shown in Example 4.9.

Example 4.9 `filter9PT_2` kernel using GPU constant memory for filter coefficients

```
        . . .
05    __constant__ fc[9];   // declaration has file scope
        . . .
10    __global__ void filter9PT_2(cr_Ptr<uchar> a,
                          r_Ptr<uchar> b, int nx, int ny)
11    {
        . . .
18      float v = fc[0]*a[idx(yl,xl)] + fc[1]*a[idx(yl, x)] +
                  fc[2]*a[idx(yl,xh)] + fc[3]*a[idx(y ,xl)] +
                  fc[4]*a[idx( y, x)] + fc[5]*a[idx(y ,xh)] +
                  fc[6]*a[idx(yh,xl)] + fc[7]*a[idx(yh, x)] +
                  fc[8]*a[idx(yh,xh)];
        . . .
21    }
        . . .
      // copy c on host to fc on device constant memory
45    cudaMemcpyToSymbol(fc, c.data(), 9*sizeof(float));
        . . .
```

Example 4.9 is a minor modification to Example 4.8; in line 10 we have removed the final argument containing the filter coefficients c and replaced them with an array fc in GPU constant memory declared at file scope. Also, in line 18 we have replaced c with fc to pick up the values in the global array. Line 45 is a line from the new main routine using `cudaMemcpyToSymbol` to copy the coefficients from the host array c to the device global array `fc`. Constant memory declared at file scope can also be initialised directly by something like `__constant__ float fc[9]` = {0,−1,0, −1,0,1, 0,1,0}.

CUDA constant memory is a block of special GPU memory, currently of size 64 KB on all NVIDIA GPUs, which is shared as read-only memory by all SM units. Constant memory has separate caching and can be efficiently read by all threads in a warp. It is intended for parameters in just the sort of case discussed here. Some constant memory is always reserved by the system but 48 KB is available for use by kernel code. Actually, all kernel arguments passed by value are stored in constant memory by the system so there is no need to explicitly do this as an optimisation. You can also use a kernel argument as a variable in kernel code, but if you do then that argument will be copied to a local register by the compiler and the advantage of constant memory is lost. There is a limit of 4 KB on the total size of all arguments passed to a kernel.

The effect of this small change is to speed up the kernel by up to ~25% for larger images. Encouraged by this quick win, we can look at ways of reading the elements of the array more efficiently.

In Examples 4.8 and 4.9 there are two issues with the way the elements of the input array a are read. Firstly, they are read from global memory as single bytes and secondly each element is read by nine different threads. We attack both issues by reading from global memory using the 32-byte uchar4 type and then placing the values in shared memory. This is a form of vector loading which has been discussed previously.

The kernel filter9PT_3 implements these ideas and is shown in Example 4.10. Our new kernel is considerably more complicated, but it does give a further speed-up of about 30%. In this kernel each thread handles four elements of a stored in the consecutive bytes of one 32-bit word. The kernel is specifically designed for 2D thread blocks of dimension 16×16 and shared memory is allocated as a 2D array of 66×18 bytes which is sufficient to hold a central core of 64×16 bytes surrounded by a halo of single bytes. The central core allows each thread to load 4 bytes as a single uchar4 and then process them as individual bytes. The external halo is 1-byte deep which is sufficient for a 3×3 filter. Note that explicitly loading the external halo used here is more complicated than implicitly loading internal halo as was done for stencil2D_sm in Example 4.2.

Description of Example 4.10

- Line 10: The kernel arguments are the same as the previous version. As before it is assumed that the filter coefficients are stored in the array __constant__ fc.
- Line 12: We allocate a 2D static shared memory array of type uchar sufficient to hold for value for each thread in a 16×16 tile and a halo of one element around all four sides of the 64×16 data set.

Note the total shared memory size is just 1188 bytes which is well below the practical limit of about 48 KB available on each SM of the GPU. However, for full occupancy, most NVIDIA GPUs require 2048 resident threads equivalent to eight thread blocks of size 256. This kernel can therefore easily run at full occupancy as the total shared memory requirement is still only 9504 bytes.

- Line 13: Here we define the lambda function idx used for 2D addressing of the arrays a and b.
- Lines 14–16: Here we define some base variables used to address the active tile in both global and shared memory:
  - Line 14: x0 and y0 are the 2D coordinates of the top left-hand corner of the tile being processed in global memory; note these are multiples of 64 and 16 respectively because 16 consecutive threads processing one horizontal line of the tile each process 4 elements.
  - Line 15: xa and ya are the starting position of the current thread in a and b.
  - Line 16: x and y are the starting position of the current thread in the shared memory array as.
- Line 17: Here we copy four bytes from a to the local uchar4 variable a4 in a single memory transaction; a reinterpret cast is needed to do this. Also because the input argument a is declared const, we must also declare a4 as const.

Example 4.10 filter9PT_3 kernel with vector loading to shared memory

```
10   __global__ void filter9PT_3(cr_Ptr<uchar> a,
                        r_Ptr<uchar> b, int nx, int ny)
11   {
        // 16 x 64 tile plus 1 element wide halo
```

```
12     __shared__ uchar as[18][66];
13     auto idx = [&nx](int y,int x){ return y*nx+x; };

       // (y0,x0) tile origin in a
14     int x0 = blockIdx.x*64; int y0 = blockIdx.y*16;
       // (ya,xa) index in a
15     int xa = x0+threadIdx.x*4; int ya = y0+threadIdx.y;
       // (y,x) in shared mem
16     int x = threadIdx.x*4 + 1; int y = threadIdx.y + 1;

17     const uchar4 a4 = reinterpret_cast
                     <const uchar4 *>(a)[idx(ya,xa)/4];
18     as[y][ x] = a4.x; as[y][x+1] = a4.y;
       as[y][x+2] = a4.z; as[y][x+3] = a4.w;


       // warp 0 threads 0-15: copy top (y0-1) row to halo
19     if(y==1){
20       int ytop = max(0,y0-1);
21       as[0][x  ] = a[idx(ytop,xa )];
         as[0][x+1] = a[idx(ytop,xa+1)];
22       as[0][x+2] = a[idx(ytop,xa+2)];
         as[0][x+3] = a[idx(ytop,xa+3)];
23       if(threadIdx.x==0) {  // top corners
24         int xleft= max(0,x0-1);
           as[0][0 ]= a[idx(ytop,xleft)]; //(0,0)
25         int xright= min(nx-1,x0+64);
           as[0][65]= a[idx(ytop,xright)];//(0,65)
26       }
27       int xlft = max(0,x0-1);
          // left edge halo
28       as[threadIdx.x+1][0] = a[idx(y0+threadIdx.x,xlft)];
29     }
       // warp 1 threads 0-15: copy bottom row (y0+16) to halo
30     if(y==3){
31       int ybot = min(ny-1,y0+16);
32       as[17][x  ] = a[idx(ybot,xa  )];
         as[17][x+1] = a[idx(ybot,xa+1)];
33       as[17][x+2] = a[idx(ybot,xa+2)];
         as[17][x+3] = a[idx(ybot,xa+3)];
34       if(threadIdx.x==0) { // bottom corners
35         int xleft = max(0,x0-1 );
           as[17][0 ]= a[idx(ybot,xleft) ];//(17,0)
36         int xright= min(nx-1,x0+64);
           as[17][65]= a[idx(ybot,xright)];//(17,65)
37       }
38       int xrgt = min(nx-1,x0+64);
          // right edge halo
```

```
39        as[threadIdx.x+1][65] = a[idx(y0+threadIdx.x,xrgt)];
40      }
41      __syncthreads();
42      uchar bout[4];
43      for(int k=0;k<4;k++){
44        float v = fc[0]*as[y-1][x-1] + fc[1]*as[y-1][x]  +
                    fc[2]*as[y-1][x+1] + fc[3]*as[y  ][x-1] +
                    fc[4]*as[y  ][x]   + fc[5]*as[y  ][x+1] +
                    fc[6]*as[y+1][x-1] + fc[7]*as[y+1][x]   +
                    fc[8]*as[y+1][x+1];

45        uint kf = (uint)(v+0.5f);
46        bout[k] = (uchar)min(255,max(0,kf)); // b in [0,255]
47        x++;
48      }
49      reinterpret_cast<uchar4 *>(b)[idx(ya,xa)/4] =
                    reinterpret_cast<uchar4 *>(bout)[0];
50    }
```

- Line 18: Individual bytes from a4 are copied to consecutive locations of shared memory using four separate 1-byte copy statements. Note at this point the 256 threads in the thread block will together have filled the entire central 64 × 16 byte tile. In comparison, lines 19–40 are needed to load the halo.

(We have experimented using a single uchar4 copy here, but this requires extra padding of the shared memory array to ensure its central tile is aligned on a 4-byte memory boundary and with the RTX 2070 GPU the resulting code is slightly less fast).

- Lines 19–29: The test on y selects threads 0–15 from warp 0. These 16 threads load the top (y=0) line of the halo (lines 20–22) and the left-hand edge of the halo (lines 27–28). Note that in line 28 threadIdx.x is used as a y index for both as and a. This is a poor, but here unavoidable, memory access pattern. A single thread, with threadIdx.x = 0, then also loads the corners of the top line of the halo (lines 23–26).
- Lines 30–40: These are similar to lines 19–29 but use threads 0–15 of warp 1 to load the bottom and right-hand edge of the halo. Because we use different warps in these two sections they can run simultaneously on the GPU. There is a tacit assumption here that every thread block has at least 2 warps.
- Line 41: A __syncthreads() is necessary here to wait until the filling of shared memory is complete.
- Lines 42–48: Here we see the actual work of the kernel; each thread will handle 4 data elements from as.
  ○ Line 42: The uchar array bout is used to store results for the for loop in line 43.
  ○ Line 43: Here we use a 4 step for loop which processes one element on each pass. The elements of data addressed by x and y in this section of code and thus we increment x at the end of each pass but leave y unchanged.
  ○ Line 44: Here finally is the actual filter calculation. The result is calculated using floating point arithmetic.

Table 4.5 *Performance of filter9PT kernels on an RTX 2070 GPU*

	Compute in GFlops			Memory bandwidth in GB/sec		
Image Size	9pt	9pt_2	9pt_3	9pt	9pt_2	9_pt3
28 × 128	98.8	104.5	99.2	58.1	61.5	58.4
256 × 256	255.6	294.0	343.5	150.4	172.9	202.1
512 × 512	434.8	554.0	817.7	255.8	325.9	481.0
1024 × 1024	524.3	708.4	1254.2	308.4	416.7	737.8
2048 × 2048	565.6	781.4	1312.0	332.7	459.7	771.8
4096 × 4096	943.1	1324.2	**2260.9**	554.8	779.0	**1330.0**

- ○ Lines 45–46: The result is rounded to the nearest integer, clamped to be in the range [0,255] and stored in one element of bout.
- • Line 49: The four results in bout are copied to the output array b in a single memory transaction using casts.

This example illustrates that although the concept of tiles with halos for stencils and filters is simple and a good fit for GPU architecture, the implementation details can be messy. Note by using external halos we have been able to ensure that the central 64 × 16 byte active tile is always correctly aligned on a 32-bit address boundary – this is essential for the use of uchar4 vector loads. Preserving correct alignment would not have been possible had we used an internal halo. The technique of using individual warps (or sub-warps in this case) to perform different tasks within a kernel is also noteworthy. This helps when there is a lot of messy detail to deal with in a kernel. Different warps can run different tasks simultaneously without thread divergence issues. The example could be changed to use cooperative groups to define 16-thread tiled partitions to clarify our intentions in lines 19 and 30.

Table 4.5 shows the performance achieved by the three versions of the filter9PT kernel. The numbers given are the compute performance in GFlops and memory throughput in GB/sec. The timings are for our RTX 2070 GPU and we have assumed 17 floating point operations and 10 bytes of global memory accesses per kernel call. For the smallest image size there is little difference between the kernels, but as image size increases while all kernels improve their performance, our final kernel (c) using shared memory does best, outperforming the original kernel by up to factor of 2.4. The memory bandwidths also increase with image size and for the largest image sizes exceed the uncached hardware limit by a factor of up to 3.

4.5 Sobel Filter

The Sobel filter is another interesting example showing the flexibility of GPUs. It is an edge finding filter based on the local image contrast gradient. The gradient operator $\nabla = (\partial/\partial x, \partial/\partial y)$ points in the direction of the maximum gradient and its magnitude is the maximum gradient. The Sobel filter estimates this gradient based on the two 6-point smoothed filters for $\partial/\partial x$ and $\partial/\partial y$ shown in Figure 4.3 (f) to evaluate Eq. 4.10 at each image pixel.

$$|\nabla| = \left[\left(\frac{\partial}{\partial x} \right)^2 + \left(\frac{\partial}{\partial y} \right)^2 \right]^{1/2}. \tag{4.10}$$

We base our Sobel kernel `sobel6PT` on the kernel `filter9PT_3` which performed fastest and can easily be adapted by changing its line 44 from a 9-point filter calculation to a function call. The fragment of the kernel `sobel6PT` which implements the Sobel filter is shown in Example 4.11. The device function `sobel` receives the values of the pixel being processed and its eight nearest neighbours. The function call is shown as a modified line 44 from Example 4.10 and the sobel function is shown in lines 60–66.

Notice that the function arguments are passed by reference; this means that this function call has very low overheads; it will use its arguments directly from the shared memory registers passed in line 44. Lines 62 and 63 show the calculation of the two derivative filters.

Example 4.11 `sobel6PT` kernel based on `filter9PT_3`

```
       __global__  void sobel6PT(cr_Ptr<uchar> a,
                     r_Ptr<uchar> b,int nx,int ny)
       {
         . . .
44       float v= sobel<uchar>(as[y-1][x-1],as[y-1][x],
                 as[y-1][x+1],as[y  ][x-1],as[y  ][x],
                 as[y  ][x+1],as[y+1][x-1],as[y+1][x],
                 as[y+1][x+1]);
         . . .
       }
         . . .
60       template <typename T> __device__ float sobel(
             T &a00,T &a01,T &a02,T &a10,T &a11,
             T &a12,T &a20,T &a21,T &a22 )
61     {
62       float dx = a02 -a00 +2.0f*(a12-a10) + a22 -a20;  // d/dx

63       float dy = a00 -a20 +2.0f*(a01-a21) + a02 -a22;  // d/dy
64       float v = sqrtf(dx*dx+dy*dy);
65       return v;
66     }
```

We will end this chapter with one more filter, the median filter which requires us to think about parallel sorting methods.

4.6 Median Filter

The Sobel filter is an example of a non-linear filter, it cannot be represented by a set of linear scaling coefficients. Another interesting filter, which cannot be represented by coefficients, is

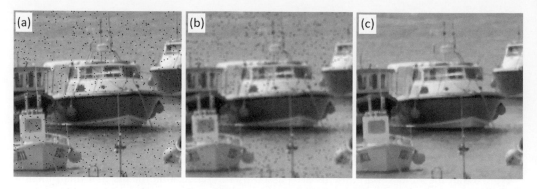

Figure 4.5 Noise reduction using a median filter

the median filter, which simply replaces a target pixel by the median value of itself and its neighbours. Median filters are especially useful for removing single pixel noise from images captured by CCD cameras often used for scientific data. This is illustrated in Figure 4.5 where we have added fake noise to our standard image by setting a random 1% of the pixels to zero. Figure 4.5 (a) shows the original noisy image and Figures 4.5 (b) and (c) show the results of applying a 3×3 smoothing filter and a 3×3 median filter. The smoothing filter has turned single black pixels into 3×3 grey squares while the median filter has eliminated them completely albeit with some slight blurring of the image.

Implementing a parallel median 3×3 filter on a GPU is moderately challenging. For image processing we would like to keep to an implementation where one thread handles one pixel. Thus each thread has to sort 9 numbers and pick the middle one. Additionally, we want to avoid conditional statements which might lead to thread divergence. Our key tool is the non-divergent swap function a_less shown in Example 4.12:

Example 4.12 The device function a_less

```
60   template <typename T> __device__ __inline__
                                     void a_less(T &a,T &b)
61   {
62       T temp = a;           // NB this is much faster than
63       a = min(a,b);         // using an if statement on
64       b = max(temp,b);      // both host and gpu
65   }                          // a ≤ b on exit
```

On a CUDA GPU this function is faster than the equivalent using an `if` statement to compare the two arguments. Notice that the function arguments are passed by reference so that they can be changed in the calling routine. The `inline` directive means that if the arguments a and b are stored in registers then these registers will be used directly and zero overheads are associated with the function call.

If we imagine the nine elements are stored in nine locations from 1 to 9, a naïve sorting algorithm would be as follows:

Step 1: Call a_less 8 times with elements 1–8 as first argument and element 9 as second argument. After this element 9 will be the largest.

Step 2: Repeat for elements 1–7 as first argument and element 8 as fixed second argument. After this element 8 is the second largest

Steps 3–8: Continue the process with one less element each time.

At the end of all the steps the entire nine elements will be sorted into ascending order. For just finding the median we can stop after five steps after which element 5 is the desired median value. The device function median9 which implements this 5-step algorithm is shown in Example 4.13; in all 30 calls to a_less are needed.

Example 4.13 median9 device function

```
70   template <typename T> __device__ __inline__ T
            median9(T a1,T a2,T a3,T a4,T a5,T a6,T a7,T a8,T a9)
72   {
73     a_less(a1,a9); a_less(a2,a9); a_less(a3,a9);
       a_less(a4,a9); a_less(a5,a9); a_less(a6,a9);
74     a_less(a7,a9); a_less(a8,a9);              // a9 1st max
75     a_less(a1,a8); a_less(a2,a8); a_less(a3,a8);
       a_less(a4,a8); a_less(a5,a8); a_less(a6,a8);
76     a_less(a7,a8);                            // a8 2nd max
77     a_less(a1,a7); a_less(a2,a7); a_less(a3,a7);
78     a_less(a4,a7); a_less(a5,a7); a_less(a6,a7);// a7 3rd max
79     a_less(a1,a6); a_less(a2,a6); a_less(a3,a6);
80     a_less(a4,a6); a_less(a5,a6);              // a6 4th max
81     a_less(a1,a5); a_less(a2,a5); a_less(a3,a5);
       a_less(a4,a5);                            // a5 median

82     return a5;
83   }
```

Notice that in median9 the input arguments a1 to a9 may have their values exchanged by calls to a_less; it is thus necessary for these arguments to be passed by value and not by reference. The actual values are stored in shared memory by the calling kernel and so their values need to be preserved for use by multiple threads.

This kernel is quite fast and can process a large image of size 4096 × 4096 in about 0.5 ms, which is more than 1000 times faster than the same algorithm running on a single core of the host CPU. Nevertheless, it is possible to improve the code by removing some unnecessary calls to a_less from the median9 kernel. It is, in fact, possible to sort 9 numbers with just 23 calls to a_less rather than 30. The scheme for doing this is shown in Figure 4.6 which shows Batcher sorting networks for four and nine numbers. Each vertical

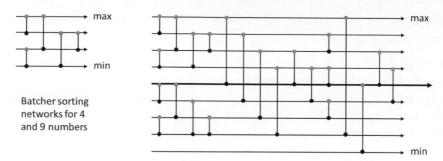

Figure 4.6 Batcher sorting networks for N = 4 and N = 9

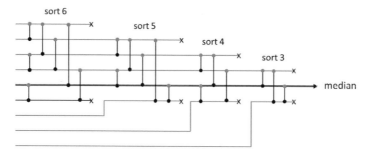

Figure 4.7 Modified Batcher network to find median of nine numbers

line in the diagram represents a call to the a_less function, after which the grey point at the top of the line is the larger of the two numbers and the black point at the bottom of the line is the lower number.

In Figure 4.6 each vertical bar represents a sort between two numbers after which the smaller (shown in black) is below the larger value (shown in grey). After the sort, the median of the nine numbers in the right-hand diagram will be on the central line. These networks have complexity of order $N\log^2(N)$ and hence become less efficient for large N.

As shown in the figure the full sort of nine numbers requires 23 pairwise tests. However, 23 tests are more than required to simply find the median. We will follow the method of Perrot et al.,[7] which is based on the observation that given a set of 2N+1 numbers a sort of any subset with N+2 or more numbers have a maximum and minimum value neither of which can be the median. Thus, to find the median of nine numbers we start with a Batcher network to sort six numbers and find and discard the max and min. We add one of the unused numbers the remaining four numbers from the original six and repeat with the resulting set of five numbers and so on discarding the max and min each time until we find the median. The resulting median finding network has 20 comparisons as shown in Figure 4.7.

The code to implement this median filter is shown in Example 4.14.

Description of Example 4.14

The device functions shown here implement the Batcher network shown in Figure 4.7 on a per thread basis.

- Line 44: This is the modified version of line 44 from Example 4.10 showing the call to the device function `batcher9` described below. Since this function returns a result of type `uchar` it can be directly stored in the output array `b`.
- Lines 70–74: The function `medsort6` implements the 6-item sort from Figure 4.7. It is called with arguments `a4-a8` in line 92. There are 7 calls to `a_less` here.
- Lines 75–87: These lines define three more functions to perform the remaining sorts of five, four and three items as shown in Figure 4.7. There are a further 13 calls to `a_less` here, making a total of 20 calls in all.
- Lines 88–97: Here we define the `__device__` function `batcher9` which takes the 9 image pixel values centred on `a5` as arguments. These are deliberately passed by value so that they can be safely modified when by `a_less`.

The times taken by the two median filter kernels, median9 and batcher9, to process a large uchar image of size 4096×4096 pixels were 0.534 and 0.374 ms respectively. These times are just the kernel run times ignoring the overheads of loading the image and storing the result. Nevertheless, the filter is impressively fast and certainly fast enough for real time applications such as real time denoising of video from CCD imaging cameras run at high frame rates and high gain for astronomical or other low light applications. The equivalent host code running of a single CPU core is about 1000 times slower, requiring 620 and 307 ms per frame for the two versions of the filter.

Batcher networks could of course also be used for simple sorting operations although for sorting a large number of values other algorithms such as a radix sort are better. In fact parallel sorting is another "classic" GPU application and like reduce is often discussed in CUDA tutorials. If you are interested in this topic the CUDA SDK is a good place to start; the `6_Advanced` directory has three examples `cdpAdvancedQuicksort`, `mergeSort` and `sortingNetworks` which illustrate some of the methods. If your application needs to sort large arrays it is probably best to start with the available libraries. For example CUDA thrust has good support for sorting arrays.

Example 4.14 `batcher9` kernel for per-thread median of nine numbers

```
         . . .
44       bout[k] = batcher9<uchar>(as[y-1][x-1],
         as[y-1][x], as[y-1][x+1], as[y  ][x-1],
         as[y  ][x], as[y  ][x+1], as[y+1][x-1],
         as[y+1][x], as[y+1][x+1]);
         . . .
70       template <typename T> __device__ __inline__
         void medsort6(T &a1,T &a2,T &a3,T &a4,T &a5,T &a6) {
```

```
71      a_less(a1,a2); a_less(a3,a4); a_less(a5,a6);
72      a_less(a1,a3); a_less(a2,a4);
73      a_less(a1,a5); a_less(a4,a6);
        // a1 and a6 are now min and max of a1-a6
74    }

75    template <typename T> __device__ __inline__
      void medsort5(T &a1,T &a2,T &a3,T &a4,T &a5) {
76      a_less(a1,a2); a_less(a3,a4);
77      a_less(a1,a3); a_less(a2,a4);
78      a_less(a1,a5); a_less(a4,a5);
        // a1 and a5 now min and max of a1-a5
79    }

80    template <typename T> __device__ __inline__
      void medsort4(T &a1,T &a2,T &a3,T &a4) {
81      a_less(a1,a2); a_less(a3,a4);
82      a_less(a1,a3); a_less(a2,a4);
        // a1 and a4 now min and max of a1-a4
83    }

84    template <typename T> __device__ __inline__
      void medsort3(T &a1,T &a2,T &a3) {
85      a_less(a1,a2);
86      a_less(a1,a3); a_less(a2,a3);
        // a1 and a3 now min and max of a1-a3
87    }

88    template <typename T> __device__ __inline__ T
89      batcher9(T a1,T a2,T a3,T a4,T a5,T a6,T a7,T a8,T a9)
90    {
91      // implement modified Batcher network as per figure 4.7
92      medsort6<T>(a4,a5,a6,a7,a8,a9);
93      medsort5<T>(a3,a5,a6,a7,a8   ); // drop a4 & a9 add a3
94      medsort4<T>(a2,a5,a6,a7      ); // drop a3 & a8 add a2
95      medsort3<T>(a1,a5,a6         ); // drop a2 & a7 add a1

96      return a5;   // return median value now in a5
97    }
```

In this chapter we have introduced the idea of stencils and image filters which both require essentially the same coding approach. Explicit use of NVIDIA GPU `constant` memory was used for the first time. In the next chapter we continue the theme of image manipulation and introduce another (and the last) type of specialised GPU memory – the texture.

Endnotes Chapter 4

1 Equal spacing is a simplifying assumption; more advanced finite element-based methods (FEM) use variable point spacings adapted to the local needs, i.e. more points in regions where more detail is needed.

2 This is not entirely true for recent GPUs. Cooperative groups provide a kernel wide function for grid synchronisation analogous to syncthreads() but this comes at the price of limiting the number of thread blocks in the kernel launch, which for many applications would lead to a performance drop outweighing the gain of needing fewer kernel launches.

3 A kernel using thread blocks of size 16×16 and shared memory can either load tiles of size 16×16 including the halo or tiles of size 18×18 including the halo. The former makes loading shared memory easy but then only 14×14 threads to perform the calculation. The latter allows all 16×16 threads to perform useful work but this approach significantly complicates the tile loading process. We can think of this as a choice between inner or outer halos.

4 In the next chapter on image processing, we will look at a number of interpolation strategies for rescaling images.

5 This indeed is the origin of the term pixel. According to Wikipedia (https://en.wikipedia.org/wiki/Pixel) the first published use was in 1963 in connection with images from space craft. These days pixel is widely used for both digital images and the screens on which they are displayed. In 3D datasets, for example, volumetric MRI scans, the term voxel has more recently been introduced for a volume element.

6 We have used a 512×512 portion of a holiday picture of St Ives harbour converted to greyscale.

7 Perrot, G., Domas, S. & Couturier, R. Fine-tuned High-speed Implementation of a GPU-based Median Filter. *Journal of Signal Processing Systems* 75, 185–190 (2014).

5

Textures

The previous chapter discussed filtering of 2D images by changing the values of individual pixels based on the values in that pixel's neighbourhood. However, many pixel image transformations, including image resizing and rotation are more complicated in that there is not a simple one-to-one correspondence between the pixels before and after the transformation.

Digital images are often used to represent mathematical distributions or scientific data. In these cases, the discrete image pixels are used as an approximation to a "real" continuous distribution and the pixel value is understood to be an average for the region represented by that pixel. A digital image will always be displayed in print or on a screen as a 2D rectangular grid of pixels having a horizontal x-axis and vertical y-axis. We follow the C++ convention of addressing a row of N pixels with an integer ix index running from 0 to N–1 and a column of M pixels with an integer iy index running from 0 to M–1. The origin is in the top left-hand corner of the image. This means that for pixels of unit size, the ix and iy coordinates are the displacements from the top left-hand corner of the image as illustrated in Figure 5.1.

Figure 5.1 shows the pixels of an image with 10×3 pixels where the integer pixel coordinates ix and iy follow the C++ index convention. If the pixels have unit size then rows are 10 units wide and the columns are 3 units deep. The centres of the pixels are at the centre positions indicated by dots. In quantitative work a digital image is regarded as a sampling of a continuous 2D function $f(x,y)$ where the value in each pixel is the integral of f over the area of the pixel.[1] In turn this means that the pixel values are estimates of the value of $f(x,y)$ at the geometric centres for each pixel which are obtained by adding 0.5 to the integer pixel coordinates as shown in Figure 5.1.

Thus, if the pixel with x and y coordinates (7,1) has a value of say 42 this means our best estimate for the underlying continuous distribution is that it has the value 42 at position (7.5,1.5) and not at (7, 1).[2] This subtlety can often be ignored in simple image manipulation tasks such as the filters used in Chapter 3. For other more complicated operations such as scaling the image size by a non-integer value or rotation by an angle that is not a multiple of $90°$ we find the centres of pixels in the transformed image do not exactly correspond to centres of pixels in the original image. In these cases, we have to calculate the transformed image by interpolating values from the original image. It is important that we work consistently with pixel centres when performing these interpolations. The main theme of this chapter is how to use the texture hardware of NVIDIA GPUs to perform very fast interpolation. Some of the applications we build around this hardware, such as image registration, are important in many fields including medical image processing.

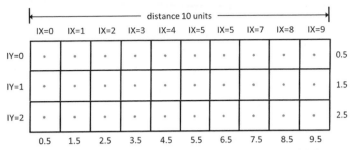

Pixel address is (ix,iy) where ix and iy are integers in ranges 0–9 and 0–2
Point in image is (x, y) where x and y are floats in ranges 0.0–10.0 and 0.0–3.0
Pixel centre is at   x = ix+0.5 and y = iy+0.5

Figure 5.1 Pixel and image addressing

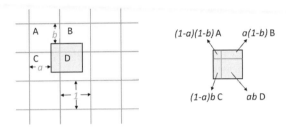

$$G = (1-a)(1-b)\, A + a(1-b)B + (1-a)b\, C + ab\, D$$

The grey pixel overlaps 4 image pixels having values A, B, C and D, it is
displaced by (*a, b*) from the A pixel. The bilinear interpolated value G in the
grey pixel is a weighted sum of the 4 image pixels.

Figure 5.2 Bilinear interpolation for image pixels

5.1 Image Interpolation

Figure 5.2 shows the calculation of the estimated value in a new image pixel displaced with respect to an original image. As written, the formula for the interpolated pixel value G requires 15 arithmetic operations and although this can be reduced to about 8 by regrouping the terms it is still a significant amount of per pixel calculation. This is obviously a great candidate for GPUs.

Linear interpolation can be performed in any number of dimensions and is referred to as *bilinear* or *trilinear* interpolation for the 2D and 3D cases. Other forms of interpolation are possible, including:

- Simple interpolation which just uses the nearest neighbour. For the grey pixel in Figure 5.2 this would mean simply setting G = D.
- Non-linear interpolation which uses more pixels thanjust the nearest neighbours and fits a second or higher order polynomial or B-splines to calculate interpolated values.

5.2 GPU Textures

NVIDIA textures are a hardware feature that provides fast linear interpolation from arrays of one, two or three dimensions. The NVIDIA hardware supports 16 and 32-bit floating point, and 8, 16 or 32-bit signed and unsigned integer formats. When interpolating integer data, CUDA converts the values to floating point and returns a 32-bit float result normalised to the range [–1,1] for signed integers and [0,1] for unsigned integers. Textures also support 2 and 4 component CUDA vector types such as `float4` and `int2`.

Very briefly the hardware texture units are used as follows:

1. Copy the arrays to be interpolated from host to GPU texture memory. Specialised versions of `cudaMalloc` and `cudaMemcpy` are used for this and the end result is a texture object which can be passed as an argument to kernels in place of the usual memory pointer. The details of texture creation are quite complicated and verbose and in this chapter we will use routines provided by `cxtexture.h` to hide much of this detail. Interested readers can find more in Appendix H.

2. In kernel code one reads interpolated values from texture memory using the *texture fetch* functions `tex1D`, `tex2D` or `tex3D`. These functions take a texture object as their first argument and then either 1, 2 or 3 floating point coordinates indicating the point at which interpolation should be performed.

Several different kinds of interpolation (or filtering in NVIDIA's jargon) can be performed depending on how the coordinates are specified and on how the texture was created.

The possible interpolation modes are illustrated in Figure 5.3 for a 1D interpolation over six pixels.

Figure 5.3 is based on a similar figure in the NVIDIA C++ programming guides. In the figure a 1D array of six pixels indexed from 0 to 5 and containing the values 1, 3, 2, 4, 5; and 3 is shown at the top. The results of interpolating a floating-point variable x in the range $0 \leq x \leq 6$ are shown in the four figures as follows:

(a) A simple "Nearest Point Sampling" method using a pixel index i = `floor(x)`, no interpolation is performed. This mode requires the value `cudaFilterModePoint` to be used for the value for the `FilterMode` parameter when the texture is created. This type of lookup could be performed directly by using `(int)x` as an array index; however, the texture hardware may still be faster due to separate texture caching and optimisation of array layout in texture memory. Modes (b) to (d) below require `filterMode` to be set to `cudaFilterModeLinear` which enables hardware accelerated linear interpolation.

(b) This is the standard CUDA texture "Linear Filtering" method using linear interpolation between the pixels and just specifying x as the coordinate in `tex1D`. *The texture hardware uses x-0.5 not x as the interpolation point.* Thus, for values of x in the range $0.5 \leq x \leq 5.5$ we see a smooth interpolation across the range of pixel values. For x < 0.5 the values of x are clamped to the value of pixel 0 and for x > 5.5 the values are clamped to the value of pixel 5. Out of range clamping is performed when `cudaAddressModeClamp` is specified as the value of `AddressMode` when the texture is initialised. The result is smoothly varying with the values at the pixel centres at x = 0.5, 1.5 . . . 5.5 equal to that pixel's value. This corresponds to the model that the

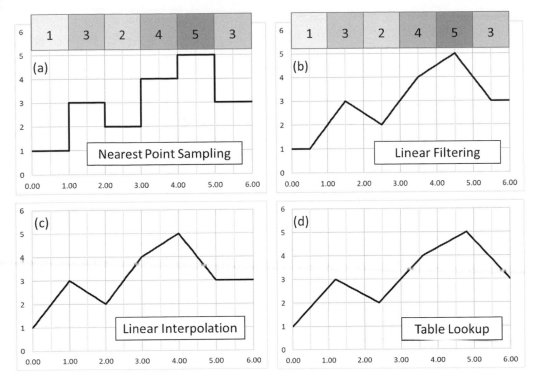

Figure 5.3 Interpolation modes with NVIDIA textures

pixel values represent values of a continuous function at their central points. Note the subtraction of 0.5 in CUDA texture image-interpolation is done by the CUDA lookup function (tex1D in this case) not the user who supplies the program x value as a function argument.

(c) This is the same as (b) but using `tex1D(tex,x+0.5)` instead of `tex1D(tex,x)`, we refer to this a "Linear Interpolation". This method is useful in applications where exact pixel values are expected at integer values of x. To use this method the user has to specify x+0.5 as an argument to the CUDA texture lookup function. The graph for mode (c) is just the graph for mode (b) shifted half a unit to the left. This is the natural mode to use for image processing because if x is set to a pixel index value i, then `tex1D` `(tex,x+0.5)` returns the value in `pixel[i]`. This method can also be used for table lookup where the texture represents a function sampled at six equally spaced points in the range [0,5].

(d) It is more natural to perform "Table Lookup" with a function sampled at six equally spaced points giving a variable range of [0,6] and we can do this with the same texture by passing the value `5*x/6+0.5` to the texture lookup function. The graph in (d) is just a stretched version of that in (c).

A nice feature of the texture hardware, illustrated in the figure, is that we do not have to perform explicit out-of-range checks on the coordinates sent to the texture lookup functions – the hardware takes care of this issue. The action performed on out-of-range coordinates depends on the setting of the `cudaAddressMode` flag used when initialising the texture. For example, to get out-of-range clamping to edge values, we must be set this flag to `cudaAddressModeClamp`.

Another issue to bear in mind is that images displayed on a screen are restricted to 8-bit values by hardware which reflects a limitation of the human visual system which is unable to distinguish more than about 200 shades of grey. The original data may, however, be floating point or integers of 16 or 32-bits. All the processing discussed here and in the previous chapter can and should be done in the native precision of the data, and conversion to 8-bits for display should be left as the last step. In many cases you may not be interested in displaying your transformed image.

Curiously CUDA textures are rarely discussed in tutorials aimed at scientific applications of CUDA; this may be because texture have their origins in gaming. Another possible reason is that the coefficients used for interpolation in CUDA texture lookups are calculated with only eight bits of precision. In practice, we have never found this to be a problem. At points which represent exact values, exact values are returned, at other points for reasonable functions interpolation errors are likely to be no more than one part in a thousand. In cases where the function varies more rapidly it must be remembered that even exact linear interpolation is only an approximation to the underlying function, so additional small errors are unlikely to be important. Another possible issue is that textures are quite verbose to setup. Here we solve that problem for you by using our cx library functions as wrappers that hide much of the complexity. We think it is a pity that textures are not more widely used because as we shall see, there are real performance gains to be had.

5.3 Image Rotation

If we want to display an image after a transformation, for example, a rotation by an angle that is not a multiple of $90°$, then for each pixel of the transformed image (the so-called *target* image) we have to find the corresponding location in the transformed *source* image and if that point does not correspond exactly to a pixel in the source image, we have to take an appropriate average of the nearby image pixels. As already discussed, the simplest method is to choose the nearest pixel from the source image. A better method is to use bilinear interpolation. Figure 5.4 Shows two images, on the left a 60×60 pixel potion of our test

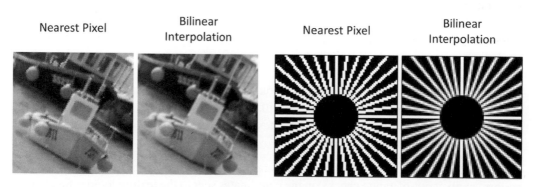

Figure 5.4 Image quality after rotation using nearest pixel and bilinear interpolations

image after a 30 degree rotation using nearest pixel and bilinear interpolation. On the right we show a composite image of a vertical bar which has been rotated about a central point in 10-degree steps. The bar has the width of 2 pixels and the original position is vertical. Again, the pair of images clearly show the results of using nearest pixel and bilinear interpolation. The jagged appearance of the lines is sometimes referred to as aliasing. Notice rotations by multiples of 90° are free from aliasing; such rotations are equivalent to simply exchanging pairs of pixels.

5.4 The Lerp Function

We are also interested in performing linear interpolation on the host and GPU without using texture hardware for both performance comparison and for case where the best possible precision is required.

The Lerp function for ID linear interpolation can be used as a building block for linear interpolation in any number of dimensions. Linear interpolation in one dimension, (for example, the x direction in Figure 5.2) is very straightforward; the formula is just:

$$I = (1 - a)A + aB \quad \text{or} \quad I = A + a(B - A), \tag{5.1}$$

where I is the interpolated value. Note the first form of the equation requires four arithmetic operations whereas the second form only requires three. The CUDA header file `helper_math.h` provides a function `lerp` to evaluate the second form as shown in the box.

```
inline __device__ __host__ float lerp(float a, float b, float t)
{
    return a + t*(b-a);
}
```

The CUDA lerp function from `helper_math.h`

We can use multiple `lerps` to build up both 2D bilinear and 3D trilinear interpolations using straightforward code. Example 5.1 shows functions for performing bilinear interpolation and nearest pixel interpolation on either the host or the GPU.

Description of Example 5.1

- Line 10: This is the declaration of template function `bilinear`. The function can be used by either the host or GPU to perform bilinear interpolation at the point (x, y) in the 2D array a. Note the arguments x and y are of type float. The array a has dimensions specified by the arguments nx and ny.
- Line 12: Declares an indexing function `idx` for the array a using stride nx.
- Line 13: Out of range checks on x and y. Note that because a tile of four pixels contributes to bilinear interpolation we have relaxed our usual check to include an additional halo one pixel wide. The index clamping in lines 25 and 26 makes this safe. If (x, y) is outside the halo, then we return 0 as the result which mimics the `cudaAddressModeBorder` mode of the texture hardware. This

sort of code always needs some sort of method for dealing with image boundaries and there is no unique best solution. Using texture hardware avoids this complication.

Example 5.1 Bilinear and nearest device and host functions for 2D image interpolation

```
10   template <typename T> __host__ __device__ T
       bilinear(cr_Ptr<T> a, float x, float y, int nx, int ny)
11   {
12     auto idx = [&nx](int y,int x){ return y*nx+x; };
13     if(x< -1.0f || x>= nx || y< -1.0f || y>= ny) return 0;

14     float x1 = floorf(x-0.5f);   // find left-hand
15     float y1 = floorf(y-0.5f);   // pixels
16     float ax = x - x1;           // a and b parameters
17     float ay = y - y1;           // from fig 5.3(c)

18     //  set indices to safe ranges
19     int kx1 = max(0,(int)x1); int kx2 = min(nx-1,kx1+1);
20     int ky1 = max(0,(int)y1); int ky2 = min(ny-1,ky1+1);

       // x interp at y1
21     float ly1 = lerp(a[idx(ky1,kx1)],a[idx(ky1,kx2)],ax);
       // x interp at y2
22     float ly2 = lerp(a[idx(ky2,kx1)],a[idx(ky2,kx2)],ax);
       // y interp of the x interpolated values
23     return (T)lerp(ly1,ly2,ay);
24   }

25   template <typename T> __host__ __device__ T
       nearest(cr_Ptr<T> a, float x, float y, int nx, int ny)
26   {
27     auto idx = [&nx](int y,int x){ return y*nx+x; };
28     if(x< 0 || x>= nx || y< 0 || y>= ny) return 0;
29     int ix = clamp((int)x,0,nx-1);
30     int iy = clamp((int)y,0,ny-1);
31     return a[idx(iy,ix)];
32   }
```

- Lines 14–15: Here we use the fast CUDA floorf function to find the two pixels with lowest x or y values for the 4-pixel tile to be used.
- Lines 16–17: The a and b parameters from Figure 5.2 are found here as ax and ay.
- Lines 19–20: The tile coordinates are calculated and clamped to the ranges [0,nx-1] and [0,ny-1].
- Lines 21–23: Calculate the desired bilinear interpolated value is calculated from 4 pixels of a using 3 lerp calls.
  - Line 21: Set ly1 to value of a interpolated for x and with y fixed to y1.

- ○ Line 22: Set ly2 to value of a interpolated for x and with y fixed to y2.
- ○ Line 23: Return value of a for y interpolated between ly1 and ly2.
- • Lines 25–32: These show the declaration of the nearest function which interpolates by simply finding the pixel in which the input point (x,y) lies.
  - ○ Line 28: Clamps to zero all pixels outside valid positions in the original image. This is different to corresponding line 13 of bilinear which allows a halo of one pixel around the valid region. This mimics the cudaAddressModeBorder addressing mode of the texture hardware.
  - ○ Lines 29–30: Here we simply round x and y down to the nearest integer which gives the pixel of the original image contained at the point (x,y). We use the clamp function from helper_math.h to ensure that the rounded value ix and iy are both valid. This precaution is not strictly necessary as line 32 has already ensured that ix and iy will be valid. However, we keep it here for future development; if line 32 was bypassed by being made conditional on a flag then the function would clamp out-of-range pixels to the nearest edge value rather than clamping them to zero. This would then mimic the cudaAddressModeClamp addressing mode of the texture hardware.

Example 5.2 shows code for image rotation consisting of the rotate1 kernel and a simple main routine. The rotate1 kernel performs image rotation and uses the bilinear function of Example 5.1. This example is a baseline and does not use hardware textures.

Example 5.2 rotate1 kernel for image rotation and simple main routine

```
40   template <typename T> __global__ void rotate1
       (r_Ptr<T> b, cr_Ptr<T> a, float alpha, int nx, int ny)
41   {
42     cint x = blockIdx.x*blockDim.x + threadIdx.x;
43     cint y = blockIdx.y*blockDim.y + threadIdx.y;
44     if(x >= nx || y >= ny) return; // range check
45     auto idx = [&nx](int y,int x){ return y*nx+x; };
46     float xt = x - nx/2.0f;   // rotate about centre
47     float yt = y - ny/2.0f;   // of image
       // rotate and restore origin
48     float xr =  xt*cosf(alpha) + yt*sinf(alpha) + nx/2.0f;
49     float yr = -xt*sinf(alpha) + yt*cosf(alpha) + ny/2.0f;
50     b[idx(y,x)] = bilinear(a, xr, yr, nx, ny);
51   }

60   int main(int argc,char *argv[])    // main routine
61   {
62     int nx      = (argc >3) ? atoi(argv[3]) : 512;
63     int ny      = (argc >4) ? atoi(argv[4]) : nx;
64     float angle = (argc >5) ? atoi(argv[5]) : 30.0f;
65     angle *= cx::pi<float>/180.0f;  // to radians

66     int size = nx*ny;
67     thrustHvec<uchar> a(size);
```

```
68     thrustHvec<uchar> b(size);
69     thrustDvec<uchar> dev_a(size);
70     thrustDvec<uchar> dev_b(size);

71     if(cx::read_raw(argv[1], a.data(), size)) return 1;
72     dev_a = a;  // copy to device
73     dim3 threads ={16,16,1};
74     dim3 blocks ={(uint)(nx+15)/16,(uint)(ny+15)/16,1};
75     rotate1<<<blocks,threads>>>(dev_b.data().get(),
                          dev_a.data().get(), angle, nx, ny);
76     b = dev_b; // get results
77     cx::write_raw(argv[2], b.data(), size);
78     return 0;
79  }
```

Description of Example 5.2

- Line 40: Declaration of the rotate1 kernel which takes two pointer arguments a and b for the input and output images, a rotation angle alpha in radians and their common dimensions nx and ny. The kernel is designed to use one thread per image pixel and expects a 2D thread grid spanning the image area.
- Lines 42–43: Here we find the (x, y) pixel position of the current thread. This position represents a pixel in the output image b.
- Line 43: Perform a range check on (x, y).
- Line 44: Define our usual idx 2D addressing function.
- Lines 46–47: We want to rotate the image around its centre point not the top left-hand corner. To do this we must rotate the current point's displacement vector from the image centre not the current point. Here we calculate (xt,yt) as that displacement.
- Lines 48–49: Perform an anti-clockwise rotation through an angle alpha. The sense of the rotation depends on which of the sin(alpha) terms has a minus sign, in this case it is the one in line 49.[3] We also translate back to the original origin. The result is stored in (xr,yr) and the rotation is clockwise for positive alpha.
- Line 50: The rotated position (xr,yr) is the position of the point in the original image a to be displayed in pixel (x,y) of image b. Here we call the device function bilinear to perform interpolation in a at that position. The result is then stored at (x,y) in b. This line can easily be changed to call different functions, for example, nearest, to perform other kinds of interpolation.
- Lines 60–79: This is a basic main routine to set up the required arrays a and b, call the rotate1 kernel and save the rotated image. Note the file names of the original and rotated image are supplied by the user as the first and second command line arguments. This is a convention we often use for command line arguments; note also that the input image name precedes the output image name in command line. If the user accidentally reverses the names when running a program there is a danger that the original image file will be overwritten.[4]

This version of the GPU code for image rotation works reasonably well delivering over 600 GFlops of compute performance and running 500 times faster than a single core CPU version. However as promised, we can do better by using the texture features of NVIDIA GPUs.

Table 5.1 *Maximum sizes for CUDA textures*

Dimension	CC 6.0 and above	CC 3.5–5.2
1D	131072	65536
2D	131072 × 65536	65536 × 65536
3D	65536 × 65536 × 65536	4096 × 4069 × 4096

5.5 Texture Hardware

Because GPUs were originally developed for computer gaming, they have special hardware to perform image interpolation operations. In our case CUDA texture memory is used for this purpose. Unlike shared memory which is fast and small but separate from global memory, texture memory is allocated on demand from standard global device memory but it is managed by dedicated texture mapping units (TMUs) which are a significant hardware feature of each SM unit on the GPU. On most NVIDIA GPUs, including those without graphics designed for HPC applications, there is one TMU for every 16 CUDA cores.

CUDA textures are arrays of up to three dimensions stored in the global device memory but formatted in a special way and managed by dedicated TMUs. The maximum sizes for CUDA textures are shown in Table 5.1. The hardware includes additional memory caching and fast interpolation units. Setting up a CUDA texture is more complex than just allocating a thrust vector; the syntax is quite verbose in that there are a confusingly large number of possible options. Our goal here is to introduce interpolation features of 2D and 3D textures for image transformation because that is where the real performance gains are to be found.[5]

Our `cxtextures.h` header file defines three objects `tsx1D`, `txs2D` and `txs3D` which act as container classes for GPU texture memory and encapsulate much of the detail required to setup and use textures. In particular, they have constructors and destructors to manage device memory allocation. However, a number of option flags still have to be supplied by the user when creating these objects. Example 5.3 uses 2D textures for fast bilinear interpolation on TMUs instead of calling the `bilinear` function in Example 5.1.

Example 5.3 `rotate2` kernel demonstrating image rotation using CUDA textures

```
40    __global__ void rotate2(r_Ptr<uchar> b,
         cudaTextureObject_t atex, float angle, int nx, int ny)
41    {
42      cint x = blockIdx.x*blockDim.x + threadIdx.x;
43      cint y = blockIdx.y*blockDim.y + threadIdx.y;
44      if(x >= nx || y >= ny) return; // range check
45      auto idx = [&nx](int y,int x){ return y*nx+x; };
46      float xt = x - nx/2.0f;   // rotate about centre
47      float yt = y - ny/2.0f;   // of the image
        // rotate and restore origin
48      float xr =  xt*cosf(angle)+ yt*sinf(angle) + nx/2.0f;
49      float yr = -xt*sinf(angle)+ yt*cosf(angle) + ny/2.0f;
        // interpolate using texture lookup
```

```
50      b[idx(y,x)] = (uchar)(255*tex2D<float>(atex,
                                 xr+0.5f, yr+0.5f));
51  }

60  int main(int argc,char *argv[]) // minimal main routine
        . . .
67      thrustHvec<uchar> a(size);
68      thrustHvec<uchar> b(size);
69.1    int2 nxy ={nx, ny};
69.2    cx::txs2D<uchar> atex(nxy, a.data(), // pass host array
        cudaFilterModeLinear,   // do linear interpolation
        cudaAddressModeBorder, // out of range pixels are zero
        cudaReadModeNormalizedFloat,  // return floats in [0,1)
        cudaCoordNatural );         // coords in [0,nx] & [0,ny]
70      thrustDvec<uchar> dev_b(size);
        . . .
75      rotate2<<<blocks,threads>>>(dev_b.data().get(),
            atex.tex, angle, nx, ny); // pass texture to kernel
        . . .
79  }
```

Description of Example 5.3

- Lines 40–51: The kernel rotate2 is a modification to the rotate1 kernel of Example 5.2; only lines 40 and 50 differ for the corresponding lines in rotate1.
  - Line 40: The second argument is now the cudaTextureObject_t atex which holds the original image data instead of a simple pointer to the data in GPU memory. Also the kernel is not a template function; it is explicitly written to process data of type uchar.
  - Line 50: Instead of calling the function bilinear to perform interpolation about the point (xr,yr) in the source array, we use the built-in CUDA tex2D function to interpolate from the texture containing a, namely atex. In order to process 8-bit uchar data the values are actually stored in GPU texture memory as floating point numbers normalised so that the largest representable native value corresponds to 1.0. This is why we specify <float> in the tex2D template argument (a default does not work here), scale the result by 255 and finally cast back to a uchar.

Another point to note is that the coordinates (xy,yr) are offset by +0.5f; this corresponds to the linear interpolation mode of texture lookup shown in Figure 5.3 (c).

- Lines 60–79: These lines are a modified version of the main routine in Example 5.2. There are only two changes. Line 69 is replaced by lines 69.1 and 69.2 and the kernel call in line 75 has been changed.
  - Line 69.1: The int2 object nxy is created and initialised to (nx,ny). It is needed in the next line as an input argument.
  - Line 69.2: Here we create the cx::txs2D texture object atex specifying the following arguments to the object constructor:
    1. nxy – an int2 containing the array sizes nx and ny.
    2. a.data() – a pointer to the source array data in host memory. This data will be copied to the GPU.

Table 5.2 *Performance of Examples 5.1–5.3 on an RTX 2070 GPU*

Image Size	Images processed per second			Bilinear Interpolation GFlops		
	Host	GPU	Textures	Host	GPU	Textures
128×128	3925	369515	414636	2.22	544	1063
256×256	989	241314	341772	2.21	787	**2936**
512×512	249	104106	185798	2.43	849	2617
1024×1024	62	30896	66149	2.23	844	2756
2048×2048	15	8052	13299	2.13	851	1693
4096×4096	4	2009	3393	1.98	835	1690

3. `cudaFilterModeLinear` – a flag specifying bilinear interpolation is required.
4. `cudaAddressModeBorder` – a flag specifying that out of range points return zero. The fact that texture lookups automatically deal with points outside the stored texture is a nice feature that simplifies the calling code by removing the need for explicit out-of-range checks.
5. `cudaReadModeNormalizedFloat` – a flag specifying that results are returned as normalised floats. This flag is necessary when using hardware interpolation for any types other than float.
6. `cudaCoordNatural` – a cx defined flag specifying normal interpretation of position coordinates. Without cx this would be specified as plain zero as there is no CUDA defined mnemonic. The alternative is the cx defined flag `cudaCoordNormalized` or 1, which specifies normalised coordinates in the range [0,1] which are automatically mapped onto the full span of the stored array.

• Line 75: Here we call the `rotate2` kernel instead of `rotate1`; the second argument is passed by value as `atex.tex` instead of the pointer `a.data()`.

If you are not familiar with CUDA textures line 69.2 may appear quite complicated; if you are familiar with CUDA textures you may feel that our modified code is rather less verbose than you expected. Either way we have gained a factor of up to 3.7 in the interpolation performance of our code. The performance of our bilinear interpolation codes is shown in Table 5.2.

The first set of columns in Table 5.2 show the number of images processed per second by using a single CPU on the host and the rotate1 and rotate2 GPU kernels. These numbers are based on the total execution times for the whole calculation and then subtracting IO and initialisation overheads. For the largest two image sizes a single CPU cannot deliver processing at video rates but either GPU implementation is more than adequate. The second set of columns in the table show the compute performance of just the bilinear interpolation part of the calculation. These numbers were found by also running equivalent jobs with bilinear interpolation replaced by simply storing fixed values in the output buffer. The difference in times was taken as the time for interpolation. We assumed each interpolation involved 20 floating point operations to convert execution times to GFlops per second. Overall, the GPU implementation is about 500 times faster than the CPU and the texture-based implementation is more than 1000 times faster. Interestingly, the best texture performance is achieved for intermediate of image sizes between 256×256 and 1024×1024. This is in contrast to our usual finding that GPU performance tends to continue to improve as dataset sizes increase. We conjecture that the different behaviour of GPU textures is because the Morton ordering scheme, which makes local x-y neighbour addressing more efficient, is

Figure 5.5 Rotations and scaling of test image

optimal for these intermediate image sizes (see Appendix H for more detail). Compared to the `rotate1` kernel, textures give a factor of 3.7 speed-up for bilinear interpolation of images having size 256 × 256 and at least a factor of 2 improvement for all image sizes.

The rotation of a rectangular image also presents the difficulty that the rotated image may not fit into the original frame. This is illustrated in Figure 5.5 which shows the test image in (a) and a 45° rotation in (b). Note that in (b) corners of the original image are missing and its corners of (b) have black regions which were outside the area of the original image and have been set to zero because `cudaAddressModeBorder` is specified in the texture initialisation in line 69.2 of Example 5.3. This issue can be fixed by padding the original image with a sufficiently wide boarder as illustrated in Figure 5.5 (c) and (d).

We can use the normalised coordinate feature of CUDA texture lookups to easily implement image rescaling. This allows an image of any size to interpolate a texture without needing to know the actual resolution of the stored image. The modifications are shown in Example 5.4.

Example 5.4 `rotate3` kernel for simultaneous image rotation and scaling

```
40   __global__ void rotate3(r_Ptr<uchar> b,
         cudaTextureObject_t utex, float angle,
         int mx, int my, float scale)
41   {
42     cint x = blockIdx.x*blockDim.x + threadIdx.x;
43     cint y = blockIdx.y*blockDim.y + threadIdx.y;
44     if(x >= mx || y >= my) return; // range check
45     auto idx = [&mx](int y,int x){ return y*mx+x; };
46     float xt = x - mx/2.0f;  // rotate about centre
47     float yt = y - my/2.0f;  // of the image
       // rotate and restore origin
48     float xr =  xt*cosf(angle)+ yt*sinf(angle) + mx/2.0f;
49     float yr = -xt*sinf(angle)+ yt*cosf(angle) + my/2.0f;
       // scale and preserve the image centre
50     float xs = (xr+0.5f)*scale/mx-0.5f*scale+0.5f;
51     float ys = (yr+0.5f)*scale/my-0.5f*scale+0.5f
       // texture lookup now using normalised coordinates
53     b[idx(y,x)] = (uchar)(255*tex2D<float>(utex, xs, ys));
54   }
```

```
      . . .
69.2  cx::txs2D<uchar> atex(nxy,a.data(), // pass host array
      cudaFilterModeLinear,    // do linear interpolation
      cudaAddressModeBorder,  // out of range pixels are zero
      cudaReadModeNormalizedFloat, // return floats in [0,1)
      cudaCoordNormalized);   // coords in [0,1.0] [0,1.0]
      . . .
75    rotate3<<<blocks,threads>>>(dev_b.data().get(),
                atex.tex, angle, mx, my, scale);
      . . .
```

Description of Example 5.4

Only a few changes to Example 5.3 are required to enable rescaling of the output image size. In the main routine we add three extra command line parameters, int mx and my, the new dimensions of the output image frame, and float scale, the factor by which to rescale the image within the new frame. If mx and my differ from the input image size nx and ny then the output image will be resampled using bilinear interpolation to fit the new output frame. Additional image scaling by a factor of scale is also applied.

- Line 40: Declaration of the rotate3 kernel. The image size arguments, previously nx and ny, have been renamed mx and my to reflect a change of use – they are now only the size of the output image frame. Because this kernel uses normalised coordinates for texture lookup there is no need for the kernel to know the actual dimensions of the image stored in the texture. There is also a new final argument scale which specifies a scaling factor for the output image within the mx x my frame. A scale value of $1/\sqrt{2}$ would allow an image rotated by 45° to fit inside its original frame.
- Lines 41–49: These lines are identical to rotate2 except that mx and my are used instead of nx and ny.
- Lines 50–51: These lines are new and set xs and ys to the rotated coordinates xr and yr but normalised to the range [0,1] and then rescaled by a factor of scale. Both steps are done by multiplying by scale/mx and scale/my. There are also terms to keep the image centre in the centre of the frame and to deal with the 0.5 offsets needed for linear interpolation mode.
- Line 69.2: The main routine is changed to use the flag cudaCoordNormalized as the last argument of the call to cx::txs2.

The images in Figure 5.1 (c) and (d) were produced using rotate3 with a scale factor of $1/\sqrt{2}$ and rotations of 0° and 45°.

Bilinear interpolation will always give a smooth result for any increase in the image size or for decreasing the size by up to a factor of 2. For larger decreases, say by a factor of 8, bilinear interpolation between adjacent pixels in the original image is equivalent to sparsely sampling that image giving a potentially noisy result.

A better approach in this case is to use average values for 8 × 8 tiles spanning the source image. Equivalently our code could be used three times to step the image size down by a factor 2 each time. The last step could be any value less than 2 for cases which are not an exact power of 2. This is illustrated in Figure 5.6 where our test image with original

Sampling   Averaging

Figure 5.6 Test image at 32 × 32 resolution

resolution of 512 × 512 pixels has been downscaled by a factor of 8 using the rotate3 kernel. The left-hand image using a single step with size = ⅛ and the right-hand image used 3 separate steps of ½.

5.6 Colour Images

The code of Example 5.1 can easily be adapted to process colour images. A standard digital colour image has 3 8-bit values for each pixel representing the red, green and blue intensity values of that pixel. There are two ways in which these bytes can be stored in memory; either the three values are stored in consecutive memory locations – such images are known as RGB formatted images, or all the R values are stored in consecutive locations followed by all the G values and then the B values – this arrangement is known as planar-RGB. Most standard digital image formats such as BMP, JPG and PNG use RGB but often adding compression. Planar-RGB is more convenient for some image processing tasks as the data is then organised as three separate 1-byte images in the 3 colours. A fourth channel "A" may also be present representing the transparencies of the pixels; in this case we have RGBA or planar-RGBA. RGBA format is interesting because the data for each pixel occupies a 32-bit word – which corresponds to naturally aligned memory accesses in many processing situations including CUDA texture processing. Example 5.5 shows the `rotate4` kernel for the rotation of RGBA images.

Description of Example 5.5

In this example we show how our previous `rotate3` kernel can be modified to process RGBA data. The main change is that the texture has been created to hold RGBA image data and is of type `uchar4`.

- Line 40: The rotate4 kernel declaration only differs from rotate3 in that the first 2 arguments now refer to `uchar4` objects instead of `uchar`. This is explicit for the output array b and implicit for the input texture `atex4`. Each element of the texture is now a 4-component vector of RGBA values for one pixel and the texture lookup will automatically perform the same interpolation on each component of the vector.
- Lines 41–51: These lines are unchanged from their equivalents in `rotate3`.

- Line 52: Here we perform the vector texture lookup which is returned as a float4 result. Since the definitions in helper_math.h do not include overloaded conversions between float4 and uchar4 we have to store the result in the temporary variable float4 fb.
- Lines 53–56: Here each component of fb is scaled and then copied to a component of an element of the output uchar4 b.

Example 5.5 rotate4 kernel for processing RGBA images

```
40   __global__ void rotate4(r_Ptr<uchar4> b,
     cudaTextureObject_t utex4, float angle, int mx,
                               int my, float scale)
41   {
42     cint x = blockIdx.x*blockDim.x + threadIdx.x;
43     cint y = blockIdx.y*blockDim.y + threadIdx.y;
44     if(x >= mx || y >= my) return; // range check
45     auto idx = [&mx] (int y, int x) { return y*mx+x; };
46     float xt = x - mx/2.0f;   // rotate about centre
47     float yt = y - my/2.0f;   // of the image

       // rotate and restore origin
48     float xr =  xt*cosf(angle)+ yt*sinf(angle) + mx/2.0f;
49     float yr = -xt*sinf(angle)+ yt*cosf(angle) + my/2.0f;

       // scale and preserve the image centre
50     float xs = (xr+0.5f)*scale/mx-0.5f*scale+0.5f;
51     float ys = (yr+0.5f)*scale/my-0.5f*scale+0.5f;

       // NB here tex2D returns floats not uchars
52     float4 fb = tex2D<float4>(utex4,xs,ys);
53     b[idx(y,x)].x = (uchar)(255*fb.x);
54     b[idx(y,x)].y = (uchar)(255*fb.y);
55     b[idx(y,x)].z = (uchar)(255*fb.z);
56     b[idx(y,x)].w = (uchar)(255*fb.w);
56   }
```

5.7 Viewing Images

One of the nice things about working with images is that one can literally look at the results to spot bugs or admire results. There are numerous software tools available to help with this. One of my favourite tools for inspecting and manipulating images is ImageJ; this is a lightweight but powerful program, freely available from US National Institutes for Health at https://imagej.nih.gov/ij/. The J stands for Java so the program runs on most systems and has a large library of additional plugins written in Java. It reads most image formats including

Figure 5.7 ImageJ dialogue for binary image IO

some medical ones such as Dicom. It also allows reading and writing of raw image data as used with the `cxbinio` routines. The program is well documented and here we will show just one image, in Figure 5.7, of the dialogue for reading binary (or raw) image data. The figure shows the main ImageJ window at the top with the menu options ImageJ→Import→Raw selected together with the raw image properties dialogue which lets you specify the raw image layout.

While separate image viewing tools are useful, incorporating image display directly into your production code is sometimes more interesting as it opens the possibility of interactive user interfaces. The tool we use here is OpenCV. This is a big project and consists of a very large function library, routines of which you can incorporate into your own C++ code. The website https://opencv.org/ is the place to go for downloading the libraries and finding documentation. One of the features we like about this package is that very few lines of code are required to directly read, display and write images of all many types including jpg, bmp and png. It also handles video formats nicely; one can treat video frames as simply a set of images. We only use a tiny number of the available features.

The host code to drive `rotate4` including the use of OpenCV is shown in Example 5.6; it is similar to the code used before except we have generalised the code to use `OpenCV` instead of `cxbinio`.

Example 5.6 `rotate4cv` with `OpenCV` support for image display

```
      .   .   .
05    #include "opencv2/core.hpp"
06    #include "opencv2/highgui.hpp"
```

```
07   using namespace cv;
     . . .
60   void opencv_to_uchar4(uchar4 *a, Mat &image)
61   {
62     int size = image.rows*image.cols;
63     for(int k=0; k<size; k++){  // BGR => RGB
64       a[k].z = image.data[3*k];
65       a[k].y = image.data[3*k+1];
66       a[k].x = image.data[3*k+2];
67       a[k].w = 255;
68     }
69   }

70   void uchar4_to_opencv(Mat &image, uchar4 *a)
71   {
72     int size = image.rows*image.cols;
73     for(int k=0; k<size; k++){  // RGB => BGR
74       image.data[3*k]   = a[k].z;
75       image.data[3*k+1] = a[k].y;
76       image.data[3*k+2] = a[k].x;
77     }
78   }

80   int main(int argc,char *argv[])
81   {
       // read and decode image file
82     Mat image = imread(argv[1],IMREAD_COLOR);
83     int nx = image.cols; // get image dimensions
84     int ny = image.rows; // from image metadata

85     float angle = (argc >3) ? atof(argv[3]) : 30.0f;
86     float scale = (argc >4) ? atof(argv[4]) : 1.0f;
87     int mx = (argc >5) ? atoi(argv[5]) : nx; // image size
88     int my = (argc >6) ? atoi(argv[6]) : ny; // is default
89     angle *= cx::pi<float>/180.0f;

90     int asize = nx*ny;  // set image sizes
91     int bsize = mx*my;
92     thrustHvec<uchar4> a(asize);
93     opencv_to_uchar4(a.data(),image);
94     thrustHvec<uchar4> b(bsize);
95     thrustDvec<uchar4> dev_a(asize);
96     thrustDvec<uchar4> dev_b(bsize);
97     dev_a = a;  // copy to device

98     int2 nxy ={nx,ny};
99     cx::txs2D<uchar4> atex4(nxy, a.data(),
           cudaFilterModeLinear, cudaAddressModeBorder,
```

```
                 cudaReadModeNormalizedFloat, cudaCoordNormalized);
100    dim3 threads ={16,16,1};
101    dim3 blocks ={ (uint)(mx+15)/16,(uint)(my+15)/16,1};
102    rotate4<<<blocks,threads>>>(dev_b.data().get(),
                          atex4.tex, angle, mx, my, scale);
103    b = dev_b; // get results
       // NB order here is rows,cols
104    Mat out_image(my,mx,CV_8UC3,Scalar(0));
105    uchar4_to_opencv(out_image,b.data());

106    // Window for image display
107    namedWindow(argv[2],WINDOW_NORMAL);
108    imshow(argv[2],out_image);    // show new image
       // wait for key here, then optional image save
109    if( waitKey(0) != ESC ) imwrite(argv[2],out_image);
110    return 0;
111  }
```

Description of Example 5.6

- Lines 5–6: Headers required for OpenCV. In addition, several library files need to be specified in the linking step.
- Line 7: The namespace cv is needed for OpenCV functions, objects and flags.
- Lines 60–69: OpenCV Mat containers hold colour images as 3-byte BGR sequences stored contiguously in memory. For use in CUDA kernels we prefer 4-byte RGBA format. The function opencv_to_uchar4 performs this conversion. Note in line 62 we get the image dimensions from the Mat object. In lines 64 and 66 we swap the R and B channels.
- Lines 70–78: The function uchar4_to_opencv performs the opposite conversion of RGBA format to BGR. Note lines 74 and 76 swap the R and B channels.
- Line 80: Declaration of main program, which takes up to 6 user supplied command line arguments.
  - Arg 1: The name of the input image which can be any of the usual colour formats such as jpg, bmp or png.[6] Note the dimensions of the input image are obtained directly from the image metadata and do not need to be specified here by the user. This is a significant simplification.
  - Arg 2: The name of the output file containing the transformed image; again this can be any of the usual image formats as specified by the file extension. The output image format does not have to be the same as the input format, so one use for our program is to simply change image formats.
  - Arg 3: The rotation angle in degrees.
  - Arg 4: The parameter scale, as before.
  - Args 5 and 6: The optional dimensions mx and my of the output image; they will default to the same values as the input image. It is not necessary to preserve the image aspect ratio.
- Line 82: The powerful imread OpenCV statement reads and decodes the image file specified in argv[1] and stores the pixel data in the OpenCV Mat object image. The Mat objects are another example of a container class for arrays. When used for RGB images the data is stored in the order BGR which can be confusing. The necessary conversion functions are shown above.
- Lines 83–84: The image dimensions are extracted from image and stored as nx and ny. The OpenCV library has its origins in C not C++ and Mat objects are simple structs whose data variables we can access directly as needed.

- Lines 85–88: Here we get the optional user parameters from command line arguments as usual. The output image dimension mx and my are now the last two arguments so that the user can specify just the angle and scale parameters without knowing the input image dimensions.
- Line 92: Here we create a familiar thrust host vector, a, of type uchar4 to hold a copy of the input image pixel data.
- Line 93: Copy the pixel data from Mat object image to the vector a using the opencv_to_uchar4 utility routine. The format is changed from BGR in the mat image object to RGBA in the thrust vector a.
- Lines 94–96: Create thrust containers for the host output image b and corresponding device vectors for both a and b.
- Lines 98–99: Create the required texture object atex4 containing the input pixel values, using the cx::txs2D function as before with the same arguments. Note the template variable is now set to uchar4 which is also the type of a.data().
- Lines 100–103: Here we run the rotate4 kernel and copy the results back to b as before.
- Line 104: Create the Mat object out_image which is used to display and save the result. The parameters specify the matrix size (mx x my), type of elements (8-bit unsigned, 3-channels) and initialise the matrix to zeros. This again is a powerful statement because it allows any array of data to be displayed and saved as an image.
- Line 105: Copy the pixel data from the thrust vector b to the Mat object out_image using the uchar4_to_opencv utility function.
- Line 107: In order for openCV to display an image, we first have to create a window in which to display that image. We do this by calling the imshow function with two parameters; the first parameter is the name given to the window and the second parameter is a defined constant indicating the window type. Here we use WINDOW_NORMAL for the window type and the name of the output file as supplied by the user for the window name. Rather unusually for this sort of package the function imshow does not return handle to the new window; instead it uses the window name, argv[2] in this case.
- Line 108: Display the Mat object out_image in the window created in line 107.
- Line 109: Here the openCV function waitkey is used to wait for the user to enter a keystroke. The keycode is returned and here we use it to save the output file unless the escape key has been used. The function imwrite is used to save the output image to disk with the user supplied name and extension contained in argv[2].

We think our final reduc4cv program is a useful piece of code, it can resize your digital images in a large variety of standard formats and convert between formats. Future enhancements would be to allow enlarged images to be cropped in windows translated from the image centre and perhaps to allow the mouse to be used for this purpose. For now, we leave these improvements as exercises for the reader.

5.8 Affine Transformations of Volumetric Images

The real power of GPUs for image processing becomes more apparent with large data sets such as 3D MRI scans or video data. Video data is really a sequential flow of 2D images, and can easily result in a large data set. For example, just 1 minute's worth of high-resolution 1920×1080 colour video at a 25 Hz frame rate is more than 9 GB of data. Although sophisticated compression algorithms are used to store digital video, the uncompressed data is still needed for most processing operations such as object tracking.

A typical MRI scan might contain $256 \times 256 \times 256$ volume elements (or *voxels* the 3D analog of 2D pixels). Commonly MRI scans are viewed as a stack of 2D slices, say 256 images. Each planar image is of dimension 256×256 and in the x-y plane represents a "slice" along the z axis. But MRI data is more than a stack of images, it is truly volumetric data and for many processing operations it is necessary to operate on complete datasets. One example is registration where two or more datasets need to be aligned with each other in 3D.

The simplest transformations of a 3D volume are rigid rotations and translations, and even these involve 6 parameters, 3 rotation angles around the x, y and z axes and displacements along these axes. In fact, the most general linear or *affine* transformation of a 3D volume involves up to 12 parameters, the six already mentioned plus three different scalings along each axis and three shear transformations. We can represent a general affine transformation using a 4×4 matrix as shown in Eq. 5.2. The vector $(x'\ y'\ z')$ is the result after the affine transform. The 3×3 matrix A in the top left-hand corner represents the combined rotation, scale and shear operations and the vector **t** with components $(t_x\ t_y\ t_z)$ in the right-hand column represents the translations.

$$\begin{bmatrix} x' \\ y' \\ z' \\ 1 \end{bmatrix} = \begin{bmatrix} a_{00} & a_{01} & a_{02} & t_x \\ a_{10} & a_{11} & a_{12} & t_y \\ a_{20} & a_{21} & a_{22} & t_z \\ 0 & 0 & 0 & 1 \end{bmatrix} \begin{bmatrix} x \\ y \\ z \\ 1 \end{bmatrix}. \tag{5.2}$$

Examples of individual affine transformation matrices are shown in Eq. 5.3

$$\begin{bmatrix} \cos\theta & -\sin\theta & 0 \\ \sin\theta & \cos\theta & 0 \\ 0 & 0 & 1 \end{bmatrix}, \quad \begin{bmatrix} s_x & 0 & 0 \\ 0 & s_y & 0 \\ 0 & 0 & s_z \end{bmatrix} \quad \text{and} \quad \begin{bmatrix} 1 & 0 & 0 \\ \alpha & 1 & 0 \\ 0 & 0 & 1 \end{bmatrix} \tag{5.3}$$

and represent a clockwise rotation of θ in the x-y plane, scalings of s_x, s_y and s_z along the coordinate axes and a shear in the x-y plane. The sub-matrix A in Eq. 5.2 is the product of a number of such matrices. Note the individual 3×3 transformation matrices do not in general commute so one must be consistent in the order in which they are multiplied to generate A.

Our next example 5.3 in an implementation of 3D volume affine transformations using the six rigid body transformations and a single scaling parameter applied isotopically (i.e. setting $s_x = s_y = s_z$ in 5.3).

```
struct affparams {
    float4 A0;    // three rows of affine
    float4 A1;    // matrix, translations
    float4 A2;    // in 4th column
    float scale;
};
```

The struct affparams is used in examples 5.7–5.13.

The stuct affparms shown in the box is used to pass the affine parameter matrix from the host to the GPU. Using a struct in this way has several advantages; it makes the kernel argument lists more compact and, because structs are passed by value, the parameters will automatically be stored in GPU constant memory. In addition, using structs in this fashion is helpful during development as function interfaces do not change if the details of the struct change. For example, if we changed `scale` to be a `float3` to allow for differential scalings, while the details of our code would change, the kernel arguments would not. The kernel `affine3D` used to implement 3D affine transformations is shown in Example 5.7. The additional parameter `scale` is used for debugging and is stored as the reciprocal of the user supplied scale factor.

Description of Example 5.7

The kernel `affine3D` is remarkably short for the range of transformations it can accomplish.

- Line 10: The kernel arguments are the 3D output array b, the 3D texture `atex` which holds the input array a, the affine transform parameters passed by value in the stuct `aff` and the dimensions of the input and output arrays passed as the `int3` variables n and m. Note the data type is fixed as `ushort`. This 16-bit type is commonly used in applications such as MRI. Since signed and unsigned data require different scalings when using normalised texture coordinates we have not attempted to make the type of b a template parameter.
- Lines 12–13: The variables `ix` and `iy` are the address of the pixel to be processed by the current thread.
- Lines 16–18: In this kernel we use normalised coordinates in the range [0,1] to address the texture; here we calculate the normalised distances between the output pixels.
- Lines 19–20: Because the affine transformation includes rotations, the origin of the normalised pixel coordinates x and y is shifted to the centre of the image.

Example 5.7 `affine3D` kernel used for 3D image transformations

```
10   __global__ void affine3D(r_Ptr<ushort> b,
         cudaTextureObject_t atex, affparams aff,
                              cint3 n, cint3 m)
11   {
12     cint ix = blockIdx.x*blockDim.x + threadIdx.x;
13     cint iy = blockIdx.y*blockDim.y + threadIdx.y;
14     if(ix >= m.x || iy >= m.y) return; // range check
15     auto mdx = [&m] (int z,int y,int x)
                            { return (z*m.y+y)*m.x+x; };

16     float dx = 1.0f/(float)m.x;  // normalized coords
17     float dy = 1.0f/(float)m.y;  // in [0,1] for textures
18     float dz = 1.0f/(float)m.z;  // with unsigned ints

19     float x = ix*dx - 0.5f;  // move origin to
20     float y = iy*dy - 0.5f;  // volume centre

21     for(int iz=0; iz<m.z; iz++){ // loop over z-slices
22       float z = iz*dz - 0.5f;
```

```
23        //      affine 3 x 3 matrix and translation
24        float xr = aff.A0.x*x+aff.A0.y*y+aff.A0.z*z +
                            dx*aff.A0.w +0.5f/n.x +0.5f;
25        float yr = aff.A1.x*x+aff.A1.y*y+aff.A1.z*z +
                            dy*aff.A1.w +0.5f/n.y +0.5f;
26        float zr = aff.A2.x*x+aff.A2.y*y+aff.A2.z*z +
                            dz*aff.A2.w +0.5f/n.z +0.5f;

27        b[mdx(iz,iy,ix)] =
            (ushort)(65535.0f*tex3D<float>(atex, xr, yr, zr));
28     }
29  }
```

- Lines 21–28: This is the loop over all z values for the fixed x-y position handled by the current thread.
  - Line 22: Get the current normalised z value; this line corresponds to lines 19–20 for x and y.
  - Lines 24–26: Here the affine transformation is performed. In each line the first three terms represent multiplication by the 3×3 A matrix in Eq. 5.2, the fourth term represents the translations by **t**, note the scaling of t_x by dx and similarly for y and z. This means the translation is measured in pixels on the input image. The final term shifts the origin of the normalised coordinates back to the (0,0,0) corner of the image.
  - Line 27: Here we perform the texture lookup with implicit trilinear interpolation. The result is stored directly into the output array b. Note the scale factor used for ushort texture lookups.

We do not show all the corresponding host code for this example because it is similar to the previous examples except that the user is able to enter seven parameters for the affine transformation. The resulting code allows users to apply 3D rotations and translations and also to enlarge the image and optionally change aspect ratios by adjusting the dimensions of the output array. Some output examples are shown in Figure 5.8 which shows single slices from a $256 \times 256 \times 256$ MRI head scan.

The slices shown in the Figure 5.8 are as follows:

(a) x-y slice from original image which is oriented in the axial or transverse direction (i.e. with the perpendicular z-axis running from head to toes).
(b) Sagittal slice obtained by rotating original image by 90 degrees around by z and y axes.
(c) Coronal (front-back) view obtained by rotating original image by 90 degrees around x axis.
(d) Skewed slice obtained by rotating image by 45 degrees around the y axis. After this rotation the new image width in the x direction exceeded the original width of 256 pixels by up to a factor of $\sqrt{2}$. The view shown was obtained by doubling the size of the output window with scaling factor of ½ and then manually cropping the result to 320×256.
(e) The coronal image in (c) is somewhat squashed in the vertical direction because the original MRI voxels dimensions were not isotropic; in (e) this is corrected by using $256 \times 320 \times 256$ for the output image. Note that while views (b) and (c) could be generated by reordering pixels in the output volume without interpolation, view (d) requires full 3D interpolation.

Table 5.3 *Performance of* affine3D *kernel using an RTX 2070 GPU*

	volumes per second		
Volume size	host	interp3D	affine3D
$128 \times 128 \times 128$	17.4	5029	27816
$256 \times 256 \times 256$	2.1	646	3253
$512 \times 512 \times 512$	0.20	78	336
$1024 \times 1024 \times 1024$	0.02	8	30

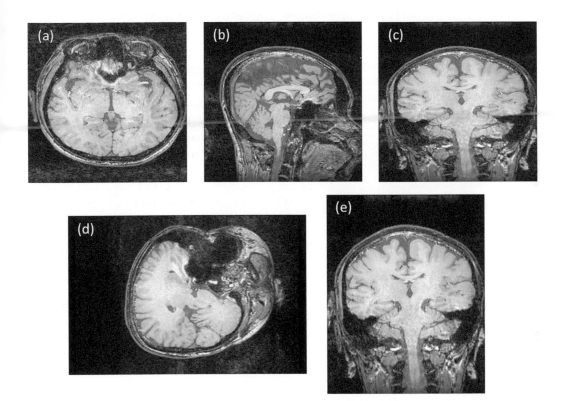

Figure 5.8 Affine transformations of a $256 \times 256 \times 256$ MRI head scan

For timing purposes, we also wrote versions of the kernel that used the lerp function instead of textures to perform 3D interpolation. The function interp3D is shown in Example 5.8; it uses two sets of bilinear interpolations in x and y similar to the interp2D kernel of Example 5.2 followed by a single lerp in z to perform full trilinear interpolation using a total of 7 lerps. Some timing results using our RTX 2070 GPU are shown in Table 5.3. The table shows the number of volumes that could be processed per second assuming the data is already on the GPU. The affine3D column shows the result for the kernel listed above, the interp3D column shows the results for a kernel identical to this except that the interpolation is performed by calling interp3D instead of using a texture lookup. The use of textures gives about a factor of 5 performance gain, which in this context is huge! The host version is about 2000 times slower than affine3D. Measurements with Nsight Compute confirm that the affine3D kernel is delivering well over a TFlop/sec of performance.

Example 5.8 `interp3D` function for trilinear interpolation

```
40   template <typename T> __host__ __device__ T
41        interp3D(cr_Ptr<T> a, cfloat x, cfloat y,
                              cfloat z, cint3 n)
42   {
43     if(x < -1.0f ||  x >= n.x || y < -1.0f ||
            y >= n.y || z < -1.0f || z >= n.z) return (T)0;

44     auto idx = [&n](int z,int y,int x)
                           { return (z*n.y+y)*n.x+x; };

45     float x1 = floorf(x-0.5f);
46     float y1 = floorf(y-0.5f);
47     float z1 = floorf(z-0.5f);

48     float ax = x - x1;
49     float ay = y - y1;
50     float az = z - z1;

51     int kx1 = max(0,(int)x1);
       int kx2 = min(n.x-1,kx1+1); // in [0,n.x-1]
52     int ky1 = max(0,(int)y1);
       int ky2 = min(n.y-1,ky1+1); // in [0,n.y-1]
53     int kz1 = max(0,(int)z1);
       int kz2 = min(n.z-1,kz1+1); // in [0,n.z-1]

54     float ly1 =
           lerp(a[idx(kz1,ky1,kx1)],a[idx(kz1,ky1,kx2)],ax);
55     float ly2 =
           lerp(a[idx(kz1,ky2,kx1)],a[idx(kz1,ky2,kx2)],ax);
56     float lz1 =
           lerp(ly1,ly2,ay); // bilinear x-y interp at z1

57     float ly3 =
           lerp(a[idx(kz2,ky1,kx1)],a[idx(kz2,ky1,kx2)],ax);
58     float ly4 =
           lerp(a[idx(kz2,ky2,kx1)],a[idx(kz2,ky2,kx2)],ax);
59     float lz2 =
           lerp(ly3,ly4,ay); // bilinear x-y interp at z2

60     float val =
           lerp(lz1,lz2,az); // trilinear interp x-y-z
61     return (T)val;
62   }
```

5.9 3D Image Registration

The affine3D kernel is essentially all the GPU code we need to implement 3D image registration. Image registration is the process of transforming one image to agree as closely as possible with another image. In this context the "images" can be either 2D images or 3D volumes. Medical imaging is one area in which registration is important, for example, registering MRI brain scans for a particular patient taken at different times is necessary for measuring progression of diseases like Alzheimer's. Registration between different subjects is also important, for example, to put a large set of images taken over time on a variety of different scanners into a common coordinate system for big-data applications.

Essentially all we have to do to the affine3D kernel is to replace line 27 with the calculation of a metric measuring the difference between the values of pixels in image b and the corresponding interpolated position in image a. The combined metric from all pixels is then a measure of how well the images correspond. The host can then run an optimisation process to vary the affine parameters until the best value for the metric is reached. An example of a simple metric is the sum of the squared differences between the values of corresponding pixels in a and b. The metric function is often referred to as a cost function in image registration code. Examples 5.9–5.13 are a simple but complete working registration program built around the modified version of affine3D. The full program can be found in our code repository.

Example 5.9 costfun_sumsq kernel: A modified version of affine3D

```
10    __global__ void costfun_sumsq(r_Ptr<float> cost,
         cr_Ptr<ushort> b, cudaTextureObject_t atex,
         affparams aff, cint3 n, cint3 m)
11    {
12       cint ix = blockIdx.x*blockDim.x + threadIdx.x;
13       cint iy = blockIdx.y*blockDim.y + threadIdx.y;
14       if(ix >= m.x || iy >= m.y) return; // range check
15       auto mdx = [&m](int z, int y, int x)
                            { return (z*m.y+y)*m.x+x; };
15.1  auto cdx = [&m](int y, int x){ return y*m.x+x; };

16       float dx = 1.0f/(float)m.x;   // normalized coords
17       float dy = 1.0f/(float)m.y;   // for texture lookup
18       float dz = 1.0f/(float)m.z;   // in a

19       float x = ix*dx - 0.5f;   // move origin to
20       float y = iy*dy - 0.5f;   // volume centre

20.1  if(cost != nullptr) cost[cdx(iy,ix)] = 0.0f;
21       for(int iz=0;iz<m.z;iz++){
22          float z = iz*dz - 0.5f;
23          // affine 3 x 3 matrix and translation
24          float xr = aff.A0.x*x+aff.A0.y*y+aff.A0.z*z +
                            dx*aff.A0.w +0.5f/n.x +0.5f;
```

```
25        float yr = aff.A1.x*x+aff.A1.y*y+aff.A1.z*z +
                            dy*aff.A1.w +0.5f/n.y +0.5f;
26        float zr = aff.A2.x*x+aff.A2.y*y+aff.A2.z*z +
                            dz*aff.A2.w +0.5f/n.z +0.5f;
27        if(cost == nullptr) b[mdx(iz,iy,ix)] =
              (ushort)(65535.0f*tex3D<float>(atex,xr,yr,zr));
27.1      else {
27.2        float bval = (float)b[mdx(iz,iy,ix)];
27.3        float aval = 65535.0f*tex3D<float>
                                      (atex,xr,yr,zr);
27.4        cost[cdx(iy,ix)] += (aval-bval)*(aval-bval);
          }
28      }
29    }
```

Description of Example 5.9

The kernel costfun_sumsq is our modified version of affine3D and is the only new GPU code needed for the registration program. It evaluates the sum of the squared differences between voxels of the input volume b after being transformed by the affine transformation in aff and the second volume a stored in the texture atex. Code that differs from affine3D is shown in bold.

- Line 10: The declaration of costfun_sumsq is the same as affine3D except that we have added a new first argument cost. This 2D array has space for each thread to store its contribution to the cost function. Since the code is mostly identical to affine3D, we have designed costfun_sum to either evaluate the cost function or to transform the volume b using the transformation aff. The latter operation is performed if cost is set to nullptr. It could be argued that using the argument cost as either an array or a flag is an example of undesirable "tricky code" that might confuse the user; we could have used the separate affine3D code instead. However, we feel that duplicating code in multiple kernels is harder to maintain, justifying our "trick".
- Line 15.1: We add a new indexing function cdx to address the 2D array cost.
- Line 20.1: We initialise the elements of cost to zero. Note the check on the pointer cost.
- Line 27: If cost is set to nullptr this line performs the same function as affine3D; the volume b is transformed and there is no cost function computation, otherwise lines 27.1–27.4 are executed.
- Lines 27.2–27.4: These lines perform the cost function evaluation in the case that cost is not nullptr.
  ∘ Line 27.2: Set bval to the value of b at its untransformed position (ix,iy,iz).
  ∘ Line 27.3: Set aval to the trilinear interpolated value of a at the transformed position (xr,yr,zr).
  ∘ Line 27.4: Calculate the square of the difference between the two values and add this to the sum for this thread in its element of cost. This sum is accumulated over all z values.

Note the sum computed here will be minimised when the transformation aff takes a into the frame of b, i.e. this code registers volume a to volume b. Volume b is the static or target volume and a is the moving or source volume. Note this is not a restriction on the code, as the volumes used for a and b depend on the order which they are specified by the user on the command line.

Also note that line 27.4 is the only line that needs changing to implement different cost functions, for example, `fabs(aval-bval)` or `powf(aval-bval, cpower)` where `cpower` is a user adjustable parameter.

The remainder of our code in examples 5.10–5.13 is host code built around the GPU kernel.

Example 5.10 The struct `paramset` used for affine image registration

```
30   struct paramset {
31     affparams p;
32     float a[7];  // 3 rotations, 3 translations & 1 scale

33     // constructor
34     paramset(float sc =1.0f, float ax =0.0f, float ay =0.0f,
35              float az =0.0f, float tx =0.0f, float ty =0.0f,
36              float tz =0.0f)
37     {
         // units are degrees and pixels
38       a[0] = ax; a[1] = ay; a[2] = az;  // rotations
39       a[3] = tx; a[4] = ty; a[5] = tz;  // translations
40       a[6] = sc;                        // global scale
41     }
42   };
```

Description of Example 5.10

The struct `paramset` holds a 12-parameter affine matrix in `affparams` p and the set of 7 physical displacements in a on which the 12 values in p depend.

- Line 31: A copy of the affine transformation matrix used by the GPU code is stored as `affparams` p, the first element of the stuct.
- Line 32: The 7 physical transformation parameters stored as elements of the array a [7]. Storing parameters in this fashion allows the optimisation code to simply loop over these parameters which reduces the complexity of that code.
- Lines 34–41: In C++ the keywords struct and class are equivalent.[7] Thus, here we can include a constructor for the struct with default values which specify an identity transformation.

Example 5.11 functor `cost_functor` for evaluation of image registration cost function

```
50   struct cost_functor {
51     ushort *b;                          // moving image
52     float *d;                           // buffer of size m.x x m.y
53     thrust::device_vector<float> dsum;  // single word
```

```
54    cudaTextureObject_t atex;   // fixed image in texture
55    int3 n, m;    // sizes of fixed and moving images
56    int calls;  // count total calls
57    cost_functor() {};  // null default constructor
      // useful constructor with arguments
58    cost_functor(ushort *bs, float *ds,
            thrust::device_vector<float> ds1,
            cudaTextureObject_t at1, int3 n1, int3 m1) {
59      b = bs; d = ds; dsum = ds1; atex = at1;
        n = n1; m = m1;
60    };
      // overloded () so can use function syntax
61    float operator()(paramset &s) {
62      make_params(s); // put this here to simplify code
63      dim3 threads(32,16,1);
64      dim3 blocks((m.x+threads.x-1)/threads.x,
                    (m.y+threads.y-1)/threads.y, 1);
65      costfun_sumsq<<< blocks,threads>>>
                         (d, b, atex, s.p, n, m);
66      dsum[0] = 0.0f;  // note warp_reduce needs this
        // from chapter 3
67      warp_reduce<<<1,256>>>(dsum.data().get(), d, m.x*m.y);
68      cudaDeviceSynchronize();
69      float sum = dsum[0];
70      calls++:
71      return sum;
72    }
73   };
```

Description of Example 5.11

The code here is a nice example of how a set of GPU kernel calls can be packaged up to look like a simple function call. This can be useful for simplifying your own code and for interfacing with external libraires. A C++ struct which includes an overloaded operator definition for () is called a *functor*. It can be used like a function but its member variables maintain an internal state between calls.

- Line 50: Here we declare our functor cost_functor; note that like other C++ objects we will need to create one or more instances of this struct to actually use the functor.
- Lines 51–56: Here we declare the variables contained in the struct; they are basically all the arguments we need to call the costfun_sumsq kernel. Hiding them in the functor means that our optimisation codes will not need to deal with them. The variable calls records the number of calls to the functor which is helpful for monitoring the efficiency of the optimisation algorithm being used.
- Line 57: This is a default constructor for the functor which does nothing. In most cases C++ provides a default constructor (which sets everything to zero), but that is not the case if an overloaded operator () is declared.

- Lines 58–60: This is a proper constructor which sets all the parameters to user supplied values.
- Lines 61–71: Here we define the functor itself.
  - Line 61: The functor takes a single argument which is a reference to a `paramset` object s.
  - Line 62: Here we calculate the `affparams` values s.p from the values stored in s.a by calling the host function `make_params`. This function is relatively expensive in CPU time as it involves several 3 × 3 matrix multiplications and computations of `sin` and `cos` for three angles. The reason for placing this call inside the functor is to simplify the calling code on the assumption that the functor is only called when at least one of the physical parameters has been changed. The function `make_params` is shown as part of Example 5.13.
  - Lines 63–64: Set the usual thread block configuration for one thread per x-y position in the 3D volume.
  - Line 65: Call the `costfun_sumsq` kernel with the first input argument set to an array d of sufficient size to hold the partial sums of each thread.
  - Lines 66–67: The warp reduce kernel described in Chapter 3 is used to sum the values in d leaving the result in `dsum[0]`, which is the required cost function value.
  - Lines 69–70: The result is copied from the GPU to the host and then returned to the caller.

A simple function to find the minimum cost function is shown in Example 5.12.

Example 5.12 Simple host-based optimiser which uses `cost_functor`

```
80   float optimise(paramset &s, cost_functor &cf, float scale)
81   {
82       // 3 rotations, 3 translations & 1 scale
83       float step[7] = {2.0f, 2.0f, 2.0f, 4.0f, 4.0f,
                                           4.0f, 0.05f };
84       paramset sl = s;      // step down
85       paramset sh = s;      // step up
86       paramset sb = s;      // best so far
87       paramset sopt = s;    // trial set

88       float cost1 = cf(s);

89       for(int k=0;k<7;k++){   // reduce delta on each pass
90           float delta = step[k]*scale;
91           sl.a[k] = s.a[k] - delta;
92           sh.a[k] = s.a[k] + delta;
93           float cost0 = cf(sl);
94           float cost2 = cf(sh);
95           if(cost0 > cost1 || cost2 > cost1){  // potential min
96               float div = cost2+cost0-2.0f*cost1;
97               if(abs(div) > 0.1) { // optimal step if parabolic
98                   float leap = delta*(cost0 - cost2)/div+s.a[k];
99                   leap = (leap < 0.0f) ?
                            std::max(leap,s.a[k]-2.0f*delta) :
                            std::min(leap,s.a[k]+2.0f*delta);
```

```
100                 sopt = s;
101                 sopt.a[k] = leap;
102                 float cnew = cf(sopt);
103                 if(cnew < cost1) sb.a[k] = leap;
104             }
105         }
106         // here if parabolic maximum, so go to smallest
107         else sb.a[k] = (cost0 < cost2) ? sl.a[k] : sh.a[k];
108     }
199     float cost3 = cf(sb);
110     if(cost3 < cost1) s = sb; // update only if improved
111     return cost3;
112 }
```

Description of Example 5.12

The basis of the optimisation function shown in Example 5.12 is that starting from a given set of parameter values stored in s, the cost function is evaluated at s and then for each parameter separately evaluated at values ±delta from the current value of that parameter. A parabola is fitted to these three values and the minimum is used as the new trial value for that parameter. If a function has values f_0, f_1 and f_2 at points x-h, x and x+h then a parabola through the three points has a max or min at:

$$x + \frac{h(f_0 - f_2)}{f_0 + f_2 - 2f_1}. \tag{5.4}$$

- Line 80: The function takes 3 arguments, the current parameter values in paramset s, a reference to the cost function functor cf and a scaling value scale for the step size.
- Line 83: Default step sizes for the parameters are held in the array step. These parameters could be tuned to improve performance and accuracy.
- Lines 84–87: Several paramsets are defined here; sl for a step down, sh for a step up, sopt for the current trial set and sb for the best set found so far.
- Line 88: The cost function value on entry is stored in cost1.
- Lines 89–109: Loop over the 7 parameters where each one is optimised in turn.
- Lines 91–94: Set sh and sl to the starting set with only parameter k adjusted up or down by an amount which depends both on the step[k] and scale. The cost function values for these parameter sets are stored in cost0 and cost2.
- Line 95: If the cost1 is greater than both cost0 and cost2 then that parabolic fit is a maximum and we go straight to line 107 and store in sb the parameter corresponding to the smaller of cost0 and cost2.
- Line 96: Here we evaluate the denominator of Eq. 5.4; the result is stored in div.
- Line 97: We check that div is not too close to zero; the cut-off used is tiny given that the cost functions have values of 10^{12} or more.
- Line 98: Here we calculate the position of the turning point from Eq. 5.4.
- Line 99: We adjust the proposed parameter step to be not more than twice the current step size. The value of 2.0 used here turns out to be quite a sensitive tuning parameter. The new parameter is stored in leap.

- Lines 100–104: Here we calculate the cost function `cfnew` using the new value for the current parameter; if this is smaller than the current value of `cost1` we update `sb`.

Next, in Example 5.13 we show that part of the main routine that calls `optimise`.

Example 5.13 Image registration main routine fragment showing iterative optimisation process

```
          . . .
150   paramset s; // default constructor used
151   cost_functor cf(dev_b.data().get(),
            dev_d.data().get(), dev_dsum, atex.tex, n, m);
152   cx::timer tim;
153   float cf2 = cf(s);     // cost function before optimisation

154   float scale = 2.0f;    // scale factor for optimise calls
155   float cfold = cf2;     // previous best cf value
156   float cfnew = cf2;     // current best estimate of cf
157   int iter =0;           // iteration counter for loop step
158   for(int k=0;k<9;k++){
159     while(iter <100){  // expect far fewer iterations
160       iter++;
161       cfnew = optimise(s, cf, scale);
162       if(cfnew > 0.99*cfold) break;
163       cfold = cfnew;
164     }
165     printf("scale %.3f iter %2d cfnew 10.3e\n",
                          scale, iter, cfnew);
166     iter = 0;
167     scale /= 1.5f;  // gently decrease step size
169   }
168   double t1 = tim.lap_ms();
          . . .
200   int make_params(paramset &s)
201   {
202     double d2r = cx::pi<double>/180.0;
        // zoom 2.0 needs scale = 0.5
203     double scale = 1.0/s.a[6];
204     double A[3][3] ={{scale,0,0},{0,scale,0},{0,0,scale}};
205     double cz = cos(s.a[2]*d2r);
        double sz = sin(s.a[2]*d2r);
206     double cx = cos(s.a[0]*d2r);
        double sx = sin(s.a[0]*d2r);
207     double cy = cos(s.a[1]*d2r);
        double sy = sin(s.a[1]*d2r);
208     double RZ[3][3] ={{cz,sz,0},{-sz,cz,0},{0,0,1}};
```

```
209    double RX[3][3] ={{1,0,0},{0,cx,sx},{0,-sx,cx}};
210    double RY[3][3] ={{cy,0,sy},{0,1,0},{-sy,0,cy}};
211    matmul3(A,RZ,A);
212    matmul3(A,RY,A);
213    matmul3(A,RX,A);
214    s.p.A0.x =A[0][0]; s.p.A0.y =A[0][1];
       s.p.A0.z =A[0][2]; s.p.A0.w =s.a[3];
215    s.p.A1.x =A[1][0]; s.p.A1.y =A[1][1];
       s.p.A1.z =A[1][2]; s.p.A1.w =s.a[4];
216    s.p.A2.x =A[2][0]; s.p.A2.y =A[2][1];
       s.p.A2.z =A[2][2]; s.p.A2.w =s.a[5];
217    s.p.scale = scale;  // NB this is 1/scale
218    return 0;
219  }
```

Description of Example 5.13

- Line 150: Create the paramset s used to hold the final transformation. The default constructor is used.
- Line 151: Create an instance cf of the cost function functor supplying the relevant device memory pointers as arguments. The cf object can now be used in our code as if it were a standard function.
- Lines 152–168: This section of code is the timed section that performs the registration by calling optimise multiple times with decreasing values of the scale parameter.
  - Line 153: cf2 is the value of the cost function at the start.
  - Lines 154–157: Declare and initialise variables used during optimisation loops.
  - Line 158: Start of outer for loop, the variable scale is reduced on each pass through this loop.
  - Line 159: Start of inner while loop where we call optimise repeatedly with a fixed value of scale until no further improvement of the cost function is found. A maximum number of calls is imposed to prevent endless loops.
  - Lines 160–163: Here we call optimise and update cfnew and cfold each time an improvement is made. Note that the paramset s is also updated by cf when an improvement is made.
  - Lines 165–167: Print progress at end of inner loop and set iter and scale to values required for next iteration of the inner loop.
- Lines 200–219: The make_parms utility function which constructs the affine transformation matrix from the physical rotation angles, translations and scaling parameters.
- Line 202: For convenience, users enter rotation angles in degrees, the factor d2r converts these values to radians.
- Line 204: The 3 × 3 matrix A will hold the affine transformation excluding translations. It is initialised to the scale times the unit matrix.
- Lines 205–207: The sins and cosines of the three rotation angles are calculated here.
- Lines 208–210: Three rotation matrices about the three coordinate axes are defined here.
- Lines 211–213: The matrix A is multiplied in turn by RZ, RY and RX using the utility function matmul3 (not shown). The first argument is set to the result multiplying the second and third arguments. It is safe for the first argument to be the same as one or both of the other arguments. Note that in general the final result depends on the order in which these matrix multiplications are performed.
- Lines 214–217: The final A matrix and translations in s.a[3–5] are copied to the parmset row vectors A0, A1 and A2.

Some typical results for this code are shown in the next section.

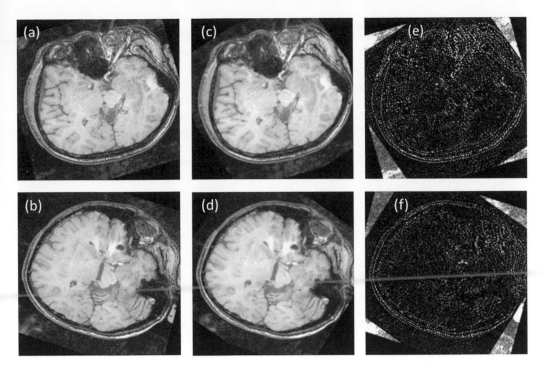

Figure 5.9 Image registration results

5.10 Image Registration Results

To test our registration code, we used the affine3D program to transform the MRI volume shown in Figure 5.8 using 2 separate transformations to generate two new volumes vol1 and vol2. The results are shown in Figure 5.9 (a) and (b).

Figure 5.9 (a) shows a central slice from vol1 which was generated using rotations of (10,20,15) degrees of the original volume about its three coordinate axes and translations by (5,3,1) voxels. Similarly, vol2 shown in Figure 5.9 (b) was produced using rotations of (−5,10,−15) degrees and translations of (−1,2,−1) pixels. Note these are large spatial transformations in the context of MRI registration.

The results of running the registration program to register vol2 to vol1 and vice versa are also shown in the Figure 5.9 (c) and (d). To highlight any residual errors the differences between (a) and (c) are shown in (e) and the differences between (b) and (d) are shown in (f). Images (e) and (f) have increased contrast. The bright wedges at the edges are portions of the volumes that have been rotated out of the field of view and set to zero for one of vol1 or vol2 but not the other. These wedges which are artefacts of the synthetic images used are a potential problem for registration and lead to a large residual cost function. Nevertheless, in this case the registration process has been successful.

The printed output from running the program is shown in Figure 5.10.

The time to run the whole program including reading and writing the data sets is about one second, the time to run the registration loop is about 650 ms. The results show that about 1000 cost function evaluations were used in each run and we estimate that these would take

```
D: >register.exe vol1.raw vol2.raw vol1to2.raw 256
file vol1.raw read
file vol2.raw read
start cf   1.48153e+14
scale 2.000 iterations  9 cf calls  206 cf  6.03421e+13
scale 1.333 iterations 20 cf calls  666 cf  6.73378e+12
scale 0.889 iterations  8 cf calls  850 cf  4.38710e+12
scale 0.593 iterations  5 cf calls  965 cf  3.50503e+12
scale 0.395 iterations  3 cf calls 1034 cf  3.33628e+12
scale 0.263 iterations  2 cf calls 1080 cf  3.29818e+12
scale 0.176 iterations  1 cf calls 1103 cf  3.29082e+12
scale 0.117 iterations  1 cf calls 1126 cf  3.28782e+12
scale 0.078 iterations  1 cf calls 1149 cf  3.28552e+12
file vol1to2.raw written
final cf 3.28552e+12 cf calls 1150 reg time 688.978 ms job time 1045.016 ms

D: >register.exe vol2.raw vol1.raw vol2to1.raw 256
file vol2.raw read
file vol1.raw read
start cf   1.48153e+14
scale 2.000 iterations 21 cf calls  482 cf  2.09059e+13
scale 1.333 iterations  7 cf calls  643 cf  9.68373e+12
scale 0.889 iterations  5 cf calls  758 cf  5.62953e+12
scale 0.593 iterations  3 cf calls  827 cf  5.14188e+12
scale 0.395 iterations  2 cf calls  873 cf  5.09413e+12
scale 0.263 iterations  1 cf calls  896 cf  5.08894e+12
scale 0.176 iterations  1 cf calls  919 cf  5.08625e+12
scale 0.117 iterations  1 cf calls  942 cf  5.08519e+12
scale 0.078 iterations  1 cf calls  965 cf  5.08422e+12
file vol2to1.raw written
final cf 5.08422e+12 cf calls 966 reg time 614.262 ms job time 992.122 ms
```

Figure 5.10 Output from registration program

about 310 ms. Thus, we conclude that firstly our code is really very fast by historic standards for this sort of registration problem, and secondly the overall time is dominated by the host code not the GPU. In Chapter 7 we show how to overlap both disk IO with host calculation and host calculation with GPU calculation. These techniques would give further speed-ups, useful for big-data applications where thousands of MRI images might need frequent registration. On this happy note we end this chapter. If you are interested in the gory details of texture creation then Appendix H4 has all the details of the cx routines and the NVIDIA C++ Programming Guide has even more information.

In the next chapter we move on to discuss random number generation and applications. Monte Carlo methods have many scientific applications including, very importantly, applications to simulation.

Endnotes Chapter 5

1 In many cases pixel values are only proportional to the sampled distribution function; this is due to the various rescaling operations that are likely to have occurred between image capture and image display.

2 As a reminder, we follow the usual mathematical convention that the point with coordinates (x, y) on some graph has a horizontal displacement of x along the x-axis and a vertical displacement of y along the y-axis. However, in our computer code an image stored in a 2D array A is addressed as A[y][x] and that is because of the C/C++ convention that it is the rightmost index that addresses adjacent memory locations. As a further source of confusion, in image processing the coordinate origin the usually taken to be the top left-hand corner of the image so that the y-axis runs downwards whereas in mathematical and most scientific work the convention is for the y axis to run upwards from an origin at the bottom left-hand corner.

3 It is quite hard to get this sign choice right. For the transformed image to have a clockwise rotation we need the pixel (xt, yt) in the original image to have an anti-clockwise rotation (or more generally apply the inverse transformation). We also need to remember that we are using left-handed axes where y points downwards from the origin.

4 Of course, in production code one can perform a check on whether a candidate output file already exists and ask the user for permission to overwrite. We do not do this routinely in our demonstration code to keep things compact.

5 On early GPUs there was a performance gain from reading data from texture memory rather than global memory, particularly for 2D arrays. Thus, there are still many examples advocating this floating around internet. On modern GPUs my own tests suggest that reading from simple pointers to global memory is faster than using textures and less is complicated. But this only true if we remember to use const __restrict__ qualifiers on the kernel input arguments.

6 We rather favour png for scientific image processing because it uses lossless image compression which makes for smaller files than bmp but does not lose information like most compressed jpg files.

7 There is one small difference, by default the member variables are public for a stuct and private for a class. In both cases the default can be overridden.

6

Monte Carlo Applications

NVIDIA GPUs can generate random numbers extremely fast and this enables their use for a vast range of applications in both Monte Carlo integration and simulation. In this chapter we explain the various ways in which the cuRAND library can be used.

6.1 Introduction

Scientific applications of Monte Carlo methods have always been important and their applications continue to grow in importance, tracking the growth and availability of computing power. Today they are a vital tool in many areas of science. To oversimplify, these applications can be classified into two groups; (a) integration – where some function is sampled over random points in its domain and (b) simulation – where the behaviour of some physical system or piece of experimental equipment is investigated using random numbers to mimic a stochastic process. A "good" random number generator (RNG) is an essential tool for many applications of computers in science.

Computers rarely use genuinely random numbers;[1] rather they use either pseudorandom numbers or quasirandom numbers. A pseudorandom number generator (PRNG or just RNG) starts with an initial bit string (the seed) and *calculates* a new string where the new bits have little correlation with the seed bits. This bit string can be converted to either an integer or a floating-point value and returned to the user as a random number. The generated bit string then becomes the seed for the next number.

A well-known example of such a generator is the `rand` function in C++, which is actually a legacy from the early days of C; it is simple to use but is now deprecated by most people. The reasons why `rand` is disliked are firstly that it returns integers in the range 0 to RAND_MAX where RAND_MAX is an implementation defined constant which is typically either $2^{15}-1$ (Visual Studio 17) or $2^{31}-1$ (gcc 4.8.4). The former value is quite small which makes it hard to scale the results for other ranges. Moreover, the quality of the random numbers is not guaranteed and unwanted correlations between sets of generated numbers may be present.

Finding good algorithms for RNGs which are both fast and which produce sequences with minimal correlations between values is an ongoing research effort in computer science, but it is fair to say that modern generators are now excellent. Both modern C++ and CUDA provide libraries for random number generation. For C++11 and later versions, including the header file `<random>` gives access to a number of powerful generators. For CUDA the header files `<curand.h>` and `<curand_kernel.h>` give access to generators for either host code or kernel code.

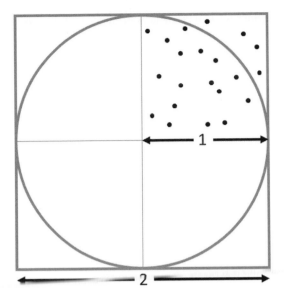

Figure 6.1 Calculation of π

Quasi-random number generators (QRNG) are similar to pseudorandom number generators but populate a defined interval more uniformly than pseudorandom numbers; hence they may be a better choice for function integration type problems. The CUDA libraries provide both types of generator.

Our first example is the calculation of π by generating random points in the unit square representing the positive quadrant of a square of side 2 and finding the fraction that fall inside the circle of radius 1, inscribed in the larger square; this is shown in Figure 6.1. The fraction inside the circle is just $\pi/4$. This example is quite common and is included in the CUDA SDK. It is good for comparing RNGs because it needs lots of random numbers but performs very little other calculation or memory access. Our first version, shown in Example 6.1, implements the calculation on the host using the C++11 `<random>` library. The idea of the calculation is shown in Figure 6.1. We simply generate random points inside a unit square and calculate the fraction that also fall into the quadrant of the circle as indicated in the figure.

In Example 6.1 we show a complete host only program, which is very compact. The C++ `<random>` library allows users to create instances of various random number generator objects which can then subsequently be used in code. The "bare" generators return 32 or 64-bit `unsigned ints` with random bit patterns and hence could be used directly in the same way as `rand`. However, it is usually more convenient to wrap the generator with a distribution function object such as the uniform floating-point distribution used in line 14 of the example.

Description of Example 6.1

- Lines 2–4: These show the required `#include` statements; note line 4 `<random>` which provides the C++11 support for random number generators beyond the basic `rand` function.
- Line 7: Here we create an instance `rd` of the C++ `random_device` generator type. This generates true random numbers based on hardware if available. Unfortunately, this generator is

slow and has poor behaviour for long sequences of numbers. It is, however, a good alternative to using the time of day clock when generating random seeds for other generators and that is why we use it here.

- Lines 8–9: Set the int variables `points` and `passes`. The code is designed to process a potentially very large number of points and so uses a doubly nested pair of loops. The inner loop in lines 17–21 processes `points` generations and accumulates the number of hits in the int variable `subtot`. The outer loop between lines 15 and 23 accumulates the values of `subtot` in the `long long` variable `pisum` which is used later to estimate pi. The number of iterations in the outer loop is controlled by the user settable variable `passes`.
- Line 10: Here we initialise the variable `seed` using a value either `rd` or user input.
- Line 11: Here we create an instance, `gen`, of an RNG having type `default_generator_engine`, and initialise it with `seed`.
- Line 12: Here we create `fdist`, a uniform distribution of floating point 32-bit numbers in the range [0,1). Notice how RNG `gen` and distribution `fdist` are used together in lines 18 and 19. The `<random>` library provides a variety of generators and distributions most of which can be combined together in this way.
- Line 13: Initialises a 64-bit integer `pisum` to count the number of points generated inside the circle.
- Line 14: Creates an instance `tim` of a timer object from the `cx` utility file `cxtimers.h`. The timer contained within `tim` starts immediately.
- Lines 15–23: These are the doubly nested loops where random points within a unit square are created in lines 18 and 19 and then tested for being inside the unit circle in line 20. The number of hits is accumulated firstly in inner loop variable `subtot` which itself is accumulated in the outer loop `long` variable `pisum`.
- Line 24: After the loops end, the time taken is stored in the variable `gen_time` in units of ms.
- Lines 25–26: Here we calculate an estimate of the value of π as four times the ratio of `pisum` and `ntot` and also the fractional error on this estimate in ppm.

Example 6.1 `piH` host calculation of π using random sampling

```
02   #include "cx.h"
03   #include "cxtimers.h"
04   #include <random>

05   int main(int argc,char *argv[])
06   {
07     std::random_device rd;    // truly random but slow
08     int points = 1000000;     // inner loop 10^6 generations
09     int passes = (argc >1) ? atoi(argv[1]) : 1;   // outer loop
10     unsigned int seed = (argc >2) ? atoi(argv[2]) : rd();

11     std::default_random_engine gen(seed);
12     std::uniform_real_distribution<float>  fdist(0.0,1.0);

13     long long pisum = 0;
14     cx::timer tim;
```

```
15      for(int n = 0; n<passes; n++){
16        int subtot = 0;
17        for(int k = 0; k < points; k++) {
18          float x = fdist(gen);  // generate point
19          float y = fdist(gen);  // in square
20          if(x*x + y*y < 1.0f) subtot++;  // inside circle?
21        }
22        pisum += subtot; // use long long for this sum
23      }

24      double gen_time = tim.lap_ms();
25      double pi = 4.0*(double)pisum /
                    ((double)points *(double)passes);
26      double frac_error = 1000000.0*
                    (pi- cx::pi<double>)/cx::pi<double>;
27      long long ntot = (long long)passes*(long long)points;
28      printf("pi = %10.8f err %.1f, ntot %lld,
                    time %.3f ms (float gen)\n",
                    pi, frac_error, ntot, gen_time);
29      return 0;
30    }

D:\>piH.exe 1000 123456
pi = 3.14152040 err -23.0, ntot 1000000000, time 74229.004 ms
```

- Line 28: Prints the results including time taken.
- The results shown at the end of this example show that a calculation using 10^9 points required 75 seconds to complete using the `std::uniform_real_distribution<float>` distribution.

We will use the 75 seconds required for this calculation as a baseline to improve on. The fractional error of 23.0 is given in parts per million. The number of generated points falling inside the circle has a binomial probability distribution, which in this case has an error of $\sqrt{\frac{\pi}{4}\left(1 - \frac{\pi}{4}\right)10^9}$ so the expected fractional error in our estimate of π is $\sqrt{(4/\pi - 1)/10^9} = 16.5 \times 10^{-6}$. The fractional error reported here, based on the deviation from the true value of π, is consistent with this.

The time taken is actually quite large and it turns out that the host code can be improved by using a different C++ distribution function. During testing we noticed by accident that the C++ uniform float distribution used in Example 6.1 is seven times slower than the corresponding integer distribution. Accordingly, we can change the code to use the faster `int` distribution by making the changes shown in Example 6.2.

Example 6.2 `piH2` with faster host RNG

```
      . . .
      // uniform ints in [0,2^31-1]
12    std::uniform_int_distribution<int>  idist(0,2147483647);
12.1  double idist_scale= 1.0/2147483647.0;
      . . .
18    float x= idist_scale*idist(gen); // uniform floats in [0,1.0)
19    float y= idist_scale*idist(gen);
      . . .
D:\>pieH2.exe 1000 123456
pi = 3.14158036 err -3.9 ntot 1000000000, time 10275.153 ms
```

Description of Example 6.2

- Line 12: Has been replaced by the creation of a uniform integer distribution `igen`, with integer values in the range $[0, 2^{31}-1]$. We also introduce a new scale factor `double idist_scale` which is set to the reciprocal of $2^{31}-1$.
- Lines 18–19: These are changed to use `idist_scale*idist(gen)` instead of `fdist(gen)`.
- The result from this modified example indicates that it is indeed about seven times faster than Example 6.1. Since the method used here is a standard way of generating a float random number from an integer random number generator, it is puzzling that the default C++ floating point generator is so slow.[2]

We can get even better performance from the host by using OpenMP to run several parallel host threads. There is, however, one issue to consider; we cannot simply share the loops between several threads as we did in Chapter 1. This is because the `fdist` or `idist` functions are likely to be called by multiple threads simultaneously and these functions may not be thread-safe.[3]

Our solution for this problem is to warp the allocation and use of the RNGs into a single function and have that function called by multiple threads. In this way, each thread will get its own instance of the generator and these multiple instances will be able to safely run simultaneously. One vital detail is to ensure that each thread uses a *different* seed when initialising its copy of the RNG. If this were not done, each thread would see the same random number sequence rather defeating the point of running multiple threads. This is an obvious point but in practice rather easy to overlook. Interestingly, our kernel code discussed below also uses one generator per thread and hence has the same issue.

Example 6.3 shows our implementation; the main change is that we have moved lines 13–25 of Example 6.1 which create and initialise the RNG and perform the required summations to the separate function, `part_sum`, as shown in lines 11–28 of Example 6.3. Each OMP thread which calls this function creates a separate instance of the RNG initialised with a seed that depends on the thread number. The main routine then sums the contributions from each thread in an OMP reduce operation. Notice the same effect could be obtained by running our single thread program several times with different seeds and averaging the results. The separate programs would run in parallel if launched

---

Example 6.3 piOMP version

```
05   #include "omp.h"

06   long long int sum_part(uint seed, int points, int passes)
07   {
08     int thread = omp_get_thread_num();
09     // NB different seed for each thread
10     std::default_random_engine gen(seed+113*thread);
11     std::uniform_int_distribution<int> idist(0,2147483647);
12     double idist_scale = 1.0/2147483647.0;

13     long long int pisum = 0;
14     for(int n = 0; n<passes; n++){
15       int subtot = 0;
16       for(int k = 0; k < points; k++) {
17         float x = idist_scale*idist(gen);
18         float y = idist_scale*idist(gen);
19         if(x*x + y*y < 1.0f) subtot++;  // inside circle?
20       }
21       pisum += subtot;
22     }
23     return pisum;
24   }

25   int main(int argc,char *argv[])
26   {
27     std::random_device rd;  // truely random but slow
28     int points = 1000000;
29     int passes =           (argc >1) ? atoi(argv[1]) : 1;
30     unsigned int seed =    (argc >2) ? atoi(argv[2]) : rd();
31     int omp_threads =      (argc >3) ? atoi(argv[3]) : 4;
32
33     omp_set_num_threads(omp_threads);
34     long long int pisum = 0;

35     cx::timer tim;
36   #pragma omp parallel for reduction (+:pisum)
37     for(int k = 0; k < omp_threads; k++) {
38       pisum += sum_part(seed,pass,passes/omp_threads);
39     }
40     double gen_time = tim.lap_ms();
```

```
41     double pi = 4.0*(double)pisum
                /((double)(passes)*(double)points);
42     double frac_error = 1000000.0*
                (pi-cx::pi<double>)/cx::pi<double>;
43     long long ntot = (long long)(passes)*(long long)points;
44     printf("pi = %10.8f err %.1f, ntot %lld,
            time %.3f ms\n", pi, frac_error, ntot, gen_time);
46     return 0;
47  }


D:\>pieOMP.exe 1000 123456 8
pi = 3.14160701 err 4.6, ntot 1000000000, time 2463.751 ms
```

together on a multi core PC. As discussed in Chapter 1, this is a standard approach used by parallel programmers for "embarrassingly parallel" code. A more detailed description of the code follows.

Description of Example 6.3

- Line 5: This include statement is needed for OMP support. (Windows users will also have to enable OMP support in Visual Studio and Linux users will have to include the appropriate library.)
- Lines 6–24: The new part_sum function that takes input arguments points, passes and seed which have the same meaning as in Example 6.1.
  - Line 8: Sets the variable thread to the OMP rank of the thread running this particular instance; this is directly equivalent to the tid or id variables used frequently in our kernel codes.
  - Line 10: Initialises an instance of the C++ default random generator for this thread using a seed which depends on the rank of the thread, thus ensuring that separate threads use different sequences of random numbers.
  - Lines 11–23: These are the same as 14–24 in Examples 6.1 and 6.2 and calculate the number of points inside the circle for passes*points generations.
  - Line 23: The final total accumulated in pisum is returned to the calling code by the function.
- Lines 27–30: These are the beginning of the main routine and are the same as the corresponding lines in Examples 6.1 and 6.2. They initialise the variables points, passes and seed using optional user input.
- Line 31: Is new and initialises the variable omp_threads to the number of OMP threads to be used.
- Line 33: Tells OMP how many threads to use with a standard library call.
- Lines 34–35: Initialise the accumulator pisum and timer tim.
- Line 36: The pragma tells OMP to split the for loop beginning at line 38 into omp_threads separate threads and, since the loop counter is also equal to omp_threads, each thread will execute a single call to sum_part in line 39. The pragma also requests a reduction operation on pisum; thus the individual return values will be summed and pisum will contain the total contribution from all threads when the loop is done.
- Lines 37–39: The for loop calls sum_part once for each OMP thread.

- Lines 40–46: Get elapsed time and print results. These lines are the same as in the previous examples.
- The results shown at the end the example are for 8 threads which was optimum for the platform used.

For our PC we found eight OMP threads gave the best performance; about 2.46 seconds were required to generate 10^9 points. The OMP version gives a speed-up by a factor of 30 compared to our initial base version. This is quite good but we can do better with the help of the GPU.

6.2 The cuRAND Library

So far we have achieved a speed-up of 30 on the original version of the code; to do better we need to use the GPU. NVIDIA provides RNGs with their cuRAND library which is part of the standard CUDA SDK. The cuRAND library can be used in two ways; firstly through the Host API, which is rather similar to the C++11 `<random>` in use except that the GPU is used to generate random numbers; and secondly the Device API where random numbers are both generated and used on the GPU. The former API is useful in problems which are difficult to port to the GPU, as it offers significantly faster generation of random numbers. Indeed in some cases, the overhead of generating random numbers can be reduced to zero. If, on the other hand, your application can be ported to the GPU, the Device API offers a potential speed-up of two orders of magnitude.

6.2.1 The cuRAND Host API

The idea of the cuRAND Host API is to generate a large set of random numbers on the GPU and then transfer them to the host for use. Example 6.4 shows how our previous Example 6.1 can be modified to do this. Unsurprisingly, we will find that time taken to transfer the numbers generated on the GPU back to the host across the PCI bus dominates the generation time. Examples 6.5 and 6.6 build on 6.4 to improve performance, in Example 6.5 we show how the overhead of PCI bus transfer can be reduced by using pinned memory on the host and Example 6.6 shows how the overhead can be effectively reduced to zero by using asynchronous memory transfers. The way the Host API works is that random numbers are generated on the GPU and then transferred to the host in blocks not individually. Large block sizes give better performance and in our examples we use a block size of 2×10^6 controlled by the variable `points`. Just like the C++ `<random>` library, the host API requires the creation of a generator and a distribution function which converts the output of the generator into values for the required distribution e.g. floats in [0,1]. Example 6.4 shows how Example 6.1 can be converted to use the cuRAND host API.

Description of Example 6.4

The example is quite similar to 6.3; thus here we only mention lines which differ.

- Line 6: Include `curand.h` to use the cuRAND host API.
- Lines 6–15: Define the function `sum_part` which calculates the contribution from one block of random numbers. This function is similar to that used in Example 6.3 except that now the required random numbers are precalculated and are passed to the function as the new first argument `rnum`.

- ○ Lines 10–11: Here we get a candidate point in the square by simply looking up a pair of values from the input random number array `rnum`.
- Lines 24–25: Here we create a pair of thrust vectors `rdm` and `dev_rdm` to hold the random numbers on the host and device. Since we process points in blocks of size `points`, these array have size `2*points`.
- Lines 29–31: These lines create and initialise an instance `gen` of a cuRAND random number generator having default type XORWOW and using the variable `seed` as the initial seed. These lines are equivalent to line 11 of Example 6.1 which uses the C++11 library `<random>` for the same purpose.
- Lines 33–37: This is a modified version of the outer loop which calls `sum_part` with a different set of random numbers on each pass.
  - ○ Line 34: This is the most import line in the whole example; here we call a cuRAND distribution function to generate a set of random numbers in GPU memory using the previously created generator `gen` sampled by the distribution implicit in the function call. In this case the function specified, `curandGenerateUniform`, produces a uniform distribution of 32-bit floats in (0,1]. The arguments passed to the distribution function are the generator `gen`, a pointer to the device memory buffer and the number of points required. Notice the library function handles all the details required to actually perform the calculation, for example, kernel launches.
  - ○ Line 35: Here we copy the random numbers back to the host.
  - ○ Line 36: Call `sum_part` with a new set of random numbers each time.
- Line 46: Here we release the CUDA resources acquired by cuRAND.

Example 6.4 `piH4` with cuRand Host API

```
      . . .
05    #include "curand.h"

06    void sum_part(float *rnum, int points, long long &pisum)
07    {
08      unsigned int sum = 0;
09      for(int i=0;i<points;i++){
10        float x = rnum[i*2];
11        float y = rnum[i*2+1];
12        if(x*x + y*y < 1.0f) sum++;
13      }
14      pisum += sum;
15    }

17    int main(int argc, char *argv[])
18    {
19      std::random_device rd;   // truly random but slow
20      int points = 1000000;    // points per inner iteration
21      int passes =          (argc >1) ? atoi(argv[1]) : 1;
22      unsigned int seed = (argc >2) ? atoi(argv[2])  : rd();
23
24      thrustHvec<float>     rdm(points*2); // host and device
```

```
25     thrustDvec<float> dev_rdm(points*2); // RN buffers

27     long long pisum = 0;
28     cx::timer tim;
29     curandGenerator_t gen;    // Host API cuRand generator
30     curandCreateGenerator(&gen,CURAND_RNG_PSEUDO_DEFAULT);
31     curandSetPseudoRandomGeneratorSeed(gen,seed);
32
33     for(int k=0; k<passes; k++) {
34       curandGenerateUniform(gen,
               dev_rdm_ptr.data().get(),points*2);
35       rdm = dev_rdm;             // copy GPU => Host
36       sum_part(rdm.data(),points,pisum); // use on Host
37     }

39     double gen_time = tim.lap_ms();
40     double pi = 4.0*(double)pisum /
                 ((double)points*(double)passes);
41     double frac_error = 1000000.0*
                 (pi- cx::pi<double>)/cx::pi<double>;
42     long long ntot = (long long)passes*(long long)points;
43     printf("pi = %10.8f err %.1f, ntot %lld,
                        time %.3f ms (float gen)\n",
44       pi,frac_error,ntot,gen_time);

46     curandDestroyGenerator(gen); // tidy up
47     return 0;
48   }

D:\ >piH4.exe 1000 123456
pi = 3.14165173 err 18.8, ntot 1000000000, time 2557.818 ms
```

The performance of Example 6.4 is similar to the previous OMP version. However, one difference is that the GPU version requires a single host thread whereas the OMP version uses all eight threads on the 4-core hyperthreading PC used. Therefore, this is already a modest improvement. The host API is limited by the need to copy data from the GPU to Host. In this example we use a total of 10^9 points which means transferring 8 GB across the PCI bus, at 6 GB/sec; this takes about 1.3 seconds. We can easily reduce this overhead by using "pinned" memory for the host random number buffer. Modern operating systems use sophisticated real-time memory management techniques which mean that the memory addresses used by a typical executing program are virtual in the sense that they may be remapped to different physical addresses from time to time during program execution. Blocks of pinned memory are guaranteed not be remapped which allows faster PCI transfer using DMA at 11 GB/sec.

We can take advantage of pinned memory very simply by changing the allocation in line 24 from using the cx defined type thrustHvec to thrustHvecPin as shown in Example 6.5.

Example 6.5 `piH5` with cuRand Host API and pinned memory

```
      // piH5 using pinned memory for host random number buffer
      . . .
24    thrustHvecPin<float> rdm(points*2);   // host pinned memory
      . . .
D:\ >example4.exe 1000 123456
pi = 3.14165173 err 18.8, ntot 1000000000, time 1737.297 ms
```

The time saving observed in Example 6.5 is about 0.8 secs consistent with the improved PCI bandwidth. The `cx` wrappers used to allocate thrust vectors hide a little bit of complexity; without them the code would look as shown in the box.

(a) standard thrust host vector
```
#include "thrust/host_vector.h"
thrust::host_vector<float> rdm(points*2);
```

(b) thrust host vector using pinned memory
```
#include "thrust/system/cuda/experimental/pinned_allocator.h"
thrust::host_vector<float,thrust::cuda::experimental::
  pinned_allocator<float>>
                        rdm(points*2);
```

Header files and native declarations for thrust host vectors.

Even with the use of pinned memory the transfer of 2×10^9 random numbers takes 720 ms, but we can hide nearly all of this cost by overlapping memory transfers with host calculation. In essence we need to write code where the host processes random numbers in block N while the GPU calculates block N+1 and transfers the data to the host in parallel with the host calculation. Fortunately, CUDA provides a `cudaMemcpyAsync` function that does exactly this. To make this code work we obviously will need two buffers, for example, a and b, for blocks of random numbers that are operated in ping-pong fashion, with the host processing one block while the GPU works simultaneously with the other block. Example 6.6 shows the resulting code. Note that Chapter 7 on CUDA Streams and Events discusses synchronous operations in CUDA in much more detail.

Example 6.6 `piH6` with cudaMemcpyAsync

```
      . . .
17    int main(int argc,char *argv[])
18    {
19      std::random_device rd;
20      int points = 1000000;
21      int passes =           (argc >1) ? atoi(argv[1]) : 1;
```

```
22    unsigned int seed = (argc >2) ? atoi(argv[2]) : rd();

23    int bsize = points*2*sizeof(float);
24    float *a; cudaMallocHost(&a, bsize);    // host buffers a & b
25    float *b; cudaMallocHost(&b, bsize);    // in pinned memory
26    float *dev_rdm; cudaMalloc(&dev_rdm, bsize); // device

      // CUDA event
27    cudaEvent_t copydone; cudaEventCreate(&copydone);

28    long long pisum = 0;
29    cx::timer tim;    // overall time
30    curandGenerator_t gen;
31    curandCreateGenerator(&gen, CURAND_RNG_PSEUDO_DEFAULT);
32    curandSetPseudoRandomGeneratorSeed(gen, seed);

33    curandGenerateUniform(gen, dev_rdm, points*2);
      // get 1st block in a
34    cudaMemcpy(a,dev_rdm,bsize,cudaMemcpyDeviceToHost);
35    for(int k = 0; k < passes; k++) {
        // generate next block and copy to b
36      curandGenerateUniform(gen,dev_rdm,points*2);
37      cudaMemcpyAsync(b,dev_rdm,bsize,cudaMemcpyDeviceToHost);
        // place event in default stream
38      cudaEventRecord(copydone,0);
39      cudaEventQuery(copydone);
        // process a while GPU works on b then swap a and b
40      sum_part(a,points,pisum); // for ping-pong processing
41      std::swap(a,b);
42      cudaStreamWaitEvent(0,copydone,0); // now wait for a
43    }
44    double t1 = tim.lap_ms();

45    double pi = 4.0*(double)pisum /
                  ((double)points*(double)passes);
46    long long ntot = passes*points;
47    double frac_error = 1000000.0*
              (pi - cx::pi<double>)/cx::pi<double>;
48    printf("pi = %10.8f err %.1f, ntot %lld, time %.3f
                ms\n", pi, frac_error, ntot, t1);
49    // tidy up
50    cudaFreeHost(a); cudaFreeHost(b); cudaFree(dev_rdm);
51    curandDestroyGenerator(gen);
52    return 0;
53  }

D:\ >piH6.exe 1000 123456
pi = 3.14165610 err 20.2, ntot 1000000000, time 1162.474 ms
```

Description of Example 6.6

The code up to line 22 is identical to the previous examples.

- Lines 23–26: We cannot perform asynchronous memory transfers using thrust copy operations, so in this example we revert to the native CUDA memory allocation method using versions of the cudaMalloc function. In lines 24 and 25 we use cudaMallocHost to allocate two host buffers, a and b, in host pinned memory. Notice that like most CUDA functions we have to allocate the pointer variables first and then initialize by passing them an argument to a CUDA function. Line 26: This is a standard memory allocation in device memory using the cudaMalloc function. Notice that unlike the C++ malloc-like functions, in CUDA the array size is *specified in bytes* not as the dimension of required array.
- Line 27: To manage asynchronous memory transfers we need to create a CUDA event copydone. As explained in detail in the next chapter, work submitted to the GPU can be sent to different streams which operate asynchronously with each other. Items of work in a single stream are run one at a time in the order they were submitted. A default stream (the null stream or 0) is used in the case where no stream is explicitly mentioned. CUDA events can be placed in streams between other pieces of work and when queried return either cudaErrorNotReady if the previous work is not yet complete or cudaSuccess if the previous work is complete. The CUDA event copydone, as its name implies, will be used to wait for the completion of the asynchronous memory transfers, analogously to the use of cudaDeviceSynchronize() to wait for kernel completion.
- Lines 28–32: These are the same as lines 27–31 of Example 6.4; they initialize a timer and set up the generator.
- Lines 33–34: Generate the first block of random numbers and then copy them to the host buffer a. In line 35 we use the standard cudaMemcpy function which is not asynchronous but blocks the host until the transfer is complete.
- Lines 35–43: This is the main loop where blocks of random numbers are generated and processed.
  - Line 36: Starts the generation of the next block of random numbers on the GPU.
  - Line 37: Starts the asynchronous copy of the new block of random numbers to the buffer b. It is important to know that the work in both this line and the previous line are sent to the default CUDA stream so that the cudaMemcpyAsync will wait for the completion of the curandGenerateUniform in line 36 before starting.
  - Line 38: Places our CUDA event in the default stream here. The stream is specified by the second argument.
  - Line 39: Immediately query the copydone event. It is not logically necessary to query the event at this point but at the time of writing this the statement is needed here, at least with the Windows WDDM driver.
  - Line 40: Here we call sum_part with the random numbers contained in buffer a. This calculation proceeds in parallel with the downloading of a new set of random numbers into buffer b. In this example the call to sum_part requires more time to execute (about 1 ms) than the download operation (about 0.7 ms) so the cost of random number generation on the GPU and downloading to the host is entirely hidden.
  - Line 41: Here we swap the pointers a and b; this implements ping-pong buffer use while keeping the rest of the code simple. This kind of pointer trickery must be used with care as it is easy to get confused. In the present program a and b are not used again until the memory they point to is freed in line 50. At that point it does not matter if the current a points to the original b and vice versa. But you need to always think about such details with care when you reassign pointers.
  - Line 42: Wait until the copydone event reports success. At that point, a will point to a complete and freshly loaded block of new random numbers, ready for the next pass through the for loop.

- Lines 44–48: Print results, these lines are the same as the corresponding lines in Example 6.4.
- Lines 50–51: Free GPU resources. Since we are not using thrust containers, we have to explicitly free memory allocations on both the host and device.

The results from Example 6.6 are good in that we have removed nearly all the overhead of random number generation for the host and our code is now about 70 times faster than the original. If we want to go faster we need to also move the host calculations to the GPU; for this we need the cuRAND Device API.

6.2.2 The cuRAND Device API

The cuRAND Device API permits the programmer to write Monte Carlo applications where much of the calculation is done on the GPU using user written kernels in the same way as the other applications in this book. The host still determines which type of RNG and its initial seed to use, but everything else is done on the GPU. In particular, each thread in a kernel has its own instance of an RNG of the chosen type, and these RNGs can persist between kernel launches. In a typical case a program will first launch a simple kernel in which each thread initialises its RNG and stores the internal state of that RNG in persistent device memory. In subsequent kernels, threads then read back these states to restore their RNGs to the state they were in at the end of the previous kernel, generate more numbers as necessary and then resave the modified state at the end of the kernel.

Note that the sequence produced by any pseudo random number generator will eventually repeat because the seed must eventually return to one of its previously used values. For example, a generator using only 32-bit values could only ever produce a sequence of length 2^{32}. GPU-based applications have the potential to consume vast quantities of random numbers so such a generator would be useless; the sequence is likely to repeat within the first second of a kernel launch. Generators for GPU code must not only produce sequences with very long repeats but also generate different *uncorrelated* sequences for thousands of different threads. Similar considerations apply to HPC applications running on many processors.

The Device API provides a number of generators with different properties, for full details you should consult the NVIDIA cuRAND Library Programming Guide which is included in the CUDA SDK documentation set. The following brief descriptions are from that document.

1. The XORWOW generator, which is a member of the xor-shift family of PRNGs, is very fast; it is a good first choice for most problems. It has a repetition period of over 2^{190} and subsequences have length 2^{67}. These two numbers are very large it is most unlikely that any current application will need more. For example, in Example 6.7 the RTX 2070 card processes nearly 2^{39} random numbers per second; this is fast, but it would still take about eight years to use one subsequence of 2^{67} random numbers, let alone 2^{190}! In CUDA code this generator has type `curandStateXORWOW` which is also aliased to `curandState`.[4] The latter is intended for the cuRAND default generator and so that might change in the future. This is also the default generator used by the host API.

2. The `MRG32k3a` generator which is a member of the Combined Multiple Recursive family of PNRGs. It also has a repetition period greater than 2^{190} and subsequence length of 2^{67}; its generator state is `curandStateMRG32k3a`. This generator produces up to $\sim 4.9 \times 10^9$ samples per second using an RTX 2070 GPU.

3. The MTGP32 generator is an adaptation of code developed at Hiroshima University. In this algorithm, samples are generated for multiple sequences, each sequence based on a set of computed parameters. cuRAND uses the 200 parameter sets that have been pre-generated for the 32-bit generator with period 2^{11214}. There is one state structure for each parameter set (sequence), and the algorithm allows thread-safe generation and state update for up to 256 concurrent threads (within a single block) for each of the 200 sequences.

4. The Philox4x32_10 generator is a member of the Philox family, which is one of the three non-cryptographic Counter Based Random Number Generators presented on the SC11 conference by D E Shaw Research. This generator has a repeat of 2^{128} and sub-sequences have a length of 2^{64}. This generator is differentiated from the other two in that it is particularly efficient at generating sets of 4 numbers in each call; thus it is a good choice when used with distributions returning `float4`, `int4` or `double2` results. Its generator state is named `curandStatePhilox4_32_10`. This generator can produce up to ~3.8×10^{10} samples per second when using its `float4` mode.

For most applications we recommend using the XORWOW generator which appears to be faster and simpler to use than any of the others. This is the generator we use in our examples; experts might favour a different generator for a specific problem but such advanced considerations are beyond the scope of this book.

In use for GPU code the XORWOW generator must first be initialised by each thread calling the cuRAND device function `curand_init`. This function takes four arguments as follows:

1. An `unsigned long int` containing the seed with which initialise the chosen RNG.
2. An `unsigned long int` containing the subsequence for this thread within the RNG.
3. An `unsigned long int` containing the offset within the sequence for the first number.
4. A pointer to a `struct` in global memory used to store the current state of the RNG.

In practice we can either use the same seed and different subsequences for all threads or we can use different seeds and the same subsequence for each thread. Note the subsequences have length of 2^{67} and there are up to 2^{133} possible subsequences, which should be more than enough. Typical calls are shown in the box.

```
int id = threadIdx.x + blockIdx.x*blockDim.x;
```
Either same seed and different subsequences, slow but statistically best.
```
(a)  curand_init(seed,id,0,&states[id]);
```
Or different seeds and same subsequence, fast but small chance of correlations.
```
(b)  curand_init(seed+id,0,0,&states[id]);
```

In case (a) where we use the same seed and hence the same generator of all threads, each thread uses a separate subsequence. The subsequences are determined by the second argument which is set to `id`, the sequential rank of each thread in the thread grid. This gives random numbers with the best statistical properties but generating the initial state for all subsequences is slow, depending linearly on the number of threads. Method (a) is about 60 times slower than method (b). In Example 6.7 initialisation for 2^{23} threads is required and takes 184 ms for method (a) but only 2.9 ms for method (b). These numbers were measured using an RTX 2070 card with CUDA SDK version 11.4, the performance of method (a) was significantly worse in earlier SDK releases.

Example 6.7 `piG` kernel for calculation of π using cuRand Device API

```
01  #include "cx.h"
02  #include "cxtimers.h"
03  #include "curand_kernel.h"
04  #include <random>

05  template <typename S> __global__ void
               init_generator(long long seed,S *states)
06  {
07    int id = threadIdx.x + blockIdx.x*blockDim.x;
08    curand_init(seed+id, 0, 0, &states[id]); // faster
      // slower but statistically better
09    // curand_init(seed, id, 0, &states[id]);
10  }

11  template <typename S> __global__ void
               piG(float *tsum, S *states, int points)
12  {
13    int id = threadIdx.x + blockIdx.x*blockDim.x;
14    S state = states[id];
15    float sum = 0.0f;
16    for(int i = 0; i < points; i++) {
17      float x = curand_uniform(&state);
18      float y = curand_uniform(&state);
19      if(x*x + y*y < 1.0f) sum++; // inside?
20    }
21    tsum[id] += sum;
22    states[id] = state;
23  }

30  int main(int argc,char *argv[])
31  {
32    std::random_device rd;
33    int shift =      (argc >1) ? atoi(argv[1])  : 18;
34    long long seed = (argc >2) ? atoll(argv[2]) : rd();
35    int blocks =     (argc >3) ? atoi(argv[3])  : 2048;
36    int threads =    (argc >4) ? atoi(argv[4])  : 1024;

37    long long ntot = (long long)1 << shift;
```

```
38    int size = threads*blocks;
39    int nthread = (ntot+size-1)/size;
40    ntot = (long long)nthread*size;

41    thrust::device_vector<float> tsum(size);  // thread sums
      // generator states
42    thrust::device_vector <curandState> state(size);
43    cx::timer tim;   // start clock
44    init_generator<<<blocks,threads>>>
                      (seed,state.data().get());
45    piG<<<blocks,threads>>>(tsum.data().get(),
                      state.data().get(), nthread);
46    double sum_inside =
              thrust::reduce(tsum.begin(), tsum.end());
47    double t1 = tim.lap_ms(); // record time
48    double pi = 4.0*sum_inside/(double)ntot;
49    double frac_error = 1000000.0*
          (pi - cx::pi<double>)/cx::pi<double>; // ppm
50    printf("pi = %10.8f err %.3f, ntot %lld, time %.3f
                      ms\n", pi, frac_error, ntot, t1);
51    return 0;
52  }


D:\ >piG.exe 40 123456 8192 1024
pi = 3.14159441 err 0.559, ntot 1099511627776, time 4507.684 ms
```

Description of Example 6.7

- Lines 1–4: These are the standard headers; note line 3 where we include the required header for the cuRAND device API.
- Lines 5–10: Here is the kernel `init_generator` which is used to initialise separate generators for each thread.
  - Line 5: The kernel arguments are the initial base seed which is the same for all threads and can be set by the user and an array `states` in device global memory where each thread stores the final state of its generator.
  - Line 7: Set `id` to the rank of the current thread in thread-grid.
  - Line 8: Call `curand_init` to initialise the default random number generator. In all versions of cuRAND to date that is the XORWOW generator and here we initialise it using the faster method (b) with a different seed for each thread. We use `seed+id` as the simplest way to provide unique seed values for each thread. In a demanding application, a better way of getting more random bit patterns might be desirable. For example, multiplying by large prime numbers or using `id` as an index to a precalculated table. Correlation between early random numbers is the most likely problem, so flushing the first 1000 or so would be another possibility (and still much faster than method (a). Note the generator's initial state is stored in the fourth argument `state[id]`.
  - Line 9: This is the initialisation for alternative method (a); it is commented out here.

- Lines 11–23: This is the kernel function piG, which is the heart of our program and is where all the time is spent.
  - Line 11: The first and third arguments are similar to the host version. The first argument tsum is a device array used to hold the partial sums accumulated by each thread. The second input argument, states, contains the RNG state for each thread as set by the previous call to init_generator. The final argument points is the number of points to be generated by each thread. Note that as the number of hits found is stored in the float array tsum the value of points should not exceed about 2^{25} otherwise there is a danger of losing hits. If this were to be a problem then tsum could be promoted to a double without incurring any significant time penalty because it is only used once at the end of the kernel to store final results. We use a floating point rather than a long integer type for tsum in order to facilitate a subsequent thrust reduce operation.

    Note also that this is a templated function where the template parameter S is the type of random number generator being used. Thus, this function does not need changing if a different cuRAND generator is used. Different generators need significantly different methods of initialisation so we cannot simply template the initialisation function curand_init, a different function would be needed to try a different generator.
  - Line 13: Set id to the current thread's rank in the thread-grid.
  - Line 14: This copies the RNG state in states[id] to a local variable state. Copying from device memory to a local variable held in a register is always worthwhile in cases like this where state is updated in an inner loop.
  - Lines 15–20: This is the main loop which for points passes generates points in the unit square and tests if they are also inside the required circle. These lines correspond exactly to the inner loop in lines 17–21 of Example 6.1. The outer loop of that example has been replaced here by parallel execution of multiple threads.
  - Line 21: The final sum for the current thread is stored in tsum[id] in device global memory. A reduction operation on this array will be performed as a subsquent step.
  - Line 22: The final state of the current thread's generator is saved in states[id]. This is not strictly necessary for this example as no further use will be made of the generators. However, it is an essential step in more complicated programs where multiple kernels use the generators. We recommend you always include a final state save in your cuRAND GPU code.
- Lines 30–52: This is the host code, which sets up the calculation using user supplied values, runs the two kernels and computes and prints the final result.
- Lines 32–36: Set the configuration parameters for the calculation using optional user input. The number of points to be generated is entered by the user as shift which is used as a power of 2. The variable seed is the base seed used to initialise the RNGs. Note our use of atoll[argv(2)] which allows the user to enter long long values if desired. The variables threads and blocks are the usual CUDA 1D thread block and grid sizes.
- Line 37: The variable ntot is the total number of points to be generated and is the power of 2 determined by shift.
- Lines 39–40: The value of ntot is rounded up to be an exact multiple of size, that is, the total number of threads in the thread-grid and points, the number of points to be generated by each thread.
- Lines 41–42: These lines create two thrust device arrays of dimension size. The first array tsum will store the number of hits inside the circle found by each thread and the second array state will hold the RNG state for each thread. We implicitly rely on tsum being initialised to zero by thrust in our kernels. Note that the array state is of type curandState which implies that the default XORWOW generator is to be used.

- Lines 43–47: This timed section is where the kernels are called to perform the entire calculation; it is equivalent to the timed loops in the previous host code examples.
  - Line 44: This calls the kernel `init_generator` to initialize the generators. This kernel is a template function which determines which generator to use from the type of its second input argument `state`.
  - Line 45: Call the `sum_part` kernel which does all the work of the calculation. After the call, the number of points found inside the circle for each thread is stored in the elements of the device array `tsum`.
  - Line 46: The elements of the array `tsum` are added together using a host call to `thrust::reduce`, which runs on the GPU using data stored in device memory, and then returns the final sum to host. This call is blocking on the host so there is no need for a final `cudaDeviceSynchronize`.

  Notice the entire calculation is done on the GPU; only the final sum needs to be copied to the host as a 4-byte float.

- Lines 48–50: Calculate and print π and the fractional error in parts per million.

The thread block and grid-block sizes of `1024` and `8192` used in this example were manually optimised for the RTX 2070. We think the final performance is very impressive; moving the entire calculation to the GPU has given a further speed-up of over 280. The speed-up compared to our baseline Example 6.1 of about 18,000. Although we have used a trivial integration for this example, the fact that we can process 10^{12} points in about 4 seconds is interesting for less trivial Monte Carlo integrations. In Chapter 8 we give a more substantial example involving simulating the detection efficiency of a Positron Emission Tomography (PET) scanner.

The timing results for Examples 6.1–6.7 are summarised in Table 6.1.

6.3 Generating Other Distributions

We often need non-uniform random number distributions, for example, random numbers from a Poisson or normal distribution. Both C++ and CUDA provide such distribution functions for a few standard cases as shown in Table 6.2. These distributions are derived from the same long integer generators as used in the previous examples.

An example illustrating the use of the cuRAND Poisson RNG can be found in the NVIDIA cuRAND Library Programming Guide. Other examples can also be found in the CUDA SDK.

In fact there is a method of generating any desired distribution from a uniform floating point distribution using the inverse transform method discussed next.

6.3.1 The Inverse Transform Method

In addition to the library functions one can in principle generate a probability distribution for any non-negative function $f(x)$ in some interval, for example, $[a, b]$. We start by defining the associated normalised cumulative distribution function $F(x)$ by:

$$F(x) = \int_a^x f(x')\,dx' \Big/ \int_a^b f(x')\,dx'. \tag{6.1}$$

If u is a random number from a uniform distribution in $[0, 1]$ then $F^{-1}(u)$ is actually a random number distributed like $f(x)$. $F^{-1}(x)$ is the inverse of $F(x)$.

Table 6.1 *Times required for random number generators using an RTX 2070 GPU*

Calculation Method	Time for 10^9 points (ms)	Random Number pairs per sec	Speed-up with respect to previous code	Speed-up with respect to original host code
Host code using the C++11 uniform_ real_ distibution	74229	2.69×10^7	1	1
Host code using the C++11 uniform_ int_ distibution	10275	1.95×10^8	7.2	7.2
Host code using the C++11 uniform_ int_ distibution and OMP 4 threads	2464	8.12×10^8	4.2	30.1
Host code using the cuRAND Host API for RNG on GPU	2558	7.82×10^8	(0.96)	29.0
Host code using the cuRAND Host API for RNG on GPU and using pinned Host memory buffer	1737	1.15×10^9	1.4	42.7
Host code using the cuRAND Host API for RNG on GPU and using pinned Host memory buffer with cudaMemcpyAsyc	1163	1.72×10^9	1.5	63.8
cuRAND Device API using XORWOW generator	4.100	4.87×10^{11}	283	18106

Table 6.2 *Random number distribution functions in C++ and CUDA*

Name	Type	Details
C++ Random Number Distributions		
Poisson	int	$P(i|\mu) = \mu^i e^{-\mu}/i!$
Binomial	int	$P(i|n,p) = \frac{n!}{i!(n-i)!} p^i (1-p)^{n-i}$
Normal	float/double	$P(x|\mu,\sigma) = e^{-(x-\mu)^2/2\sigma^2}/\sigma\sqrt{2\pi}$
Log-normal	float/double	$P(x|\mu,\sigma) = e^{-(\ln x - \mu)^2/2\sigma^2}/\sigma x\sqrt{2\pi}$
Exponential	float/double	$P(x|\lambda) = \lambda e^{-\lambda x}$
CUDA Random Number Distributions		
Poisson	int	$P(i|\mu) = \mu^i e^{-\mu}/i!$
Standard Normal	float/double	$P(x) = e^{-x^2/2}/\sqrt{2\pi}$
Log-normal	float/double	$P(x|\mu,\sigma) = e^{-(\ln x - \mu)^2/2\sigma^2}/\sigma x\sqrt{2\pi}$

An important simple case is the function $f(x) = x$:

$$F(x) = \int_a^x x'\, dx' / \int_a^b x'\, dx' = (x^2 - a^2)/(b^2 - a^2), \tag{6.2}$$

which can easily be solved for x to find the inverse function:

$$F^{-1}(u) = \left[u\left(b^2 - a^2\right) + a^2 \right]^{1/2}. \tag{6.3}$$

We shall need this formula later in Chapter 8, but here it is worth noting that in the special case a = 0 the right-hand side of Eq. 6.3 becomes $bu^{1/2}$. This is useful for directly generating points inside a circle because the density of points at a distance r from the centre of the circle is proportional to r and not constant as would be the case for points inside a square. Thus to generate a point uniformly distributed inside a circle of radius R, use polar coordinates and set the radius to $r = Ru_1^{1/2}$ and the polar angle to $\phi = 2\pi u_2$ where u_1 and u_2 are random numbers taken from a standard uniform distribution. This is a much more GPU friendly method than the common alternative of generating Cartesian coordinates inside a square of side R and rejecting those samples that are not also inside the circle. This is because in the first case all threads get valid points whereas in the second case some threads get invalid points and have to wait while other threads in the same warp process their valid points.

In many cases, notably the Gaussian distribution, it is not possible to find an analytic form for the inverse function; in these cases a numerical solution in the form of a lookup table can be used. On GPUs such lookup tables could be accessed using texture fetches for extra speed. The lookup table itself is just the set of $\{x_0, x, , x_2, \ldots, x_n\}$ such that $F(x_i) = i/n$, where the equations are solved numerically. This approach might also be useful in cases where an analytic expression for the inverse function does exist but is slow to calculate.

6.4 Ising Model

The final example in this chapter is another simple but more interesting simulation – the Ising model. This model is well known in solid state physics and concerns the evolution of spin one-half particles arranged on an equally spaced grid in any number of dimensions. Here we will discuss 3D grids which are appropriate for solids. At each grid point we place an object of spin S where S can be ± 1. Each spin is acted on by its neighbours such that the parallel spins have lower energy than antiparallel spins and the resulting energy for a spin grid position *(x ,y ,z)* can then be taken to be:

$$E = J\left(S_{x-1,y,z} + S_{x+1,y,z} + S_{x,y-1,z} + S_{x,y+1,z} + S_{x,y,z-1} + S_{x,y,z+1}\right) S_{x,y,z}. \tag{6.4}$$

Eq. 6.4 is the simplest possible Ising model where we only consider interactions between nearest neighbours. The constant J measures the strength of the spin-spin interactions and in our simulation we set it to one. Notice that E will be positive if most of the neighbouring spins are parallel to $S_{x,y,z}$ and negative if they are mostly antiparallel. In the simulation we test a single arbitrary spin and flip it according to the criteria shown in the box.

Monte Carlo Simulation of Ising Model

Flip spin at (x,y,z) if

Either $E < 0$

Or $\quad e^{-E/T} > R$

where R is a random number sampled from a uniform distribution in [0,1] and T is temperature.

The criteria in the box correctly simulate the thermodynamics of a physical system at an absolute temperature proportional to T. The most interesting feature of the Ising model is that it has a phase transition at about $T_c = 4.5115$ in the system of units used here. For temperatures below T_c large scale domains of parallel spins form; above T_c they do not. Interested readers can find more detail on solid state physics in standard texts or online.

An Ising model simulation demands that any given spin be updated independently of other spins. Consider a 2D Ising model on a square grid. If we colour the spin sites alternately white and black like a chessboard then the nearest neighbours of the white squares are all black squares and vice versa. Thus, we can implement a parallel simulation by updating all the white sites in parallel and then in a separate step updating all the black sites. This idea can easily be extended to 3D models provided that alternate slices in z have opposite colours in each x-y position. The advantage of this approach is that we can update spins in place reducing the memory needed for the simulation.

Our code to simulate a 3D Ising model is shown in Example 6.8. We use our standard approach to 3D grids and use one thread per x-y position and a loop over z values. The array of spins is implemented using type `char` which can hold values in the range [−128,127]. We actually only need two values, namely 1 and −1 so a single bit would do, but unless we need a very large grid, using `char` is better because it leads to much simpler code. The kernels are implemented as template functions but only type `char` is used.

The code is shown below and described in Examples 6.8, 6.9 and 6.10 below. This example has two features; firstly it shows an implementation of a 3D Ising model in straightforward kernel code. That code is quite similar to the image processing stencils discussed in previous chapters. The performance is fast but no doubt tricks like vector loading could squeeze a bit more performance from the kernels. The second shows how OpenCV can be used to create a simple interactive program that allows you to visualise the progress of the spin flipping in the model and see the responses to changes in the model temperature in real time.

Description of Example 6.8

- Lines 1–5: Include statements required to use cuRAND in kernel code.
- Lines 7–10: Include statements required to use OpenCV in host code.
- Lines 14–27: The kernel `setup_randstates` is called to initialise the random number generator used by each thread. The input parameters are the array `state`, which holds the current generator state for each thread, and the number of threads in the x and y directions. Note that while `ny` is the dimension of the spin array in the y-direction, `nx` is only half the dimension of the spin array in the x-direction. The kernel performs the following 2 functions:
  ○ Line 20: Initialise a separate generator for each thread using the fast method (b).
  ○ Lines 24–26: For each thread, flush the first 100 numbers produced by the generator and then store in resulting state in the device array `state`. This process reduces the chances of correlations between generators and is still much faster than using method (a).
- Lines 40–56: The kernel `init_spins`, which randomly initialises the spins in the 3D device array `spin` to either +1 or −1. The input arguments are the generator states in `state`, the spin array `spin` and the dimensions of the spin array. Note that although the type of the spin array is a template parameter, the code will only work for signed integer types. Type `char` is obviously the

best choice to economise on memory for large spin systems. Also note that to implement the chess
board update scheme the actual dimensions of the spin array are 2nx × ny × ny. In this kernel
and the flip_spin kernel the input parameter nx refers to the number of spins in the x-direction
that are updated on a single call. The variable nx2 is used for array addressing purposes.

∘ Line 45: Set id to the current threads position in the x-y plane of the spin array.
∘ Line 46: Set nx2 to 2 × nx as explained above.
∘ Line 47: Define an idx lambda function to address the array spin; note we use nx2 for the
  x dimension.
∘ Lines 49–54: A loop over all z values where the current thread initialises elements of spin for its
  value of x and y and all values of z. This is also done for x+nx and y to allow for the fact that nx
  is only half the x dimension. Here the probabilities of spin up and down are equal and random.
  Other initialisation schemes are possible here, for example, setting a block of spins to the same
  value to study melting at edges.

Example 6.8 3D Ising model setup_randstates and init_spins kernels

```
01  #include "cx.h"
02  #include "cxtimers.h"
03  #include "cxbinio.h"
04  #include <curand_kernel.h>
05  #include <random>

07  #include "Windows.h"
08  #include "opencv2/core/core.hpp"
09  #include "opencv2/highgui/highgui.hpp"
10  using namespace cv;

12  // NB because of 2-pass checkerboard update pattern
13  // the nx parameter in the GPU code is NX/2 where NX
    // is x dimension of volume
14  __global__ void setup_randstates
        (r_Ptr<curandState> state,cint nx,cint ny,cllong seed)
15  {
16    int x = threadIdx.x + blockIdx.x*blockDim.x;
17    int y = threadIdx.y + blockIdx.y*blockDim.y;
18    if(x >= nx || y >= ny) return;
19    int id = nx*y+x;
20    curand_init(seed+id,0,0,&state[id]);
21
22    // flush values to remove any early correlations
23    curandState myState = state[id];
24    float sum = 0.0f;
25    for(int k=0;k<100;k++) sum += curand_uniform(&myState);
26    state[id] = myState;
27  }
```

```
40   template <typename T> __global__ void
        init_spins(r_Ptr<curandState> state, r_Ptr<T> spin,
                   cint nx, cint ny, cint nz)
41   {
42     int x = threadIdx.x + blockIdx.x*blockDim.x;
43     int y = threadIdx.y + blockIdx.y*blockDim.y;
44     if(x >= nx || y >= ny) return;

45     int id = nx*y+x;
46     int nx2 = 2*nx;   // actual x-dimension NX of volume
47     auto idx = [&nx2,&ny,&nz](int z,int y,int x)
                           { return (ny*z+y)*nx2+x; };

48     curandState myState = state[id];
49     for(int z=0; z<nz; z++){  // random initial states
50       if(curand_uniform(&myState) <= 0.5f)
                   spin[idx(z,y,x)] = 1;
51       else
                   spin[idx(z,y,x)] = -1;
52       if(curand_uniform(&myState) <= 0.5f)
                   spin[idx(z,y,x+nx)] = 1;
53       else
                   spin[idx(z,y,x+nx)] = -1;
54     }
55     state[id] = myState;
56   }
```

Example 6.9 3D Ising 2D model flip_spins kernel

```
60   template <typename T> __global__ void
        flip_spins(r_Ptr<curandState> state,r_Ptr<T> spin,
        cint nx, cint ny, cint nz,cfloat temp, cint colour)
61   {
       // NB thread x here not spin x
62     int xt = threadIdx.x + blockIdx.x*blockDim.x;
63     int y = threadIdx.y + blockIdx.y*blockDim.y;
64     if(xt >= nx || y >= ny) return;

65     int id = nx*y+xt;
66     int nx2 = 2*nx;       // NB nx2 is volume x dimension
67     auto idx = [&nx2,&ny,&nz](int z,int y,int x)
                           { return (ny*z+y)*nx2+x; };
68     // lambda functions for cyclic boundary conditions
69     auto cyadd = [](int a,int bound)
                   { return a < bound-1 ? a+1 : 0; };
```

```
70    auto cysub = [](int a,int bound)
                 { return a > 0 ? a-1 : bound-1; };

71    curandState myState = state[id];

72    int yl=  cysub(y,ny);    // l low
73    int yh = cyadd(y,ny);    // h high
74    for(int z = 0; z < nz; z++){
75      int zl = cysub(z,nz);
76      int zh = cyadd(z,nz);
        // In our 3D chess board voxel (0,0,0) is white
77      int x = 2*xt+(y+z+colour)%2;
78      int xl = cysub(x,nx2);
79      int xh = cyadd(x,nx2);

80      float sum = spin[idx(z,y,xl)] + spin[idx(z,y,xh)] +
                    spin[idx(z,yl,x)] +
                    spin[idx(z,yh,x)] + spin[idx(zl,y,x)] +
                    spin[idx(zh,y,x)];

81      float energy = 2.0f*sum*(float)spin[idx(z,y,x)];
82      if(energy <= 0.0f ||
          expf(-energy/temp) >= curand_uniform(&myState)) {
83              spin[idx(z,y,x)] = -spin[idx(z,y,x)];
84      }
85    }
86    state[id] = myState;
87  }
```

Description of Example 6.9

- Lines 60–87: This is the kernel `flip_spin` which implements the Ising model. A chessboard approach is used and either white squares or black squares are updated using the nearest neighbours of opposite colour. The colour updated depends on the value of the last input argument `colour`. The other arguments are the random number states, the spin array and its dimensions and the Ising temperature in the variable `temp`. Note that nx is half of the x-dimension of the spin array.
  - Lines 62–64: xt and y are set to index a single colour in a slice of the spin-array.
  - Line 67: Declare a lambda index function `idx` to index the spin-array; note the use of `nx2` for the x dimension.
  - Lines 69–70: Two additional lambda functions for cyclic addition or subtraction by 1 are defined here.
  - Lines 72–73: Here the y-indices for the nearest neighbours are found using cyclic arithmetic. These do not depend on the slice index z.
  - Lines 74–85: This is the loop over slices in z where we do all the work; note that for our 3D chessboard the positions of white and black squares will flip depending on whether z is even or odd.

- Lines 75–79: In line 77 we find the x coordinate for the current thread depending on its values of y, z and `colour`. The other lines determine its nearest neighbours in the x and z directions.
- Line 80: Here we simply add the spins of the six nearest neighbours.
- Lines 81–83: Here we implement the thermodynamic-based spin flipping of the Ising model.

The main routine is shown in Example 6.10 and shows the use of OpenCV to implement a simple interactive visualisation of the model.

Example 6.10 3D Ising model main routine

```
90   int main(int argc,char *argv[])
91   {
92     std::random_device rd;    // many parameters here
93     int nx = (argc >1) ? atoi(argv[1]) : 256;   // image nx
94     int ny = (argc >2) ? atoi(argv[2]) : nx;   // image ny
95     int nz = (argc >3) ? atoi(argv[3]) : nx;   // image nz
96     llong seed = (argc >4) ? atoll(argv[4]) : rd(); // seed
97     seed = (seed > 0) ? seed : rd(); // random seed if 0
                         ;// Ising temperature
98     double temp  = (argc >5)  ? atof(argv[5]) : 4.4
                         // Ising iterations
99     int steps    = (argc >6)  ? atoi(argv[6]) : 100;
                         // save result
100    int   dosave =   (argc >7) ? atoi(argv[7]) : 1;
101    uint threadx = (argc >8)  ? atoi(argv[8]) : 32;
102    uint thready = (argc >9)  ? atoi(argv[9]) : 8;
                         // view progress ?
103    uint view    = (argc >10)  ? atoi(argv[10]) : 0;
                         // ms delay per frame if viewing
104    uint wait    = (argc >11)  ? atoi(argv[11]) : 0;

105    if(nx%2==1)   nx += 1; // force nx even
106    int nxby2   = nx/2;    // index for checkerboard
107    int volsize = nx*ny*nz;
108    int slice   = nx*ny;

109    double tc = 4.5115;   // critical temperature
110    double tstep = 0.2;   // temperature step for +/- key

111    // define thread blocks
112    dim3 threads ={threadx,thready,1};
113    dim3 blocks ={(nxby2+threads.x-1)/threads.x,
                      (ny+threads.y-1)/threads.y,1};
114    int statesize = blocks.x*blocks.y*blocks.z*
                       threads.x*threads.y*threads.z;
```

```
115    thrustDvec<char> dspin(volsize);  // dev  3D spins
116    thrustHvec<char> hspin(volsize);  // host 3D spins
117    thrustDvec<char> dslice(slice);   // x-y slice of
118    thrustHvec<char> hslice(slice);   // spin array

119    // openCV image
120    Mat view_image(ny,nx,CV_8UC1,Scalar(0));
121    if(view) namedWindow("Spins",WINDOW_NORMAL |
                  WINDOW_KEEPRATIO | WINDOW_GUI_EXPANDED);

122    // per thread buffer for random generator state
123    curandState *dstates;
124    cx::ok( cudaMalloc((void **)&dstates,
                  statesize*sizeof(curandState)) );

125    cx::timer tim;
126    setup_randstates<<<blocks,threads>>>
                  (dstates,nxby2,ny,seed);
127    cudaDeviceSynchronize();
128    double state_time = tim.lap_ms()
129    init_spins<char><<<blocks,threads>>>
                  (dstates, dspin.data().get(), nxby2, ny, nz);
130    cudaDeviceSynchronize();
131    double init_time = tim.lap_ms();

132    for(int k = 0; k<steps; k++){
          // white squares
133      flip_spins<char><<<blocks,threads>>>(dstates,
              dspin.data().get(), nxby2, ny, nz, temp, 0);
          // black squares
134      flip_spins<char><<<blocks,threads>>>(dstates,
              dspin.data().get(), nxby2, ny,nz, temp, 1);

135      if(view > 0 && (k%view==0 || k==steps-1)){
            // use thrust to copy one x-y slice to host
136        thrust::copy(dspin.begin()+slice*nz/2,
              dspin.begin()+(slice+slice*nz/2), hslice.begin());
137        for(int i=0;i<slice;i++) // copy to openCV
                  view_image.data[i] = hslice[i];
138        imshow("Spins", view_image);
139        char key = (waitKey(wait) & 0xFF); // mini event loop
140        if(key == ESC) break;
141        else if(key =='s'){
142          char name[256];
143          sprintf(name,"ising_%d_%.3f.png",k,temp);
144          imwrite(name, view_image);
145        }
146        else if(key== '+'){temp += tstep;
                  printf("temp %.3f\n",temp);}
```

```
147        else if(key== '-'){temp = std::max(0.0,temp-tstep);
                printf("temp %.3f\n",temp);}
148        else if(key== 'c'){temp = tc;
                printf("temp %.3f\n",temp);}
149    }     // end mini event loop
150  }       // end spin update loop

151    cudaDeviceSynchronize();
152    double flip_time = tim.lap_ms();
153    printf("timing setup %.3f ms, init %.3f ms,
          fliping %.3 fms\n", state_time,init_time,flip_time);
154    if(dosave > 0){
155      hspin = dspin;
156      cx::write_raw<char>("ising.raw",hspin.data(),volsize);
157    }

158    std::atexit( []{cudaDeviceReset();} ); // safe reset
159    return 0;
160  }

D:\ >ising.exe 512 512 512 123456   3.5115 1000   1 32 8
timing - setup 0.163 ms, init 0.713 ms, fliping 3422.359 ms
```

Description of Example 6.10

- Lines 92–104: Here we set a large number of optional parameters which are as follows.
  - nx, ny and nz: The dimensions of the spin-array. These should be even numbers.
  - seed: The initial seed for the cuRAND random number generator. Note a value of zero specifies that truly random seed will be chosen.
  - temp: This is the temperature in the Ising model. The critical temperature is known to be 4.5115 for the system of units used here.
  - steps: The number of update cycles required. This can be set to a very large number if the interactive display is being used.
  - dosave: The final volume will be written to disk if this flag is non-zero.
  - threadx and thready: The 2D thread block dimension for the flip_spins kernel launches.
  - view: If this is set to a value greater than zero, a window will be opened showing the state of the central z slice of the spin array. The window will be updated each time view update cycles are completed. Note updating the window is relatively time consuming so set view to a small number (1–10) if you want to inspect the early stages of the evolution or a large number (try 100) if you want to inspect asymptotic behaviour.
  - wait: This is the pause in ms to wait for user input on the current frame. If set to a large value (say 5000) you can press any key on the keyboard to move to the next frame. If set to a low value (say 50) you effectively see a real-time movie.
- Lines 105–108: Adjust the x-dimension nx to be an even number and set nxby2 to be half of nx. The variable nxby2 is used as the number of black or white squares along the x-axis in some kernel calls.

- Line 109; Set `tc` to be the critical temperature of this 3D Ising model.
- Line 110: Set `tstep` to be the temperature step for the interactive "+" and "-" commands.
- Lines 112–113: Set the launch configuration for the main kernels.
- Lines 115–118: Allocate thrust arrays on host and device for the 3D spin array and for a single x-y slice of that array. The latter is used for display purposes.
- Lines 120–121: Create an OpenCV `Mat` object `view_image` to hold a single spin-array slice and, if view is set, create a named display window `Spins`.
- Lines 123–124: Create a device array `dstates` to hold the cuRAND generator states for each thread. Use of the type `curandState` implicitly selects the XORWOW generator. The size of the array `statesize` is equal to the total number of threads in the launch configuration.
- Lines 125–128: Timed block which calls the kernel `setup_randstates` to initialise the generators. The variable `seed` is an argument to the kernel.
- Lines 129–131: Timed block which calls `init_spins` to initialise the device spin-array `dspin`.
- Lines 132–150: This is the loop where the Ising model is implemented and spins are tested and randomly flipped according to the model. The loop is repeated `steps` times. Only the first two lines of the loop are needed to implement the model; the remaining lines implement a simple visualisation of the progress.
  - Lines 133–134: Here we call `flip_spins` twice, once for white squares and once for black squares.
  - Line 135: If the current step through the for loop is to be displayed, the code in lines 136–150 is executed. The user settable variable `view` controls how often this occurs.
  - Line 136: Use thrust to copy a single x-y slice of the 3D array `dspin` to the 2D host array `hslice`.
  - Line 137: Next copy `hslice` to the OpenCV Mat object `view_image`.
  - Line 138: Display the copied slice in the named window `Spins` using the OpenCV function imshow.
  - Line 139: In OpenCV a window filled by a call to `imshow` only becomes visible when followed by a call to `waitKey`. Here the user settable parameter `wait` specifies the time in ms to wait for user input before proceeding. A value of zero indicates an indefinite wait. This function returns on any keystroke and its return value is the code corresponding to the key pressed.
  - Lines 140–148: This is a mini event-loop where different actions are taken in response to different keys. The actions are as follows:
  ESC: (the escape key defined as 127 in `cx.h`). Close window and exit program.
  s: Save the current view to .png file with temperature and step count in name.
  +: Rise temperature.
  -: Lower temperature
  c: Set temperature to critical temperature.
- Lines 151–159: This is the end for the Ising simulation and here we print timing information and optionally save the final spin array to disk then finally exit.

The timing results shown at the end of Example 6.10 correspond to about 4×10^{10} spins processed per second and Nsight Compute reports about 180 GFlops/sec of compute performance. This is a good but not outstanding result for the RTX 2070 GPU. The performance is being held back by memory latency so improvement could be expected if vector loading were used. Performance might also be improved if shared memory were used, although as each spin value is shared by at most seven threads, probably native caching is just as effective. Another optimisation that would improve the locality of memory access is

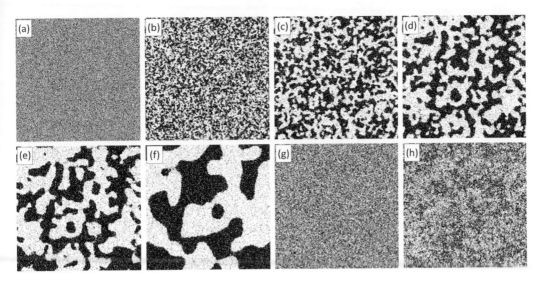

Figure 6.2 3D Ising model results showing 2D x-y slice at central z

the use of separate 3D arrays for the white and black voxels. Nevertheless, the performance from this very straightforward code is fast enough to allow the study and visualisation of large 3D systems at excellent frame rates. Some results from the simulation are shown in Figure 6.2.

The images shown in Figure 6.2 are a central slice from the simulation of a volume with $512 \times 512 \times 512$ spins. In (a) the starting configuration with random spins is shown, (b) shows steady state after 500 iterations at Tc+1, (c) shows the steady state after 100 iterations at Tc. Images (d) to (h) show the evolution of the state at Tc−1 after 5, 20, 50, 100 and 500 iterations. Where Tc is the critical temperature of 4.5115 and +1 spins are shown black and −1 spins are shown white. The states at temperatures Tc and above persist indefinitely with fluctuations but no emerging structure. The states below Tc develop persistent clusters of like spins which grow and merge over time. Thermal "noise" from individual spin flips can be seen on these clusters. This noise increases as we approach Tc from below.

As a final comment on visualisation, the OpenCV implementation shown here is inefficient in that several, logically unnecessary, copies of the image data across the PCI bus are performed. The slice data originally in the GPU array dspin is copied to the host array hspin and then again to another host array in the OpenCV Mat file view_image. Finally, the call to imshow triggers another copy of the data back across the PCI bus to a separate GPU memory buffer maintained by OpenCV. These overheads are not important for our example but might be for more demanding visualisations.

For visualisation, an alternative to OpenCV is the use of the OpenGL which has been well integrated with CUDA from the very first release. The key advantage is that CUDA kernels can operate directly on OpenGL memory buffers. However, the resulting code is quite verbose and opaque; interested readers can find out more in the Chapter 3 of the NVIDIA C++ Programming Guide. The SDK volumeRender example is a good example to study. Interestingly, the most recent versions of OpenCV have introduced GpuMat objects which interact well with thrust.[5] We feel this is probably a better way to go for new projects.

Our next chapter will show you how to speed up calculations by overlapping operations. Then in Chapter 8 we return to random numbers and develop code to simulate a medical imaging system.

Endnotes Chapter 6

1 This is possible on modern PCs using either special hardware which uses thermal noise or some other hardware stochastic process to generate truly randomnumbers. The C++ standard for <random> actually includes the generator, random_device, that uses such a source if available. The random_device generator is quite slow and in practice is best used to seed other RNGs. Actually, true randomness is often a bad idea during program development, because it is impossible to repeat a sequence to check fixes for issues arising from a particular set of generated numbers.

2 This said we have also run this code using the gcc 4.8.4 under the ubuntu 14.04.4 shell in Windows 10. In that case we find the opposite behaviour! The float version runs in about 8.2 seconds and the int version in about 120 seconds.

3 Thread safety is an important consideration when writing multithreaded host code. Many functions might fail if multiple threads access the same instance of the function simultaneously. One solution is to implement a locking and queuing mechanism so that a resource can only be used by one thread at once. However, queueing would defeat the aim of speeding up code by sharing a task across multiple threads. In CUDA code, paradoxically, this is less of an issue as resources potentially accessed simultaneously by multiple threads, such as shared memory, are explicit and tools such as syncthreads() are available to help. Needless to say, CUDA intrinsic functions are thread-safe.

4 A lot of the objects used in cuRand have typedef aliases defined by appending _t to their actual name, for example `curandStateXORWOW_t`. There is a convention used by some programmers that _t indicates a type rather than an object, but it makes no difference to the compiler. The cuRand examples in the NVIDIA SDK mostly follow that convention, but I prefer brevity and omit the _t.

5 See for example https://docs.opencv.org/master/d8/db9/tutorial_gpu_thrust_interop.html.

7

Concurrency Using CUDA Streams and Events

A typical CUDA job involves three steps:

1. Transfer data from the host to the GPU global memory using `cudaMemcpy`, `cudaMemcpyAsync` or thrust.
2. Run one or more kernels to process the data and leave the results in GPU memory.
3. Transfer the results in GPU global memory back to the host using the same functions as 1.

These steps are run sequentially on the GPU, in the order they were sent by the host, and each process must complete before the next process starts. This is of course the only correct behaviour for this simple job, but it leaves the GPU processing cores idle during IO operations and vice versa.

7.1 Concurrent Kernel Execution

In fact, the hardware of modern NVIDIA GPUs is capable of running multiple kernels and data transfers in parallel and this chapter explains how CUDA streams are used to unlock this potential. Typical applications where this is useful are:

A) Repetitive processing on a large volume of data, for example, running an image processing filter on every frame of a long movie. It would be nice if the GPU kernel could be processing frame n while the results from frame n–1 were being sent back to the host and the next frame n+1 was being sent to the GPU. In an ideal case, where each process requires about the same amount of time, the overlapping suggested will give a factor of 3 in performance. This is an example of a 3-step pipeline.

B) Running a memory bound kernel and a processor bound kernel simultaneously on the same GPU. This is particularly helpful for computer centres where the same hardware is used to service multiple users. The hardware of recent GPUs such as Ampere natively supports GPU resource sharing. We do not need to discuss those details here as they do not affect the way individual kernels are written.

We have already discussed how the run code in parallel on the host and GPU, using the fact that kernel launches and calls to `cudaMemcpyAsync` are non-blocking on the host. This allows useful work to be done on the host in parallel with data transfers and kernel execution on the GPU. An example of this, using `cudaMemcpyAsync`, was shown in Example 6.6 of the previous chapter.

The key to running multiple workloads in parallel on the GPU is the use of CUDA *streams*. A CUDA stream is a queue of work (i.e. device IO and kernels) that is to be done

Table 7.1 *CUDA stream and event management functions*

Stream Management	Description
cudaStreamCreate (cudaStream_t *pStream)	Creates a new asynchronous stream with handle copied to pstream.
cudaStreamSynchronize (cudaStream_t stream)	The host waits for all current tasks in stream to complete.
cudaStreamQuery(cudaStream_t stream)	Returns cudaSuccess if all operations on stream are complete; otherwise returns cudaErrorNotReady.
cudaStreamDestroy(cudaStream_t stream)	Deletes a stream object and frees resources.
Event Management	
cudaEventCreate(cudaEvent_t *event)	Creates a new event with handle copied to event.
cudaEventRecord(cudaEvent_t event, cudaStream_t stream)	Places the event in next position of streams's FIFO work queue. The status of the event changes to not completed until the queue completes all work preceding the insertion point. The event status then changes to complete and the completion time is recorded in the event.
cudaEventElapsedTime(float *tdiff, cudaEvent_t start, cudaEvent_t end)	Computes the elapsed time between a pair of completed events. The result is stored in tdiff in units of ms with an accuracy of about 0.5 microsecs.
cudaEventQuery(cudaEvent_t event)	Queries an event's status, returns cudaSuccess if work captured by event is complete otherwise returns cudaErrorNotReady.
cudaEventSynchronize(cudaEvent_t event)	Host waits for the stream in which event has been placed to reach to event.
cudaEventDestroy(cudaEvent_t event)	Deletes the event and frees resources.
Both	
cudaStreamWaitEvent(cudaStream_t stream, cudaEvent_t event, unsigned int flags)	Blocks future work on stream until the event reports completion. N.B. stream does not have to be the CUDA stream in which event is placed. This is useful for interstream synchronisation. Does not block the host.

serially. The host can then send packages of independent work to different GPU streams and the streams can then run them in parallel. In the host code, a CUDA stream is represented by a cudaStream_t object. Kernel launches and calls to cudaMemcpyAsync can include a cudaStream object as an optional final argument to place different pieces of work into different cuda streams. If this argument is omitted or set to zero, then the so-called *default stream* is used. Most of the previous examples in the book have in fact implicitly used this default stream. CUDA streams are created and managed by the host and the most important functions are shown in Table 7.1.

For each stream, the CUDA API creates a separate queue of work, the items in a particular queue are completed in FIFO order and their execution does not overlap. In contrast operations in different queues are unordered and their executions can overlap. Specifically, modern GPUs can support concurrent simultaneous IO from host to device (H2D) on one stream, IO from device to host (D2H) on another stream and execution of multiple kernels on additional streams. CUDA events (discussed below) provide tools for managing work on multiple streams, for example, by allowing one stream to wait for work on a second stream to be complete.

We have seen in previous chapters that running a kernel with a large number of thread blocks can be advantageous as this allows the hardware to better hide memory latency. This is achieved by constantly switching between warps as their memory requirements become available. In fact the GPU can also do this by switching between warps belonging to different *concurrently executing kernels* which can further improve latency hiding. For example, if a CPU bound kernel is run concurrently with a memory bound kernel then execution time for both might be no more that for the memory bound kernel run on its own. NVIDIA GPU hardware can typically support up to 32 concurrently executing kernels but to save resources this is reduced to 8 by default. This number can be changed at runtime using the environment variable `CUDA_DEVICE_MAX_CONNECTIONS`, as will be illustrated in Example 7.1.

A CUDA stream is created using `cudaStreamCreate` as shown in the box:

```
// create CUDA stream
cudaStream_t stream1;
cudaStreamCreate(&stream1);
```

Having created a stream object, we can then add work to it by using it as an argument in kernel launches or `cudaMemcpyAsync` calls.

7.2 CUDA Pipeline Example

In Example 7.1, `pipeline`, we consider the case where the host has a large amount of data that needs to be copied to GPU memory, then processed by a kernel and then the final the results are copied back to the host. If the data can be separated into a number of independent subsets (or frames) we can set up a pipeline corresponding to scenario (A) above. Processing video frames would be a real-world example, but in Example 7.1 we just process each word of data independently with the kernel `mashData`. A large data block of size N words can be processed as F separate frames each of size N/F. Each frame is processed on a separate CUDA stream with the intention that processing on different streams will overlap on the GPU giving a speed-up. The code is written to allow users to experiment with different values of N and F. A nice way of checking that our code is working properly is to use the NVIDIA Visual Profiler NVVP which displays timelines for all processes running on the GPU during the execution of a given kernel. NVVP is discussed in more detail in Chapter 10 and is well documented in the NVIDIA CUDA Profiler Users Guide which is part of the

SDK documentation set. Examples of NVVP timelines for this example are included in the following discussion.

Notice that the optimisation in this example is not the same as the overlapping host computation with GPU processing which we have discussed previously. That optimisation could be added to this example if there was useful additional host work to perform.

Example 7.1 Pipeline data processing

```
01  #include "cx.h"
02  #include "cxtimers.h"
03  #include "helper_math.h"
    . . .
08  __global__ void mashData(cr_Ptr<float> a, r_Ptr<float>,
                   uint asize, int ktime)
09  {
10    int id =      blockDim.x*blockIdx.x + threadIdx.x;
11    int stride = blockDim.x*gridDim.x;
12    for (int k = id; k<asize; k+=stride) {
13      float sum = 0.0f;
14      for (int m = 0; m < ktime; m++) {
15        sum += sqrtf(a[k]*a[k]+
                (float)(threadIdx.x%32)+(float)m);
16      }
17      b[k] = sum;
18    }
19  }

20  int main(int argc, char *argv[])
21  {
22    int blocks  = (argc >1) ? atoi(argv[1]) : 256;
23    int threads = (argc >2) ? atoi(argv[2]) : 256;
24    uint dsize  = (argc >3) ? 1 << atoi(argv[3]) :
                          1 << 28;  // data size
25    int frames  = (argc >4) ? atoi(argv[4]) : 16; // frames
26    int  ktime  = (argc >5) ? atoi(argv[5]) : 60; // workload
                          // max connections
27    int maxcon  = (argc >6) ? atoi(argv[6]) : 8
28    uint fsize = dsize / frames;  // frame size

29    if (maxcon > 0) {
30      char set_maxconnect[256];
31      sprintf(set_maxconnect,
              "CUDA_DEVICE_MAX_CONNECTIONS=%d", maxcon);
32      _putenv(set_maxconnect);
33    }
34    thrustHvecPin<float>  host(dsize); // host data buffer
35    thrustDvec<float>   dev_in(dsize); // dev input buffer
36    thrustDvec<float>   dev_out(dsize); // dev output buffer
```

```
37    for (uint k = 0; k < dsize; k++) host[k] =
                            (float)(k%77)*sqrt(2.0);


      // buffer for stream objects
38    thrustHvec<cudaStream_t> streams(frames);
39    for (int i = 0; i < frames; i++)
                  cudaStreamCreate(&streams[i]);

40    float *hptr    = host.data();  // copy H2D
41    float *in_ptr  = dev_in.data().get();  // pointers
42    float *out_ptr = dev_out.data().get(); // used in loop

43    cx::timer tim;
44    // data transfers & kernel launch in each async stream
45    for (int f=0; f<frames; f++) {
46      if(maxcon > 0) {  // here for multiple async streams
47          cudaMemcpyAsync(in_ptr, hptr, sizeof(float)*fsize,
               cudaMemcpyHostToDevice, streams[f]);
48        if(ktime > 0)
              mashData<<<blocks,threads,0,streams[f]>>>
                          (in_ptr, out_ptr, fsize, ktime);
49        cudaMemcpyAsync(hptr, out_ptr, sizeof(float)*fsize,
               cudaMemcpyDeviceToHost, streams[f]);
50      }
51      else {  // here for single synchronous default stream
52        cudaMemcpyAsync(in_ptr, hptr, sizeof(float)*fsize,
               cudaMemcpyHostToDevice, 0);
53        if(ktime > 0)mashData<<<blocks,threads,0,0>>>
                          (in_ptr, out_ptr, fsize, ktime);
54        cudaMemcpyAsync(hptr, out_ptr, sizeof(float)*fsize,
               cudaMemcpyDeviceToHost, 0);
55      }
56      hptr    += fsize;  // point to next frame
57      in_ptr  += fsize;
58      out_ptr += fsize;
59    }
60    cudaDeviceSynchronize();
61    double t1 = tim.lap_ms(); printf("time %.3f ms\n",t1);

62    . . . // continue host calculations here

63    std::atexit( []{cudaDeviceReset();} )
64    return 0;
65  }

D:\ >pipeline.exe 256 256 28 1 60 0
time 229.735 ms
D:\ >pipeline.exe 256 256 28 8 60 8
time 122.105 ms
```

Description of Example 7.1

- Lines 8–19: This is the `mashdata` kernel which uses thread linear addressing to perform some GPU calculations on each element of the input array `a` with the result being stored in the output array `b`. The arrays have size given by the third argument `asize`. The actual calculation in lines 13–16 is fairly meaningless but mimics a real calculation and the time required is proportional to the input argument `ktime`. We can use `ktime` to vary the relative amount of time required by the kernel and IO operations.

- Lines 22–28: Here, at the start of the main routine, we set a number of parameters which control the calculation; they can be set by command line values supplied by the user or from defaults. The variables `blocks` and `threads` are the usual configuration parameters for all the kernel launches. The third variable `dsize` is the full size of the data set used for the calculations and is specified as a power of 2. For processing, the full dataset is divided into a number of equally sized frames specified by the variable `frames` which should also be a power of 2. The size of each frame is calculated in line 28 and stored in `fsize`. The parameter `ktime` controls the time used by the mashdata kernel and the final parameter `maxcon` controls the number of CUDA connections. We use the convention that if `maxcon≤0` the default stream is used for all work but the environment variable `CUDA_DEVICE_MAX_CONNECTIONS` is not changed. This allows for baseline performance measurements.

- Lines 29–33: Configure the number of CUDA connections used to process multiple streams in parallel. The default is 8 but can be increased up to 64 for Turing GPUs or 32 for earlier generations. This is done by setting `maxcon` or the local environment variable `CUDA_DEVICE_MAX_CONNECTIONS` to the desired number. The appropriate text string (for Windows) is created in line 31 and used as an argument for the system function `_putenv()` in line 32. This portion of code is only executed if `maxcon>0`.

- Lines 34–36: Allocate the required memory buffers for the working dataset on both the host and GPU using thrust vectors as containers. Notice the host vector `host` is created using pinned memory. This is a *necessary requirement* for any asynchronous data transfers between the host and GPU. Pinned memory also allows faster data transfers between the host and GPU.

- Line 37: Fills the host data buffer `data` with some fairly arbitrary numbers.

- Lines 38–39: Creates and initialises the thrust container array `streams` which holds a set of CUDA streams, one for each frame. As usual in CUDA, separate steps are needed to perform the declarations and initialisations.

- Lines 40–42: Copy the pointers to the start of the data buffers. These pointers are incremented in the processing loop to select successive portions of data for each frame.

- Line 43: Start timed section of code.

- Lines 45–59: Here we do the actual work of the kernel. This section starts with a `for` loop over the frames where for each frame `f` the code in either lines 46–58 or 51–53 is executed depending on the value of `maxcon`. Note that because we use `cudaMemcpyAsync` everywhere, all passes through this loop will execute on the host without any delay so all the work is queued on CUDA streams immediately.

- Lines 47–49: This block of three statements is executed for `maxcon>0` and sends work to CUDA stream `streams[f]`.
  - Line 47: Uses `cudaMemcpyAsyc` to transfer this frame of data from the host to the GPU.
  - Line 48: Launches the kernel `mashdata` to process that data, specifying the required stream as a fourth parameter in the launch configuration.
  - Line 49: This uses `cudaMemcpyAsyc` to transfer the results for frame `f` back to the host. Note that this transfer overwrites the original contents of the host array data for that frame.

Notice this set of three statements will be run sequentially on a particular stream; the use of `cudaMemcpyAsync` permits the overlap of operations in different streams on the GPU not within the same stream.

- Lines 52–54: These are the same as lines 47–49 but using the default stream for all frames. These statements are selected for the case `maxcon≤0`. We expect no asynchronous behaviour on the GPU in this case although the `cudaMemcpyAsyc` calls will still not be blocking on the host.
- Lines 56–58: Here we increment all data pointers to point to the next frame.
- Line 60: A `cudaDeviceSynchronize` call is made here which causes the host to wait for work on all streams to be done before proceeding. This is necessary for timing purposes and for the host to be able to use the results copied from the GPU. Note that if we were using simple synchronous `cudaMemcpy` calls these would be blocking and this call would be unnecessary. If you are using asynchronous GPU operations you have to be more careful with explicit synchronisations.
- Line 61: Here we print the time taken for the processing. The really interesting features of the code can only be investigated using a profiling tool like NVVP.
- Line 62: This is the placeholder indicating where code to process the results now in the host array `data` could be further processed or written to disk.
- Line 63. This is the end of the program where we need to "tidy up" to free any resources allocated during execution.

The timing results at the end of this example show a factor of 2 speed-up between running all work on the default stream (`maxcon=0` case) and eight streams (`maxcon=8` case).

The complicated nature of line 63 has an interesting explanation which is explained in the next section as a little digression before we move on to the results.

7.3 Thrust and cudaDeviceReset

Tidying up at the end of a C++ program (and elsewhere) is always a bit of a chore and easy to forget. This is why we use thrust as a container class for our host and device arrays – the memory allocations are automatically freed on exit. However, other allocated CUDA resources also need to be deallocated. In simple cases you rely on the operating system to tidy up after you exit a CUDA program; however, this is always poor practice. Here where we intend to use a profiling tool it is necessary to call `cudaDeviceReset` before exiting for the profiler to get correct information. The reason for the complicated way we do this has to do with an incompatibility we discovered between thrust and `cudaDeviceReset`.

The incompatibility between `cudaDeviceReset` and thrust vectors is that by default the thrust destructors run during the program exit phase *after* all statements in your program have been executed including `cudaDeviceReset`. This means that the device has been reset and so the context in which the device memory allocations originally took place has been lost. This turns out to mean that (on Windows systems) the program crashes when the destructors are implicitly called during the exit stage. This crash in turn causes NVVP to fail completely – which is ironic as the reason we used `cudaDeviceReset` was to improve the nvvp reporting. Fortunately, there is a fix for the apparent incompatibility between thrust and `cudaDeviceReset` and that is to use the C++11 `atexit` function to move the `cudaDeviceReset` call to the final step of the operating system clean-up after main has exited and any implicit calls to destructors have occurred.

The `atexit` function takes a single argument which is a pointer to the function contain-ing the code to be run on exit. In line 63 we supply the anonymous C++11 lambda function

$$[ ] \{ \text{ cudaDeviceReset}(); \}$$

as the argument. This provides a nice solution to the incompatibility issue. The `atexit` function can in fact be placed anywhere in your code, but in this case placing it just before the exit is the natural choice.

7.4 Results from the Pipeline Example

Some results from running the pipeline example are printed at the bottom of Example 7.1. The program was run several times on an RTX 2070 with `blocks` and `threads` both set to 256, `dsize` set to 2^{28} (1 GB of data for floats) and `ktime` set to 60. The results show that the times for running the same task in just the default stream with `frames` = 1 and in 8 streams with `frames` = 8 were about 230 and 122 ms respectively. Using `frames` = 8 gives about a factor of 2 improvement. In our previous timing tests, we found the PCI bus transfer rate to be about 11.5 GB/sec for pinned host memory, thus we might expect it to take about 175 ms to transfer 1 GB of data from host to GPU and then back again. Since the total time for our 8-frame run is only 130 ms this confirms that IO in both directions and GPU computation all overlap.

We can more gain more insights from the actual CUDA timelines obtained by running `pipeline` with NVVP. In Figure 7.1 we show timelines for four runs of the program with different values of `ktime` and `frames`. The first run (a) used one frame and the default stream; this sets our baseline performance, the remaining three runs (b-d) used `frames` = 8 and `ktime` = 60, 1 or 400. These three values of `ktime` give GPU computation times roughly equal to the IO time in one direction for `ktime` = 60, much less than the IO time for `ktime` = 1 and much more than the IO time for `ktime` = 400.

In each part of the figure NVVP shows three timelines, one for IO from host to device (H2D), one for IO from device to host (D2H) and one for kernel computation. These timelines are then shown twice; once at the top with one line for each of the three activities summed over all active streams and then again at the bottom with one line per stream showing when each activity occurs in the individual streams. The bottom set has just one line for first case (a) using the default stream and frames = 1 and eight lines for the three other cases (b-d) which use eight streams. (Note these are called streams 14–21 in the figure although we index the *handles* for these streams with an index going from 0–7).

Figure 7.1 (a) for the default stream shows the processing of the data as a single frame. There is no overlap between the 3-steps and the total time required for `ktime` = 60 is about 230 ms, equal to the sum of the times for the individual steps.

Figure 7.1 (b) shows the results when processing the same data with eight frames and eight streams. All three steps of the pipeline overlap on different streams for most of the time. The total time required is reduced to about 125 ms. Notice that, except at the start and end, data is being continuously streamed in both directions between the host and GPU; thus the kernel computation is effectively "free". Using 16 frames (not shown) reduces the total runtime further, down to about 115 ms.

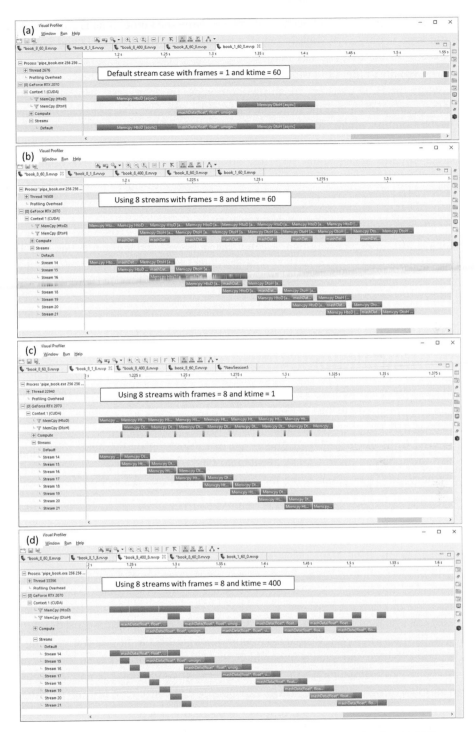

Figure 7.1 Timelines for three-step pipeline code generated using NVVP

Figure 7.1 (c) shows the timelines for `ktime=1`. Now the kernel time is almost negligible but the run time is only very slightly reduced to about 116 ms. The H2D and D2H IO still overlap except for the first and last frames.

Figure 7.1 (d) the kernel time is now much longer than the time to transfer a frame, so we see that, while the H2D transfers are still without gaps, there are increasing delays opening between their completion and the dependant kernel launch. We also note that there are now places in the timeline where two kernels are running simultaneously. Running this calculation on the default stream with one frame takes about 500 ms whereas running with 32 frames on separate streams takes about 315 ms, so in this case it is the IO time which is almost "free".

7.5 CUDA Events

A CUDA event is an object with two possible states: completed and not completed. CUDA event objects have type `cudaEvent_t` and are created with cudaEventCreate as shown in the box:

```
cudaEvent_t event1;
cudaEventCreate(&event1);
```

A CUDA event is created with its initial status set to completed. The event's subsequent status can be queried using `cudaEventQuery(event1);` which returns either `cudaSuccess` if the event is completed or `cudaErrorNotReady` if the event is not yet complete.[1] Calls to `cudaEventQuery` are non-blocking on the host.

The host program can insert CUDA events into CUDA streams between kernel execution and/or memory copy operations using the `cudaEventRecord` function. For example:

```
cudaEventRecord(event1);

or

cudaEventRecord(event2,stream3);
```

If the stream argument is omitted or set to zero, then the default stream is used. Like kernel launches, calls to `cudaEventRecord` are non-blocking on the host and in general it will take some time before the stream into which the event has been placed catches up and processes the record instruction. During this interval the event's status is not completed. The host can monitor progress using `cudaEventQuerey(event)`. When all pending operations preceding the event in the relevant stream have been completed the event will change its status back to completed and the completion time will be stored in the event. The host code can also use `cudaEventSychronise(event)` to wait until a particular event has been completed, note that while this call is blocking on the host it does not affect operations on any active CUDA streams and thus it is a better choice than `cudaDeviceSynchronize()`

or `cudaStreamSynchronize()`. The time held in a completed event cannot be accessed directly, but the difference in the times held in two completed events can be found using `cudaEventElapsedTime`.

The interactions between CUDA events and streams are explored in examples 7.2 and 7.3. In Example 7.2 we reuse the `mashData` kernel to show how kernel execution times can be measured on the host using both conventional C++ timers and CUDA events. Then in Example 7.3 we show some of the complications that can arise when attempting to time events on multiple asynchronous streams. Only part of the main routine is shown in Example 7.2; the missing code is similar to Example 7.1.

Example 7.2 `event1` program showing use of CUDA events with default stream

```
         . . .
         // kt1 & kt2 control kernel execution times
25       int kt1 = (argc >4) ? atoi(argv[4]) : 100;
26       int kt2 = (argc >5) ? atoi(argv[5]) : kt1;

27       thrustHvecPin<float> host(dsize);
28       thrustDvec<float>    dev_in(dsize);
29       thrustDvec<float>    dev_out(dsize);
30       for(int k=0; k<dsize; k++) host[k] =
                              (float)(k%77)*sqrt(2.0);
31       dev_in = host;      // copy H2D

32       // run kernel twice timing with host timers
33       cx::timer tim;
34       mashData<<<blocks,threads>>>(dev_in.data().get(),
                         dev_out.data().get(), dsize, kt1);
35       cudaDeviceSynchronize();  // wait
36       double host_t1 = tim.lap_ms();
37       mashData<<<blocks,threads>>>(dev_out.data().get(),
                          dev_in.data().get(), dsize, kt2);
38       cudaDeviceSynchronize();  // blocks host
39       double host_t2 = tim.lap_ms();

         // now repeat using CUDA event timers
40       cudaEvent_t start1; cudaEventCreate(&start1);
         // need two events for each time measurement
41       cudaEvent_t stop1;  cudaEventCreate(&stop1);
42       cudaEvent_t start2; cudaEventCreate(&start2);
43       cudaEvent_t stop2;  cudaEventCreate(&stop2);

44       cudaEventRecord(start1);  //time at first launch
45       mashData<<<blocks,threads>>>(dev_in.data().get(),
                         dev_out.data().get(), dsize, kt1);
46       cudaEventRecord(stop1);   //time at first finish
```

```
47   cudaEventRecord(start2);   //time at second launch
48   mashData<<<blocks,threads>>>(dev_out.data().get(),
                  dev_in.data().get(), dsize, kt2);
49   cudaEventRecord(stop2);   //time at second finish

50   . . . // extra asynchronous host work possible here

     // after this sync the event based timers are ready
51   cudaEventSynchronize(stop2);

52   float event_t1 = 0.0f;
53   float event_t2 = 0.0f;
     // times for first & seconds kernel runs
54   cudaEventElapsedTime(&event_t1,start1,stop1);
55   cudaEventElapsedTime(&event_t2,start2,stop2);
56   float diff = host_t1 + host_t2 - event_t1- event_t2;

57   printf("times %.3f %.3f %.3f %.3f diff %.3f ms\n",
              host_t1,host_t2,event_t1,event_t2,diff);
     . . .
D:\ >event1.exe 256 256 26 10 10
times 3.462 3.462 3.387 3.380 diff 0.157 ms
```

Description of Example 7.2

- Lines 25–26: Set the user defined parameters `kt1` and `kt2` which control the kernel execution times; the other parameters are as in Example 7.1.
- Lines 27–31: Declare and initialise the data buffers as for Example 7.1.
- Lines 33–39: Run the `mashData` kernel from Example 7.1 twice, using the cx timer routines to measure the time for each kernel run.
  - Line 33: Declares cx timer `tim`, the constructor initialises the timer to the current time.
  - Line 34: Runs `mashData` kernel with time control parameter `kt1`.
  - Line 35: Performs a `cudaDeviceSynchronize` so that the host waits for all pending CUDA work to complete. In this case, only the kernel from line 34 is pending.
  - Line 36: Stores elapsed time since initialisation or last reset of `tim` in variable `host_t1`. This also resets the timer.
  - Line 37: Runs kernel `mashData` a second time with time control parameter `kt2`.
  - Lines 38–39: Wait for completion of second kernel and store elapsed time in `host_t2`.
- Lines 40–55: This is an alternative version of the two-kernel timing code using CUDA events to perform the timing; this is more verbose but does not use `cudaDeviceSynchronize`.
  - Lines 40–43: Declare and initialise the 4 CUDA events `start1` and 2 and `stop1` and 2; these will be used to measure the time intervals required for running the two kernels.
  - Line 44: Places a `cudaEventRecord` for `start1` in the default CUDA work stream.
  - Line 45: Runs the `mashData` kernel.
  - Line 46: Places a `cudaEventRecord` for `stop1` in the default CUDA work stream.

○ Lines 47–49: These are the same as 45–47 but using the events `start2` and `stop2` for timing the second run of the `mashdata` kernel. Notice that there are no host blocking instructions between line 38 and this point.

○ Line 50: This is a place holder; at this point in the code, extra host work can be performed which will run asynchronously with the kernels launched in lines 45 and 48.

○ Line 51: At this point, all asynchronous work has been added to the default CUDA stream and any extra host work has been done so we resynchronise operations of the host and GPU issuing a `cudaEventSynchronise` for the `stop2` event. The host will be blocked until the CUDA stream reaches the `stop2` event. We choose `stop2` because it is the last event to have been inserted into the default stream; thus we can be sure that it, together with all the preceding tasks in that stream, have been completed. Note the host is only blocked for work in the CUDA default stream; any work in other active CUDA streams would continue asynchronously. This is different to `cudaDeviceSynchronize` which blocks the host until work on *all* CUDA streams is complete.

○ Lines 52–55: Here we find the execution times for the two kernels using `cudaEventElapsedTime` to store the `stop1-start1` and `stop2-start2` time differences in `event_t1` and `event_t?`; the units are ms.

• Line 56: Calculates difference between first and second sets of timing measurements.

• Line 57: Prints the measured times.

A typical result for a kernel run time of about 3.4 ms is shown at the bottom of Example 7.2. In this case we find that timing using CUDA events is consistently about 0.15 ms faster than using host-based timers needing `cudaDeviceSynchronize()`. This difference, although small, is quite interesting. It shows that `cudaDeviceSynchronize()` has a significant overhead and using CUDA events can give more accurate kernel timings. In more complex cases, where multiple CUDA streams are being used, `cudaDeviceSynchonize()` will block the host's progress until all active streams complete their work whereas CUDA streams allow the host to wait for a specific point on a single stream.

This last point is illustrated in Example 7.3 which is a modification of the previous example to run the two kernels on two different CUDA streams rather than running both on the default stream.

Example 7.3 `event2` program CUDA events with multiple streams

```
      . . .
25    int kt1   =   (argc >4) ? atoi(argv[4]) : 100;
26    int kt2 =     (argc >5) ? atoi(argv[5]) : kt1;
27    int sync =    (argc >6) ? atoi(argv[6]) : 0;

28    // allocate sets of buffers for two CUDA stream
29    thrustHvecPin<float> host1(dsize);
30    thrustDvec<float>    dev_in1(dsize);
31    thrustDvec<float>    dev_out1(dsize);
32    thrustHvecPin<float> host2(dsize);
33    thrustDvec<float>    dev_in2(dsize);
```

```
34   thrustDvec<float>     dev_out2(dsize);

     // create two CUDA streams
35   cudaStream_t s1;  cudaStreamCreate(&s1);
36   cudaStream_t s2;  cudaStreamCreate(&s2);

37   // initialise buffers
38   for(uint k=0; k<dsize; k++) host2[k] = host1[k] =
                      (float)(k%77)*sqrt(2.0);
39   dev_in1 = host1;  dev_in2 = host2;  // H2D transfers

40   // test1: run kernels sequentially on s1 and s2 and
     // time each kernel using the host-blocking timers
     // host_t1 and host_t2
42   cx::timer tim;
43   mashData<<<blocks,threads,0,s1>>>(dev_in1.data().get(),
                    dev_out1.data().get(), dsize, kt1);
44   cudaStreamSynchronize(s1);  // blocking on s1 only
45   double host_t1 = tim.lap_ms();
46   mashData<<<blocks,threads,0,s2>>>(dev_in2.data().get(),
                    dev_out2.data().get(), dsize, kt2);
47   cudaStreamSynchronize(s2); // blocking on s2 only
48   double host_t2 = tim.lap_ms(); // both kernels done

49   // test2: run kernels asynchronously and measure
     // combined time host_t3
50   mashData<<<blocks,threads,0,s1>>>(dev_in1.data().get(),
                    dev_out1.data().get(), dsize, kt1);
51   mashData<<<blocks,threads,0,s2>>>(dev_in2.data().get(),
                    dev_out2.data().get(), dsize, kt2);
52   cudaDeviceSynchronize();   // wait for all steams
53   double host_t3 = tim.lap_ms();

54   // test3: create CUDA events for GPU based timing of
     // asynchronous kernels
55   cudaEvent_t start1; cudaEventCreate(&start1);
56   cudaEvent_t stop1;  cudaEventCreate(&stop1);
57   cudaEvent_t start2; cudaEventCreate(&start2);
58   cudaEvent_t stop2;  cudaEventCreate(&stop2);

59   // test3: launch and time asynchronous kernels
     // using CUDA events
60   cudaEventRecord(start1,s1);
61   mashData<<<blocks,threads,0,s1>>>(dev_in1.data().get(),
                    dev_out1.data().get(), dsize, kt1);
62   cudaEventRecord(stop1,s1);
```

```
      // optional pause in s2
63    if(sync != 0) cudaStreamWaitEvent(s2,stop1,0);

64    cudaEventRecord(start2,s2);
65    mashData<<<blocks,threads,0,s2>>>(dev_in2.data().get(),
                      dev_out2.data().get(), dsize, kt2);
66    cudaEventRecord(stop2,s2);
67    // all work now added to CUDA streams

68    cudaEventSynchronize(stop1); // wait for s1
69    float event_t1 = 0.0f;
70    cudaEventElapsedTime(&event_t1, start1, stop1);
71    cudaEventSynchronize(stop2); // wait for s2
72    float event_t2 = 0.0f;
73    cudaEventElapsedTime(&event_t2, start2, stop2);

74    float hsum = host_t1+host_t2;
      float hdiff = hsum-host_t3;
75    printf("host : ht1+ht2 %.3f ht3 %.3f diff %.3f\n",
                           hsum,host_t3,hdiff);
76    float esum = event_t1+event_t2;
      float ediff = esum-host_t3;
77    printf("event: et1+et2 %.3f et1 %.3f et2 %.3f
          diff %.3f ms\n",esum,event_t1,event_t2,ediff);
      . . .

>event2.exe 256 256 28 1000 1000 0     (sync is set to 0)
host : ht1+ht2 1542.569 ht3 1416.593 diff 125.975
event: et1+et2 2211.594 et1 805.213 et2 1406.381 diff 795.001 ms


>event2.exe 256 256 28 1000 1000 1     (sync is set to 1)
host : ht1+ht2 1533.053 ht3 1409.700 diff 123.353
event: et1+et2 1534.690 et1 767.489 et2 767.200 diff 124.989 ms
```

In Example 7.3 we show three different strategies for measuring the kernel times, the first two are on the host, and the third uses events on the GPU. The first host method uses a cudaStreamSynchronize immediately after each kernel launch so that the two kernels actually run sequentially, albeit on different streams. The second host method uses a single cudaDeviceSychronize after both kernels have been launched. If there is any overlap in the execution of the two kernels we would expect the time measured by the second method to be less than the time measured by the first. Finally, the third method uses CUDA events instead of host timers to measure the times taken by the two asynchronous kernels. To show the effect of cudaStreamWaitEvent, there is an optional call to this function in line 63 between two calls to cudaEventRecord and the two sets of results shown illustrates its effect.

Description of Example 7.3

- Lines 25–27: Get user settable parameters. As before, `kt1` and `kt2` control the execution times for the `mashData` kernel and in line 27 a new parameter, `dosync`, is set which controls the `cudaStreamWaitEvent` statement in line 57.
- Lines 28–34: Allocate data buffers for the host and kernel code. Note we use two sets of buffers, one set for each of the kernel launches. Buffer sharing would be a bad idea in this program as the kernels are now asynchronous and kernel executions might overlap. Note that in the previous Example 7.2 we were sure that the kernels would run sequentially so we could use the same buffers for both kernel launches.
- Lines 35–36: Create and initialise two CUDA streams `s1` and `s2`.
- Lines 38–39: Initialise the host buffers and copy them to the device input buffers.
- Line 42: Initialises and starts the host cx timer `tim`.
- Lines 43–48: Time the two kernel launches in the separate CUDA streams `s1` and `s2`. The use of `cudaStreamSynchronize` in lines 44 and 47 means that the host will wait at line 44 until the first kernel launch is complete; hence the two kernels are run sequentially and thus the measured times are expected to reflect the actual kernel execution times. This implements our first host timing method.
  - Line 43: Launches the `mashData` kernel in CUDA stream `s1` using the first set of buffers.
  - Lines 44–45: Wait for all pending work in `s1` to complete and then store the time taken in `host_t1`.
  - Lines 45–47: Launch `mashData` on stream `s2` using the second set of buffers, wait for completion using a second `cudaStreamSynchronize` and then store the time taken in `host_t2`.
- Lines 49–53: Repeat the kernel launches in CUDA stream `s1` and `s2` but now without calling `cudaStreamSynchronize`; hence this time the two kernels may execute simultaneously on the GPU. If this does occur, we expect that the measured time to complete both executions, `host_t3`, to be less than the sum of `host_t1` and `host_t2` times from the sequential runs. Note that we use `cudaDeviceSynchronize` in line 52 to ensure that the pending work in all streams is complete before measuring `host_t3`, in line 53. This implements our second host timing method.
- Lines 54–66: In this section we implement our third timing method using CUDA events instead of host-based timers.
  - Lines 55–58: Declare and create `start` and `stop` events for the two streams.
  - Lines 60–62: Run the `mashData` kernel in stream `s1` bracketed by calls to `cudaEventRecord` for events `start1` and `stop1`. The difference between the times held by these events will be the wall-clock time taken to run the kernel.
  - Line 63: This call to `cudaStreamWaitEvent` will block the activity on stream `s2` until the pending event, `stop1`, on stream `s1` completes. This call is dependent on the user settable parameter `sync`. If this call is made, we would expect nothing to be done on stream `s2` until all work on `s1` is finished and thus the execution of the two kernels is sequential, therefore, the same as the first host-based timing method.
  - Lines 64–66: These are the same as lines 60–62 but now run the kernel in stream `s2` bracketed by calls to `cudaEventRecord` for events `start2` and `stop2`.
    If `cudaStreamWaitEvent` is not called, the `start2` event in line 64 will immediately complete in stream `s2` but the `mashData` kernel launched in the next line may not start running on `s2` until some later time because the GPU is fully occupied with previously added work on stream `s1`. Thus, the measured time interval between `start2` and `stop2` may be greater that the running time for the kernel on `s2`. This is always a potential pitfall when using CUDA events for

timing purposes when multiple streams are active. The call to `cudaStreamWaitEvent` can partially solve this problem by forcing the steps in streams `s1` and `s2` to run sequentially rather than asynchronously. However, this does not give us any information about timing in the asynchronous case.

- Lines 68–73: Here we use the timing information recorded in the `start` and `stop` events. Note that the statements in lines 54–66 are not blocking on the host; to ensure that all events have been properly recoded before attempting to use `cudaEventElapsedTime`, we use `cudaEventSynchronize` in lines 68 and 71.
- Lines 74–77: Here we print the results; two example sets of results are shown at the bottom of the figure.

The timing results shown at the end of Example 7.3 are for running `event2` with and without the calling `cudaStreamWaitEvent` (line 63 above). In the first case (no wait) both ht3 and et2 are the net time for overlapped execution of the two kernels. In the second case the et1 and et2 each measure the time for individual kernel executions with no overlap. Hence et1+et2 is about the same value as ht1+ht2 and both give the time required for executing the two kernels without overlap. For the `mashData` kernel running two instances of the kernel simultaneously on the GPU gives roughly an 8% speed-up.

To illustrate this more clearly, Figure 7.2 shows the timelines obtained using NVVP for the two cases.

The `cudaStreamWaitEvent` is only one of many functions available for managing activity on multiple CUDA streams, possibly spread across multiple GPUs. A few of these functions are shown in Table 7.1 and the CUDA Runtime API Reference Manual contains full details on all the functions for stream management in Section 5.4 and for event management in Section 5.5.

7.6 Disk Overheads

Asynchronous data transfers between host and GPU memory as shown in Example 7.1 are well worthwhile if the data to be processed is generated on the host. However, for many real-world, data-flow problems the data to be processed will be stored on disk and hence needs to be transferred to the host before the processing. Likewise, the final results may need to be written back to disk at the end of the calculation. Typical PC hard drives have read and write speeds of about 100 MB/sec which is much less than the 11.5 GB/sec transfer speeds between the host and GPU. Thus, any real-world, data-flow problem is likely to be limited by disk transfers not GPU transfers. In the case of Example 7.1, transferring 1 GB of data from conventional disk to the host and vice versa adds about 18 seconds to the total time. This makes the hundreds of ms saved overlapping GPU IO and computation negligible.[2] An SSD drive is roughly a factor of five times faster than a conventional hard drive; on our system 1 GB transfers take about 3.8 seconds, but even this is much larger than the gains found in Example 7.1.

In this section we will show a scheme for overlapping disk IO with host computation. There is no analogue of `cudaMemcpyAsync` for IO in C++, but a good portable approach is to the C++ `<threads>` library which permits the launch of asynchronous threads that can perform IO in parallel with host computation. The features of the thread library which we need to use are shown in Table 7.2 and the method we use is quite similar to Example 7.1.

Table 7.2 *C++ `<threads>` library*

Element	Comment
`std::thread t;`	Create thread object t using default constructor. The thread is created but inactive.
`t(fun,arg1,arg2,...);`	Activate the thread t to run `fun(arg1,arg2,...)` asynchronously with parent code.
`bool t.joinable();`	Test to see if thread t is active.
`void t.join();`	Wait for thread t to finish.

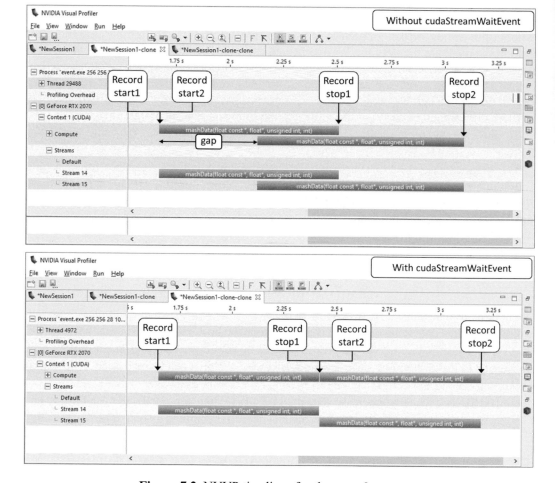

Figure 7.2 NVVP timelines for the event2 program

The idea is to run a set of steps, where each step processes different pipeline stages for a number of frames. A typical step might run the computation for frame n and also handle IO steps for frames n–1 and n+1. The actual scheme we use is shown in Figure 7.3. To process N frames, it turns out we need N+3 steps in total to cater for an initial read before any computation and a final write after the computation has finished. Since we are going to read

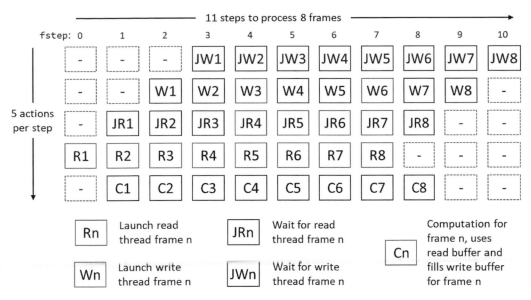

Figure 7.3 Scheme for asynchronous host disk IO

and write different frames of data using asynchronous threads, we must take care that one read has completed before the next one is launched. That is why in the table each read Rn is preceded by a JRn−1 and likewise each write Wn is preceded by JWn−1 in the scheme. (Here R stand for read, W stands for write and J stands for join, the C++ threads equivalent of `cudaStreamSynchronize`).

The `asyncdiskIO` code corresponding to Figure 7.3 is shown in Examples 7.4 and 7.5.

Example 7.4 asyncDiskIO program support functions

```
20   template <typename T> int read_block
                   (FILE *fin, T *buf, uint len)
21   {                   // read frame
22     uint check = fread(buf,sizeof(T), len, fin);
23     if(check != len) {printf("read error\n"); return 1;}
24     return 0;
25   }


26   template <typename T> int write_block
                   (FILE *fout, T *buf, uint len)
27   {                   // write frame
28     uint check = fwrite(buf,sizeof(T), len, fout);
29     if(check != len) {printf("write error\n"); return 1;}
30     return 0;
31   }


32   template <typename T> int swork
```

```
        (thrustHvecPin<T> &inbuf, thrustHvecPin<T> &outbuf,
         thrustDvec<T> &dev_in, thrustDvec<T> &dev_out,
         int blocks, int threads, uint fsize, int ktime)
33  {
34    dev_in = inbuf;  // copy H2D
35    mashData<<<blocks,threads,0,0 >>>
        (dev_in.data().get(), dev_out.data().get(),
                    fsize, ktime);    // do some work
36    cudaDeviceSynchronize();   // wait for kernel
37    outbuf = dev_out;   // copy D2H

38    return 0;
39  }
```

Description of Example 7.4

Example 7.4: Shows the support functions `read_block`, `write_block` and `swork` used in the main portion of the host code. These are similar to the `cx::read_raw` and `cx::write_raw` functions but differ in that here the caller maintains the file handles `fin` and `fout`.

- Line 20: Declaration of the template function `read_block`, which reads a block of `len` words of type `T` from the file pointed to by `fin` into the data buffer `buf`. These parameters are the function arguments. The function assumes that `fin` points to a file that has been successfully opened for binary read operations.[3]
- Line 22: Use the old C function `fread` to read a block of data; the number of words actually read is stored in `check`.
- Line 23: Check that the correct amount of data has been read. Although, for clarity, we don't usually include error checking in our code listings, we do so in this case because it is particularly important for IO operations as errors with data files at run time can never be excluded.
- Lines 26–31: The template function `write_block` is similar to `read_block` but performs a write operation instead of a read operation.
- Line 32: Declaration of the host function `swork`. Calls to `swork` implement the Cn blocks of GPU work shown in Figure 7.3. The version of `swork` implemented here does the same work as was done in Example 7.1. The arguments are the input and output host buffers `inbuf` and `outbuf` and the corresponding device buffers `dev_in` and `dev_out`. These arguments are received as references to the caller's thrust vector objects not bare pointers.
- Line 34: Copy input data to GPU, for simplicity; we have replaced the calls to `cudMemcpyAsync` used in Example 7.1 with host blocking thrust-based copy operations.
- Line 35: The `mashData` kernel called here is the version shown in Example 7.1.
- Lines 36–37: A call to `cudaDeviceSynchronize()` is necessary to ensure the kernel has completed before copying the output buffer back to the host in line 37.

The main routine is shown in Example 7.5.

Example 7.5 asyncDiskIO program main routine

```
   // this program is based on figure 7.3 in the book
50 int main(int argc,char *argv[])
51 {
52   int blocks =   (argc >3) ? atoi(argv[3]) : 256;
53   int threads =  (argc >4) ? atoi(argv[4]) : 256;
54   uint dsize =   (argc >5) ? 1 << atoi(argv[5]) :
                                   1 << 28; // data size
55   int frames =   (argc >6) ? atoi(argv[6]) : 16;
56   int ktime =    (argc >7) ? atoi(argv[7]) : 100;
57   int flush =    (argc >8) ? atoi(argv[8]) : 0;
58   uint fsize = dsize/frames;  // frame size

     // optional flush of OS disk cache a file size
     // of 1 GB needs flush=10 on test PC
59   if(flush>0){
60     uint flsize = 1<< 28;
61     thrustHvec<float> flbuf(flsize);
62     char name[256];
       // use file names A1.bin A2.bin etc.
63     for(int k=0;k<flush;k++){
64       sprintf(name,"A%d.bin",k+1);
65       cx::read_raw(name,flbuf.data(),flsize,0);
         // use data to fool smart compliers
66       printf(" %.3f",flbuf[flsize/2]);
67     }
68   }

69   thrustHvecPin<float> inbuf1(fsize);
70   thrustHvecPin<float> inbuf2(fsize);
71   thrustHvecPin<float> outbuf1(fsize);
72   thrustHvecPin<float> outbuf2(fsize);
73   thrustDvec<float>    dev_in(fsize);
74   thrustDvec<float>    dev_out(fsize);

75   FILE *fin =  fopen(argv[1],"rb"); // open input file
76   FILE *fout = fopen(argv[2],"wb"); // open output file

77   std::thread r1; // read  thread for odd steps
78   std::thread w1; // write thread for odd steps
79   std::thread r2; // read  thread for even steps
80   std::thread w2; // write thread for even steps
81   int fstep = 0;  // column counter
82   while(fstep<frames+3) {
```

```
83      // even fsteps here (= 0,2,4...)
84      if(w2.joinable()) w2.join();   // wait for w2 & r2
85      if(r2.joinable()) r2.join();   // to complete

86      if(fstep>=2)        // async write blocks w1,w3,w5...
            w1 = std::thread(write_block<float>,
                        fout,outbuf1.data(),fsize);
87      if(fstep<frames)  // async read blocks r1,r3,r5...
            r1 = std::thread(read_block<float>,
                        fin,inbuf1.data(),fsize);
88      if(fstep >0 && fstep<=frames) // do work c2,c2,c4...
            swork<float>(inbuf2,outbuf2, dev_in, dev_out,
                        blocks,threads, fsize,ktime);
89      fstep++;

90      // odd fsteps here (= 1,3,5...)
91      if(w1.joinable()) w1.join();   // wait for w1
92      if(r1.joinable()) r1.join();   // wait for r1

93      if(fstep>=3)  // async write blocks w0,w2,w4...
            w2 = std::thread(write_block<float>,
                        fout, outbuf2.data(),fsize);
94      if(fstep < frames) // async read blocks r0,r2,r4...
            r2 = std::thread(read_block<float>,
                        fin, inbuf2.data(),fsize);
95      if(fstep >0 && fstep<=frames) // do work c1,c3,c5...
            swork<float>(inbuf1,outbuf1, dev_in,dev_out,
                        blocks,threads, fsize,ktime);
96      fstep++;
97    }

98    fclose(fin);
99    fclose(fout);
100   std::atexit( []{ cudaDeviceReset(); } );
101   return 0;
101 }
```

Description of Example 7.5

- Lines 52–58: Set all the control parameters from optional user input, using default values as necessary. These parameters are the same as used in Example 7.1 except for flush which is used in line 59 to control flushing of the operating system's disk cache.
- Lines 59–67: Modern operating systems go to considerable lengths to hide the high latency and relative slowness of hard drives. Copies of recently read files are stored in both main memory and higher-level caches and possibly even in hardware buffers on the disk unit itself. This makes timing measurements involving disk IO unreliable. One solution is to read a large volume of new data from disk before reading

or (especially) re-reading the file of interest. We find that on our test PC 10 GB is sufficient. The flushing process takes about 90 seconds so it is useful to have a flag to turn this on or off.

- ○ Line 60: Sets the buffer size for reading flush files.
- ○ Line 61: Creates temporary buffer for reads.
- ○ Lines 64–65: For each of the flush files create a filename and read the file. This version assumes the files A1.bin etc. are on the current working directory, but the `sprintf` statement on line 64 could include path names as required.
- ○ Line 66: After reading each file it might be necessary to use the data in some way to prevent a smart compiler from optimising out this section of code. We choose to print one word from each file. This also gives you a simple progress indicator to watch while waiting.
- Lines 69–74: Allocate the host and device input and output buffers as thrust vectors. Notice the buffer sizes are one frame which may be considerably less than the size of the full dataset. Although Figure 7.3 appears to suggest we need a separate set of buffers for each frame, it turns out that only two are sufficient, one for the even columns in the figure and another for the odd columns.
- Lines 75–76: Here we open the input and output data files for binary reading and writing. If errors occur, the file pointers fin and/or `fout` will be set to `nullptr`. It is really important to include error checking in production code at this point.
- Lines 77–80: Here we declare four host thread variables `r1`, `r2`, `w1` and `w2` which are used for asynchronous read and write operations.

  Lines 81–102: This is the most interesting part of the code and implements the scheme of Figure 7.3. The implementation is a `while` loop based on the step counter `fstep`, the body of the loop has two sections where each section represents one column in Figure 7.3. The first section (lines 84–88) corresponds to even columns in the figure and the second section (lines 91–95) corresponds to the odd columns.
- Line 81: Initialises the variable `fstep` which serves as a column counter in the following `while` loop.
- Line 82: This is the start of our `while` loop over `fstep`. On entry `fstep` has the value zero. Note the termination condition is `fstep=frames+3` to allow for extra steps at the start and end of the process. The conditional clauses on lines 86–88 and 93–95 are used to cater for the blank boxes in Figure 7.3.
- Lines 84–85: Here we check on and if necessary wait for completion of the pending read and write operations corresponding to JRn and JWn for even n. In the C++ <threads> library `join` and `joinable` are member functions of thread objects like `w1`. The join function waits for an active thread to complete or returns immediately if the thread is not active. The function `joinable` returns `true` if the thread is active and not detached.
- Line 86: Here we launch thread `w1` to write the result of the previous step to `outbuf1`. This corresponds to Wn for odd n in Figure 7.3. Notice the deceptively simple syntax for launching a host thread. We assign a thread newly created by the class initialiser constructor to `w1`. This thread executes the function call specified in the constructor argument. In this case we pass a call to our `write_block` function.
- Line 87: Launch thread `r1` to read data for the next step into `inbuf1`. This corresponds to Rn for odd n in Figure 7.3.
- Line 88: Here we call `swork` using `inbuf2` for input and `outbuf2` for the result. This call is blocking on the host thread but not on the asynchronous threads `w1` and `r1`. This corresponds to Cn for even n in Figure 7.3.
- Line 89: Increment `fstep` to move on to the next column of Figure 7.3.
- Lines 91–86: These are the same as lines 84–89 but for the odd columns; thus `r1` and `w1` are replaced by `r2` and `w2` and vice versa. Likewise, `inbuf2` and `outbuf2` are replaced by `inbuf1` and `outbuf1`.
- Lines 98–100: Tidy up at the end of the while loop and exit.

Table 7.3 *Results from* `asyncDiskIO` *example using 1 GB data sets*

Kernel Times	Baseline		Kernel Overlap		Full Overlap	
	Case A	Case B	Case A	Case B	Case A	Case B
0.19	20.16	12.17	21.09	10.21	22.36	10.43
8.45	29.33	20.93	23.08	10.25	21.11	10.14
16.77	36.08	29.20	25.83	17.65	22.07	16.98
25.17	**44.36**	37.72	**33.18**	25.10	**25.29**	24.86
			Speed-ups compared to Baseline			
0.19	–		−0.93 (−5%)	1.96 (16%)	−2% (−11%)	1.74 (14%)
8.45	–		6.25 (21%)	10.68 (51%)	8.22 (28%)	10.79 (52%)
16.77	–		10.25 (28%)	11.55 (40%)	14.01 (39%)	12.22 (42%)
25.17	–		11.18 (25%)	12.62 (34%)	19.07(43%)	12.86 (34%)

Note that we have omitted the performance timing code from these listings but it is present in the versions in our code repository.

Some results obtained from running Example 7.5 on out test PC are shown in Table 7.3. All the tests were run using a 1 GB dataset and 4 values of the `ktime` parameter. All the times are shown in seconds. Three pairs of columns are shown: baseline is the case with no overlap of disk IO and kernel execution; kernel overlap is the case where only a single thread was used to overlap IO operations with the kernel execution but with no overlap between read and write operations. The last pair of columns are for the `asyncDiskIO`, Example 7.5 with full overlap of kernel execution and of read and write IO operations.

It turned out to be quite tricky to get reliable timing measurements for this example; the reason is that modern operating systems go to great lengths to hide the latency and slow read/write speeds of hard drives. For read operations they cache recently read files in memory so that, after an initial slow first read operation, subsequent reads of the same file are fast. Write operations are also cached, in that data is not written directly to the hard drive but is queued for writing using caches in host memory and the drive hardware. In experiments on my Windows 10 PC we found that the read cache worked for up to 10 GB of recently read files and for write operations a command line driven program writing a large file might appear to complete quickly but then the OS would wait for the write operation to finish before responding to the next command. Thus, to mimic a pipeline processing situation, we used a script file to run 12 jobs each using different pairs of input and output files with command line timing steps between each job. This tactic defeats both the read and write caching. The times of single jobs still showed significant fluctuations due to other background activity on the system and the results in Table 7.3 are the median job times from each batch of 12 jobs. It is possible that other operating systems might behave differently. This tactic is better than simply flushing the read cache as discussed above.

The four rows of Table 7.3 show results for four different values of the `ktimes` parameter namely 10, 6400, 12800 and 19200. The GPU times including thrust transfers between the host and GPU is shown in the first column;[4] these times were measured using a separate program. Results for two different disk configurations are shown in the table; Case A uses the same conventional hard drive for both the read and write operations whereas Case B uses separate drives, a fast SSD drive for reading files and a conventional hard drive for writing files. In the past when disk IO was uncached attempting to read and write to the same physical drive simultaneously, it could have a catastrophic impact on performance as the mechanical read/write heads would be constantly in motion. However, we see no evidence for this problem in our results for Case A – a good demonstration that caching is working. Most of the differences between cases A and B are due to the SSD drive being five times faster than the conventional drive. In the four rows of results, we see the following:

- GPU time 0.19 seconds: There is little difference between the three cases which is not surprising as there is almost no GPU time to overlap with disk IO.
- GPU time 8.45 seconds: Now the GPU time is about the same as the time to read or write the data to the hard drive. Here we see speed-ups of 21% and 28% for case A and 51% and 52% for case B. For both cases this is equivalent to the entire GPU computation being hidden and for fully overlapped IO there is an additional saving of about 2 seconds.
- GPU time 16.77 seconds: Here the GPU time is about the same as needed for the sequential reading and writing of data to the hard drive in Case A. The results show that for the fully overlapped IO of Example 7.5, the kernel execution dominates the computation time with disk IO adding about 5.3 seconds for case A and only 0.21 seconds for case B. Without the overlapping of disk IO these overheads rise to 9.06 for case A and 0.88 seconds for case B.
- GPU time 25.17 seconds: Here the GPU time dominates the calculation time for fully overlapped disk IO which is now essentially free. For serial disk IO in case A there is still a time penalty of about 8 seconds.

As a final remark it is worth noting that, while the compute task in our Example 7.5 involved GPU computation, any CPU-based computation would also benefit from the overlapping of computation and disk IO as shown here. One approach would be to simply change the function `swork` as necessary.

7.7 CUDA Graphs

CUDA Graphs were introduced with CUDA 10.1 in 2018 and are actually a method of packaging a piece of work consisting of multiple kernel launches, including possible kernel interdependencies, into a single *graph object* which captures all the details of the required work. Graphs are described in Section 3.2.6.6 of the version 11.0 CUDA C++ Programming Guide which explains the purpose of graphs as follows:

> Separating out the definition of a graph from its execution enables a number of optimisations: first, CPU launch costs are reduced compared to streams, because much of the setup is done in advance; second, presenting the whole workflow to CUDA enables optimisations which might not be possible with the piecewise work submission mechanism of streams.

Graphs are also convenient in more complex situations, such as deep learning applications because once created, a graph can be launched multiple times or embedded as a single node in another (parent) graph. Some possible graph topologies are shown in Figure 7.4.

In this figure the nodes in a graph represent activities and can be a kernel call, a `cudaMemcpy` or `cudaMemset` operation, a CPU function call, an empty node or child

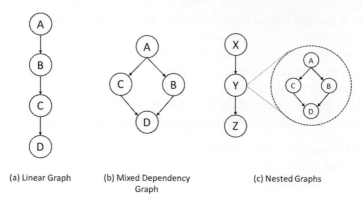

(a) Linear Graph   (b) Mixed Dependency   (c) Nested Graphs
                              Graph

Figure 7.4 Possible topologies for CUDA graph objects

graph. The edges in the graph represent dependencies. Graph (a) shows a simple linear case where each node depends on the previous node, for example H2D `memcpy`, kernel1, kernel2 and D2H `memcpy`. Graph (b) shows a case where nodes B and C do not depend on each other but do depend on node A. Here nodes B and C can run concurrently and will be automatically launched to do so when the grid is run. Graph (c) shows a three-step linear graph where the middle node Y is actually the whole of graph (b) embedded as a child graph. This figure is based on the NVIDIA C++ Programming Guide.

CUDA graphs can actually be created in two ways. In simple cases, such as a linear graph without complex dependencies, an existing workflow can be "captured" as a graph. The resulting graph can then be run, possibly multiple times, or be embedded in a more complex parent graph. If there are more complex dependencies, then the second method is better and uses CUDA API functions to explicitly state inter-node dependencies while leaving the details of organising concurrent execution to the system.

Example 7.6 is based on the "Getting Started with CUDA Graphs" blog post by Alan Gray[5] and shows how a simple workflow involving many kernel launches can be captured and how the kernel launch overhead is then reduced when the workflow is run as a graph as compared to being run directly.

Example 7.6 CUDA graph program

```
02   __global__ void scale(r_Ptr<float> dev_out,
        cr_Ptr<float> dev_in, int size, float lambda)
03   {
04     int tid = blockIdx.x*blockDim.x+threadIdx.x;
05     while(tid<size) {
06       dev_out[tid] = lambda*dev_in[tid];  // scale & save
07       tid += blockDim.x*gridDim.x; }
08   }

10   int main(int argc,char *argv[])
11   {
```

```
12    int blocks  = (argc >1) ? atoi(argv[1]) : 256;
13    int threads = (argc >2) ? atoi(argv[2]) : 256;
14    int size    = (argc >3) ? 2 << atoi(argv[3])-1 :
                                 2 << 15;
15    int steps   = (argc >4) ? atoi(argv[4]) : 1000;
16    int kerns   = (argc >5) ? atoi(argv[5]) : 20;

17    thrustHvec<float> host_data(size);
18    thrustDvec<float> dev_out(size);
19    thrustDvec<float> dev_in(size);

20    for(int k=0;k<size;k++) host_data[k] = (float)(k%419);
21    dev_in = host_data; // H2D
22    float lambda = (float)pow(10.0,
                       (double)(1.0/(steps*kerns)));
23    cudaStream_t s1;  cudaStreamCreate(&s1);

24    cx::MYTimer tim;
25    for(int n=0; n<steps; n++){
26      for(int k=0; k<kerns/2; k++){    // ping pong
27        scale<<<blocks,threads,0,s1>>>
                (trDptr(dev_out),trDptr(dev_in),size,lambda);
28        scale<<<blocks,threads,0,s1>>>
                (trDptr(dev_in),trDptr(dev_out),size,lambda);
29      }
30    }
31    cudaStreamSynchronize(s1);
32    double t1 = tim.lap_ms();
33    float x1 = dev_in[1];
34    printf("standard    time %8.3f ms check %f
             (expect %f)\n",t1,x1,host_data[1]*10.0);

35    dev_in = host_data;  // restore dev_in
36    tim.reset();  // capture work on stream s1
37    cudaStreamBeginCapture(s1,cudaStreamCaptureModeGlobal);
38    for(int k=0; k<kerns/2; k++){
        scale<<<blocks,threads,0,s1>>>
39          (trDptr(dev_out),trDptr(dev_in),size,lambda);
40      scale<<<blocks,threads,0,s1>>>
            (trDptr(dev_in),trDptr(dev_out),size,lambda);
41    }
42    // end capture, create graph then instantiate as g
43    cudaGraph_t graph;
      cudaStreamEndCapture(s1,&graph);
44    cudaGraphExec_t g;
      cudaGraphInstantiate(&g,graph,nullptr,nullptr,0);
```

```
45      // now launch graph g steps times in stream s2
46      cudaStream_t s2;  cudaStreamCreate(&s2);
47      for(int n=0; n<steps; n++)cudaGraphLaunch(g,s2);
48      cudaStreamSynchronize(s2);
49      double t2 = tim.lap_ms();

50      float x2 = dev_in[1];
51      printf("using graph time %8.3f ms check %f
            (expect %f)\n",t2,x2,host_data[1]*10.0);
52      return 0;
53 }


>graphs.exe 256 256 16 1000 50
standard     time   142.644 ms check 9.980973 (expect 10.000000)
using graph time    89.686 ms check 9.980973 (expect 10.000000)
```

Description of Example 7.6

There are three blocks of code in the main function of this example. Lines 12–19 set variables used by both subsequent processing blocks. Lines 24–34 are the first processing block which uses conventional kernel launching and lines 36–52 are the second processing block which uses a CUDA graph to replace the inner loop used in the first processing block. A significant speed-up is achieved.

- Lines 2–8: This is the kernel scale; it simply multiplies each element in the input vector dev_in by a factor lambda and stores the results in the vector dev_out. Standard linear thread addressing is used here.
- Lines 12–16: Here we set user supplied parameters. The variables blocks and threads are self-explanatory, size is the array size, entered as a power of 2. The variables steps and kerns together define the total number of kernel launches which are grouped together as steps sets each of size kerns by the pair of for loops in lines 25 and 26.
- Lines 17–19: Here we define the host and device arrays used for data processing.
- Line 20: This fills the host array host_data with test data. Note host_data[1] is set to 1.0f.
- Line 21: Use thrust to copy host_data to the device array dev_in.
- Line 22: Set the parameter lambda to the Nth root of 10 where N = steps*kerns. The idea here is that the final result of scaling the data by lambda N times by using the scale kernel, will be multiplication by a factor of 10.
- Line 23: It is recommended not to use the default stream for defining CUDA graphs; therefore we define the CUDA stream s1 to use for processing.
- Lines 24–32: This is a timed block of code that repeatedly calls the kernel scale in the conventional way:
  - Line 24: Define and start host timer tim.
  - Lines 25–26: A pair of nested for loops, the outer loop has steps iteration and the inner loop has kerns/2 iterations.
  - Lines 27–28: These two kernel calls are the body of the loops. The kernel scale is called twice using the arguments dev_in and dev_out in ping-pong so that after each pair of calls the contents of dev_in have been multiplied by $lambda^2$. Note we launch the kernels using the non-default stream s1.

- Line 31: Wait for the work on stream `s1` to finish before checking the host timer.
- Line 32: Store the time for the double loop in `t1`.
- Line 33: Copy the value of `dev_in[1]` to the host variable `x1` implicitly using thrust. This should have been scaled up from 1.0 to 10.0 by the kernel calls.
- Line 34: Print `t1` and `x1`.
- Line 35: Restore `dev_in` to its original starting value, prior to repeating the calculation in the second processing block.
- Line 36: Reset the host timer at start of second timed block.
- Lines 37–43: Capture the CUDA work contained in the inner loop (lines 26–29) of the first processing block to the `cuda_graph_t graph` CUDA graph object.
  - Line 37: Begin capturing work from CUDA stream `s1` by calling `cudaStreamBeginCapture`
  - Lines 38–41: These lines are exactly the same as lines 26–29 for the first processing block, but here they are being captured *not executed*.
  - Line 43: End the capture using `cudaStreamEndCapture` and store the result as the CUDA graph `graph`.
- Line 44: The `cuda_graph_t graph` object cannot be launched directly; instead a separate `cudaGraphExec_t` object has to be derived (or instantiated) from it by using `cudaGraphInstantiate`. This is done here to create the launchable object `g`.
- Line 46: Create a second CUDA stream `s2` which will be used to launch `g`. Note it is not necessary to use a different stream to the one used for capture and we could use either `s1` or `s2` in line 47.
- Line 47: This single line replaces the outer loop in the previous block (lines 25–30) and launches the graph `g` steps times in stream `s2` using `cudaGraphLaunch`.
- Lines 50–52: Display the results from the second processing block, similar to lines 32–34 from the first block.

The results shown are for processing arrays of 2^{16} 4-byte floats using 50,000 kernel calls grouped into 1000 sets of 50 calls. The time per kernel measured on the host was typically 2.853 µs for the first method reducing to 1.793 µs for the second method where sets of 50 calls were launched as a CUDA group. This is a reduction of 1.059 µs or 37%.[6] Note that at present the performance gain is only significant for kernels with microsecond execution times. This is because at present CUDA graphs mainly reduce kernel launch overheads. However, this is a relatively new feature and may become more powerful in future versions of CUDA.

A summary of the functions needed to create a CUDA graph using capture is shown in Table 7.4.

CUDA also provides an alternative set of API functions to allow a graph to be defined directly rather than using capture. This alternative is considerably more verbose than the capture approach. Nevertheless, it might be useful in situations where there are complex dependencies between nodes in the graph because those dependencies can be defined directly not implicitly via events. We will not give an example here but interested readers should look at the `simpleCudaGraphs` example in recent versions of the CUDA SDK.

This chapter has focused on overlapping IO operations with kernel and/or CPU activity as a means of further accelerating parallel code. We have looked at both transfers between the host and GPU and between the host and external disk drives. The latter case is not really a CUDA topic but is discussed here because this is often a bottleneck in data processing pipelines.

In the next chapter, we return to random numbers with a substantial example based on a modern medical imaging positron emission (PET) scanner. These scanners work be detecting

Table 7.4 *API functions needed for creation of CUDA graphs via capture*

```cudaStreamBeginCapture(``` `    cudaStream_t s,` `    cudaStreamCaptureMode mode )`	Start capture on CUDA stream `s`. Mode is typically `cudaStreamCaptureModeGlobal`.
```cudaStreamEndCapture(``` `    cudaStream_t s,` `    cudaGraph_t * graph)`	End capture on CUDA stream `s`. A pointer to the resulting graph is placed in `graph`.
```cudaGraphInstantiate(``` `    cudaGraphExec_t* gexec,` `    cudaGraph_t graph,` `    cudaGraphNode_t* errornode,` `    char* errorlog,` `    size_t errorlogsize )`	The argument `gexec` is set to an executable version of the graph in graph. The last three arguments provide detailed error information and can be set to `nullptr`, `nullptr` and 0 if this information is not needed
```cudaGraphLaunch(``` `    cudaGraphExec_t gexec,` `    cudaStream_t s )`	Launch the executable graph `gexec` in stream `s`. The launch stream does not have to be the same as the capture stream.

simultaneous pairs of gammas from decays of a tracer taken up by various anatomical regions in a patient. We will give examples both describing the simulation of the event detection by the scanner and the subsequent tomographic reconstruction of the distribution of the activity in the patient. We think these examples are interesting both for the particular problem described and a model for simulation of other scientific data acquisition systems. The tomographic reconstruction method described is the well-known maximum likelihood expectation maximisation (MLEM) algorithm which also has many other applications. We will find that GPUs are enormously helpful in speeding up both these aspects of the problem.

Endnotes Chapter 7

1 The function `cudaEventQuery` can also return some other error codes indicating problems with the input event argument. See the CUDA Runtime API documentation for details.

2 PCs do a lot of data caching when reading from disk. Thus, reading a large file for a second time is often much faster than reading it for the first time. These caches may be many GB, in order to time disk IO realistically we have to read up to 10 GB of data from other files between each test run in order to "flush" the cache and force the PC to actually read data from disk each time we run a test.

3 As is our custom no error checking is shown in the listings for these functions. However, the real-world code does indeed contain error checking which is particularly important for IO operations as problems with data files at run time can never be excluded.

4 In a previous example we have shown you how to overlap these transfers with kernel execution, but we have not included this refinement in Example 7.4 in order not to overcomplicate the code. In fact the thrust IO takes a total of about 180 ms in this example, which is small compared to the disk transfer overheads which are about 17 seconds.

5 Getting Started with CUDA Graphs, Alan Gray https://devblogs.nvidia.com/cuda-graphs/, 5 September, 2019.

6 Note these are typical numbers for my RTX 2070 GPU running on Windows 10. There is quite a lot of variation between individual runs.

8

Application to PET Scanners

In this chapter we show how CUDA can be used with a much more substantial calculation with features typical of many research applications. Specifically, we exploit the use of fast random number generation to perform a simulation. The simulation of experimental equipment is now an important tool in many areas of research.

In this application chapter we show how the GPU can be used to greatly speed up both calibration and image reconstruction in clinical positron emission tomography (PET) scanners. Developing this code will illustrate points of general interest in designing GPU code, specifically the mapping of symmetries to GPU threads and careful design of memory layout. The host code needed for this application is more complicated than in our previous chapters but the GPU code (which does nearly all the work) is all contained in a small number of short kernels. Full details, including all the host code, are available on our code repository.

Section 8.1 sets up the problem in some detail including important details of how the data is organised to take advantage of the symmetries in the system. This section is quite long and could be skimmed over in a first reading. Our simulation code in Section 8.2 is quite straightforward and will help readers to simulate other systems without needing to master all the details in Section 8.1.

8.1 Introduction to PET

A clinical PET scan works by first injecting the subject with a pharmaceutical containing a short-lived radioactive isotope such as ^{18}F which decays by emission of a positron. An emitted positron will annihilate with a nearby electron in the subject's tissue to produce a pair of back-to-back gamma rays which can be detected as a coincidence event in a surrounding array of gamma detectors. The principle of PET is shown in Figure 8.1.

Figure 8.1 shows an example of a PET detector having four rings with 48 detectors per ring. A tilted 3D view on the left shows the general arrangement and a transverse view is shown on the right. A positron annihilation event in the subject (indicated in the centre) produces two back-to-back gamma rays with paths shown by the line. The gammas are shown passing through detectors in the second and fourth rings. The positions of these detectors define a line of response or LOR. Many such LORs are recorded in a typical scan and at the end the full set of LORs is used to perform a tomographic reconstruction of the distribution of radioactivity in the subject.

A typical detector used in PET scanners consists of scintillating crystals viewed by photomultipliers. The crystals absorb the energy of a gamma ray and convert it to photons

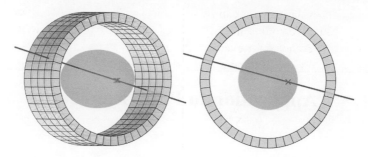

Figure 8.1 PET detector showing four rings of 48 detectors

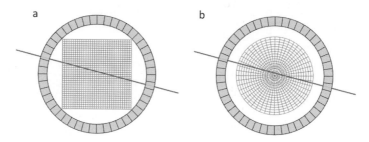

Figure 8.2 Transverse views of coordinate systems used for PET

in the visible range which in turn produce signals in the photomultipliers. The two detectors in a coincidence event define a line of response (or LOR) along which the decay event occurred. Older PET detectors have timing resolutions of a few nanoseconds which is good enough to find coincidences between events from genuine annihilation events while rejecting most other sources of background. This timing, however, is not good enough to give any useful information about where on the line of response a particular decay event occurred. A clinical PET scan may involve the acquisition of billions of LORs so that a statistical analysis to reconstruct the most probable distribution of activity in the subject is feasible. The reconstructed activity is usually displayed as a 3D Cartesian grid of voxels with the x-y plane in the transverse plane of the scanner with the z-axis aligned along the axis of the cylinder formed by the detectors. This x-y coordinate system is shown in Figure 8.2 (a). A rarely used but interesting alternative is to use polar coordinates in the transverse plane yielding wedge shaped voxels of varying size as illustrated in Figure 8.2 (b).

Figure 8.2 (a) shows a Cartesian voxel grid defining the subject volume in a PET scanner. An x-y slice is shown; there are one or more such slices for each detector ring in the axial z-direction. The grid has an 8-fold symmetry (about the horizontal and vertical axes and the main diagonals). In (b) the figure shows a plane polar coordinate grid in the x-y plane. This grid has a symmetry equal to the number of detectors in the PET ring (48 in the case shown here) greatly reducing the number of distinct elements in the PET system matrix required for tomographic reconstruction.

A popular image reconstruction algorithm is the maximum likelihood expectation maximisation method (MLEM) which is theoretically optimum if the number of decays observed in each LOR follows the Poisson distribution of the underlying radioactive decay process.

An early description of the method can be found in Linda Kaufman's paper.[1] This paper is also interesting because it contains an early discussion of the advantages of using polar rather than Cartesian voxel geometry for event reconstruction.

The MLEM method is iterative and uses the deceptively simple formula shown in eqn 8.1:

$$a_v^{n+1} = \frac{a_v^n}{\sum_{l'=1}^{N_l} S_{vl'}} \sum_{l=1}^{N_l} \frac{m_l S_{vl}}{\sum_{v'=1}^{N_v} a_{v'}^n S_{v'l}}, \tag{8.1}$$

where a_v^n is the estimated activity in voxel v at iteration n, m_l is the measured number of decays in LOR l, and S_{vl} is the PET system matrix (SM). The SM elements, S_{vl}, are defined as the probabilities that a decay in voxel v is detected in LOR l. The iteration is usually started by assigning equal values to all the a_v^0. The summation limits N_l and N_v are the total numbers of LORs and voxels involved.

Applications of Eq. 8.1 are not confined to PET; it is applicable to all tomographic applications and more generally to any problem where a set of detected measurements from multiple sources is used to estimate the strength of those sources,[2] Another example of one such application is given at the end of this chapter.

There are three summations involved in Eq. 8.1 each of which has a direct physical interpretation.

The denominator term $FP_l = \sum_{v'} a_{v'}^n S_{v'l}$ is the net contribution of all the currently estimated voxel activities $a_{v'}^n$ to the LOR l. This is referred to as *forward projection* (FP) of subject activity into the detector. The middle term can then be written as $BP_v = \sum_l m_l S_{vl}/FP_l$ which is the *backward projection* (BP) of all the detected decays m_l back into the voxels. As the iteration proceeds we expect a_v^n to tend to m_l so that the BP_v factor will tend to a constant which is just the overall probability that a decay in voxel v is detected somewhere in the detector; therefore, it is the detection efficiency for that voxel. The final summation term $\sum_{l'} S_{vl'}$ is also just this detection efficiency, so that the overall factor multiplying a_v^n tends to one as the iterations proceed.

The problem with the MLEM method is that for a useful PET system, the matrix S_{vl} is enormous – but this is just what makes it an interesting challenge for GPU code. We will consider a clinical system with 400 detectors per ring and 64 rings and assume each detector has a face 4×4 mm in size. This leads to an inner ring radius of about 256 mm (enough for a head or thin subject).

8.2 Data Storage and Definition of Scanner Geometry

For clarity, our description of the ideas and code in this section will use explicit values for the various scanner parameters such as the number of detectors, namely 400 per ring and 64 rings. However, all the production code uses parametrised constants defined in the file scanner.h, for example, cryNum and zNum for the number of detectors per ring and the number of rings.

Our first task and most important task is to think about storing the required data:

- The voxel array a_v is quite straightforward, we will use a polar grid with 400 angular positions to match the detectors, 100 radial sectors with 2 mm spacing and 64 z slices (one per ring). The final array size is $N_v = 400 \times 100 \times 64 = 2,560,000$ words corresponding to $\sim 10^7$ bytes if we use floats to store the values. This is not a problem.

- The LOR array is more difficult. Each detector is defined by two numbers, "c" (for crystal) the angular position around the ring in the range 0–399 and "z" the detector ring number in the range 0–63. A LOR is defined by a pair of detectors $(c1,z1)$ and $(c2,z2)$. The total number of possibilities is therefore potentially $(400 \times 64)^2 \sim 6.55 \times 10^8$ which requires over 2.6×10^9 bytes to store as 4-byte integers – this is a problem. We can reduce the size somewhat by noting that LORs have no preferred direction; thus we can adopt the convention that $z1 \leq z2$. Furthermore, if $z1=0$ there are 64 possibilities for $z2$, if $z1 = 1$, there are 63 possibilities for $z2$ and so down to one possibility for $z2$ if $z1=63$. Thus, the total number of $(z1, z2)$ pairs is only $64+63+\cdots+1 = 2080$. Having adopted our convention for $z1$ the associated $c1$ must be allowed to have all 400 possible values, but for each $c1$ value we can impose a restriction on the corresponding $c2$, namely that it differs from $c1$ by at least 100. This restricts $c2$ to 201 possibilities and effectively puts $c2$ into the opposite half of the detector in the transverse plane.[3] For example, if $c1=0$ then $100 \leq c2 \leq 300$. Finally, we note that all four values can be packed into a single 4-byte field allowing 9-bits for $c1$ and $c2$ and 7 bits for $z1$ and $z2$. The resulting storage requirement is now $N_l = 2080 \times 400 \times 201 = 167,232,000$ words, corresponding to $668,928,000$ bytes, still a big number, but the best we can do. It will turn out that the performance of our code is limited by access to this array.

- The system matrix s has a nominal size of $N_v \times N_l$ which is about 4.28×10^{14} (we did mention it was enormous), but fortunately s is a very sparse matrix and has many symmetries.

  ○ Polar voxels express the rotational symmetry of the scanner; therefore, the LORs $(z1,c1,z2,c2)$ and $(z1,c1+c,z2,c2+c)$ have identical s values for any integer c. Here we assume that addition of detector c values is done modulo 400. This symmetry will be mapped to our GPU code by allocating *adjacent GPU threads to adjacent* $c1$ *values*. Note this in an important design choice and will drive the way we write both the host and GPU code. This is also why we choose to use polar voxel geometry rather than the more conventional Cartesian geometry.[4] The voxel polar angle is also adjusted by c when applying this symmetry. Using polar symmetry in this way greatly reduces the size of the system matrix and simplifies our kernel code compared to using Cartesian voxels.

  ○ Z translation symmetry, i.e. the LORs $(z1,c1,z2,c2)$ and $(z1+z,c1,z2+z,c2)$ have identical s values for all z such that $z1+z \geq 0$ and $z2+z \leq 63$. This symmetry is exploited by loops over z in our kernels. The voxel position is also adjusted by z when applying this symmetry.

  ○ Other symmetries exist for example reflection symmetry about the vertical axis in the x-y plane so that the LORs $(z1,c1,z2,c2)$ and $(z1\ 399-c1,z2,399-c2)$ have the same **s** values for correspondingly reflected voxel positions. In order to keep our kernel code as simple as possible we have not used these additional symmetries. Had we been using Cartesian coordinates, the use of these more complicated symmetries would have been essential for managing the size of the system matrix.

We will store the SM matrix as a list of 8-byte items, the first item is a 4-byte packed LOR as described above but with $z1$ and $z2$ representing the displacements to the left and right from

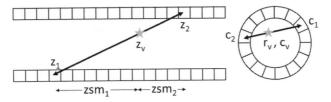

A voxel is defined by 3 integer coordinates r (radial distance from axis), c detector angle, (clockwise from vertical in 400 steps) and z (detector ring number)

A detected lor consists of $(z_1,c_1,z_2,c_2,$counts$)$ with unknown decay position

A System Matrix element consists of $(zsm_1,c_1,zsm_2,c_2,$probability$)$ where the decay point z value is implied by giving a value to zsm1 or zsm2. The decay point c value is implicitly zero if c1 and c2 are used or c if c1+c and c2+c are used. The r value is implied by indexing the SM array.

In the code the coordinates are packed into a 32-bit key:

z_1/zsm_1	c_1	z_2/zsm_2	c_2
31	25 24	16 15	9 8	0

Figure 8.3 Encoding scheme for lines of response in PET scanner

the voxel z position and not absolute detector positions. This change is helpful when applying the z-translation symmetry. The last 4 bytes are the floating-point value of the detection probability calculated by our simulation. It will turn out that for each voxel ring sector we need to store about 1.3×10^5 values resulting in a total SM size of about 1.2×10^8 bytes, an order of magnitude less than what we need for the LORs.

On a conventional system each MLEM iteration requires many minutes of CPU time and, as usually a large number of iterations are required, a full MLEM PET reconstruction takes hours. To speed up the process people often use a subset of the LORs for each MLEM interaction and on each iteration a different subset is used. This so-called ordered subsets expectation maximisation method (OSEM) was introduced by Hudson and Larkin in 1994.[5] We will show examples of reconstruction using both the full MLEM method and OSEM.

Figure 8.3 Illustrates the coordinates and storage methods for both detected LORs and system matrix elements.

Figure 8.3 Shows a sketch of the longitudinal and transverse views of a detected decay in the PET scanner. For a detected event, the LOR contains the c and z of the two detectors that fired in coincidence and the total number of times this occurred (counts). For the SM the LOR contains the z displacements from the known decay voxel and the c values of the LOR when the decay voxel has c=0. The packed key format used allows for a maximum of 128 detector rings each having up to 512 crystals. (More precisely a PET scanner could have more than 128 rings but only use detected LORs with a maximum z difference of 127).

The code described in this chapter has a number of components including:

1. Calculation of the SM of the scanner using a Monte Carlo method. The PET scanner is defined by the header file `scanner.h` which contains parameters defining the detector elements and the polar voxel grid used by the programs. All the programs in this chapter use this file and the code should work for other scanners and voxel grids if this file is changed (but note the limits on ring and detector numbers implicit in the 32-bit key

format). The constants are defined using C++11 `constexpr` and not with C/C++ macros. This has the advantage that all derived values are evaluated at compile time and that the parameters are treated as `const`.

The system matrix is calculated by simulating the detector response to decays in representative voxels using the `fullsim` program. The file `fullsim.cu` contains all the necessary host code and kernels. On its own this program provides a nice example of a physics simulation.

2. The `fullsim` program is designed to be run separately for each different set of radial distances of voxels from the central axis of the scanner. All the results from `fullsim` are then assembled into a system matrix. The is done with the short `readspot` program which just uses host code contained in `readspot.cpp`.
3. We implement a full MLEM reconstruction for the scanner. For this we need a test or *phantom* data set. The creation of such datasets is implemented as an option in the `fullsim` program. This is done rather easily by extending the simulation volumes used by `fullsim` from single polar voxels to other volumes such as ellipsoids.
4. We implement MLEM from Eq. 8.1 efficiently in GPU code; this is done with the `reco` program in the file `reco.cu`. The core kernel code in this program is fast and requires less than 60 lines. There are many real-world applications of MLEM so this example should be of interest for many tomographic and other applications.
5. For further speed-up and to compare with common practice we also implement an OSEM version of our PET reconstruction. For this we need to sort the system matrix into subsets and that is done with the host program `smsplit.cpp`.
6. Implementing OSEM with the modified system matrix is just a simple modification to `reco.cu` and is contained in the separate `recosem` program contained in the file `recosem.cu`.
7. To inspect our reconstructed images, we have to remap the polar voxel reconstructions back to a Cartesian grid for display and potential quantitative analysis. This is done by the simple host `poluse` program contained in `poluse.cpp`. This program uses a simple lookup table which is precalculated using another simulation on the GPU by the `pol2cart` program in `pol2cart.cu` file.

The file `scanner.h` defines the following basic scanner parameters:

```
constexpr int   cryNum   = 400;  // number of crystals in one ring
constexpr float crySize  = 4.0f; // size of square face 4 x 4 mm
constexpr float cryDepth = 20.0f; // depth of crystal 20 mm
constexpr int   zNum = 64;        // Number of rings in detector
```

The scanner is defined by `cryNum` the number of detectors per ring (set to 400), `crySize` the dimensions of the square detector faces (set to 4 mm) and `zNum` the number of detector rings (set to 64). In addition, the depth of the detectors in the transverse plane `cryDepth` is specified as 20 mm; this parameter will be used if we include depth of interaction in our simulation. We use the prefix `cry` for detector size parameters because most usually the

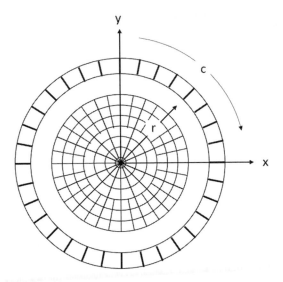

Figure 8.4 PET (c, r) and (x, y) coordinates

detectors are in fact scintillating crystals, in this case having size 4 × 4 × 20 mm.[6] This is also why we use c for the angular position of detectors around the rings.

Numerous secondary parameters can then be derived, for example the inner radius of the system is

```
detRadius = cryNum*crySize/cx::pi2<>.
```

Note this formula assumes that the inner faces of the detectors form a perfect circle which is an approximation for real PET systems.

In Figure 8.4 we show a possible coordinate systems for voxels in transverse plane for a small PET system having 32 detectors per ring and a polar voxel grid of 7 rings. The grid shown has 32 voxels per ring. Optionally adjacent voxels in the same ring can be merged to maintain approximately equal volumes for all voxels. In the figure in the outer three rings are shown with the full 32 voxels per ring and the inner four rings are shown with 16 voxels per ring. The integer ring coordinate r starts at zero for the innermost ring. The angular coordinate c is the detector number within each detector ring starts at zero at the top of the ring and increases with clockwise rotation. The voxels are arranged in a 3D stack of z-slices with typically either one or two slices per detector ring. The integer z coordinate determines which slice the voxel belongs to. Thus overall, we use 3D cylindrical polar coordinates (r, c, z) for the voxel grid. Conventionally the coordinate origin is on the central axis at one end of the scanner so that z coordinate would run from 0 to 15 for a 16-ring scanner. In the examples presented here we do not merge voxels at smaller r. This keeps our code simple and means that the values of the integer polar coordinates (c, z) are also used to identify individual detectors in the PET scanner. Floating point versions of these coordinates are also extensively used in the simulations for exact positions of decay events within a voxel and interaction points within a detector. Note our polar angle is unconventional in that it starts at zero for directions parallel to the y-axis and then increases clockwise.

Table 8.1 *Coordinate ranges for PET simulation*

Symbol	Coordinate range	Physical range of one voxel	Description
r	$0 - 99$	$2r - 2(r+1)$ mm	Radial position
c	$0 - 399$	$2\pi c/400 - 2\pi(c+1)/400$ radians	Polar angular position
z	$0 - 63$	$4z - 4(z+1)$ mm	Axial position

For the scanner simulated in our code we use a conventional z coordinate either running from 0 to 63 for integer detector numbers or continuously from 0.0 to 256.0 for exact axial positions. In the simplest simulation we use 64 axial voxel slices of thickness 4 mm to exactly match the detector rings. Thus, the voxel dimensions are typically $2 \times 2 \times 4$ mm in the r, c and z directions. The c dimension is approximate and varies with ring position as the voxels are wedge shaped not cubical. These details are summarised in Table 8.1. In real-world clinical PET scanners, it is usual to use voxel z-dimensions of half the detector z dimension to give a more uniform resolution in all directions. In this case the z slices are usually arranged so that alternate slices are centred on either detector centres or detector edges. In our case this would lead to 127 z slices where the first and last slices have widths of 3 mm and the other slices have widths of 2 mm.

The following parameters are defined in `scanner.h` to assist in creating and managing data storage:

```
constexpr int mapSlice = cryNum*zNum; // number of c1-z1 combinations
constexpr int detZdZNum = zNum*(zNum+1)/2; // number of z1-z2
  combinations
constexpr int cryCdCNum = cryNum*(cryDiffMax-cryDiffMin+1);
// c1-c2 combinations
```

The parameter `mapSlice` is the number of detectors in one ring times the number of rings. This is just the total number of detectors in the system, therefore, 400*64 = 25,600. When we generate LORs in our simulation, we choose to accumulate the results in an array large enough to hold all possible combinations. This requires an array of 4-byte `uints` of size $mapSlice^2$, amounting to about 2.6 GB. The array `map` is used in our code on the GPU while generating events in the `fullsim` program. Thus, to run the examples in this chapter a GPU with a minimum of about 4 GB of main memory is required. The simulations are done separately for each detector ring, which in our case means 100 different simulations are required to generate a complete system matrix. Were we to simply copy all the resulting map files back to host disk space, that would require ~260 GB which would be slow and wasteful.

Some compression of the map file is possible. As explained above, the number of valid z1-z2 combinations is given by `detZdzNum` which is 2080 and the number of valid c1-c2 combinations is `cryCdVNum` which is $400 \times 201 = 80,400$. Both these numbers are used extensively in the simulations and their product, 167,232,000 is the maximum number of different valid LORs that can occur in the detector simulation; this is the value of N_l in Eq. 8.1. Using this compression reduces the map file size by nearly a factor of 4, and this method is used in our code where we refer to it as *zdz format*.

The symmetries in the detector mean that we can fully simulate the system using a single voxel from each ring. In our simulation we will use the 100 voxels with integer coordinates $c_v = z_v = 0$ and r_v in the range $0 - 99$. Note the ranges for c_v and z_v match the arrangement of detectors in the physical scanner but the r_v range is simply chosen to give a good coverage of the useful volume of the scanner.

As explained above, lines of response are specified by four coordinates $(z1,c1,z2,c2)$ which define the detectors at the start and end point of the LOR. The start point of a LOR is located at detector $(z1,c1)$ and at the end point $(z2,c2)$ where $z1 \leq z2$. The symmetries of the system mean that any two LORs with the same values of $dz = z2-z1$ and $dc = c2-c1$ $(mod\ 400)$ will have the identical values for the system matrix element for corresponding voxels. We can think of a particular pair of (dz,dc) values as defining a "*base-LOR*" (BL) from which many actual detector LORs are derived by rotation (400 positions) and translation (32 positions on average depending on the value of dz). A typical derived LOR would be defined by $(z1,c1,z1+dz,c1+dc)$ where the final addition is understood to be modulo 400. Since there are 400 choices for $c1$ and $64-dz$ choices for $z1$, this is on average about $400 \times 32 = 12800$ detector LORs coming from each unique BL. The number of unique base BLs is $64 \times 201 = 12462$ where the number of $c2$ values (201) depends on our convention that $100 \leq dc \leq 300$.

In the `fullsim` simulation program we find all LORs going through a polar voxel having coordinates $c_v=0$, $z_v=63$ and $r_v=n$ where $0 \leq n \leq 99$. We use an overlong scanner with 127 rings so that the dz range of the generated LORs can reach the maximum allowed value of 63 in the real scanner with 64 rings. These LORs have the same rotation and translation symmetries as the base-LORs discussed above except that they also have an associated voxel with a definite position. The associated voxel must move with the base-LOR under any transformation. We can treat the LORs found by `fullsim` as "*base–LORs with voxel*" (BLV) defined in Eq. 8.2,

$$\text{Base LOR with Voxel: } (zsm1,c1,zsm2,c2)\{r_v = r, c_v = 0, z_v = zsm1\} \qquad (8.2)$$

where `zsm1` is the displacement from the start of the LOR to the voxel and `zsm2` is the displacement from the voxel to the end of the LOR. The extent of the LOR along the z-axis is then `dz=zsm1+zsm2`. The associated decay voxel coordinates are shown in the braces{}. In the code the voxel r value is implicit because voxels with the same r value are grouped together. The results of the `fullsim` program are the probabilities that a decay in the voxel is detected in the set of base-LORs associated with that voxel. These probabilities are invariant when the BLV is translated along the z-axis or rotated in the x-y plane. The set of LORs derived from the BLV defined in 8.2 is shown in Eq. 8.3.

$$(z,c1+c,z+dz,c2+c)\{r,c,z+zsm1\}$$
$$\text{where } dz = zsm1+zsm2 \quad \text{and} \quad 0 \leq z \leq 63 - dz \quad \text{and} \quad 0 \leq c \leq 399. \qquad (8.3)$$

8.3 Simulating a PET Scanner

After this rather long introduction we can finally dive into some code, we start with the `fullsim` program which generates the BLVs used for the system matrix. Example 8.1 shows some basic structs defined in `scanner.h` and used in the program.

Example 8.1 structs used in `fullsim`

```
10   struct Lor {    // detected Line of response (lor)
11     int z1;       // leftmost z of physical LOR
12     int c1;       // corresponding c for Z1
13     int z2;       // rightmost z of physical LOR
14     int c2;       // c2-c1 (mod 400) or position
15   };

// Same as Lor except names of z variables changed
16   struct smLor {
17     int zsm1;     // displacement to left of decay voxel
18     int c1;       // corresponding c for zsm1
19     int zsm2;     // displacement of right of decay voxel
20     int c2;       // corresponding c for zsm2
21   };

22   struct Ray {    // specifies 3D line r = a+λn
23     float3 a;
24     float3 n;
25     float lam1;   // first end point λ₁
26     float lam2;   // second end point λ₂
27   };

// can define polar voxel or complete cylinder etc.
28   struct Roi {
29     float2 z;     // z.x & z.y start and end z
30     float2 r;     // r.x & r.y start and end r
31     float2 phi;   // phi.x & phi.y start and end phi in radians
32   };
```

Description of Example 8.1

- Lines 10–15: Defines the `stuct Lor` which represents a detected line of response which following our convention has its leftmost detected point at the detector (z_1, c_1) and its rightmost point at the detector (z_2, c_2).
- Lines 16–21: Defines the `struct smLor` used for LORs with implied voxel. The variables $zsm1$ and $zsm2$ are the z displacements to the left and right of the voxel z position.
- Lines 22–27: The `stuct Ray` defines a line in 3D space. The line goes through the point **a** and has vector direction **n**. Up to two specific points on the ray can be defined by setting the values of lam1 and lam2. In our code a is a generated decay point, n is the direction in which the gammas travel and `lam1` and `lam2` indicate the two points at which the gammas meet the inner surface of the surrounding detectors. If **n** is normalised, `lam1` and `lam2` measure the distances from **a** to the detection points.

This type of geometric object is common in simulation software.

- Lines 28–31: Here we define a region of interest (ROI) within which decay events will be generated. The volume is specified as ranges of cylindrical polar and z coordinates. The r range is r.x to r.y and similarly for the polar angle phi and axial distance z.

The heart of the code is the kernel voxgen which generates decays in a given scanner voxel or other ROI and tracks the resulting back-to-back gammas to the points where they hit the inner surface of the scanner. The gamma-pair directions are generated isotropically in 3D and the decay positions are generated uniformly within the voxel volume. Such event generation is fundamental to many simulations. The voxgen kernel code is shown in Example 8.2 and a supporting kernel function ray_to_cyl in Example 8.3.

Example 8.2 voxgen kernel for PET event generation

```
40  template <typename S> __global__ void voxgen
        (r_Ptr<uint> map, r_Ptr<double> ngood, Roi roi,
                            S *states, uint tries){
41    int id = threadIdx.x + blockIdx.x*blockDim.x;
42    S state = states[id];
43    Ray g;      // generate rays
44    Lor lor;   // find Lor where ray meets detector
45    uint good = 0;
46    float r1sq = roi.r.x*roi.r.x;       // r1^2
47    float r2sq = roi.r.y*roi.r.y-r1sq; // r2^2 - r1^2
48    float dphi = roi.phi.y-roi.phi.x;  // phi range
49    float dz =   roi.z.y-roi.z.x;       // z range
50    for (uint k=0; k<tries; k++){
51      // generate point in cylindrical roi
52      // uniform in z, phi & annulus between r1 and r2
53      float phi = roi.phi.x + dphi*curand_uniform(&state);
54      float r =   sqrtf(r1sq +r2sq*curand_uniform(&state));
55      g.a.x = r*sinf(phi); // Cartesian x y
56      g.a.y = r*cosf(phi); // from r and phi
57      g.a.z = roi.z.x + dz*curand_uniform(&state);

58      // generate isotropic back to back gammas
59      phi_gam = cx::pi2<>*curand_uniform(&state);
60      // theta from acos of cos sampled uniformly in [-1,1]
61      float theta_gam = acosf(1.0f-2.0f*
                            curand_uniform(&state));
62      g.n.x = sinf(phi_gam)*sinf(theta_gam);
63      g.n.y = cosf(phi_gam)*sinf(theta_gam);
64      g.n.z = cosf(theta_gam);
```

```
65       // find & save hits in scanner detectors
66       if(ray_to_cyl(g, lor, detLongLen)){
67         good++;
68         uint zsm2 = max(0,lor.z2-zNum+1); // zsm2
69         uint zsm1 = max(0,zNum-lor.z1-1); // zsm1
70         uint index = (zsm1*cryNum+lor.c1)*mapSlice +
                             zsm2*cryNum+lor.c2;
71         atomicAdd(&map[index],1); // Histogram hits
72       }
73     }  // end generate loop
74     ngood[id] += good;  // count good hits for each thread
75     states[id] = state; // save cuRand state
76   }
```

Description of Example 8.2

- Line 40: The templated kernel function `voxgen` is the heart of the fullsim program, it generates a large number of decay events at random uniformly distributed points inside a voxel. The back-to-back gammas from these events are projected to the surrounding PET detector rings and the hit points are saved as a LOR. We expect to generate 10^{11} or more LORs for each voxel; thus we accumulate totals for the number of times each LOR occurs rather than just outputting individual events.[7] The arguments used by `voxgen` are as follows:
  - The array `unit *map` which is used to store the generated LORs. This is a large array of dimensions $(zNum \times cyrNum)^2$ which in our case is about 2.6 GB of GPU memory. In the code this array is addressed as the 4D array `hits[z1][c1][z2][c2]`. This choice is an important design decision for our code and rules out low end CUDA GPUs with smaller memories but yields fast straightforward code.

    The `map` array is used to hold integer numbers of hits; hence the choice of `uint` for the array type. This allows us to accumulate counts of up to $2^{32}-1$ for individual LORs whereas a `float` type is good only for up to $\sim 2^{25}$. The choice of `ushort` was also considered to save memory but the need to check for and deal with potential overflows in some bins would slow down and complicate the code. Also, CUDA support of 16-bit `atomicAdd` is only available in the latest GPUs (compute capability 7.0 and above).

    This array is actually bigger than it needs to be, the size could be reduced by a factor of nearly four by exploiting the constraints $z1 \leq z2$ and $dc \leq 201$. These constraints are used in the MLEM reconstruction code, `reco`, discussed later in Section 8.5. Here we are addressing elements of the very large map array randomly using results of a Monte Carlo simulation – this is a worst-case scenario for CUDA and it is not clear that adding extra code to compress the array would be worthwhile.

    We also note that while performance is important for the `fullsim` program, it is only needed once to generate the system matrix. Thus, it is better to spend our time optimising the later reconstruction code which will be run many times and for clinical applications needs to be as fast as possible.
  - The array `double* ngood`, has size equal to the total number of threads in the grid of thread blocks and is used to store the total number of good events found by individual threads. The type

double is used for storing individual thread's contributions in global memory so that the final `thrust::reduce` operation used to find the grand total of good hits is done with adequate precision, bearing in mind that the total might exceed the maximum value of the `uint` variables used to accumulate the contributions from individual threads.

○ The struct `Roi roi` which defines the volume within which decays are to be generated.[8] This `struct` is defined in `scanner.h` and is shown in Example 8.1(a), it contains the `float2` variables `r`, `phi` and `z`. The x and y components of each of these members specifies the range of values to be used in the simulation, for example, the range of radial values is `roi.r.x` ≤ `r` ≤ `roi.r.y`.

○ The template array `S *states` is used to store the cuRAND states used by each thread as in our previous Monte Carlo examples.

○ Finally `uint tries` which holds the number of generations to be attempted by each thread; it is typically in the range 10^4–10^6.

- Line 41: Determines a unique rank number `id` for each thread using our standard 1D linear thread addressing method.
- Line 42: Copy the current cuRAND state into the local variable `state`
- Lines 43–44: Declare the `structs Ray g` and `Lor lor` which are used later in the code.
- Line 45: Declare the variable `ngood` which counts the number of good hits generated by the thread.
- Lines 46–49: Initialise constants specifying the range of voxel coordinates r, phi and z to be used in the simulation loop.

Lines 50–73: These are the main event generation loop which is executed `tries` times by each thread.

- Lines 53–57: Here we generate a random point within the region specified by `roi`. The points need to populate space uniformly; this is easy to do with cubes but harder for other objects. The inverse transform method discussed in Chapter 6 is needed to do this correctly for the radial coordinate. The voxel r range goes from `roi.r.x` to `roi.r.y` but because of the wedge shape we need more points for larger values of r than for smaller values of r. The formula we need is actually Eq. 6.3 in Chapter 6 and involves the square root of a uniformly generated random number.
  ○ Line 53: Set `phi` to a uniform random value in desired range [`roi.phi.x,roi.phi.y`]
  ○ Line 54: Set `r` to a random value in the desired range [`roi.r.x,roi.r.y`] but biased so that large values occur more often and the resulting spatial distribution is uniform, Eq. 6.3 is used here.
  ○ Lines 55–56: Store the Cartesian x-y coordinates corresponding to r and phi in `g.a`.
  ○ Line 57: Store a z coordinate in `g.a` where z is generated uniformly in range [`roi.z.x, roi.z.y`].
- Lines 58–64: Simulate the production of a pair of back-to-back gamma rays at the decay point by generating a normalised 3D direction vector `g.n`. This direction is also random and we use appropriately generated random spherical polar coordinates (θ, ϕ) for this purpose. In these coordinates an area element on the unit sphere (or solid angle) is $\sin\theta \, d\theta \, d\phi$.
  ○ Line 59: Generates `phi_gam` uniformly in $[0, 2\pi]$
  ○ Line 61: For `theta_gam` but we must again use the inverse transform method of Chapter 6 to deal with $\sin\theta$. Since the integral of $\sin\theta$ is $\cos\theta$ we need to generate u uniformly in $[-1, \ 1]$ and find $\cos^{-1}(u)$.
  ○ Lines 62–64: Store the Cartesian components of the direction vector in g.**n**.
- Line 66: Find the two points where the random Ray g, constructed by the previous steps, meets the inner surface of the scanner. The calculation is done by calling the function `ray_to_cyl` with arguments g, `lor` and `detLongLen` (the detector length in mm, 508 in our case). If the ring difference between the hits points is found to be less than `zNum` (64 in our case) the function stores

the calculated (z, c) pairs in the second argument `lor` and returns 1 to indicate that a detected event has been generated. Lines 67–71 are then executed for good hits.

- Line 67: Increments the local variable `good` to keep track of successful hits. This is important as it will allow us to calculate the efficiency of the PET system for detecting gammas from the ratios of good hits to all generated gamma pairs.
- Lines 68–69: reformat the `z1` and `z2` LOR positions from absolute values in the long scanner to displacements from the source voxel at `z=zNum−1`. This `zsm1` and `zsm2` format used in the system matrix.
- Lines 70–71: Increment the appropriate element of the `map` array using `atomicAdd` in line 71. The index mimics a 4D `map[zms1][c1][zms2][c2]` layout. Note what we are doing here is effectively creating a frequency histogram of how often each possible LOR is generated for the particular voxel geometry used. Histograming is a worst-case scenario for GPU memory access as all 32 threads in any warp could be accessing 32 widely different memory locations. There is no chance of nicely coalesced memory access patterns here. On early GPU generations elaborate schemes, involving buffering in shared memory and other tricks, might have been used to try and improve performance. Fortunately, modern GPUs are more forgiving and we think it is best to take the performance hit on the chin and keep your code simple.
- Lines 74–75: For each thread store the final values of the local variables `good` and `state` in the global arrays `ngood` and `states`. Notice we use `+=` for `ngood` so that values are properly accumulated over repeated calls to the kernel.

A listing of the function `ray_to_cyl` which is used by `voxgen` to find the points at which a ray meets the cylindrical detector barrel is shown in Example 8.3.

Example 8.3 `ray_to_cyl` device function for tracking gammas to cylinder

```
80   __device__ int ray_to_cyl(Ray &g, Lor &l,  float length)
81   {
82     // find interection of ray and cylinder, need to
       // solve quadratic solve quadratic Ax²+2Bx+C = 0
83     float A = g.n.x*g.n.x +g.n.y*g.n.y;
84     float B = g.a.x*g.n.x +g.a.y*g.n.y;
85     float C = g.a.x*g.a.x +g.a.y*g.a.y -detRadius*detRadius;
86     float D = B*B-A*C;
87     float rad = sqrtf(D);
88     g.lam1 = (-B+rad)/A;   // gamma1
89     float z1 = g.a.z+g.lam1*g.n.z;
90     g.lam2 = (-B-rad)/A;   // gamma2
91     float z2 = g.a.z+g.lam2*g.n.z;

92     if (z1 >= 0.0f  && z1 < length && z2 >= 0.0f &&
                      z2 < length && abs(z2-z1) < detLen){
93       float x1  = g.a.x+g.lam1*g.n.x;
94       float y1  = g.a.y+g.lam1*g.n.y;
```

```
95      float phi = myatan2(x1,y1);
96      l.z1 = (int)(z1*detStep);
97      l.c1 = phi2cry(phi);
98      float x2 = g.a.x+g.lam2*g.n.x;
99      float y2 = g.a.y+g.lam2*g.n.y;
100     phi = myatan2(x2,y2);
101     l.z2 = (int)(z2*detStep);
102     l.c2 = phi2cry(phi);

103     if (l.z1 > l.z2){ // enforce z1 <= z2 here
104        cx::swap(l.z1,l.z2);
105        cx::swap(l.c1,l.c2);
106     }
107     return 1; // 1 indicates success - good hits in scanner
108   }
109   return 0;   // 0 indicates failure - miss scanner
110 }
      . . .
120 // NB x and y reversed compared to usual atan2
121 template <typename T> __host__ __device__
                                    T myatan2(T x, T y)
122 {
123   T angle = atan2(x,y);
124   if(angle <0) angle += cx::pi2<T>; //  0 ≤ angle ≤ 2π
125   return angle;
126 }

    // convert phi in radians to integer crystal number
127 __host__ __device__ int phi2cry(float phi)
128 {
129   while(phi < 0.0f) phi += cx::pi2<float>;
130   while(phi >= cx::pi2<float>) phi -= cx::pi2<float>;
131   return (int)( phi*cryStep );
132 }
```

Description of Example 8.3

• Line 80, The function declaration with three arguments – the input ray g, the output LOR l and the length the length of the scanner in mm. This function solves Eq. 8.4 and returns floating point values for λ the two solutions of the quadratic equation and integer values for the (z, c) values of the hit detectors. These values are all stored in the output argument l.

If the ray is $\mathbf{r} = \mathbf{a} + \lambda \mathbf{n}$ and the radius of the cylinder is R, than the equation to solve is a quadratic equation for λ as shown in Eq. 8.4.

$$\text{given} \quad \mathbf{r} = \mathbf{a} + \lambda\mathbf{n} \quad \text{find} \quad \lambda \text{ such that } r_x^2 + r_y^2 = R^2$$

$$\text{thus} \quad \lambda^2(n_x^2 + n_y^2) + 2\lambda(a_x n_x + a_y n_y) + a_x^2 + a_y^2 - R^2 = 0$$

$$\text{and} \quad \lambda = \frac{-B \pm \sqrt{B^2 - 4AC}}{2A} \tag{8.4}$$

$$\text{where} \quad A = (n_x^2 + n_y^2), \quad B = 2(a_x n_x + a_y n_y) \quad \text{and} \quad C = a_x^2 + a_y^2 - R^2$$

Intersection of ray with cylinder aligned along z-axis.

- Lines 83–85: Calculate the parameters A, B and C for Eq. 8.4; note the factors of 2 and 4 shown in the equation are not present in our code because they cancel in the final answer.
- Lines 86–87: Calculate the square root (radical) used in the solution of a quadratic equation. Since the point **a** is always inside the cylinder, we know the quadratic equation will always have real roots so D must be positive and no check is needed before taking the square root. In a more general case, where **a** might be outside the cylinder, a check would be necessary as negative values of D occur when the ray misses the cylinder.
- Lines 88–91: Calculate the `lam1` and `lam2` values for the hit points using positive D for `lam1` and negative D for `lam2`. The results are stored in g. The z coordinates, `z1` and `z2`, of the hit points are also calculated here.
- Line 92: Checks that `z1` and `z2` are both inside the finite length scanner, that is in the range `[0,length]` (length is 508 mm in our case) and that the difference between their values is consistent with the length of the short physical scanner (256 mm in our case). LORs which have a small inclination with respect to the z-axis will fail this test.
- Lines 93–97: Calculate the integer detector `z1` and `c1` values at the point given by `lam1`. Two small utility functions `myatan2` and `phi2cry` shown in 8.3 are used for this purpose.
- Lines 98–102: The same calculation for the second hit point.
- Lines 103–106: Here we swap detector elements if `z1 > z2` to ensure `z1 ≤ z2` in the subsequent processing.
- Line 107: Returns 1 to indicate success.
- Line 109: Returns 0 to indicate failure, meaning that one or both gammas escape the scanner.
- Lines 121–126: This is the support function `myatan2`. It is based on the standard C++ `atan2` math library function but is called with the arguments reversed, therefore, (x, y) indeed of the usual (y, x). It returns an angle following our PET convention, 0 for a vector parallel to the y axis and increasing with clockwise rotation up to 2π. It is good programming practice to isolate special conventions like this in a single function because then changes are easily made. If the code were repeated in multiple places, bugs are more likely if you change your convention. A particularly nice feature of CUDA is that we can use literally the same function on both the host and device, further reducing the chances of bugs.
- Lines 128–132: The function `phi2cry` converts the angle `phi` in radians to a detector number in the range 0–399 following our numbering convention for the detectors as shown in Figure 8.4.

The host code, which is not shown here, is straightforward and follows the usual pattern of our examples: read parameters, allocate and initialise memory buffers, call kernels, collate results and finish up. To compare the performance of our GPU code to similar CPU code we can replace the kernel voxgen with some similar host code running on a single CPU thread. Some typical results are shown in the box.

GPU event generation:

```
D:\ >fullsim.exe 1 144 2048 10000 12344 88 89 0 1
len 508.0 radius 254.648 rings 127 crystals/ring 400 zstep 4.000
 phistep 0.900
Roi  phi (0.000 0.016)  r (176.0 178.0)  z (252.0 256.0)  a (1.39
 176.99 254.00)
file big_map088.raw written
ngen 10000465920 good 5054418255 gen 2.056, io 25.999, total 28.059 sec
```

Single core CPU event generation:

```
D:\ >fullsim.exe 3 100 12344 88 89 0 1
len 508.0 radius 254.648 rings 127 crystals/ring 400 zstep 4.000
 phistep 0.900
Roi  phi 0.000 0.016)  r (176.0 178.0)  z (252.0 256.0)  a (1.39
 176.99 254.00)
file host_big_map088.raw written
ngen 100000000 good 50540716 gen 25.306, io 22.324, total 47.631 sec
```

Timing results for the `fullsim` code run on both the GPU and a single core of host PC. Event generation on the GPU is over 1200 times faster than on the CPU.

The GPU version of `fullsim` runs on an RTX 2070 GPU and is capable of generating about 5×10^9 events per second with isotropic orientations. About half of these interact with the PET detectors for our specific geometry. This information itself is interesting as it allows the user to calculate the geometrical efficiency of the PET scanner as a function of voxel position. The detailed information in the output file will let us go further and create the full system matrix. The same code running on a single CPU of the host PC is well over 1000 times slower. This is in spite of the fact that analysis of the GPU performance with Nsight Compute suggests the GPU code is limited by memory access and delivering "only" about 450 GFlops.

The entire system matrix requires 100 such generations corresponding to an overall generation time of only a few minutes of GPU time for reasonable statistical accuracy. Note again that the use of polar voxels is critical here. An equivalent 200×200 Cartesian grid has 8-fold symmetry and would require about 5000 separate runs of `fullsim`, a 50 fold increase in both computing time and disk space for results.

If we were to write the full 2.6 GB output map array to disk, the disk IO would take significantly longer than the time required to generate its contents. The program does have an option to do this because these files are useful for debugging. For each fixed (`c1,zsm1`) pair one slice of the map is a 2D plot of all the associated (`c2,zsm2`) hits. Now all these LORs must pass through both the 4×4mm area of the first detector and the fixed source voxel of appropriately 2 mm^3 and this restricts their possible directions to a narrow cone diverging from the source voxel towards the second detector. The divergence of these cones

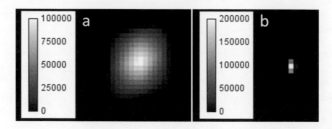

Figure 8.5 PET detector spot maps for second gamma from LOR

increases as the distance between the source voxel on the first detector decreases. Two examples corresponding to the extremes of spot sizes are shown in Figure 8.5.

Figure 8.5 shows spot maps with (c2,zsm2) distributions for fixed (c1,zsm1)=(6,5). The zsm2 axis is vertical and the c2 axis is horizontal. In 8.5 (a) the source voxel is near the scanner surface with $198 < r < 200$ mm and $0 < \phi < 7.5°$; here the spot is large with 278 non-zero values centred at (c2,zsm2)=(247,35). The peak value is 95518 for 10^{10} generated decays. In 8.5 (b) the source voxel is near the scanner centre with $0 < r < 2$mm and $0 < \phi < 7.5°$; this time the spot is small with six non-zero values centred at (c2,zsm2)=(206,5). The peak value is 182121 for 10^{10} generated decays. The "lever arm", zsm2/zsm1, is equal to 7 for (a) and 1 for (b) which accounts for the difference in spot sizes.

Apart from debugging, it is unnecessary to output the entire `400x64` (`c2,zsm2`) array for each fixed (`c1,zsm1`) pair. In fact, a square of dimension 24×24 is big enough to accommodate each "spot". It is easy to calculate the centre of the spots using the known positions of (`zsm1,c1`) and the source voxel. The calculation is similar to that of Eq. 8.4 except that as it is known that one of the points on the desired ray is already on the surface of the scanner, we only need to solve a linear equation; the result is shown in Eq. 8.5 in the box.

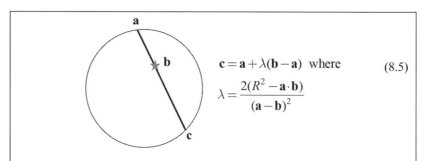

$$\mathbf{c} = \mathbf{a} + \lambda(\mathbf{b} - \mathbf{a}) \quad \text{where} \tag{8.5}$$

$$\lambda = \frac{2(R^2 - \mathbf{a} \cdot \mathbf{b})}{(\mathbf{a} - \mathbf{b})^2}$$

A LOR through **b** meets detectors at **a** and **c**. If **a** is known then **c** is given by the above formula where R is the radius of the circle.

In order to compress the output files, a kernel, find_spot, was written which reduces the volume of data that needs to be transferred back to the host and written to disk from 2.6 GB to 59 MB. The kernel is shown in Example 8.4. This kernel is not particularly elegant nor particularly efficient; rather it demonstrates that, once one knows a bit of CUDA, it is relatively easy to write kernels to do specific programming tasks for which a bespoke library function is unlikely to exist. Since the kernel has to process 400×64 separate frames of size also 400×64 we allocate one CUDA thread per frame by using 64 blocks of 400 threads. Having made this design choice no further tuning of launch block sizes is possible.

Example 8.4 find_spot kernel used to compress full_sim results

```
140   __global__ void find_spot(r_Ptr<uint> map,
                         r_Ptr<uint> spot, Roi vox) {
141     // MUST be called with zNum blocks of cryNum threads
142     float c1 = threadIdx.x; // use floats for (z1,c1) as
143     float z1 = blockIdx.x;  // they are used in calculations
144     if (c1 >= cryNum || z1 >= zNum) return;

145     float3 a; // LH hit on scanner
146     float phi = (cx··pi?c> / cryNum)*(c1 ᵢ 0.5f),
147     a.x = detRadius * sinf(phi); // phi = 0 along y axis
148     a.y = detRadius * cosf(phi); // and increases clockwise
149     a.z = crySize * (z1 + 0.5f); // use slice centre

150     float3 b;   // source voxel centre
151     phi = 0.5f*(vox.phi.y + vox.phi.x);    // mean phi
152     float rxy = 0.5f*(vox.r.y + vox.r.x); // mean r
153     b.x = rxy * sinf(phi);         //
154     b.y = rxy * cosf(phi);          // source voxel
155     b.z = 0.5f*(vox.z.y + vox.z.x);// mean x,y,z

156     // find λ₂ and point c where ray hits scanner again
157     float lam2 = -2.0f*(a.x*b.x + a.y*b.y -
            detRadius*detRadius)/((b.x-a.x)*(b.x-a.x) +
                            (b.y-a.y)*(b.y-a.y));
158     float3 c = lerp(a,b,lam2); // c = a + λ₂(b-a)
159     phi = myatan2(c.x,c.y);
160     int c2 = phi2cry(phi);  // calculated end point
161     int z2 = c.z / crySize; // of LOR starting at (z1,c1)

162     // copy the 24x24 tile at (z2,c2) from map to spot
163     int zsm1 = zNum-1 - (int)z1;
164     int zsm2 = z2 - zNum+1;
165     zsm2 = clamp(zsm2,0,zNum-1);   // could be out of range
        // map slice
166     size_t m_slice = (zsm1*cryNum + c1)*mapSlice;
        // spot slice
167     size_t s_slice = (zsm1*cryNum + c1)*spotNphi*spotNz;

168     int sz = max(0,zsm2 - spotNz/2); // tile z offset
169     for (int iz=0; iz<spotNz; iz++) {
170       int sc = cyc_sub<cryNum>(c2,spotNphi/2); // c offset
```

```
171        for (int ic=0; ic<spotNphi; ic++) {
172          uint val = map[m_slice + sz * cryNum + sc];
173          spot[s_slice + iz * spotNphi + ic] = val;
174          sc = cyc_inc<cryNum>(sc);
175        }
176        sz++;
177        if (sz >= zNum) break;
178      }

179      // store offsets in top LH corner of tile
180      spot[s_slice] = max(0,zsm2-spotNz/2) );
181      spot[s_slice+spotNphi] = cyc_sub<cryNum>(c2,spotNphi/2);
182    }
       // utility functions used above
       //   cyclic addition: returns i+step modulo cryNum
190    __host__ __device__ int cyc_add(cint i,cint step) {
191        return i+step < cryNum ? i+step : i+step-cryNum;
192    }

       //   cyclic subtraction: returns i-step modulo cryNum
193    __host__ __device__ int cyc_sub(cint i,cint step) {
194        return i >= step ? i-step : i-step+cryNum;
195    }

       //   cyclic increment: returns i+1 modulo cryNum
196    __host__ __device__ int cyc_inc(cint i) {
197        return i+1 < cryNum ? i+1 : 0;
198    }

       //   cyclic decrement: returns i-1 modulo cryNum
199    __host__ __device__ int cyc_dec(cint i) {
200        return i >= 1 ? i-1 : cryNum-1;
201    }
```

Description of Example 8.4

- Line 140: The kernel declaration has three input arguments, `uint` arrays `map` and `spot` and a `Roi` `vox` describing the voxel used in the simulation. The output array `spot` receives tiles of size 24x24 copied from the relevant region of `map`.
- Lines 142–143: The position of the left-hand end of the LOR being processed, $(z1, c1)$, is set here using thread and block ranks. Note that we use type `float` for these variables.
- Lines 145–149: Here we compute the coordinates of the point **a** on the surface of the scanner.
- Lines 150–155: Here the coordinates of the centre of the source voxel, **b**, are calculated.
- Lines 156–161: We use the result in Eq. 8.5 to calculate the end point of the LOR at **c.**
  ◦ Line 157: We calculate `lam2` using the formula in Eq. 8.5.

- ○ Line 138: This performs the linear interpolation $\mathbf{c} = \mathbf{a} + \lambda(\mathbf{b} - \mathbf{a})$ using the utility function `lerp` defined in the CUDA file `helper_math.h`.
- ○ Lines 139–141: Here we calculate the integer detector coordinates (`z2`,`c2`) for the mid-point of the "spot".
- Lines 163–165: Convert the `z1` and `z2` measured from LH end of scanner to the source voxel displacements `zsm1` and `zsm2` used in indexing the `map` and `spot` arrays. Note we clamp `zsm2` to the allowed range [`0`,`zNum-1`] and continue. This is because although `zsm2` might be out of the valid range for the scanner, some of the halo LORs in the associated spot could still be detectable.
- Lines 166–167: Find indices to the relevant (`zsm1`,`c1`) slice in `map` and `spot` for the current thread.

The rest of the code concerns copying the correct tile from `map` to `spot`.

- Lines 168–178: Loop over 24 × 24 tile centred at the calculated hit point (`zsm2`,`c2`) in `map` and copy values to `spot`. For index calculations involving the angular `c` coordinate we use modular arithmetic implemented by the utility functions `cyc_inc` and `cyc_sub`.
- Lines 180–181: Finally we store the position of the tile in the first two elements of the first column of the tile in `spot`. There is a tacit assumption here that the tile is big enough to prevent any useful data being overwritten. Obviously a more robust strategy could be used, for example, writing these numbers to a separate file, but here we want to keep our code as simple as possible.
- Lines 190–201: A set of small support functions to perform modular addition and subtraction with respect to `cryNum`. Since `cryNum` has been defined as `constexpr` in `scanner.h` its value is known at compile time aiding the compilation of efficient inline functions.

The host code used to call these kernels is not fully discussed here, but it is straightforward and can be found in our repository. Basically, the user can specify which subset of voxels to simulate and the dimensions of each voxel. Most of the parameters used by the simulation are actually defined in the `scanner.h` file and changes to these parameters would require recompilation of the whole program.

Each voxel simulated is saved in a separate binary file comprising a stack of 400 × 64 24 × 24 tiles. These files are named `spot_map000.raw` to `spot_map099.raw` for the full set of 100 voxels at different radii. On my system using 10^{11} generations per voxel (a lot!) all the files can be generated in about 36 minutes. Using an older GTX 970 GPU is about 2.5 times slower, needing about 90 minutes. Interestingly our results for the RTX 2070 card are about 160 times faster than results I was able to achieve using a cluster of 32 dual processor Xeon 3.2 GHz PCs for a similar project in 2007.[9] That system was not cheap to buy or run; it was noisy, required a full-time system manager and lots of air conditioning.

The full data set is still quite large at just under 6 GB. However, there are still a substantial number of zeros (most spots are much smaller than 24 × 24) or tiny values in the files. Since these can be discarded when building a useful system matrix, this size can be further reduced.

8.4 Building the System Matrix

The elements of the system matrix, $\mathbf{S}_{vl}$, needed for MLEM image reconstruction are the probabilities that a decay in voxel v is detected on LOR l. These are simply the numbers accumulated in the spot-map files from our simulations normalised by the number of generations. Specifically, a base-LOR with values (`zsm1`,`c1`,`zsm2`,`c2`) is proportional to the decay probability of that LOR for the voxel with $c=0$, $z=zsm1$ and $r=r_s$ where r_s in $[0,99]$ depends on which of the 100 spot-map files is used. The integer values in the spot-map files need to be divided by the total number of decays, N_{gen} used in the simulation to obtain the actual probability. As an implementation detail, in our code the scaling by N_{gen} is performed by the reconstruction code which reads unscaled values stored in the system matrix.[10]

Combining the 100 spot-map files into a single system matrix is relatively quick and straightforward; we simply concatenate all the spot-map files into a single file and compress the data to minimise storage requirements. We compress the four integer values defining a base LOR into a single 32-bit word using seven bits for the z values and nine bits for the c values as previously illustrated in Figure 8.3.

In the code we refer to the compressed values as "keys" and for each spot-map file the keys are *sorted into ascending key value order* when stored in the system matrix file. This is an important detail.

The actual system matrix file is a stack of smPart objects which hold the key values and associated number of decays converted to a 32-bit float.[11] The definition is shown in Example 8.5 together with functions for packing and unpacking keys.

Example 8.5 smPart object with key2lor and lor2key utility functions

```
// 8-byte system matrix element. Each matrix element is the
// probability that a decay in voxel v is detected in a
// particular lor. The probability is given by val and the lor
// and decay voxel are given the 4 zsm1, c1, zsm2, c2 values
// compressed into key. The voxel is at z=zsm1, c = 0 and
// r = rs. The lor goes from  z=0 & c1 to z=zsm1+zsm2 & c2.
// The matrix elements are invariant under rotation and
// translation. The rs values are implicit as sm elements are
// stored by ring number.

struct smPart {
  uint key;
  float val;
};

__device__ __host__ inline smLor key2lor(uint key)  {
  smLor sml;
  sml.c2 = key & 0x000001ff;          // bits  8-0
  sml.zsm2 = (key>>9) & 0x0000007f;   // bits 15-9
  sml.c1 = (key>>16) & 0x000001ff;    // bits 24-16
  sml.zsm1 = (key>>25);               // bits 31-25
  return sml;
}

__device__ __host__ inline uint lor2key(smLor &sml) {
```

```
  uint key = 0;
  key = (sml.zsm1<<25) | (sml.c1<<16) | (sml.zsm2<<9)
                                        | (sml.c2);
  return key;
}
```

A straightforward host code program `readspot` is used to convert the 100 spot-map files into a single system-matrix file; the code is available in our repository. The outputs from this program are two files. The first file, `sysmat.raw`, is the system matrix itself and it contains all the `smParts` from valid lines of response in the spot-map files. Importantly, the entries are sorted first in ascending order of the radial voxel position and then the data for each radial subset are sorted into ascending `key` order. The sorting by key affects memory access patterns in the reconstruction code. Using sorted keys has the consequence that `zsm1` and `c1` vary more slowly than `zsm2` and `c2` when stepping through `sysmat.raw`. Kernel code is constructed with an awareness that array indices that `zsm1` or `c1` correspond to large strides and `zsm2` or `c2` correspond to smaller strides, thus threads in the same warp should tend to use the same values for `zsm1` and `c1`. This improves the memory caching performance when running the kernels.

The `readspot` program can reject some of the LOR data in the spot-map files using user settable cuts. In particular, the user can specify a maximum value for `zsm1+zsm2`, that is the maximum scanner-ring difference for the LORs. This is useful in real-world scanners where LORs with large ring differences give less precise information. The other cut is a probability value cut on the LORs – we have found that there is a large tail of very small values which contribute nothing to the accuracy of reconstruction. For each `zsm2-c2` spot we find the maximum value and then reject LORs with values less than a fixed fraction of that value. For example, a value cut of 3% reduces the size of the `sysmat` file by 34%. After such cuts the `sysmat` file holds about 6×10^6 base-LORs requiring just 48 MB of memory.

The second file produced by the `readspot` program is `systab.raw`, a small index file containing pointers to the start and end of data for each radial subset in the `sysmat` file. The `systab` file contains one `smTab` object per radial subset, the `smTab` structure is shown in Example 8.6. The integer `start` points to the first entry in `sysmat` for this ring and `end` is one greater than the final index for this ring. The other values are for possible development and are not used at present, but they do pad the size of `smTab` to 16 bytes which matches GPU L1 cache lines.

Example 8.6 smTab structure used for indexing the system matrix

```
struct smTab {
  int ring;     // voxel radial position
  uint start;   // pointer to sysmat start of data
  uint end;     // pointer to sysmat end of data
  int  phi_steps;
};
```

8.5 PET Reconstruction

We can now implement a PET image reconstruction program using the MLEM method shown in Eq. 8.1. The program, `reco`, will reconstruct images from "*digital phantoms*" designed to simulate actual LOR image data from real scanners. The format of the phantom data files is a compressed version of the very large map array used by the `fullsim` program. The LORs are defined by sets of (`z1,c1,z2,c2`) values. However, these are not base-LORs and they do not "remember" the parent voxel where the decay occurred so this is why we use variable names `z1` and `z2` not `zsm1` and `zsm2`. Because of our conventions that `z1` $\leq$ `z2` and $100 \leq |$`c2-c1`$| \leq 300$, we must allow for all possible values of `z1` and `c1` but then the corresponding values of `z2` are restricted to `64-z1` possibilities and `c2` is restricted to `201` possibilities. The total number of combined `z1-z2` possibilities summed over the `64` possible values of `z1` is just $1 + 2 + \cdots + 64 = 2080$ hence the size of a digital phantom is `400*2080*201` corresponding a size of ~668 MB for 4-byte `uint` data. We compute a unique index value for any valid (`z1,z2`) pair as `z1+zdz_slice(z2-z1)` where the support function `zdz_slice` is shown below in Example 8.7. We will refer to such a combined z index as the `zdz` index. In the code the phantom data is indexed as `phant[zdz][dc][c1]`.

The MLEM iteration scheme shown in Eq. 8.1 involves three separate summation terms:

1. The denominator term $\mathrm{FP}_l^n = \sum_{v'=1}^{N_v} a_{v'}^n S_{v'l}$; this is the forward projection of the activity in voxel v at iteration n into LOR l obtained as the sum over all voxels of the activities $a_{v'}^n$ multiplied by $S_{v'l}$ the probability they contribute to LOR l. This sum is performed by the kernel `forward_project` shown in Example 8.7. The implementation involves an outer loop over l values and an inner loop over the subset of v' with non-zero values of $S_{v'l}$. This term is evaluated first in each MLEM iteration.
2. The numerator term $\mathrm{BP}_v^n = \sum_{l=1}^{N_l} M_l^n S_{vl}$ where $M_l^m = m_l/\mathrm{FP}_l^n$ and m_l is the measured activity in LOR l. This term is the backward projection of the detected counts in LORs to activity values in voxels. The summation is performed by the kernel `backward_project` shown in Example 8.8 which also uses an outer loop over l values.
3. The final step involves multiplication of the current activity estimate a_v^n by $\mathrm{BP}_v^n/\sum_{l'}^{N_l} S_{vl'}$ where the denominator is a normalising constant depending only on v and needs only to be calculated once. This step is performed by the kernel `rescale` also shown in Example 8.8.

Note both projection kernels use thread block sizes reflecting the angular symmetry of our polar voxel design – 400 in this case. This means that each `sysmat` element is only processed by one thread block which handles the phi symmetry by using one thread per phi value and these threads then loop over the possible z displacements. With this design the kernel code required to implement Eq. 8.1 is straightforward and is shown in Examples 8.7–8.9.

Example 8.7 `forward_project` kernel used for MLEM PET reconstruction

```
      // calculate c2-c1 rotating clockwise from c1 (modulo 400)
01    __host__ __device__ int c2_to_dc2(cint c1, cint c2) {
02      return cyc_sub(c2,c1)-cryDiffMin;
03    }
```

```
04    __host__ __device__ int  zdz_slice(int z) {
05      return detZdZNum - (zNum-z)*(zNum-z+1)/2;
06    }
      . . .
10    __global__ void forward_project(cr_Ptr<smPart> sm,
          uint smstart, uint smend, cr_Ptr<float> a,
          int ring, r_Ptr<float> FP, int dzcut, float valcut)
11    {
12      int phi = threadIdx.x;  // assumes blockDim.x = cryNum
13      uint smpos = smstart+blockIdx.x;

14      while (smpos < smend) {
15        smLor tl = key2lor(sm[smpos].key); // sysmat key
16        tl.c1 = cyc_add(tl.c1, phi); // rotate base-lors
17        tl.c2 = cyc_add(tl.c2, phi); // c1 and c2 by phi
18        int dc = c2_to_dc2(tl.c1,tl.c2);
19        int dz = tl.zsm1+tl.zsm2;

20        float val= sm[smpos].val; // sysmat value
21        if(dz > dzcut || val <valcut)
                      {smpos += gridDim.x; continue; }

22        uint lor_index = zdz_slice(dz)*cryCdCNum +
                                  dc*cryNum + tl.c1;
23        uint vol_index = (ring*zNum + tl.zsm1)*cryNum + phi;
24        for (int zs1 = 0; zs1 < zNum-dz; zs1++) {
25          float element = a[vol_index]*val;
26          atomicAdd(&FP[lor_index],element);
27          lor_index += cryCdCNum;  // lor index for z-step
28          vol_index += cryNum;     // vol index for z-step
29        }
30        smpos += gridDim.x;  // next sysmat element
31      }
32    }
```

Description of Example 8.7

Each call to this kernel adds the contribution from one ring of voxels to the FB values. The host code calls the kernel using a loop over r values and sets the smstart and smend arguments to span the range of sm elements appropriate to the particular r for each call.

- Lines 1–3: The support function c2_to_dc2 calculates a dc index from c1 and c2. The difference c2-c1 is calculated modulo 400 going clockwise from c1 to c2 and then subtracting 100 to get an index in the range [0,200].

- Lines 4–6: The support function `zdz_slice` which returns the starting index for a given `dz` value for the compressed LOR file format.
- Line 10: The declaration of the `forward_project` kernel; its arguments are as follows:
  - `sm` – this is the system matrix passed as a device pointer to an array of `smPart` objects. In our tests the `sm` array had a size of about 16.5×10^6 elements.
  - `smstart` and `smend` – integer pointers to the range of `sm` values to be processed for the current voxel ring.
  - `a` – a pointer to the `float` array holding the current estimate of voxel activities a_v^n. The voxel array size is `radNum` $\times$ `phiNum` $\times$ `zNum` $= 100 \times 400 \times 64 = 2.56 \times 10^6$.
  - `ring` – an `int` value of the voxel ring to be processed on this call; it is needed when indexing the voxel array `a` and its value is implicit in the range of `sm` elements used.
  - `FP` – an output array that holds the forward projected values. The forward projected detected LORs due to the current activities in `a`. This array is initialised to zeros by the host and gets incremented on each subsequent call for different rings.
  - `dzcut` and `valcut` – optional user defined cut values to skip some `sysmat` values for faster processing. Can be used for tuning purposes.
- Line 12: Set the voxel radial position, `phi`, to the local thread number. This is where we use the 400-fold symmetry of the voxels defined using polar coordinates. Had we used Cartesian coordinates our code would have had to be significantly more complicated.
- Line 13: Set a `uint` pointer `smpos` to the first entry in the system matrix `sm` to be used by this thread block. We need to process elements of `sm` in the range `[smstart,smend-1]` and use the thread block `id` for this purpose. This approach is just a version of the linear thread addressing mode used in many examples, but here we use thread block ids not individual thread ids.
- Lines 14 and 31: This is the processing loop over `sm` elements; notice the index `smpos` is incremented by the number of thread blocks in line 30. This design means that thread blocks with adjacent ids will process `sm` elements adjacent in memory and although in principle we have no control over the order in which thread bocks are scheduled on the GPU, it is likely that in practice adjacent thread blocks are mostly run together improving the memory caching efficiency for `sm`.
- Line 15: The key in `sm[smpart]` is decoded and the four elements are stored in the local `smLor` object `tl`.
- Lines 16–17: The `c1` and `c2` polar angles from the `sm key` are adjusted for each thread's `phi` value. This is where a single `sm` element is expanded to 400 elements.
- Line 18: The int variable `dc` is set to the angular difference between the end of the LOR using the utility function in lines 1–3.
- Line 19: The int variable `dz` is set to the z-length of the LOR, `zsm1+zsm2`.
- Line 20: The value stored in the `sm` element is stored in the local `float` variable `val`. Notice that it is correct to use the same value for all 400 threads in the thread block.
- Line 21: Here processing of the current `sm` element is skipped if it fails the cuts supplied at runtime by the user. Notice there is no thread divergence within a thread block as all the threads use the same `sm` element. This feature allows users to rapidly experiment with cuts, but for production purposes it is better to prune the system matrix in the `readspot` program, in which case this line could be removed.
- Lines 22–23: We are about to start performing the required calculation to update elements of `FP` using elements of the volume array `a`. In these lines we calculate the starting indices `lor_index` which corresponds to `FP[zdz_slice(dz)][dc][tl.c1]` and `vol_index` which corresponds to `a[ring][tl.zsm1][phi]`. Notice that within a thread block the right-hand indices `tl.c1` and `phi` are consecutive in adjacent threads leading to efficient memory caching. The index `[ring]` is also constant in the kernel. Unfortunately, the other indices are quite variable between thread blocks which means that memory access is still the performance limiting feature of this kernel.

- Lines 24–29: Here we loop over all the valid z positions for the translationally invariant sm element. In the `for` loop the variable `zs1` represents the position of the left-hand end of the LOR and has the range `[0,63-dz]`. The corresponding positions of the voxel are `[tl.zsm1,63-tl.zsm2]`.
- Lines 25–26: Here we finally do the required calculation adding $a_v S_{vl}$ to FP_l using `atomicAdd` to perform the addition. The `atomicAdd` is necessary because many voxels contribute to each LOR. Experiments suggest that on modern GPUs this use of `atomicAdd` does not have a strong effect on performance.
- Lines 27–28: Here we increment the array pointers appropriately for the LOR and voxel z positions.
- Line 30: In the last line of the kernel we increment the `smpos` index by the number of thread blocks to prepare for the next iteration.

In this kernel all the real work is done in lines 25–26 inside the for loop over `zsm1`; all the rest of the code is a wrapper designed to loop over all the entries in the system matrix.

In Example 8.8, we show the code for the `backward_project` kernel which uses the same wrapper code as the `forward_project` kernel but calculates `BP` as the second step of the MLEM iteration formula.

Example 8.8 `backward_project` and `rescale` kernels

```
40   __global__  void backward_project(cr_Ptr<smPart> sm,
         uint smstart, uint smend, cr_Ptr<uint> meas,
         int ring, cr_Ptr<float> FP, r_Ptr<float> BP,
         int dzcut, float valcut)
41   //
...  // These lines identical to lines 11-24 in forward_project
55   //
         // no division by zero
56       float FPdiv = max(1.0f,FP[lor_index]);
         // one term in sum
57       float element = val*meas[lor_index]/FPdiv;
58       atomicAdd(&BP[vol_index],element); // add
59   //
...  // These lines identical to lines 27-32 in forward_project
64   //

         . . .

     // perform rescale step - scale estimated activities
70   __global__ void rescale(r_Ptr<float> a,
                 cr_Ptr<float> BP, cr_Ptr<float> norm)
71   {
72     int id = blockIdx.x*blockDim.x + threadIdx.x;
73     while(id < zNum*radNum*cryNum){
74       a[id] *= BP[id]/norm[id/cryNum];
75       id += blockDim.x*gridDim.x;
76     }
77   }
```

Description of Example 8.8

- Line 40: The kernel declaration includes the BP and `meas` arrays instead of `FP` and the estimated activity array a. The `meas` array contains the LOR data from the digital phantom. In a real PET-scan this would be the measured number of counts in each LOR, which is commonly referred to as list-mode data.[12]
- Lines 56–58: These three lines inside the inner `zs1` loop replace lines 26–27 of the forward project example and calculate BP_v instead of FP_l.
  - Line 56: The calculation of an element of the BP array involves division by elements of FP. In this statement we guard against the case of division by zero in cases when an element of FP is zero by setting the local copy `FPdiv` to a minimum value of 1. This heuristic is based on the observation that valid values of FP are always large.
  - Line 57: Sets the local variable `element` as the required contribution to BP.
  - Line 58: Adds `element` to BP using `atomicAdd`.

  The check in line 56 is necessary because on the GPU, division by zero silently sets the result to `nan` and in our iterative calculation any `nan` elements in BP will then propagate throughout the calculation. Zeros in FP can arise because some of the measured values in the array `meas` used in line 57 can legitimately be zero.

- Lines 70–77: The Final `rescale` kernel needed to calculate Eq. 8.1 is shown here. This kernel simply scales each element a_v by the factor $BP_v/\sum_l S_{vl}$. The values of the denominator are calculated once on the host and passed to the `rescale` kernel in the kernel argument `norm`.

8.6 Results

We have tested our code with simulated decays from a Derenzo rod phantom; these phantoms are commonly used for studying PET reconstruction and consist of a number of cylinders of varying diameters grouped into a hexagonal pattern as shown in Figure 8.6.

Figure 8.6 shows the cylinder pattern of the generated Derenzo phantom; the cylinder diameters are 24.5, 17.1, 9.8, 8.6 and 6.1 mm and their lengths are 128 mm. The layout in the transverse plane is shown in (a) and a 3D rendering is shown in (b). The LORs from simulated decays in the phantom were generated using a modified version of the `fullsim` program; the activity per unit volume was assumed to be constant everywhere at about 2.5×10^5 decays per mm^3 amounting to a total activity of about 2.3×10^{10} decays. The

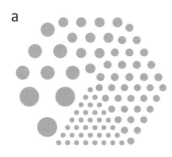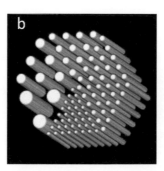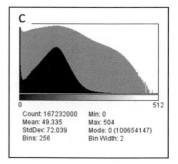

Figure 8.6 Derenzo Phantom transverse and 3D views and generated counts per LOR

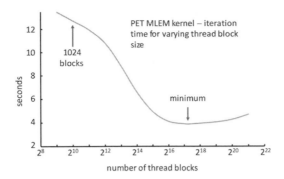

Figure 8.7 MLEM iteration time as a function of the number of thread blocks

number of detected decays in the list-mode data set used for reconstruction was about 8.25×10^9 corresponding to a geometric detection efficiency of 36% for this object. Over half the LORs in the data set had zero detected counts. Figure 8.6 (c) is a histogram of the numbers of detected decays in each LOR; about 60% of the possible LORs have zero counts; the maximum number of counts in a single LOR was 504. The grey distribution corresponds to a log-scale.

Our initial testing showed that while the code worked and gave potentially excellent reconstructions the time required was disappointingly large. For a launch configuration of 1024 thread blocks with 400 threads per block, each iteration required 12.7 seconds. About 50–100 iterations taking 10–20 minutes were required to give high-quality results. Although this was about 40 times faster than the equivalent code running on a single CPU, the GPU was running at well under its potential – the code was clearly limited by memory access. After spending some time experimenting, unsuccessfully, with different memory organisations we tried optimising the number of thread blocks while keeping the number of threads per block fixed at the design value of 400. It turned out that our standard assumption, that 1024 blocks was about right for most problems, is wildly wrong for this problem; the optimal number is around 156,000! Figure 8.7 shows how the execution time per iteration varies as a function of block size. Thus, simply using the optimal number of blocks reduces the time per iteration to about 3.9 seconds; a speed-up of a factor of 3.3.

We can estimate the performance of the code by noting that the inner loops of the forward and backward projection kernels contain about 20 arithmetic instructions including one division and two atomic adds. These inner loops over `zsl` are executed an average 32 times per system matrix element. For this test we used a system matrix with about 12.8×10^6 elements and each element is used by 400 threads. Thus, the total number of arithmetic operations performed in one iteration is about `20x400x32x12.8` $10^6 \sim 3.3 \ 10^{12}$, or just under 10^{12} operations per second which is reasonable for a memory intensive problem.

This is an excellent example of the GPU hiding memory latency when it has enough threads. This result is for an RTX 2070 GPU; other architectures may have different optima.

For comparison, running the same code on a Maxwell generation GTX 970 GPU gave an optimal execution time of 23.5 seconds per iteration, which is eight times slower. This card also required a large number of thread blocks for best performance. Here we found about 50,000 thread blocks gave the best results but the improvement over using 1024 thread blocks was only a factor of 1.2 or 20% compared to the 330% speed-up obtained with the RTX 2070. This is an unexpected and dramatic difference between cards that are only two generations apart.

8.7 Implementation of OSEM

This is as far as we can go in performance tuning our kernel code. However, we can get faster results by processing fewer system matrix elements in each iteration. For PET there is a well-known method of doing this involving the processing of different subsets of the LOR data in each iteration; the method is known as ordered subset expectation maximisation or OSEM. If we divide measured LORs into B subsets, then the modified version of Eq. 8.1 is shown in Eq. 8.6.

$$a_v^{n+1} = \frac{a_v^n}{\sum\limits_{l' \in Set_b}^{N_l} S_{vl'}} \sum\limits_{l \in Set_b}^{N_l} \frac{m_l S_{vl}}{\sum\limits_{v'=1}^{N_v} a_{v'}^n S_{v'l}} \qquad \text{for subsets } b = 1, 2, \ldots, B. \qquad (8.6)$$

In this equation it is understood that in successive iterations the subsets are processed in order so that after B iterations all the measured LOR data has been used. We will refer to the result of B such iterations as a full OSEM-B iteration. The idea is that one full OSEM-B iteration should take the same time as a single MLEM iteration but converge a factor of B times faster. In practice, while OSEM works well for early iterations it may not ultimately converge to quite the same final state as MLEM. The number of subsets, B, is known as the OSEM factor and relatively high values such as 16 are widely used in the PET community.

OSEM can be easily implemented in our code, with no changes to the kernels, by appropriate partitioning of system matrix elements into subsets and using the host code to set the kernel arguments `smstart` and `smend` to span one subset on each iteration. Similarly, the `norm` pointer used by the `rescale` kernel is set by the host to the appropriate subset sum on each iteration. However, our method, which exploits rotational symmetry, means that our definition of the OSEM subsets requires care. For the OSEM method to work it is important that each subset of LORs covers the entire region of interest in a fairly uniform way; normally this is done using *parallel projections* which are sets of LORs parallel to each other in the transverse x-y plane. In standard PET image reconstruction, each such parallel projection can be used as an OSEM subset.

In our approach, however, each thread in a thread block processes the same LOR but rotated to 400 different angles in the x-y plane. Moreover, each physical LOR occurs in potentially many system matrix elements with differing voxel radii or `c1` offsets. Helpfully, in our implementation the value of `c1+c2` obtained from the system matrix `key` defines the angle of a LOR in the transverse plane and this is different for all threads in a thread block which add an integer between 0 and 399 to both `c1` and `c2`. However, all threads in a given thread block will agree on whether `c1+c2` is even or odd – we can use this to divide our system matrix into two mutually exclusive subsets for B=2 OSEM processing. To go further we can use the even or oddness of `c1` itself to subdivide both of these subsets for B=4 OSEM or the value of `c1%m` for B=2m subsets. Using `c1` in this way ensures that all instances of a particular physical LOR in our system matrix are mapped to the same subset

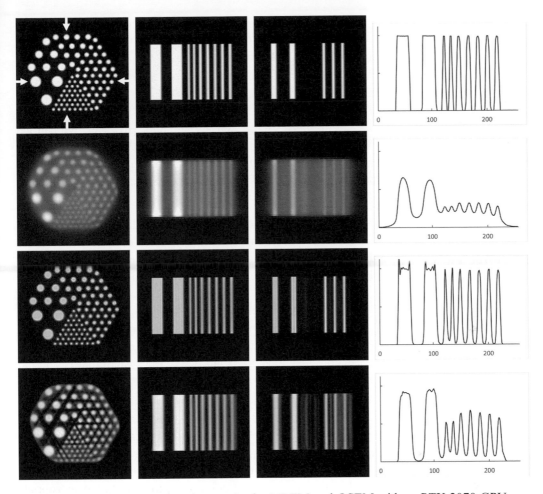

Figure 8.8 PET reconstruction results for MLEM and OSEM with an RTX 2070 GPU

but does not ensure complete coverage of the region of interest, particularly for larger B values. OSEM-1 is clearly identical to MLEM and, in practice, we find B=2, 4 and 8 gives good convergence, but higher B values do not. The execution times for full OSEM iterations are 3.8, 4.6 and 5.9 seconds for B =2, 4 and 8 respectively. Some results for the Derenzo phantom are shown in Figures 8.8 and 8.9. For OSEM factors above 8 we find that reconstructions start to lose quality and the time per full iteration increases.

The fact that good quantitative and excellent qualitative image data can be reconstructed in less than one minute using iterative methods with OSEM factors up to 8 is very helpful in some clinical applications. The fact that this can be done using inexpensive commodity GPUs compatible with a clinical environment is also significant.

Figure 8.8 shows a row of images for a central slice of the Derenzo phantom. The top row shows original activity distribution, the second row shows a reconstruction with 5 MLEM iterations (15.8 secs), the third row shows a reconstruction with 5 OSEM iterations B=8 subsets (24.3 secs) and the final row shows the reconstruction after 100 MLEM iterations (312.5 secs). The four images in each row are firstly a slice in the x-y plane, secondly a slice

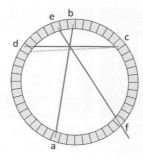

Figure 8.9 PET depth of interaction errors

in the x-z plane, thirdly a slice in the y-z plane and finally a profile of counts along a horizontal line in the x direction. The y-position of the x-z slices in column two and the profiles in column four is indicated by the horizontal arrows shown in the top left image. The x-position of the y-z slices shown in column three is shown by the vertical arrows in the top left image.

All the host code required to run the kernels described in this section can be found in our code repository. So far we have only simulated an idealised PET gamma detector; for more accurate results it is necessary to do more sophisticated simulations as discussed in the next section. Interestingly, while these complications effect the size of the system matrix and the time taken to generate it, the reconstruction code shown here does not need changing.

8.8 Depth of Interaction (DOI)

So far, we have only simulated the geometry of an idealised PET scanner, assuming that the detector where a gamma ray first reaches the inside surface of the detector array is the place where that gamma interacts. In fact, the physics of radiation transport means that gammas penetrate some depth into the detecting medium before detection and hence might be detected by the "wrong" detector or might escape without detection. These possibilities are illustrated in Figure 8.9 which shows three LORs coming from decays at the point where they intersect. The gammas defining the LOR from (a) to (b) interact in the detectors they meet first; hence the detector pair (a, b) defines a geometrically correct LOR. The second LOR from (c) to (d) has a gamma detected in a detector that is not the one it first met; hence this LOR will be incorrectly treated as if it was the dotted line shown in the figure. This causes a depth of interaction (DOI) blurring of the reconstructed image. Although illustrated here for the transverse plane, gammas can also cross detector boundaries in the axial direction. The third LOR from (e) to (f) has a gamma which passes through the (f) detector and hence no LOR event will be recorded; however, the signal from the (e) detector will contribute to the "singles" background count rate observed in PET systems. In a practical system only a fraction, typically around 50%, of the gammas that reach detectors are recorded.

The physics of radiation transport is that a beam gamma rays propagating through a uniform medium is exponentially attenuated – specifically if the initial intensity is I_0 then after travelling a distance x through the medium the surviving intensity is $I_0 e^{-x/\lambda_{attn}}$ where

λ_{attn} is a property of the medium called the *attenuation length*. Many clinical PET systems use BGO (bismuth germanate) for their detectors; BGO has as an attenuation length of ~10.1 mm. A gamma ray entering perpendicularly into a 20 mm deep layer of this material has an 86% chance of interacting. For PET both gammas need to be detected with a joint probability of 74%. This is a reasonable value for clinical PET systems. In practice most gammas enter the material at an oblique angle (as in Figure 8.9) and hence have greater change of detection albeit at the price of possible DOI errors if a system matrix based on entry points is used.

We can straightforwardly modify our `fullsim` simulation to include DOI effects resulting in a physically accurate system matrix which is then used by the unmodified reconstruction code. The detectors used for PET use arrays of dense scintillating material to absorb gammas and then emit light which is detected by photomultipliers. Two commonly used scintillators for PET are LSO and BGO which have attenuation lengths of 11.4 and 10.4 mm respectively. These values are defined in `scanner.h` as `LSO_atlen` and `BGO_atlen`. The probability distribution function for a gamma to interact after traveling a distance x through the material is:

$$P(x) = \frac{1}{\lambda_{\text{attn}}} e^{-x/\lambda_{\text{attn}}}, \tag{8.7}$$

and the probability that the gamma interacts before exceeding the distance x is

$$f(x) = \int_0^x \frac{1}{\lambda_{\text{attn}}} e^{-x'/\lambda_{\text{attn}}} dx' = 1 - e^{-x/\lambda_{\text{attn}}}. \tag{8.8}$$

Applying our inverse transform method from Chapter 6 to this function gives the following formula for generating values distributed like *f(x)*:

$$x = -\lambda_{\text{attn}} \ln(1 - U), \tag{8.9}$$

where U is a uniform random number in [0,1].

To simulate depth of interaction we model the PET detector array as a cylindrical shell of material with inner radius `detRadius` and outer radius `detRadius + cryDepth` where `cryDepth` is just the thickness of the material in the radial direction. These constants are defined in `scanner.h`, where the additional constant `doiR2` is defined as the square of the outer radius.

Example 8.9 shows the modifications to the `voxgen` and `ray_to_cyl` kernels from Example 8.1 needed to include DOI.

Example 8.9 `ray_to_cyl_doi` and `voxgen_doi` device functions

```
40   template <typename S> __global__ void voxgen_doi
         (r_Ptr<uint> map, r_Ptr<double> ngood, Roi roi,
                                S *states, uint tries) {

41       int id = threadIdx.x + blockIdx.x*blockDim.x;
42       S state = states[id];
         . . .
```

```
65     // find & save hits in scanner detectors
66     if (ray_to_cyl_doi(g, lor, detLongLen, state)) {
       . . .
76     }
       . . .
80     template <typename S> __device__ int ray_to_cyl_doi
                       (Ray &g,Lor &l, float length, S &state)
81     {
82     // track lor to cylinder
       // solve quadratic solve quadratic Ax²+2Bx+C = 0
83     float A = g.n.x*g.n.x + g.n.y*g.n.y;
84     float B = g.a.x*g.n.x + g.a.y*g.n.y;
85     float C = g.a.x*g.a.x + g.a.y*g.a.y
                             - detRadius*detRadius;
86     float D = B*B-A*C;
87     float rad = sqrtf(D);
88     g.lam1 = (-B+rad)/A;   // gamma1
88.1   float path1 = -BGO_atlen*
                         logf(1.0f - curand_uniform(&state));
88.2   g.lam1 += (g.lam1 >= 0.0f) ? path1 : - path1;
88.3   float x1 = g.a.x + g.lam1*g.n.x;
88.4   float y1 = g.a.y + g.lam1*g.n.y;
88.5   if(x1*x1+y1*y1 > doiR2) return 0;   // fail ray escapes
89     float z1 = g.a.z+g.lam1*g.n.z;
90     g.lam2 = (-B-rad)/A;   // gamma2
90.1   float path2 = -BGO_atlen*
                         logf(1.0f - curand_uniform(&state));
90.2   g.lam2 += (g.lam2 > 0.0f) ? path2 : - path2;
90.3   float x2 = g.a.x + g.lam2*g.n.x;
90.4   float y2 = g.a.y + g.lam2*g.n.y;
90.5   if (x2*x2+y2*y2 > doiR2) return 0;   // fail ray escapes
91     float z2 = g.a.z+g.lam2*g.n.z;
92     if (z1 >= 0.0f && z1 < length && z2 >= 0.0f
                     && z2 < length && abs(z2-z1) < detLen){
       . . .
107      return 1; // 1 indicates success
108    }
109    return 0;   // 0 indicates failure - gammas escaped
110  }
```

Description of Example 8.9

- Line 66: The only change between the original voxgen kernel and voxgen_doi is this line where the function to ray_to_cyl_doi is called instead of the original ray_to_cyl.
- Lines 80–110: This is the modified version of the ray_to_cyl function in Example 8.3.

- Line 80: Notice there is an extra argument – the cuRAND state object &state. The argument is passed as reference because it is important that the caller receives the updated version of state after the function call.
- Lines 88.1–88.5: These have been inserted to add an interaction point sampled from an exponential probability distribution along the first gamma's path inside the detector material and check if it escapes before interacting.
  - Line 88.1: Generates a random step from an exponential distribution with mean BGO_atlen; the result is stored in path1.
  - Line 88.2: The Ray object holds both gammas for the annihilation event associated with a decay and they share the same direction vector g.n; therefore, one of g.lam1 and g.lam2 will be positive and the other negative. The conditional assignment here caters for either possibility.
  - Lines 88.3–4: Calculate the x and y coordinates, x1 and y1, of the gamma interaction point in the detector. These coordinates were not needed in the original version.
  - Line 88.5: Here we test if the radial distance of the interaction point from the origin is less than the outer radius of the detector. The square of this radius is stored in consexpr doiR2 to avoid having to take a square root here. If the point is outside the detector the gamma has escaped and we return the failure flag.
- Lines 90.1–90.5: These perform the same interaction point check for the second gamma.
- Lines 91–110: These are the same as Example 8.3. Note the z1 and z2 coordinates now also depend on the generated interaction points.

8.9 PET Results Using DOI

The time taken to generate a complete system matrix including DOI effects actually decreased slightly to 1925 seconds for 10^{11} generations per voxel compared to 2041 seconds using the version of fullsim without DOI. This is because some previously detected gammas now escape without detection so the detector efficiency falls from 45.8% to 34.8% – hence fewer memory writes using atomicAdds are required during execution of the DOI kernel. This is not really a saving of time; it just means that we should generate more than 10^{11} events to get the same statistical errors on elements of the system matrix.

Even though there are fewer detected events, the size of the new system matrix including DOI is more than twice that of the original. This is because the set of gammas reaching any particular detector might now trigger one of the neighbouring detectors instead of the one it first met. This causes an increase in the size of the "spots". In fact, the number of distinct LORs rises from 1.64×10^6 to 3.58×10^6; a factor of ~2.2. Potentially this will slow the reconstruction program reco by the same factor. In practice, the effect is less than this because a large number of the added LORs have extremely low probabilities and can be discarded; in fact, 48% of the LORs in the new system matrix contribute only a total of 1% to the overall probability sum in the matrix and it was found that discarding these LORs made no discernible difference to the quality of the reconstructions.

Adding DOI is, however, important for simulating a real scanner where the effect is necessarily present. If we create a digital Phantom also using the DOI simulation and compare its reconstruction using system matrices with and without DOI then the original version without DOI underestimates the reconstructed activities by 25%, whereas the new version with DOI gives correct results.

Our tracking of gammas through material using samples from an exponential distribution is typical of the code used in many simulations of radiation transport problems. An important feature of our kernel code is that the only thread divergence occurs when a thread exits because its gamma misses the detector or exits though the outer surface of the detector ring without interacting. However, we have still simplified the geometry and the next sections present some ideas for the simulation of more complex cases. As the geometry becomes more complex, gammas have more opportunity to follow different paths and preventing thread divergence becomes harder. The code presented in the next section is just one approach, we do not claim it is necessarily the best.

8.10 Block Detectors

In reality PET detectors are not arranged as a perfect circle; rather the detector is a ring of blocks where each block is a set of rectangular scintillating crystals; in our simulations we are using crystals of dimension $4 \times 4 \times 20$ mm. If we now assume they are arranged into blocks of 8×8 crystals each block will have a dimension of $32 \times 32 \times 20$ mm. In the complete detector sets of 50 blocks arranged as 50-sided polygons in the x-y plane and 8 such block-rings are stacked in z to give a total of 64 detecting crystals in the z direction.

Figure 8.10 shows a close-up transverse view of three blocks in the new arrangement and illustrates the various trajectories that might occur. LOR A is detected in the same crystal where it entered the block, LOR B escapes detection by passing through the narrow gap between blocks, LOR C enters in the central block but is detected in an adjacent block, LOR D escapes detection by passing through the full crystal depth and LOR E is detected in the block it entered but by a different crystal. Our original entry-point simulation is adequate for LORs A and D and the DOI simulation is adequate for LOR E, but a full block simulation is needed for LORs B and C. Notice small gaps between blocks are unavoidable in any practical design. The dotted line indicates the "touching cylinder" which just touches the block centres. In our improved simulation the point where a gamma crosses this cylinder is used as a first guess for the block and crystal where the gamma meets the detector.

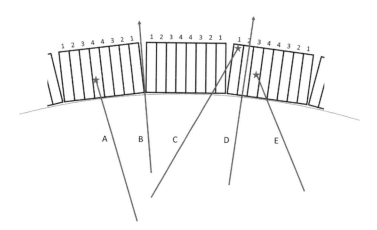

Figure 8.10 LOR paths in blocked PET detectors

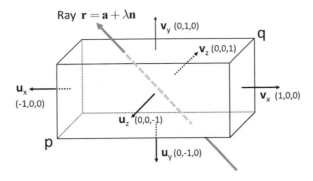

Figure 8.11 Ray tracing through a coordinate aligned block

For a full block simulation, we have to trace the paths of individual gammas first to a particular block and then through that block. The latter is actually a standard problem for all ray tracing code: the basic geometry is shown in Figure 8.11.

The block is aligned parallel to the coordinate axes and is defined by its corner points **p** and **q**. The normals at the faces point outwards and are labelled $\mathbf{u}_x$, $\mathbf{u}_y$ and $\mathbf{u}_z$ for the faces at **p** and $\mathbf{v}_x$, $\mathbf{v}_y$ and $\mathbf{v}_z$ for the faces at **q**. A typical ray is shown entering at the lower face and leaving at the upper face.

A straight line or *ray* in 3D space is defined by the equation $\mathbf{r} = \mathbf{a} + \lambda\mathbf{n}$ where **r** is the position vector of a point on the ray, **a** is a fixed point on the ray, **n** is the direction vector of the ray and λ is a parameter measuring the distance of **r** from **a**. If **n** is a unit vector then λ measures actual distance otherwise the distance is $\lambda|\mathbf{n}|$.

A plane in 3D space is defined by the equation $\mathbf{r} \cdot \mathbf{m} = d$ where **r** is the position vector of a point on the plane, **m** is the normal to the plane and d is the perpendicular distance of the plane from the origin.

To find the points where a LOR defined by the ray $\mathbf{r} = \mathbf{a} + \lambda\mathbf{n}$ meets the planes in Figure 8.11, we need to find values of λ that are solutions of the equations $\mathbf{r} \cdot \mathbf{m} = \mathbf{p} \cdot \mathbf{m}$ or $\mathbf{r} \cdot \mathbf{m} = \mathbf{q} \cdot \mathbf{m}$ where **p** and **q** are the block corners indicated in Figure 8.11 and **m** is the normal to one of the planes touching that corner We can solve these equations by noting that for the common point:

$$(\mathbf{a} + \lambda_p\mathbf{n}) \cdot \mathbf{m} = \mathbf{p} \cdot \mathbf{m} \Rightarrow \lambda_p = (\mathbf{p} - \mathbf{a}) \cdot \mathbf{m}/\mathbf{n} \cdot \mathbf{m} \quad \text{and}$$
$$(\mathbf{a} + \lambda_q\mathbf{n}) \cdot \mathbf{m} = \mathbf{q} \cdot \mathbf{m} \Rightarrow \lambda_q = (\mathbf{q} - \mathbf{a}) \cdot \mathbf{m}/\mathbf{n} \cdot \mathbf{m}. \tag{8.10}$$

In our case **m** represents one of the $\mathbf{u}_i$ or $\mathbf{v}_i$ normals to the faces of the block; these normals are all parallel to the coordinate axes thus only one component of the vector **m** is non-zero. Hence, we can express the six solutions as

$$\lambda_i^p = (p_i - a_i)/n_i \quad \text{and} \quad \lambda_i^q = (q_i - a_i)/n_i \quad \text{for} \quad i = x, y, z. \tag{8.11}$$

Notice the values of the non-zero components of $\mathbf{u}_i$ and $\mathbf{v}_i$ have cancelled so that the directions chosen for these vectors (namely in or out of the block) did not matter. If n_i is zero, then the ray is parallel to the plane in question and there is no solution.

We can exploit the fact that the overloaded operators defined for the CUDA float3 data type perform operations component-wise. Thus, if a ray is defined by the float3 vectors **a** and **n** and a coordinate aligned block has corners defined by float3 vectors **p** and **q,** then the expressions for λ in Eq. 8.7 can be evaluated in just two lines of code as shown in the box.

```
    . . .
    float3 lam_p = (p-a)/n;   // λp 3-componensts for 3 p faces
    float3 lam_q = (q-a)/n;   // λq 3-componensts for 3 q faces
    . . .
```

Fragment Showing Eq. 8.7 implemented in CUDA kernel code.

Unfortunately finding the 6 λ values is not enough; we also have to find which two points on the ray are actually on a surface of the physical block and not on an extension of a plane beyond the block. This means finding all six space points and checking that their coordinates are in the right range.

Actually, the problem of finding if and where a ray meets a rectangular block is fundamental in ray-tracing applications. A block with its sides aligned with the coordinate axes as in Figure 8.11 is often called an Axes Aligned Bounding Block (AABB) and such blocks are used to build hierarchical trees of objects contained in the scene being rendered. It is easy to show that if Eq. 8.7 are solved for a given ray and block then that ray will miss the block if and only if all the components of `lam_p` are either greater than or smaller than all the components of `lam_q`; otherwise the ray intersects the block. This test can be performed using `max` and `min` functions. It is useful in situations where many rays miss the block.

For our GPU code it is not worth including this test because for each 32-thread warp it is very likely that some of the threads will have gammas that do intersect with their target block and those threads would simply be slowed down by such a test – thus the overall simulation time would be increased even though some threads were doing less work overall. This is an example of how a different mindset is needed for GPU program optimisation as opposed to single thread CPU optimisation.

The rest of our calculation is not as elegant as the above fragment – from the six calculated values of λ we have to find the two values λ_{in} and λ_{out} that correspond to the required entry and exit points. This involves checking all six λ values in turn. Either no candidates will be found – in which case the gamma misses the block – or two candidates will be found. In our simulation the ray direction vector **n** is such that λ increases from zero as we move from the decay point **a**; thus the smaller of the two candidates will be the entry point λ_{in} and the larger the exit point λ_{out}. In addition, the difference between λ_{out} and λ_{in} is the path length travelled through the block and this can be used for DOI probability checks. Our code is shown in Example 8.10.

Example 8.10 `ray_to_block` device function

```
10  __device__ int ray_to_block(Ray &g, cfloat3 &p, cfloat3 &q)
11  {
12      // find points were ray meets the 6 planes that define
        // the block. NB all overloaded operations are
        // performed on corresponding components.
13      float3 lam_p = (p-g.a)/g.n;
```

```
14    float3 lam_q = (q-g.a)/g.n;

15    float lmin =  1.0e+06f;  // this is lam-in
16    float lmax = -1.0e+06f;  // this is lam-out
17    int exit_plane = 0; // return code, zero means missed

18    float3 b = g.a + lam_p.x * g.n;  // y-z left side plane 1
19    if(b.y >=p.y && b.y <=q.y && b.z >=p.z && b.z <=q.z) {
20      lmin = fminf(lmin,lam_p.x);
21      if(lam_p.x > lmax){exit_plane = 1; lmax =lam_p.x;}
22    }
23    b = g.a + lam_p.y * g.n;  // x-z  bottom plane 3
24    if(b.x >=p.x && b.x <=q.x && b.z >=p.z && b.z <=q.z) {
25      lmin = fminf(lmin, lam_p.y);
26      if(lam_p.y > lmax){ exit_plane = 3; lmax =lam_p.y; }
27    }
28    b = g.a + lam_p.z * g.n;  // x-y front plane 5
29    if(b.x >=p.x && b.x <=q.x && b.y >=p.y && b.y <=q.y) {
30      lmin = fminf(lmin, lam_p.z);
31      if(lam_p.z > lmax){ exit_plane = 5; lmax =lam_p.z; }
32    }
33    b = g.a + lam_q.x * g.n;  // y-z right side plane 2
34    if(b.y >=p.y && b.y <=q.y && b.z >=p.z && b.z <=q.z) {
35      lmin = fminf(lmin, lam_q.x);
36      if(lam_q.x > lmax){ exit_plane = 2; lmax =lam_q.x; }
37    }
38    b = g.a + lam_q.y * g.n;  // x-z top plane 4
39    if(b.x >=p.x && b.x <=q.x && b.z >=p.z && b.z <=q.z) {
40      lmin = fminf(lmin, lam_q.y);
41      if(lam_q.y > lmax){ exit_plane = 4; lmax =lam_q.y; }
42    }
43    b = g.a + lam_q.z * g.n;  // x-y back plane 6
44    if(b.x >=p.x && b.x <=q.x && b.y >=p.y && b.y <=q.y) {
45      lmin = fminf(lmin, lam_q.z);
46      if(lam_q.z > lmax){ exit_plane = 6; lmax =lam_q.z; }
47    }

48    g.lam1 = lmin;  // set hit points
49    g.lam2 = lmax;  // for caller

50    return exit_plane;  // zero is failure, 1-6 success
51 }
```

Description of Example 8.10

- Line 10: The function declaration with 3 input arguments, the Ray g to be tested and the float3 variables p and q defining the block. All arguments are passed by reference. The λ values for the entry and exit points will be stored in g on exit. The plane through which the ray exits is the function return value. The planes are numbered 1–6 and a return value of zero indicates that the ray misses the block.
- Lines 13–14: In the fragment shown above, the six values of λ are stored in lam_p and lam_q.
- Lines 15–16: Initialise the variables lmin and lmax; these will hold λ_{in} and λ_{out}.
- Line 17: Initialise exit_code which returns the exit plane coded in the range 1–6 if found; otherwise zero indicates that the ray misses the block. In this routine we do not return the entry plane to the user as our code does not need it, but the code could easily be modified if necessary.
- Lines 18–22: Check if the ray meets the left side face of the block at the point on the ray defined by lam_p.x and update λ_{in} and λ_{out} if it does.
  - Line 18: Gets the point **b** on the plane containing **p** with normal parallel to the x-axis using the ray equation $\mathbf{b} = \mathbf{a} + \lambda_x^p \mathbf{n}$.
  - Line 19: Check that $p_y \leq b_y \leq q_y$ and $p_z \leq b_z \leq q_z$, therefore, that point is on left-side face of the block.
  - Line 20: If point is on the face then update lmin using fminf.[13]
  - Line 21: If point is on the face also update lmax and exit_plane; this requires an if statement rather than fmaxf.
- Lines 23–47: Repeat the fragment in lines 18–22 for the other 5 points with appropriate changes to components and exit_plane codes. I usually try to avoid this kind of code repetition as it is ugly and error-prone, but this time it is hard to avoid and for GPU code the NVCC compiler actually likes code repetition and will, for example, unroll for loops. Lines 33–47 are almost identical to lines 18–32, simply replacing lam_p with lam_q and adding one to the exit_plane codes. Example 8.11 takes advantage of this to encapsulate that part of the code in a C++11 lambda function; if you like modern C++ you may prefer that version.
- Lines 48–49: Return the final λ_{in} and λ_{out} to the caller stored in g.
- Line 50: Ends the function and returns the final exit_plane value.

This function has a lot of if statements but there are no else clauses; hence there is a lot of conditional execution going on resulting in idle periods for many threads but at least there is no genuine thread divergence in the code. Minimising genuine thread divergence is a key design aim of our simulation code. The code contains 6 evaluations of the form:

```
float3 b = g.a + lam.x * g.n;
```

Each of the three components of b requires one floating point multiply and one addition making a total of 36 floating point instructions. However, in each case we use only two of the three components of b so 12 instructions are wasted. This suggests it should be more efficient to abandon the elegant vector expressions using overloaded operators to evaluate all three components and instead explicitly evaluate just the required components, this would involve replacing line 18 above with:

```
float3 b;
b.y = g.a.y + lam.x * g.n.y;
b.z = g.a.z + lam.x * g.n.z;
```

and similarly, for the other 5 evaluations of b. This should reduce the instruction count to 24 floating point operations which is significant. However, before making this change, it is interesting to look at the ptx code generated by the CUDA NVCC compiler for Example 8.10. The generated code for line 23 of Example 8.10 is shown in the following box:

```
//   float3 b = g.a+lam_p.x*g.n;   // y-z left side plane
     .loc 1 184 11
     fma.rn.ftz.f32   %f338, %f35, %f34, %f32;
     fma.rn.ftz.f32   %f339, %f16, %f35, %f12;
```

PTX code for line 23 of example 8.10; note that just two fused multiply and add instructions are generated. The compiler does not calculate b.x because that value is not used in the subsequent code.

We see that just two machine code instructions are generated, each of these instructions is a fused multiply and add taking three inputs (g.a.y/z, lam_p.x and p.n.y/z) and storing one output (b.y/z). This is the best possible code that can be generated; the unused competent of b is NOT calculated and moreover a single fused multiply and add is being used to combine the addition and multiply into one instruction. There is no need to change our code from the elegant vector equations used and only a total of 12 instructions are generated, not the 36 we feared and actually better than the 24 we expected after our proposed optimisation. In this case the compiler is at least as clever as we are and, as is so often the case, straightforward code is best.

The code in Example 8.10 is still verbose with a lot of error prone repetition. Example 8.11 is the same as 8.10 but replacing lines 18–47 with the lambda function lam_check which is defined in lines 21–38 and then called twice in lines 40 and 41.

Example 8.11 ray_to_block2 illustrating C++11 lambda function to reduce code duplication

```
10   __device__  int ray_to_block2(Ray &g, const float3 &p,
                                             const float3 &q)
11   {
12     // find points were ray meets the 6 planes that define
       // the block. NB all overloaded operations are
       // performed on corresponding components.
13     float3 lam_p = (p - g.a) / g.n;
14     float3 lam_q = (q - g.a) / g.n;

15     float lmin = 1.0e+06f;    // this is lam-in
16     float lmax = -1.0e+06f;   // this is lam out
17     int exit_plane = 0; // return code, zero means missed

18     // lambda function (C++11) Capture 6 items
19     auto lam_check = [&lmin, &lmax, &exit_plane, g, p, q]
```

```
        (float3 &lam, int side)
 20     {
 21       float3 b = g.a + lam.x * g.n;   // y-z l/r side plane
 22       if(b.y >=p.y && b.y <=q.y && b.z >=p.z && b.z <=q.z) {
 23         lmin = fminf(lmin, lam.x);
 24         if(lam.x >lmax){ exit_plane = 1+side; lmax =lam.x; }
 25       }
 26       b = g.a + lam.y * g.n;   // x-z  bottom/top plane
 27       if(b.x >=p.x && b.x <=q.x && b.z >=p.z && b.z <=q.z) {
 28         lmin = fminf(lmin, lam.y);
 29         if(lam.y >lmax){ exit_plane = 3+side; lmax =lam.y; }
 30       }
 31       b = g.a + lam.z * g.n;   // x-y front/back plane
 32       if(b.x >=p.x && b.x <=q.x && b.y >=p.y && b.y <=q.y) {
 33         lmin = fminf(lmin, lam.z);
 34         if(lam.z >lmax){ exit_plane = 5+side; lmax =lam.z; }
 35       }
 36     };

 37     lam_check(lam_p, 0);  // Faces 1, 3 and 5
 38     lam_check(lam_q, 1);  // Faces 2, 4 and 6

 39     g.lam1 = lmin;  // set hit points
 40     g.lam2 = lmax;  // for caller

 41     return exit_plane;  // zero is failure
 42   }
```

Description of Example 8.11

- Lines 10–17: These are identical to Example 8.10.
- Line 18: Declare the lambda function lam_check which replaces the two blocks of code lines 18–32 and lines 33–47 of Example 8.10 with a single block in lines 21–35. The lambda captures 6 local variables and takes two arguments. The first argument is lam which is set to either lam_p or lam_q in lines 37 and 38 duplicating the first and second blocks of code in Example 8.10. The second argument is side which is used to adjust the value of exit_plane depending on if the plane in question is on p or q. This trick only works if the planes are numbered in a particular order.
- Lines 21–34: This is the body of the function and is similar to either of the blocks in Example 8.10.
- Lines 37–38: Here we call lam_check twice to check all 6 planes.
- Lines 39–41: These are the same as lines 48–51 in Example 8.10.

Example 8.12 shows the kernel function track_ray which calls the ray_to_block2 function and plays the same role as the ray_to_cyl kernel shown in Example 8.3 and ray_to_cyl_doi in Example 8.9.

Example 8.12 `track_ray` device function which handles calls to ray_to_block2

```
60   __device__ int track_ray(Ray &g, cfloat length, float path)
61   {
62     //swim to touching cylinder: solve Ax^2+2Bx+C = 0
63     float A = g.n.x*g.n.x + g.n.y*g.n.y;
64     float B = g.a.x*g.n.x + g.a.y*g.n.y;
65     float C = g.a.x*g.a.x + g.a.y*g.a.y - bRadius * bRadius;
66     float D = B * B - A * C;
67     float rad = sqrtf(D);

68     float lam_base = (-B + rad) / A; // this is +ve root
       // b at inner surface of block centres
69     float3 b = g.a + lam_base * g.n;
70     float phi = myatan2(b.x, b.y);
71     int block = (int)(phi*bStep);
72     block = block % bNum; // nearest block to b

73     // rotated ray rg meets AABB aligned block
74     float rotback = rbStep * ((float)block + 0.5f);
75     Ray rg = rot_ray(g, rotback);

       // block p  and q corners
76     float3 p { -bcHalf, bRadius, 0.0f);
77     float3 q {  bcHalf, bRadius + cryDepth, length };

78     // find rg intersection with block
79     int exit_plane = ray_to_block2(rg, p, q);
       // gamma is detected
80     if(exit_plane > 0 && rg.lam2-rg.lam1 >= path ){
81       g.lam1 = rg.lam1;
82       g.lam2 = rg.lam1+path;// interaction point defines LOR
83       return exit_plane;
84     }
85     if(exit_plane > 2) return 0;   // gamma not detected

86     // try adjacent block if not absorbed
87     if(exit_plane > 0)  path -= rg.lam2-rg.lam1;
       // enters on RH side of block
88     if (rg.n.x < 0.0f)  rotback -= rbStep;
       //enters on LH side of block
89     else                rotback += rbStep;
90     rg = rot_ray(g, rotback);
91     exit_plane = ray_to_block2(rg, p, q);
92     if(exit_plane > 0 && rg.lam2-rg.lam1 >= path) {
93       g.lam1 = rg.lam1;
```

```
94        g.lam2 = rg.lam1+path;// interaction point defines LOR
95        return exit_plane;
96      }
97    return 0;   // not detected
98  }
```

Description of Example 8.12

- Line 60: The declaration of the device function `track_ray` has three arguments; the first two are g the ray being processed and the other is `length` the length of the scanner in in the z-direction. These are the same as in the previous versions, but the use of g has been changed. Previously a single g was used to represent both of the back-to-back gammas from a decay event with `g.lam1` and `g.lam2` being their distances to the inner surface of the cylinder. In this version, g represents a single gamma with `g.lam1` and `g.lam2` being set to the entry point and interaction or exit point of that gamma in the block. There is also a new third argument `path` which is the path length that the gamma has to travel before interacting. The path argument is the same as the `path1` and `path2` variables used in `ray_to_cyl_doi` but here it is passed as an argument rather than being calculated locally.
- Lines 63–67: Calculate the point at which the ray meets the surface of a "touching cylinder" of radius `bRadius`.[14] Since we are now inside a 50-sided polygon, not a true cylinder, this is the distance from the origin to the centre of the inner surface of one of the defining blocks.
- Line 68: This sets `lam_base` to the positive root of the quadratic equation solved in lines 63–67. In this function, it is necessary to know that as the ray parameter – lambda – increases, the associated point moves in the ray direction outwards through the detecting block. Getting this right is the responsibility of the kernel calling `track_ray`.
- Line 69: Calculates the point b where the ray meets the touching cylinder.
- Line 70: Finds the polar angle `phi` of the point b with respect to with the y-axis.
- Lines 71–72: From `phi` determine block that corresponds to the point b, (a few rays will actually "hit" the small gap between blocks). The variable `block` will be in the range [0,49].
- Lines 73–77: Calculate a rotated ray `rg` which meets an AABB aligned block with the same geometry as the original ray. Because of rotational invariance, the distances `lam1` and `lam2` that we calculate for the AABB aligned block will also be valid for the original ray g.
- Line 79: Call `ray_to_block` for the ray `rg` using the corner values set in lines 76–77.
- Lines 80–84: If the ray has actually met the block (`exit_code >0`) and the path length through the block is at least as big as `path` then it has successfully been detected. In this case we reset `g.lam1` to the entry point of the block and `g.lam2` to the detection point within the block and return with a positive exit code.
- Line 85: If `exit_code` is positive and greater than 2, the ray has passed through the block and exited either through the top, the front or the back side of the block. In these cases further interactions are impossible so that the gamma has not been detected and we return a value of zero to indicate failure.
- Lines 87–96: Here we deal with the case that the ray has either passed through the gap between blocks or exited from the left or right side of its block without interaction. In these cases, it is possible that the ray might be detected by an adjacent block, so we continue the calculation using an adjacent block.

- Line 87: If we have actually passed through a block the value of `path` is adjusted down appropriately as it is the total distance travelled through both blocks that will determine if this gamma will be detected.
  - Lines 88 and 89: Here we use the sign of `rg.n.x` to determine if the gamma is traveling towards the left or right-hand side of the AABB aligned block. If the gamma is travelling to the left, we remake `rg` to use the block one to the right of the original so that the gamma can enter its right-hand side and vice-versa for gamma travelling to the right of the original block. This is slightly counterintuitive.
  - Lines 90–96: This is simply repetition of lines 79–85 to see if the gamma interacts in the new block and passes the result back to the caller.
- Line 97: If we arrive here the ray has gone through a gap between blocks.

This illustrates a general difficulty with MC radiation transport calculations on GPUs – as particles travel through material, they acquire different histories leading to increasing thread divergences. Fortunately, in our problem the geometry is such that a valid ray cannot ever travel through more than two blocks. Here at most two calls to `ray_to_block` are required and the code shown here is complete.[15]

The final code modification that is needed is to the top level kernel `voxgen_block` which calls `track_ray`; this modified code is shown in Example 8.13. Note much of this kernel is identical to `voxgen` in Example 8.2.

Example 8.13 `voxgen_block` kernel for event generation in blocked PET detector

```
110   template <typename S> __global__ void voxgen_block
        (r_Ptr<uint> map, r_Ptr<double> ngood, Roi roi,
                                S *states, uint tries) {

111     int id = threadIdx.x + blockIdx.x*blockDim.x;
112     S state = states[id];
        // NB now using separate rays for the two gammas
113     Ray g1, g2;
114     Lor lor;
115     uint good = 0;
116     float r1sq = roi.r.x*roi.r.x;          // r1^2
117     float r2sq = roi.r.y*roi.r.y - r1sq;   // r2^2 - r1^2
118     float dphi = roi.phi.y - roi.phi.x;    // phi range
119     float dz = roi.z.y - roi.z.x;          // z range
120     for (uint k = 0; k < tries; k++) {
121       float phi = roi.phi.x + dphi*curand_uniform(&state);
122       float r = sqrtf(r1sq + r2sq*curand_uniform(&state));
123       g1.a.x = r*sinf(phi);
124       g1.a.y = r*cosf(phi);
125       g1.a.z = roi.z.x + dz*curand_uniform(&state);
126       phi = cx::pi2<float>*curand_uniform(&state);
127       float theta = acosf(1.0f-2.0f*curand_uniform(&state));
128       g1.n.x = sinf(phi)*sinf(theta);
129       g1.n.y = cosf(phi)*sinf(theta);
```

```
130        g1.n.z = cosf(theta);

131        g2.a = g1.a;   // copy ray to g2
132        g2.n = -g1.n;  // and flip direction

133        float path1 = -BGO_atlen*
                              logf(1.0f-curand_uniform(&state));
134        float path2 = -BGO_atlen*
                              logf(1.0f-curand_uniform(&state));
135        int ex1 = track_ray(g1, detLongLen, path1);
136        int ex2 = track_ray(g2, detLongLen, path2);
137        if (ex1 > 0 && ex2 > 0) {
138           float3 p1 = g1.a + g1.lam2*g1.n;
139           float phi = myatan2(p1.x, p1.y);   // here now
140           lor.z1 = (int)(p1.z*detStep);
141           lor.c1 = phi2cry(phi);
142           float3 p2 = g2.a + g2.lam2*g2.n;
143           phi = myatan2(p2.x, p2.y);
144           lor.z2 = (int)(p2.z*detStep);
145           lor.c2 = phi2cry(phi);
146           if (abs(lor.z2 - lor.z1) < zNum) {
147              if (lor.z1 > lor.z2) {
148                 cx::swap(lor.z1, lor.z2);
149                 cx::swap(lor.c1, lor.c2);
150              }
151              uint zsm2 = max(0, lor.z2-zNum+1);
152              uint zsm1 = max(0, zNum-lor.z1-1);
153              uint index = (zsm1*cryNum+lor.c1)*mapSlice +
                                  (zsm2*cryNum+lor.c2);
154              atomicAdd(&map[index], 1);
155              good++;
156        } } }
157     ngood[id] += good;
158     states[id] = state;
159   }
```

Description of Example 8.13

- Line 110: The arguments of voxgen_block are the same as voxgen; this enables the same host code to be used to call either of these kernels.
- Lines 112–130: These lines are almost identical to lines 42–64 of Example 8.2 and find random a and n values for the ray g1. The name change from the g of the original version is because we now want to use g1 to represent a single gamma whereas before it was used to represent both gammas.
- Lines 131–132: Here we create the second gamma of the pair g2 by simply copying g1 to g2 and then reversing the sign of g2.n. Both gammas now travel in the positive direction of g1.n or g2.n when moving away from the decay point towards different points on the detector rings.

Table 8.2 *Performance of event generators*

Program version	Fraction of good events in simulation (%)			Typical good events/sec
	Ring 0	Ring 70	Ring 99	
fullsim	46.9	48.1	52.7	$2.3 \ 10^9$
fullsimdoi	32.8	36.9	42.8	$1.8 \ 10^9$
fullblock	30.6	35.3	41.1	$1.8 \ 10^9$

- Lines 133–134: Here we calculate the random distances, `path1` and `path2`, to be travelled in the detectors before generating a decay point.
- Lines 135–136: Here we call `track_ray` twice to see if the gammas will be detected or not. The return values `ex1` and `ex2` are set to zero if their gamma is not detected.
- Lines 137–155: These lines are executed when both gammas are detected; they build a LOR to add to the system matrix.
  - Line 138: The point `p1` is set to the detection point for `g1` using `g1.lam2`.
  - Line 139: The polar angle `phi` in the transverse plane is calculated here from the x and y coordinates of `p`.
  - Lines 140–141: The LOR coordinates `c1` and `z1` are found here.
  - Lines 142–145: The LOR coordinates `c2` and `z2` for the `g2` gamma are found here in the same way.
  - Line 146: If the two points in the candidate LOR have a z difference less than the number of detector rings, lines 147–151 are executed. If necessary the two ends of the LOR are swapped and then appropriate element of `map` is incremented using `atomicAdd`.
- Lines 157–158: The number of good LORs and final random number state for the current thread are stored in the global memory at the end of the generation loop.

The extra steps required to accurately simulate a blocked detector do not have much impact on the rate at which events are generated by the code, the performance of the three versions is shown in Table 8.2.

Note the efficiencies in Table 8.2 reflect the real-world efficiencies of the PET geometry and detectors for capturing decay events and not the software. In fact, these efficiencies are in themselves useful results and our fast simulations could be a useful aid in optimising hardware design.

This essentially completes our discussion of the code for this section on PET; however, there is quite a lot of additional work needed on the host code to support the use of blocked detectors. Careful inspection of Figure 8.10 reveals that introducing block detectors breaks the 400-fold geometrical symmetry of the system matrix. A 100 fold symmetry remains; crystal detectors having the same number in this figure have the same values for their system matrix elements. Here we are using rotational symmetry and reflection symmetry with respect to the centres of the blocks. This means the system matrix will increase by a factor of 4 in size and the reconstruction kernels become more complicated.

We have also neglected gamma scattering events where the angle of the ray might change as it passes though material. For PET, the scatter of gammas in the detectors is not much of problem. Scatter and absorption within the subject before the gamma pair reach the detectors is an important issue, but that is another story beyond the scope of the present chapter. However, here again simulation can play a big role.

8.11 Richardson–Lucy Image Deblurring

The MLEM method is not just for PET it turns up in many applications. One interesting application, well suited to GPUs, is image deblurring, for example, to undo blurring on images caused by defects of an imaging system. In this context it is known as the Richardson–Lucy algorithm or Lucy–Richardson deconvolution It is named after William Richardson and Leon Lucy, who described it independently.[16] The algorithm effectively uses MLEM iterations where the blurred image corresponds to detected LORs in a PET scanner and the underlying true image corresponds to the unknown voxel activities. The PET system matrix is replaced by a known image filter represented by some 2D kernel, very often Gaussian blurring. This is usually called the *point spread function* of the imaging system. One important simplification is that for linear optics the same kernel is used for all pixels. This is a big simplification compared to PET where the system matrix is voxel dependent.

Eqs. 8.7–8.9 summarise the algorithm.

If an image has true pixel values p_i, then observed image has pixel values q_i given by the forward projection:

$$q_i = \sum_{\{j\}} K_{ij} p_j. \tag{8.12}$$

Where K_{ij} is the blurring filter which gives the contribution to q_i from pixel p_j, it is understood that both i and j represent 2D ranges of x and y coordinates and the notation $\{j\}$ in the summation indicates that j covers a 2D neighbourhood of pixels centred on i. The RL iteration method is then given by:

$$p_j^{n+1} = p_j^n \sum_{\{i\}} \frac{q_i}{c_i} K_{ij}, \tag{8.13}$$

where p_j^n is our estimate of p_j at iteration n and c_i is given by

$$c_i = \sum_{\{j\}} K_{ij} p_j^n. \tag{8.14}$$

Eqs. 8.7, 8.8 and 8.9 are clearly the same MLEM algorithm that we used for PET. The summation in Eq. 8.8 is the backward projection from the measured image pixels q_i to the true image but with q_i weighted by c_i, as $c_i \to q_i$ the ratio tends to one and the iteration has converged.

Examples 8.14 and 8.15 show our implementation.

Example 8.14 Richardson–Lucy FP and BP device functions

```
10   __device__  void convolve(int &x, int &y, float *kern,
         int &nkern, float *p, float &q, int &nx, int &ny)
11   {
12     int offset = nkern/2;
13     float sum = 0.0f;
14     for(int ky=0;ky<nkern;ky++){
```

```
15      int iy = y+offset-ky;
16      iy = clamp(iy,0,ny-1);    // clamp to edge values
17      for(int kx=0;kx<nkern;kx++){
18        int ix = x+offset-kx;
19        ix = clamp(ix,0,nx-1); // clamp to edge values
20        sum += p[nx*iy+ix]*kern[ky*nkern+kx];
21      }
22    }
23    q = sum; // qᵢ is sum Kᵢⱼ*Pⱼ over neighbourhood of i
24  }
30  __global__ void rl_forward(float *kern, int nkern,
        float* p1, float *c,float *q, int nx, int ny)
31  {
32    int x = blockDim.x*blockIdx.x +threadIdx.x;
33    int y = blockDim.y*blockIdx.y +threadIdx.y;
34    if(x >= nx || y >= ny) return;
35    float f= 0.0f;  // single element of c
36    convolve(x,y,kern,nkern,p1,f,nx,ny);
37    c[y*nx+x] = (abs(f) > 1.0e-06) ? q[y*nx+x]/f : q[y*nx+x];
38  }

40  __global__ void rl_backward(float *kern, int nkern,
        float *p1, float* p2, float *c, int nx, int ny)
41  {
42    int x = blockDim.x*blockIdx.x +threadIdx.x;
43    int y = blockDim.y*blockIdx.y +threadIdx.y;
44    if(x >= nx || y >= ny) return;
45    float f=0.0f;
46    convolve(x,y,kern,nkern,c,f,nx,ny);
47    p2[y*nx+x] = p1[y*nx+x]*f;
48  }
```

Description of Example 8.14

- Line 10: Declaration of the GPU function `convolve`; this function is used for the summations in Eqs. 8.8 and 8.9. The arguments x and y correspond to the point around which the summation is to be performed; this is the index i for Eq. 8.9 and j for Eq. 8.8. The arguments `kern` and `nkern` are the kernel and its size, the array p is the array to be convolved with the kernel and nx and ny are the image dimensions.
- Line 12: The variable `offset` is the maximum distance in either x or y that the centre of the kernel can move from the target point (x, y) and still contribute to the sum.
- Line 13: The variable `sum` is used to accumulate contributions from the convolution.
- Lines 14–16: These lines organise the loop over y displacements of the kernel centre; it is assumed that the kernel centre starts at a y position +`offset` from the target y coordinate and then moves in the direction of decreasing y. Line 15 calculates the y index of the element in p at the kernel centre and line 16 clamps this value to be in the allowed range.[17]

- Lines 17–19: These organise the x loop similarly to the above for y.
- Line 20: The only line that does any real work – here we add the contributions for elements of p in the neighbourhood of the target weighed by the appropriate kernel values.
- Line 23: Here we store the final result in q. Notice q is a scalar in this function; this is because convolve is called separately by each thread in the kernel; in corresponding host code q would be an array.
- Line 30: This is declaration of the rl_forward kernel which handles the forward projection of Eq. 8.9. The arguments are the convolution kernel, (kern & nkren), the current estimated activity p1, the output c array and q the measured image and finally the image dimensions.
- Lines 32–34: Find the point (x-y) about which the current thread performs convolution (i.e. the index i in Eq. 8.9).
- Lines 35–36 Perform the convolution for Eq. 8.9 with the result being placed in the temporary variable f.
- Line 37 Stores the result as q_i/c_i in the output array c. It is this ratio that is required for the next step so this is more efficient than simply storing c.
- Line 40: This is the declaration of the rl_backward kernel which handles the backward projection of Eq. 8.8. The kernel arguments are the convolution kernel, (kern & nkren), the current estimated activity p1, the improved estimate p2, the c array as computed by rl_forward and the image dimensions.
- Lines 42–44: Find the image point (x, y) for this thread.
- Lines 45–46: Perform the convolution step corresponding to Eq. 8.8.
- Line 47: Saves the result.

Example 8.15 rl_deconv host function

```
50   int rl_deconv(thrustHvec<float> &image,
              thrustHvec<float> &kern, int nx, int ny,
              int nkern, int iter, dim3 &blocks, dim3 &threads)
51   {
52     int size = nx*ny;
53     thrustDvec<float> p1(size,1.0f); // ping-pong buffers
54     thrustDvec<float> p2(size);      // for RL iterations
55     thrustDvec<float> c(size); // forward proj denominator
56     thrustDvec<float> q(size); // device copy of blurred image
57     thrustDvec<float> kn(nkern*nkern); // kernel
58     q = image;
59     kn  = kern;

60     for(int k=0;k<iter;k+=2){ // ping-pong pairs of iterations
61       rl_forward <<<blocks,threads>>>(kn.data().get(),
            nkern, p1.data().get(), c.data().get(),
                          q.data().get(), nx, ny);
62       rl_backward<<<blocks,threads>>>(kn.data().get(),
            nkern, p1.data().get(), p2.data().get(),
                          c.data().get(), nx, ny);
63       rl_forward <<<blocks,threads>>>(kn.data().get(),
```

```
              nkern, p2.data().get(), c.data().get(),
                       q.data().get(), nx, ny);
64       rl_backward<<<blocks,threads>>>(kn.data().get(),
              nkern, p2.data().get(), p1.data().get(),
                       c.data().get(), nx, ny);
65     }
66     image = p1;
67     return 0;
68 }
```

Description of Example 8.15

- Line 50: Declaration of the host function `rl_deconv` that performs the necessary calls to CUDA kernels to implement RL deconvolution. The function arguments are `image`, a host array that initially contains the blurred image and receives the final deblurred result at the end, the image filter `kern` and `nkern` (this is either known or estimated), the image dimensions `nx` and `ny`, the number of RL iterations `iter` and the kernel launch configuration `blocks` and `threads`.
- Lines 53–54: This pair of image sized device arrays hold the p_j^n and p_j^{n+1} image buffers using in the calculation. Only two buffers are necessary as they are used in a ping-pong fashion as the calculation proceeds. Notice the elements of `p1` are initialised to 1.0. This is our starting estimate for the final image.
- Lines 55–56: The `c` and `q` device arrays hold the forward projected image and observed blurred image following the notation of Eqs. 8.7, 8.8 and 8.9.
- Line 57: The device array `kn` holds a copy of the blurring kernel K_{ij}.
- Lines 58–59: Copy `image` and `kern` to device arrays.
- Lines 60–65: The main iteration loop performing `iter` iterations of the RL algorithm.
  - Lines 61–62: Call `rl_forward` and then `rl_backward` to perform one complete RL iteration. Initially `p1` holds the estimated image and afterwards `p2` holds the improved estimate. It is important to note that we must use two separate kernels here. This is because the calculation by a single thread in `rl_backward` may depend on values of `c` calculated by multiple thread blocks in `rl_forward`. Thus, the entire calculation of `c` by `rl_forward` must be complete before `rl_backward` can safely commence.
  - Lines 63–64: These are the same as 61–63 except that the roles of `p1` and `p2` are interchanged. Thus at the end of both pairs of calls, `p1` contains the result of two iterations.
  - Line 66: Copies the final result from GPU to host.

Figure 8.12 shows results from running this example on some blurred text. The computation time taken to run the program on the GPU corresponds to about 360×10^9 fused multiply and add instructions per second. Since there is also a relatively high demand for memory, using vector-loading techniques might give a modest further speed-up. However, it is very doubtful that using shared memory for the kernel would help due to the large halos required for larger kernels. Compared to a single CPU on the host PC the GPU version is about 450 times faster. It is also interesting to note that that image quality continues to improve for up to at least 10^6 iterations. This might be helpful for difficult images.

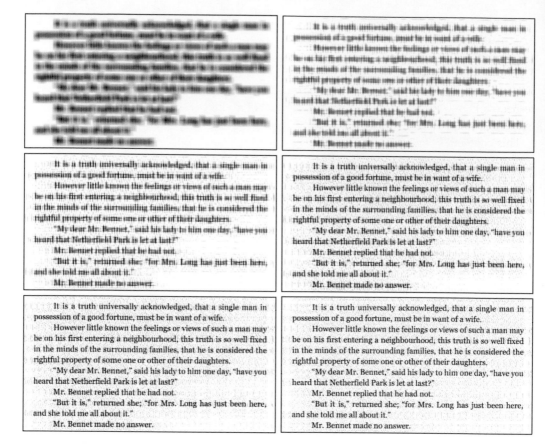

Figure 8.12 Image deblurring using the Richardson–Lucy MLEM method

We slightly cheated with this example in that we were able to use exactly the same kernel for devolution of blurring as was used to create the blurred image. In a real-world case, the original kernel might not be known, but this is exactly where the GPU speed-up helps. We can quickly try lots of kernels to find which gives the best result. We could envisage automatic searches for kernels that maximise image derivatives, for example. So-called "blind-deconvolution" is an ongoing research topic and clearly GPUs have an important role to play.

The original blurring operation in Eq. 8.7 is of course just the convolution of the image **p** with the kernel K. There are other faster deconvolution methods available, for example, taking ratios of the image and kernel in Fourier space. However, these methods are less robust against noise than the RL method. More interestingly, standard convolution-based methods assume that the filter K is position independent. MLEM-based methods do not have this restriction and will work if K depends on the position of the image pixels **p**. The system matrix used in our PET examples depends strongly on voxel positions. It would be easy to extend our RL example to allow threads to calculate the elements of K when necessary. This could be used to remove rotation smearing from long exposure images, for example, in astrophotography where the arc lengths of star trails depend on their position on the image.

In Figure 8.12 the images show some well-known text. These images have a size of 600×320 pixels. The top left image shows the original text after blurring with a truncated Gaussian filter having standard deviation of 10 pixels embedded in a 15×15 pixel kernel. The remaining five images show the results after 10^2, 10^3, 10^4, 10^5 and 10^6 iterations of our GPU kernel. The times required were 204 ms, 434 ms, 2.4 sec, 22.1 secs and 230 secs respectively. An RTX 2070 GPU was used for this example. The text is just readable after only 100 iterations and excellent after 10^6.

This concludes Chapter 8; in the next chapter we look at techniques for getting even more performance by using multiple GPUs.

Endnotes Chapter 8

1 Kaufman, L. Implementing and accelerating the EM algorithm for positron emission tomography. *IEEE Transactions on Medical Imaging* 6, 37–51 (1987).

2 MLEM is essentially a linear method which assumes that the detectors record a linear response to the received signals.

3 This is actually a commonly applied restriction. LORs with a small c1-c2 difference enter the detectors at shallow angles and may penetrate several crystals before interacting. This leads to larger depth of interaction blurring effects from these LORs.

4 Equipping readers with the necessary insights to efficiently map the particular details of their own research problems into GPU code is my key motivation for writing this book.

5 Hudson, H.M. and Larkin, R.S. Accelerated image reconstruction using ordered subsets of projection data. *IEEE Transactions on Medical Imaging*, 13(4), pp.601–609 (1994).

6 For clarity in this section we will use the defined values of the scanner parameters, e.g. 400, not the parameter name e.g. cryNum. However, in the code the parameter names are always used.

7 The is a fundamental design choice in many simulation events. Here we need a very large array to accumulate the totals for each for every possible LOR. In this case a histogram with $\sim 6.5\ 10^8$ bins, however this is small compared to the space that would be required for say 10^{12} generated LORs. In other simulations where the number of generated events is small compared to the number of event configurations it would be efficient to save individual events rather than a histogram.

8 The acronym ROI is commonly used in medical imaging circles and means region of interest.

9 Ansorge, R. "List mode 3D PET reconstruction using an exact system matrix and polar voxels." In *2007 IEEE Nuclear Science Symposium Conference Record*, vol. 5, pp. 3454–3457. IEEE, 2007. Ansorge, R. et al. "Very high resolution 3D list-mode PET reconstruction using polar voxels." In *2008 IEEE Nuclear Science Symposium Conference Record*, pp. 4112–4114. (2008).

10 The overall normalisation of the in the system matrix turns out to cancel in the expression for MLEM interactions, so in the code we normalise the probabilities to 10^6 instead of 1 to avoid tiny numbers in S. The important point is that the same number of generation attempts is made for each spot file used.

11 Converting from unsigned int to float for int values $> 2^{25}$ will introduce rounding errors, but these are completely negligible compared to the Poisson statistics on the actual values found in the simulation and the sort of accuracy needed in real PET scans. We choose to use float because 32-bit floating point calculations are faster on most NVIDIA GPUs. The most recent Turing cards have better support for integer arithmetic.

12 A great deal of older PET literature discusses sinogram data rather than list-mode data. A sinogram is simply a version of list-mode data where groups LORs are summed together to form a Radon transform of the actual activity. Sinograms both reduce the size of the measured activity data set and enable fast analytical approaches such as filtered back projection (FBP) for the reconstruction of the activity. Unfortunately, these approaches are approximate, particularly for 3D data sets which use all or most of the detected LORs not just those in the plane of a single detector ring. As modern computing

hardware becomes increasingly powerful computationally expensive methods based on the fully 3D MLEM method are increasing used.

13 While developing this code we observed that using `minf` with floats in kernel code occasionally appeared to use an integer overload and hence round floats down giving hard to find bugs. To avoid ambiguity, we switched to using explicit versions of these generic functions, `fminf` in this case.

14 We had some fun figuring out how to define `bRadius` as a `constexpr` since the expression involves a tangent but `constexpr` objects are evaluated at compile time and cannot use the standard maths library. We wrote our `constexpr` trig functions using power series to do the job, these can be found in `cxconfun.h`.

15 Actually, we have assumed that there are no gaps between detectors along the z-axis. For most scanners this is not true, so we might also have to search for neighbouring blocks in the z direction as well as phi.

16 See for example the online article in Wikipedia.

17 Dealing with edges always needs consideration when applying image filters, by clamping to the edges here we are tacitly assuming the illumination beyond the borders of the image is the same as at the edges. This is a reasonable starting guess.

9

Scaling Up

Sometimes one GPU is not enough and CUDA contains tools that allow you to spread a big calculation over more than one GPU. At this point you are moving into the world of high-performance computing (HPC) and are probably more interested in using existing applications rather than developing your own code from scratch. However, you may need to write additional code to tailor a standard application to your specific problem. In addition, we think that it is always helpful to have some understanding of what is going on to enable multiple GPUs to share a big task. There are two stages in the scaling up:

Stage 1 A single workstation with multiple GPUs

This can simply involve plugging a second GPU into an existing PC or buying a pre-configured high-end workstation with four or eight GPUs. Key considerations are how the host code manages workflows on these GPUs and how the GPUs can access each other's data.

If you are moving up to large scale GPU computing, then it is probably time to use Linux rather than Windows. This is because currently NVIDIA does not support some of the best features for managing multiple GPUs in Windows. Most dedicated workstations with multiple GPUs can be supplied running a version of the Linux operating system.

Figure 9.1 (a–c) shows 3 levels of scaling up from a basic system with just one GPU. Figure 9.1 (a) shows the first step up – a single PC with two GPUs on the PCIe bus. Figure 9.1 (b) shows an advanced workstation with a 20 core CPU and four high-end GPUs connected with two PCIe buses and additional multiway connections between pairs of GPUs using NVIDIA's proprietary NVLINK. The final scaling step is shown in Figure 9.1 (c) where multiple workstations of the types shown in Figures 9.1 (a) or (b) are linked together by a switched network that can route data between any pair of workstations.

In advanced HPC systems the network interconnect is likely to be InfiniBand rather than ethernet. In this context a single workstation is often referred to as a *node*. The topology of the network interconnect can also become complicated with communication between "close" nodes having less latency than communication between "distant" nodes. The network shown in Figure 9.1 (c) has two levels of latency; each group of 18 nodes is connected to a single InfiniBand L2 switch that allows those nodes to communicate with each other directly. Communication between different 18-node groups is possible using the second layer of L1 switches. The L1 layer has slightly higher latency and less aggregate bandwidth. The L2 connections to the nodes are 40 Gbits/sec and the connections between the L1 and L2 switches are 2×40 Gbits/sec. Figure 9.1 (c) is taken from the Mellanox website: (https://community.mellanox.com/s/article/designing-an-hpc-cluster-with-mellanox-infiniband-solutions). This company, which is now owned by NVIDIA, manufactures InfiniBand equipment and interested readers can find out much more from their website.

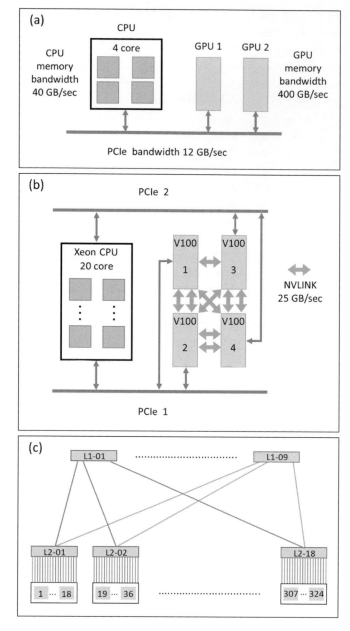

Figure 9.1 Topologies of HPC systems with multiple GPUs

At the time of writing three of the five most powerful supercomputers in the November 2020 TOP500 list: (www.top500.org/lists/top500/2020/11/) included Volta or Ampere GPUs. Number 2 on the list is the Summit machine at Oak Ridge: (www.olcf.ornl.gov/olcf-resources/compute-systems) which has 4608 nodes. Each node on Summit has two IBM Power9 CPUs and six NVIDIA V100 GPUs. Interestingly, the latest NVIDIA GPUs have hardware features to enhance IO between these specific IBM CPUs and the GPUs.

Versions of the Linux operating system dominate in the world of HPC and some recent NVIDIA CUDA developments such as demand paged virtual unified memory management are currently only supported on Linux.

This chapter discusses the additional programming tools and techniques that are used to scale up a calculation from a single GPU to these more powerful systems.

The simplest programming paradigm for a single workstation, such as that shown in Figure 9.1 (a) or (b), is for the host to control all data flow to and from the GPUs; in such cases, essentially, the only code modification required is for appropriate calls to the `cudaSelectDevice` function to be used in host code to specify which GPU subsequent CUDA calls that run kernels or access GPU memory refer to. For larger scale systems such as shown in Figure 9.1 (b) this approach becomes cumbersome and NVIDIA provides tools to manage both peer-to-peer communication between GPUs over either PCIe or NVLINK and also various unified memory addressing modes that allow the programmer to treat CPU and GPU memories as a single entity without needing explicit `cudaMemcpy` calls. This is discussed below, in our section on Unified Memory. Finally, the management of communication between HPC systems with large numbers of interconnected nodes as shown in Figure 9.1 (c) is best manged using MPI; a section on MPI is also included in this chapter. Although MPI is not strictly a CUDA topic, it shares many of the same ideas and indeed, because MPI emerged in the early 1990s, well before CUDA, it almost certainly influenced the design of CUDA. MPI is an acronym for message passing interface.

9.1 GPU Selection

Example 9.1 features the use of CUDA device management routines that are used by the host code of a multi-GPU CUDA program to manage which tasks are dispatched to which GPU. Table 9.1 shows a list of some of the more commonly used management functions and a full list with more detailed documentation can be found in Chapter 5 of the CUDA API Reference Manual. In passing we note that our old friends `cudaDeviceSynchronize()` and `cudaDeviceReset()` are included in this set of functions. These two functions, along with others in Table 9.1 do not take any arguments and always apply their actions to the currently active GPU. In CUDA programs the default active GPU is GPU zero, which has therefore been used as the correct default in most of our previous single-GPU examples. However, in the present case, where we are using multiple GPUs, we have to be careful to make the relevant GPU active before using it implicitly with any of the other device management functions.

Example 9.1 Using multiple GPUs on single host

```
10  __global__ void copydata(float *a, float *b, int n, int gpu)
11  {
12    int id = blockIdx.x*blockDim.x + threadIdx.x;
13    while(id < n){
14      b[id] = a[id];    // copy a to b
15      id += blockDim.x*gridDim.x;
16    }
17    if(threadIdx.x==0 && blockIdx.x ==0)
              printf("kernel1 gpu = %d\n",gpu);
```

```
18  }

19  int main(int argc,char *argv[])
20  {
21    int blocks = (argc >1) ? atoi(argv[1]) : 256;
22    int threads =(argc >2) ? atoi(argv[2]) : 256;
23    uint dsize = (argc >3) ? 1 << atoi(argv[3]) : 1 << 28;
24    uint bsize = dsize*sizeof(float);   // size in bytes

25    int ngpu = 0;
26    cudaGetDeviceCount(&ngpu);
27    printf("Number of GPUs on this PC is %d\n",ngpu);

28    std::vector<float *> host_buf;
29    std::vector<float *> dev_a;
30    std::vector<float *> dev_b;

31    for(int gpu=0; gpu<ngpu; gpu++){
32      cudaSetDevice(gpu);    // must select gpu before use
33      float *a = (float *)malloc(bsize); host_buf.push_back(a);
34      cudaMalloc(&a,bsize); dev_a.push_back(a);
35      cudaMalloc(&a,bsize); dev_b.push_back(a);
36      for(uint k=0;k<dsize;k++) host_buf[gpu][k] =
                                        (float)sqrt((double)k);
37      cudaMemcpy(dev_a[gpu], host_buf[gpu], bsize,
                                  cudaMemcpyHostToDevice);
38      copydata<<<blocks,threads>>>
                    (dev_a[gpu],dev_b[gpu],dsize,gpu);
39    }

40    // do host concurrent work here ...

41    for(int gpu=0; gpu<ngpu; gpu++){
42      cudaSetDevice(gpu);    // select gpu before use
43      cudaMemcpy(host_buf[gpu], dev_b[gpu], bsize,
                                  cudaMemcpyDeviceToHost);
44    }
45    // do host work on kernel results here ...

46    for(int gpu=0; gpu<ngpu; gpu++){ // tidy up
47      cudaSetDevice(gpu);         // select gpu before use
48      cudaDeviceSynchronize(); // In case of pending work
49      free(host_buf[gpu]);
50      cudaFree(dev_a[gpu]);
51      cudaFree(dev_b[gpu]);
52      cudaDeviceReset();     // reset current device
53    }
54    return 0;
55  }
```

Table 9.1 *CUDA device management functions*

`cudaGetDeviceCount(int *count)`	Returns available number of CUDA GPUs.
`cudaSetDevice(int *dev)`	Select active GPU in range 0 to `count-1`.
`cudaGetDevice(int *dev)`	Get currently active GPU.
`cudaDeviceReset(void)`	Reset current GPU.
`cudaDeviceSynchronize(void)`	Block host until all work on current GPU finished.
`cudaGetDeviceProperties(` `cudaDeviceProp *prop, int dev)`	Get device properties for GPU `dev`.

`cudaChooseDevice(`
`int *dev, const cudaDeviceProp`
`*prop)`
	Choose best match GPU based on properties
	`prop`, return result in `dev`.

`cudaDeviceSetCacheConfig(` `cudaFuncCache cacheConfig)`	Set L1 cache/shared memory allocation on devices that support this option.
`cudaDeviceGetCacheConfig(` `cudaFuncCache **pCacheConfig)`	Get current L1 cache/shared memory allocation on devices that support this option.
`cudaDeviceSetSharedMemConfig(` `cudaSharedMemConfig config)`	Set shared memory bank width to either 4-bytes or 8-bytes.
`cudaDeviceGetSharedMemConfig(` `cudaSharedMemConfig *pConfig)`	Get current shared memory bank width.
`cudaSetDeviceFlags(uint flags)`	The argument flags is a bit field specifying various runtime properties. For full details see reference manual.
`cudaGetDeviceFlags(uint *flags)`	Get current set of runtime flags.

Description of Example 9.1

- Lines 10–18: A simple test kernel `copydata` that copies n words from the input array b to the output array a. It also takes the argument gpu that is printed by the lowest ranking thread as a verification.
- Lines 21–24: Standard initialisation of user settable parameters. The variable `dsize` is the number of words of data to be processed and `bsize` is the corresponding number of bytes. The latter is convenient as array sizes in bytes are required by many CUDA functions.
- Lines 25–27: Here we set the `int` variable ngpu to the number of GPUs on the host system. This is done by calling `cudaGetDeviceCount()` in line 26. The value of ngpu is printed out in line 27 as a check.
- Lines 28–30: Here we allocate standard vectors of type `float*` to hold the pointers to actual data buffers. The index used with these vectors will correspond to the GPU being used. Here we need three buffers for each GPU, one for the host (host_buf) and two for each GPU (dev_a and dev_b).
- Lines 31–39: This loop is executed once for each GPU on the system. On each pass, we create a set of data buffers and store their pointers in elements of the buffer vectors. Specifically:
  - Line 32: Sets the current GPU to the loop variable gpu. This is critical for getting the code to work; the steps in the remainder of the loop body will apply to this GPU.
  - Line 33: Create a host buffer using good old-fashioned `malloc` rather than a container class. This will allow a more natural transition to CUDA managed memory in later examples. The pointer is held in the temporary variable `float *a` and is then stored in the host_buf vector using push_back.

- ○ Lines 34–35: Create and store pointers to the device a and b data buffers. Note, that like many CUDA functions, the syntax of cudaMalloc means that a temporary variable must be used for the result, here we reuse a for this purpose.
- ○ Line 36: Fill the host buffer host_buf[gpu] with some random data. In a real-world example host_buf[gpu] would receive different data for different values of the index gpu.
- ○ Line 37: Copies the contents of host_buf to the device buffer dev_a.
- ○ Line 38: Launches a kernel using the newly created buffers. The kernel will be run on the currently active GPU, in this case gpu. This call is not blocking on the host and we proceed to the next pass through the loop using gpu+1 while work is still running on gpu.
- • Line 40: Additional host work running in parallel with the kernels executing on the GPUs could be placed here.
- • Lines 41–44: Loop over GPUs to wait for the pending kernel to complete and then copy the device results buffer, dev_b, back to the host. Note the call to cudaSetDevice(gpu) at the start of each pass through the loop.
- • Line 45: Additional host work to process the results from the kernels could be done here.
- • Lines 46–53: Tidy up at the end of the main program. We use yet another loop over the GPUs; free the allocated host and device memory blocks and reset each device.

The code in Example 9.1 will work but it is rather ugly; in more complicated situations it would be easy to overlook a necessary cudaSetDevice causing hard to find bugs. In addition, for many problems, for example, iterative grid PDF solvers, data needs to be exchanged between GPUs as the calculation progresses. While this can always be done by copying data back and forth between the host and GPUs, a better solution would be a direct exchange of data between the GPUs bypassing the host. Such direct inter GPU or peer-to-peer communication is indeed possible over the PCI bus or NVLINK (if present). This will be explained in the next section as part of a more general discussion of CUDA support for the management of the multiple memory subsystems on a typical GPU-based workstation.

9.2 CUDA Unified Virtual Addressing (UVA)

Once you start writing programs for more than a single GPU you may want to treat their combined memory as a single entity rather than manage individual GPU memories separately. CUDA provides tools for this, albeit with some potential loss of performance.

A feature called Unified Virtual Addressing (UVA) was introduced in 2011 as part of the CUDA SDK version 4.00 release. UVA is supported on all devices of CC $\geq$ 2.0. An application *must* be compiled as a 64-bit application to take advantage of UVA; this is because 32-bit wide addressing is too limited to address the total memory space of modern workstations.

The effect of UVA is that all CUDA memory pointers allocated at run time refer to a single virtual address space within which the physical memories of the host and attached GPUs occupy separate regions. This is illustrated in Figure 9.2. When supported, UVA pointers are *always* returned by functions like cudaMalloc and cudaMallocHost but are obviously not returned by non-CUDA functions like malloc.

The main direct benefit of UVA is the simplification of calls to the cudaMemcpy family of functions which take a final argument of type cudaMemcpyKind specifying whether the

Table 9.2 *Values of the CUDA* cudaMemcpyKind *flag used with* cudaMemcpy *functions*

Flag	Source	Destination	Comment
cudaMemcpyHostToDevice	Host	Active GPU	H2D copy
cudaMemcpyDeviceToHost	Active GPU	Host	D2H copy
cudaMemcpyDeviceToDevice	Active GPU	Active GPU	Source and destination restricted to same GPU
cudaMemcpyHostToHost	Host	Host	Useful for cudaMemcpy2D and 3D
cudaMemcpyDefault	Defined by pointer	Defined by pointer	Requires UVA, source and destination can be different GPUs

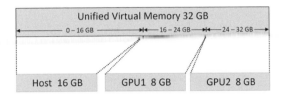

Figure 9.2 CUDA unified virtual memory

source and destination memory pointers refer to the host or GPU memory. The allowed values of this flag are shown in the Table 9.2.

Using cudaMemcpyDefault whenever possible is recommend as this makes your code more portable and removes a potential source of bugs when this flag is specified incorrectly which leads to undefined behaviour. The other important change is that using cudaMemcpyDefault allows cudaMemcpy to copy data directly between two different GPUs on the same system. The data flow in such transfers will be directly over NVLINK (if available) or the PCIe bus. Such transfers are usually referred to as peer-to-peer or P2P transfers and do require a little extra preparation in CUDA programs as discussed next.

9.3 Peer-to-Peer Access in CUDA

By default, a GPU will not allow another device to access its memory – this is a sensible precaution against bugs elsewhere in the system. Also, some older GPUs may not be capable of P2P access. Thus before performing P2P operations between a pair of GPUs a CUDA program should first check that P2P is supported on the GPUs and if so then enable P2P operations between the pair. The relevant code is shown in the box:

Example 9.2 p2ptest kernel demonstrating P2P operations between two GPUs

```
10   __global__ void p2ptest(float *src, float *dst, int size) {
11     for(int id = blockIdx.x*blockDim.x+threadIdx.x; id<size)
                              id += blockDim.x*gridDim.x;
```

```
12    dst[idx] = 2.0f*src[idx];
13  }
    . . .
20  // check for p2p access
21  int p2p_1to2;
    cudaDeviceCanAccessPeer(&p2p_1to2, gpu1, gpu2);
22  int p2p_2to1;
    cudaDeviceCanAccessPeer(&p2p_2to1, gpu2, gpu1);
23  if(p2p_1to2 == 0 || p2p_2to1 == 0) return 1;
24  cudaSetDevice(gpu1);
    cudaDeviceEnablePeerAccess(gpu2, 0);
25  cudaSetDevice(gpu2);
    cudaDeviceEnablePeerAccess(gpu1, 0);

26  cudaMemcpy(gpu1_buf, gpu2_buf, size*sizeof(float),
                                    cudaMemcpyDefault);
27  p2ptest<<<256,256>>>(gpu1_buf,gpu2_buf,size)
    . . .
30  cudaSetDevice(gpu1);
    cudaDeviceDisablePeerAccess(gpu1);
31  cudaSetDevice(gpu2);
    cudaDeviceDisablePeerAccess(gpu2);
```

Description of Example 9.2

- Lines 10–13: The p2ptest kernel is shown here; it multiplies the elements of the input array src by 2 and stores the results in the array dst. Nothing in the kernel code depends on whether the src and dsc pointers address memory in the same or different GPUs. Routing data across the NVLINK or PCIe connection, if necessary, will be decided at runtime by the driver during its translation of the unified virtual addresses in src and dst to true device memory address.
- Line 21: The code fragment assumes the int variables gpu1 and gpu2 refer to valid GPUs on the system, for example, gpu1 = 0 and gpu2 = 1. Here we check the gpu1 device supports P2P transfersto the gpu2 device. The variable p2p_1to2 will be set to zero if support is not available.
- Line 22: This is the corresponding check that the gpu2 device supports P2P transferswith the gpu1 device.
- Line 23: Abandon the test if there is no support for P2P transfers.
- Lines 24–25: Enable P2P transfers in both directions. This is essential for P2P to work.
- Line 26: Use cudaMemcpy to copy data from gpu2 to gpu1 using P2P transfers. Note the use of cudaMemcpyDefault as the fourth argument.
- Line 27: Use the p2ptest kernel to process the data received in gpu1_buf and copy the results back to gpu2_buf again using a P2P copy. This demonstrates that P2P transfers can be used directy in kernel code as well as by using cudaMemcpy calls in host code.
- Lines 30–31: Release the P2P resources allocated by the enabling calls in lines 24–25. This is not mandatory or necessary in small projects but is useful in larger projects where CUDA resources might be scarce.

Table 9.3 *CUDA host memory allocation functions*

Allocation Function	Comment
cudaHostAlloc(void **buf, size_t size, uint flags) **cudaMallocHost**(void **buf, size_t size, uint flags=0)	Identical except the second version permits a default value for flags. The first version is preferred when using non-default flags.
cudaHostGetDevicePointer(&dev_buf, buf,0)	Set dev_buf to the device pointer corresponding to buf.
cudaFreeHost(buf)	Free previously allocated memory

Possible values of flags	Comment
cudaHostAllocDefault	Allocate pinned memory on host
cudaHostAllocMapped	Maps the allocation into the CUDA address space accessed by dev_buf set by calling cudaHostGetDevicePointer.
cudaHostAllocPortable	The memory returned will be considered to be pinned memory by all CUDA contexts.
cudaHostAllocWriteCombined	Allocates the memory as write-combined. Gives faster writes but slower reads

Note these flags can be combined with each other using the arithmetic OR operator "|"

It is also possible to go further and allow the Host and all attached GPUs to use the same region of host memory directly without the need for explicit transfers using CUDA zero-copy memory.

9.4 CUDA Zero-Copy Memory

While UVA simplifies the use of the cudaMemcpy family of functions and extends them to P2P operations the programmer still needs to use cudaMemcpy calls to manage the flow of data between the Host and GPU. CUDA has an alternative mode of operation where a region of pinned memory on the host can be configured to be read or written *directly* by the system's GPUs. In this configuration the pinned memory is referred to as zero-copy or mapped memory. The key to configuring this option is the cudaHostAlloc function as shown in Table 9.3

More details of the functions in Table 9.3 can be found in the CUDA Runtime API documentation.

To set up zero-copy operation a host memory pool needs to be allocated by calling cudaAllocHost with the cudaHostAllocMapped flag. A separate device pointer is still needed for passing to kernel calls and this is set by calling cudaHostGetDevicePointer as indicated in the box. If the flag cudaHostAllocPortable is used, then the same memory pool can be used by all the devices on the system, but each device will need to have its own device memory pointer. If the cudaHostAllocWriteCombined flag is set then the host reads and writes will bypass the standard PC L1 and L2 memory caches, this has the effect of speeding up host writes to the memory at the expense of greatly slowing down host reads from the memory. Note write combining is an Intel PC feature not a CUDA feature, it is likely to be useful in cases where the host often writes to the pooled memory but rarely if ever reads from it.

Notice that when using zero-copy memory care must be taken to properly synchronise writing and reading from that memory by the host and devices. There will be not any `cudaMemcpy` calls to provide implicit synchronisation. Thus, extra care needs to be taken with appropriate use of `cudaDeviceSynchronize` and CUDA events to ensure that no read after write errors occur.

9.5 Unified Memory (UM)

Even when using zero-copy memory the programmer still needs to keep track of separate data pointers for the host and each GPU despite the fact that all these pointers refer to the same block of host memory. CUDA Unified Memory (UM) was first introduced in 2013 with CUDA 6.0. In the UM model the *same* data pointer is used for both host and device accesses to a block of memory. However, the memory block itself is managed by CUDA and is automatically copied between the host memory and device memory when necessary. In essence the host and all attached GPUs have a separate copy of the memory block in their local memory spaces and CUDA ensures that any block is up-to-date with the previous write operations between the host and attached GPUs. The system keeps track of write operations to a block of unified memory and performs a copy whenever a different device subsequently accesses that memory.

In the original release of UM the automatic copying of memory between device was always the whole block; thus using UM needed some care to avoid excessive overheads from automatic copying of large blocks of data in situations where only a few words have been changed. Also, the system automatically triggered a D2H transfer on the first host access to the UM memory block even if the programmer's intention was for the host to initialise that memory. Nevertheless, using UM dramatically simplifies pointer management in CUDA programs and might be a good initial choice for porting existing material to CUDA code.

UM is also helpful on workstations with multiple GPUs such as illustrated in Figure 9.2. In these cases, the system will automatically route the transfers by the fastest route, using NVLINK for inter-GPU transfers. There is no need for explicit management of peer-to-peer communications between the GPUs. To use UM the host merely needs to allocate a block of memory using `cudaMallocManaged` and then use the resulting pointer for all host *and* GPU accesses instead of using separate pointers allocated by, for example, `cudaHostAlloc` and `cudaMalloc`.

For systems of CC$\geq$6.0 (the Pascal generation and above) there is more fine-grained page-faulting system for managing migration of data between devices; this potentially reduces much of the inefficiency in the first release of UM and could lead to its wider adoption. However, at the time of writing, this more sophisticated memory management is only available on Linux operating systems and not in Windows. Nevertheless, this is an interesting feature which, where available, has the potential to greatly reduce the present execution time overhead encountered when using the present methods of using managed memory.

More details on managed memory can be found in an appendix of the NVIDIA CUDA C++ Programming Guide.

The performance of the various memory allocation methods is explored with the set of Examples 9.3–9.10. In these examples we use our best reduce kernel from Chapter 3 with these different methods.

Example 9.3 shows the reduce_warp_vl kernel and the simple main routine that performs all the tests.

Example 9.3 Managed memory timing tests reduce_warp_vl kernel and main routine

```
02   __global__ void reduce_warp_vl(r_Ptr<uint> sums,
                                     cr_Ptr<uint> data,uint n)
03   {
04     auto b = cg::this_thread_block();      // thread block
05     auto w = cg::tiled_partition<32>(b);  // warp
06     int4 v4 ={0,0,0,0};
07     for(int tid = b.size()*b.group_index().x +
                  b.thread_rank(); tid < n/4;
08                   tid += b.size()*gridDim.x)
09       v4 += reinterpret_cast<const int4 *>(data)[tid];
10     uint v = v4.x + v4.y + v4.z + v4.w;
11     w.sync();

12     v += w.shfl_down(v,16);
13     v += w.shfl_down(v,8);
14     v += w.shfl_down(v,4);
15     v += w.shfl_down(v,2);
16     v += w.shfl_down(v,1);
17     if(w.thread_rank() == 0)
             atomicAdd(&sums[b.group_index().x],v);
18   }

19   double fill_buf(uint *buf, uint dsize)
20   {
21     double sum = 0.0;
22       for(uint k=0;k<dsize;k++) {
23         buf[k] = k%419;   // some test data
24         sum += buf[k];    // host sum to check correctness
25       }
26     return sum;
27   }

30   int main(int argc, char *argv[])   // used for all tests
31   {
32     int test   =   (argc > 1) ? atoi(argv[1]) : 0;   // choose test
33     int blocks =   (argc > 2) ? atoi(argv[2]) : 256;
```

```
34    int threads = (argc > 3) ? atoi(argv[3]) : 256;
      // data size is
35    uint dsize =  (argc > 4) ? 1 << atoi(argv[4]) : 1 << 24;
      // a power of 2
36    double t2 = 0.0;   // kernel time
37    cx::MYTimer tim;

38    if(test==0)
          reduce_classic(blocks,threads,dsize,t2);
39    else if(test==1)
          reduce_classic_pinned(blocks,threads,dsize,t2);
40    else if(test==2)
          reduce_thrust_standard(blocks,threads,dsize,t2);
41    else if(test==3)
          reduce_thrust_pinned(blocks,threads,dsize,t2);
42    else if(test==4)
          reduce_thrust_hybrid(blocks,threads,dsize,t2);
43    else if(test==5)
          reduce_zerocopy(blocks,threads,dsize,t2);
44    else if(test==6)
          reduce_managed(blocks,threads,dsize,t2);

45    double t1 = tim.lap_ms();
46    printf("test %d total time %.3f kernel time %.3f
                                    ms\n",test,t1,t2);
47    std::atexit([]{cudaDeviceReset();});
48    return 0;
49  }
```

Description of Example 9.3

- Lines 1–18: This is our best version of the reduce function `reduce_warp_vl` and was described in Chapter 3.
- Lines 19–27: The utility host function `fill_buf` fills its array argument `buf` with `dsize` items of test data. The sum of the values is also accumulated in line 24 and returned to the caller in line 26.
- Lines 32–35: Here the main routine sets the run configuration from optional user inputs. The first user parameter, `test`, is used to select which test function is called.
- Line 36: The double variable `t2` will be set to the kernel execution time.
- Lines 37–45: This is a timed block of code which calls one of the 7 available test functions. In line 45 the variable `t1` is set to the total time taken by the called function.
- Lines 46–48: Print the times, tidy up and exit.

Example 9.4 shows our first test which uses standard `cudaMalloc` for device memory allocation. This sets our performance baseline.

Example 9.4 Managed memory test 0 using `cudaMalloc`

```
50   int reduce_classic(int blocks,int threads,uint dsize,
                                                double &t)
51   {
52     uint *host_buf = (uint *)malloc(dsize*sizeof(uint));
53     uint *dev_buf;
       cudaMalloc(&dev_buf,dsize*sizeof(uint));
54     uint *dev_sum;
       cudaMalloc(&dev_sum,blocks*sizeof(uint));
55     uint host_tot;
56     uint *dev_tot;
       cudaMalloc(&dev_tot,1*sizeof(uint));
57     double check = fill_buf(host_buf,dsize);
58     cx::MYTimer cuda;      // timed block start
59     cudaMemcpy(dev_buf, host_buf, dsize*sizeof(uint),
                                cudaMemcpyHostToDevice);
60     reduce_warp_vl<<<blocks,threads>>>(dev_sum,dev_buf,dsize);
61     reduce_warp_vl<<<    1,blocks>>>(dev_tot,dev_sum,blocks);
62     cudaMemcpy(&host_tot, dev_tot, sizeof(uint),
                                cudaMemcpyDeviceToHost);
63     cudaDeviceSynchronize();
64     t = cuda.lap_ms(); // timed block end
65     if(check != host_tot)
          printf("error classic: sum %u check %.0f\n",
                                host_tot,check);
66     free(host_buf);
67     cudaFree(dev_buf); cudaFree(dev_sum); cudaFree(dev_tot);
68     return 0;
69   }

D:\temp>memtests.exe 0 256 256 24
test 0 total time 176.503 kernel time 13.147 ms
```

Description of Example 9.4

- Line 50: The `reduce_classic` function uses the standard combination of `malloc` and `cudaMalloc` to manage memory buffers and `cudaMemcpy` transfer data between the host and GPU. The function arguments are the launch parameters for running the kernel (`blocks` and `threads`), the size of the data buffer and the argument `double` t passed by reference to return the time taken to the caller.
- Lines 52–56: Allocate all the memory buffers required using `malloc` for the host buffers and `cudaMalloc` for the device buffers. The arrays `host_buf` and `dev_buf` have size `dsize` to equal to that of the total dataset. The device array `dev_sum` has size `blocks` (the number of thread blocks used) and is used as an output array to hold the individual block sums in the first kernel call (line 40) and as an input array in the second kernel call (line 61).

- Line 57: Here we call `fill_buf` the fill the host array `host_buf` with data. The sum of these values is returned by the function and stored in `check`.
- Line 58: Starts a timed block of code ending at line 64.
- Line 59: Copies the host data to the device using an explicit `cudaMemcpy` call.
- Line 60–61: Call the `reduce_warp_v1` kernel twice, first to get thread block sums into the device array `dev_sum` and then a second time to sum the elements of `dev_sum` to the first (and only) element of the array `dev_tot`. Note there is no need for a host array corresponding to `dev_sum`.
- Line 62: Copy the final total from `dev_tot` to `host_tot` using cudaMemcpy to copy one word back to the host.
- Line 63: Call `cudaDeviceSynchronize()` prior to the timing call in the next line. This call is not strictly necessary because the previous cudaMemcpy call is blocking on the host.
- Line 64: Find the time taken to run the kernels and perform the memory transfers and store the result in `t`.
- Line 65: Check the GPU reduce calculation agrees with the direct calculation on the host.
- Lines 66–68: Explicitly free all allocated memory buffers and return to caller.

As discussed previously the performance of the memory bound kernels, such as this reduce example, can be improved by a factor of two by using pinned memory on the host. The pinned memory version is shown in Example. 9.4. We note the kernel execution time is reduced from about 12.7 ms down to about 5.9 ms. This is due to the speed-up of cudaMemcpy transfer in lines 79 and 82.

Example 9.5 Managed memory test 1 using cudaMallocHost

```
70   int reduce_classic_pinned(int blocks, int threads,
                                  uint dsize, double &t)
71   {
72      uint *host_buf;
        cudaMallocHost(&host_buf, dsize*sizeof(uint));
73      uint *dev_buf;
        cudaMalloc(&dev_buf,dsize*sizeof(uint));
74      uint *dev_sum;
        cudaMalloc(&dev_sum,blocks*sizeof(uint));
75      uint host_tot;
76      uint *dev_tot;
        cudaMalloc(&dev_tot,1*sizeof(uint));
77      double check = fill_buf(host_buf,dsize);
78      cx::MYTimer cuda; // timed block start
79      cudaMemcpy(dev_buf, host_buf, dsize*sizeof(uint),
                                      cudaMemcpyDefault);
80      reduce_warp_v1<<<blocks,threads>>>(dev_sum,dev_buf,dsize);
81      reduce_warp_v1<<<    1,blocks>>>(dev_tot,dev_sum,blocks);
82      cudaMemcpy(&host_tot, dev_tot,sizeof(uint),
                                    cudaMemcpyDefault);
83      cudaDeviceSynchronize();
84      t = cuda.lap_ms(); // timed block end
```

```
85      if(check != host_tot)
            printf("error classic pinned: sum %u check %.0f\n",
                                          host_tot,check);
86      cudaFreeHost(host_buf);
87      cudaFree(dev_buf); cudaFree(dev_sum); cudaFree(dev_tot);
88      return 0;
89   }


D:\temp>memtests.exe 1 256 256 24
test 1 total time 176.023 kernel time 6.194 ms
```

Description of Example 9.5

This example is identical to Example 9.4 except for two statements.

- Line 72: Here we use `cudaMallocHost` instead of `malloc` for the allocation of the large host buffer `host_buf`. This creates a pinned memory allocation.
- Line 86: Here we use `cudaFreeHost` to free the memory allocated to `host_buf` rather than using `free` as was done in the previous version.

Using pinned memory gives a factor of 2 speed-up for this kernel which is limited by the speed of memory access. These are the same results we found in Chapter 3.

The next Example 9.6 uses `thrust` vectors as containers for the memory allocations. This is our standard practice for most examples so it is shown here for the sake of completeness. The vector `host_buf` is again allocated using pinned host memory.

Example 9.6 Managed memory test 3 using thrust for memory allocation

```
90   int reduce_thrust_pinned(int blocks,int threads,
                                  uint dsize, double &t)
91   {
92      thrustHvecPin<uint> host_buf(dsize);
93      thrustDvec<uint>    dev_buf(dsize);
94      thrustDvec<uint>    dev_sum(blocks);
95      thrustHvecPin<uint> host_tot(1);
96      thrustDvec<uint>    dev_tot(1);
97      double check = fill_buf(host_buf.data(),dsize);
98      cx::MYTimer cuda; // timed block start
99      dev_buf = host_buf;
100     reduce_warp_vl<<<blocks,threads>>>
            (dev_sum.data().get(), dev_buf.data().get(),dsize);
101     reduce_warp_vl<<<     1,blocks>>>
            (dev_tot.data().get(),dev_sum.data().get(),blocks);
102     host_tot = dev_tot;
```

```
103    cudaDeviceSynchronize();
104    t = cuda.lap_ms(); // timed block end
105    if(check != host_tot[0])
            printf("error pinned thrust: sum %u check %.0f\n",
                                          host_tot[0],check);
106    return 0;
107 }


D:\temp>memtests.exe 3 256 256 24
test 3 total time 175.360 kernel time 5.887 ms
```

Description of Example 9.6

- Lines 91–96: Perform the same memory allocation as in the previous version but using thrust as a container class. The advantages are that we do not have to manage additional pointer variables nor do we have to remember to free the memory at the end of the function. The host buffer `host_buf` is allocated in pinned memory.
- Line 99: A simple copy between thrust arrays replaces the explicit `cudaMemcpy` used in the previous versions. Note that thrust will still use `cudaMemcpy` or an equivalent "under the hood" to actually perform the transfer.
- Lines 100–101: The kernel calls are the same as before; the required memory pointers are obtained from using the thrust member functions `.data()` and `.data().get()` for the host and device thrust vectors.
- Line 102: The final result is transferred back to the host from device memory. Note that in this version `host_tot` has been declared as a thrust vector of length 1 so that it can be used for thrust data copies between host and device.
- Lines 105–106: These final lines are the same as before but there is no need to use `free` or `cudaFree`.

The next Example 9.7 is new and illustrates the use of zero-copy memory where the device directly accesses a block of host pinned memory, removing the need for any data transfer between the host and device.

Example 9.7 Managed memory test 5 using `cudaHostMallocMapped`

```
110    int reduce_zerocopy(int blocks,int threads,
                                      uint dsize,double &t)
111    {
112      uint *host_buf; cudaHostAlloc(&host_buf,
                     dsize*sizeof(uint), cudaHostAllocMapped);
113      uint *host_sum; cudaHostAlloc(&host_sum,
                     blocks*sizeof(uint), cudaHostAllocMapped);
114      uint *host_tot; cudaHostAlloc(&host_tot,
                        1*sizeof(uint), cdaHostAllocMapped);
```

```
115    uint *dev_buf; cudaHostGetDevicePointer(&dev_buf,
                                   host_buf,0);
116    uint *dev_sum; cudaHostGetDevicePointer(&dev_sum,
                                   host_sum,0);
117    uint *dev_tot; cudaHostGetDevicePointer(&dev_tot,
                                   host_tot,0);

118    double check = fill_buf(host_buf,dsize);

119    cx::MYTimer cuda;      // timed block start
120    reduce_warp_vl<<<blocks,threads>>>
                               (dev_sum,dev_buf,dsize);
121    reduce_warp_vl<<<    1,blocks >>>
                               (dev_tot,dev_sum,blocks);
122    cudaDeviceSynchronize();
123    t = cuda.lap_ms();    // timed block end

124    if(check != host_tot[0]) printf("error zero-copy:
               sum %u check %.0f\n",host_tot[0],check);

125    cudaFreeHost(host_buf);
126    cudaFreeHost(host_sum);
127    cudaFreeHost(host_tot);
128    return 0;
129  }

D:\temp>memtests.exe 5 256 256 24
test 5 total time 170.782 kernel time 6.010 ms
```

Description of Example 9.7

- Lines 112–114; Allocate the same three host memory buffers as before, but this time using cudaHostAlloc with the flag cudaHostAllocMapped. Just like cudaMallocHost, this allocates blocks of pinned host memory, but the extra flag tells CUDA that this memory can also be used by the GPU via special device pointers.
- Lines 115–117: Create the same three device memory pointers as before, but this time we do not allocate any memory on the GPU; rather we create three device pointers using cudaHostGetDevicePointer that associates the device pointers with the corresponding host memory buffers. Any use of these pointers by the GPU will result in data flow on the PCIe bus. The GPU main memory is not involved, although GPU memory caching may still occur.
- Lines 120–121: Run the reduce kernel as before, but without the need for any explicit copying of data to or from the GPU.
- Lines 125–127: Free the pinned memory allocations as before.

Finally, in Example 9.8 we illustrate the use of managed memory, where the same pointer is used on both the host and the GPU.

Example 9.8 Managed memory test 6 using `cudaMallocManaged`

```
140   int reduce_managed(int blocks,int threads,
                                  uint dsize,double &t)
141   {
142     uint *buf; cudaMallocManaged(&buf,dsize*sizeof(uint));
143     uint *sum; cudaMallocManaged(&sum,blocks*sizeof(uint));
144     uint *tot; cudaMallocManaged(&tot,sizeof(uint));
145     double check = fill_buf(buf,dsize);
146     cx::MYTimer cuda;

// timed block start
147     reduce_warp_vl<<<blocks,threads>>>(sum,buf,dsize);
148     reduce_warp_vl<<<   1,blocks >>>(tot,sum,blocks);
149     cudaDeviceSynchronize(); // necessary
150     t = cuda.lap_ms();       // timed block end
151     if(check != tot[0])
            printf("error managed: sum %u check %.0f\n",
                                     tot[0],check);
152     cudaFree(sum);
153     cudaFree(buf);
154     cudaFree(tot);
155     return 0;
156   }

D:\temp>memtests.exe 1 256 256 24
test 6 total time 647.316 kernel time 51.985 ms
```

Description of Example 9.8

This example has the simplest code; the *same* memory pointers are used for both the host and GPU code. The CUDA driver will automatically transfer data between the host and GPU to ensure code correctness. Presently on Linux systems with devices of $CC \geq 6.0$ memory transfers are manged using a relatively efficient demand paged virtual memory scheme. On Windows and all $CC < 6.00$ devices the entire memory block is always transferred between host and device resulting in lower performance.

- Lines 142–144: Allocate the same three blocks of memory as before, but this time we use `cudaMallocManaged` which means that the *same pointer* is used for both the host and device code. Thus, in this version we have left off the prefixes `host_` and `dev_` used for pointers in the previous versions. On Windows and $CC < 6.00$ devices full size blocks of pinned host memory and GPU memory will be allocated. On Linux and $CC \geq 6.0$ demand page virtual memory is used and these will be mapped to physical host or GPU memory by the driver when read or written.
- Line 145: Fills `buf` on the host. Note that the driver assumes that managed memory allocations are initially valid on the GPU. Thus on Windows and $CC < 6.00$ devices the entire memory block `buf`

is copied from the GPU to the host before being written to by the host. This accounts for most of the performance drop observed in our test.

- Line 147: This is the first kernel call and the contents of buf will be copied back to the GPU before the kernel starts. There is no copying associated with the array sum because the driver assumes that this array is valid on the GPU on first use.
- Line 148: This second kernel call does not cause any implicit memory transfers.
- Line 151: This use of tot[0] by the host will trigger the array tot to be copied from the GPU to the host.
- Lines 152–154: Use cudaFree to release the managed memory allocations.

The full version of the code for these tests includes additional tests 2, 4 and 7 which are not shown here. Tests 2 and 4 are variations on the thrust test 3 which perform similarly to either test 1 or test 3. Test 7 uses advanced memory management currently only available on Linux.

The timing tests included in the above examples demonstrate that:

1. Using pinned host memory gives a performance boost of roughly a factor of 2 as compared to using normal memory.
2. Zero-copy memory works just as well as explicit copying data between the host and GPU memory for the reduction example.
3. Managed memory is significantly slower on a Windows platform.

The reason that we did not see a significant performance hit when using zero-copy memory (test 5) in Example 9.7 is that we used a single data copy from the host to the GPU across the PCIe bus. When using zero-copy memory this is done implicitly when the first kernel reads the input data buffer. We have designed this kernel to read the input data very efficiently, so this operation is essentially about the same speed as cudaMemcpy. If, however, the GPU reads the input data several times during processing, then the zero-copy version of our example would perform worse because multiple reads across the PCIe bus would be necessary. In contrast, in the cudaMemcpy version of the example (test 1) only a single read across the PCIe bus is necessary. This is because afterwards the input data is stored in GPU memory.

We can illustrate this by adding two additional kernel calls to our example as illustrated in Example 9.3. The added kernels first replace the content of the device data buffer by the square root of their original values rounded back to an integer and then the second new kernel squares this result. Thus, both new kernels read and write to the whole device data buffer. The execution times of the timed block and kernels in Examples 9.2 and 9.3 are summarised in Table 9.3.

As can be seen from Table 9.3 adding the two extra kernels to Example 9.2 makes little difference to the kernel execution times except for the case of zero-copy memory where total kernel time has increased from about 6.5 ms to 19.4 ms, about a factor of 3. The increase is entirely due to the fact that in 9.3 the kernels have to read the 16 MB memory buffer three times and write it twice instead of reading it just once as in Example 9.2. The additional kernel computation takes only about 0.8 ms.

Example 9.9 Extended versions of tests 1 and 5

```
10   __global__ void intsqrt(r_Ptr<uint> data, uint n)
11   {
12     uint tid = blockDim.x*blockIdx.x+threadIdx.x;
13     while(tid <n){
14       float val = data[tid];
15       data[tid] = (int)sqrtf(val);
16       tid += blockDim.x*gridDim.x;
17     }
18   }

19   __global__ void intsq(r_Ptr<uint> data, uint n)
20   {
21     uint tid = blockDim.x*blockIdx.x+threadIdx.x;
22     while(tid <n){
23       uint val = data[tid]*data[tid];
24       data[tid] = val;
25       tid += blockDim.x*gridDim.x;
26     }
27   }
       . . .
       // main call additional kernels
100a   intsqrt<<<blocks,threads>>>(dev_buf,dsize);// read/write
100b   intsq<<<blocks,threads>>>(dev_buf,dsize);   // read/write
100    reduce_warp_vl<<<blocks,threads>>>
                         (dev_sum,dev_buf,dsize);
101    reduce_warp_vl<<<     1,blocks >>>
                         (dev_tot,dev_sum,blocks);
       . . .

D:\temp>memtests2.exe 1 256 256 24
test 1 total time 192.078 kernel time 6.471 ms

D:\temp>memtests2.exe 5 256 256 24
test 5 total time 236.591 kernel time 19.412 ms
```

Table 9.3 shows times measured by the host code timers, the main features are 3-fold increase in kernel time between the 2-kernel and 4-kernel cases for the zero-copy memory (test 5) and the 4-fold increase in time for the managed memory case (test 6).

We can get more precise information from nvprof and as shown in Table 9.4. The values shown in this table are the averages of 5 separate runs.

In Table 9.5 we see more accurate estimates of the true individual kernel execution times. In all cases except for test 5 the time required to run all four kernels is only about 0.91 ms. This should be compared to the values of about 6 ms obtained from the host-based

Table 9.4 *Timing results for CUDA memory management methods*

	Test	Timed block 9.2 versions (ms)	Ex 9.2 (2 kernel) time (ms)	Timed block 9.3 versions (ms)	Ex 9.3 (4 kernel) time (ms)
Classic `cudaMalloc` memory	0	190.152	13.351	180.869	14.325
Classic host pinned memory	1	182.921	5.917	178.193	6.666
Thrust host pinned memory	3	185.859	5.882	188.162	6.567
Zero-copy memory	5	175.548	6.065	194.633	**20.174**
Managed memory	6	**720.358**	61.362	**732.192**	64.397

Table 9.5 *Additional timing measurements using NVPROF*

Kernels and memory transfers	test 0	test 1	test 3	test 5	test 6
insqrt	409 us	409 us	411 us	**6.837 ms**	408 us
insq	388 us	386 us	385 us	**6.771 ms**	385 us
reduce (blocks = 256)	167 us	166 us	166 us	**5.646 ms**	166 us
reduce (blocks = 1)	2 us	2 us	2 us	5 us	2 us
Memcopy H2D (64 MB in all)	12.220 ms	5.536 ms	5.369 us	–	**34.930 ms**
Memcpy D2H (1 4-byte word)	806 ns	787 ns	538 ns	–	**290.875 ms**
Kernel launch overhead	80 us	82 us	145 us	102 us	**60.513 ms**
Device Synchronisation	13 us	14 us	**6.920 ms**	**19.555 ms**	1.147 ms
Thrust	–	–	163 us	–	–

NB for Test 6 the automatic H2D memory transfer was performed as 512 separate transfers of 128 KB blocks and the (unnecessary) initial D2H transfer was performed using 70 blocks of up to 1 MB in size.

timers. This difference is due to various overheads such as kernel launch and device synchronisation that occur when CUDA kernels are run. Note that some of these overheads increase significantly for tests 3–6. The device synchronisation overheads for tests 3 and 5 have a significant impact on the total job time for the short duration kernels being tested in Examples 9.2 and 9.3 but are still only a few ms and thus would be less important for longer duration kernels expected in real-world applications. In the case of test 6 however the Memcpy overheads are significant and mean that, at least with the present Windows driver, managed memory is only practical for applications where data is resident in GPU memory for the duration of the calculation.

9.6 A Brief Introduction to MPI

MPI is an acronym for Message Passing Interface and is a function library designed to enable parallel programming on computing systems with distributed compute nodes such as shown in Figure 9.1. The original version, now known as MPI 1.0, was released in June 1994. This was an era when researchers, troubled by the high cost for traditional "supercomputing"

Table 9.6 *MPI version history*

Version	Date	Bindings	Comment
MPI 1.0	June 1994	C & FORTRAN	Initial release
MPI 1.1	June 1995	C & FORTRAN	
MPI 1.2	June 1997	C & FORTRAN	
MPI 1.3	May 2008	C & FORTRAN	
MPI 2.1	Sept 2008	C++, C & FORTRAN	Limited shared memory support
MPI 2.2	Sept 2009	C++, C & FORTRAN	
MPI 3.0	Sept 2012	C & FORTRAN	Better shared memory support
MPI 3.1	Sept 2015	C & FORTRAN	
MPI 4.0	draft	C & FORTRAN ?	Under development

systems, were starting to exploit clusters of inexpensive PCs for the same purpose. MPI was very influential in the success of so-called Beowulf PC clusters which started in 1998. These clusters are arguably the blueprint for all present-day HPC computer systems which can have a vast number of nodes. MPI is still the dominant software tool used for inter-node communication in these systems. Table 9.6 shows the evolution of MPI over time.

A key feature of distributed systems is that each node has its own separate host memory. If nodes need to see each other's data, then that data must be copied across the network connections. The bandwidth of the interconnect between nodes is often the limiting factor in overall compute performance. The role of MPI is to optimally manage these transfers. From the beginning MPI provided a comfortable and intuitive programming paradigm for coding parallel programs and this explains its rapid uptake and continuing popularity. In fact, the MPI paradigm is essentially the same as that used by present-day NVIDIA CUDA code; it is reasonable to argue that MPI is the mother of CUDA. This is good news for readers of this book – you essentially already know the ideas used in MPI.

- The first shared idea is that an MPI program is run by launching a number of cooperating processes that run on the nodes of the distributed system. A common configuration would be a number of processes equal to the total number of compute cores on the system. MPI would then ensure that each compute core would run one process. Thus, if each node has a 20 core CPU it would be natural to use 20 x (number of nodes) as the required number of processes when launching an MPI job. This is directly analogous to choosing the number of thread blocks and thread block size when launching a CUDA program.
- The second shared idea is that you only write one program and that program runs on all MPI processes just like a CUDA kernel is one piece of code that is run by all GPU threads.
- The third shared idea is that each MPI process can find its own rank in the MPI job. If there are a total of np MPI processes in the job then a process's rank is an integer in the range 0 to np−1. This is analogous to finding a CUDA thread's rank using the built-in `threadIdx` and `blockIdx` constants or simply `grid.rank()` if using cooperative groups.
- The fourth shared idea is that some calls to some MPI functions which involve data transfers are blocking in the sense that the calling MPI process will wait until the transfer is complete. For example, the `MPI_Send` function, which sends data from the calling

process to one or more other process, will wait until the transfer is complete before it continues.[1] This is analogous to cudaMemcpy being blocked on the host in CUDA code. There is also a non-blocking MPI_Isend call which is analogous to cudaMemcpyAsync and an MPI_Wait call which is analogous to cudaDeviceSynchronize.

* Finally, most MPI functions return error codes to indicate success or failure; this again is the same approach as used by most CUDA functions.

An important difference between MPI and CUDA is that MPI uses a distributed memory model whereas CUDA uses a shared memory model. Originally, MPI had no direct support for shared memory, thus each process had its own copy of all MPI managed memory even if these processes were running on the same CPU. In MPI the only way to process shared information was by using the interconnect to transfer data. In the 1990s that was a perfectly reasonable model as all PCs would have had a single CPU with one processing core. More recent versions of MPI will recognise cases where two or more processes are on the same PC and will implement data exchange using direct memory copies to implement the exchange whenever possible. There is now also some support for shared host memory access.

Since about 2013[2] some versions of MPI are "CUDA-aware" which means that MPI will use NVLINK to transfer data directly between GPU memories on the same workstation. In this case CUDA unified virtual addressing (UVA) and MPI are used together, making programming very straightforward.

The full MPI library contains literally hundreds of functions but fortunately straightforward applications can be built using only a small subset of these functions. Some of these core functions are shown in Table 9.7.

More detailed information on MPI is readily available online. The full specifications can be obtained from www.mpi-forum.org/docs/ and tutorials are available from https://mpitutorial.com/ and many other websites.

The first four functions in Table 9.7 will appear in every MPI program; the MPI documentation recommends that MPI_Init is called at the very start of a program and is necessary before any other MPI function is used. The arguments allow command line parameters to be passed to MPI, but in practice they are not used. The next four commands, Bcast, Scatter, Gather and Reduce are examples of MPI collective commands which involve collaboration between all the calling processes. In the mid-1990s, MPI was my introduction to parallel programming and I was immediately struck with the elegance and simplicity of this approach – the same piece of code runs on all processors which share a given task in a symmetrical way. One consequence of this paradigm is that speeding up a calculation by adding more processors is in principle trivial, as no code needs to be changed.[3] Of course, as discussed elsewhere, not all algorithms deliver a speed-up proportional to the number of processors. In particular, communication and other overheads limit the speed-up that can be achieved by adding more processors for any particular parallel computing task.

A simple complete MPI program to perform reduction (what else) is shown in Example 9.4:

It is important to keep in mind that MPI programs are like CUDA kernels; an instance of the code will be run on each of the processors used.

Table 9.7 *Core MPI functions*

For brevity we show examples of function calls in column 1 not the function prototypes. The functions all return an integer error code which is zero (`MPI_SUCCESS`) if no error has occurred or positive otherwise. We use standard names for the arguments as explained at the bottom of the table.

`MPI_Init(&argc, &argv)`	Mandatory initialisation, should be first statement in `main`.
`MPI_Finalize()`	Close MPI on this node, usually last statement.
`MPI_Comm_size(MPI_COMM_WORLD, &procs )`	Sets `int procs` to the number of processes in this job.
`MPI_Comm_rank(MPI_COMM_WORLD, &rank )`	Sets `int rank` to this process's rank in the job.
`MPI_Bcast(sbuf, size, type, root, comm)`	Process `root` sends the data in its copy of `sbuf` to all other processes' copy of `sbuf`.
`MPI_Scatter(sbuf, size1, type1, rbuf, size2, type2, root, comm)`	Process `root` sends subsets of the data in its copy of `sbuf` to all processes' copy of `rbuf`.
`MPI_Gather(sbuf, size1, type1, rbuf, size2, type2, root, comm)`	Process `root` accumulates subsets of the data from each process's copy of `sbuf` to its copy of `rbuf`.
`MPI_Reduce(sbuf, rbuf, size, type, op, root, comm)`	Each element of `root`'s copy of `rbuf` is set to the sum (or other function depending on `op`) over all nodes of the corresponding element of `sbuf`. The resulting vector `rbuf` is thus the result of a vector operation `op`. Set op to `MPI_SUM` for summation.
`MPI_Allreduce(sbuf, rbuf, size, type, op, comm)`	Same as `MPI_Reduce` except all processes get the result in their copy of `rbuf`. The argument `root` is not needed.

In the argument lists `sbuf` and `rbuf` are pointers to arrays containing the send and receive buffers for operations. The data type of these buffers is indicated by the `type` arguments which are set to a defined MPI keyword, for example, `MPI_FLOAT`. MPI defines keywords for all the usual data types and additionally allows user defined types. If this keyword occurs twice in the argument list then `sbuf` and `rbuf` can be different data types and MPI will perform type conversion during the operation. The argument `root` is an integer indicating the sending node for send functions like `Bcast` and `Scatter` or the receiving node for operations like `Gather` and `Reduce`. The argument `op` can be set to `MPI_SUM` in the reduce function to indicate a classic addition of elements is required but other operations are available. The final argument `comm` is an MPI communicator which specifies which of the available processes will participate in this call. The most commonly used communicator is `MPI_COMM_WORLD` which uses all processors. Other user defined communicators for subsets of the nodes are possible, for example, in the case of multi core nodes, communicators could be used to group together MPI processes running on the cores of a single node.

Example 9.10 Reduction using MPI

```
03 #include <stdio.h>
04 #include <stdlib.h>
05 #include <string.h>
06 #include <mpi.h>
```

```
07 #include <vector>

10 int main(int argc, char *argv[])
11 {
12    // Initialize the MPI environment
13    MPI_Init(&argc,&argv);

14    // get number of processes and my rank
15    int nproc;   MPI_Comm_size(MPI_COMM_WORLD,&nproc);
16    int rank;    MPI_Comm_rank(MPI_COMM_WORLD,&rank);
17    int root = 0;

18    int frame_size = (argc >1) ? atoi(argv[1]) : 100;
19    int size = nproc*frame_size;
20    if(rank==root)printf("dataset size %d frame size %d
            number of processes %d\n",size,frame_size,nproc);

21    std::vector<int> sbuf(size);        // full data buffer
22    std::vector<int> rbuf(frame_size);  // frame buffer

23    int check = 0;
24    if(rank==root) { // fill with test data
25      for(int k=0;k<size;k++) sbuf[k] = k+1;
26      for(int k=0;k<size;k++) check += sbuf[k];
27    }

28    // partition data into nproc frames
29    MPI_Scatter(sbuf.data(), frame_size, MPI_INT, rbuf.data(),
            frame_size, MPI_INT, root, MPI_COMM_WORLD);

30    // start work for this process
31    int procsum = 0;
32    for(int k=0;k<frame_size;k++) procsum += rbuf[k];
33    // end work for this process

34    // sum values for all nodes and print result
35    int fullsum = 0;
36    MPI_Allreduce(&procsum, &fullsum, 1, MPI_INT, MPI_SUM,
            MPI_COMM_WORLD);
37    printf("rank %d: procsum %d fullsum %d check %d\n",
            rank,procsum,fullsum,check);

38
39    MPI_Finalize(); // tidy up

40    return 0;
41 }
```

Description of Example 9.10

- Lines 1–7: Here we include some standard headers; note line 6 which includes `mpi.h`. This is the only change needed when writing MPI code. Note also line 7 where we include the C++ `vector` header. Although we use the C bindings for MPI these can be used in C++ code, we do not have to revert to using C for everything.

- Line 13: This is the mandatory initialisation of MPI. The standard command line interface variables `argc` and `argv` are passed as arguments. This is because some implementations might manipulate them to aid the launch process. If necessary `MPI_Init` will undo any such changes.

- Lines 15–16: Here we set the variables `nproc` to the total number of processes being run and `rank` to the rank of each particular process. The value of rank is an integer in the range `[0,nproc−1]`.

- Line 17: While it is true that in both CUDA and MPI all threads or processes are equal, there is usually one thread or rank that is more equal than the others. In simple MPI, this thread may be responsible for distributing external data to all the processes and printing etc. Here we use `int root` for this process and initialise it to zero.

- Lines 18–19: For the reduction example we are going to sum a set of integers; the total number of integers `size` is set to `nproc*frame_size` where `frame_size`, a user supplied parameter, is the number of integers to be summed by each process.

- Line 20: Here we print information for the user. The `if` statement means that only the single process with rank `root` performs this operation. Without the `if` clause each process would print this line.

- Lines 21–22: Here we allocate send and receive buffers `sbuf` and `rbuf` using standard vector containers. The send buffer `sbuf` has dimension `size` so that it can hold all of the data. As implemented, this is wasteful, as only the root process needs this array to hold data and the other processes just use it as a placeholder in line 29. In a real-world program, we would fix this issue. The receive buffer `rbuf`, on the other hand is necessary for all processes but it has a smaller dimension `frame_size`.

- Lines 23–27: Here we initialise the contents of `sbuf` in the root processes with a simple count and accumulate the sum in `int check`. In a real-world case, the data might be read from disk or be the result of a previous calculation.

- Line 29: This is an example of MPI doing real work; data in the source buffer of the process specified by the seventh argument (`root` in this case) will be divided into `nproc` contiguous frames and these frames with be distributed to the receive buffer of each process. The source buffer, frame size and data type are specified by the first three arguments; the receive buffer frame size and data type are specified by arguments 4–6. The final argument (`MPI_COMM_WORLD`) specifies that all processes are to take part.

Notice the frame size and data type of the receive buffer can be different to those of the source buffer. In this case they are the same (`frame_size` and `MPI_INT`). Obviously the receive buffer frame size need not be larger than the send buffer frame size allowing for any implicit type conversions. Notice also that we do not need to specify either the number of processes (which MPI knows) or the full size of `sbuf` (which MPI assumes is large enough). Finally, since only the version of `sbuf` in the root process is actually needed we could replace line 29 by:

```
if(rank==root)MPI_Scatter(sbuf.data(), frame_size, ..., root,
  MPI_COMM_WORLD);
else MPI_Scatter(nullptr, frame_size, ..., root,
  MPI_COMM_WORLD);
```

`MPI_Scatter` is an example of a one-to-many collective operation.

- Lines 30–33: This is the place in the program where all processes do unique work in parallel. In this example, we do very little work; the elements of `rbuf` are summed to `int framesum`. In a real-world example, considerably more work might be done here.
- Line 36: Here we use the many-to-many MPI operation `Allreduce`. The first and second arguments are vectors of equal length specified by the third argument and types specified by the fourth and fifth arguments. In our case the vectors are actually scalars of length one and so the sum of the values of `procsum` across all processes is placed in the value in `fullsum` for all the processes. The fifth argument `MPI_SUM` specifies the type of reduction operation required. Other options for this variable include `MPI_MAX`, `MPI_MIN` and `MPI_PROD`. Had the value of the third argument been greater than one, the first two arguments would have been vectors, say **a** and **b** then each element i the sum of the a[i] elements over all processors would be placed in b[i].

  A many-to-one version of `MPI_Allreduce` also exists and is simply called `MPI_Reduce`. In this version only a single process has its receive buffer updated with the summed values and the rank of that process is specified by an additional argument placed just before the communicator.
- Line 37: Here we print some results; there is no if clause attached to this printf so each process will print a line.

An example of compiling and running an MPI program is shown in Example 9.11. Here we are using the Linux Bash shell running under Windows 10 with OpenMPI installed using SUDO. This provides the compiler `mpic++` (a front end to g++) which compiles and links MPI code and an executable `mpirun` to launch MPI jobs.

Example 9.11 Compiling and running an MPI program in Linux

```
01 real@PC:~/mpi$  mpic++ reduce_book.cpp -o mpireduce
02 real@PC:~/mpi$  mpirun -np 8 mpireduce 1000

03 dataset size 8000 frame size 1000 number of processes 8
04 rank 6: procsum 6500500 fullsum 32004000 check 0
05 rank 7: procsum 7500500 fullsum 32004000 check 0
06 rank 0: procsum  500500 fullsum 32004000 check 32004000
07 rank 1: procsum 1500500 fullsum 32004000 check 0
08 rank 2: procsum 2500500 fullsum 32004000 check 0
09 rank 3: procsum 3500500 fullsum 32004000 check 0
10 rank 4: procsum 4500500 fullsum 32004000 check 0
11 rank 5: procsum 5500500 fullsum 32004000 check 0
```

Description of Example 9.11

- Line 1: Building `mpireduce` using bash shell in Windows 10, using the `mpic++` compiler which is provided by OpenMPI.
- Line 2: Running the program with 8 MPI processes using `mpirun`. The `-np 8` option specifies the total number of processes to be launched. The last two options are the task to be run by each process and its single argument. Thus, here each process sets `frame_size` from the value of `argv[1]`. In this case all the processes actually run on the same machine but will be shared equally between the

Table 9.8 *Additional MPI functions*

`MPI_Scan(sbuf, rbuf, count, op, comm)`	For each process, the result vector `rbuf` is an element-wise inclusive prefix scan operation on the vectors `sbuf` ordered by process rank. The scan operation in indicated op, e.g. `MPI_SUM`.
`MPI_Alltoall(sbuf, size1, type1, rbuf, size2, type2, comm)`	For each process, `sbuf` is partitioned into subblocks of size `size2` with stride `size1` and these blocks are distributed between processes such that process p sends its subblock q to process p's subblock position in `rbuf` of process q.
`MPI_Send(buf, size, type, dest, tag, comm)` `MPI_Recv(buf, size, type, source, tag, comm, &status)`	These two functions are used together to allow two processes to exchange data; one process uses `MPI_Send` to send data to a receiving process which must use a matching `MPI_Recv` call. The int variables `source` and `dest` are set to the ranks of the sending and receiving processes respectively. The values of int `tag` must be the same for both processes
`MPI_Barrier(comm)`	Waits for all processes in communicator `comm` to reach this point in the code. Similar to `cudaDeviceSynchronize`
`MPI_Comm_split(comm, color, key, &newcomm)`	Create new communicators `newcomm` from subsets of processes in communicator `comm` where processes specifying the same value of `color` are in the same new communicator. The variable int `key` controls the rank order in the `newcomm` communicators, using the process `rank` for `key` is a common choice which maintains the original rank ordering.

cores of a multicore PC. In more complicated situations involving distributed processors a configuration file can be specified containing the names and network addresses of the hosts to be used.

- Line 3: The output from line 20 of Example 9.10; notice that only output from the root process appears here.
- Lines 4–11: The output from line 37 of Example 9.10; now there is one line of output for each process, but the order in which the lines appear is effectively arbitrary. The value of check is only correct for the process of rank zero. That is expected because only process root sets this value. All processes report the correct value for fullsum.

Some additional MPI functions are shown in Table 9.8.

The function `MPI_Scan` is similar to `MPI_Reduce` but performs a scan operation rather than a reduce operation. The function `MPI_Alltoall` is an example of a many-to-many parallel operation where each process shares subsets of a buffer with all processes. An example showing how `MPI_Alltoall` can be used to transpose a matrix is shown as Example 9.12.

Example 9.12 Use of `mpialltoall` to transpose a matrix

```
01  void showmat(const char *tag, std::vector<int> &m,
                                   int nx, int ny)
02  {
03    printf("\n%s\n",tag);
04    for(int y=0;y<ny;y++){
05      for(int x=0;x<nx;x++) printf(" %3d",m[nx*y+x]);
06      printf("\n");
07    }
08  }

10  int main(int argc,char * argv[])
11  {
12    // Initialize the MPI environment
13    MPI_Init(&argc,&argv);

15    // get number of processes and my rank
16    int nproc; MPI_Comm_size(MPI_COMM_WORLD,&nproc);
17    int rank;  MPI_Comm_rank(MPI_COMM_WORLD,&rank);
18    int root = (argc >1) ? atoi(argv[1]) : 0;

20    int N = nproc;  // matrix size is number of processes
21    int size = N*N;
22    std::vector<int> row(N);
23    std::vector<int> col(N);
24    std::vector<int> mat;  // empty placeholders

26    if(rank==root) {  // mat gets bigger only on root node
27      for(int k=0;k<size;k++) mat.push_back(k+1);
28      showmat("matrix",mat,N,N);
29    }
30    MPI_Barrier(MPI_COMM_WORLD); // just in case

32    // copy one row to each process
33    MPI_Scatter(mat.data(),N,MPI_INT,row.data(),N,MPI_INT,
                                  root,MPI_COMM_WORLD);

35    // get per process column data by sharing row data
36    MPI_Alltoall(row.data(),1,MPI_INT,col.data(),1,MPI_INT,
                                  MPI_COMM_WORLD);

38    // gather all columns to get transpose in root process
39    MPI_Gather(col.data(),N,MPI_INT,mat.data(),N,MPI_INT,
                                  root,MPI_COMM_WORLD);
40    if(rank==root) showmat("transpose",mat,N,N);
```

```
42      MPI_Finalize();   //  tidy up
43
42      return 0;
43    }
```

Description of Example 9.12

- Lines 1–9: A simple function to print a matrix of size nx × ny. The first argument is a title.
- Lines 13–17: Initialise MPI and set the number of processes and rank of current process in nproc and rank.
- Line 18: Sets the value of the root process in root using optional user input.
- Lines 20–24: Allocate arrays to process a N × N matrix where N is set equal to the number of MPI processes nproc. For each process, the vectors row and col will contain one row and one column of this matrix. In addition, for the root process only, the vector mat will store the whole matrix. In line 24 an empty vector mat is created for each process.
- Lines 26–29: For the root process only we create the full matrix by storing elements in root's copy of mat using the push_back member function of std::vector. The matrix is filled with integers in the range $1 - N^2$ and then printed. Non-root processes retain zero sized versions of mat.

C++ tip.

The use of push_back() to dynamically allocate space for std::vector objects is often a convenient programming technique – but it is potentially inefficient for large arrays. If you know the size of the array use one of

```
        std::<vector> bigv(size);
```

or

```
        std::<vector> bigv;  bigv.reserve(size);
```

The former will allocate memory and initialise all elements of bigv to zero. The latter will allocate memory but not perform any initialisation; hence it might be faster.

- Line 30: MPI_Barrier is used here to ensure that all processes have been launched and are ready for the subsequent MPI_Scatter operation in line 33. This is probably not strictly necessary, as all the core MPI routines used in our examples are themselves locally blocking on their process. However, unlike the CUDA case we might be synchronising across a network with heterogeneous processors. If in doubt I recommend using lots of synchronisation calls while developing MPI code – the unnecessary ones can be removed later in production code.
- Line 33: MPI_Scatter is used here to send blocks of N elements from root's copy of mat to the vector row in each process including the sending process root. At this point each process has one row of the matrix in its row vector.
- Line 36: The MPI_Alltoall call used here is the key element of this example. For each process, individual elements of its row vector are sent to an element of the col vector in each process.

Specifically, process p will send its element row[q] to the element col[p] in processes q. This results in the vectors col containing the columns of the original matrix.
- Line 39: This MPI_Gather copies the col vector of each process to a row of the original matrix mat on the root process. This results in the original columns of mat now being its rows.
- Line 40: We print mat again to check the result.

The results of compiling and running the program with eight processes is shown in Example 9.13.

Example 9.13 Results of matrix transposition program

```
real@PC:~/mpi$ mpic++  -std=c++11 all2all.cpp -o mpialltoall
real@PC:~/mpi$ mpirun -np 8 mpialltoall

matrix
    1    2    3    4    5    6    7    8
    9   10   11   12   13   14   15   16
   17   18   19   20   21   22   23   24
   25   26   27   28   29   30   31   32
   33   34   35   36   37   38   39   40
   41   42   43   44   45   46   47   48
   49   50   51   52   53   54   55   56
   57   58   59   60   61   62   63   64

transpose
    1    9   17   25   33   41   49   57
    2   10   18   26   34   42   50   58
    3   11   19   27   35   43   51   59
    4   12   20   28   36   44   52   60
    5   13   21   29   37   45   53   61
    6   14   22   30   38   46   54   62
    7   15   23   31   39   47   55   63
    8   16   24   32   40   48   56   64
```

While the results of running mpialltoall are as expected, one could argue that using eight processors to transpose an 8×8 matrix is overkill for a small problem. However, there is an interesting scaling feature here; we need N processors to handle N^2 data elements. Moreover, although we used alltoall to transfer single ints between processors, we could modify the code to transfer sub-matrices of a much larger matrix. Large problems in linear algebra are indeed an important application area for MPI.

This is a brief introduction to MPI but hopefully it will help you get started with the mixed CUDA and MPI applications. In the next chapter we discuss tools for profiling and debugging your code.

Endnotes Chapter 9

1 Actually, this is not quite true, the MPI_Send call uses a data buffer argument which is an array in the calling process's local memory. The call causes this buffer to be copied across the interconnect to a corresponding buffer in the receiving processor's local memory space. MPI_Send will return once that data buffer in the calling process is no longer required and can be safely reused. An MPI implementation may choose to copy the sender's data buffer to another system buffer on the local host which would allow a faster return as compared to time taken to directly transfer the data across an interconnect. In neither case is there a guarantee that the reading process has actually got the intended data. There are a number of alternative versions of MPI_Send which cater for various synchronisation needs. For example, MIP_Ssend will block the sending process until the data really has reached the receiving process.

2 See the NVIDIA blog "*What is CUDA Aware MPI*" https://devblogs.nvidia.com/introduction-cuda-aware-mpi/

3 In the 1980s I had been involved in projects at CERN and elsewhere using multiple processors to speed-up real-time event data processing. This involved chaining several processors into a pipeline through which event data flowed and where each processor performed a different step in the processing chain. Here one needed a different program for each processor and all the programs had to be tuned to take the same amount of time. Hence here the programming complexity increased with every additional processor added to the chain.

10

Tools for Profiling and Debugging

Sadly, not all newly written code works perfectly the first time it is run. Debugging and performance tuning of code often takes a significant proportion of code development time. Fortunately, the NVIDIA SDK provides many tools for profiling and debugging both host and GPU code. Some of these tools, such as nvprof, have been around since early releases of CUDA and some, such as Nsight Systems, are more recent. The tools used for Windows and Linux systems are somewhat different in detail but in general give similar information. In this chapter, our examples will mostly be taken from the Windows toolset as this is the system used to develop the code for this book. Exactly the same methods can also be used for Linux development; it is just that the user interfaces for some of the tools differ.

10.1 The gpulog Example

The example code used in this chapter is a variation of our very first example in Chapter 1 where we used a power series to evaluate a mathematical function $f(x)$ many times over a range of x values using one thread per x value. The function values are then summed to produce an estimate of $\int f(x)\,dx$ over the range of x values. In this chapter, we will use the more slowly converging series for $\log(x)$. Example 10.1 shows our model example for evaluating the natural logarithm $\log(x)$ over the range $1 \leq x \leq 2$ using the series expansion:

$$\log{(1+x)} = x - \frac{x^2}{2} + \frac{x^3}{3} - \frac{x^4}{4} + \frac{x^5}{5}\cdots. \tag{10.1}$$

This series actually converges really slowly and much faster algorithms for finding log(1+x) are available. However, here we use it as an interesting example of a computationally intensive kernel. Using floating point kernels, we find the fractional error on log(2) is about 0.7% for 100 terms and 0.008% for 10,000 terms.

Description of Example 10.1

- Lines 11–22: The function logsum defined here for both the host and device takes input arguments x and terms and returns the value of log(1+x) by summing the power series for the first terms terms.
  - Line 11: The input arguments are the x, the required x value and terms the required number of terms.
  - Line 15: Sets termsum to the first term x.
  - Lines 16–20: This simple for loop adds the remaining terms to termsum using floating point arithmetic.

- Lines 23–31: The kernel function gpu_log calls logsum for the required number of x values using thread linear addressing.
  - Line 23: The input arguments are logs a floating point array that holds the calculated log(1+*x*) values, terms the required number of terms to be used when summing the power series, steps the number of different uniformly spaced x values to be used and step_size the spacing between x values. We expect the calculation time to be directly proportional to the product of steps and terms.

Example 10.1 gpulog program for evaluation of log(1+x)

```
10   // gpulog calculate log(1+x)  series valid for  -1 < x <= +1
11   __host__ __device__  inline float logsum(float x, int terms)
12   {
13     float xpow = x;
14     float xn = 1.0f;
15     float termsum = x;
16     for(int k=1;k<terms;k++) {
17       xn += 1.0f;
18       xpow *= -x;
19       termsum += xpow/xn; // x - x^2/2 + x^3/3 - x^4/4 ...
20     }
21     return termsum;
22   }
23   __global__ void gpu_log(r_Ptr<float> logs, int terms,
                               uint steps, float step_size)
24   {
25     int tid = blockIdx.x*blockDim.x+threadIdx.x;
26     while(tid < steps){
27       float x = step_size*(float)tid;
28       logs[tid] = logsum(x,terms);
29       tid += gridDim.x*blockDim.x;
30     }
31   }

32   float host_log(int terms, uint steps, float step_size)
33   {
34     double sum = 0.0;  // double necessary here
35     for(uint k=0; k<steps; k++){
36       float x = step_size*(float)k;
37       sum += logsum(x,terms);
38     }
39     return (float)sum;
40   }

41   __global__ void reduce_warp_v1(r_Ptr<float> sums,
                       cr_Ptr<float> data, uint steps)
     . . . // same code a chapter 3


51   // identical to above, different name helps profiling
```

```
52    __global__ void reduce_warp_vlB(r_Ptr<float> sums,
                           cr_Ptr<float> data, uint steps)
53    . . . // same code a chapter 3

60    int main(int argc, char *argv[])
61    {
62      int  shift =   argc >1 ? atoi(argv[1]) : 16;
63      uint steps = 2 << (shift-1);
64      int blocks =   argc >2 ? atoi(argv[2]) : 256;
65      int threads = argc >3 ? atoi(argv[3]) : 256;
66      int terms =   argc >4 ? atoi(argv[4]) : 1000;
67      int hterms =  argc >5 ? atoi(argv[5]) : terms;

68      float *logs = (float *)malloc(steps*sizeof(float));
69      cx::timer gpuall;
70      float *dev logs;
        cudaMalloc(&dev_logs, steps*sizeof(float));
71      float *dev_sums;
        cudaMalloc(&dev_sums, blocks*sizeof(float));
72      float *dev_tot;
        cudaMalloc(&dev_tot,1*sizeof(float));
73      float step_size = 1.0f/(float)(steps-1);
74      cx::timer tim; // start cuda block timer
75      gpu_log<<<blocks,threads>>>(dev_logs,terms,steps,
                                            step_size);
76      cudaMemcpy(logs,dev_logs,steps*sizeof(float),
                                    cudaMemcpyDeviceToHost);
77      reduce_warp_vl<<<blocks,threads>>>(dev_sums,dev_logs,
                                            steps);
78      reduce_warp_vlB<<<   1,blocks >>>(dev_tot,dev_sums,
                                            blocks);
79      float gpuint = 0.0f;
80      cudaMemcpy(&gpuint,dev_tot,1*sizeof(float),
                                    cudaMemcpyDeviceToHost);
81      cudaDeviceSynchronize();
82      double tgpu= tim.lap_ms();  // end cuda block timer
83      // trapezoidal rule correction
84      gpuint -= 0.5f*(logsum(0.0f,terms)+logsum(1.0f,terms));
85      gpuint *= step_size;  // scale by dx
86      double gpujob = gpuall.lap_ms(); // end cuda work
87      double log2_gpu = logs[steps-1]; // gpu calc of log(2)
88      double log2 = log(2.0);         // true value of log(2)
89      double logint = 2.0*log2 - 1.0;// true value of integral
90      double ferr = 100.0f*(log2-log2_gpu)/log2;// log(2) error
91      printf("gpu log(2) %f frac err %e%%\n",log2_gpu,ferr);
92      ferr = 100.0f*(logint-trapsum)/logint;// gpu error
93      printf("gpu  int %f frac err %e %% \n",trapsum,ferr);

94      // flush denormalized to zero on host needs <float.h>
```

```
95      _controlfp_s(nullptr,_DN_FLUSH,_MCW_DN);

96      tim.reset();                   // start host timer
97      double hostint = host_log(hterms, steps, step_size)
                                               *step_size;
98      double thost = tim.lap_ms();   // end host timer

99      hostint -= 0.5f*(logsum(0.0f,hterms)+logsum(1.0f,hterms))
                                               *step_size;
100     ferr = 100.0f*(logint-hostint)/logint; // host error
101     printf("host int %f frac err %e %%\n",hostint,ferr);
102     double ratio = (thost*terms)/(tgpu*hterms); // speedup
103     printf("times gpu %.3f host %.3f gpujob %.3f ms
                speedup %.1f\n", tgpu, thost, gpujob, ratio);

104     free(logs); // tidy up
105     cudaFree(dev_logs);
106     cudaFree(dev_sums);
107     cudaFree(dev_tot);
108     cudaDeviceReset();   // no thrust
109     return 0;
110   }
```

- ○ Line 25: Set `tid` to the rank of this thread in the grid-block using standard thread linear addressing.
- ○ Lines 26 and 29: Standard loop where the threads share the work for a total of `steps` passes.
- ○ Lines 27–28: Calculate the current x value directly from `tid`; there is a tacit assumption here that the first x value is zero. Then store the result in `logs[tid]`.
- • Lines 32–40: The function `host_log` uses the host to perform the same calculations as the GPU using the same `logsum` function for the calculation of individual vales of log(1+x) and performing the sum of these values directly in line 37. Notice the accumulation value `sum` is declared `double` not float. This is necessary to avoid excessive rounding errors when `steps` is large. As noted before, the equivalent parallel reduction operation performed on the GPU is more robust in this respect.
- • Lines 41–53: Here we have two copies of our parallel reduction code as discussed in previous chapters; the code details are not repeated here. Two copies with different names are used in this example to simply trick the profiler into giving separate information for the two different calls in lines 77 and 78. This would not be necessary in production code.

The remainder of the code from line 60 is the main routine.

- • Lines 62–67: Here the user can optionally set parameters for the job. These parameters are:
  - ○ `steps`: This defines the number of x steps spanning the range [0,1]. The computation time should be directly proportional to the number. This value is set to the power of 2 entered by the user in line 62.
  - ○ `blocks` and `threads`: These are CUDA grid configuration; our standard defaults of 256 and 256 work well in this example.
  - ○ `terms`: Is the number of power series terms used in the evaluation of each log value by the GPU.
  - ○ `hterms`: This is the same as `terms` but controls the number of terms used by the host calculation. Since it turns out that the host is much slower than the GPU, it is convenient to use a separate value.

- Line 68: Uses `malloc` to allocate the host array `logs` to hold GPU calculated log values.
- Line 69: Declares and starts the timer `gpuall` intended to measure the time for all CUDA steps.
- Lines 70–72: Declare device arrays for the calculation. We choose to use `cudaMalloc` here rather than `thrust` to avoid complications with the profiling and debugging tools. The arrays `logs` and `dev_logs` are of size `steps` and will hold the full set of log values evaluated by the GPU. The device array `dev_sums` has size of `blocks` and will hold the block sums produced by the first reduce step in line 77. The variable `dev_tot` will hold the final sum of all log values from the second reduce step in line 78.
- Line 73: This sets the step size required to span a unit range in `steps` steps. Notice we divide by `steps-1` not `steps`; there is a good chance of a hard-to-spot, off-by-one error here if you get this wrong.
- Lines 74 and 82: These lines, which bracket the CUDA calculation, define and use the host-based timer `tim`. This measures the time to run the kernels and transfer results back to the host but excludes time for `cudaMalloc`.
- Lines 75–81: This is the code CUDA calculation that we are interested in profiling and debugging.
  - Line 75: Calls the `gpu_log` kernel to fill `dev_logs` with steps values of $\log(1+x)$ based on the power series using `terms` terms.
  - Line 76: Copies the values back to the host array `logs`. Notice that although we only use the single value `logs[steps-1]` in the later code, here we choose to copy the whole array – this makes the profile more interesting.
  - Lines 77–78: Perform a 2-step summation of the values in `dev_logs` down to the single value `dev_tot` using our standard reduction kernel.
  - Line 80: Copies the sum `dev_tot` back to the host variable `gpuint`.
  - Line 81: Finally uses `cudaDeviceSynchonize` to ensure all operations are complete before the time measurement in line 82.[1]
- Lines 84–85: Here we turn the sum `gpuint` into the actual integral required by making the trapezoidal rule correction in line 84 and then scaling the result by `step_size` which represents `dx` in the integral. Notice in line 83 we call the `gpulog` function directly from the host.
- Line 86: Sets `gpujob` to the time required for all CUDA steps including the `cudaMalloc` statements.
- Line 87: Copies the GPU calculated value of log(2) from last element of `logs` to `log2_gpu`.
- Lines 88–89: Here we store the values of log(2) and the integral in `log2` and `logint` using the accurate C++ log function.
- Lines 90–93: Find the fractional errors in the GPU calculated quantities and print the results.
- Line 95: This is a bit of obscure Microsoft magic to switch on hardware flushing of denormalised floating point numbers to zero (FTZ). This fixes a problem with the host code which otherwise slows down dramatically for larger values of `terms`. The header file `<float.h>` is required for this to work.[2]
- Lines 96–101: Here we perform and time the calculation using a single host CPU. The number of terms used is `hterms`. The host-based calculation of the integral is stored in `hostint` and the calculation time is stored in `thost`. The fractional error is printed in line 101.
- Line 103: Here we print the times: GPU kernel time, host time, time for all the CUDA steps and ratio of GPU to host time as calculated in line 102. Note this calculation corrects for different values of `terms` and `hterms`.
- Lines 104–108: Tidy up at the end of the program; this helps the profiler.

Some results from running the code are shown in Example 10.2. One feature of these results is a significant overhead of several hundred ms in addition to running the kernels in the CUDA section of the code. This reflects the cost of `cudaMalloc` in lines 76–78. To understand what is going on here in more detail we need profiling.

Example 10.2 Results of running `gpulog` on an RTX 2070 GPU

(a) A small job with 2^{16} steps and 100 terms for both GPU and host. This is too small a calculation to demonstrate the full power of the GPU.

```
D: >gpulog.exe 16 256 256 100 100
gpu log(2) 0.688172 frac err   7.178e-01%
gpu  int   0.386245 frac err   1.269e-02%
host int   0.386245 frac err   1.268e-02%
times gpu 0.400 host 12.167 gpujob 177.555 ms speedup 30.4
```

(b) Same as (a) but using 2^{24} steps. The accuracy of the results are unchanged but the GPU is now about 100 times faster than the host.

```
D: >gpulog.exe 24 256 256 100 100
gpu log(2) 0.688172 frac err   7.178e-01%
gpu  int   0.386245 frac err   1.267e-02%
host int   0.386245 frac err   1.267e-02%
times gpu 27.611 host 3160.105 gpujob 202.490 ms speedup 114.5
```

(c) The number of GPU terms is increased from 100 to 10^5. Now the GPU is fully utilized and outperforms the host by a factor of about 1600. The accuracy of the GPU calculation of log(2) and the integral has also increased.

```
D: > gpulog.exe 24 256 256 100000 100
gpu log(2) 0.693134 frac err   1.874e-03%
gpu  int   0.386294 frac err  -8.701e-06%
host int   0.386245 frac err   1.267e-02%
times gpu 1861.515 host 3079.824 gpujob 2049.234 ms speedup 1654.5
```

10.2 Profiling with nvprof

The NVIDIA nvprof profiler has been available since the launch of CUDA in 2007 The simplest use of nvprof is to run it from the command line as indicated in the box.[3]

Simple use of `nvprof`

(a) navigate to build directory of exe file
```
> cd /mycode/x64/release
```

(b) run program as usual but add leading `nvprof`
```
> nvprof  myprog.exe arg1 arg2
```

(c) `nvprof` options can be added
```
> nvprof --timeout 10 myprog.exe arg1 arg2
```

(d) see all options with `--help`
```
> nvprof --help
```

The results of running the `gpulog` example with nvprof are shown as Example 10.3. Accurate times are reported for each of the six steps in the CUDA pipeline (lines 68–81 of Example 10.1). For any particular function, nvprof reports the number of times it occurred in the pipeline, the total time for all calls and the maximum and minimum times for particular calls. Since the D2H cudaMemcpy operation is used twice (lines 76 and 80), it is easy to infer that the first memcpy of 10,000 words took 26.232 ms and the second copy of a single word took 704 ns. The remaining 4 steps each occurred once so their times are unambiguous. These six times are shown in bold in Example 10.3. The sum of these times is 244.838 ms which is in good agreement with the host reported GPU time of 245.732 ms. However, it would have been quite tedious to have written host code to obtain the times for the individual steps – nvprof makes this task simple. Another point to note is that the host reported time for running gpujob is 655.452 ms, about 200 ms more that the time reported when running without nvprof. The increase is due to the overhead of running the nvprof profiler.

One apparently puzzling feature of the profile is the value of 245.61 ms reported for the 2 API cudaMemcpy operations. These are the same operations as reported for the GPU but apparently taking 10 times longer. This puzzle is solved by inspecting the actual timeline for the process involved when it becomes clear that the GPU values are timed from the beginning to end of execution for the process whereas the API values are the time between the process being added to the CUDA stream queue and the completion of the process. Another feature to note is that both cudaMalloc and cudaDeviceReset are relatively expensive operations for short jobs taking 66 and 44 ms respectively.

Example 10.3 nvprof output for `gpulog` example

```
D:\ >nvprof gpulog.exe 24 256 256 100000 100
==5008== NVPROF is profiling process 5008 ...
gpu log(2) 0.693134 frac err  1.874e-03%
gpu  int   0.386294 frac err -8.701e-06%
host int   0.386245 frac err  1.267e-02%
times gpu 1834.348 host 3051.117 gpujob 2284.805 ms speedup 1663.3

==5008== Profiling application: gpulog.exe 24 256 256 100000 100
==5008== Profiling result:
Type Time(%) Time  Calls  Avg    Min     Max     Name
GPU 98.55%  1.816s   1   1.80s  1.806s  1.806s  gpu_log
     1.44%  26.4ms   2   13 ms  640ns   26.4ms  [CUDA memcpy ]
     0.01%  158 us   1   158 us 158 us  158 us  reduce_warp_vl
     0.00%  1.20us   1   1.24us 1.24us  1.24us  reduce_warp_vlB
API 88.36%  1.831s   2   917 ms 273 us  1.833s  cudaMemcpy
     9.69%  201 ms   3   67.0ms 16.9us  200 ms  cudaMalloc
     1.93%  40.0ms   1   40.0ms 40.0ms  40.0ms  cudaDeviceReset
     0.02%  437 us   3   145 us 21.5us  256 us  cudaFree
     0.01%  120 us   3   40.0us 17.8us  61.6us  cudaLaunchKern
     0.00%  43.2us   1   43.2us 43.2us  43.2us  cuDeviceTotalMe
     0.00%  17.5us  97   180ns  100ns   2.70us  cuDeviceGetAtt
```

```
  0.00%   9.90us   1   9.90us   9.90us 9.90us  cudaDeviceSync
  0.00%   5.20us   3   1.73us    200ns 4.40us  cuDeviceGetCount
  0.00%   1.50us   2    750ns    200ns 1.30us  cuDeviceGet
  0.00%    500ns   1    500ns    500ns  500ns  cuDeviceGetName
  0.00%    400ns   1    400ns    400ns  400ns  cuDeviceGetLuid
  0.00%    200ns   1    200ns    200ns  200ns  cuDeviceGetUuid
```

Nvprof run from command line using default parameters. The reported values are ordered by execution time. The API operations may overlap those on the GPU. The profile GPU times are accurate and agree with the host code reported GPU time, but the host code reported `gpujob` time has increased by about 200 ms compared to running without nvprof; this is due to profiling overheads. The reported memcpy time of 26.4 ms is about right for transferring 2^{24} 4-byte floats using unpinned host memory. The API reported value of 1.83 seconds is misleading because it includes the time this call was pending in the CUDA stream.

For larger projects nvprof can generate a great deal of output unrelated to the features that you wish to explore. A simple way to limit profiling to a block code is to warp the statements `cudaProfilerStart();` and `cudaProfilerStop();` around that block. The header file `cuda_profiler_api.h` contains the necessary definitions and must be added to the include statements at the head of your code. Example 10.4 shows how to restrict profiling to a few lines of the CUDA code. The more limited results of running the modified program are also shown.

Example 10.4 nvprof with `cudaProfilerStart` and `Stop`

```
   . . .
   #include "cuda_profiler_api.h"
   . . .
75 gpu_log<<<blocks,threads>>>(dev_logs,terms,steps,step_size);
76 cudaMemcpy(logs,dev_logs,steps*sizeof(float),
                                  cudaMemcpyDeviceToHost);
   cudaProfilerStart();
   // 2 step reduce
77 reduce_warp_vl<<<blocks,threads >>>(dev_sums,dev_logs,steps);
78 reduce_warp_vlB<<<    1,threads >>>(dev_tot,dev_sums,
                                  threads);
79 float gpuint = 0.0f;
80 cudaMemcpy(&gpuint,dev_tot,1*sizeof(float),
                                  cudaMemcpyDeviceToHost);
81 cudaDeviceSynchronize();
   cudaProfilerStop();
   . . .

D: >nvprof --profile-from-start off gpulog.exe 24 256 256 10000 100
==31592== NVPROF is profiling process 31592
```

```
gpu log(2) 0.693092 frac err  7.988e-03%
gpu  int   0.386294 frac err -8.701e-06%
host int   0.386245 frac err  1.267e-02%
times gpu 2456.137 host 3111.062 gpujob 2708.699 ms speedup 126.7
==31592== Profiling application: gpulog.exe 24 256 256 10000 100
==31592== Profiling result:
Type Time(%) Time Calls Avg       Min     Max        Name
GPU  98.66% 165 us 1    165 us    165 us  165.00us   reduce_warp_vl
      0.98% 1.63us 1    1.63us    1.63us  1.6320us   reduce_warp_vlB
      0.36%  608ns 1     608ns     608ns     608ns   [CUDA memcpy
API  94.88% 4.69ms 2    2.34ms    8.60us  4.6858ms   cudaLaunchKern
      4.76% 235 us 1    235 us    235 us  235.70us   cudaMemcpy
      0.26% 12.7us 1    12.7us    12.7us  12.700us   cudaDeviceSync
      0.10% 4.80us 1    4.80us    4.80us  4.8000us   cuDeviceGetCount
```

Code fragment of gpulog with profiling restricted to lines 77 81 of the program. The nvprof output is reduced as expected. It is necessary to use the profile-from-start off switch for the embed statements to work. Note also that the overheads of running with nvprof have increased by a factor of 10 compared to before. If the modified program run directly without nvprof there is no performance loss.

The header file `cuda_profiler_api.h` is actually quite limited; it just contains the two start and stop functions used above.

The NVIDIA Tools Extension Library (NVTX) is a much more elaborate suite of functions allowing you to customise the output for the visual profiler in many ways. However, these tools are quite verbose and are beyond the scope of this book. More information can be found in NVIDIA Profiler Users Guide https://docs.nvidia.com/pdf/ CUDA_Profiler_Users_Guide.pdf.

10.3 Profiling with the NVIDIA Visual Profiler (NVVP)

The NVIDIA Visual Profiler, NVVP, can be launched either from a desktop shortcut or from the command line by typing nvvp. The box shows a possible command line approach.

Running nvprof to generate a profile file and then launching NVVP to view the timeline.

```
> nvprof --export-profile prof.nvvp gpulog.exe 24 256 256 10000 100
> nvvp prof.nvvp
```

Additional nvprof options can be used if desired .e.g. --profile-from-start off

As indicated the visual profiler can be launched from the command line specifying the name of an input file; the timeline will then be displayed as shown in Figure 10.1. If no arguments are specified, nvvp will still launch and you will be presented with a dialogue

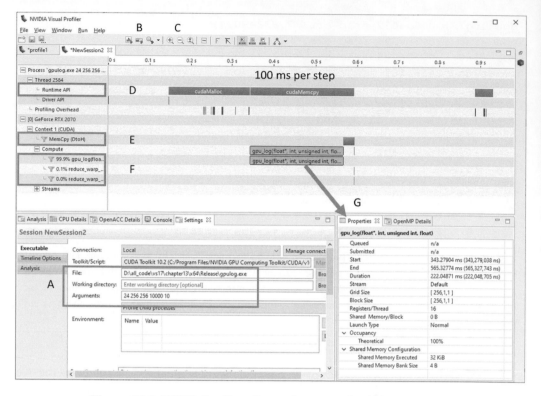

Figure 10.1 NVVP timelines for gpulog example: 100 ms per step

enabling you to choose the exe file to run and to supply the command line arguments. The program will then be automatically run to collect a profile for display. The visual profiler can also be launched from a desktop shortcut in the usual way.

Figure 10.1 shows the nvvp output for the above job; we have zoomed the timeline view a couple of steps using the control at C. The main window shows the timelines for all the CUDA processes run in the job. The three most interesting sections are the runtime API (D), the cudaMemcpy operations (E) and the kernels (F). It is possible to click on any of the displayed tasks to view many details in the properties window (G). In the figure, the details of the gpu_log kernel call (line 75 in Example 10.1) are shown and we can see that this kernel call took 222.049 ms. The two reduce kernels which are much faster appear as vertical bars on this view.

In the bottom left-hand corner, we can see the session settings window giving details of the exe file and program arguments. Both of these can be changed manually and then the session can be rerun using the control at B. I find this very convenient when exploring effects of parameter changes. It is also possible to recompile the program, for example, with Visual Studio, while the nvvp window is open and then use the control at B to see results with the new version of the exe file.

The runtime API line (D) shows kernel and cudaMemcpy events starting when they are added to the CUDA stream pipeline and finishing when they are complete. In this example kernels, which are non-blocking on the host, are added at lines 75, 77 and 78 and cudaMemcpy

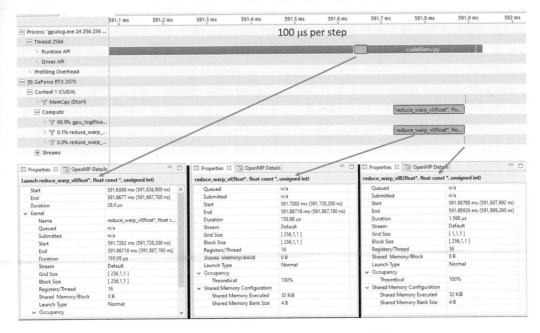

Figure 10.2 NVVP timelines for gpulog example: 100 μs per step

operation, which is blocking on the host, is added at line 80. Thus from the API point of view the first cudaMemcpy operation begins at the same time as the first kernel. However, this operation does not actually start until the first kernel has completed because operations on a given CUDA stream are blocking with respect to each other on the GPU. This explains the apparently long duration of this operation in the API section of the nvprof output. In more complicated situations with multiple asynchronous CUDA streams the API information is a useful aid for checking that the behaviour is as expected. Figures 10.2 and 10.3 show portions of the same NVVP timelines but with the main window zoomed in further to show better detail of the short duration reduce kernels and 4-byte cudaMemcpy operation.

In detail Figures 10.1–10.3 show portions of the timelines for gpulog generated using the Nsight Visual Profiler NVVP for Windows 10. Figure 10.1 shows about 0.9 seconds of execution giving an overview of all steps. Interesting features are:

A: The executable program and command line arguments are entered in this the panel.
B: Once set up in A the job can be run or rerun using the tool at B.
C: Timelines can be expanded in or out using the controls at C.
D–F: Timelines for runtime API, cudaMemcpy operations and kernels are shown separately here. Each different kernel has a separate timeline.
G: Clicking on any object allows you to inspect its properties. Here we show the properties for the gpu_log kernel including the run time of 222.048 ms. It is possible to zoom in and then to inspect details of short duration events using the controls at C as illustrated in Figures 10.2–3.

Figure 10.2 shows the NVVP timeline zoomed by a factor of 100 to show details of the reduce kernels. The full width is now about 0.9 ms. The lower panels show details of the

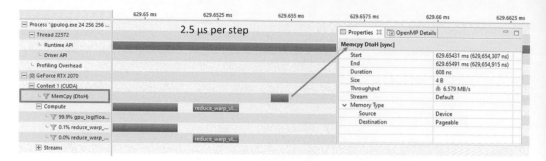

Figure 10.3 NVVP timelines for gpulog example: 2.5 μs per step

launch and execution times of the `reduce_warp_v1` kernel. The reported execution times for the two runs of this kernel are 158.98 μs and 1.568 μs respectively.

Figure 10.3 shows an even deeper zoom; the fullwidth is now about 12.5 μs. The figure shows detail of the `reduce_warp_v1B` kernel and the subsequent 4-byte cudaMemcpy operation. This `memcpy` is reported to take 608 ns.

Both nvprof and NVVP are first generation NVIDIA products and work with early GPUs. Recent GPUs of CC≥6.0 have extra hardware features to support profiling and in 2018 NVIDIA introduced a next generation pair of tools to better support these GPUs. The new tools are Nsight Systems and Nsight Compute and these are discussed next.

10.4 Nsight Systems

Nsight Systems can be downloaded from the NVIDIA developer web pages,[4] at the time of writing the following link to the place to start is: https://developer.nvidia.com/nsight-systems. On my Windows 10 machine the install directory is `C:\Program Files \NVIDIA Corporation\Nsight Systems 2020.3.1` where the version number will obviously change with time. The executable is `nsight-sys.exe` in the `host-windows-x64` subdirectory. You may have a shortcut installed on your desktop or if not a Windows search for Nsight Systems will find it.

When launched, its use is similar to NVVP. You start by using the `File` control to start a new project and are then presented with a window similar to that shown in Figure 10.4.

The first action is at A and selects a machine on which the code to be profiled is to run. Here we have selected the local host. On both Linux and Windows, it is possible to select remote machines instead. Details of how to configure communication with the remote machine are in the NVIDIA documentation.

Your next action is to choose the `exe` file and associated command line arguments that define the job to profile. This is done at B in the figure.

Next choose which tasks to profile using the tick boxes at C. The large number of options gives a hint of the power of this new program and here we only discuss a subset of the possibilities related to profiling small jobs running on a single GPU. To this end we have selected the first 3 options which provide all the CUDA information we are interested in and also some information about host activity.

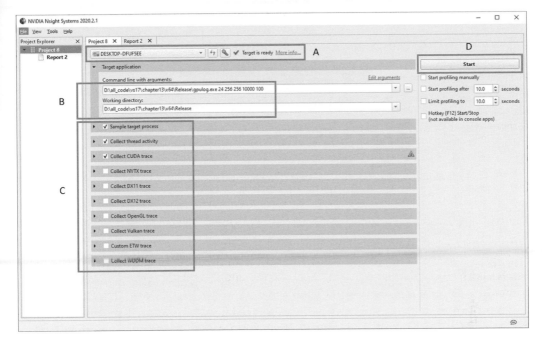

Figure 10.4 Nsight Systems start-up screen

Some of the other options shown in Figure 10.4 are primarily of interest to games developers; these include DX11, DX12, OpenGL and Vulcan trace. The WDDM driver trace is also mainly of interest for graphics applications. The NVTX option is of interest and is discussed below. The ETW (Event Tracing for Windows) is somewhat specialised. More details of all the tracing options can be found at the NVIDIA web page: https://docs.nvidia .com/nsight-systems/tracing/index.html.

The results of running Nsight Systems with the options in Figure 10.4 are shown in Figures 10.5. and 10.6.

Figure 10.5 shows the Nsight Systems timeline display. Many timelines are shown, of which, those at A, B and C are directly relevant to the `gpulog` CUDA job. The CUDA API calls are shown at A, the kernel and `cudaMemcpy` calls at B and the device memory allocation is shown at C. The timing detail of the events in B can be displayed in D by right clicking as indicated. More details of individual items can be displayed at E. To zoom in to the timeline, drag the cursor horizontally. Note the tool at F simply enlarges everything rather than expanding the timeline. Figure 10.6 shows the timeline from Figure 10.5 expanded by factor of $\sim 6 \times 10^5$ to show detail for reduce kernels.

Comparing the results from NVVP and Nsight Systems we can see that the complete timelines in Figures 10.1 and 10.5 contain similar information. This is also true for the expanded timelines. Nsight Systems is a suitable replacement for the NVVP. There is one caveat to this, whereas nvprof is a good command line alternative to the GUI driven NVVP, there is no equivalent command line interface for Nsight Systems on Windows. In Linux the nsys command line tool is available as a command line driven profiler.[5] Nsight Systems will also work well with NVTX code annotations.

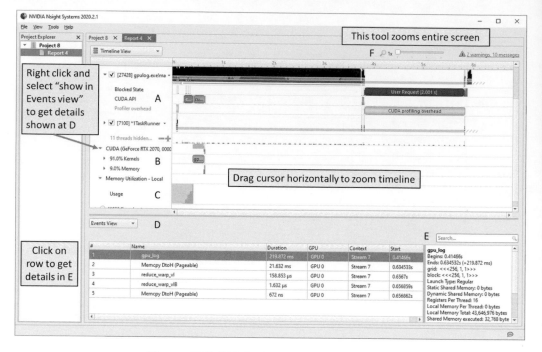

Figure 10.5 Nsight Systems timeline display

Figure 10.6 Timeline from Figure 10.6 expanded by a factor of ~6 × 10⁵

10.5 Nsight Compute

Nsight Compute is a powerful new tool that complements Nsight Systems and allows you to examine the performance of each kernel in your code in great detail. The performance metrics are divided into sections and you have the opportunity to select which metric sections to use when the program is launched. Once started you are presented with the dialogue shown in Figure 10.7.

Pressing the Launch button will run the profiling process and when complete the results of all selected sections will be presented displayed as shown in Figure 10.8. This figure shows a summary of the profiling results for the three active sections. Each section can then be expanded using the control to the left of its title. Results are displayed for the kernel selected in the indicated box at the top of the screen. Several kernels can be displayed on the same plots by selecting them as baselines.

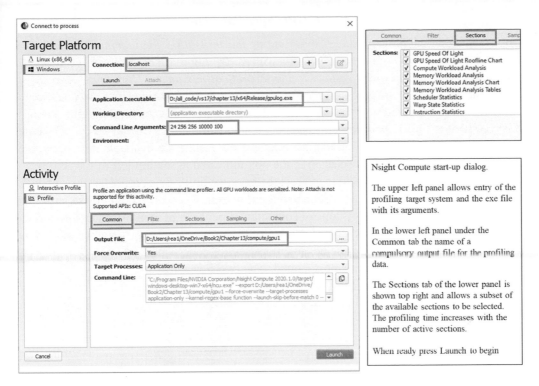

Figure 10.7 Nsight Compute start-up dialog

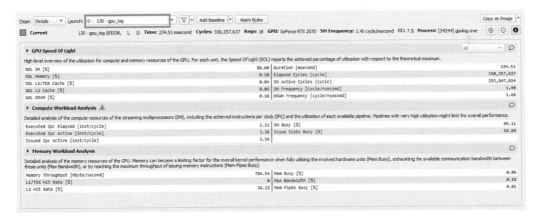

Figure 10.8 Profiling results from Nsight Compute

10.6 Nsight Compute Sections

In this section we show the on-screen descriptions and examples of results for each of the currently available Nsight Compute sections. Once again, the results are for profiling our `gpulog` program compiled in release mode. In the plots below, we show the `gpu_log` kernel together with the `reduce_warp_v1` kernel using the latter as a baseline.

10.6.1 GPU Speed of Light

On-screen description: *"High-level overview of the utilisation for compute and memory resources of the GPU. For each unit, the Speed Of Light (SOL) reports the achieved percentage of utilisation with respect to the theoretical maximum. High-level overview of the utilisation for compute and memory resources of the GPU presented as a roofline chart."*

Figure 10.9 shows charts of the compute and memory performance for individual kernels. It is clear that the `gpu_log` kernel is compute bound while the `reduce_warp_vl` kernel is memory bound. In this section like many others the results are available on a per kernel basis. The kernel to display is selected in the box indicated at the top left of the screen.

A "roofline" chart is often used to indicate the resource limits on a particular piece of code. Such charts are produced in this section and are shown in Figure 10.10. On these charts the horizontal axis is the number of flops of computation per byte of memory access performed by the code and the vertical axis is the number of flops per second. The diagonal line on the left of the chart is the maximum achievable flops/sec for code which performs few flops per memory access and hence is memory bound. The two horizontal lines to the right are the maximum flops/sec achievable by the hardware for 4-byte float and 8-byte double operations. The performance of our two kernels is shown on these plots and we note that both are essentially on their limiting lines. By hovering over the makers with the mouse pointer we can get popup boxes showing numerical values. This shows that the `gpu_log` kernel is delivering 2.87 TFlops/sec and the `reduce_warp_vl` kernel is delivering 432 GFlops/sec of performance.

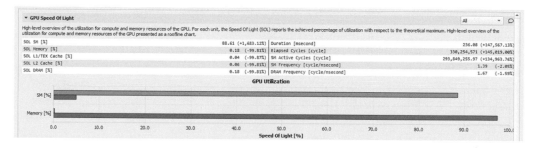

Figure 10.9 GPU Speed of Light: kernel performance

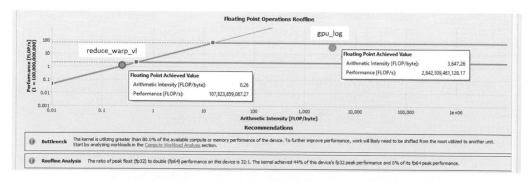

Figure 10.10 GPU Speed of Light: roofline plot for two kernels

Figure 10.9 shows the compute and memory use for the `gpu_log` (upper bar) and `reduce_warp_vl` (lower bar) kernels. It is clear that the first kernel is compute bound and the second kernel is memory bound.

Figure 10.10 shows the floating-point performance for the two kernels as points on a "roofline" plot. Right clicking on a point gives a mini-summary box showing Flops per byte and Flops per second. The `gpu_log` kernel achieves a compute performance of 2.84 TFlops/sec and 3.67 kFlops/byte whereas the `reduce_warp_vl` kernel achieves 107.8 GFlops/sec and 0.26 Flops/byte.

10.6.2 Compute Workload Analysis

On-screen description: "*Detailed analysis of the compute resources of the streaming multi-processors (SM), including the achieved instructions per clock (IPC) and the utilisation of each available pipeline. Pipelines with very high utilisation might limit the overall performance.*"

In this section we see the utilisation of the various SM resources. The display shows that the `gpu_log` kernel makes much more use of the XU and FMA than the `reduce_warp_vl` kernels whereas the opposite is true of the LSU resource. That suggests that in some situations they might be run simultaneously to make better use of all SM resources.

An example of this analysis for our two kernels is shown in Figure 10.11.

10.6.3 Memory Workload Analysis

On-screen description: "*Detailed analysis of the memory resources of the GPU. Memory can become a limiting factor for the overall kernel performance when fully utilising the involved hardware units (Mem Busy), exhausting the available communication bandwidth between those units (Max Bandwidth), or by reaching the maximum throughput of issuing memory instructions (Mem Pipes Busy). Detailed chart of the memory units. Detailed tables with data for each memory unit.*"

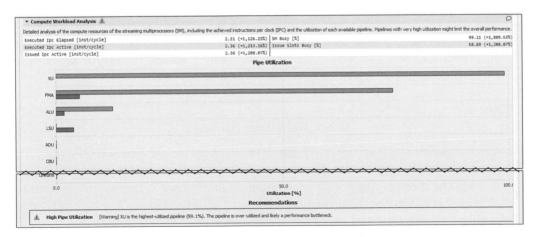

Figure 10.11 Compute workload analysis: chart for two kernels

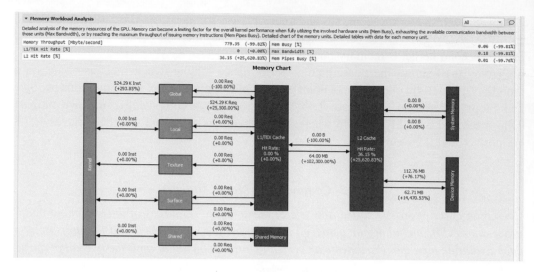

Figure 10.12 Memory workload analysis: flow chart for gpu_log kernel

Figure 10.12 Shows the Nsight Compute memory workload analysis chart for the gpu_log kernel. A flow of 64 MB from L1 cache to system memory can be seen.

10.6.4 Scheduler Statistics

On-screen description: *"Summary of the activity of the schedulers issuing instructions. Each scheduler maintains a pool of warps that it can issue instructions for. The upper bound of warps in the pool (Theoretical Warps) is limited by the launch configuration. On every cycle each scheduler checks the state of the allocated warps in the pool (Active Warps). Active warps that are not stalled (Eligible Warps) are ready to issue their next instruction. From the set of eligible warps the scheduler selects a single warp from which to issue one or more instructions (Issued Warp). On cycles with no eligible warps, the issue slot is skipped and no instruction is issued. Having many skipped issue slots indicates poor latency hiding."*

Figure 10.13 shows statistics for both gpu_log and reduce_warp_v1. From the Slot Utilisation issues boxes we see the warp scheduler issues one instruction every 1.7 cycles for the gpu_log kernel and one every 22.9 cycles for the reduce_warp_v1 kernel. The second kernel thus has very poor memory latency hiding.

10.6.5 Warp State Statistics

On-screen description: *"Analysis of the states in which all warps spent cycles during the kernel execution. The warp states describe a warp's readiness or inability to issue its next instruction. The warp cycles per instruction define the latency between two consecutive instructions. The higher the value, the more warp parallelism is required to hide this latency. For each warp state, the chart shows the average number of cycles spent in that state per issued instruction. Stalls are not always impacting the overall performance nor are they completely avoidable. Only focus on stall reasons if the schedulers fail to issue every cycle.*

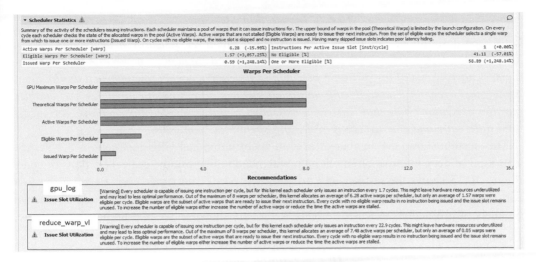

Figure 10.13 Scheduler statistics

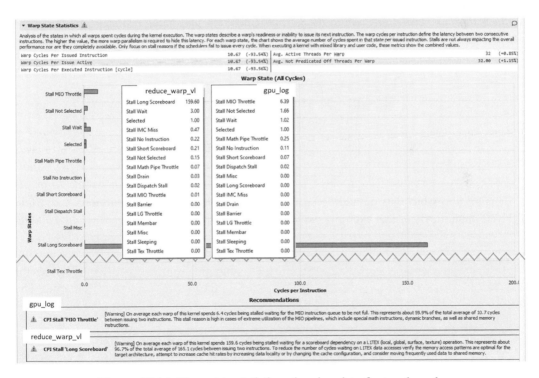

Figure 10.14 Warp state statistics: showing data for two kernels

When executing a kernel with mixed library and user code, these metrics show the combined values."

The detailed information in Figure 10.14 includes recommendations which might help experienced GPU programmers improve the design of their code.

10.6.6 Instruction Statistics

On-screen description: *"Statistics of the executed low-level assembly instructions (SASS). The instruction mix provides insight into the types and frequency of the executed instructions. A narrow mix of instruction types implies a dependency on few instruction pipelines, while others remain unused. Using multiple pipelines allows hiding latencies and enables parallel execution. Note that 'Instructions/Opcode' and 'Executed Instructions' are measured differently and can diverge if cycles are spent in system calls."*

This section shows the number of executions of individual GPU instructions per kernel. This kind of deep information might help with hand tuning of time critical portions of code. Figure 10.15 shows the results for `reduce_warp_vl` and `gpu_log`. Because the first kernel runs for much less time than the second, it is barely visible on the chart. The actual numbers of instructions executed for each kernel are shown in the pop-up box in the figure.

10.6.7 Launch Statistics

On-screen description: *"Summary of the configuration used to launch the kernel. The launch configuration defines the size of the kernel grid, the division of the grid into blocks, and the GPU resources needed to execute the kernel. Choosing an efficient launch configuration maximises device utilisation."*

Grid Size	256
Block Size	256
Threads	65,536
Waves per SM	1.78
Registers per Thread	16

This section which has no additional charts reports the launch configurations and a few derived quantities. For this example, we get the values shown in the box.

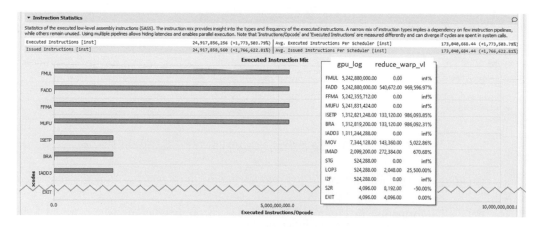

Figure 10.15 Instruction statistics: statistics for two kernels

Table 10.1 *Tuning the number of thread blocks for the gpulog program*

Blocks	Waves	gpu_log		reduce_warp_vl	
		TFlops/sec	time ms	TFlops/sec	Time μs
256	1.78	2.847	235.73	0.107	160
512	3.56	3.067	218.79	0.110	160
1024	7.11	3.143	213.47	0.114	163
288	2	3.161	212.31	0.108	160
576	4	3.193	210.16	0.101	176
1152	8	3.190	210.35	0.117	160

The value reported for threads which is simply the product of the grid size and block size is as expected and the number of registers per thread has been decided by the compiler and is safely below 32, the limit for full occupancy. However, the value for waves is interesting and helpful. In CUDA a wave of threads refers to the set of all threads launched on all SMs at a given time. For full occupancy this is either 2048 or 1024 times the number of SMs on the GPU depending on the CC level of the GPU. For current GPUs with CCs in the range 3.5 to 8.0 only Turing GPUs with CC=7.5 have SMs which support up to 1024 resident threads; for all others the maximum is 2048.

The Turing RTX 2070 GPU used here has 36 SMs so the wave size is $1024 \times 36 = 36864$ threads and the launch configuration corresponds to $65536/36864 = 1.78$ waves. This means two waves will be launched to process the job; the first wave achieves full occupancy, but the second wave only achieves 78% occupancy. This may or may not affect performance depending on the kernels. Nsight Compute allows you to easily experiment with this and some results for the `gpulog` program are shown in Table 10.1.

As is clear from the table using a launch configuration with an integer number of waves is significantly better than our first choice for the `gpu_log` kernel. Using exactly four waves gives a performance of 3.19 TFlops/sec, a gain of 12%. A final wave with less than full occupancy is sometimes referred to as the "*tail*" by CUDA programmers, and while I was always aware that such a tail exists using a standard launch configuration like 256×256 I had assumed that any effect on CPU bound kernels would be small. After all a single GPU SM unit only has enough hardware to process two or four warps at a given instant, the advantage of full occupancy is latency hiding – it would appear that full occupancy is hiding more than just the latency of external memory access. We have experimented with other kernels used in this book and find that using an integer number of waves for the number of thread blocks instead of a power of 2 does not always make a significant difference. We recommend experimenting with this for each of your GPU projects.

10.6.8 Occupancy

On-screen description: "*Occupancy is the ratio of the number of active warps per multiprocessor to the maximum number of possible active warps. Another way to view occupancy is the percentage of the hardware's ability to process warps that is actively in use. Higher occupancy does not always result in higher performance, however, low occupancy always reduces the ability to hide latencies, resulting in overall performance degradation. Large*

discrepancies between the theoretical and the achieved occupancy during execution typic-
ally indicates highly imbalanced workloads."

This section gives the achieved kernel occupancy and has charts showing how this might vary with registers per thread and shared memory use. Figure 10.16 shows the chart produce for the gpulog program.

10.6.9 Source Counters

On-screen description: "*Source metrics, including warp stall reasons. Sampling Data metrics are periodically sampled over the kernel runtime. They indicate when warps were stalled and couldn't be scheduled. See the documentation for a description of all stall reasons. Only focus on stalls if the schedulers fail to issue every cycle.*"

The details under this section allow inspection of kernel performance at the level of single hardware instructions. Figure 10.17 shows how this section can be used to view the assembly code associated with each line of GPU code. The line selected is line 19 from Example 10.1 and is the expensive division in the `for` loop of the `logsum` device function. (This is reported as line 24 in the figure.) We can see that different SASS code is generated with and without using the `fast_math` option. Note that to get this source code view the `exe` file must be compiled in debug mode. This in turn makes generation of the profile much slower and it is a good idea to greatly reduce the problem size. We used arguments of `20 288 256 1000 1` in this case. The box indicated at A on the top left of the figure allows one to switch between viewing SASS or PTX code.

This source counters section can also provide a great deal of detail about how often each instruction is used. The use of such information is an advanced topic beyond the scope of this book.

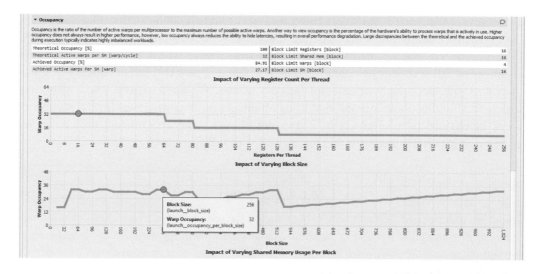

Figure 10.16 Occupancy: theoretical and achieved values for gpulog program

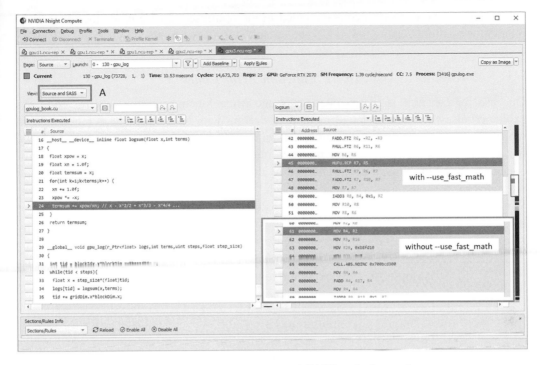

Figure 10.17 Source counters: source and SASS code for gpulog program

In summary, Nsight Systems and Nsight Compute are really powerful tools for investigating the performance of your GPU code. We highly recommend their use in situations where you suspect your code is not performing as well as it might.

Since fast code is no use if it does not actually work, it is now time to consider debugging.

10.7 Debugging with Printf

Bugs in computer code are inevitable and finding them is an art; you will get better as your experience grows. It is a very good idea to write new code with debugging in mind, thus keeping your code simple, and to break it down so that each task is a separate function. The main routine should simply organise function calls and data flow. Try to debug your functions one by one as you progress. I like to add `printf` statements in critical places as I write code. This allows you to check progress function by function as you proceed. Remember you can use `printf` in both your host and kernel code.

In kernel code it is a good idea to make all printing conditional on block and thread values – otherwise far too much output will be produced. Also, `printf` is expensive in all code, so do not keep active `printf` statements in blocks of code while you are trying to tune the performance.

One disadvantage of `printf` is that code will need to be recompiled every time you think of something else to print. On the other hand, in a debugging session you will probably be recompiling a lot anyway. That said, larger CUDA programs tend to be slower to compile and the other methods described below might be more effective. Note what while `printf` debugging can be done with code compiled in the optimised release mode the other more interactive methods require the code to be compiled in debug mode.

10.7.1 Function Error Codes

One use for `printf` is to generate a message when function returns an error code. As explained elsewhere our preferred method of dealing with errors in a C++ function is to return a non-zero integer flag indicating that an error has occurred. In most of our code we just return 1 after printing an error message rather than developing sets of different error codes which might or might not be checked by the caller. If no errors are found, the function returns zero. NVIDIA uses a similar approach, albeit with an elaborate set of error codes. Most host callable CUDA functions return a value of type `cudaError_t` which is a set of enum defined error codes. The return value `cudaSuccess` (which has numerical value zero) indicates success. Typical uses are shown in Example 10.5:

Example 10.5 Checking the return code from a CUDA call

```
10    cudaError_t cudaStatus = cudaSetDevice(0);
11    if (cudaStatus != cudaSuccess) {
12        printf("cudaSetDevice failed!\n");
13        goto Error;
14    }

20    cudaError_t cudaStatus = cudaSetDevice(0);
21    if (cudaStatus != cudaSuccess) {
22        printf("CUDA Error %s\n",
                    cudaGetErrorString(cudaStatus));
23        exit(1);
24    }

30    checkCudaErrors( cudaSetDevice(0) );

40    cx::ok( cudaSetDevice(0) );

50    kernel<<<blocks,threads>>>(a,b,c);
51    cx::ok( cudaGetLastError() ); // check for launch error
52    cudaDeviceSynchronize();
53    cx::ok( cudaGetLastError() ); // check for run time error
```

Description of Example 10.5

- Lines 10–14: This code fragment is taken from the kernel.cu template code used by the NVIDIA CUDA project add-in for Visual Studio.
  - Line 10: The variable `cudaStatus` is declared as type `cudaError_t` as set to the code returned by the CUDA function `cudaSetDevice()`. This function will return an error code if there is no CUDA GPU available; hence it is good practice to check for this error.

- ○ Line 11: Here we check `cudaStatus`, if it is equal to `cudaSuccess` then there is a CUDA device present and we can bypass the `if` clause and proceed with the rest of the program.
- ○ Line 12: An error has occurred so print a warning message.
- ○ Line 13: We cannot continue after this error so the code uses a `go to` statement to jump a shared fragment code that performs a tidy-up and then exits. The use of `go to` in this way dates from the FORTRAN II era and should *never* be used in modern software. It is always possible to avoid `go to`, for example, by encapsulating sections of code in a sub-function and returning with an error code. The routines in `cxbinio.h` are an example of this.
- • Lines 20–24: This is a slightly improved version of the above. We have used `cudaGetErrorString` in the `printf` on line 22 to convert the value of `cudaStatus` to a readable description of the error. We have also replaced the `go to` with `exit(1)` which ends the program and returns an error code of 1 to the operating system. For simple programs we can rely on the operating system to clean up allocated resources in the case of fatal errors, but this should not be relied on for high-quality production code. Using `exit` in this way may also prevent profiling or debugging tools such as Nsight Compute from working properly.
- • Line 30: This is a more compact version of lines 20–24. The CUDA SDK uses the function `checkCudaErrors` for checking return codes in many of the SDK examples. It performs the same task as lines 20–24 including exiting the program if an error is found. The function is defined in `cuda_helper.h`.
- • Line 40: This is similar to using `cudaCheckErrors` except that `cx::ok` as defined in `cx.h` is used and hence is easy for you to edit and change the `exit(1)` to `return 1` for situations where you may need to continue after an error has been detected. It is also slightly less verbose improving the readability of your kernel code.

  Lines 50–53 These lines show how to use the same method with kernel code, given that a kernel cannot directly return an error code to the caller. However, the CUDA system maintains a flag containing the *last* reported runtime error from either host or device code. The flag can be read using the `cudaGetLastError` function as shown in this fragment of code.
- ○ Line 50: Here we launch a kernel and want to check for errors.
- ○ Line 51: Here we check for kernel errors using `cx::ok` with `cudGetLastError` – this will now behave just like the code in lines 30 or 40 albeit with one subtle difference. The kernel launch is asynchronous with the host execution so probably this call will not pick up any errors that occur during kernel execution, except possibly at the very start. What it will do is to pick up any errors from the kernel launch itself, for example, insufficient shared memory or a thread block size which is too large. A side effect of calling `cudaGetLastError` is to reset the internal error to `cudaSuccess` so repeated calls will only detect a given error once. (There is also a `cudaPeekAtLastError` which returns the most recent error without resetting the error state.)
- ○ Line 52: The `cudaDeviceSynchronize` call now suspends host execution until the kernel launched in line 50 has completed. After this call the last of any errors reported by the kernel will be available to check.
- ○ Line 53: Here we check for errors during kernel execution.

10.8 Debugging with Microsoft Visual Studio

Even diehard Linux devotees will admit that Microsoft Visual Studio is an excellent (and free) tool for both writing and debugging C++ code. There is extensive documentation readily available on the web so here we will just give a basic introduction emphasising support for CUDA.

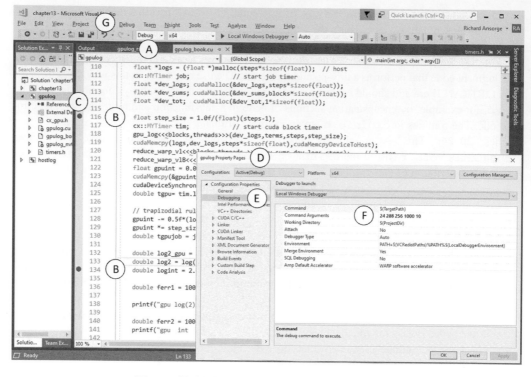

Figure 10.18 Preparing a VS-debugging session

To debug in Visual Studio, all that is needed is to select debug mode compilation, set one or more break points and then press F5. This is illustrated in Figure 10.18 which also explains how to set the command line arguments and make the desired project the target for debugging.

The procedure for starting a debugging session in Visual Studio as shown in Figure 10.18 is as follows:

1. Select debug mode at A.
2. Set one or more break points by clicking to the left of appropriate statement line numbers. The selected statements are shown by markers indicated by B for lines 116 and 134 in the figure.
3. Press F5 to start the session.
4. If you have more than one project in your solution then, before starting debugging, the project concerned must be set as the default startup project by right clicking on the project name at C. The default startup project name is shown in bold.
5. Right clicking on the project name also allows you to open the project properties pages as shown at D.
6. The debugging tab at E is where you set the command line arguments for the program being debugged as shown at F.

Once the debugging session has started, the program will run as far as the first break point and then wait for user input. At this point the debug menu option at G in Figure 10.18 will be populated with many options as shown in Figure 10.19.

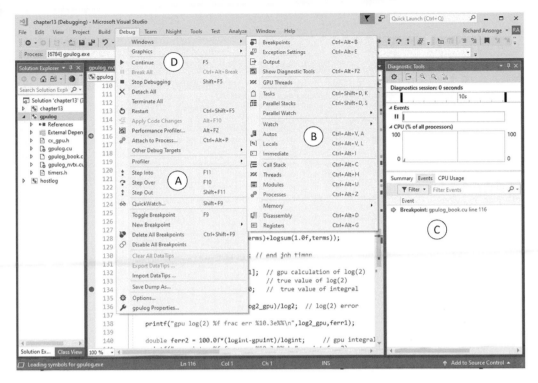

Figure 10.19 Start of VS debugging after pressing F5

Interesting commands are F10 and F11 shown at A; these run the next line in your code with the option to step into or over called functions. Note that a called function is still executed even if stepped over and this applies to CUDA functions as well as host functions.

You can also open the Locals window at B which displays the current values of local variables. These values are dynamically updated as you step through your code, with newly changed values being highlighted in red. The current value of a variable can also be inspected by hovering over that variable with the mouse pointer. This is obviously very powerful and an alternative to using printf.

Pressing F5 shown at D will cause the program to run on until the next breakpoint is reached (this could be at the same place in the code, if inside a loop). The line number corresponding to the current break point is shown at C.

A more in-depth treatment of the Visual Studio debugger can readily be found on the web, for example, https://docs.microsoft.com/en-us/visualstudio/debugger/getting-started-with-the-debugger-cpp?view=vs-2019.

Figure 10.20 shows the result of stepping the through the `gpulog` code up to the second break point at line 134 (at A). The Locals window now displays values of variables calculated up to this point. We can see at B that both the `log2` and `log2_gpu` variables have correct values indicating that the GPU code has run successfully by this point. The host array `logs` will also have been filled by the first `cudaMemcpy`. The contents of large arrays can be inspected by opening a Watch window using the menu option at B in Figure 10.18 and then typing in the array element to view, this is illustrated at C in

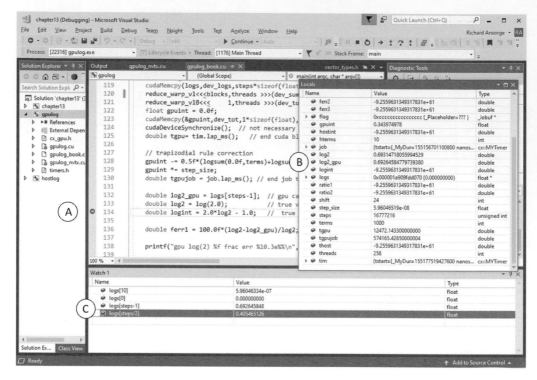

Figure 10.20 VS debugging at second break point

Figure 10.19. Note simple index arithmetic using valid variables is allowed, for example, `logs[steps/2]` is fine.

10.9 Debugging Kernel Code

The CUDA code in the program will run perfectly well inside the VS debugger but it is not possible to step into GPU code and inspect kernel variables using the native debugger. However, the NVIDIA Nsight Visual Studio Edition addon adds just this support. The code installs as a Visual Studio plugin and is part of the standard Windows SDK or it can be obtained separately from the NVIDIA website at https://developer.nvidia.com/nsight-visual-studio-edition. Once installed a number of options are available under the new `Nsight` menu option as illustrated at B in Figure 10.21. You can use this menu to start a new debugging session including support for CUDA kernels. Choose either "`Start CUDA Debugging (Next Gen)`" for recent Pascal and above GPUs or "`Start CUDA Debugging (Legacy)`" for older GPUs. This menu also allows you to run Nsight Systems, Nsight Compute and CUDA `memchk` from within Visual Studio.

Breakpoints can now be inserted in kernel code as shown at A in the Figure F5 can then be used as before to run your code until you reach the desired breakpoint. Once a breakpoint inside a kernel is reached, the Windows menu option shown at B in the figure allows you to open the Warp Info and Lanes panels shown in Figure 10.22. Note that your still cannot step into a CUDA kernel from a host function using F11. F5 is the only way to get to a kernel

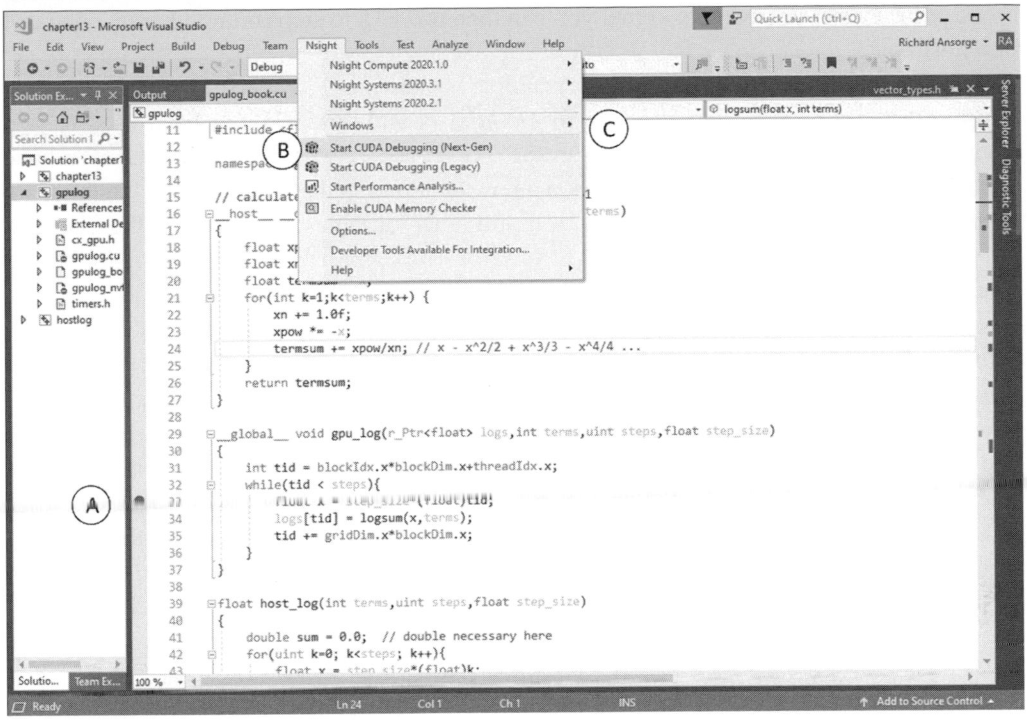

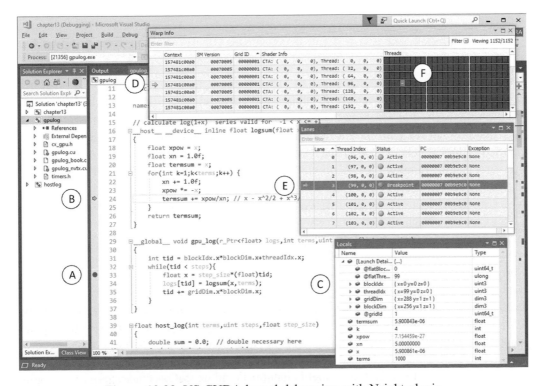

Figure 10.21 VS debugging: using Nsight for kernel code

Figure 10.22 VS CUDA kernel debugging with Nsight plugin

break point, however once in a kernel you can then use F11 to step through kernel code just like host code.

A debugging session for our `gpulog` example is shown in Figure 10.22. In this example the program has been run up to the break point at A and then F11 has been used to step through the kernel code up to line 24 in the `logsum __device__` function. We have actually then stepped through the `for` loop a few iterations so that k is equal to 4 at the point shown in the figure. The current values of k and other variables are shown in the `Locals` window at C. Note that the CUDA built in variables are included here and we are looking at thread 99 in block 0. By default, the CUDA debugger will show values for thread 0 in block 0 but this can be changed by using the CUDA `Warp Info` and `Lanes` windows which are shown at D and E. To select a particular thread one can just click on an element of the matrix shown at F in the `Warp Info` window. The selected thread will have a different colour as can be seen for thread 99 near F in our figure. Alternatively, one can select a particular warp and lane by clicking in the left-hand columns in the Warp Info and Lanes windows. The selected rows are indicated by the arrows at D and E.

More information on CUDA debugging with Visual Studio can be found on the NVIDIA website, for example, at https://docs.nvidia.com/nsight-visual-studio-edition/index.html.

10.10 Memory Checking

Memory leaks and out-of-range pointers can cause program crashes or more subtle hard-to-find errors. Fortunately, NVIDIA provides a number of tools specifically designed to help find such errors.

10.10.1 Cuda-memcheck

Another useful tool is the NVIDIA CUDA memory checker `cuda-memcheck.exe` which can help diagnose hard-to-find array-addressing errors in kernel code. Such errors often manifest themselves by crashing the program. Sometimes the `cx::ok` return code checker will also pick up these errors but that is not always true and `cuda-memcheck` provides better diagnostics. The `cuda-memcheck` program is like nvprof in that it is a command line wrapper for running CUDA programs. As an example, let us introduce a bug in our Example 10.1 `gpulog` code as shown in Example 10.6 below. The new kernel mem_put writes to one element of the input array and the host code uses the user-defined parameter `loc` to specify which element to overwrite.

The results of testing different values of `loc` are also shown in Example 10.6. For case (a), the code is run without any checks, no error is reported for any value of `loc` up to $2^{31}-1$. Correct results are still obtained but the execution time for the GPU code has increased. In case (b) we use conventional error checking with the `cx::ok` wrapper around the `cudaDeviceSynchronize` in line 81. In this case we do detect errors but only when `loc` is about a factor of 8 times larger than the valid index range. The nature of the error is correctly reported but the offending kernel is not identified. The program is terminated when the first error is detected.[6] In case (c) using cuda-memcheck the error found when `loc` $\geq$ `steps+blocks`, the offending kernel is identified and execution continues.

Example 10.6 Use of cuda-memcheck

```
01  __global__ void mem_put(float *a,int loc)
02  {
03    if(threadIdx.x==0 && blockIdx.x==0) a[loc] = 12345.0f;
04  }
     . . .
67    int hterms = argc >5 ? atoi(argv[5]) : terms;
67.5  int loc =    argc >6 ? atoi(argv[6]) : steps;
     . . .
79    float gpuint = 0.0f;
80    cudaMemcpy(&gpuint,dev_tot,1*sizeof(float),
                            cudaMemcpyDeviceToHost);
80.5  mem_put<<<1,1>>>(dev_logs,loc);
81    cudaDeviceSynchronize();
```

(a) **With no checks**
```
D:\> gpulog.exe 6 288 256 1000 10 2147483647
gpu log(2) 0.692646 frac err  7.233e-02%
gpu  int   0.386294 frac err  1.225e-04%
host int.  0.382179 frac err  1.065e+00%
times gpu 15.939 hostjob 1.169 gpujob 182.347 ms speedup 7.3
```

(b) With cx::ok(cudaDeviceSynchronize()); at line 81
```
D:\> gpulog.exe 16 288 256 1000 10 524288
cx::ok error: an illegal memory access was encountered at
                gpulog_book.cu:132 cudaDeviceSynchronize()
```

(c) **With cuda-memcheck**
```
D:\ >cuda-memcheck.exe gpulog.exe 16 288 256 1000 10 65824
===== CUDA-MEMCHECK
gpu log(2) 0.692646 frac err  7.233e-02%
gpu  int   0.386294 frac err  1.302e-04%
host int   0.382179 frac err  1.065e+00%
times gpu 120.462 host 1.261 gpujob 342.407 ms speedup 1.0
===== Invalid __global__ write of size 4
===== at 0x000000a0 in mem_put(float*, int)
===== by thread (0,0,0) in block (0,0,0)
===== Address 0x700e40480 is out of bounds
===== Device Frame:mem_put(float*, int)(mem_put(float*, int)
===== Saved host backtrace up to driver entry point at kernel
===== Host Frame:C:\WINDOWS\system32\nvcuda.dll ...
===== Host Frame:D:\...\gpulog.exe(cudart::cudaApiLaunchKernel+
===== Host Frame:D:\...\gpulog.exe(cudaLaunchKernel + 0x1c4)
[0x1654]
===== Host Frame:D:\...\gpulog.exe mem_put + 0xbd) [0xfcfd]
===== Host Frame:D:\...\gpulog.exe(main + 0x3a6) [0x10346]
===== . . .
```

Note that in case (c) using `cuda-memcheck` we only detect errors when `loc` exceeds `steps+blocks-1`, then the offending kernel is correctly identified and program execution is allowed to continue. Even `cuda-memcheck` is not perfect for finding out-of-range index errors. We conjecture that in our example the two large GPU memory allocations for `dev_logs` and `dev_sums` made in lines 70 and 71 of Example 10.1 are actually allocated as contiguous blocks with `dev_sums` after `dev_logs`. Thus, it is only when the index used in `dev_logs` exceeds the combined size of both arrays that an out-of-range error is flagged by the hardware.[7]

Note the GPU execution times are always increased when using `cuda-memcheck` irrespective of whether an error is detected but this is not really a problem as no code changes are necessary when using this tool and you would not use `cuda-memcheck` for production runs of code.

10.10.2 Linux Tools

Nsight Eclipse Edition is included in the Linux version of the CUDA SDK and offers essentially the same profiling and debugging tools as discussed above for windows. The "Nsight Eclipse Edition Getting Started Guide" is included in the SDK documentation and is also available from https://developer.nvidia.com/nsight-eclipse-edition. This toolkit includes Linux versions of Nsight Systems and Nsight Compute.

Linux also offers an alternative command line debugging tool `cuda-gdb` which is based on the popular Linux `gdb` debugger. This might be a good choice if you are already familiar with gdb. More information can be found at https://developer.nvidia.com/cuda-gdb.

The command line-based memory checking tool `cuda-memcheck` is also available on Linux.

10.10.3 CUDA compute-sanitizer

The CUDA `mem-check` program is quite old and has recently been superseded by the more capable CUDA `compute-sanitizer` application. In simple cases, both programs perform the same check and produce similar output. In more complex situations, the `compute-sanitizer` is recommended. Both programs have extensive documentation available from https://docs.nvidia.com/cuda/sanitizer-docs/ and https://docs.nvidia.com/cuda/pdf/CUDA_Memcheck.pdf.

This ends our chapter on profiling and debugging. The next chapter discusses the relatively new tensor-core hardware of recent NVIDIA GPUs.

Endnotes Chapter 10

1 This final `cudaDeviceSynchronize` is not strictly necessary as the previous `cudaMemcpy` (D2H) is always blocking on the host. (But note that H2D copies with data sizes of less than 64K might not be blocking on the host.)

2 On Linux you may be able to use the compiler switch `-ftz` or on Windows with the Intel C++ compiler the `/Qftz` switch.

3 You may get a missing dll error message when you first try this, e.g. missing `cupti64_2020.1.1.dll`. On Windows this can be fixed by adding `%CUDA_PATH%/extras/CUPTI/lib64` to the system PATH.

4 You may need a (free) developer account to access these pages – you should not have a problem with this; just follow the instructions to register for one.

5 It seems that differences in CUDA support tools for Windows and Linux are emerging. The Windows tools being more focused on gaming and graphics while the Linux tools are more focused on HPC.

6 This behaviour can be modified by editing the definition of `cx::ok` in the `cx.h` include file.

7 If we are being picky, then there is also a third allocation of just one word in line 72 of example 10.1 (b). Maybe that allocation is not contiguous and so does not contribute to the size of larger contiguous block. We can actually print the GPU pointers (using `%lld`) to check this and indeed find that whereas the first two allocations are contiguous the third allocation is offset by an additional 96 bytes. This in turn is because each cudaMalloc array is aligned on a 512 byte boundary and the size of the dev_sums array for 288 blocks is not a multiple of 512.

11

Tensor Cores

The Volta CC 7.0 generation of GPUs, launched in June 2018, included new *Tensor Core* hardware to accelerate matrix multiplication. The capabilities of this hardware were increased in June 2020 with the launch of the Ampere GPU generation. Although intended specifically for applications in artificial intelligence, we feel this hardware may be more generally useful and is well worth looking at even if AI is not your primary focus.

11.1 Tensor Cores and FP16

These special purpose hardware units are known as Tensor Cores which are specifically designed to perform fast multiplication of two matrices A and B with addition of a third a matrix C and storing the result in a fourth matrix D. All the matrices are 4×4 and C and D hold standard 4-byte floats (FP32) whereas A and B hold 2-byte floats (FP16 or *half*). This is shown in Eq. 11.1 where the suffices indicate the bit-size of the elements:

$$\mathbf{D}_{32} = \mathbf{A}_{16} \times \mathbf{B}_{16} + \mathbf{C}_{32}. \tag{11.1}$$

The hardware supports the case where C and D are the same matrix resulting in

$$\mathbf{C}_{32} = \mathbf{A}_{16} \times \mathbf{B}_{16} + \mathbf{C}_{32}. \tag{11.2}$$

The hardware is designed to support tiled matrix multiplication of large matrices, where the tiles A and B sweep along the rows and columns of two large matrices and their product is accumulated in a fixed tile C as shown in Eq. 11.3:

$$\begin{aligned}
\mathbf{C}_{ij}^0 &= 0, \\
\mathbf{C}_{ij}^k &= \mathbf{A}_{ik} \times \mathbf{B}_{kj} + \mathbf{C}_{ij}^{k-1}
\end{aligned} \tag{11.3}$$

where the index k sweeps along the rows or columns.

The FP16 format supported by tensor cores is the IEEE format which uses 5-bits for the exponent and 10 bits for the faction giving an accuracy of about one part in 2000.[1] The 5-bit exponent covers the range of roughly $10^{-4.5}$–$10^{4.8}$. The lower precision of the 2-byte floats is obviously a concern, but it turns out that that there are interesting applications where the precision is adequate and that gain in speed from the new hardware is really useful. One notable case is machine learning where NVIDIA tensor cores are rapidly being adopted as essential hardware. Indeed, it seems that NVIDIA hardware is starting to dominate this major new field. The tensor cores also support single byte integer types (variously referred to as char and uchar or int8 and uint8 or u8 and s8) for A and B and 32-bit integers for C and D.

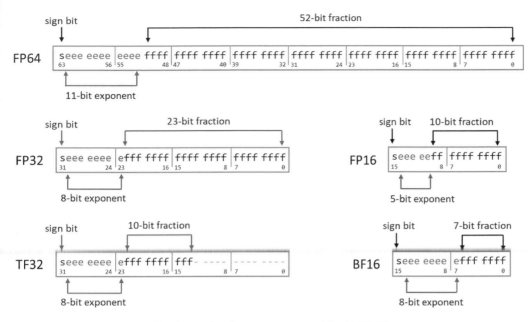

Figure 11.1 Floating-point formats supported by NVIDIA tensor cores

The Turing generation of GPUs with CC = 7.5 were launched shortly after Volta in August 2018 and have tensor cores upgraded to include processing of 4-bit and 1-bit integers. In June 2020, NVIDIA launched its CC 8.0 Ampere generation of GPUs which include upgraded third generation tensor cores. These are a factor of 2 or more faster and support two additional short floating-point types, BF16 and TF32. Both new types have an 8-bit exponent, the same as used in FP32 and either a 7-bit or a 10-bit fraction. The hardware layout of all these floating-point numbers is shown in Figure 11.1. The BF16 format is a variant of the IEEE standard FP16 format allowing more dynamic range at the expense of reduced precision. The TF32 format is a variant of the IEEE FP32 format with the same exponent range but with fewer fraction bits. Importantly, standard FP32 values can be used as inputs for the A and B matrices and will be internally converted to TF32 values. This greatly simplifies porting existing matrix code to tensor cores because format conversions on the host are not required. Ampere also has other enhancements closely targeted at machine learning or AI applications; we recommend the interested reader to look at the NVIDIA *nvidia-ampere-architecture-whitepaper* document which can be found in PDF form at www.nvidia.com/content/dam/en-zz/Solutions/Data-Center/nvidia-ampere-architecture-whitepaper.pdf.

In Figure 11.1 the FP64, FP32 and FP16 are standard IEEE formats but TF16 and BF16 are proprietary to NVIDIA. Only FP16 is supported on first generation CC = 7 GPUs (Volta and Turing) while all formats are supported on third generation CC = 8 (Ampere) GPUs. Although FP32 and FP64 can be used for the A and B matrices on third generation tensor cores there is no performance gain.

11.2 Warp Matrix Functions

In software, NVIDIA CUDA supports tensor cores with a set of *warp matrix functions* which use definitions in the CUDA mma.h include file. With this header file included, the type half is defined to represent FP16 numbers and can be used like other numeric types in GPU code and to a limited extent in host code.[2] There are large sets of intrinsic functions available for both FP16 and BF16 which are accessed from the include files cuda_fp16.h and cuda_bf16.h. Note most of these intrinsics are only available for device code but those involving conversion between native 4-byte and 2-byte types are available for both host and device code. The full set of these intrinsics can be found in the NVIDIA CUDA Math API Reference Manual.

The warp matrix functions use the 32-threads in a warp to cooperatively perform the matrix multiplications shown in Eqs. 11.2 and 11.3 but with matrices of size 16×16 rather than 4×4. Although not stated explicitly in the documentation, this must involve a total of 64 hardware tensor core operations to perform the tiled 16×16 matrix multiplication using 4×4 tiles. The full set of functions is shown in Table 11.1 taken from the NVIDIA CUDA C++ Programming Guide. In the descriptions the tiles A, B, C and D are represented by

Table 11.1 *CUDA warp matrix functions*

template<typename Use, int **m**, int **n**, int **k**, typename **T**, typename **Layout**=void> class fragment;	Creates objects of type fragment. The parameter Use must be one of the keywords matrix_a, matrix_b or accumulator. Layout is one of row_major or col_major.
void **load_matrix_sync** (fragment<...> **&a**, const T* **mptr**, unsigned **ldm**, layout_t **layout**);	Load a 16×16 tile of data into fragment a from array at mptr using a stride of ldm between rows or columns depending on layout. This version is for accumulator fragments
void **load_matrix_sync** (fragment<...> **&a**, const T* **mptr**, unsigned **ldm**);	As above but for matrix type fragments with known layouts.
void **fill_fragment**(fragment<...> **&a**, const T& **v**);	Set all elements of fragment a to the value v.
void **mma_sync**(fragment<...> **&d**, const fragment<...> **&a**, const fragment<...>**&b**, const fragment<...> **&c**, bool **satf**=false);	This evaluates D=A*B+C for the fragments. If satf is true overflows are set to ±max_norm and nan is replaced by 0.
void **store_matrix_sync**(T* **mptr**, const fragment<...> **&a**, unsigned **ldm**, layout_t **layout**);	The fragment a is written to a 16×16 tile in the array at lptr using a stride of ldm.
operator [] e.g.for(k=0; k<**frag_a.num_elements**; k++) frag_a[k] = p*frag_a[k] + q;	Elements of fragments can be accessed using standard array index notation, but fragments of different types cannot be mixed in expressions. All threads in the warp must perform the same for loop operation.

Note these functions must be called with the same arguments by all threads in a warp which implicitly share the same set of fragments.

fragment objects of sizes given by three integers n, m and k. NVIDIA's convention is that if c and d are m × n matrices, then a is n × k and b is k × n. The warp matrix functions in fact support three geometries {m,n,k} = {16,16,16} or {32,8,16} or {8,32,16}. In other words, k must always be 16 but m and n can either both be 16 or one can be 8 while the other is 32. The include file mma.h defines the warp matrix functions and a fragment class. Functions are provided to fill, multiply and store fragments.

Some functions take an optional last argument layout. If specified this must be one of the keywords row_major or col_major. Layout is specified when declaring fragments for the a and b matrices but not for c and d. However, layout is necessary when c or d are used with the load_matrix_sync or store_matrix_sync functions.

Example 11.1 shows how to perform matrix multiplication using tensor cores. It is similar to our early Example 2.13 in that both use tiled matrix multiplication. The difference is that in 2.13 each thread in a thread block evaluates one element of a tile whereas in Example 11.1 one warp evaluates one tile; thus, here a thread block of 256 threads evaluates eight 16 × 16 tiles instead of one. In Example 2.13 we used one thread block for each tile in the output matrix c whereas in Example 11.1 we use warp-linear addressing to span all the tiles in c. The code assumes that the matrix dimensions are multiples of 16 so that edge effects can be ignored. The tile sizes for the tensor core calculations are set explicitly to 16 × 16 rather than being parametcrised using NVIDIA's m, k and n parameters to help with the clarity of the code.

Example 11.1 matmulT kernel for matrix multiplication with tensor cores

```
05   #include "mma.h"
06   using namespace nvcuda;
     . . .
10   __global__ void matmulT(r_Ptr<float> C, cr_Ptr<half> A,
                             cr_Ptr<half> B, int Ay, int Ax, int Bx)
11   { //  warp rank in grid
12     int warp = (blockDim.x*blockIdx.x+threadIdx.x)/warpSize;
13     int cx = warp%(Bx/16);  // (x,y) location if active tile
14     int cy = warp/(Bx/16);  // for current warp in C matrix

15     int Atile_pos = cy*16*Bx; // start x (row) for first A tile
16     int Btile_pos=  cx*16;    // start y (col) for first B tile

17     // Declare the fragments as 16 x 16 tiles
18     wmma::fragment<wmma::matrix_a,16,16,16,half,
                               wmma::row_major> a_frag;  // A
19     wmma::fragment<wmma::matrix_b,16,16,16,half,
                               wmma::row_major> b_frag;  // B
20     wmma::fragment<wmma::accumulator,16,16,16,
                                       float> c_frag;  // C
21     wmma::fill_fragment(c_frag,0.0f);  // set C = 0
```

```
         // accumulate sum of row*column tiles.
22       for(int k=0;k<Ax/16;k++){
             // load A as 16x16 tile
23           wmma::load_matrix_sync(a_frag,&A[Atile_pos], Ax);
             // load B as 16x16 tile
24           wmma::load_matrix_sync(b_frag,&B[Btile_pos], Bx);
             // C = A*B + C
25           wmma::mma_sync(c_frag,a_frag,b_frag,c_frag);
26           Atile_pos += 16;      // step along row of A
27           Btile_pos += 16*Bx;   // step down column of B
28       }
29       wmma::store_matrix_sync(&C[(cy*Bx+cx)*16], c_frag,
                                 Bx,wmma::mem_row_major);
30   }

D:\ >matmulT.exe 100 1024 1024 1024
GPU time 229.631 TC time 55.756 ms GFlops GPU 935.2 TC 3851.6
speedup 4.12
```

Description of Example 11.1

- Lines 5–6: The warp matrix functions are accessed from the CUDA mma.h include file and are in the nvcuda.wmma namespace. The convention used here and in the SDK examples is hide the nvcuda namespace but leave the remaining wmma qualifier explicit.
- Line 10: The declaration of kernel matmulT, the arguments are pointers to the arrays holding the A, B and C matrices and the matrix dimensions. Ax and Ay are the number of columns and rows of A, thus A is Ay × Ax. Finally, Bx is the number of columns of B, hence B is Ax × Bx and C is Ay × Bx.
- Line 12: Here, for the current thread, we set warp to the rank of its warp in the grid. It is assumed that the launch configuration will have a total number of 32-thread warps equal to the number of 16 × 16 tiles needed to span the output matrix C. The host code calculates the required number of thread blocks based on user supplied thread block size, typically 256.
- Lines 13–14: Calculate the position (cx, cy) of the tile in C corresponding to the current warp. This is a form of warp-linear addressing analogous to the thread-linear addressing used in many of our previous examples.
- Lines 15–16: To perform the multiplication we need the dot product of a row of A tiles with a column of B tiles. Here we calculate the starting row for A (Atile_pos) and column for B (Btile_pos).
- Lines 18–20: Declare warp matrix fragments for tiles in A, B and C. Fragments for A and B hold f16 values and C holds f32 values. Both A and B are specified as row_major, the usual C++ convention. The types of the fragments match those of the input arguments.
- Line 21: The call to fill_fragment sets all 256 values of that fragment to the same value; in this case the values of c_frag are set to zero. This initialises the accumulator.
- Lines 22–28: This loop evaluates the tile C by summing matrix products of tiles along a row of A with tiles down a column of B.

- ○ Line 22: Store next A tile in a_frag, the values are read from the argument A which points to global GPU memory. Note the entire warp participates in this operation and control passes to the next statement only when all threads in the warp are ready.
- ○ Line 23: Like the previous line but stores the next B tile in b_frag.
- ○ Line 23: This is where the tensor cores perform matrix multiplication on the 16 × 16 A and B tiles and accumulate the result in the accumulator C tile.
- ○ Lines 26–27: Here we advance the A and B tile pointers to the next position along a row of A or column of B.
- Line 29: At the end of the process we copy the result in c_frag to the output array C. Note all threads in the warp specify the same address in C.

The result shown in the figure for 1024 × 1024 matrices shows a speed-up of about a factor of 4 compared to the standard GPU version in Example 2.13 and a factor of over 8000 compared to using unoptimised code with three for loops on a single host CPU. The results agree to 4-significant figures for matrices filled with random numbers taken from a uniform distribution between 0 and 1. The performance of Example 11.1 is about 3.8 TFlops/sec. This excellent performance can be improved further by noting that A and B tiles read from GPU memory in lines 23–24 are only used to evaluate a single C tile and are actually reread Ax times by different warps. We can use shared memory to hold a single A tile which can then be used by the 8 warps in a single thread block of size 256 to multiply 8 different B tiles. This version is shown in Example 11.2 where we also buffer the 8 B tiles in shared memory.[3] This code uses thread blocks of size 256 and firstly all the threads in a thread block cooperatively set up one tile from the matrix A in shared memory and then secondly each of the eight warps separately loads a different tile from the B matrix into the shared memory.

Example 11.2 matmulTS kernel for matrix multiplication with tensor cores and shared memory

```
10   __global__ void matmulTS(r_Ptr<float> C, cr_Ptr<half> A,
                          cr_Ptr<half> B, int Ay, int Ax, int Bx)
11   {
12     __shared__ half as[256];
13     __shared__ half bs[8][256];

14     if(blockDim.x != 256) return; // block is 256 threads

15     int warp = (blockDim.x*blockIdx.x+threadIdx.x)/warpSize;

16     int cx = warp%(Bx/16); // (x,y) location if active tile
17     int cy = warp/(Bx/16); // for current warp in C matrix

18     int Atile_pos = cy*16*Bx; // start x (row) for first A tile
19     int Btile_pos=   cx*16;    // start y (col) for first B tile

20     int wb =   threadIdx.x/32; // warp rank in block  in [0,255]
```

```
21      int trw = threadIdx.x%32;  // thread rank in warp
22      int txw = trw%16;          // thread x in warp    in [0,15]
23      int tyw = trw/16;          // thread y in warp    in [0, 1]

24      int idx = threadIdx.x%16;  // assign 256 threads to span
25      int idy = threadIdx.x/16;  // the 16 x 16 x-y values in tile

26      // Declare the fragments
27      wmma::fragment<wmma::matrix_a,16,16,16,half,
                                wmma::row_major> a_frag;   // A
28      wmma::fragment<wmma::matrix_b,16,16,16,half,
                                wmma::row_major> b_frag;   // B
29      wmma::fragment<wmma::accumulator,16,16,16,float>
                                                 c_frag;   // C
30      wmma::fill_fragment(c_frag,0.0f);  // set C = 0

31      for(int k=0;k<Ax/16;k++){
32        as[idy*16+idx] = A[Atile_pos+idy*Ax+idx]; // 256 threads here
33        __syncthreads();
34        for(int p=0;p<8;p++) bs[wb][p*32+tyw*16+txw] =
                  B[p*2*Bx+Btile_pos+tyw*Bx+txw]; // 32 threads fill tile
35        __syncwarp();
36        wmma::load_matrix_sync(a_frag,&as[0],16); // load A as
              16x16 tile
37        wmma::load_matrix_sync(b_frag,&bs[wb][0],16);// load B as
              16x16 tile
38        wmma::mma_sync(c_frag,a_frag,b_frag,c_frag); // C = A*B + C
39        Atile_pos += 16;      // move along A row
40        Btile_pos += 16*Bx;   // move down B cols
41      }
42      wmma::store_matrix_sync(&C[(cy*Bx+cx)*16], c_frag,
                                Bx,wmma::mem_row_major);
43  }

D:\ >matmulTS.exe 100 1024 1024 1024
GPU time 264.390 TS time 38.350 ms GFlops GPU 812.2 TC 5599.7
speedup 6.89
```

Description of Example 11.2

- Line 10: The declaration of matmulTS is the same as for matmulT in the previous example.
- Lines 12–13: Here we declare the shared memory arrays as, which holds one tile from the A matrix, and bs which holds eight tiles from the B matrix – one for each warp in the thread block.
- Line 14: A sanity check on the thread block size.
- Lines 15–19: These are identical to lines 12–16 in Example 11.1.

- Lines 20–25: These lines have been added and are used to organise the loading of the shared memories.
  - Line 20: The variable wb is set to the rank of the current warp in the thread block. For 256 threads wb will be in the range [0,7] and is used as the leftmost index of the shared array bs.
  - Line 21: The variable trw is set to the current thread's rank in its warp.
  - Lines 22–23: The 32 warp-local variables trx and try are set in the ranges 0–15 and 0–1 respectively. These variables are used to address rows of the 16 × 16 B tiles in line 34.
  - Lines 24–25: The 256 block-wide variables idx and idy are both set in the range 0–15 and are used to address a complete A tile in line 32.
  - Lines 27–30: Define the required fragments and initialise c_frag to zero. These lines are identical to lines 18–21 from the previous example.
- Lines 31–41: Loop over the pairs of A and B tiles and sum their matrix products to find the required C tile.
  - Line 32: The entire A tile is copied to the shared memory array as. Each thread in the thread block copies one element.
  - Line 33: The use of __syncthreads is required here before warps are allowed to progress independently for the rest of the iteration.
  - Line 34: Each warp copies a different B tile to bs[wb][0–225] where wb is the rank of the warp in the thread block. Since now there are only 32 cooperating threads an 8-pass loop is required.
  - Line 35: This __syncwarp is necessary before using the contents of bs[wb].
  - Lines 36–40: These lines are almost identical to lines 23–27 of the previous example. We use the warp matrix functions to load A and B tiles to a_frag and b_frag and then accumulate their product to c_frag. The only change is that in lines 36 and 37 we load a_frag and b_frag from shared memory instead of device global memory. Note the strides are also changed to 16 in these lines.
- Line 42: Copy the completed C tile to global memory; this line is the same as line 29 of the previous example.

The performance of our matmulTS kernel at around 6 TFlops is approaching the 8.8 TFlops we found in Chapter 2 using the optimised cuBlas library routines. The matmulTS kernel uses a fixed thread block size of 256, but this can easily be changed to 512 or 1024 which would allow the A tile to be shared by 16 or 32 warps. In fact, the number of warps can be made a template parameter. We have experimented with this and find that on our platform eight warps gives the best performance. Performance could be further improved if we find a way of sharing the B tiles as well as A tiles between warps. The CUDA SDK 11.0 example cudaTensorCoreGemm does just this and archives around 15 TFlops on my platform. However, that code is more complicated than our example.

11.3 Supported Data Types

The warp matrix functions also support other data types and tile shapes and the options (as of SDK version 11.2) are shown in Table 11.2. The theoretical peak performance for both the V100 and A100 GPUs is shown in Table 11.3. The data from this table were taken from the *nvidia-ampere-architecture-whitepaper* pdf document.

Table 11.2 *Tensor cores supported data formats and tile dimensions*

Min CC	A tile	B tile	C accumulator	Layout n-m-k
7.0	half	half	float	$16 \times 16 \times 16$ or
7.0	half	half	float	$32 \times 8 \times 16$ or
7.0	uint8	uint8	int32	$8 \times 32 \times 16$
7.0	int8	int8	int32	
8.0	bf16	bf16	float	
8.0	tf32	tf32	float	$16 \times 16 \times 8$
8.0	double	double	double	$8 \times 8 \times 4$
7.5	uint4	uint4	int32	$8 \times 8 \times 32$
7.5	int4	int4	int32	$8 \times 8 \times 32$
7.5	b1	b1	int32	$8 \times 8 \times 128$

For a description of the specialised float types `bf16` and `tf32` and the sub-byte types `u4`, `s4` and `b1`, see the most recent CUDA C++ Programming Guide.

Table 11.3 *Tensor core performance*

GPU	A & B tiles	C accumulator	TOPS	Speed-up w.r.t GPU
V100	fp16 (half)	fp32	125	8
A100	fp16 (half)	fp32	312	16
A100	fp64	fp64	19.5	1
A100	BF16	fp32	312	16
A100	TF32	fp32	156	8
A100	int8	int32	624	32
A100	int4	int32	1248	64
A100	b1	int32	4992	256

Data taken from nvidia-ampere-architecture-whitepaper.pdf

11.4 Tensor Core Reduction

NVIDIA has designed the features of tensor cores specifically for machine learning and matrix intensive HPC applications and they have indeed become very popular in large data centres. However, most users of these centres are interested in running existing software packages rather than developing new CUDA kernels to do the same thing. This book is aimed at readers who are interested in developing software to perhaps further analyse or visualise data from these centres or to experiment with new ideas on the scale of their own desktop or local group-based facilities. With this is in mind, it is interesting to ask if tensor cores can be used in other ways for scientific computing. The answer is yes for tasks that involve a lot of repeated matrix multiplication; one example turns out to be our old friend reduction. If one of the matrices in the matrix product **AB** has all its elements set to 1 then all the rows or columns of the product will be the sums of the columns or rows of the other matrix as shown in Eq. 11.4.

$$\text{If} \quad \mathbf{C} = \mathbf{A} \cdot \mathbf{B} \quad \text{or} \quad C_{ij} = \sum_k A_{ik} B_{kj} \quad \text{then}$$

$$C_{ij} = \sum_k B_{kj} \quad \text{if} \quad A_{ij} = 1 \quad \text{for all} \quad i \ j \quad \text{and} \qquad (11.4)$$

$$C_{ij} = \sum_k A_{ik} \quad \text{if} \quad B_{ij} = 1 \quad \text{for all} \quad i \ j.$$

Thus, to partially sum a large set of numbers, we can modify the matrix multiplication in Example 11.1 by setting all elements of fragment A to 1 and stream sets of 256 numbers to fragment B for each warp and accumulate the column sums in C. At the end of the process, we simply need to sum the 16 values along a row of the accumulator C to get that warp's contribution to the sum. Note we can choose any row as all the 16 rows of C will contain the same column sums. Of course, we have done 16 times more work than is strictly necessary for reduction so this would be a crazy method without very fast matrix multiplication. The resulting code is show in Example 11.3.

Example 11.3 reduceT kernel for reduction using tensor cores

```
10   __global__ void reduceT(r_Ptr<float> sums,
                             cr_Ptr<half> data, int n)
11   {
12     extern __shared__ float fs[][256]; // one tile per warp

13     auto grid  = cg::this_grid();
14     auto block = cg::this_thread_block();
15     auto warp  = cg::tiled_partition<32>(block);

16     int tid    = grid.thread_rank(); // thread rank in grid
17     int wid    = warp.thread_rank(); // thread rank in warp
18     int wb     = warp.meta_group_rank(); // warp rank in block
19     int wpoint = (tid/32)*256;        // warp offset in data
20     int wstep  = grid.size()*8;       // total warps*256

21     // Declare the fragments
22     wmma::fragment<wmma::matrix_a,16,16,16,half,
                        wmma::row_major> a_frag; // A
23     wmma::fragment<wmma::matrix_b,16,16,16,half,
                        wmma::row_major> b_frag; // B
24     wmma::fragment<wmma::accumulator,16,16,16,
                        float> c_frag; // C
25     wmma::fill_fragment(c_frag,0.0f); // C = 0
26     wmma::fill_fragment(a_frag,(half)1.0); // A = 1

27     // stream data through tensor cores, each warp handles
       // batches of 256 values
28     while(wpoint < n){ // warp linear addressing used here
```

```
      // load B from data
29    wmma::load_matrix_sync(b_frag,&data[wpoint],16);
      // C = A*B + C
30    wmma::mma_sync(c_frag,a_frag,b_frag,c_frag);
31    wpoint += wstep;
32  }
33  wmma::store_matrix_sync(fs[wb],c_frag,16,
                        wmma::mem_row_major); // copy c to fs
34  //reduce first row which holds column sums
35  float v = fs[wb][wid];
36  v += warp.shfl_down(v,8);
37  v += warp.shfl_down(v,4);
38  v += warp.shfl_down(v,2);
39  v += warp.shfl_down(v,1);
40  if(wid==0) atomicAdd(&sums[block.group_index().x],v);
41 }

D:\ >reduceT.exe 1000 28 256 256
reduceT  times Host 533.517 reduceT 1269.198 reduce7_vl 2525.858 ms
```

Description of Example 11.3

- Line 10: The declaration of reduceT uses the same arguments as the previous reduce kernels discussed in Chapters 2 and 3. The kernel argument sums is used for the results and is of size equal to the number of thread blocks; it will hold the partial sums from those thread blocks on exit. The array data holds the values to be summed and contains n elements specified by the third argument. A significant difference is that here data is declared as half whereas previous reduction kernels use float.

- Line 12: A 2D shared memory array fs is declared to hold one 256-word tile of floats for each warp. Dynamic shared memory is used here so that the thread block size can be varied for tuning purposes.

- Lines 13–15: We use cooperative groups in this kernel as the warp_shfl function is used in lines 36–39.

- Lines 16–18: Here we find warp and thread ranks to use in the subsequent calculation.

- Lines 19–20: The variables wpoint and wstep are initialised here and are used to implement warp-linear addressing of the array data in chunks of 256 words in lines 28–32.

- Lines 22–25: Here the a, b and c fragments to be used in the calculation are declared as in Examples 11.1 and 11.2.

- Line 26: This line differs from before as now we now fill a_frag with the value 1 instead of matrix data.

- Lines 28–32: This loop implements warp linear addressing to step through the input array data with each warp processing a chunk of 256 words on each step through the loop. There is a tacit assumption that the array size n is a multiple of 256.

  ○ Line 29: Loads the next chunk of data into b_frag; note we use a stride of 16 here to load 256 consecutive values from the array data.

  ○ Line 30: Performs matrix multiplication and accumulates the resulting column sums to c_frag.

- ○ Line 31: Increments the data pointer `wpoint` by the amount of data used by all warps in this pass.
- Line 33: The final accumulated values of the column sums are copied to the shared memory 2D array `fs` here. The first index `wb` is the rank of the current warp in the thread block.
- Lines 35–39: Here we perform warp-level reduction on the copy of the first 16 elements (i.e. the first row) of each warp's `c_frag` array. The method is the same as used in Chapter 3. We note that on GPUs with CC $\geq$ 8 we could effectively use the new warp-level reduce function to replace these lines.
- Line 40: Here the warps add their contributions to elements of the output array sums.

The timing results shown at the end of the example are for the reduction of 2^{28} values. One calculation was used for the host CPU calculation and 1000 repeated calculations were used for `reduceT` and the comparison `reduce7_vl` kernels.

Another interesting detail in Example 11.3 is that in line 29 we are reading a 512-byte chunk of data from GPU main memory. In this case neither using shared memory nor using the vector-loading technique improves performance. This is because the `load_matrix_sync` call is performed cooperatively by all threads in the warp and is designed to load this size chunk of data very efficiently. Note that because the loaded data is only used by one warp, shared memory is not helpful.

The new `reduceT` kernel runs twice as fast as our previous best `reduce7_vl` kernel. This improvement is in fact due to using type `half` instead of `float` for the input array `data` which halves the number of bytes that we have to read from GPU main memory. This is not a trivial observation, NVIDIA's hardware support for the new type is because it is used by tensor cores and AI applications where the limited precision is usually adequate. This suggests we could just use the method from Chapter 3 with the new half data type and get a similar speed-up. Example 11.4 shows the resulting `reduce7_vl_half` kernel.

Example 11.4 `reduce_half_vl` kernel for reduction using the FP16 data type

```
10    __global__ void reduce_half_vl(r_Ptr<float> sums,
                                      cr_Ptr<half> data, int n)
11    {
12        // This kernel assumes the array sums is pre-set to zero
13        // and blockSize is multiple of 32

14        auto grid  =  cg::this_grid();
15        auto block = cg::this_thread_block();
16        auto warp  = cg::tiled_partition<32>(block);

17        float v = 0.0f;
18        half v8[8] = {(half)0.0f,(half)0.0f,(half)0.0f,
                                           (half)0.0f};
19        for(int tid = grid.thread_rank(); tid < n/8;
          tid += grid.size()) {
20            reinterpret_cast<int4 *>(v8)[0] =
                      reinterpret_cast<const int4 *>(data)[tid];
```

```
21        for(int k=0;k<8;k+=2)v += (float)__hadd(v8[k],v8[k+1]);
22    }
23    warp.sync();

24    v += warp.shfl_down(v,16); // warp level
25    v += warp.shfl_down(v,8);  // reduce only
26    v += warp.shfl_down(v,4);  // here
27    v += warp.shfl_down(v,2);
28    v += warp.shfl_down(v,1);  //atomic add sums over blocks
29    if(warp.thread_rank()==0)
              atomicAdd(&sums[block.group_index().x],v);
30 }
```

```
D:\ >reduce_half.exe 1000 28 256 256
reduceTH  times Host 533.517 reduceT 1269.198 reduce7_half_v1
1264.910 ms
```

Description of Example 11.4

This example illustrates how the type half can be used in kernel code. Since this is not a native C++ type it turns out that an explicit cast to or from the type is nearly always needed to prevent the compiler complaining. Also, it is best to use NVIDIA intrinsic functions to perform arithmetic with this type because they are very fast, often compiling to a single machine code instruction.

- Lines 10–16: The only change from Example 3.7 is that the input data array data is declared as half not float.
- Line 17: Here we declare float v which will be used by a thread to accumulate its contribution to the overall sum. In Example 3.7, this was the float4 variable v4 which has a size of 128 bytes suitable for optimal vector loading and support for vector arithmetic operations.
- Line 18: Declare v8 as an 8-element vector of type half for each thread. This will play the same role as v4 in Example 3.7 but does not have overloaded operators to support arithmetic operations.
- Lines 19–22: This for loop accumulates contributions for each thread using vector loading to load eight elements of sums in one step.
  - Line 20: We use reinpterpret_casts to the int4 data type to copy 128 bytes from sums to v8 in a single operation.
  - Line 21: Here we add the eight values in v8 to v. We use a hybrid approach to precision by using the intrinsic __hadd to add pairs of values from v8 to get their sum as another half value and then adding this to the float accumulator v. There are many variations one could try here but adding too many half values to another half accumulator is likely to rapidly lead to a loss of precision. The cast (float) could be replaced by the intrinsic function __half2float() but hopefully the compiler is performing this sort of optimisation for us.
- Lines 23–30: This last section of code is identical to lines 20–27 of Example 3.7.

Our conclusion from the reduction examples is that switching from 4-byte to 2-byte variables gives a factor of 2 speed-up as we would expect for this memory access dominated problem. This reinforces a key message of this book that memory access is often the limiting performance factor on both GPU- and CPU-based computations and using *float rather than double where possible* is really important. We can now add the recommendation *use half rather than float when possible* – but obviously the limited precision makes this impossible in many cases. From the timings above it is not clear if using tensor cores to perform addition is faster than simply using thread-based additions. This is because the GPU is good at hiding computational cost in memory bound calculations. We have, however, shown the method works and is not slow.

Another interesting feature added to the third generation tensor cores of Ampere (CC 8) GPUs is a *sparsity feature* involving the automatic dropping of small values from the A fragments to gain another factor of two in performance. Specifically, this feature is implemented in hardware by dropping the smallest two elements out of each set of four elements along the rows of the A matrix. This feature is intended for training neural networks where the A matrix holds weights applied to the node inputs. In large problems there are initially many such weights, most of which become unimportant during training. If the sparsity feature is used appropriately during training, the process will be faster with no loss of correctness. I have to say this is interestingly close to natural neural evolution where synaptic connections get stronger with use or atrophy when not used. In the spirit of Example 11.3, we speculate that this sparsity feature might also be used for sorting or at least finding the maximum values in large datasets.

11.5 Conclusion

This is the end of the last main chapter in our book and we seem to have ended where we began – with yet another variation of the reduction problem. This is not because we are obsessed with adding up lots of numbers really fast, but because reduction is an exemplar for any memory bound GPU problem. Such memory bound problems are often hard to port effectively to GPUs. In other chapters we have explored a variety of interesting real-world problems and presented fully working GPU code which often gives impressive speed-ups for what I consider to be relatively little effort.

Importantly, all our code is available online for readers to use as starting points for their own problems. In developing these examples, we learnt a lot and had some surprises. We were surprised by the erratic performance of built-in C++ random number generators using both Visual Studio and g++. We were astonished by how badly denormalised floating point numbers slow down Intel CPUs. On the other hand, in Chapter 8 we were gratified by the unexpected performance gains achieved in our PET reconstruction code by using $50,000 \times 256$ threads instead of the more normal 256×256 or 1024×256.

We plan to extend some of the examples presented here and to update the code repository from time to time and to add material for new versions of CUDA – so please check for this.

Finally, this book is not really finished yet; there is more interesting material in the appendices.

Endnotes Chapter 11

1 Remember that floating-point fraction starts with an implicit 1 so the 10-bit fraction can represent 11 bit values.

2 On the host, these arithmetic operations are not supported by the hardware and have to be emulated by software, they are hence quite slow. On the GPU they are supported by hardware. In both cases a large set of intrinsic functions are available and should be used whenever possible.

3 Buffering the B tiles, though apparently unnecessary, does give further small speed-up. However, more importantly, we found that loading A tiles from shared memory but B tiles directly from GPU main memory did not work on our platform (Windows 10 home edition, CUDA SDK 11.0 and RTX 2070 GPU). The program ran but gave incorrect results which varied from run-to-run indicative of a race condition which we were unable to resolve.

Appendix A

A Brief History of CUDA

CUDA was launched by NVIDIA in 2007 as a high-level programming tool for enabling scientific computation on their GPUs developed for gaming on PCs. Prior to this there had been at least a decade of efforts by individuals to use the then-available and rather primitive GPUs for this purpose. The acronym GPGPU (general-purpose computation on graphics processing units) was coined to describe these efforts, and an influential website (www .gpgpu.org) was set up to document and share ideas.[1] Although there were some successes, progress was limited by lack of floating-point support and small graphics memories. The actual programming of these early GPUs was also difficult; the general idea was to trick the hardware shader and texture units into calculating scientifically useful results. The resulting code tended to be specific to one GPU and hence difficult to port between different GPUs; this was frustrating, as types of GPUs were evolving very rapidly in that era.

NVIDIA CUDA actually replaced the earlier NVIDIA Cg computing language, which, while not general purpose, was being used for GPGPU applications and offered some degree of portability. Cg had a C-like syntax but was not actually C and was really intended as a tool for game developers. Cg continued to be supported by NVIDIA until 2012, and at present (2022) it is still available as a deprecated legacy product on their website.[2]

CUDA changed everything; it enabled GPGPU programming in C by adding a few (and, in my opinion, very elegant) extensions. Moreover, it was a strong statement by NVIDIA that they wanted to support GPGPU applications on their GPUs. Since that launch, GPU computing has changed from a niche to a mainstream activity, and NVIDIA has become a dominant force in high-end supercomputing. This is the reason why we have chosen to write a GPU programming book about CUDA rather than possible alternatives such as OpenCL or OpenMP. We think CUDA code is simpler and more elegant and thus facilitates the creation and maintenance of better code. Also, because CUDA is vendor-specific, it gives better access to NVIDIA hardware features such as texture lookup with interpolation and recent innovations such as the tensor cores.

A.1 Evolution of NVIDIA GPUs

The initial CUDA release supported the GeForce GTX 8800 card with 128 cores and 768 MB of graphics memory. For its time, this was a fast card, and CUDA was eagerly adopted for GPGPU applications. The hardware capabilities of this card define the so-called compute capability 1.0 feature set; compute capability (CC) level is used by NVIDIA to differentiate between different GPU generations, with the more recent generations having higher values. The recent Turing generation of GPUs has CC 7.5; CC is backwards compatible, so, for example, a Maxwell GPU with CC 3.5 has all the features of GPUs up to that level but not some of the features of later GPUs with higher values of CC. The details of which features go with which CC levels are specified in an appendix of the "NVIDIA CUDA C Programming Guide", which is included in the documentation set for each release of CUDA.[3]

The software supporting CUDA is provided by the NVIDIA SDK, and this also evolves in time and has a similar but different numbering scheme. Thus, while the initial SDK release was CUDA 1.0, the numbering scheme then evolved differently to the GPU CC level. For example, as of December 2020, the most recent Ampere GPUs have CC level 8.6 but the most recent CUDA SDK is version 11.5 (or CUDA 11.5 for short). The associated hardware drivers also need to be updated from time to time to match changes in CUDA hardware and software.

Although the arrival of CUDA was a huge step for GPGPU programming, some restrictions in the early hardware and software and their associated workarounds have lingered on and even now are overemphasised in many tutorials. Firstly, accessing early GPU memory was slow, and strict coalesced memory accesses (i.e. neighbouring threads access neighbouring 4-byte words) were essential for decent performance. This meant that early CUDA examples, including those supplied in the initial CUDA SDK, emphasised the use of fully coalesced memory access or use of shared memory when this was not possible. Additionally, the use of the dedicated texture and constant memory spaces was recommended to reduce latency where appropriate. The end result produced some really complicated examples, which juggled these various tricks to maximise performance. While this was important in the early days, it has become increasingly less important as successive generations of GPUs brought in better and bigger caching of GPU memory. Unfortunately, much of the current learning materials, including both CUDA SDK examples and some textbooks, have not kept pace with these changes and can make CUDA development appear to be more complicated than necessary. In developing the examples for this book, we have found that in many cases straightforward code that does not use shared memory or other complicated tricks performs just as well as, or better than, tricky code based on early SDK examples.[4]

The second legacy problem is that the SDK examples in the first CUDA release were written in essentially ANSI C. Hence the code was littered with bare pointers managed with explicit `malloc` and `free` statements, and was quite verbose. Sadly, although the NVCC compiler now supports C++ up to C++17, many examples have not caught up.[5] In this book we have used modern C++ to simplify our code while keeping the style straightforward and readable and avoiding excessive use of abstraction.

So far NVIDIA have released eight generations of GPUs named after famous physicists or mathematicians. Within each generation different cards exist for gaming, HPC and workstation applications. With each generation, the hardware and software capabilities of the GPUs have increased. Tables A.1 and A.2 show a summary of naming details and the evolution of hardware performance. Table A.2 is a nice illustration of the dramatic consequences coming from a decade of Moore's law evolution – all the capabilities of the GPUs have increased. The total number of cores on a GPU has increased steadily by a factor of 20 from 512 on the Fermi GTX580 to 10,496 on the Ampere RTX3090 – the individual cores have also become more powerful. Interestingly the number of cores per streaming multi-processor (SM), while

Table A.1 *NVIDIA GPU generations, 2007–2021*

Generation	Compute Capability	GeForce (gaming)	Tesla (HPC)	Quadro (workstation)	Chipset Codes
Ampere (2020)	8.0–8.6	RTX 3090	A100	A6000	GA100, GA102, GA104, GA106
Turing (2018)	7.5	RTX 2080	T4	RTX 8000	TU102, TU104, TU106
Volta (2017)	7.0–7.2	TITAN V	V100	GV100	GV100
Pascal (2016)	6.0–6.2	GTX 1080	P100, P40	P6000 P100	GP100, GP104, GP106
Maxwell (2014)	5.0–5.3	GTX 980	M60, M40	M6000	GM200, GM204, GM206
Kepler (2012)	3.0–3.7	GTX 680 GTX 780	K40, K80	K4000	GK104, GK110, GK210
Fermi (2010)	2.0–2.1	GTX 480GTX 580	C2070	Quadro 4000	GF100, GF102, GF107, GF110
Tesla (2007)	1.0–1.3	GTS 8800	C1060	FX 5800	G80, G92, GT200

remaining a multiple of the warp size 32, has had a different trajectory. The number of warps per SM peaked at six (192 cores) in the early Kepler generation and then fell back to two (64 cores) by the Pascal generation. This is because many kernels have their performance limited by the number of SMs rather than the number of cores. For this reason, Kepler often failed to deliver a significant real-world performance enhancement over Fermi in spite of the greatly increased number of cores.[6]

The fall in power consumption per TFlop over 10 years is a dramatic and welcome reduction. This is especially true for high-end supercomputers that use literally thousands of GPUs. For example, the second ranked machine in the November 2001 TOP500 list is the Oak Ridge Summit system. It has 27,648 V100 GPUs and delivers about 150,000 TFlops on a high-performance Linpack benchmark.

Of course, not just the number of cores but also their computational capabilities have improved over time. Much of this is due to detailed changes such as improved atomic operations, faster memory and better caching strategies.

The Volta generation introduced a step change in design of the compute cores. As in previous generations, each core can perform both FP32 and INT32 arithmetic operations, but in Volta a core can perform both types of operation simultaneously, whereas in previous generations a core could only perform one of these operations in a cycle. Another important change is to move away from the strict SIMT principle where all 32 threads in a warp execute the same instruction in lockstep. Starting from Volta, individual threads now have individual PCs instead of having a single program counter (PC) used by all threads in the warp.[7] This breaks older kernel code, which assumes there is an implicit synchronisation between the 32 threads of a warp and hence omits the calls to __syncthreads() that would otherwise be logically necessary. From Volta onwards an explicit synchronisation is necessary, as now the threads may not be executing in lockstep. However, the lightweight

Table A.2 *NVIDIA GPUs from Kepler to Ampere*

Generation Chip GPU		Kepler GK110B K40	Maxwell GM200 M40	Pascal GP100 P100	Volta GV100 V100	Ampere GA100 A100	Ampere GA102 A40	Ampere GA102 RTX3090	Turing TU102 RTX 2080Ti	Turing TU106 RTX 2070
Compute capability		3.5	5.2	6.0	7.0	8.0	8.6	8.6	7.5	7.5
Date		10/2013	11/2015	06/2016	06/2017	05/2020	10/2020	09/2020	09/2018	10/2018
Total cores		2880	3072	3584	5120	6912	8704	10496	4352	2304
SMs		15	24	56	80	108	84	82	68	36
Cores per SM		192	128	64	64	64	128	64	64	64
Floating point	FP16	–	–	21.2	31.4	78	37.4	35.6	28.5	15.8
peak	**FP32**	**5.2**	**6.1**	**10.6**	**15.7**	**19.5**	**37.4**	**35.6**	**14.2**	**7.9**
performance	FP64	2.6	3.1	5.3	7.8	9.7	0.584	0.508	0.420	0.247
(TFlop)	TC 16/32	–	–	–	125	156	149.7	71	113.8	31.5
Maximum memory size (GB)		12	12	16	32	40	48	24	11	8
Memory bandwidth (GB/s)		**288**	**288**	**703**	**877**	**1215**	**696**	**936**	**616**	**448**
Registers per SM (K)		64	64	64	64	64	256	256	64	256
L1+Shared per SM (KB)		64	24+96	24+64	128	164	128	128	96	96
L2 cache (KB)		1536	3072	4096	6114	40,000	6144	6144	5632	4096
Fabrication (nm)		28	28	16	12	7	8	8	12	8
Transistors ($\times 10^9$)		7.1	8	15.3	21	52.2	28.3	28.3	18.6	10.8
Max power (Watts)		235	250	300	300	400	300	350	260	185
Watts per FP32 TFlop		45	41	29	20	20.5	8.0	9.8	18.3	12
Relative performance		**0.4**	**0.5**	**2.1**	**3.9**	**6.7**	**7.4**	**9.4**	**2.5**	**1.0**

__syncwarp() function, which is local to each warp, can be used for this purpose instead of the expensive __syncthreads() function, which has thread block wide effect. More details about this are in Chapter 3 on cooperative groups.

From Table A.1 we see that the more recent GPUs have higher compute capabilities. In most generations the same generic architecture is available as a low-end GeForce gaming card, a Tesla HPC card without graphics capability but much enhanced double-precision performance or a Quadro workstation card with both graphics and good double-precision performance. The named cards are examples of high-end cards in their class; other versions with fewer or sometimes more cores are available. For example, the RTX 2080 has 2944 cores, whereas the RTX 2070 has 2304 cores and the RTX 2080 Ti has 4352 cores. The codenames in the last column refer to the underlying chipset architecture. Compute capabilities are backwards compatible, but recent drivers no longer support CC levels 1 or 2.

The GPU used for performance measurements in this book is the RTX 2070, which is a relatively inexpensive gaming card. The last row of Table A.2 shows the relative performance of other GPUs using the product of FP32 GFlops/sec and memory bandwidth in GB/sec as a metric. The RTX 3090, launched in January 2021 at an initial price of about £1400, performs a factor of 10 better on this metric.

An interesting recent advance, starting with Pascal, is the introduction of hardware support for FP16 calculations at twice the speed of FP32. Although a single FP16 variable can be used in code, the speed advantage is only gained by using intrinsic functions operating on pairs of FP16 variables stored in 32-bit words. The reason for this is that the hardware implements FP16 operations using the existing FP32 registers modified to operate on such pairs in parallel. This is actually an example of thread-wise SIMD operations supported by CUDA. The Volta and later architectures massively extend the usefulness of FP16 calculations by introducing *tensor cores* (TCs) to support mixed FP32 and FP16 arithmetic for 4×4 matrix multiplication, which can deliver a peak of over 100 TFlops of computation, as shown in the TC 16/32 line of Table A.2. Although the introduction of TCs and FP16 support is intended for machine learning applications, it is likely that other application areas will be found.

The important area of inter-GPU communication has also seen recent advances. It is now common for a single workstation to have more than one GPU installed, and in the past they would have been managed by the host passing data back and forth to the GPUs across the PCIe bus. Recent Tesla and Quadro cards have NVLINK, a much faster direct GPU-to-GPU interconnect.

A.2 The CUDA Toolkit

CUDA developers need to install the free NVIDIA Toolkit or SDK appropriate to their system from NVIDIA's website.[8] The Toolkit actually has four components: a device driver, the CUDA Toolkit itself, a set of about 150 examples (referred to as "samples" in the documentation) and complete documentation in both PDF and HTML formats.

The CUDA toolkit contains all the software needed to compile CUDA code; this includes header files, libraries and the NVCC compiler. Table A.3 summarises the history of CUDA Toolkit releases from 2007 to 2020. A new Toolkit is released whenever new hardware with a new CC level appears. The Toolkit version numbers are not the same as the maximum

Table A.3 *Evolution of the CUDA toolkit*

Version	Date	CC support	Added features
11.0	May 2020	3.0 – 8.0	**Ampere** support
10.0	Sept 2018	3.0 – 7.5	**Turing** support. 10.1 (Feb 2019) and 10.2 (Nov 2019)
9.2	May 2018	3.0 – 7.0	Maintenance release.
9.1	Dec 2017	3.0 – 7.0	Passing __restrict__ references to __global__ functions supported
9.0	Sept 2017	3.0 – 7.0	**Volta** support. Tensor cores, simultaneous FP32 & INT32 per core. Warp shuffle supports 8-byte fields. Cooperative groups introduced. __syncwarp() or __syncthreads() now mandatory for warp level programming. New synchronising versions of warp vote functions introduced, __activemask() added. Ended support for Fermi and below.
8.0b	Feb 2017	2.0 – 6.2	**Pascal** support. AtomicAdd for FP64 in global and shared memory.
7.5	Sept 2015	2.0 – 5.3	C++11 support. 8.0a (Sep 2016). Maintenance release
7.0	Mar 2015	2.0 – 5.2	Ended support for Tesla (CC < 2.0). CUSOLVER library introduced.
6.5	Aug 2014	1.1 – 5.0	Maintenance release.
6.0	Apr 2014	1.0 – 5.0	**Maxwell** support.
5.5	Jul 2013	1.0 – 3.5	Maintenance release.
5.0	Oct 2012	1.0 – 3.5	Dynamic Parallelism. FP16 operations on device. Funnel shift.
4.2	Apr 2012	1.0 – 3.0	**Kepler** support. Unified memory programming. Warp shuffle functions __shfl() etc. introduced for CC ≥ 3.0.
4.1	Jan 2012	1.0 – 2.1	CUBLAS library introduced.
4.0	May 2011	1.0 – 2.1	cuRAND, cuFFT, cuSPARSE, NPP and THRUST libraries introduced.
3.2	Nov 2010	1.0 – 2.1	Maintenance release.
3.1	Jun 2010	1.0 – 2.0	Maintenance release.
3.0	Mar 2010	1.0 – 2.0	**Fermi** support. Atomic functions for FP32 in global and shared memory and INT64 in shared memory. Limited FP16 support in textures. 3D thread block grids. Surfaces introduced.
2.3	Jun 2009	1.0 – 1.3	Some C++ support, including function templates and operator overloading.
2.2	May 2009	1.0 – 1.3	Pinned Memory support.
2.1	Jan 2009	1.0 – 1.3	cudaMalloc3D() and cudaMalloc3DArray() added.
2.0	Aug 2008	1.0 – 1.3	Atomic functions for INT64 in global memory and for INT32 in shared memory. Support for FP64 in device code. Warp vote functions __all(), __any() and __ballot() introduced.
1.1	Dec 2007	1.0 – 1.1	Atomic functions for INT32 in global memory.
1.0	June 2007	1.0	**Tesla** support. Initial release.

GPU CC level supported. Support for the early Tesla and Fermi generations ended with Toolkit versions 7.0 (2015) and 9.0 (2017), respectively.

Of particular note is Toolkit 9.0, which introduced support for Volta (CC 7.0) requiring significant changes in the management of warp-level programming that may break older codes. Toolkit 7.5 is also interesting in that it introduced good support for C++11

```
C:\Program Files\NVIDIA GPU Computing Toolkit\CUDA\v10.2>dir
 Volume in drive C has no label.
 Volume Serial Number is C294-8079

 Directory of C:\Program Files\NVIDIA GPU Computing Toolkit\CUDA\v10.2

31/08/2019  14:19    <DIR>          .
31/08/2019  14:19    <DIR>          ..
31/08/2019  14:19    <DIR>          bin
29/07/2019  06:27            56,048 CUDA_Toolkit_Release_Notes.txt
31/08/2019  14:19    <DIR>          doc
29/07/2019  06:27            60,244 EULA.txt
31/08/2019  14:19    <DIR>          extras
31/08/2019  14:19    <DIR>          include
31/08/2019  14:19    <DIR>          lib
31/08/2019  14:18    <DIR>          libnvvp
31/08/2019  14:19    <DIR>          nvml
31/08/2019  14:19    <DIR>          nvvm
31/08/2019  14:19    <DIR>          src
31/08/2019  14:19    <DIR>          tools
29/07/2019  06:28                23 version.txt
               3 File(s)        116,315 bytes
              12 Dir(s)  202,170,028,032 bytes free
```

Figure A.1 ToolKit version 10.2 install directory on Windows 10

features – sadly, many CUDA tutorial examples in NVIDIA's own example set and elsewhere do not yet take advantage of C++11 to simplify code. One feature of our examples is the use of such features where they simplify our code.

On a Windows machine, the Toolkit is typically installed under `C:\Program Files\`. On my system, this is `C:\Program Files\NVIDIA GPU Computing Toolkit \CUDA\v10.1`, as indicated in Figure A.1.

The top-level install directory contains release notes and licence information in .txt files and directories for all the essential components; some of these directories will be added to the system search path at installation time. The more important directories are:

- bin: Executable files, including the CUDA NVCC compiler nvcc.exe and profiler nvprof. exe. A large number of .dll files are also held in this directory.
- doc: Comprehensive documentation in both HTML and PDF formats. The "CUDA C++ Programming Guide" is a good place to start, but there are detailed guides for those who want to go deeper. There are also guides for the various libraries, such as cuRAND and THRUST. The "CUDA_Samples" guide tells you all about the samples included in the SDK.
- include: A large number of .h files are necessary to compile CUDA code. Most user code in .cu file only needs to explicitly include `cuda_runtime.h`. This file will load other .h files as necessary. If your code mixes .cu and .cpp files, then the .cpp files (which are not compiled by NVCC) may need to include `vector_types.h` to access the definitions of CUDA types such as float3.
- lib: A large number of .lib files support various CUDA options. For example, you will need `curand.lib` if you make use of cuRAND in your code.
- src: A small number of files for Fortran support.
- tools: A single file, "CUDA_Occupancy_Calculator.xls", which, as the name implies, can be used for occupancy calculations.

On Windows, the toolkit installation process will add a plugin to Visual Studio C++, enabling you to create CUDA projects directly without needing to use the process described in the "CUDA_Samples" guide. For this to work, Visual Studio must be installed prior to the installation of the CUDA SDK.

A.3 The CUDA Samples

On a Windows system the examples are typically installed under `C:ProgramData`. On my system this is `C:\ProgramData\NVIDIA Corporation\CUDA Samples\v10.1`; details are shown in Figure A.2. Curiously, by default this is a hidden directory on Windows – I recommend you unhide it as soon as you can.[9]

The Samples directories contain Visual Studio the project and solution files used to build the examples from source. On Windows the installer also adds a plugin to Visual Studio which helps create new CUDA projects.

There are over 150 example programs in the sample directories, and these are a natural starting point for people wishing to develop their own code. Indeed, this is what we have done with some of the examples in this book. However, while the examples do illustrate the full range of CUDA features, they are often very verbose and written in a basic C style which can make the whole process seem to be much more complicated than it really is. In this book, we have recast the ideas in the SDK code using modern C++ style which is more compact, simpler to understand and we think elegant.

If you are using Linux, the Toolkit can be installed using the standard Linux tools and detailed instructions are on the NVIDIA website. Makefiles for building the SDK samples are included in the SDK.

```
C:\Program Files\NVIDIA GPU Computing Toolkit\CUDA\v10.2>dir
 Volume in drive C has no label.
 Volume Serial Number is C294-8079

 Directory of C:\Program Files\NVIDIA GPU Computing Toolkit\CUDA\v10.2

31/08/2019  14:19    <DIR>          .
31/08/2019  14:19    <DIR>          ..
31/08/2019  14:19    <DIR>          bin
29/07/2019  06:27            56,048 CUDA_Toolkit_Release_Notes.txt
31/08/2019  14:19    <DIR>          doc
29/07/2019  06:27            60,244 EULA.txt
31/08/2019  14:19    <DIR>          extras
31/08/2019  14:19    <DIR>          include
31/08/2019  14:19    <DIR>          lib
31/08/2019  14:18    <DIR>          libnvvp
31/08/2019  14:19    <DIR>          nvml
31/08/2019  14:19    <DIR>          nvvm
31/08/2019  14:19    <DIR>          src
31/08/2019  14:19    <DIR>          tools
29/07/2019  06:28                23 version.txt
               3 File(s)        116,315 bytes
              12 Dir(s)  202,170,028,032 bytes free
```

Figure A.2 CUDA samples directory on Windows 10

Appendix A Endnotes

[1] Sadly, this historic website has now gone but "gpgpu" is still a very useful keyword for web searches.

2 Somewhat confusingly for people with long memories, recent versions of CUDA contain a cg namespace which is used for cooperative groups. The eagle eyed will notice "c" is not capitalised in this case.

3 Since the 2019 CUDA 10.1 release, the documentation covers compute capabilities between 3.0 and 7.5; support for CC levels 1 and 2 has now ended.

4 This is, of course, an oversimplification; there are still some cases where shared memory is very helpful. However, constant memory is now automatically used by the compiler for kernel arguments which are declared const, so explicit use of constant memory is less necessary.

5 For instance, the CUDA SDK addon for Visual Studio helpfully provides a code sample, kernel.cu, when creating a new CUDA project. Unfortunately, even in 2022 this sample is written in essentially early C and even uses the dreaded goto statement for error handling.

6 To be fair to NVIDIA, the extra cores on Kepler cards did function well for gaming purposes and at that stage gaming was NVIDIA's main focus. A decade later Turing cards are superb for both gaming and HPC and have new hardware features for both, Tensor cores for AI and ray tracing (RT) units for graphics.

7 The Volta and Turing hardware typically requires two register slots per thread for the thread's PC. This might impact code with demanding per-thread register requirements.

8 The web link is https://developer.nvidia.com/cuda-toolkit. Versions are available for Windows, and Linux. Support for MacOs ended with version 10.2.

9 Explorer, (renamed File Explorer in Windows 10) is a venerable and much-loved tool replicated in MacOS and Linux GUIs. However, Microsoft has some curious default choices, one of which is making ProgramData a hidden directory. An even worse default is "hiding extensions for known file types" which makes it much more likely that the naïve user will click on an evil .exe file planted by a virus. On Windows 10 these options can and should be changed using "change folder and search options" under File Explorer->view->options.

Appendix B

Atomic Operations

The essence of parallel programming is that many threads run simultaneously and cooperatively to solve a problem – so what happens if two or more threads try to write to the same memory location simultaneously? This is a generic problem for any parallel system using *shared memory*, that is, where multiple active threads can access the same block of memory at the same time. Reading from shared memory alone is not a problem and indeed NVIDIA GPUs feature a dedicated block of constant memory for just this purpose. But writing to shared memory raises two difficult issues:

1. What happens if two or more threads write to the same memory location simultaneously? On NVIDIA hardware one thread will succeed and the others will silently fail. This produces incorrect results in most cases.
2. The so-called read-after-write problem. If some threads are writing to memory while others are reading from it, how can we be sure the necessary write operations have completed before other threads perform reads. This problem is greatly complicated by the hierarchy of caching levels used in modern computing systems – how can we ensure main memory and all caches are kept in synchronisation? This is the cache–coherency problem.

Problem 1 is solved by implementing atomic operations in hardware or software. If two or more threads use an atomic function to write to the same memory location simultaneously, the requests are queued in hardware and executed one at a time. They all succeed but there is no guarantee about the order in which they are executed. Such queued operations are known as *atomic operations* and CUDA provides a range of atomic functions that run on the GPU. This appendix describes these functions.

We should point out that problem 2 is much harder to solve and basically it is up to the programmer to synchronise threads so as to avoid read-after-write errors – the various CUDA sync functions are the key to doing this.

B.1 AtomicAdd

The CUDA atomicAdd function is typical and the version for 32-bit integers is shown in the box.

Table B.1 *Atomic functions*

Atomic Functions **type** atomic**Fun**(**type *acc, type val**)		
Fun	Supported Types	Effect
Add	int, uint, ullong, float, double, half, half2, nv_bfloat16, nv_bfloat162	acc = acc + val
Sub	int, uint	acc = acc - val
Exch	int, uint, ullong, float	acc = val
Min	int, uint, llong, ullong	acc = min(acc, val)
Max	int, uint, llong, ullong	acc = max(acc, val)
Inc	int	acc = (acc >= val) ? 0 : acc+1;
Dec	int	acc = (acc==0 || acc>val) ? val : acc-1
CAS	ushort, int, uint, ullong	acc = (acc == comp) ? val : acc
And	int, uint, llong, ullong	acc = acc & val (logical AND)
Or	int, uint, llong, ullong	acc = acc | val (logical OR)
Xor	int, uint, llong, ullong	acc = acc ^ val (logical exclusive OR)

The variable `acc` accumulates the result of all calls to an atomic function. Atomic functions return the value of `acc` before the current thread's successful update of `acc`. Note this is likely to vary from thread to thread.

The CAS (compare and swap) atomic function is an exception in that it takes 3 arguments:

```
atomicCAS(type *acc, type comp, type val)
```

The atomic functions in this table are atomic for all threads on a single GPU in the kernel launch. For recent GPUs with CC ≥ 6.0, the following additional forms are valid:

`atomicFun_block`: The operation is atomic for all threads in one thread block but not between thread blocks.
`atomicFun_system`: The operation is atomic across multiple GPUs and also host memory in managed memory scenarios.

This table is valid for CUDA SDK 11.5 (November 2021).

```
int atomicAdd(int *old, int val);
   where
                 old  is variable to added to
                 val  is the variable to be added to
   result:       old = old+val
   return value: original value of old;
```

This function has been available to all GPUs with CC ≥ 1.1 but on the early GPUs it required the variable being updated is in device global memory. On all modern GPUs (CC ≥ 3.5) shared memory can also be used. Over GPU generations additional variable types have been added to those supported by the atomic functions. AtomicAdd now supports more types than any of the other atomic functions and the full set (up to CC 11.2) is shown in Table B.1. Note that atomic functions are not template functions; they use standard C/C++ compiler function selection based on argument types. Some types require more recent GPUs for support; 64-bit integers require $CC \geq 3.5$, double, half2 and nv_bfloat162 require $CC \geq 6.0$, half requires $CC \geq 7.0$ and nv_bfloat16 requires $CC \geq 8.0$.

On early GPUs, atomic functions were slow and were avoided by programmers wherever possible. On more recent GPUs, they are significantly faster especially when only a few threads actually compete to perform the operation. A good example is our fast reduce kernel where only one thread in a warp competes to perform an addition to an element of the output array.

B.2 AtomicCAS

The atomicCAS function is interesting because it can be used to make new atomic functions. Example B.1 shows an implementation of integer atomicAdd using atomicCAS:

Example B.1 Use of atomicCAS to implement atomicAdd for ints

```
// myatomic_add example of atomic function constructed using
// atomicCAS. This code is based on the example in section
// B14 of the CUDA C++ Programming Guide (SDK version 11.2)

10  __device__ int myatomic_add(int *acc, int val)
11  {
12    int acc_now = acc[0];
13    while(1) {
14      int acc_test = acc_now;  // current accumulator value
15      acc_now = atomicCAS(acc, acc_test, acc_now+val);
16      if(acc_test == acc_now) break;  // CAS test succeeded
17    }
18    return acc_now;
19  }
```

Description of Example B.1

- Line 10: The arguments and return value for myatomic_add are the same as for the standard atomicAdd function.
- Line 12: The value of the output argument acc[0] at the start of execution for this thread is stored in acc_now. Note the value stored in acc[0] may constantly change during the execution of this code as other threads add their contributions.
- Lines 13–17: The current thread will repeatedly execute the three lines of code in this loop until its attempt to use atomicCAS succeeds.
  - Line 14: The value currently in acc[0] is copied to acc_test.
  - Line 15: This is where we use atomicCAS; if the value in acc_test is equal to acc[0] then the CAS test succeeds and the value that was stored acc[0] is replaced by acc[0]+val. This is trivial in the case where only one thread calls atomicCAS, but if many threads call

simultaneously only at most one thread will be allowed to succeed by the atomicCAS function. Importantly, the value returned by atomicCAS is used to update acc_now and this is the value that was used by atomicCAS in the comparison with acc_test for this thread.

    ◦ Line 16: If after calling atomicCAS the updated value of acc_now is equal to acc_test the CAS test must have succeeded, so this thread now exits the while loop.

- Line 18: On exiting the function we return the value in acc[0] used at the start of this thread's successful call to atomicCAS.

I would rate this function as being quite tricky code; we need to know that atomicCAS and all the other built-in atomic functions only ever let one thread succeed at any one time. We have to be very aware that this code is being executed in parallel. The code is also very inefficient if called simultaneously by many threads as their accesses will be effectively serialised. In our fast reduce examples we used warp level reduction and then only one thread from each warp called atomicAdd. This turns out to be as good as, if not better than, any other approach. Obviously, you should avoid letting all 32 threads in a warp call atomic functions simultaneously. The warp shuffle functions are helpful here.

Another point to make is that the above version of atomicAdd is likely to always be less efficient than the standard version because modern GPU hardware directly supports common atomic operations.

Interestingly, atomicCAS only takes integer type for its arguments so how can we implement something like atomicAdd for floats or doubles? The answer is to notice that atomicCAS either does nothing if the CAS test fails, or if it succeeds the third argument is simply the address pointed to by the first argument. There is no arithmetic performed so we can make atomicCAS work for floats if we do some gymnastics with type casting. The result is shown in Example B.2.

Example B.2 Use of atomicCAS to implement atomicAdd for floats

```
// myatomic_add example of atomic function constructed using
// atomicCAS. This code is based on the example in section
// B14 of the CUDA C++ Programming Guide (SDK version 11.2)

20   __device__ float myatomic_add(float *acc, float val)
21   {
22     float acc_now = acc[0];
23     while(1) {
24       float acc_test = acc_now; // current accumulator
25       acc_now = uint_as_float( atomicCAS( (uint *)acc,
                         __float_as_uint(acc_test),
                         __float_as_uint(acc_now+val) ) );

26       if( __float_as_uint(acc_test) ==
               __float_as_uint(acc_now)) break; // OK?
27     }
28     return acc_now;
29   }
```

Description of Example B.2

Most of this example is identical to Example B.1 except that arguments of type int are now of type float.

- Line 20: Here we declare myatomic_add with arguments of type float.
- Line 22: The current accumulator value acc_now is also of type float.
- Lines 23–27: This while loop is the same as before.
  - Line 24: acc_test is also of type float.
  - Line 25: The arguments we wish to use for the atomicCAS call are now all of type float instead of the necessary uint. Fortunately, we can use casts to make NVCC compile this statement.

    For the first argument we can use a standard C/C++ cast to cast the pointer type to uint: (uint *)acc. This cast tells the compiler to treat the pointer as a pointer to a uint object but does not change the bit pattern in that object. There is, however, an implicit assumption that both objects use the same number of bytes in memory – 4 bytes in this case. (The equivalent routine for doubles would use unsigned long long as both objects would then be 8 bytes long. Helpfully unsigned long long is another valid input type for atomicCAS.)

    For the second and third arguments which are passed by value and not pointers, we cannot use any of the standard C/C++ casts. For example, our standard C style cast (uint)acc_test would cause the compiler to convert the value of acc_test to an actual uint and pass that new value to the function; thus 3.145 would be passed as 3. Instead, we have to use the CUDA device-only intrinsic casting function __float_as_uint(). This does exactly what we need and tells the compiler to pass by value the unchanged float object to a function expecting a uint argument. We use this cast for both the second and third arguments.

    This is tricky code used to work around a problem with the user interface of an externally supplied library function. Unless we are really careful, we are likely to get bugs. Here we know (or rather we hopefully assume) that atomicCAS will not perform any actual arithmetic with its arguments. It will firstly *compare* the first and second arguments and secondly it will *copy* the third argument to the first on success. Both steps work fine for any bit patterns of equal size.
  - Line 26: Here we test if the CAS test has succeeded for the current thread. Again we do the comparison treating the bit patterns as unsigned ints. This is done for a different reason to line 25. Both of these floats just might be set to nan, and (nan == nan) returns false! This has the potential to cause an infinite loop so we use the casts to work around the problem.
- Line 28: When it is done we return the value of acc[0] before the successful update as a float.

This version of atomicAdd is likely to be less efficient than the standard one. Note the use of the CUDA built-in cast __float_as_uint().This is an instruction to the NVCC compiler to treat the bit pattern as a uint; the bit pattern is not changed. Since we only copy or compare two floats, both of which use this cast, correct results are obtained. It is, however, necessary that uint and float both have the same size (4 bytes).

The atomicCAS function can also be used to provide a MUTEX (mutual exclusive access) flag that a group of threads can use to serially execute any piece of code but care is required to avoid deadlock between divergent threads. Serialising single thread execution in CUDA is very slow and should obviously be avoided.

Appendix C

The NVCC Compiler

CUDA programs are compiled using the NVIDIA NVCC compiler; this is either done implicitly in Visual Studio using the NVIDIA supplied build tools or explicitly on the command line in Windows or Linux using the NVCC command.

C.1 Build Command

NVCC expects kernel code to be contained in files with extension .cu and for simple cases the entire program can be contained in a single .cu file. This is what we do in most of our examples. NVCC will deal with all the GPU code but pass the remaining host to a local C++ compiler, typically VC on windows or gcc on Linux. Like all modern compilers there are a great many options that can be specified to configure the compilation. If you are using an NVIDIA supplied project template on Visual Studio or a makefile on Linux then a suitable set of options will be supplied for you and this is certainly the best way to begin using CUDA. Indeed, for this book we have stuck with default options for nearly all the examples except for the non-default --use_fast_math option which we use frequently. An example of a full NVCC command line generated by Visual Studio is shown in Example C.1

Example C.1 Build command generated by Visual Studio

```
10   "%CUDA_PATH%\bin\nvcc.exe"
11   -gencode=arch=compute_75,code=\"sm_75,compute_75\"
12   --use-local-env
13   -ccbin "%VS2017INSTALLDIR%\VC\Tools\MSVC\14.16.27023\bin
             \HostX86\x64"
14   -x cu
15   -I"D:\Users\real\OneDrive\Code\inc"
16   -I"%NVCUDASAMPLES_ROOT%\common\inc"
17   -I"%CUDA_PATH%\include"
18   --keep-dir x64\Release
19   -maxrregcount=0
20   --machine 64
21   --compile
22   -cudart static
23   --use_fast_math
```

```
24    -DWIN32 -DWIN64 -DNDEBUG -D_CONSOLE -D_MBCS
25    -Xcompiler "/EHsc /W3 /nologo /O2 /Fdx64\Release\vc141.pdb
                 /FS /Zi  /MD "
26    -o x64\Release\reduce4.cu.obj
27    "D:\all_code\vs17\Chapter2\reduce4\reduce4.cu"
```

Description of Example C.1

Note the symbols shown between % signs are defined in the Windows command line environment variables and will be shown expanded to their actual values in the VS output. The command can be entered either as a single line or split into several lines by using the DOS ^ continuation indicator at the end of all but the last line.

- Line 10: Runs `nvcc` using an explicit path to the exe file.
- Line 11: GPU code for a CC=7.5 (Turing) device is to be generated (this choice is not a default).
- Line 12: Tells NVCC that the local environment variables have been set to run the local C++ compiler (VC in this case).
- Line 13: Path to local C++ compiler.
- Line 14: The input is a .cu file.
- Lines 15–17: These are extra directories to search for include files; they are specified by prefixing `-I`.
- Line 18: Relative path to output directory for .exe file.
- Line 19: Maximum number of registers per thread. The value zero is a default leaving the compiler free to choose. Specifying a value greater than 32 might reduce the maximum occupancy of the kernel. 32 is usually the best choice but this is one flag you may want to tune for optimal performance. For more information see the NVCC reference manual.
- Line 20: Compile for 64-bit OS.
- Line 21: Compile all files in argument list after options (this is a default).
- Line 22: Specify CUDA run-time library; possible choices are `none`, `shared` and `static`. The default is `static`.
- Line 23: This is our favourite option – it makes your kernel code faster but it is not a default. The `--use_fast_math` flag also implies the additional options `--ftz=true`, `--prec-div=false`, `--prec-sqrt=false` and `--fmad=true`.
- Line 24: This is a standard list of definitions passed to the VC compiler.
- Line 25: The keyword `Xcompiler` introduces a list of options for the host C++ compiler; in this case VC.
- Line 26: The option `-o` names the output files. If omitted the files `a.obj` and `a.exe` arc created. This flag should always be used.
- Line 27: This is the file to be compiled which come after the options. It is not prefixed with `--` or `-` and a list of several files can go here.

Note that in simple cases the complexity of Example C.1 is not needed; on my Windows10 system I can perform the same compilation with the command shown in the box:

```
D:\> nvcc -I"D:\Users\real\OneDrive\Code\inc" ^
          -I"%NVCUDASAMPLES_ROOT%\common\inc" ^
       -o reduce4.exe --use_fast_math reduce4.cu
```

where the "^" indicates that a continuation line follows. The include from line 17 is a default. On Linux the environment variables NVCC_PREPEND_FLAGS and NVCC_APPEND_FLAGS can be defined to hold commonly used strings. Note that Visual Studio generates a separate -I for each path but a single "I" followed by a comma separated list of paths is also valid. A space between the "I" and filename is also allowed:

```
D:\ >nvcc -I path1,path2 ^
          -o reduce4.exe --use_fast_math reduce4.cu
```

A commonly used set of options can be read from a text file using -optf <file>:

```
D:\ >nvcc -optf include.txt -o reduce4.exe reduce4.cu
where the file include.txt contains:
    -I "D:\Users\real\OneDrive\Code\inc"
    -I "C:\ProgramData\NVIDIA Corporation\CUDA
Samples\v11.2\common\inc"
    --use_fast_math
```

Note that Windows parameters such as NVCUDASAMPLES_ROOT are not expanded when read from text files and thus would have to be replaced by their actual values.

The process of building an executable program file from a .cu file is quite complex. Device code is first compiled by NVCC producing an assembly language PTX for the GPU code. The PTX file is then converted in machine code for the target device and merged with code from the host compiler to finally produce an executable file. Interested readers can find more detail in the NVIDIA NVCC Reference guide.

C.2 NVCC Options

The full set of options available in NVCC can be found in the *CUDA Compiler Driver NVCC Reference Guide* which is included in the SDK documentation set. The options are grouped according to function of these groups and a subset of options are listed below. NVCC calls the NVLINK program to perform the step of linking compiled code with libraries to build an executable file. Options for NVLINK should also be included on the NVCC command line by users. A subset of NVLINK options is included in the following list.

Options for NVCC and NVLINK

- Compilation phase.
  - `--ptx` or `-ptx` Compile all .cu/.gpu input files to device-only .ptx files. This step discards the host code for each of these input files.
  - `--compile` or `-c`: Compile each .c/.cc/.cpp/.cxx/.cu input file into an object file.
  - `--link` or `-link`: This option specifies the default behaviour: compile and link all inputs.
  - `--lib` or `-lib`: Compile all inputs into object files (if necessary) and add the results to the specified output library file.
  - `--run` or `-run`: This option compiles and links all inputs into an executable file and runs it. Or, when the input is a single executable file, it is run without any compilation or linking. This step is intended for developers who do not want to be bothered with setting the necessary environment variables; these are set temporarily by NVCC.
- File and path specifications.
  - `--output-file <file>` or `-o <file>`: Specify name and location of the output file. Only a single input file is allowed when this option is present in NVCC non-linking/archiving mode.
  - `--library <library>,...` or `-l <library>,...`: Specify libraries to be used in the linking stage without the library file extension. The libraries are searched for on the library search paths that have been specified using option `--library-path`.
  - `--include-path <path>,...` or `-I <path>,...`: Specify include search paths.
  - `--cudart <opt>` or `-cudart <opt>`: Specify the type of CUDA runtime library to be used: no CUDA runtime library, shared/dynamic CUDA runtime library, or static CUDA runtime library. Allowed values for this option are `none`, `shared` or `static`. The default value is `static`.
- Options for specifying behaviour of compiler/linker.
  - `--profile` or `-pg`: Instrument generated code/executable for use by gprof (Linux only).
  - `--debug` or `-g`: Generates debug information for host code.
  - `--device-debug` or `-G`: Generates debug information for device code. Turns off all optimisations. Isn't used for profiling; it is better to use `-lineinfo` instead.
  - `--generate-line-info` or `-lineinfo`: Generates line-number information for device code.
  - `--optimize <level>` or `-O`: Specifies optimisation level for host code.
  - `--no-exceptions` or `-noeh`: Disables exception handling for host code.
  - `--shared` or `-shared`: Generates a shared library during linking. Use `--linker-options` when other linker options are required for more control.
  - `--std <opt>` or `-std <opt>`: Where opt is one of `c++03`, `c++11`, `c++14` or `c++17`, Used to select a particular C++ dialect. Note that this flag also turns on the corresponding dialect flag for the host compiler.
  - `--machine <opt>` or `-m <opt>`: Where opt is either `32` or `64`, used to specify 32 or 64-bit architecture. The default value is `64`.
- Options for passing specific phase options.
  - `--compiler-options <options>,...` or `-Xcompiler <options>,...`: Used to specify options directly to the host compiler or pre-processor.
  - `--linker-options <options>,...` or `-Xlinker <options>,...`: Used to specify options directly to the host linker.
- Miscellaneous options for guiding the compiler driver.
  - `--dryrun` or `-dryrun`: Do not execute the compilation commands generated by nvcc. Instead, list them.

○ `--verbose` or `-v`: List the compilation commands generated by this compiler driver, but do not suppress their execution.

○ `--keep` or `-keep`: Keep all intermediate files that are generated during internal compilation steps.

○ `--keep-dir <dir>` or `-keep-dir <dir>` Keep all intermediate files that are generated during internal compilation steps in this directory.

○ `--save-temps` or `-save-temps`: This option is an alias of `--keep`.

○ `--clean-targets` or `-clean`: This option reverses the behaviour of NVCC. When specified, none of the compilation phases will be executed. Instead, all of the non-temporary files that NVCC would otherwise create will be deleted.

○ `--run-args <arg>,...` or `-run-args <arg>,...`: Used in combination with option `--run` to specify command line arguments for the executable.

- Options for steering GPU code generation.

○ `--gpu-architecture <arch>` or `-arch <arch>`: Specify the CC level of the target GPU, for example, `-arch=sm_75` for Turing CC=7.5 devices. The resulting exe file will run on all devices of the specified CC level and higher. The current (December 2021) minimum supported CC level is CC=3.0 but levels below 5.2 are deprecated. This is an important parameter to get right; we recommend always explicitly using the CC level of your target device.

○ `--gpu-code <code>` or `-code <code>`: This controls the CC level of the actual GPU code generated. If omitted the value set by -arch is used which is usually what you need. See the NVIDIA documentation for more information.

○ `--maxrregcount <value>` or `-maxrregcount <value>`: This is the maximum number of registers that GPU functions can use. This parameter is actually obsolete and should not be used. The compiler and run time system will normally optimise this for you. Experienced users can also use the Launch Bounds feature, described in Appendix B of the CUDA Programming Guide, in kernel code to give hints to the compiler.

○ `--use_fast_math` or `-use_fast_math`: This is the one option we use nearly all the time. If in doubt about accuracy, try with and without using this switch and compare numerical results. In some case the performance effect is dramatic; in others it makes little difference. Experienced users can omit this switch and explicitly mix fast intrinsic functions with slower standard versions in kernel code to optimise both speed and accuracy. This option also implies `--ftz=true`, `--prec-div=false`, `--prec-sqrt=false` and `--fmad=true`.

○ `--extra-device-vectorization` or `-extra-device-vectorization`: This option enables more aggressive device code vectorisation in the NVVM IR[1] optimiser. We have not experimented with this option.

- Options for steering cuda compilation.

○ `--default-stream <value>` or `-default-stream <value>` one of `legacy` or `null` or `per-thread`: Specifies the default stream on which GPU work will be queued. We recommend the default `per-thread` which refers to CPU threads not GPU threads. This is the only flag in this section.

- Generic tool options.

○ `--disable-warnings` or `-w`: Suppresses all warning messages.

○ `--source-in-ptx` or `-src-in-ptx` Interleaves source in PTX code. May only be used in conjunction with `--device-debug` or `--generate-line-info`.

○ `--restrict` `-restrict`: Treat all kernel pointer arguments as restrict pointers. We do this explicitly in all our examples.

- ◦ `--resource-usage` or `-res-usage` Shows resource usage such as registers and memory for the GPU code. This option implies `--nvlink-options --verbose` when `--relocatable-device-code=true` is set. Otherwise, it implies `--ptxas-options --verbose`.
  - ◦ `--help` or `-h` Prints this help information.
  - ◦ `--version` or `-V` Prints version information.
  - ◦ `--options-file <file>` or `-optf <file>`: Reads command line options from specified file.
- NVLINK Options.
- Note a number of NVCC options also apply to NVLINK, for example, `-arch`. Here we only list NVLINK-specific options.
  - ◦ `--library-path <path>,...` or `-L <path>,...` Specifies library search paths.
  - ◦ `--library <library-file>,...` or `-l <library-file>,...`: Specifies library files to be used in the linking stage. The libraries are searched for on the library search paths given by the `-L` option.
  - ◦ `--link-time-opt` or `-lto`: Performs link-time optimisation.

Appendix C Endnotes

1 The NVIDIA NVVM IR compiler is a version of the LLVM IR project compiler. More information can be found in the NVIDIA NVVM IR Specification Reference Manual which is part of the SDK documentation set. More details of the LLVM compiler infrastructure project can be found at https://llvm.org/.

Appendix D

AVX and the Intel Compiler

In this section we discuss how best to access the SIMD capabilities of an Intel CPU. As mentioned in Chapter 1 Intel added hardware to perform SIMD operations on vectors of floats and integers beginning with the MMX instruction on the Pentium II in 1977.[1]

On a computer an operation such as x = y * z is performed by the hardware, first loading y and z into hardware registers, then performing multiplication using the ALU with the result appearing in another register and finally storing the result in x. The registers used typically only have enough bits to hold a single variable, for example 32-bits for a 32-bit variable. The idea of SIMD hardware is to support vector operations such as X = Y * Z where multiplication is performed on corresponding components of the vectors simultaneously. For this to work with vectors of say, four 32-bit floats the registers need to be 128 bits wide to hold all the components of the vectors and the ALU needs to be upgraded to perform four 32-bit multiplications simultaneously. For cost reasons the SIMD-ALU needs to only support the most important operations. The original MMX hardware used registers that were 64 bits wide and only supported integer arithmetic. Thus, the supported vector types were two component 32-bit integers (I32) or four component 2-byte integers (I16) or eight component 1-byte integers (I8). Later hardware versions use wider registers which support more components. The most recent architecture AVX-512 uses 512-bit wide registers and supports simultaneous operations on 16 component 4-byte vectors. Table D.1 gives a brief overview of the history and more details can be found online, https://en.wikipedia.org/wiki/Advanced_Vector_Extensions for example.

In the table most generations are backwards compatible with earlier versions. Successive generations include numerous other improvements such as wider instruction sets that are not detailed here.

D.1 MMX

The first MMX (standing for MultiMedia Extensions) instructions were added to the Pentium II in 1997 to support graphics and audio processing and only worked with integers. It is interesting to note that like GPUs the original intent was to support entertainment on PCs not "serious" computing. The new MMX registers were 64 bits and thus supported simultaneous operations on two 4-byte integers or four 2-byte integers or eight 1-byte integers. Floating point capability was added soon after with the upgrading to SSE (streaming SIMD extensions) on the Pentium III in 1999. For SSE the register width was increased to 128 bits but the only supported operations were for 32-bit floats. However, MMX could still be used for integers.

Table D.1 *Evolution of the SIMD instruction set on Intel processors*

Model	Year	Name	Bits	Supported Data Types					
				F64	F32	I64	I32	I16	I8
Pentium II	1997	MMX	64	-	-	-	yes	yes	yes
Pentium III	1999	SSE	128	-	yes	-	yes in 64-bit MMX		
Pentium IV	2000	SSE2	128	yes	yes	yes	yes	yes	yes
Prescott	2004	SSE3	128	yes	yes	yes	yes	yes	yes
Core 2 Duo	2006	SSSE3	128	yes	yes	yes	yes	yes	yes
Penryn	2007	SSE4	128	yes	yes	yes	yes	yes	yes
Sandy Bridge	2011	AVX	256	yes	yes	yes	yes	yes	yes
Haswell	2013	AVX2	256	yes	yes	yes	yes	yes	yes
Knights Landing	2016	AVX-512	512	yes	yes	yes	yes	yes	yes

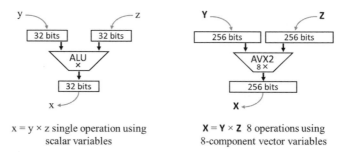

x = y × z single operation using scalar variables   **X** = **Y** × **Z** 8 operations using 8-component vector variables

Figure D.1 Normal scalar and AVX2 eight-component vector multiplication

Successive generations not only increased the width of the operation registers but also added to the available instruction set. The more recent instruction sets are very rich; the details are not discussed here, but, if you are interested, more information can be found on Intel's website: https://software.intel.com/content/ www/us/en/develop/home.html ; try searching for avx2.

Figure D.1 illustrates multiplication using the 256-bit wide registers of AVX2 which allow eight simultaneous operations on 4-byte variables.

Initially, the new hardware was difficult for programmers to use directly; essentially bits of hand-crafted assembly code had to be inserted into programs. Gradually libraries for linear algebra and the like began to appear which gave programmers an easier route to exploiting SIMD. Library developers, however, struggled to keep up with the frequent updates to hardware while retaining support for older versions so even this route was somewhat limited. More recently compilers have started to automatically vectorise code during compilation, but this only works for pieces of code where it is easy for the compiler to figure out that vectorisation is possible. Nevertheless, it is likely that much of the software running on your current PC is exploiting SIMD to some extent.

D.2 Intel ICC

Intel offers a compiler, ICC, which (not surprisingly) gives the best support for the SIMD instructions. The ICC compiler is available as part of the Intel System Studio development

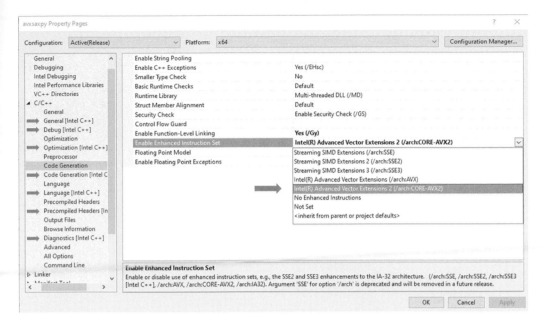

Figure D.2 Visual Studio with ICC installed

package available from https://software.intel.com/content/www/us/en/develop/tools/system-studio.html and a free annual licence is available. On Windows 10 the package installs plugins for Visual Studio 17 and 19 so that it can be used as an alternative to the Microsoft compiler. In Figure D.2 we show an example of a VS properties page with ICC integration. The grey arrows on the left panel point to ICC specific options and the grey arrow on the right shows where support for SIMD can be turned on and off. Note the default for this option is "Not Set" which experiments suggest is the same as "No Enhanced Instructions".[2]

If you are keen to ensure that your code really does use the SIMD instructions, then the Intel SIMD intrinsic function library is a good choice. This is a C++ callable function library and does not require any fancy use of assembly. We illustrate use of this library in Example D.1 which computes the saxpy formula, x = a*x+y, for vectors x and y of length size using reps repeats.

Example D.1 sets the baseline for the calculation; it uses straightforward C++ and achieves about 3.5 GFlops/sec when compiled with the Intel ICC compiler.[3]

Example D.1 Comparison of Intel ICC and VS compilers

```
01  // cpusaxpy:  a*x + y for vectors x and y
02  #include <stdio.h>
03  #include <stdlib.h>
04  #include "cxtimers.h"

05  int main(int argc,char *argv[])
06  {
07    signed int size = (argc >1) ? 2 << atoi(argv[1])
                                  : 1 << 10;
```

```
08    int reps = (argc >2) ? atoi(argv[2]) : 1000;

09    float a = 1.002305238f;  // 1000th root of 10

10    float *x = (float *)malloc(size*sizeof(float));
11    float *y = (float *)malloc(size*sizeof(float));
12    for(int k=0;k<size;k++) {x[k] = 1.0f;  y[k] = 0.0f;}

13    cx::timer tim;  // note order of loops
14    for(int i=0;i<reps;i++) for(int k=0;k<size;k++)
                                    x[k] = a*x[k]+y[k];
15    double t1 = tim.lap_ms();
16    double gflops = 2.0*(double)(size)*(double)rep
                                    /(t1*1000000);
17    printf("cpusaxpy: size %d, time %.6f ms check %10.5f
                GFlops %.3f\n", size,t1,x[129],gflops);
18    free(x); free(y); // tidy up
19    return 0;
20  }


D:\ >cpusaxpy.exe 21 3000  (using Intel ICC compiler)
cpusaxpy: size 2097152, time 3635.091200 ms check 1000.09351
GFlops 3.462


D:\ > saxpy_vs.exe 21 3000 (using Microsoft VS compiler)
saxpy_vs: size 2097152, time 8080.932400 ms check 1000.09351
GFlops 1.557
```

Description of Example D.1

- Lines 7–8: Set values of size and reps with optional user input.
- Line 9: Set the saxpy constant a to the 1000th root of 10.
- Lines 10–12: Allocate float arrays x and y of length size and initialise to 1 and 0 respectively. We use plain malloc here rather than a container class because in the later avx versions of this example we found using std::vector as a container significantly reduced performance.
- Lines 13–15: A timed loop that performs size*reps saxpy computations. Note the value of x[k] is changed in line 15 which means that the loop cannot be parallelised for the reps index i, but the loop could be parallelised with respect to the steps index k. In practice, this version of the example does have better performance with the order of the loops as shown here.
- Line 16: Here we calculate the performance assuming two operations for each evaluation.
- Line 17: Print results including a sample element of x.

Results are shown for the elements of x and y initialised to 1 and 0 respectively. The constant a is set to $10^{1/1000}$; thus for reps=3000 we expect the elements of x to be 1000 after the loops in line 15. When compiled with the Intel ICC compiler the program runs more than twice as fast as it did when using the Microsoft Visual Studio compiler. The GPU is not used in this example.

The results show a performance of about 3.5 GFlops/sec using the Intel ICC compiler and 1.6 GFlops/sec using Visual Studio. The ICC result is somewhat dependent to the value of `size`; smaller values of `size` giving a better performance, presumably due to improved memory caching. The VS compiled code is much less sensitive to the value of `size`.

D.3 Intel Intrinsics Library

Example D.2 is a modification of D.1 using the Intel intrinsics library, explicitly using AVX2 to perform the calculation with SIMD vector operations of length eight. The basic idea is to subdivide the long vectors x and y into contiguous groups of eight and call the relevant intrinsic functions with these groups as arguments. We can use the library defined type __m256 for this purpose. The type __m256 defines an object of length 256-bytes aligned on a 256-byte memory boundary containing eight 4-byte floats. There are equivalent definitions for other kinds of data, for example, __m256i for eight 4-byte `ints` and __m256d for four 8-byte `doubles`.

Example D.2 Intel intrinsic functions for AVX2

```
01   // avxsaxpy: a*x + y for vectors x and y
02   #include <stdio.h>
03   #include <stdlib.h>
04   #include <immintrin.h>   // Intel Intrinsics Library
05   #include "cxtimers.h"

06   int main(int argc,char *argv[])
07   {
08      signed int size = (argc >1) ? 1 << atoi(argv[1]) :
                                        1 << 10;
09      int reps = (argc >2) ? atoi(argv[2]) : 1000;

        // 1000th root of 10
10      __m256   ma = _mm256_set1_ps(1.002305238f);

11      __m256 *mx = (__m256 *)malloc(sizeof(__m256)*size/8);
12      __m256 *my = (__m256 *)malloc(sizeof(__m256)*size/8);
13      for(int k=0;k<size/8;k++) mx[k] = _mm256_set1_ps(1.0f);
14      for(int k=0;k<size/8;k++) my[k] = _mm256_set1_ps(0.0f);

15      cx::timer tim;
16      for(int k=0;k<size/8;k++){
17        for(int i=0;i<reps;i++){       // x = a*x+y
18            mx[k] = _mm256_fmadd_ps(ma,mx[k],my[k]);
19          }
20        }
21      double t1 = tim.lap_ms();
```

```
                                        // get 8 elements
22    float check[8];  _mm256_storeu_ps(check,mx[7]);
23    double gflops = 2.0*(double)(size)*(double)reps/
                                          (t1*1000000);
24    printf("avxsaxpy: size %d, time %.6f ms check %10.5f
                 GFlops %.3f\n",size,t1,check[7],gflops);
25    free(mx); free(my);  //tidy up
26    return ;
27  }


D:\ > avxsaxpy.exe 21 3000 (using Intel ICC compiler)
avxsaxpy: size 2097152, time 1302.000100 ms check 1000.09351
GFlops 9.664
```

Description of Example D.2

- Line 4: This added include of immintrin.h is necessary to use the Intel intrinsic functions.
- Line 10: This creates the __m256 object ma containing eight copies of the scaling constant a. This is equivalent to line 9 of (a). The function _mm256_fmadd_ps returns an __m256 object with eight copies of its input argument. If we want to fill a vector with different numbers then the function _mm256_set_ps can be used; this function takes eight separate arguments specifying the required values.
- Lines 11–12: These are the equivalent of lines 10–11 of (a) and create arrays mx and my of __m256 objects of dimension size/8 which is enough to hold size 4-byte floats. Here again we use plain malloc rather than a container class. We found using std::vector here leads to a drop in performance, possibly due to memory alignment issues.
- Lines 13–14: Here we fill the mx and my vectors with values 1 and 0 respectively again using the _mm256_fmadd_ps function.
- Lines 15–21: This is the timed saxpy loop equivalent to lines 13–15 of Example D.1. Note the outer loop of the array index k only needs size/8 iterations as we process eight floats per step. The actual saxpy calculation is performed in line 18 using the _mm256_fmadd_ps function which returns product of its first 2 arguments plus the third. A single 8-fold fused multiply and add instruction (FMA) will be used if supported by the hardware.
- Line 22: Here we extract a set of eight result values from the eighth element of the mx vector, mx[7], using the function _mm256_storeu_ps. The values are stored in the float array check. The "u" in this function name stands for unaligned, which means the function is designed to work even if the array check is not aligned on a 256-byte memory boundary. If we were sure that the first element of check was properly aligned, then the "u" in the function name can be omitted. The intrinsics library contains many functions with and without "u" functionality.

  A "feature" of the library is that when numbers are stored to __m256 objects their order is reversed in memory. But when the numbers are subsequently extracted an order reversing operation is *not* done. Thus check[7] from mx[7] actually corresponds the 129th element of the vector x used in Example D.1. In this particular example all the values in x and y are the same. However, in real code where they would be different this feature is a rich breeding ground for bugs.
- Lines 23–27: These lines are the same as 16–20 in Example D.1.

There are many more functions in the Intel intrinsics library which we have not described here. A good place to look is https://software.intel.com/sites/landingpage/IntrinsicsGuide/, which lists all the functions and provides numerous check boxes to select the ones of interest. Individual function names can then be clicked to get details of their arguments.

We can get more CPU performance by parallelising the loop over `size/8` in D.2 using OpenMP. This is well supported by ICC and requires adding just one extra line as shown in Example D.3. We also have to specify support for OpenMP in the project properties page (`C/C++ => Language [Intel C++] => openMP Support`).

Example D.3 Multithreaded version of D.2 using OpenMP

```
. . .
15    cx::timer tim;
15.5  #pragma omp parallel for    // OpenMP
16    for(int k=0;k<size/8;k++){
. . .


D:\ > ompsaxpy.exe 21 3000
ompsaxpy: size 2097152, time 171.055100 ms check 1000.09351
GFlops 73.561
```

The CPU performance of D.3 at over 70 GFlops/sec is quite impressive for my 4-core Haswell i7 4790 CPU.

As a final step we compare with a GPU implementation shown in Example D.4.

Example D.4 gpusaxpy kernel for comparison with host-based versions

```
10   __global__ void gpusaxpy(r_Ptr<float> x, cr_Ptr<float> y,
                                 float a, int size, int reps)
11   {
12     int tid = blockDim.x*blockIdx.x+threadIdx.x;
13     while(tid < size){
14       for(int k=0;k<reps; k++) x[tid] = a*x[tid]+y[tid];
15       tid += gridDim.x*blockDim.x;
16     }
17   }


18   int main(int argc, char* argv[])
19   {
20     signed int size = (argc >1) ? 1 << atoi(argv[1]) :
                                       1 << 10;
21     int blocks  = (argc >2) ? atoi(argv[2]) : 288;
22     int threads = (argc >3) ? atoi(argv[3]) : 256;
23     int reps    = (argc >4) ? atoi(argv[4]) : 100;
```

```
24      float a = 1.002305238f;   // 1000th root of 10

25      thrustDvec<float> dev_x(size,1.0f); // set device vectors
26      thrustDvec<float> dev_y(size,0.0f); // x and y

27      cx::timer tim;
28      gpusaxpy<<<blocks,threads>>>(dev_x.data().get(),
                        dev_y.data().get(), a, size, reps);
29      cx::ok( cudaDeviceSynchronize() );
30      double t1 = tim.lap_ms();

31      float gpu_check = dev_x[129]; // copy D2H
32      double gflops = 2.0*(double)(size)*(double)reps/
                                        (t1*1000000);
33      printf("gpusaxpy: size %d, time %.6f ms check %10.5f
                GFlops %.3f\n", size, t1, gpu_check, gflops);
34      return 0;
35  }

D:\ > gpusaxpy.exe 24 576 512 6000
gpusaxpy: size 16777216, time 31.711400 ms check 1000187.81250
GFlops 6348.713

D:\ > gpusaxpy.exe 28 1152 512 6000
gpusaxpy: size 268435456, time 391.937800 ms check 1000187.81250
GFlops 8218.716
```

Description of Example D.4

This is a very standard CUDA program; only the headers are omitted from the listing.

- Lines 10–17: These define the kernel function gpusaxpy which takes five input arguments, the data vectors x and y, the scaling constant a and the iteration counts reps and size. One thread performs the entire loop over reps and different threads process different elements of the vectors. We use our usual thread-linear addressing to process the whole vector.
- Line 14: This is the for loop over reps which performs the saxpy calculation.

  As an important detail we point out that our code appears to be using x[k] and y[k] as variables in the loop even though they are references to GPU main memory and not local variables stored in registers. In general, this must be avoided in CUDA kernels as it degrades performance. However, in this case tests have shown that the compiler is smart enough to have done the work of copying these array elements to local registers for us. Explicitly using temporary variables for the loop turns out to make no difference in this case, but in other cases it might, so you need be alert to this issue.
- Lines 18–39: This is the main program which is pretty standard and just prepares the data and launches the kernel.
- Lines 20–23: The user supplied parameters as before but with threads and blocks added.

- Lines 25–26: These create and initialise device thrust vectors `dev_x` and `dev_y` for x and y. Note that for this simple case where all the elements of a vector are equal we can initialise using the class constructor. There is no need for matching host vectors in this case.
- Lines 27–30: This is the timed loop that runs the kernel.
- Lines 31–33: Print results.

The results show that the for size = 2^{24} the GPU is delivering over 6.3 TFlops/sec which is about 85 times faster than the best CPU-only version. For the larger problem with size = 2^{28} the GPU delivers 8.2 TFlops/sec a speed-up of about 110.

If we compare the code in our host and GPU versions, to my eyes the CUDA version actually seems cleaner than the AVX versions. But obviously where host code must be used, Example D.3 is a big improvement on the single core version without AVX support. Note, however, that the Intel intrinsics library is limited to linear algebra type problems whereas CUDA kernels can be written to cover many additional problem types. It is the generality of CUDA that accounts for its success. The potential for huge gains in performance is, of course, another incentive.

One final lesson from this appendix is that it is well worth while trying the ICC compiler on your host code, you may well get a performance gain simply by recompiling.

Appendix D Endnotes

1 Amiri, Hossein, and Asadollah Shahbahrami. "SIMD programming using Intel vector extensions." Journal of Parallel and Distributed Computing 135 (2020): 83–100.
2 Note if you are compiling just for one machine it makes sense to choose the highest option supported by that machine. On the other hand, if you are compiling to distribute to a heterogeneous set of PCs it might make more sense to turn this option off or choose the lowest option likely to be supported by all the machines, maybe SSE2. See also our caveat about code making extensive use of the Intel intrinsic SIMD functions where, counterintuitively, it might be best to turn this option off.
3 It turned out to be quite tricky to get the best result from either ICC or the VS compiler. For example, the order of the two for loops in line 15 matters. For this problem, the VS compiler was consistently worse than ICC.

Appendix E

Number Formats

This appendix explains how numbers (and other data) are actually held in computer storage. In principle, you could write good code without knowing this. However we strongly recommend that you look at this material because it will help you understand features such as the differences between unsigned verses signed integer variables, floating point accuracy and why boundary alignment matters.

All information in a computer is represented by the states of a set of switches. Each switch can be either open or closed (but NOT in-between). The state of the switch is one *bit* of information which represents the values 0 or 1. In practice, computer DRAM requires one transistor[1] and one capacitor to represent one bit of information. If the transistor is open (conducting) or closed (non-conducting) then the voltage across the capacitor will be either low or high, so for electrical reasons we might choose "open" to represent the 1 and "closed" to represent 0.

A set of eight bits is called a byte and is the smallest addressable unit of computer memory. Using the conventions of binary arithmetic, a single byte can represent integers in the range 0–255 as illustrated in Figure E.1. Notice the bits within a byte are numbered from 0 to 7 from right to left, the *most significant* byte, worth 128 if set, is on the left.

E.1 Hexadecimal Notation

The bit pattern in a single byte can also be represented by two hexadecimal digits. The hexadecimal digits [0-9, A-F] represent the numbers [0–15] as illustrated in Figure E.2. Thus, the value of a single byte can be represented by two hex digits, for example:

$$[1001\ 1100] = 9C = 9 \times 16 + 12 = 156.$$

Hexadecimal notation can be extended to more digits:

$$[0001\ 1111\ 0010\ 1100] = 1F2C = 1 \times 16^3 + F \times 16^2 + 2 \times 16^1 + C = 7980.$$

Hexadecimal notation was introduced to computing by IBM in the 1960s when their dominant 360 series of mainframe computers, which were 8-bit byte based, imposed de facto standards on the world.[2] At that time doing hexadecimal arithmetic by hand was a necessary programming skill as a hexadecimal print out of a core dump was the only debugging information produced when your program crashed.

Binary arithmetic works just like base-10 arithmetic but using $1+1 = 10$ (i.e. $1+1$ equals zero carry 1), for example,

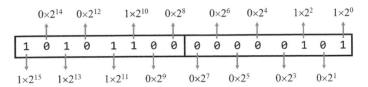

Figure E.1 16-bit pattern corresponding to AC05 in hexadecimal

$$
\begin{array}{ccc}
5 & & 0000\ 0101 \\
+7 & \text{or} & +0000\ 0111 \\
\hline
12 & = & 0000\ 1100 \ = \ 12_{10}
\end{array}
$$

where the subscript indicating that base 10 is being used.

Multiplication by 2 shifts the bit left by one position if the topmost bit was 1 it is lost – this is an *overflow* error producing a mathematically incorrect result. Similarly, division by 2 shifts all the bits one position to the right and the rightmost bit is lost. This is an *underflow* event and means that integers are rounded down to the nearest integer on division. In general underflows are less serious than overflows causing loss of precision rather than potentially catastrophic errors. Overflow can also happen using addition; an interesting case, using one-byte of data, is that 255+1=0. What happens here is that all the bits are set in 255 so that adding 1 causes arithmetic carry 1 to ripple all the way left clearing all the bits and then being lost as an overflow. As is often the case in computing we turn the bug into a feature by noticing that since in normal arithmetic -1+1=0 we can decide 255 represents -1 not +255 and indeed all values > 127 (i.e. those with the leftmost bit set to 1) are negative numbers. This is *twos complement* representation where the leftmost bit is a sign bit. You can go from any integer n to -n by flipping the values of each bit *and then adding one*. In C++ we can declare integer variables to be either signed or unsigned depending on if we want bigger positive integers or want to allow positive and negative values in our variable. Note this is more than cosmetic; the computer hardware will in fact execute different machine instructions for signed and unsigned variables. One example is that the test [0100 0000] > [1000 0000] is true or false depending on whether the variables concerned are char (true) or unsigned char (false).

Large integers and floating-point numbers require more than one byte to hold their values. In practice, this means 2, 4 or 8 bytes are used (notice always powers of 2). The C++ values are shown in Table E.1. The internal representation of integers is straightforward; the bytes on the left representing higher powers of two than the bytes on the right. Figure E.1 shows a 2-byte example.

In the figures the bit pattern can be written as AC05 in hexadecimal and if interpreted as a 16-bit integer corresponds to the value of -4493710 if signed or 4378110 if unsigned. On modern computers integers can be represented 1, 2, 4 or 8-bytes as shown in Table E.1. This table also include details of the float and Boolean intrinsic types.

E.2 Integer and Boolean Types

In C and C++ Boolean, false is always represented by zero and *all* other values are considered to represent true. This leads to a lazy programming style where numerical rather

Table E.1 *Intrinsic types in C++ (for current Intel PCs)*

name	Alternate Name	Can be Unsigned	bits	bytes	Values
bool	-	×	8	1	Either true or false
char	-	✓	8	1	Use for characters or short integers
short	short int	✓	16	2	integer $[-2^{15},+2^{15}]$ or $[0,+2^{16}-1]$
int	-	✓	32	4	integer $[-2^{31},+2^{31}]$ or $[0,+2^{32}-1]$
long	long int	✓	32	4/8	integer $[-2^{31},+2^{31}]$ or $[0,+2^{32}-1]$
long long	long long int	✓	64	8	integer $[-2^{63},+2^{63}]$ or $[0,+2^{64}-1]$
float	-	×	32	4	float $\pm 3.4\ 10^{\pm 38}$ (about 7 sig figs)
double	-	×	64	8	float $\pm 1.710^{\pm 308}$ (about 16 sig figs)
long double	-	×	64	8	80 bits possible on Intel CPUs

than Boolean values are tested in if statements. I have some sympathy for this style; it has always seemed wasteful to me for a function to return a Boolean error code rather than a potentially more useful numerical error code. In CUDA and my own code many functions return zero to indicate success and other values as error codes.

The `long int` type is something of a C legacy feature; the C/C++ standards do not specify unique value for the length of this type. Rather they specify that the length (and hence accuracy) of this type is *at least* the same at `int`. In early C implementations, `int` variables had a length of 2 bytes, the same as modern `short`, and `long int` variables had a length of 4 bytes. In modern implementations, `int` is now 4 bytes and the new type `long long` is 8 bytes, thus `long int` is arguably redundant. Another problem with `long int` is that it is likely to compile to 4-bytes in 32-bit code and 8-byte in 64-bit code. I think it is best to make your intentions explicit and stick to `int` and `long long`.

E.3 Floating Point Numbers

The representation of floating-point numbers is more complicated. Nowadays, nearly all systems conform to the IEEE standard 754 which has precise specifications for both single precision 32-bit and double precision 64-bit floating point numbers. The bit-pattern for 32-bit values is shown in Figure E.2. The least significant bits 0–22 contain the actual value expressed as a sum over negative powers of 2 (i.e. fractions), an 8-bit exponent in bits 23–30 and a sign bit 31. The precise formula for recovering the value is also shown.

Note the leading 1 in the summation over the fraction bits; this implicitly adds an extra most significant bit to the sum. Thus 32-bit floating point values are accurate to $\log_{10}[2^{24}] = 7.225$ significant figures. Also implicit in the definition is that integers, positive and negative, up to and including 2^{24} are represented exactly by 32-bit floats. This is helpful for CUDA applications where it is desirable to use float variables whenever possible. Within the safe range integer values can be reliably stored and recovered from float variables. Simple calculations such as addition will also be fine using float.

Another important detail to note is that the 8-bit exponent is biased by 127 to allow positive and negative exponents. The case where the exponent bits 23–30 are all zero is special and represents the smallest possible exponent of 2^{-127}. These numbers are

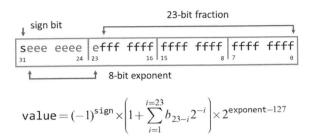

$$value = (-1)^{sign} \times \left(1 + \sum_{i=1}^{i=23} b_{23-i} 2^{-i}\right) \times 2^{exponent-127}$$

Figure E.2 IEEE 32-bit floating-point format

denormalised (or unnormalised) floating point numbers. In this case, if some of their leading fraction bits are also zero the number represented has a value less than 2^{-127} and is represented less accurately. For example, if bits 13–22 of the fraction are also zero then the value is the binary fraction represented by bits 0–12 multiplied by 2^{-137}. As we have seen previously, a denormalised number appearing in the calculations can have a catastrophic impact on performance of host code and they should be automatically flushed to zero by the hardware using either a compiler or run time switch. For GPU code flush to zero is enabled as one of the –use_fast-math options.

Double precision 64-bit floats have a similar layout with 1 sign bit, 11 exponent bits and 52 fraction bits. Their accuracy is $\log_{10}\left[2^{54}\right] = 16.256$ significant figures. Integers up to 2^{54} are held exactly in this format. The details are summarised in Table E.1. The use of double variables in a CUDA program always requires care; the cheaper cards can perform far fewer double precision operations per clock-cycle than float and for all cards double the memory bandwidth is needed.

Recent releases of CUDA have introduced a 16-bit floating point type half and other specialised variants for optimised tensor core calculations. These types are discussed in Chapter 11.

Appendix E Endnotes

1 At the time of writing 1 GB of DRAM can be bought for £10.0, so you are getting ~10,000,000 transistors for one penny. These must be the cheapest objects ever manufactured.

2 At that time most non-IBM computers used paper tape having 7 useful bits per row and hence favoured base 8 (or octal) notation. Fierce arguments raged; one story circulating at the time was that Greek scholars favoured the term sexadecimal but that IBM were too timid to adopt it. An echo from this era is found in the ASCII character encoding table, where the basic character set uses only 7-bits.

Appendix F

CUDA Documentation and Libraries

NVIDIA provide extensive documentation to support CUDA developers. The documentation is readily available online at https://docs.nvidia.com. It can be read online or downloaded in the form of pdf manuals. Up till SDK 11.1, a complete set of PDF manuals was automatically installed on your local machine in both HTML and PDF formats in the doc folder. Since SDK 11.2 this is no longer done (presumably to save space) but individual manuals are very quick to download. This appendix is a brief guide to what is available. The CUDA SDK includes many helpful examples on using these libraries. The manuals listed below are from the CUDA Toolkit Documentation section of the above website.

F.1 CUDA Programming Support

- The CUDA C++ Programming Guide: This manual is absolutely the best place to start and we have made frequent references to it throughout our book.
- SDK Release Notes.
- Installation guides for Windows and Linux.
- Best Practices Guide: This guide is highly recommended; it covers many of the ideas discussed in this book but also has interesting details about explicit NVCC features to micro optimise your code. For example, it confirms that expressions like x=index%256; y=index/256; will be evaluated using fast shift operations for any explicit power of 2 rather than the slower % and / functions.
- Compatibility: Available for each supported architecture.
- Tuning Guides: Available for each supported architecture. These guides are well worth reading.

F.1.1 PTX Documentation

PTX (Parallel Thread Execution) is the GPU assembly language created by NVCC. A detailed knowledge of this is for experts going beyond the scope of this book but it does give one a better understanding of what the hardware is really capable of doing.

- Inline PTX Assembly: The NVCC compiler lets you inject lines of PTX code directly into GPU code using the asm("PTX instructions"). You may see asm used in "expert" code or in some of the CUDA library header files. This short manual explains how this works with examples.

406

- The PTX ISA Application Guide: This is a detailed explanation of the individual PTX operations and the associated ISA (instruction set architecture). Essentially it explains in detail all the machine code operations exposed in CUDA. This is a reference manual, not light reading.
- PTX Interoperability: This is the guide you need to write GPU assembly level kernels without the help of CUDA and NVCC. It explains the Application Binary Interface (ABI) which allows your code to compile and interface correctly with the linker to run on specific devices. This is a relatively short manual.

F.1.2 CUDA API References

An API is an application programming interface which in most cases amounts to a set of callable functions which perform specific tasks. These guides are quite long and while useful for looking up specific functions are definitely not bedtime reading.

- CUDA Runtime API: This is a big manual and contains full details of all the CUDA functions you can use in either host or GPU code. I find the online version is easiest to use as one can find specific functions quickly by keyword searching.
- CUDA Driver API: This manual is the same as above but for the CUDA driver API. The CUDA driver API is an alternative to the runtime API which we have used throughout this book. The runtime API makes launching kernels simple using the host `kernel<<< >>> (arguments);` interface. This has the disadvantage that managing the loading and removal of kernel code from GPU memory is handled automatically. The driver API gives you fine control of this and other management tasks but at the price of significantly more complicated code. Since the message of this book is to keep things simple we recommend always using the runtime API.
- CUDA Math API: This is an important document relevant for scientific code; it describes the intrinsic maths functions available in GPU code. This document is well worth browsing; in addition to the functions you might expect like `sin` and `cos` there are lots of very fast niche functions which might be helpful. One example used in the book is `__ffs()` which finds the position of the least significant bit set to 1 in a 32-bit integer.
- PTX Compiler API: This gives you more information about the various PTX operations.

F.2 CUDA Computational Libraries

NVIDIA provide a number of important libraries to perform specific computational tasks. In most cases these functions are called directly from host code with no need to write kernels. There is also a set of open-source examples additional to those in the SDK (the CUDA Library Samples) at https://github.com/NVIDIA/CUDALibrarySamples.

- cuBLAS: This provides the BLAS library functions on the GPU. There are three APIs providing the user with different degrees of control over the management of device memory.
- NVBLAS: This library is designed to work with existing CPU-based projects using BLAS dependent code. If the NVBLAS library is included in the link step before the native BLAS library then certain level-3 BLAS functions will be replaced by versions from the cuBLAS library and automatically run on the GPU instead of the CPU.

- cuFFT: A suite of fast Fourier transform routines run on the GPU.
- cuRAND: This is the random number library which is discussed in detail in Chapter 6.
- cuSPARSE: This library is a set of host callable functions to perform GPU enabled linear algebra on sparse matrices having typically at leady 95% of their elements set to zero.
- cuSOLVER: This is a host callable set of functions for GPU accelerated decomposition and linear system solution for both dense and sparse matrices. It provides a high-level interface to the cuBLAS and cuSPARSE libraries.
- NPP: This library is devoted to 2D image processing including the kinds of image filtering discussed in the main text. It consists of a large set of host callable functions.
- NVRTC (Runtime Compilation): This library provides tools allowing a running host program to dynamically compile and run GPU kernel code. This is in contrast to the normal (and simpler) approach of compiling everything with NVCC before execution. There are a number of useful examples included in this manual.
- cuTensor: This is a library of host functions that use the GPU tensor cores to perform operations like contraction and reduction on matrices and tensors of higher degree. This library is a possible alternative to Thrust and the warp matrix functions discussed in Chapter 11. It is not included as part of the standard SDK but can be downloaded from https://developer.nvidia.com/cutensor and HTML documentation can be found at https://docs.nvidia.com/cuda/cutensor/index.html. Some examples using this library are included in the open source CUDA Library Samples mentioned above.

F.3 NVIDIA OptiX

Recent NVIDIA GPUs, specifically those based on the Turing TU102 and Ampere GA102 chipsets have new raytracing (RT) hardware in the form of one RT unit per SM. These units are intended to accelerate the high-quality rendering of 3D scenes for gaming and other visualisation purposes. CUDA itself does not directly expose the RT hardware to programmers but does support its use by means of function calls to objects in the additional OptiX library. The OptiX SDK can be download from https://developer.nvidia.com/designworks/optix/download. Documentation and example code are included in the download.

The RT units are designed to accelerate the tests of where and if a ray meets an object's bounding block. This is exactly the problem we discussed in Section 8.8 with CUDA code to find intersections with an axis aligned bounding block in Example 8.21. It is likely that use of RT cores could accelerate this step further. This is potentially useful for both simulation of systems for detecting ionising radiation and for both the forward and backward projection steps in tomographic reconstruction. As yet we have not explored this in detail but expect applications to emerge soon. One caveat is that present GPUs have only one RT unit per SM so the performance boost might be modest.

F.4 Third Party Extensions

- Thrust: Thrust provides a C++ vector class similar to `std::vector` but supporting vectors in both host and GPU memory. Vectors can be copied between the memory spaces. GPU accelerated algorithms similar to those in the C++ algorithms library are supported and can be run on GPU vectors. We use thrust as a container class throughout this book. While distributed with the CUDA SDK, thrust is actually an independent project and more details can be found at https://thrust.github.io/.

- CUB: This is another open-source project providing host level functions to perform operations such as reduce. Its aims are similar to thrust but unlike thrust, CUB is not included in the CUDA SDK. The short NVIDIA documentation essentially points to the official website https://nvlabs.github.io/cub/.
- CUDA C++ Standard: This refers to the `libcu++` project which aims to provide the kernel code equivalents to many of the C++ standard library (std) functions. It is a set of include files which are included in the CUDA SDK. The website https://nvidia.github.io/libcudacxx/ gives more details. We have not made use of these functions in this book.

The above list includes most of the guides and reference manuals you will need to develop you own GPU applications. However, NVIDIA provides much more documentation aimed at a wider range of audiences from games developers to administrators of large scale HPC facilities. Much of this can be accessed directly from the link at the start of this appendix.

Appendix G

The CX Header Files

Our examples use a collection of header files developed for our own use over a period of time with some additions for this book. They contain many useful functions, either utilities or wrappers to simplify some of the more complicated bits of CUDA (textures, for example). Most of the material is in the cx (CUDA Examples) namespace. When used, this namespace is explicit in the examples. A small number of commonly used definitions in the main cx.h file are not in any namespace (e.g. uint); this helps to keep our code compact. The five header files are shown in Table G.1 and complete listings are given. Obviously when compiling our examples, the cx headers should be in the path used by the compiler.

Each of these header files are shown in Examples G.1–10 and discussed in detail in the following sections.

G.1 The Header File cx.h

This base header file is needed by essentially all our examples. It defines short aliases for many arithmetic data types for example "ullong" for "unsigned long long". These are used widely in our examples, in part to reduce verbosity. Other useful definitions are wrappers for pointer types used as function arguments. A description of the code and a full listing of the file follows.

Example G.1 Header file cx.h, part 1

```
02   #pragma once

     . . .
11   // these for visual studio
12   #pragma warning( disable : 4244)// vebose thrust warnings
13   #pragma warning( disable : 4267)
14   #pragma warning( disable : 4996)// warnings: unsafe calls
15   #pragma warning( disable : 4838)// warnings: size_t to int

16   // macro #defines for min & max are usually bad news,
17   // the native CUDA versions compile to single instructions
18   #undef min
19   #undef max
```

Table G.1 *The CX header files*

File	Contents
cx.h	Basic definitions used by all examples, short type names and wrappers for pointers. cx::ok is defined here.
cxbinio.h	Simple C style binary IO, we use these a lot for transferring data to and from disk.
cxtimers.h	A simple timer class with a very compact interface.
cxtextures.h	Wrappers to simplify the use of CUDA textures.
cxconfun.h	Just a bit of fun, defines a few maths functions as constexpr so that they can be evaluated at compile time. Used once in scanner.h in the PET chapter.

```
20   // cuda includes
21   #include "cuda_runtime.h"
22   #include "device_launch_parameters.h"
23   #include "helper_cuda.h"
24   #include "thrust/host_vector.h"
25   #include "thrust/device_vector.h"
26   #include "thrust/system/cuda/experimental/
                                 pinned_allocator.h"
27   // C++ includes
28   #include <stdio.h>
29   #include <stdlib.h>
30   #include <string.h>
31   #define _USE_MATH_DEFINES
32   #include <math.h>
33   #include <algorithm>
34   #include <float.h>    // for _controlfp_s

35   // for openCV GUI etc (ASCII escape)
36   #define ESC 27
```

- Lines 12–15: Suppress certain irritating warning messages from Visual Studio C++.
- Lines 18–19 Remove #define style definitions of min and max. These do more harm than good. We use either std versions in host code or the fast built-in CUDA intrinsics in kernel code.
- Lines 21–26: Include most (but not all) of the commonly required CUDA and thrust support files.
- Lines 28–34: Host C++ includes.
- Line 36: Defines a symbol for ASCII escape, used once in the Ising example.

Example G.2 Header file cx.h, part 2

```
37   // these mimic CUDA vectors, e.g uchar4

38   using uchar  = unsigned char;
39   using ushort = unsigned short;
40   using uint   = unsigned int;
```

```
41  using ulong  = unsigned long;
42  using ullong = unsigned long long;
43  using llong  = long long;

44  // const versions of above

45  using cuchar  = const unsigned char;
46  using cushort = const unsigned short;
47  using cuint   = const unsigned int;
48  using culong  = const unsigned long;
49  using cullong = const unsigned long long;

50  // const versions of native types
51  using cchar   = const char;
52  using cshort  = const short;
53  using cint    = const int;
54  using cfloat  = const float;
55  using clong   = const long;
56  using cdouble = const double;
57  using cllong  = const long long;

58  // for CUDA (incomplete add as necessary)
59  using cint3 = const int3;
60  using cfloat3 = const float3;
61  // These to reduce verbosity in pointer arguments
62  // pointer variable data variable
63  template<typename T> using r_Ptr = T * __restrict__;
64  // pointer variable data constant
65  template<typename T> using cr_Ptr = const T *
                                          __restrict__;
66  // pointer constant data variable
67  template<typename T> using cvr_Ptr = T *
                                    const __restrict__;
68  // pointer constant data constant
69  template<typename T> using ccr_Ptr = const T *
                                    const __restrict__;

71  // thrust vectors aliases
72  template <typename T> using thrustHvecPin =
      thrust::host_vector<T,thrust::cuda::experimental::
                              pinned_allocator<T>>;
73  template <typename T> using thrustHvec =
                              thrust::host_vector<T>;
74  template <typename T> using thrustDvec =
                            thrust::device_vector<T>;

75  // get pointer to thrust device array
76  template <typename T> T * trDptr(thrustDvec<T> &a)
                            { return a.data().get(); }
```

```
77  //template <typename T> T * trDptr(thrustDvec<T> &a)
78  //   { return thrust::raw_pointer_cast(a.data()); }
```

- Lines 37–57: Lots of aliases for unsigned and const versions of native types. The use of the prefix u for unsigned is common; the use of c for const is less common. These definitions help keep function declarations compact.
- 59–60: Similar aliases for two CUDA types; you can add more if necessary.
- Lines 62–69: Define four templated aliases for C++ pointers using the restrict keyword combined with const in all possible ways.
  - Line 63: r_Ptr is defined without either the data or pointer constant. We often use this with arrays intended for output.
  - Line 65: cr_Ptr is defined for constant data but the pointer can be variable. We often use this for input array data.
  - Lines 67 and 69: Define cvr_Ptr and ccr_Ptr where the pointer itself is a constant and the data is either variable or constant. These versions are not used in our code.
- Lines 72–73: Define templated aliases thrustHvec and thrustDvec for creation of thrust host and device vectors and thrustHvecPin for host vectors in pinned memory. These are often used in our code.
- Line 76: Most array container classes including std::vector and thrust::host_vector have a member function data() which returns a raw pointer to the start of the data array. This is occasionally useful for passing to functions which expect a pointer, one example being the legacy fread and fwrite functions used for binary IO in cxbinio. h. However, if possible passing a reference to the actual container object is better. In the case of kernel calls passing a reference is not allowed and a data pointer must be passed. There is an issue with thrust which is that, although thrust_device vectors do have a data() member function, this function does not return a raw pointer for passing to kernels. If a is a thrust device vector then a.data().get() does return a suitable raw pointer. The function trDptr uses this to return a raw data point from a thrust_device vector passed by reference. This function is intended to be used on the host.
- Line 78: The a.data().get() function is undocumented and the recommended alternative is to use thrust::raw_pointer_cast() with either a.data() or &a[0] as an argument. An alternative definition of trDptr is shown here using the raw_pointer_cast. It is commented on in this version of cx.h but can be uncommented if you do not like using undocumented features.

  In our examples we don't make use of trDptr but prefer to use a.data().get() directly as a kernel argument as this use matches our practice with host container classes. If we were to use the raw_pointer_cast alternative version, the trDptr wrapper defined here would significantly reduce the verbosity of the resulting kernel calls.
- Line 79: Everything else in this header and all other cx headers is inside the cx namespace.
- Lines 81–83: Define templated constexpr symbols pi, pi2 and piby2 for π, 2π and $\pi/2$. Many scientific programs do something like this for π but using constexpr here means that the evaluations are done with maximum precision at compile time. The default

template type is set to float so that `cx::pi<>` and `cx::pi<double>` can be used for float or double values.

- Lines 84–88: The utility function `tail` returns the portion of the cstring s after the last appearance of the delimiter character c. It is used in the function `codecheck` below to strip the path from a complete file name.

Example G.3 Header file `cx.h`, part 3

```
79   namespace cx {// NB these are inside cx namespace

80   // fancy definition of pi, (default float)
81   template<typename T=float> constexpr T pi =
                          (T)(3.1415926535897932385L);
82   template<typename T=float> constexpr T pi2 =
                                  (T)(2.0L*pi<T>);
83   template<typename T=float> constexpr T piby2 =
                                  (T)(0.5L*pi<T>);
     // strip path from file name
84   const char *tail(cchar *s,char c)
85   {
86     const char *pch = strrchr(s,c);
87     return (pch != nullptr) ? pch+1 : s;
88   }

89   // Based on NVIDIA checkCudaErrors in helper_cuda.h
90   inline int codecheck(cudaError_t code, cchar *file,
                                  cint line, cchar *call)
91   {
92     if(code != cudaSuccess){
93       fprintf(stderr,"cx::ok error: %s at %s:%d %s \n",
           cudaGetErrorString(code), tail(file,'/'),
           line, call);
94       exit(1);     // NB this to quit on error
95       //return 1; // or this to continue on error
96     }
97     return 0;
98   }

99   // this during development
100  #define ok(cuda_call) codecheck((cuda_call),
                    __FILE__, __LINE__, #cuda_call)
101  // or this for final release code
102  //#define ok(cuda_call) cuda_call;
     } // end namespace cx and file cx.h
```

- Lines 90–100: Here we define the macro cx::ok which can be used to check for CUDA errors. It is closely based on the NVIDIA checkCudaErrors function in helper_cuda.h. It is slightly less verbose and can be changed to return instead of directly exiting the program.
  - Line 90: Declares the function codecheck which does all the work. The arguments are code the cuda call to be carried out, file a cstring containing the fully qualified name of the file containing the code, line a cstring containing the line number in the code where the call to cx::ok occurs and call a cstring containing the CUDA call.
  - Line 92: Performs the CUDA function call code and checks the return code.
  - Lines 93–94: If an error occurs it prints an informative message and exits the program. Note the use of cudaGetErrorString to convert the CUDA error code to a meaningful text string.
  - Line 95: An alternative to directly exiting is to return with a non-zero error code here.
  - Line 100: The definition of cx::ok as a macro. We have used very few macros in our code, but here the compiler adds a lot of extra value, by providing both the file name and line number where cx::ok detected the error.
  - Line 102: An alternate definition of cx::ok which does nothing; this could be used in debugged code to give slightly better performance.

G.2 The Header File cxbinio.h

If you aren't familiar with binary IO, this is the most efficient way to transfer data between host memory and disk; only the binary data is transferred without any formatting. This means that no accuracy is lost for data types such as double. The output file sizes are usually smaller than for formatted data.

Binary IO requires three simple steps, "open" the file for read or write, perform one or more read or write operations and then "close" the file. If you forget to close an open file, the operating system will do that for you when the program finishes – but that is poor practice as the handles created for open files are a scarce resource. Table G.2 show the functions defined in this header file.

We have used the old C functions fopen, fread and fwrite to implement these routines because they have simpler error handling than the C++ iostream equivalents. Proper error checking is essential when reading or writing files, for example, users might input wrong file names or the disk might fill when writing.

For serious GPU problems, file size may be many GBytes which means that 32-bit integers may be unable to hold their size. Hence, we use size_t instead of int or uint for the len and skip arguments in our functions and the compiler will silently promote user supplied arguments to size_t if necessary.

One disadvantage of simple binary IO is that users must know the size of a file before reading it. Most standard binary file formats start with a few bytes of header material specifying the length of following data set and the header often includes other information. Instead of using headers, we supply a function length_of which will return the length of an existing file in bytes.

Table G.2 *IO functions supplied by* `cxbinio.h`

`template <typename T> int` **`read_raw`** `(const char *name, T *buf, size_t len, int verbose=1)`	Read `len` words from named file to `buf`.
`template <typename T> int` **`write_raw`** `(const char *name, T *buf, size_t len, int verbose=1)`	Write `len` words to named file from `buf`. An existing file will be overwritten.
`template <typename T> int` **`append_raw`** `(const char *name, T *buf, size_t len, int verbose=1)`	Append `len` words to named file from `buf`. A new file is created if necessary.
`template <typename T> int` **`read_raw_skip`**`(const char *name, T *buf, size_t len, size_t skip, int verbose=0)`	Read `len` words from named file to `buf` starting after `skip` bytes.
`template <typename T> size_t` **`length_of`**`(const char *name, int verbose=0)`	Returns length of named file in words of size T bytes.
`int` **`can_be_opened`**`(const char *name)`	Returns 1 if named file can be opened otherwise returns 0.

Another issue with binary files is that they might not be portable between computers of different architectures. Specifically moving between little and big-endian will cause byte-swapping errors.

Some care is needed when opening named files for writing or appending. We use the parameters `"wb"` or `"ab"` in the open statements which will cause any existing file of the same name to be overwritten. If this is what you want, as is often the case when developing code, that is fine but in other situations care must be taken. In our examples, command line arguments are always arranged so the input file name is specified before the output file name. Since C++11, it is possible to use `"wbx"` which causes an error when opening an existing file. This could then be used to ask the user if they wanted to continue. Our function `can_be_opened` can be used to check if a file exists before passing it to a cx read or write function.

The functions are widely used in our examples but here we include another example illustrating their use to merge a set of files. This example is followed by a detailed description of the cxbinio code.

Example G.4 Use of `cxbinio.h` to merge a set of binary files

```
01   #include "cx.h"
02   #include "cxbinio.h"

03   int main(int argc,char *argv[])
04   {
05     if(argc < 3){
```

```
06        printf("Usage binio <input tag> <output file>
                              <input size>\n");
07        return 0;
08      }
09    // argv[1] is input file head - e.g. "test"
      // for test0000.raw to test0099.raw
10    // argv[2] is output file
      // argv[3] is input size in words
11    int size = (argc >3) ? atoi(argv[3]) : 1024;

      // define data type here, then implicit elsewhere
12    std::vector<ushort> buf(size);
13    int file = 0;
      // "9" is for head + nnnn.raw + \0
14    std::vector<char> name(strlen(argv[1])+9);
15    sprintf(&name[0],"%s%4.4d.raw",argv[1],file);

16    while(cx::can_be_opened(&name[0])){
17      if( cx::read_raw(&name[0],buf.data(),size,0)==0)
18        cx::append_raw(argv[2],buf.data(),size);
19      file++;
        // next file in sequence
20      sprintf(&name[0],"%s%4.4d.raw",argv[1],file);
21    }

22    printf("good files copied to %s\n",argv[2]);
23    return 0;
24  }
```

Description of Example G.4

This program merges a set of N files with names like `slice0000.raw`, `slice0001.raw` ... `slice0099.raw` for the case N=100 to a single output file. The files must all have the same data type and size.

- Lines 1–2: Include `cx.h` and `cxbinio.h`.
- Lines 5–8: Check if sufficient user arguments are present, if not print a helpful message and exit. We use this method of documenting for program arguments in the full versions of many of our examples.
- Lines 9–11: Three user supplied arguments are required, a header name for the input files, the full name of the single output file and the size in words of the input files. The data type (`ushort`) is hard wired into this simple example code.
- Line 12: Here we create a vector `buf` to hold the contents on one input file. Note the template type argument (`ushort` here) implicitly defines the data type used in the rest of the code. The compiler will automatically use the type of `buf.data()` as the template type for the `cxbinio` functions used in lines 16–18.
- Line 13: The variable `file` is used as the rank number of the file currently being processed.

- Line 14: Create a vector name of type char to hold the name of the current input file. It will be just big enough to hold the string generated by sprintf in lines 15 and 20. Note we need to include an extra character to hold the "0" byte that terminates a C-string. This approach is better than declaring a fixed size array, for example, "char name[256];" and hoping the user does not input a very large string.
- Lines 15: Uses sprintf to create the full name for the first file and store the result in the C string name. Note the use of %4.4d to create a zero padded value.
- Lines 16–21: This while loop processes each file in the sequence.
  ◦ Line 16: Checks if the current input file exists using cx::can_be_opened; the loop will terminate if it does not.
  ◦ Line 17: Calls cx::read_raw to read the current file and check the return value for success. We use the optional fourth argument to suppress the function's "file read" message.
  ◦ Line 18: Calls cx::append_raw to append the contents of buf to the output file.
  ◦ Line 19: Increment file to point to the next file in the sequence.
  ◦ Line 20: Uses sprintf to update the file name in name ready for the next pass through the while loop.
- Lines 22–23: Print a final message and exit.

Output from running the binio program on a set of 10 test files is shown in the box below.

```
D:\ >binio.exe test test_all.raw 1024
file test_all.raw appended
file test_all.raw appended
file test_all.raw appended
file test_all.raw appended
file test_all.raw appended
bad read on binio_test0005.raw got 3 items expected 1024
file test_all.raw appended
file test_all.raw appended
file test_all.raw appended
file test_all.raw appended
good files copied to test_all.raw
```

Results of running binio example on the set of 10 files test0000.raw – test0009.raw. The files are expected to have a length of 1024 words. The file test0005.raw too short and is not appended to the output file.

Example G.5 Header file cxbinio.h, part 1

```
    . . .
06  #include <stdio.h>
07  #include <stdlib.h>
08  #include <string.h>
    . . .
```

```
20   namespace cx {
21   // read an existing file.
22   template <typename T> int read_raw(const char
            *name, T *buf, size_t len, int verbose=1)
23   {
24     FILE *fin = fopen(name,"rb");
25     if(!fin) { printf("bad open on %s for read\n",
                                  name); return 1; }
26     size_t check = fread(buf,sizeof(T), len, fin);
27     if(check != len) {
28       printf("bad read on %s got %zd items expected
                        %zd\n", name, check, len);
29       fclose(fin); return 1;
30     }
31     if(verbose)printf("file %s read\n", name);
32     fclose(fin);
33     return 0;
34   }

35   // write to new file (CARE overwrites any existing
     //   version without warning)
36   template <typename T> int write_raw(const char
            *name, T *buf, size_t len, int verbose=1)
37   {
38     FILE *fout = fopen(name,"wb");
39     if(!fout) { printf("bad open on %s for write\n",
                                  name); return 1; }
40     size_t check = fwrite(buf, sizeof(T), len, fout);
41     if(check != len) {
42       printf("bad write on %s got %zd items expected
                        %zd\n", name, check, len);
43       fclose(fout); return 1;
44     }
45     if(verbose)printf("file %s written\n", name);
46     fclose(fout);
47     return 0;
48   }

50   // append to existing file or create new file
51   template <typename T> int  append_raw(const char
            *name, T *buf, size_t len, int verbose=1)
52   {
53     FILE *fout = fopen(name,"ab");
54     if(!fout) { printf("bad open on %s for append\n",
                                  name); return 1; }
55     int check = (int)fwrite(buf,sizeof(T),len,fout);
56     if(check != len) {
```

```
57        printf("bad append on %s got %d items expected
                                %zd\n", name, check, len);
58        fclose(fout);
69        return 1;
60     }
61     if(verbose)printf("file %s appended\n", name);
62     fclose(fout);
63     return 0;
64  }
65  // read len WORDS skipping first skip BYTES
66  template <typename T> int read_raw_skip(const char
            *name, T *buf ,size_t len, size_t skip,
                                        int verbose=0)
67  {
68     FILE *fin = fopen(name,"rb");
69     if(!fin) { printf("bad open on %s for read\n",
                                    name); return 1; }
70     if(fseek(fin,(long)skip,SEEK_SET)) {
71       printf("seek error on %s skip =%lld\n",
                            name,skip); return 1; }
72       size_t check = fread(buf,sizeof(T),len,fin);
73      if(check != len) {
74        printf("bad read on %s got %d items expected
                                %zd\n", name, check, len);
75        fclose(fin);
76        return 1;
77      }
78     if(verbose)printf("file %s read skiping %lld
                                bytes\n", name, skip);
79     fclose(fin);
80     return 0;
81  }
82  // returns length of file as bytes/sizeof(T)
    //i.e. type-T words
83  template <typename T> size_t length_of(const char
                                            *name)
84  {
85     FILE *fin = fopen(name,"rb");
86     if(!fin) { printf("bad open %s\n",name);
                                    return 0; }
87     fseek(fin,0,SEEK_END);
88     long offset = ftell(fin);
89     size_t len = offset/sizeof(T);
90     fclose(fin);
91     return len;
92  }
93  // test if file exists and is available for reading
```

```
 94  int can_be_opened(const char *name)
 95  {
 96    FILE *fin = fopen(name,"r");
 97    if(fin==nullptr) return 0;
 98    else fclose(fin);
 99    return 1;
100  }
```

A listing of the file cxbinio.h and detailed description follow.

Description of cxbinio.h

- Lines 6–8: Standard include files.
- Line 20: Everything is inside the cx namespace.
- Line 22: Declaration of the read_raw template function. The arguments are name a cstring containing the name of the file to be read, buf a pointer to an array of type T holding the data to be read, len the number of words to be written and verbose a flag to control printing. Note name can include a path.
- Line 24: Open the file for binary read, the handle fin will be null if an error occurs (e.g. the file does not exist).
- Line 25: print message and return if open was unsuccessful.
- Line 26: Perform the read operation using fread. Note two parameters specify the amount of data to be read, the word length (sizeof(T) here) and the number of words (len here). The function returns the number of words actually read.
- Lines 27–30: If the correct number of words has not been read, we print an error message, tidy up and return with a non-zero error code.
- Lines 31–33: If the correct number of words have been read, then we optionally print the filename and return with a zero error code.
- Lines 36–48: The function write_raw is almost identical to the read_raw except we open the file for binary write using "wb" instead of "rb" and call fwrite in line 40 instead of fread.
- Lines 50-64: This is the code for the function append_raw. This function is almost identical to write_raw() except that the output file is opened with "ab" instead of "wb" which means that data is appended to the end of the file instead of overwriting any previous contents. If the file does not already exist, it will be created as if "wb" had been specified.
- Lines 65–81: The code for the function read_raw_skip. This function is nearly the same as read_raw except that read process starts after the first skip bytes of data. The parameter skip is an additional input argument to this function. Note it is the user's responsibility to ensure the skip is a multiple of sizeof(T), otherwise memory alignment issues may occur.
- Lines 83–92: The function length_of which returns the length of the named file in words of size determined by the template parameter T. The function is implemented by using fseek to move the file position point to the end of the file and then using ftell to find the value of the pointer.
- Lines 94–100: The function can_be_opened does what you expect; it tries to open the named file for read and if successful returns one, otherwise it returns zero.

Before ending our discussion of binary IO it is worth mentioning that the ImageJ program discussed in Section 5.7 is a great tool for viewing the contents on binary files. One of its options is to replicate our Example G.4 and import a sequence of 2D images to a 3D stack. Such 3D stack can then be viewed and manipulated in many ways.

G.3 The Header File cxtimers.h

This short header file implements a simple timer object using the modern C++ `<chrono>` header. Like most PC timers this library allows you to record the wall clock times at various stages of your code and hence from time-differences infer the duration of code segments.

Unlike the early C and C++ PC timers which had a poor resolution on only 25 ms, chrono-based timers have a typical resolution of a microsecond or better.

Example G.6 Header file `cxtimers.h`

```
          . . .
16   // provides a MYTimer object for host bast elapsed time
        measurements.
17   // The timer depends on the C++ <chrono>
18   // usage: lap_ms() to returns interval since previous lap_ms(),
19   // start or reset.

21   #include <cstdio>
22   #include <cstdlib>
23   #include <chrono>

25   namespace cx {
26     class timer {
27     private:
28     std::chrono::time_point<std::chrono::high_resolution_clock>lap;
29     public:
30       timer(){ lap =
                   std::chrono::high_resolution_clock::now(); }
31       void start() { lap =
                   std::chrono::high_resolution_clock::now(); }
32       void reset() { lap =
                   std::chrono::high_resolution_clock::now(); }

34       double lap_ms()
35       {
36         auto old_lap = lap;
37         lap = std::chrono::high_resolution_clock::now();
38         std::chrono::duration<double,std::milli>
                             time_span = (lap - old_lap);
39         return (double)time_span.count();
40       }
```

```
42      double lap_us()
43      {
44        auto old_lap = lap;
45        lap = std::chrono::high_resolution_clock::now();
46        std::chrono::duration<double,std::micro>
                              time_span = (lap - old_lap);
47        return (double)time_span.count();
48      }
49    };
50  }
```

Description of cxtimers.h

- Line 23: The necessary header file `<crono>` is included here.
- Line 26: Declaration of the timer class.
- Line 28: The single member variable `lap` is declared here. It is of a type suitable to hold a single time measurement. This is intended to hold the start time for an interval measurement.
- Line 30: This is the default and only constructor. It sets `lap` to the current time. Thus, in simple use cases the statement `cx::timer tim;` both creates the timer object `tim` and sets the start time for an interval measurement.
- Lines 31–32: The two member functions `start` and `reset` both have the same effect of resetting the start time for an interval measurement to the current time. In a later release they may have different functions. These functions allow you to reuse a previously created timer.
- Lines 34–40: The member function `lap_ms` updates `lap` with the current time and returns the time interval between the new and old values of `lap`. The time interval is returned as a `double` in units of ms. Notice `lap` is reset to the current time by this call.
- Lines 42–49: This function is identical to `lap_ms` except the time interval is returned in units of microseconds.

For measuring overlapping time intervals, for example, the total job duration and the times of individual sections within the job, one can simply create multiple timer objects.

G.4 The Header File cxtextures.h

CUDA textures were introduced in Chapter 5 but those examples depended on the `cxtextures.h` header file to create and fill textures. Here we show the moderately verbose code needed to do these jobs.

On the device a texture is ultimately just a region of device global memory that has been allocated and filled by the host. This is just like the device arrays we use in many examples. However, data in the array is organised to be optimal for 2D nearest neighbour interpolation and is read via the special texture lookup (or fetched in NVIDIA's jargon) hardware. The device memory is memory allocated by the host and passed to the device wrapped in a texture object. The memory allocation is performed using either `cudaMallocArray` for 1D or 2D texture or `cudaMalloc3DArray` for 3D textures. Neither the ordinary

Table G.3 *Possible flags used in* `cudaTextureDesc`

mode	name	comment
address	cudaAddressModeWrap	The coordinate modulo the allowed range is used (normalized coordinates only).
	cudaAddressModeClamp	Coordinates are clamped to valid range.
	cudaAddressModeMirror	Like wrap but reflected i.e. x→1-x.
	cudaAddressModeBorder	Out of range coordinates return 0.
filter	cudaFilterModePoint	Nearest point.
	cudaFilterModeLinear	Linear interpolation.
read	cudaReadMode	Return native values.
	cudaReadModeNormalizedFloat	Returns floats in range [-1, 1], or [0, 1] for signed or unsigned 8 and 16 bit int types. Return values normalised so that 1 corresponds to max possible value.
coordinate	cudaCoordNormalized[†] (or 1)	Coordinates are normalised. For N pixels the range is [0, 1-1/N].
	cudaCoordNatural[†] (or 0)	Natural pixel range of values are used. For N pixels range is [0, N-1].
arraytype	cudaArrayDefault	Standard Texture.
	cudaArrayLayered	Stack of 1D or 2D textures.
	cudaArraySurfaceLoadStore	Similar to standard texture but can also be written to by kernels.
	cudaArrayCubemap	Specialized texture intended for graphics.
	cudaArrayTextureGather	Specialized texture intended for graphics.

More details can be found in the NVIDIA CUDA C++ Programming guide.
[†]These names are defined in cxtextures.h; standard CUDA simply uses 0 or 1.

`cudaMalloc` nor thrust can be used for this purpose. A total of five separate steps on the host are needed to create a texture object:

1. Allocate device memory using `cudaMallocArray` or `cudaMalloc3DArray`. The array dimensions and type are specified by creating a special `cudaChannelFormatDesc` structure and passing it as an argument to the allocation function. Note that this is where we specify the array type as a template parameter (T in our code) to the `cudaCreateChannelDesc` function. Allowed types are float, half and 1,2 or 4-byte integers. Built in vectors of length 2 or 4 are also allowed, e.g. `float2` and `float4` but not `float3`.

2. Copy host data to the allocated device memory using either `cudaMemcpyToArray` (1D or 2D) or `cudaMemcpy3D` (3D). The layout of your data after transfer to the device may be different.

3. Create a `cudaResourceDesc` stuct which holds the array pointer created in step 1.

4. Create a `cudaTextureDesc` struct which contains fields specifying various optional properties of your texture. The possible flags as shown in Table G.3 with brief descriptions.

5. Declare an instance of a `cudaTextureObject` and set its properties by calling `createTextureObject` with arguments that include the `structs` created in step 3 and step 4.

As indicated in the table there are several possible types of texture supported by the hardware and CUDA. In addition to the standard texture type used in our examples there are also layered textures and surfaces. A layered texture can be thought of as a stack of 1D or 2D textures with each slice separately addressable. A layered 2D texture would be suitable for processing a set of movie frames or MRI slices where each slice needed similar but separate processing. A surface texture is similar to a standard texture but can be written to be in kernel code. There is no attempt to maintain texture cache coherency between reads and write during kernel execution so in general any given kernel should only read or write to a surface.

The maximum sizes of standard textures are shown in Table 5.1 of Chapter 5. For a device of CC ≥ 6 the maximum dimensions for 1D or 2D layered textures are 16384 or 16384 × 16384 with up to 2048 layers. Full details of the limits for other texture types and required CC levels is given in the Compute Capabilities section of the NVIDIA CUDA C++ Programming Guide.

Kernels read from standard textures using the templated functions tex1D, tex2D and tex3D as discussed in Chapter 5. Other texture types use similar functions which are explained in the CUDA Programming Guide.

The cxtextures.h header provides objects txs1D, txs2D and txs3D which create standard textures and act as container classes for the cudaArray allocated in device memory to hold the textures. To use these classes, you only need to provide a pointer to the host array containing your data. The interface is similar for the three classes. To create a texture, provide the constructor with the array dimensions as an int1, int2 or int3 variable and a list of option flags as shown in the box:

```
cx::txsND<T> mytexN(m, data, filteropt, addressopt, readopt,
  normopt, arrayopt);
```

Where m has type intN and N is 1, 2 or 3. The options are selected from Table G.3. The final option defaults to cudaArrayDefault and should not be changed. T is the desired array type, for example, float, and data is a pointer to a host array of type T.

The member functions copyTo(T *data) and copyFrom(T *data) can be used by mytexN to transfer data between the host and GPU texture memory. Also, the public variables n and tex give access to the texture dimensions and the texture object itself. Thus one can use mytexN.n and mytexN.tex as kernel arguments.

A listing of cxtextures.h and descriptions follow.

Example G.7 Header file cxtextures.h, part 1

```
        . . .
06   #include "cuda_runtime.h"
07   #include "device_launch_parameters.h"
08   #include "helper_cuda.h"

09   #include <stdio.h>
```

```
10  #include <stdlib.h>
11  #include <string.h>

12  //============================================================
13
14  // Provides the C++ classes txs1D, txs2D and txs3D which
15  // hold CUDA textures of the indicated dimension. These
16  // classes have a simple interface for creating textures.
17  // The user supplies data for the texture as a simple
18  // pointer to a host array. The class allocates and manages
19  // the device texture memory held in a texture object which
20  // can be passed to CUDA kernels. The user also specifies
21  // values for the five CUDA texture options:

22  // cudaTextureFilterMode:  Point or Linear
23  // cudaTextureAddressMode: Wrap, Clamp, Mirror or Border
24  // cudaTextureReadMode:    ElementType or NormalizedFloat
25  // cudaCoordMode:          Normalised or Natural (or 0 or 1)
26  // cudaArray:              Default, Layered, SurfaceLoadStore,
27                             CubeMap or TextureGather
28
29  //============================================================

37  // CUDA does not define names for cudaCoordMode values
38  // which can be 0 or 1. Here cx defines names for these
39  // following the spirit of the other 4 options.
40  #define cudaCoordNormalized 1
41  #define cudaCoordNatural    0

42  namespace cx {  // the classes are in cx namespace
```

Example G.8 Header file `cxtextures.h`, part 2 – class `txs2D`

```
50  // class txs2D 2D-texture
51  template <typename T> class txs2D {
52    private:
53      cudaArray * carray;
54    public:
55      int2 n;
56      cudaTextureObject_t tex;

      // default constructor
57    txs2D(){ n ={0,0}; carray = nullptr; tex = 0; }

58    txs2D(int2 m, T *data,  // full constructor
```

```
                 cudaTextureFilterMode filtermode,
                 cudaTextureAddressMode addressmode,
                 cudaTextureReadMode readmode,
                 int normmode, int arrayType=cudaArrayDefault)
59  {
60    n = m; tex = 0; carray = nullptr;
61    cudaChannelFormatDesc cd = cudaCreateChannelDesc<T>();
62    cx::ok(cudaMallocArray(&carray,&cd,n.x,n.y,arrayType));

63    if(data != nullptr){
64      cx::ok(cudaMemcpyToArray(carray, 0, 0, data,
              n.x*n.y*sizeof(T), cudaMemcpyHostToDevice));
65    }

66    cudaResourceDesc rd ={};   // make ResourceDesc
67    rd.resType = cudaResourceTypeArray;
68    rd.res.array.array = carray;

69    cudaTextureDesc td ={};   // make TextureDesc
70    td.addressMode[0] = addressmode;
71    td.addressMode[1] = addressmode;
72    td.filterMode     = filtermode;
73    td.readMode       = readmode;
74    td.normalizedCoords = normmode;
75    cx::ok(cudaCreateTextureObject
                        (&tex, &rd, &td, nullptr));
76  }
77  // copy constructor
78  txs2D(const txs2D &txs2){ n = txs2.n; carray = nullptr;
                                        tex = txs2.tex; }

79  void copyTo(T *data) {
80    if(data != nullptr && carray != nullptr)
        cx::ok( cudaMemcpyToArray(carray, 0, 0, data,
            n.x*n.y*sizeof(T), cudaMemcpyHostToDevice) );
81    return;
82  }

83  void copyFrom(T *data) {
84    if(data != nullptr && carray != nullptr)
        cx::ok(cudaMemcpyFromArray(data, carray, 0, 0,
            n.x*n.y*sizeof(T), cudaMemcpyDeviceToHost) );
85    return;
86  }

    // destructor does nothing if this instance is a copy
87  ~txs2D() {
```

```
88      if(carray != nullptr){
89        if(tex != 0) cx::ok(cudaDestroyTextureObject(tex));
90        cx::ok(cudaFreeArray(carray));
91      }
92    }
93  };  // end class txs2D
```

Example G.9 Header file `cxtextures.h`, part 3 – class `txs3D`

```
100 // class txs3D 3D-texture
101 template <typename T> class txs3D {
102   private:
103     cudaArray * carray;
104   public:
105     int3 n;
106     cudaTextureObject_t tex;
107 // default and copy constructors
108   txs3D(){ n ={0,0,0}; carray = nullptr; tex = 0; }
109   txs3D(const txs3D &txs2){ n = txs2.n; carray = nullptr;
                                 tex = txs2.tex; }
    // copy to or from data
110   void copy3D(T* data, cudaMemcpyKind  copykind)
111   {
112     cudaMemcpy3DParms cp ={0};
113     cp.srcPtr   =
            make_cudaPitchedPtr(data,n.x*sizeof(T),n.x,n.y);
114     cp.dstArray = carray;
115     cp.extent   = make_cudaExtent(n.x,n.y,n.z);
116     cp.kind     = copykind;
117     cx::ok(cudaMemcpy3D(&cp));
118   }
119   txs3D(int3 m, T *data,
             cudaTextureFilterMode filtermode,
120          cudaTextureAddressMode addressmode,
             cudaTextureReadMode readmode,
121          int normmode, int arrayType=cudaArrayDefault )
122   {
123     n = m; tex = 0; carray = nullptr;

124     cudaChannelFormatDesc cd =   // make ChannelDesc
                      cudaCreateChannelDesc<T>();

125     cudaExtent cx =    // make cudaExtent
              {(size_t)n.x,(size_t)n.y,(size_t)n.z};
```

```
126       cx::ok(cudaMalloc3DArray(&carray,&cd,cx,arrayType));
127       if(data != nullptr)
                  copy3D(data, cudaMemcpyHostToDevice);

128       cudaResourceDesc rd ={};   // make ResourceDesc
129       rd.resType = cudaResourceTypeArray;
130       rd.res.array.array = carray;

131       cudaTextureDesc td ={};   // make TextureDesc
132       td.addressMode[0] = addressmode;
133       td.addressMode[1] = addressmode;
134       td.addressMode[2] = addressmode;
135       td.filterMode     = filtermode;
136       td.readMode       = readmode;
137       td.normalizedCoords = normmode;

138       cx::ok(
             cudaCreateTextureObject(&tex, &rd, &td, nullptr) );
139     }
140   void copyTo(T *data) {  // copy from data to texture
141     if(data!=nullptr && carray!=nullptr)
                  copy3D(data,cudaMemcpyHostToDevice);
142   }
143   void copyFrom(T *data) {  // copy to data from texture
144     if(data!=nullptr && carray!=nullptr)
                  copy3D(data,cudaMemcpyDeviceToHost);
145   }
146   ~txs3D() { // destructor does nothing if this instance is a copy
147     if(carray != nullptr) {
148       if(tex != 0) cx::ok(cudaDestroyTextureObject(tex));
149       cx::ok(cudaFreeArray(carray));
150     }
151   }
152 }; // end class txs3D
```

Description of cxtextures.h

Note this header file also contains the definition of the class tex1D which is almost identical to tex2D. In fact, CUDA implements a 1D texture of length nx as a 2D texture having dimensions nx ×1. Therefore, the class tex1D is omitted from the listings and discussion here. The full listing is of course in our code repository.

- Lines 1–39: These lines are self-explanatory.
- Lines 40–41: Define names for the two types of coordinate normalisation mode following NVIDIA's model for other texture modes.
- Line 42: The cx namespace (re)starts here for everything else in the header file.

- Lines 51–97: Contain the definition of the `txs2D` template class. The class `txs1D` (not shown here) is almost identical to `txs2D` except that n becomes an `int1` variable and `n.y` is replaced by 1.
- Lines 52–53: The single private variable `carray` is declared here. This is a pointer to the `cudaArray` used to hold the texture. The caller does not need to access this array directly.
- Lines 54–56: Here the two public class variables are declared; n is an `int2` variable that holds the dimensions of the 2D texture and `tex` is the 2D texture object to be created and is suitable for passing to GPU kernels as an argument.
- Line 57: This is the default class constructor; it is not intended to be used.
- Lines 58–79: This is the constructor used to create instances of `txs2D` objects.
- Line 58: The constructor arguments are as follows:
  - `int2 m`: `m.x` and `m.y`: These are the dimensions of the 2D array.
  - `T *data`: This is the pointer to a host array used as the source of the texture data. Note the template parameter T for the data type.
  - `cudaTextureFilterMode filtermode`: the required filter mode
  - `cudaTextureAddressMode addressmode`: the required address mode
  - `cudaTextureReadMode readmode`: the required read mode
  - `int normmode`: the required normalisation mode
  - `int arrayType`: the required array type. Note a default value of `cudaArrayDefault` is supplied for this parameter so it can be omitted by the caller. This argument is intended for future development and should not be changed.
- Line 60: The class variable n is set to m and the other class variables are cleared.
- Line 61: Declare and initialise the `cudaChannelFormatDesc` variable `cd` using `cudaCreateChannelDesc<T>()`. The only parameter is T, but the apparent simplicity here is misleading; CUDA supplies different objects using specialised instances of the function `cudaCreateChannelDesc` for all valid choices of T. Code using early versions of the SDK may be more verbose here.
- Line 62: Allocates a 2D CUDA array in GPU memory and copies a pointer to `carray`. Note we have wrapped the allocation in `cx::ok` to get feedback on errors. This is done for most of the critical CUDA calls in this header file.
- Lines 63–65: The host data is copied to the GPU here; changes to the layout in memory may occur.
- Lines 66–68: Make a `cudaResourceDesc rd` to hold the pointer `carray`.
- Lines 69–74: Make a `cudaTextureDesc td` to hold the texture mode options.
- Line 75: Create the texture object `tex` using `rd` and `td`.
- Line 78: Definition of a copy constructor. The copy will hold current copies of the public variables but `carray` is set to null so that the copy's destructor will not attempt to free resources.
- Lines 79–82: The member function `copyTo` which allow users to change the data stored in the texture – obviously this call is only used between kernel calls. Note the texture does not need to be recreated to do this.
- Lines 83–86: The member function `copyFrom` which allows data to be copied back from the texture to the host. This is not normally useful for standard textures but would be useful for similar code using surfaces.
- Lines 87–92: The class destructor which frees the resources allocated by the call. This automatic freeing of resources is the reason container classes help simplify your code. Note copies of the class made using the copy constructor will not free resources when they go out of scope. Thus there is a tacit assumption that the parent instance of this class will go out of scope last. A copy count could be used here if you wanted to be extra careful.
- Lines 101–152: These are the body of the `txs3D` class which provides support for 3D textures.

- Lines 101–106: The start of this class is the same as `txs2D` with the corresponding declarations of the member variables `carray`, `n` and `tex` except that `n` is `int3` rather than `int2`.
- Lines 108–109: The default and copy constructors are declared here.
- Lines 110–118: This is a new member function `copy3D` for copying data between the host and GPU. For 3D textures GPU memory needs to be allocated using `cudaMalloc3DArray` rather than `cudaMallocArray`. Transferring data to or from such 3D arrays is more verbose than the just calling one of `cudaMemcpyToArray` or `cudaMemcpyFromArray`. For 3D we need `cudaMemcpy3D` and this function takes a `cudaMemcpy3DParms` object as its one argument. Since we need this operation several times we have written a separate function for this task.
  - ◦ Line 110: The arguments are `data`, the pointer to the host data, and a `cudaMemcpyKind` flag `copykind` indicating the direction of transfer. The class member variables `carray` and `n` are also used.
  - ◦ Line 112: Create and clear the `cudaMemcpy3DParms` object `cp`.
  - ◦ Lines 113–116: Set the various fields in `cp` according to the CUDA recipe book. Both 2D and 3D cudaArray types are actually allocated with the x-dimension rounded up to be a multiple of 512 bytes; the `PitchedPtr` created in line 113 allows for this. Notice `n.z` is not used here but is used in line 115.
  - ◦ Line 117: Call `cudaMemcpy3D` – the actual call is nicely concise.
- Lines 119–139: This is the constructor used to create instances of `txs3D` objects. The arguments are identical to those of `txs2D` except the array dimensions `m` are specified with an `int3` variable instead of `int2`.
- Lines 123–124: These are the same as 60–61 for `txs2D`.
- Line 125: Here we create a `cudaExtent` object which holds the array dimensions in bytes. Such objects are only used for the 3D case.
- Line 126 Here we allocate the array using `cudaMalloc3DArray` instead of `cudaMallocArray`.
- Line 127: Here we call `copy3D` to transfer host data to the newly allocated GPU array. Note the transfer direction flag is `cudaMemcpyHostToDevice`.
- Lines 128–137: Here we create resource and texture description objects this is the same as before except that `td` has a third dimension specified in line 134.
- Line 138: Here we finally create the texture.
- Lines 140–150: The two data copy functions and class destructor are the same as before except that we use our `copy3D` function instead directly calling CUDA transfer functions.

Elements in 2D textures and slices of 3D textures are laid out to optimise local 2D addressing with small strides between elements. This is discussed next.

G.5 Morton Ordering

According to the CUDA documentation, data stored in GPU texture memory is ordered to optimise 2D addressing. The layout is unspecified and is subject to change between SDK releases. However, it is likely that some version of Morton ordering is used.

In most of this book we use row-major ordering where the index values increase monotonically along the x-axis or row and jump by the value of the x-dimension along the y-axis or between rows. In Morton ordering, a linear address is used but the address bits for x and y are interleaved, thus for an address contained in `int k`, x is defined by the even bits of `k` and y is defined by the odd bits of `k`. This is illustrated in Figures G.1 and G.2.

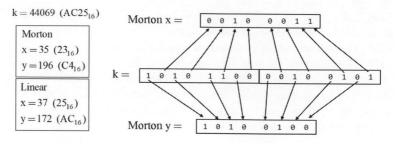

Figure G.1 Interpretation of 2D array index as Morton and row-major order

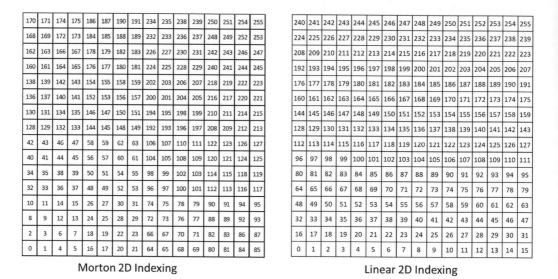

Figure G.2 2D array addresses in Morton and row-major order

Figure G.2 Two 16×16 arrays are shown with each element's position in memory shown in the boxes. Morton indexing is shown on the left and conventional row-major indexing is shown on the right. In the Morton case the indices for nearest neighbours in x and y tend to have similar values but when using conventional linear addressing the indices differ by 16. In the Morton case increasingly larger index jumps occur at increasingly large power of 2 boundaries.

G.6 Header File cxconfun.h

This is a small collection of maths functions which return `constexpr` values and thus can be used to calculate derived values in header files at compile time. The standard intrinsic functions cannot be used for this purpose because they do not return values declared as constexpr. The power series we use to calculate the functions converge well but these functions may not be as accurate as the runtime intrinsics.

Example G.10 Header file cxconfun.h

```
14 //==================================================================
15 // small set of constexpr math functions to be evaluated at
16 // compile time. Power series for sin and cos good for angles
17 // in [-2pi,2pi]. The tan function cuts off singularity at
18 // 10^9. We need to specify a fixed number of terms or
19 // iterations to keep compiler happy.
20 //==================================================================
21  namespace cx {
       // factorial n only works for n <= 12
22     constexpr int factorial_cx(int n)
23     {
24       int k = 1;
25       int f = k;
26       while(k <= n) f *= k++;
27       return f;
28     }
       // sin(x) x in radians
29     constexpr double sin_cx(double x)
30     {
31       double s = x; int nit = 1;
32       double fnit = 1.0;
33       double term = x;
34       while(nit < 12) {  // compile time evaluation
35         term *= -x * x / (2.0*fnit*(2.0*fnit + 1.0));
36         s += term;
37         nit++; fnit++;
38       }
39     return s;
40     }
       // cos(x) x in radians
41     constexpr double cos_cx(double x)
42     {
43       double s = 1;
44       int nit = 1; double fnit = 1.0;
45       double term = 1.0;
46       while(nit < 12) {   // compile time evaluation
47         term *= -x * x / (2.0*fnit*(2.0*fnit - 1.0));
48         s += term;
49         nit++; fnit++;
50       }
51       return (float)s;
52     }
       // tan(x) x in radians
53     constexpr double tan_cx(double x)
54     {
```

```
55        double s = sin_cx(x);
56        double c = cos_cx(x);
57        double t = 0.0;
58        if(c > 1.0e-9 || c < -1.0e-09) t = s/c;
59        else if(c >= 0.0) t = s/1.0e-9;
60        else t = -s/1.0e-09;
61        return t;
62      }
     // square root of abs(x)
63      constexpr double sqrt_cx(double x)
64      {
65        // return root of abs
66        if(x < 0) x = -x;
67        // NB sqrt(x) > x if x < 1
68        float step = (x >= 1.0) ? x/2.0 : 0.5;
69        float s =     (x >= 1.0) ? x/2.0 : x;
70        int nit = 32;   // explicit for compile time evaluation
71        while(nit >0) {
72          if(s*s > x) s -= step;
73          else        s += step;
74          step *= 0.5;
75          nit-;
76        }
77        return s;
78      }
69    }
80  //  end file cxconfun.h
```

The code in these functions is straightforward. We use repeated multiplication for factorial n. The integer data type used in lines 24 and 25 means the result will have overflow errors for $n > 12$. This could be improved by changing the type to double which gives exact value up to n=18 and 15 significant figures of accuracy thereafter. The `unsigned long long` data type could also be used to extend the precise range slightly further.

The sin and cos functions sum the first 12 terms of the standard power series which gives accurate results for small angles, ideally adjusted to be in the range $[-\pi,\pi]$. The tan function is evaluated from the ratio of sin and cos with a cut-off near the singularity where cos is zero.

The square root function uses a binary chop iteration with 32 steps starting from a guess. A different guess is used for the cases $x < 1$ and $x > 1$.

The examples in our book use the tan function once in the PET chapter. The other functions are not used at all and we do not claim any of these functions are efficient.

Appendix H

AI and Python

One of the most important current applications of GPUs is the field of artificial intelligence (AI) or more precisely machine learning (ML) or deep learning. In this field, a training data set is used to train a neural network to perform some data analysis task, for example, recognising cats in digital images. Once trained, the neural network can be used to process new data. Such trained networks are in daily use now for a large and growing variety of tasks. Recent NVIDIA GPU hardware innovations, including tensor cores, have been aimed specifically at these applications.

AI developers for the most part use high-level programming tools, usually Python-based, to link pre-existing modules to build neural networks of varying complexity and then train and deploy them. The low-level tools themselves are doubtless written in C++ and use carefully optimised CUDA kernels, but most users will not be exposed to those details. In this appendix we list some of the rich library of AI tools available from NVIDIA for AI developers.

Finally, we also mention some ways in which Python programs can write kernel code directly, bypassing C++. It turns out that the resulting kernels are written in the same CUDA as we use throughout this book; it is just that Python maintains the interface arrays. We think our book is certainly useful for such developers.

H.1 NVIDIA Tools and Libraries for AI

The following snapshot of available tools from the NVIDIA website was taken in January 2021: https://docs.nvidia.com/deeplearning/index.html.

- **Optimised Frameworks**
  The NVIDIA Optimised Frameworks such as Kaldi, NVIDIA Optimised Deep Learning Framework, powered by Apache MXNet, NVCaffe, PyTorch, and TensorFlow (which includes DLProf and TF-TRT) offer flexibility with designing and training custom deep neural networks (DNNs) for machine learning and AI applications.

- **cuDNN**
  The NVIDIA CUDA Deep Neural Network (cuDNN) library is a GPU-accelerated library of primitives for deep neural networks. cuDNN provides highly tuned implementations for standard routines such as forward and backward convolution, pooling, normalisation, and activation layers. Deep learning researchers and framework developers worldwide rely on cuDNN for high-performance GPU acceleration.

- **TensorRT**

  The NVIDIA TensorRT is an SDK for high-performance deep learning inference. It includes a deep learning inference optimiser and runtime that delivers low latency and high throughput for deep learning inference applications. The core of NVIDIA TensorRT is a C++ library that facilitates high-performance inference on NVIDIA GPUs. TensorRT takes a trained network, which consists of a network definition and a set of trained parameters and produces a highly optimised runtime engine which performs inference for that network.

- **Triton Inference Server**

  The NVIDIA Triton Inference Server (formerly TensorRT Inference Server) provides a cloud inferencing solution optimised for NVIDIA GPUs. The server provides an inference service via an HTTP or GRPC endpoint, allowing remote clients to request inferencing for any model being managed by the server.

- **NCCL**

  The NVIDIA Collective Communications Library (NCCL) is a library of multi-GPU collective communication primitives that are topology-aware and can be easily integrated into applications. Collective communication algorithms employ many processors working in concert to aggregate data. NCCL is not a full-blown parallel programming framework; rather, it is a library focused on accelerating collective communication primitives.

- **DALI**

  The NVIDIA Data Loading Library (DALI) is a collection of highly optimised building blocks, and an execution engine, to accelerate the pre-processing of the input data for deep learning applications. DALI provides both the performance and the flexibility for accelerating different data pipelines as a single library. This single library can then be easily integrated into different deep learning training and inference applications.

H.2 Deep Learning Performance and Documentation

GPUs accelerate machine learning operations by performing calculations in parallel. Many operations, especially those representable as matrix multiplication will see good acceleration right out of the box. Even better performance can be achieved by tweaking operation parameters to efficiently use GPU resources. The performance documents present the tips that we think are most widely useful.

- **DIGITS**

  The NVIDIA Deep Learning GPU Training System (DIGITS) can be used to rapidly train highly accurate DNNs for image classification, segmentation and object detection tasks. DIGITS simplifies common deep learning tasks such as managing data, designing and training neural networks on multi-GPU systems, monitoring performance in real time with advanced visualisations, and selecting the best performing model from the results browser for deployment.

- **NVIDIA GPU Cloud**

  The NVIDIA GPU Cloud (NGC) is a GPU-accelerated cloud platform optimised for deep learning and scientific computing. NGC empowers AI researchers with fast and easy access to performance-engineered deep learning framework containers, pre-integrated and optimised by NVIDIA.

- **DGX Systems**

  NVIDIA DGX Systems provide integrated hardware, software, and tools for running GPU-accelerated, HPC applications such as deep learning, AI analytics, and interactive visualisation.

Additional Deep Learning Resources

Another useful NVIDIA resource is the developer web pages at https://developer.nvidia .com/deep-learning which include the following links:

- **Deep leaning SDKs**: https://developer.nvidia.com/deep-learning-software.
- **Deep Learning Frameworks**: https: //developer.nvidia.com/deep-learning-frameworks.
- **Tensor Core Optimised Model Scripts**: https://developer.nvidia.com/deep-learning-examples.

NVIDIA's Python Toolkit

NVIDIA supports CUDA development in Python as an alternative to C++. This support is based on the Anaconda Python distribution and details can be found at the web page: https:// developer.nvidia.com/how-to-cuda-python. You will also need the standard CUDA SDK used elsewhere in our book to run these tools.

- **PyCUDA**

  This is an alternative route to kernel programming in Python and allows you to write full C++ kernels as used thought this book. The place to start is: https://documen.tician.de/pycuda/ but this project is now supported by NVIDIA and is linked to from https:// developer.nvidia.com/pycuda.

- **NeMo**

  NVIDIA NeMo is a flexible Python toolkit enabling data scientists and researchers to build state-of-the-art speech and language deep learning models composed of reusable building blocks that can be safely connected together for conversational AI applications.

Appendix I

Topics in C++

This section is not intended to teach you C++; rather it highlights a few topics that we have found to be useful in our, rather long, programming life. C++ is an enormous language and continues to grow with each new revision. I expect readers to have some familiarity with the basics of C (which is a subset of C++) and C++ but by no means expert knowledge. This book is about writing code for scientific applications – that means processing data, simulation of experiments and perhaps theoretical calculations. We only use a few of the advanced features of modern C++; we do use some of the features introduced with C++11 but little beyond that. We do not use OOP (object orientated programming) in any real sense; we have a few classes with their own methods but there are no class hierarchies here. On the other hand, we like template functions and some details like giving function arguments default values. Our programming is mostly algorithmic and we do not think anyone with some basic programming experience will find our code difficult to follow. Each piece of code that we present is accompanied by a rather detailed line-by-line discussion.

I.1 Coding Style

There is no such thing as a unique "best" coding style for any computer language, although there are probably lots of poor styles around. In this book, we use a rather more compact style than, for example, the CUDA SDK. This reflects the fact that we are not writing code for complex projects with large teams; rather we are crafting quite modest programs to do defined single computational tasks often of a mathematical nature. Thus, in particular we favour short variable names e.g. P for a matrix instead of say `image_point_spread_function`. This makes our code read more like a conventional mathematical text and importantly allows substantial pieces of code to be displayed on a single page of the book. Seeing a whole routine on one page improves one's ability to quickly understand how it works. We would actually go even further; we think CUDA kernel code can be an exceptionally expressive and elegant way of encapsulating parallel algorithms and these qualities are best captured by presenting kernels using a good but compact coding style.

We favour using single letter `int` or `uint` variables from the list i, j, k, l, m and n as loop counters. This follows ancient Fortran traditions and mathematical notation for subscripts in matrix work and similar applications. Again, we think this makes algorithmic code easy to understand.

We also like the RAII (resource acquisition is allocation). In practice, this means that our variables are declared and initialised in a single statement whenever possible. Annoyingly, CUDA SDK functions are often used to initialise variables passed as function arguments; in these cases we try to put both declaration and initialisation on the same line of code:

Use:
```
      float *a; cudaMalloc(&a, asize*sizeof(a));
```
rather than;
```
      float *a;
      cudaMalloc(&a, asize*sizeof(a));
```

For this reason, we also rather like the C/C++ ternary operator (? :) even though it can make code look rather opaque until you get used to it. The interesting feature of the ternary operator is that it returns a value and hence can be used anywhere a value is required which is not the case for an `if/else` statement. A good example of its use is setting variables from the user settable command line parameters. This is shown in section I.1.3 below.

Try as we may we are unable to warm to the C++ `<iostream>` classes. If you care about the layout of results from a calculation and want fine control of the number of significant figures, then these classes are simply too verbose. Instead, we use `printf` which is compact and gives good control over the final layout.

I.1.1 The RAII principle

RAII stands for resource acquisition is initialisation; in practice, it means that we like to initialise our variables and objects at the point they are declared. We dislike the older Fortran style declaration of variable names at the start of functions away from their point of first use. This includes `for` loops where we like to declare the loop counter in the loop header, e.g. `for(int k=0;k<10;k++)`.

II.1.2 Argc and Argv

We always declare our main routine in the form type `main(int argc, char *argv[])`. This allows us to give our programs very simply implemented command line user interfaces. This is in fact the mechanism used by commands in the original Unix operating system which were written as C programs; that legacy lives on in modern Linux operating systems and no doubt also in many Windows command line launched applications. In case you are not already a fan of these parameters, `argc` is the number of white-space separated options specified on the command line when the program was launched and `argv` is an array of cstrings where the strings contain the individual options in the order they were specified. The first element of `argv` is always the program name used to launch the job; this includes any explicit path used. An example is shown in the box.

```
Command:
    C: >prog1.exe infile outfile 256 128
Values in main:
    argc    = 5
    argv[0] = prog1.exe  argv[1] = infile    argv[2] = outfile
    argv[3] = 256        argv[4] = 128
```

II.1.3 The C++ Ternary Operator

This operator inherited from C is something of an oddity, it takes the form:

$$(test) \; ? \; val1 \; : \; val2$$

Where `test` is a logical test returning either Boolean `true` or `false` and the expression evaluates to either `val1` if the test is true or `val2` if the test is false. The box shows an example of how we use the ternary operator to set a parameter from either the command line option if present or a default if not.

```
Using ternary operator
    int asize   =   (argc >4) ? atoi(argv[4])  :  256;
Using if/else
    int asize = 0;
    if(argc >4) asize = atoi(argv[4]);
    else        asize = 256;
```

This example shows how one might set an array size parameter from fourth user supplied parameter on the command using a default value of 256. Most of our examples have this style of user interface. One disadvantage of this simple method is that users have to specify options in the correct order and have to give explicit values for all options preceding any option whose default value is to be changed. A more robust approach is obviously desirable for production code; the `cxoptions.h` code in our repository is one possibility.

I.2 Function Arguments and Return Values

C++ functions can have any number of input arguments and can return a single item. In our code the returned item is usually a numerical value typically an `int` or `float`, but in other cases it could be a C++ object or pointer. Arguments are passed to functions in one of three ways:

1. By **value** – in this case, when the function is called, the compiler makes a copy of the item being passed and passes that copy to the function. During execution a function may change the value it received but since these are changed in a copy, the caller's version of the item passed will not be changed when called function returns. This method is good for passing single numerical values but problematic for passing arrays as the entire array would need to be copied and that is expensive or impossible for large arrays.

2. As a **pointer** – in this case a pointer to the item in the caller's memory space is passed. If the argument is the array a then the pointer is passed as `*a` and the function can access the elements as `a[index]`. If the argument is a single variable then the argument can be accessed as either `*a` or `a[0]`. If pointers are used the function can change the caller's version of the item by simply writing to it. This can be prevented if the function declares the contents of the item as constant by using `int * const a` instead of simply `int * a` in the function argument list.

3. As a **reference** – here the function receives a reference to the item in the caller's memory space. If the reference is passed as say `int &a` then if a is an array its elements can be accessed as `a[index]` just like the pointer case. If a is just a simple variable it can be read or written to as if it had been passed by value, but any change will be seen by the caller because the caller's version of a is directly accessed by the function. Changing the contents of a can be prevented by declaring the argument `const int &a`. Passing by reference is better than passing by value for large objects unless there is a specific reason for making a copy, for example, the function makes changes which should not be seen by the caller.

Note that in CUDA programs, the arguments passed by the host to a kernel function must be either passed by value or as a pointers to previously allocated GPU main memory. Items passed by value are automatically copied to GPU memory. GPU constant memory space will be used for these items if possible. Arguments cannot be passed by reference. A CUDA kernel cannot return a value back to the host via the arguments or a return value (which must be declared `void`). If you are using CUDA managed memory allocations then some of these restrictions are implicitly lifted because the same physical memory might be used by both the host and the GPU.

I.3 Container Classes and Iterators

Many problems in scientific computing involve dynamically allocated arrays and we very much like using container classes such as `std::vector` to hold such arrays. This is because they automatically free the memory allocations when allocated objects go out of scope. This removes the need for programmers to remember to explicitly free allocated memory. In our examples, we use thrust vectors for both host and device arrays. This results in more compact code with no impact on kernel performance. Thrust device vectors differ from std::vector in one detail; if A is either a `std::vector` or a `thrust::host_vector` then the member function `A.data()` returns a pointer to the memory buffer holding the array. However, if A is a `thrust::device_vector` then the member function `A.data()` exists but does not return a pointer, we have to use the cast `thrust::raw_pointer_cast(a.data())` or `thrust::raw_pointer_cast(&a[0])`; both these casts actually use the undocumented function `A.data().get()` and we use this directly in most of our examples for kernel arguments thus saving the need to clutter code with otherwise unnecessary pointer variables.

For numerical work we think the good old for loop cannot be bettered and, therefore, we have used simple for loops throughout this book. However, C++ introduced the concept of an iterator as a generalisation for the traditional integer loop counter. Our Example I.1 shows three ways of looping over the elements of a vector in modern C++.

Example I.1 Iterators in C++

```
01   #include <stdio.h>
02   #include <stdlib.h>
03   #include <vector>

04   int main(int argc, char *atgv[])
05   {
06     std::vector<int> a(100); // vector of 100 elements
07     // set elements of a to (0,1,2...,99)

08     // Traditional for loop
09     // at each step k is an index to an element of the array
10     for(int k=0;k<100;k++) a[k] = k;
11     printf("a[20] = %d\n",a[20]);

12     // C++ iterator over the elements of a
13     // at each step iter is a pointer to an element of a
14     int k=100;
15     for(auto iter = a.begin(); iter != a.end();
                                  iter++) iter[0] = k++;
16     printf("a[20] = %d\n", [20]);

17     // C++11 range-based loop,
18     // at each step iter is a reference to an element
19     for (auto &iter : a) iter = k++;
20     printf("a[20] = %d\n", a[20]);

21     return 0;
22   }


D:\  >iter.exe
a[20] = 20
a[20] = 120
a[20] = 220
```

Description of Example I.1

- Lines 1–3: Include files.
- Line 6: Declares a as an array of 100 `ints`.
- Line 10: Initialises the elements of a to the values 0,1,2,...,99. Notice the loop counter k is being used both as an arithmetic value and an index here. This is common practice in numerical work but arguably it is bad style. If we change between C++ and FORTRAN indexing which starts at 1 not 0 then we have to remember to change the expressions involving k by adding or subtracting 1. This is a big potential source of off-by-one bugs. The alternative looping styles in lines 15 and 19 do not use an explicit arithmetic loop counter so there is less chance of confusion.
- Line 11: Print element a[20] as a check; we expect 20.
- Line 14: Introduce an explicit arithmetic variable k for use in loop calculations.
- Line 15: This is an iterator style for loop in C++. It will work for any container class in the standard library and indeed should work for anything claiming to be a container class, including thrust classes. The iterator variable `iter` is typically implemented as pointer to elements of the container class and then the loop is just a standard for loop using the pointer variable as the loop counter. At the end of each pass `iter` will be incremented using pointer arithmetic. The member functions `begin()` and `end()` return pointers to the first element of the array and one beyond the last element of the array, respectively.

  Because on each pass `iter` is a pointer to the current element we address it using `iter[0]` for all elements of the vector a. The variable k is explicitly incremented here, decoupling the arithmetic required by the program logic from that required by the loop.
- Line 16: Prints element a[20] as a check; we expect 120.
- Line 19: This is C++11 range-based for loop which effectively reads as "for `iter` ranging over all elements of a execute the dependent statement". Notice in this version `iter` is a reference to an element of a not a pointer; thus we set its value without using an index.
- Line 20: Prints element a[20] as a check; we expect 220.

Notice the range-based loop in line 19 hides all the details of the order in which elements are processed. This is just the sort of syntax we might use in a parallel program. Assigning values using k++ is arguably a potential bug in line 19; it will only work if elements are in fact accessed in their natural order – in fact the current C++ standard currently guarantees statements will be executed sequentially in the same order as a standard for loop.

Container classes have other uses in C++, `std::vector` objects can contain any type including any built-in or user defined class. The standard library contains other types of container class such as maps, lists and queues, these are intended for non-numerical work and more information can be found online or in any good book on C++. We do not need any of these features in this book.

Templates

We really like C++ templated functions; they are an elegant solution to the problem of writing a set of functions that perform the same operation on different data types. Suppose we want to write a function to calculate a saxpy-like linear combination a*X+Y where X and Y are one type and a is either the same type or a different type. The box shows two versions of the function, one standard version for the case where X and Y are floats and a is an int and one templated version which works for all types for which the (possibly overload) operators * and + are defined.

Standard function

```
float saxpy1(float x, float y, int a) {return a*x+y;}
e.g.  float z = saxpy1(x,y,5); where x and y have type float.
```

Templated function

```
template <typename T, typename S> T saxpy2(T x, T y, S a) )
  {return a*x+y;}
e.g.  float z = saxpy2(x,y,5); where x and y have type float.
or   float3 z = saxpy2(x3,y3,5); where x and y have type float3.
```

The way template functions work is that whenever the compiler finds a call to saxpy2 in your code it will examine the arguments and replace T with whatever common type x and y have and replace S with the type of a throughout the function. Note in this case the return type of the function is specified as T. The compiler will generate separate functions for each different combination of types encountered in the complete program. Often short template functions will be automatically inlined. Sometimes the compiler needs help deciding on which types to use, and in that case you can specify the types explicitly, for example, saxpy2<float3,int>(x,y,5). CUDA kernels and device function can be templated and it is always necessary to supply explicit template parameters when launching templated kernels.

Template parameters can either be types preceded by the keyword typename (or class for historic reasons) or an integer preceded by the keyword int. Templated integer values are useful in cases where the compiler needs to know their values, for example, fixed array dimensions or const values and also in cases where a hint for unrolling for loops or other optimisations is useful.

Templates can also be applied to class or struct definitions and to constexpr definitions.

I.4 Casts

In C/C++ a cast is used in expression to change the type of the value held in an object, for example, to convert a float value to an int value. Note it is the value that is converted not the declared type of the object concerned. (Beware Python is not the same; here the type of a named variable can change.)

For arithmetic work this is conceptually straightforward, although care is required to avoid unintended conversions. In C++ casts can also be used to change class objects typically moving them up and down class hierarchies – this can get really complicated but fortunately we need none of this in our book. A simple example of float to int casing is shown in the box:

```
float pi = 3.145;

(a)  int p = pi;              // implicit cast
(b)  int p = (int)pi;        // C cast convert float value to int value
(c)  int p = int(pi);        // C cast alternative style
(d)  int p = static_cast<int>(pi);   // C++ recommended style
```

In line (a) the value in `pi` is implicitly rounded to an integer and the result stored is stored in p. Rounding occurs towards zero; thus p will hold the value 3. The statement `p = -pi;` would store the value -3 in p.

Line (b) has the same effect as (a) and would suppress any compiler warning. Very importantly it tells anyone reading the code that the programmer intended a conversion to take place. We use this form of cast in numerical expressions throughout the book.

Line (c) is an alternative version of (b) available in C++; we prefer (b) because (c) is too easily confused with function syntax.

Line (d) is the recommended C++ version for this case. Most books on C++ will tell you that casting is undesirable and the ugly syntax is intended to discourage use of casts. This may well be true when playing with classes but it is certainly not true when crafting mixed precision expressions to achieve maximum compute performance on CPUs or GPUs. We unashamedly use C casts of type (b) throughout our code.

The C casting style will also work on pointers but in C++ we need to use `reinterpret_cast` instead of `static_cast`. In some cases, we do choose the verbose C++ version to emphasise the slightly tricky nature of the code. Our vector-loading kernels are an example of this.

C++ also has `const_cast` for changing the const nature of objects and `dynamic_cast` for playing with classes. Neither of these are used in this book.

I.5 Cstrings

The C and C++ types `char` and `unsigned char` are 8-bit integer types on an equal footing with the other 16, 32 and 64-bit integer types. With renewed interest in mixed precision arithmetic, they have an important role to play.

Arrays of type `char` containing ASCII character codes have long been used to represent character strings in C; such strings are terminated by the first zero character encountered when reading the string sequentially from the start. In a bug-free world of benign users such strings are perfectly acceptable. In the real world, the fragile termination convention used by cstrings has been the source of many bugs and enabled hostile attacks. C++ introduced a proper string class with a much more robust management of string operations. Hence cstrings are now rather deprecated. Nevertheless, we make some use of cstrings in our book, mainly to handle command line arguments via the argc and argv variables.

One example where cstrings are useful is passing filenames to the `cx::binio` routine `read_raw`:

```
(a)  cx::read_raw("indata.raw",inbuf,1000);
(b)  cx::read_raw(argv[1],inbuf,1000);
```

Where read_raw is declared as

```
(c)  int read_raw(const char *name, float *buf, int size);
```

In line (a): We call `read_raw` with an explicit string literal as the name of the file to be read. Note in both C and C++, string literals like this are cstrings.

Line (b): This is similar except the cstring is contained in `char * argv[1]`. This is used with command line arguments.

Line (c): Shows the declaration of `read_raw` for data of type float; the first argument which receives the cstring is declared as `const char *name`. The `const` qualifier is mandatory in modern C++ and mitigates some of the dangers inherent in cstrings.

I.6 Const

The const keyword can be used in both C and C++ to qualify the type in a declaration; this means that once initialised the declared object cannot be changed. A full discussion of all the gory details surrounding `const` can be found in textbooks; here we briefly describe what is done in this book.

Some C++ texts are very keen to emphasise *const correctness* in code, which roughly means all items that are not changed in a function must be declared `const`. Our experiments suggest that adding `const` to kernel or device function arguments does not yield any performance gains. This is in contrast to the `restrict` keyword which can make a big difference. In fact, we do try to use `const` with pointers to input data buffers, but we may sometimes omit it for scalar parameters such as array dimensions. The use of `const` for such parameters is to protect programmers from accidently changing them; this is certainly good practice but in simple cases, especially if these parameters are not passed to other functions, the compiler can presumably tell that these parameters do not get changed and so make the same optimisations it would have done if they had been declared `const`.

The use of `const` to protect code from accidental side-effects when calling functions is much more important in large projects with multiple programmers contributing to the code.

I.7 Max/Min

These simple functions are widely used, particularly in numerical code. Curiously, in early versions of C++, they were not available as intrinsic functions. Linux programmers using gcc relied on the built-in macro definitions:

```
Either this

    #define max(a, b) ( a > b) ? a : b
    #define min(a, b) ( a < b) ? a : b

Or this:

    #define max(a, b) ( (a) > (b)) ? (a) : (b)) )
    #define min(a, b) ( (a) < (b)) ? (a) : (b)) )
```

The macros were not automatically supplied on Windows platforms using Visual Studio, leading to portability issues. The upshot was that macros like this proliferated across many software packages. There are several problems with these macros; firstly they involve branching and thus might not be the most efficient way of implementing these functions on some architectures. This applies to NVIDIA GPUs which can perform these operations in a single instruction. The second problem is that macros are too powerful; they are expanded by the preprocessor and thus if defined, they prevent any superior intrinsic versions of these functions being used. Thirdly they do not always work if embedded in complex expressions or if expressions are used for arguments, the second form in the box with extra brackets is an attempt to solve this, but even this does not always work.

Modern C++ provides the max and min functions as part of the standard library so we use std::min and std::max in our host code to be sure of getting the best versions. For device code, CUDA supplies generic max and min functions that work for all standard arithmetic types using the appropriate built-in functions. If you are worried they might be overwritten by lurking macros you can use fmaxf and fminf for a pair of floats, fmax and fmin for a pair of doubles and umax and umin for unsigned ints.

Note our cx.h include file undefines the symbols max and min to help protect your code from these macros but depending on what other include files you use and in what order they are included, these macros might get redefined.

More generally macros are deprecated in modern C++; they can usually be replaced by some combination of the C++ using statement for types, constexpr for values and lambda functions for expressions.

Index